SENTENCING AND MODERN REFORM

SENTENCING AND MODERN REFORM

The Process of Punishment

Liz Marie Marciniak

ASSOCIATE PROFESSOR OF CRIMINAL JUSTICE
UNIVERSITY OF PITTSBURGH AT GREENSBURG

CAROLINA ACADEMIC PRESS
Durham, North Carolina

Library of Congress Cataloging-in-Publication Data

Names: Marciniak, Liz Marie, author.
Title: Sentencing and modern reform : the process of punishment / Liz Marie
  Marciniak.
Description: Durham, North Carolina : Carolina Academic Press, [2016] |
  Includes bibliographical references and index.
Identifiers: LCCN 2016033573 | ISBN 9781611637229 (alk. paper)
Subjects: LCSH: Sentences (Criminal procedure)--United States. | Law
  reform--United States. | Mandatory sentences--United States. | Sentences
  (Criminal procedure)--Philosophy. | Punishment--United States.
Classification: LCC KF9685 .M343 2016 | DDC 345.73/0772--dc23
LC record available at https://lccn.loc.gov/2016033573

Carolina Academic Press, LLC
700 Kent Street
Durham, North Carolina 27701
Telephone (919) 489-7486
Fax (919) 493-5668
www.cap-press.com

Printed in the United States of America

Dedication

To Ellie,
My sweet little girl who will live in my heart forever.

CONTENTS

ACKNOWLEDGMENTS

As I finish writing my first book, I feel humbled by the support I have received from the wonderful staff at Carolina Academic Press, my family, my friends, and my colleagues. When I began work on this project years ago, I really didn't know how much work it would require. I also didn't realize how important so many people would be to providing me with guidance, encouragement, and love. Words can't do justice to how much I appreciate the support of so many people in my life.

I first thank the great people at Carolina Academic Press. I met Beth Hall a few years ago when she came to my campus to share with me new and exciting titles. I discussed my book idea with her and wrote up a proposal. From the day I met Beth until today, she has been so encouraging, professional, and pleasant to work with. I am indebted to her for offering me a contract and working with me for many months. Thanks to Tasha Gervais for answering all my questions during the writing process. I thank Ryland Bowman for his editorial work and extreme attention to detail. Special thanks go to Grace Pledger and Sara Hjelt for their work on my page proofs. I also thank Meredith Jones for working with me on the Instructor's Manual. Her insights and guidance are much appreciated. Thanks to Rae Meade and Davis Alderson for assisting with my Powerpoint slides. I would also like to thank anonymous reviewers for providing feedback throughout the process.

My parents gave me the opportunity to go to college and instilled the importance of perseverance and hard work. I would never have been able to attend graduate school with an assistantship and earn a doctorate at the University of Maryland without those values. My parents have also been extremely patient throughout the time I have been writing. I look forward to spending much more quality time with them now!

I also thank Uncle Raymond and Aunt Debbie for their encouragement and support and I am so blessed to have such a cool aunt and uncle.

The professors I had while attending the University of Maryland were simply the best. And without the superb education I received from my graduate school professors, I wouldn't have the tools needed to write this book. Thanks to Colin Loftin, Larry Sherman, Ray Paternoster, Denise Gottfredson, Charles Wellford, and David McDowall for being such amazing professors, scholars and role models.

Then there are my former colleagues, who I consider friends who gave me their professional expertise while I researched and wrote this book. Tim Kinlock, my dear friend from University of Maryland (who now teaches at the University of Baltimore) shared with me his expertise in substance abuse research and pointed to some good resources.

Randy LaGrange from University of North Carolina at Wilmington gave me some great pointers on writing a textbook … and balancing that with life.

My past and present criminal justice colleagues from the University of Pittsburgh at Greensburg are simply the best. Their friendship and encouragement mean the world to me. Thanks to Tom Horan, Greg Kerpchar, Nick Hall, and Tim Holler for being the coolest colleagues a girl could ask for. And a special thanks to Neil Guzy, who offered me his legal expertise for the book and offered me time and friendship, even when he really didn't have the time.

Special thanks to Tony Boldurian and Martha Koehler for reading reviewers' remarks and giving me great advice on writing a book. Thanks to my former co-division chairs, Mark Stauffer and Bill Rued for being supportive of my writing and understanding why I had to step down to write my book. And thanks to some very special people at Pitt-Greensburg—Lori Jakiela, Melissa Marks, Steve Murabito, and Judy Vollmer. Their scholarly accomplishments are truly inspirational and their support for me during this project is much appreciated.

My friends have been amazing and so encouraging. One really realizes who is truly a friend when writing a book. Thanks to Mylene Samek, Kelly Myers, Suzanne Weightman, Jameson Bowden, and Jennifer Dunlap for being there for me and celebrating the good things in life and being there for the not so good things. True friendship is a true blessing.

And special thanks to people who have been both my friends and colleagues at University of Pittsburgh. Thanks to Mike Lucci, the truest friend a girl could ask for. He has always offered me sweet support and love. Mike is the one of the most caring, giving people I've ever met. I treasure our friendship.

I also thank Michael Spithaler, who is also both my colleague at Pitt and a friend. Michael's wisdom is truly a gift. His support for my writing meant the world to me.

And thanks to Steve Dworkin, my friend and former colleague at UNCW. I'm so glad we kept in touch. Steve is an amazing researcher, a supportive friend, and cool guy!

My student research assistants were incredibly dedicated and a joy to work with. Two students made a difference. Steve Reddy worked on tables for the book and performed legal research. He was always enthusiastic and extremely hard working and always went the extra mile. I just know he is going to have an amazing career as a lawyer. I was also blessed to have had Michelle Duffy work very hard on performing literature searches, checking references, and obtaining permissions. Michelle also got me into country music along the way!!! I totally appreciate that (I'm now a super Dan + Shay fan!!) and her sweet disposition.

The people I interviewed for my book were so gracious to give me their time. Thanks to the Honorable Judge Debra Pezze and Mr. Wayne McGrew for giving me their perspectives on sentencing in Pennsylvania. Their time is so precious which makes their contributions to my book even more special. They both also served on a panel discussion at Pitt—Greensburg on Pennsylvania's sentencing guidelines. They, along with the Honorable Judge Christopher Feliciani, Assistant District Attorney Jim De Floria, and Dr. Eric Kocian gave their time in providing Pitt students with their perspectives on

ACKNOWLEDGMENTS xxv

sentencing. I also thank Dr. Sharon Smith, President of the University of Pittsburgh at Greensburg for attending this event and encouraging me throughout my writing.

Special thanks to "Serena," a formerly incarcerated person. I so admire her willingness to talk to me and admire her courage and fortitude in life.

The librarians, past and present, at the University of Pittsburgh at Greensburg helped me so much and I am indebted to them. Thanks to Anna Mary Willford, Pat Duck, and Amanda Folk.

I must also thank the New Hanover County Criminal Justice Advisory Board for accepting me as a member back in 1994. I first became interested in sentencing when I served on this board. My position on the board helped me secure a grant to evaluate the day sentencing center that was established by the board. I don't think I'd ever have thought of writing a book on sentencing if I didn't have this opportunity. Special thanks to Andy Atkinson, who served as chair.

And before I began writing, I needed a home office. Thanks to Bob and Joella, who helped me put together a beautiful office in my home. None of this would be possible without a computer desk, carpeting, and painting!

I also thank my puppies, past and present for showing me unconditional love. I dedicated my book to Ellie, who passed shortly after I finished writing my book. She must have known how important the book was to me and she was the sweetest girl ever. I thank Bumper and Rebel, who are also at the rainbow bridge and were amazing companions. And my current pups, Jackson and my wild child puppy Jessa for being sweet.

And last but not least, I must give a very special thank you to Shawn. He was there for me from the time I signed my contract and to the day I signed off on the last page proof. He was always there for me for the time in between, even when I didn't make it so easy to be! His kindness and love are unmatched.

These acknowledgements only scratch the surface as to how many people (and dogs) helped me writing this book. I am so appreciative of so many people in my life. Now that the book is done, I can start thanking them in person and playing more with Jackson and Jessa. I have a lot of thanking (and playing) to do!

SENTENCING AND MODERN REFORM

An Overview of Sentencing in the United States

Chapter Objectives:

- To understand the considerable variation in states' sentencing practices.
- To learn what is meant by the terms "indeterminate sentencing," "determinate sentencing," "mandatory minimum sentencing laws," "truth-in-sentencing," and "three strikes laws."
- To gain an overview of the population under correctional supervision in the United States.
- To grasp the fundamentals of various sentencing goals of corrections and differentiate them in terms of their assumptions about crime causation.

Sentencing: The Link between Courts and Corrections

The process of sentencing begins after an offender has been found guilty in criminal court or has pleaded guilty to a crime. Sentencing links two stages of the criminal case processing—courts and corrections. As federal judge Marvin Frankel stated in the preface of his book *Criminal Sentences: Law Without Order* (1973), "The sentence is also critical because it is (or should be) the fundamental judgment determining how, where, and why the offender should be dealt with and what may be much or all of his remaining life."

The actions of many criminal justice actors, including police, prosecutors, defense attorneys, and the judge and jury, lead up to the sentencing stage. Police are responsible for apprehending suspects under the law. Prosecutors review criminal cases in terms of evidence and decide whether and how to charge criminal suspects. As we will discuss, the discretion of the prosecution, regarding number and types of charges, has important ramifications for the sentencing process. Most cases (approximately 90 percent) are not decided by jury trial, but result from plea bargains reached between the prosecution and defense (Siegel & Worrall, 2016).

The prosecutor and defense attorney's knowledge of potential sentences facing the accused may affect the decision of the defendant to agree on a plea or to go to trial. Sentencing reforms, such as sentencing guidelines, mandatory sentencing laws, and three strikes laws, may persuade the defendant to "take a chance" at a trial. This is because under these sentencing schemes, the offender would receive a certain harsh sentence if he or she was to plead guilty to an offense that carries a long prison sentence.

The process of sentencing varies considerably among states and the federal system. Some states give judges broad discretion in imposing a sentence in terms of sentence type (incarceration or community based sentences) and sentence length. In these states, judges may choose a prison term from a wide range dictated by state statute, for example 5–99 years for a serious felony. The exact amount of time that the offender serves in prison will depend on the decision of a parole board. After the offender serves a proportion of his or her sentence (which also varies by state), he or she may have a parole hearing, in which the board decides if the offender should be released back into society. Other states use sentencing guideline schemes that involve the mathematical calculation of offense severity, prior record, and aggravating and mitigating factors to place the offender in a grid cell that defines the type and length of the sentence. In these states, the judge has limited discretion. The minimum and maximum sentences are determined at the time of sentencing.

Clearly, there is no "American" sentencing system. The above describes extremes on continuums of judicial discretion and parole board authority. Every state is different in the way it sentences offenders. Even sentencing practices between states with commission-based guidelines vary in important ways.

A Comparison of Sentencing in Four States

The following hypothetical case is used to illustrate the differences between states in sentencing an individual convicted of the same crime. Note that even the designation of the crime—whether it's defined as an "aggravated sexual assault" or a "first degree rape" or some other term varies by state. Let's now take a look at sentencing procedures followed in four different states—Texas, South Carolina, North Carolina, and Ohio.

The Crime

Consider the case of Justin, who committed a horrific crime—forcible rape on October 11, 2011. Justin, age 35, walked around a park around sunset one early fall night with one purpose—to find a victim.[1] Justin's violence was fueled by a hatred of women. He decided that night in a fit of anger that he was going to look for a woman who was alone, hold a gun to her head, and rape her. And that night, Justin did what he set out to do—he committed a forcible rape of a 25-year-old woman.

What Justin did not know was that a passerby witnessed part of the crime and called the police. The police responded quickly and apprehended Justin at the far end of the park after they attended to the victim. Both the victim and the witness identified Justin. After a jury trial, Justin was convicted of forcible rape. Justin has a prior felony conviction for first degree burglary five years ago.

What would happen to Justin next would depend on where he committed the offense. The sentence length that Justin could receive and the amount of time Justin could spend in prison would depend on the state in which he committed the offense.

We will compare the sentencing procedures in four states: (1) Texas, which has "indeterminate sentencing" and a parole board, but has special provisions for parole release for the type of crime Justin committed; (2) South Carolina, a state that has recently categorized felonies in a way that provides upper limits of incarceration sentences for each category and also has a parole board, but which considers Justin's crime a "no parole" offense; (3) North Carolina, where sentences are calculated by rigid commission-based sentencing guidelines; and (4) Ohio, where the sentencing guidelines are more flexible and allow greater judicial discretion in setting minimum sentences.

Now let's consider how Justin would be sentenced in the four states and compare and contrast sentencing processes in each of the states.

Texas

According to the Texas Penal Code, Title 5, "Offenses Against the Person," Chapter 22, "Assaultive Offenses," Justin would have been convicted of **aggravated sexual assault** (Section 22.021) (Texas Attorney General). The elements of the crime that qualify him to be convicted of this offense include that "the person intentionally or knowingly causes the penetration of the anus or sexual organ of another person by any means, without that person's consent" and that the offender "uses or exhibits a deadly weapon in the course of the same criminal episode."

Aggravated sexual assault in Texas is considered a felony of the first degree, second in seriousness only to a capital felony. According to Section 12.32 — First Degree Felony Punishment (Texas Penal Code, Title 3, "Punishments," Chapter 12, "Punishments," Subchapter A, General Provisions), "An individual adjudged guilty of a felony of the first degree shall be punished by imprisonment in the Texas Department of Criminal Justice for life or for any term of **not more than 99 years or less than 5 years.**" The law allows an extremely broad range of time that an offender convicted of an aggravated sexual assault could serve.

The Penal Code Title 3, "Punishments," Chapter 12, "Punishments," Subchapter A, General Provisions, Section 12.42 states the penalties of **repeat and habitual felony offenders** on trial for a first, second, or third degree felony. Since Justin had been previously convicted of a first degree burglary, his sentence would be "imprisonment in the Texas Department of Criminal Justice for life, or for any term of **not more than 99 years or less than 15 years.**" If he had a prior conviction for a sexual offense against a child or a previous aggravated sexual assault, his sentence would have jumped to life without parole.

In Texas, most prisoners are released to a plan of parole supervision through discretionary parole release. The vote of members of the Texas Board of Pardons and Paroles determines whether the offender can be released to serve the remainder of his or her sentence under community supervision with conditions after serving a portion of the sentence.

South Carolina

In South Carolina, Justin's crime would be considered a **criminal sexual assault in the first degree**, which falls under Section 16-3-652 of the South Carolina Code of Laws, Title 16—Crimes and Offenses (Chapter 3, "Offenses Against the Person"). Justin's crime falls under Section 16-3-652, because he engaged in sexual battery with the victim using "aggravated force to accomplish sexual battery," in his case, with the use of a deadly weapon. The South Carolina Code of Laws, Title 16—Crimes and Offenses (Chapter 1, "Felonies and Misdemeanors; Accessories"), Section 16-1-90 ("Crimes Classified as Felonies"), classifies criminal sexual conduct in the first degree as a Class A felony, the most serious felony except murder and which according to Section 16-1-20(A) requires imprisonment of "not more than thirty years."

There are six categories of felonies defined in the state of South Carolina that range from Class A (the most serious) to Class F (the least serious) and three categories of misdemeanors—Class A (the most serious), B, and C (the least serious). Maximum penalties for each class of crime are defined by Section 16-1-20 (A) as follows: Class A felonies "not more than thirty years," Class B felonies "not more than twenty-five years," Class C felonies "not more than twenty years," Class D felonies "not more than fifteen years," Class E felonies "not more than ten years," Class F felonies "not more than five years," Class A misdemeanors, "not more than three years," Class B misdemeanors "not more than two years," and Class C misdemeanors "not more than a year."

Class A, B, and C felonies are considered "no parole" offenses, according to South Carolina Code of Laws, Title 24—"Corrections, Jails, Probation, Paroles, and Pardons," Chapter 13, "Prisoners Generally," Section 24-13-100. An offender convicted of a "no parole offense," and who "has not been subjected to punishment for misbehavior, is entitled to a deduction from the term of his sentence beginning with the day on which the service of his sentence commences to run, computed at the rate of three days for each month served" (South Carolina Code of Laws, Title 24—"Corrections, Jails, Probation, Paroles, and Pardons," Chapter 13, "Prisoners Generally," Section 24-13-210). This constitutes a small "credit given inmates for good behavior" for offenders convicted of "no parole offenses."

In Justin's case, let's assume the judge sentences him to twenty years in prison for the first degree criminal sexual conduct offense, although we know he could get up to thirty years by law. Because he committed a criminal sexual conduct offense, he will not be eligible for work release. A person convicted of a "no parole offense" "is not eligible for early release, discharge, or community supervision as provided in Sections 24-21-560, until the inmate has served at least eighty-five percent of the actual term of imprisonment imposed." Eighty-five percent of Justin's sentence of 20 years is 17 years in prison. And remember the judge could have sentenced him to 30 years in prison, which would have made him ineligible for release before serving 25.5 years. After serving a minimum of 85 percent of his 20-year sentence, Justin would be required to participate in a community supervision operated by the Department of Probation, Parole, and Pardon program for up to two years.

Under Section 16-1-120 of South Carolina Code of Laws, Title 16—"Crimes and Offenses," Chapter 1, "Felonies and Misdemeanors; Accessories," increased sentences for repeat offenders are detailed. Sentence add-ons are indicated for persons convicted of Class A, B, or C felonies who completed their sentences and subsequently are convicted of another felony offense. The amount of add-on time depends on how closely the subsequent offense was committed after release. If it was committed within forty-five days of release, five years is added to the sentence for the new conviction. The time to be added on to the new sentence decreases as the amount of time post initial conviction increases to 365 days, when one year is added on to the sentence. Since Justin's conviction was five years ago, there is no sentence enhancement.

North Carolina

If Justin had committed the offense in North Carolina, the conviction would have been for **first degree rape**. In North Carolina, his sentence would be determined by a series of steps, which essentially would come down to a mathematical calculation, with a little bit of discretion on the part of the judge. Justin would be placed on a "Felony Punishment Chart" (North Carolina Sentencing and Policy Advisory Commission, 2009) that would reflect offense seriousness and the extent and gravity of his prior record.

In North Carolina, first degree rape is considered a Class B1 felony—the most serious crime, except for murder (which is a Class A felony). Felony offense classes range from A to I in decreasing seriousness. The Felony Punishment Chart that appears in the *Structured Sentencing Training and Reference Manual for Offenses Committed on or after December 1, 2009* (North Carolina Sentencing and Policy Advisory Commission, 2009) indicates that the minimum number of months that Justin could spend in prison according to the North Carolina Structured Sentencing Guidelines is 144 months, or 12 years. That minimum sentence would be if Justin had the *lowest level of prior record* and there were *mitigating factors* in his case. The minimum term he could spend could also be life without parole. That scenario would be possible if Justin had the *highest possible prior record level* and *aggravating factors* in the case.

Justin had a prior conviction for one Class D felony—first degree burglary which gives him 6 prior record points. This would mean he would be categorized into prior record level III (6–9 points). The grid cell that Justin would fall into (B1 felony with prior record level of III) indicates three ranges of minimum sentences. The middle range is the presumptive minimum range (254–317 months, which corresponds to 21.2–26.4 years). The top range is the aggravated minimum range (317–397 months, which corresponds to 26.4–33.1 years). The judge will choose this minimum sentence if aggravating factors are present and/or outweigh mitigating factors. The bottom range is the mitigated range (190–254 months, which corresponds to 15.8–21.2 years). The judge will choose a minimum sentence from this range if mitigating factors are present and/or outweigh aggravating factors. In Justin's case, the judge decides to set the minimum sentence in the presumptive range and hands down a minimum sentence of 260 months.

The corresponding maximum sentence to a 260-month minimum sentence is automatically set by another table in the guidelines and is 317 months. This represents 120 percent of the minimum sentence (rounded to the next highest month) plus an additional nine months for post-release supervision. Justin must serve at least 260 months (21.6 years) in prison. He may accrue enough "earned time" in prison (as awarded by the Department of Corrections) to be released upon his completion of the minimum sentence, but cannot be released before the minimum term is completed. If he fails to get any "earned time," he will max out his sentence at 317 months or 26.4 years. The judge must impose an active prison sentence because of the seriousness of the crime and his prior record.

The judge has limited discretion in sentencing Justin. He or she has no part in deciding offense seriousness—this is established in the North Carolina Sentencing Commission. The judge also has no discretion in assigning prior record. This is calculated by adding points assigned to prior convictions. Once the individual is placed in a grid cell, the judge can consider aggravating and mitigating circumstances and choose which range (presumptive, aggravated, or mitigated) from which to set a minimum sentence. The number of months for the maximum sentence, however, is automatically set by a table which lists maximum terms that correspond to each number of minimum terms. After he completes his sentence, Justin will be automatically placed on "post-release supervision" for 9 months. During this time he would follow the conditions dictated by the court.

Ohio

Justin's offense is labeled **rape** in Ohio, a first degree felony. Section 2907.02 of Ohio's Criminal Code defines rape in Section (A) (2) states, "No person shall engage in sexual conduct with another when the offender purposely compels the other person to submit by force or threat of force."

In Ohio, judges are afforded wider ranges from which to choose sentence length. Senate Bill 2 established sentencing guidelines in 1996, and House Bill 86 made some revisions to the original bill. Pursuant to these bills, felony sentences are categorized from first degree (the most serious) to fifth degree (the least serious) (Woolredge & Griffin, 2005). The range of basic prison terms for each category is set. Prison is favored for first and second degree felonies. Community punishment is considered the appropriate sentence for fourth and fifth felonies if the offense is not violent and the offender has no prior record (Diroll, 2011).

Persons convicted of first degree felonies are to receive sentences between 3–11 years in prison. Ohio law (Ohio Rev. Code Ann § 2907.01, Anderson, 2002), however, requires a sentence of at least 5 years for rape "if victim compelled through force, threat, or controlled substance." Ohio also sets ranges of years of enhancement for repeat violent offenders. Since Justin's prior offense is a property crime (burglary) and not a violent crime, he would not be subject to this enhancement. If Justin was a repeat violent offender, he could get 1–10 years added on to his base sentence for the rape. If Justin committed the rape in Ohio and had a prior conviction for a violent crime, he could face anywhere from 6–21 years in prison.

However, since we assumed the judge in North Carolina chose his minimum sentence from the presumptive (middle) range, let's assume the judge in Ohio picks a sentence towards "the middle" too. Justin would be given 6 years for the basic prison term and no "repeat violent offender enhancement."

Justin may not accrue any earned credit pursuant to H.B. 86, because Justin committed a sexually oriented offense after September 30, 2011. If he had committed the offense before that date, or had committed a different first or second degree felony, he would have been able to earn a credit of one day off per month for participation in educational programs, vocational training, prison industries work, substance abuse treatment, and other miscellaneous programs (other than sex offender treatment). In Ohio, no prisoner can earn credits that account for 8 percent or more of the prison term handed down by the judge (Diroll, 2011).

Accounting for the Differences

There are many differences between these four states in the potential sentence length, criteria upon which sentences are based, when and how prior record can be incorporated, the amount of discretion afforded the judge, and the role (if any) of a discretionary parole board in determining actual time served. These systems cannot be exactly compared because they determine the ranges of minimum and maximum sentences differently, however, we can make a few observations. **Figure 1.1** highlights the differences in the minimum sentence that Justin could receive for the crime in the four states.

Figure 1.1 Potential Sentences for Hypothetical Rape Case

✓ In Texas the minimum sentence is 15 years and the maximum sentence is 99 years.

✓ South Carolina does not indicate a minimum sentence, but sets the maximum at "no more than thirty years."

✓ In North Carolina, the minimum sentence would depend on prior record, but in our scenario—with one prior conviction—it would be between approximately 21–26 years. The maximum sentence for someone with one prior in our scenario would be 26.4 years.

✓ In Ohio, the minimum is 5 years and the maximum is 11 years.

The minimum sentence length for the hypothetical case varies from 5 years in Ohio to approximately 21 years in North Carolina. South Carolina does not indicate a minimum sentence, but sets the maximum at "no more than thirty years." The maximum in Ohio is 11 years. The maximum sentence in North Carolina given the case characteristics would be 26.4 years. And the maximum sentence in Texas for the described crime is 99 years. Clearly there is no "typical" sentence for forcible rape in the United States. The state in which one is convicted has an enormous impact on sentence length.

Where prior record is considered in the sentencing process also varies. In Texas, if one is on trial for a first degree felony and has a prior felony conviction (violent or not), the minimum sentence increases from five to fifteen years, with the maximum sentence remaining at 99 years. In Ohio, a sentencing enhancement is imposed for those convicted of a first degree offense only if the prior was a violent offense. In North Carolina, the prior record score comprises one axis of the sentencing grid (the other axis is offense seriousness) and the class of the prior felony and number of prior felonies are used to calculate this number. Thus, in North Carolina, a prior record score is computed for each offender and affects grid cell placement and thus the length of sentence. In South Carolina, convicted serious felons receive an add-on number of years for prior felonies depending on how close in time the current offense was to the prior felony.

North Carolina and Ohio use sentencing guidelines to direct judges to what is considered appropriate terms through prescribed ranges based on offense class and prior record. In comparison to North Carolina, Ohio allows for wider ranges in setting minimum terms. In South Carolina, maximums are indicated.

Ohio has fewer steps and calculations, compared to structured sentencing in North Carolina. Whereas prior record level is intricately calculated in North Carolina and determines (with offense severity) the grid cell in which an offender falls, in Ohio a prior conviction for a violent offense can enhance a basic sentence term from a set range. And we can certainly see that Justin's sentence in Ohio would be shorter regardless of where within the range the judge sentences, compared to the requirements of structured sentencing in North Carolina.

Texas sets statutory maximums and employs indeterminate sentencing. The judge has greater discretion in setting maximum prison terms, compared to Ohio, South Carolina, and North Carolina. The role of the parole board (if any) varies in each state. In South Carolina for less serious and non-violent felonies, these boards decide when to release an offender, after he or she has served a portion of his or her sentence. For an offender convicted of a rape, like Justin, however, the parole board plays less of a role. In South Carolina, whereas offenders convicted of a wide range of offenses will be released by a parole board, criminal sexual assault in the first degree is considered a "no parole" offense and the convicted offender must complete at least 85 percent of the sentence. And in Texas, an offender like Justin won't even be eligible for parole until he has served half of his sentence, after which the parole board may or may not release him. North Carolina eliminated discretionary parole release in 1994 and instead, after an offender has served at least 85 percent of the sentence, he or she is put on "post-release supervision."

How can the process of sentencing for the same crime (according to legally relevant characteristics) be so different in various states? The answer lies in the type of sentencing schemes which the states have currently adopted. The 1994 North Carolina Structured Sentencing Act overhauled the way sentences were calculated and literally collapsed the sentencing process for criminal offenders into a serious of mathematical calculations. North Carolina's system of sentencing is based on clear guidelines for felonies and misdemeanors that are to be stringently followed by judges within the state. Ohio indicates a narrower range of appropriate sentence length, according to felony class. South Carolina sets upper limits by felony class. Conversely, Texas relies on indeterminate sentencing, in which statutes set broad ranges of time which the judge can sentence for most crimes, and the ultimate time that the offender will serve will be determined by a parole board.

Sentencing Approaches and Terms

Indeterminate Sentencing

Indeterminate sentencing refers to the strategy by which judges sentence a convicted offender within a broad range of possible punishments set by the legislators of the jurisdiction (most often the state) in which the offender committed the crime. Within indeterminate sentencing schemes, there is often a large range of sentences from which the judge can choose. Judges may have many alternatives available and be able to decide between relatively lenient sentences to be served in the community and prison sentences as long as the punishment lies within the broad range established by the legislature. As Alarid and Reichel (2013) noted, state legislatures set a minimum and maximum time one could receive for each offense defined by law, for example one to five years for auto theft. The judge would have to impose a minimum and maximum sentence within that range.

The actual time spent, however, would be determined by a discretionary parole board. Although there is much variation by state regarding the qualifications of the parole board and the exact proceedings of the board, this body's job is to determine if the offender is ready to re-enter society. The members may base their decision on a myriad of factors, including the seriousness of the conviction, the behavior of the inmate in prison, an inmate's statement of plans upon release, evidence that they have been "rehabilitated," and the victim's statements. Under indeterminate sentencing, the parole board decides the exact length of a prison sentence.

Indeterminate sentencing allows judges to "individualize" punishments, taking into account characteristics that they deem relevant to sentencing, including, but not limited to, prior record, community ties, family ties, perceived dangerousness, evidence of substance abuse, and the offender's plans for the future. The focus is on rehabilitating the offender. While serving the sentence, the offender's specific needs are to be understood and treated. Thus, indeterminate sentencing and rehabilitation go hand in hand. Some states, such as Texas, with indeterminate sentencing schemes, however, also note deterrence and public safety as relevant considerations in their penal codes.

Spotlight — Parole in Texas

According to *Parole in Texas: Answers to Common Questions* (Texas Department of Criminal Justice Parole Division and Texas Board of Pardons and Parole, 2012), the members of the parole board consider the following before granting parole:

> Parole panel members look at the circumstances and seriousness of the offense; prior prison commitments; relevant input from victims, family members, and trial officials; adjustment and attitude in prison; the offender's release plan; and factors such as alcohol or drug use, violent or assaultive behavior, deviant sexual behavior, use of a weapon in an offense, institutional adjustment, and emotional stability. Based on the entirety of the available information, the parole panel then determines whether the offender deserves the privilege of parole. (p. 54)

Parole guideline levels are also computed for each individual approaching parole in Texas. This level is calculated by two main factors — a risk assessment instrument and an offense severity class. Although this score is calculated for inmates coming up for parole, the parole board still makes the ultimate decision as to whether to release the individual on parole.

Determinate Sentencing

Determinate sentencing is a broad term used to describe sentencing schemes in which the length of the sentence is fixed by the judge at the time of sentencing, with the maximum term being prescribed by the legislature (Siegel & Bartollas, 2011). The statutory limits in determinate sentencing are narrower than in indeterminate sentencing (Alarid & Reichel, 2013).

An example would be that a judge sentences an offender to a term of 10 years in prison for aggravated assault, if the law, as established by the state legislature, allows for sentences of 9 to 11 years. Sentence length is therefore "determined" at the time of sentencing. Often, the offender can accrue limited "good time" to reduce the time served, but this is usually only a small percentage of one's sentence. As we will discuss in Chapter 2, when prisons were first used as distinct criminal sanctions in the United States, judges sentenced offenders to fixed (what are now called "determinate") sentences.

Commission-Based Sentencing Guidelines

One approach to structuring judicial decision making is the development of **commission-based sentencing guidelines**. Sentencing commissions are independent bodies given the task of coming up with model sentences (or narrow ranges) for offenses. Commission-based guidelines grade offenses in terms of seriousness. The seriousness score serves as one axis of a sentencing grid. The commission also creates a mathematical scoring system to count prior record, based on the number and seriousness of priors. Prior record score forms the other axis of the sentencing grid. A sentence or narrow sentencing range is indicated within each grid cell. Although commission-based guidelines schemes vary in how aggravating and mitigating factors can raise or lower the sentence, all such systems include a consideration of these factors. The judge is to impose a sentence indicated by the guidelines. As we will discuss in Chapter 4, in most jurisdictions the judge can depart from the guidelines, but must indicate why he or she chose a sentence greater than or less than a within-guidelines sentence.

Mandatory Minimums

Since sentencing reform gained momentum in the 1980s, every state has enacted some type of **mandatory minimum sentencing law** (Tonry, 1996). Mandatory minimum sentencing laws require the judge to impose a particular sentence (usually incarceration) or an add-on sentence for offenses (often violent, gun, and/or drug offenses) with specific case attributes (Seigel & Bartollas, 2011).

In 1973, the New York State legislature enacted mandatory sentencing laws for drug offenders, deemed the Rockefeller Drug Laws (named after then-governor Nelson Rockefeller, who initiated them). The laws mandated minimum sentences of fifteen years to life in prison for offenders convicted of possession of four or more ounces of narcotics or the selling of two or more ounces of narcotics (Gray, 2009). The sentences for drug law violations were harsh and on par with sentences for murder and rape. The enactment of the Rockefeller Drug Laws in 1973 was, in part, a reaction to heroin epidemic in the late 1960s and early 1970s. Although major revisions to the laws have occurred since 1973, with some parts of the laws being outright repealed, the Rockefeller Drug Laws provide an example of the most stringent mandatory sentencing regarding drug offenses in the United States. Chapter 6 documents the updates to the Rockefeller Drug Laws to date and details other mandatory sentencing laws.

In 1978, Michigan passed the "650 Lifer Law," which mandated that judges imprison anyone convicted of delivering more than 650 grams of narcotics to life (Gray, 2009). In 1994, Oregon residents voted to pass Measure 11, which mandated lengthy prison terms for offenders who were convicted of any of 16 specific violent and/or sexual offenses. The minimum prison term for those sentenced under Measure 11 ranged from 70 months for assault in the second degree to 300 months for murder (Austin, Clark, Hardyman, & Henry, 1999).

What mandatory minimum sentencing laws have in common is that **judicial discretion is eliminated**. That means if an offender is convicted of an offense that carries a mandatory sentence, the judge must impose that sentence. What the judge might otherwise deem relevant case characteristics (like if the offender had no prior record) may not be considered and the sentence must be carried out, as defined by law.

In most cases, these laws have been promoted by politicians who endorsed "get tough on crime" policies in their campaigns. They supported these laws with the assumption that the more certain that a sentence of incarceration was for a given crime, and the longer the mandated prison term was for the crime, the less likely potential offenders would be to commit the crime. Mandatory minimum sentencing laws rested on the notion that strict punishments deter crime.

"Truth-in-Sentencing" Laws

Truth-in-sentencing laws require offenders to serve a substantial proportion (usually 85 percent) of their prison sentence. Many such laws were enacted in states in the mid-nineties. The impetus for the laws was the fact that offenders typically were only serving a small proportion of the sentence handed down to them and there was public outcry that the criminal justice system was too easy on criminals. Although sentencing guidelines and mandatory minimum sentencing laws were developed to result in more certainty in sentencing, release of prisoners due to prison overcrowding, good time allowances, and earned time reduced the amount of time the offender would actually serve in prison. The purpose of truth-in-sentencing laws was to decrease the difference between the prison term handed down upon sentencing and the actual time the offender would serve in prison (Ditton & Wilson, 1999).

Part of the Violent Crime Control and Law Enforcement Act of 1994 (commonly known as President Clinton's Crime Bill) involved the United States Congress authorizing funding for states to build or expand prisons and local jails through the Violent Offender Incarceration and Truth-in-Sentencing Incentive Grants Program (Pub. L. No. 103-322, 108 Stat. 1796 (1994)). To be eligible to receive these funds, states had to require offenders convicted of Part 1 (Index) Violent Crimes (murder and non-negligent manslaughter, forcible rape, robbery, and aggravated assault) to serve at least 85 percent of their prison sentences. By 1998, 27 states and the District of Columbia met the eligibility criteria and were awarded grants. By 1999, an additional 13 states adopted versions of truth-in-sentencing laws that required offenders to serve certain proportions of their sentences (Ditton & Wilson, 1999). There are variations among states in the definition of "truth-in-sentencing," the percentage of the offender's sentence one must serve, and the offenses that are mandated to be sentenced under the state's truth-in-sentencing laws. Washington State enacted the first truth-in-sentencing law in 1984.

Three Strikes Laws

The Essence of Three Strikes Laws

Three strikes laws describe the sentencing practices that many states have initiated which mandate lengthy prison sentences (often 25 years to life) for offenders upon their third conviction for a felony — which usually has to be considered a violent and/or serious felony. These laws first sprang up in Washington and California in the mid-nineties. They followed society's concerns about violent crime and the public perception that the criminal justice system was ineffective in preventing crime and unwilling to punish habitual offenders. These followed widely publicized cases involving offenders with long violent and serious criminal records, who were released from prison and proceeded to commit heinous violent crimes.

California's Strikes Laws

Washington State was the first to enact three strikes laws. California's strikes laws, which were passed in 1994, however, have justifiably earned the reputation of being the most severe strikes laws in the United States. The most publicized component of the original California's strikes law was that it mandated, upon conviction of a third felony (with two prior convictions of "strikeable offenses") an indeterminate life sentence in which the offender would not eligible for parole for at least 25 years. This meant if the offender had "three strikes," the sentencing judge was required to sentence the offender to a lengthy prison term. The purpose of the law was to punish repeat serious and/or violent offenders harshly with lengthy prison sentences. The judge's discretion to impose probation, suspend the sentence, or divert the offender from the criminal justice system was eliminated. Simply put, those sentenced under California's strikes laws had to serve very lengthy sentences in a California state prison. There have been some revisions to California's original strikes laws, which are detailed in Chapter 6.

The Population under Correctional Supervision in the United States

To take a meaningful look at sentencing practices in the United States, we need to know how many people are sentenced and put under some form of correctional supervision in the country. The population under correctional supervision in the United States is comprised of those individuals in prison, in jail, on probation, or on parole. From the late 1970s and 1980s (which is when modern sentencing reforms began to spread in this country) through the 2000s, the populations in prison, in jail, on probation, and on parole have all skyrocketed dramatically. Recently, however, we have seen these populations beginning to decrease slightly.

The Prison Population

The growth of the prison population in the last 35 years has been striking. In the mid-seventies, the number of individuals incarcerated in state and federal prisoners was approximately 240,000 (Cullen & Jonson, 2012). By the mid-eighties, there were about 500,000 men and women incarcerated in state and federal prisons, and by the year 1996, approximately 1.1 million persons were incarcerated in state or federal prisons in this country (Bureau of Justice Statistics, 1999). The correctional population continued to increase from the mid-1990s through the 2009 when at year-end there were 1,555,600 state and federal prisoners in the United States. After year-end 2009, the United States prison population began to decrease a little. From 2009 to 2010 the overall prison population fell 0.3%, reflecting a small decrease in the state prison population (.5%) and a small increase in the federal prison population (0.8%).[2] There were more prison releases than prison admissions in 2010 — for the first time since 1977. The federal and state prison population rose a little between 2012 and 2013. Most recently we saw a decline of over one percent from year-end 2013 to year-end 2014 (Carson, 2015 September).

On December 31, 2014, the overall prison population (federal and state combined) was 1,561,500. **Figure 1.2** shows the state and federal prison population from 1978 to 2013. The population of those incarcerated more than quadrupled during this time frame

Figure 1.2 Total State and Federal Prison Populations, 1978–2013

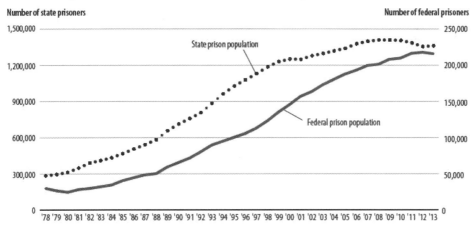

Note: Counts based on all prisoners under the jurisdiction of state and federal correctional authorities.
Source: Bureau of Justice Statistics, National Prisoner Statistics Program, 1978–2013.

Source: Carson, E. A. (2014 September). *Prisoners in 2013*, (NCJ Publication No. NCJ 247282). p. 1, Figure 1, Washington, DC: U.S. Department of Justice, Bureau of Justice Statistics. Retrieved from http://www.bjs.gov/content/pub/pdf/p14.pdf

Table 1.1 Imprisonment Rate of Sentenced State and Federal Prisoners per 100,000 U.S. Residents, by Demographic Characteristics, December 31, 2014

Age group	Total[a]	Male					Female				
		All Male[a]	White[b]	Black[b]	Hispanic	Other[b]	All Female[a]	White[b]	Black[b]	Hispanic	Other[b]
Total[c]	471	890	465	2,724	1,091	968	65	53	109	64	93
18–19	169	317	102	1,072	349	542	14	8	32	17	12
20–24	746	1,365	584	3,868	1,521	1,755	96	72	152	94	109
25–29	1,055	1,912	958	5,434	2,245	2,022	170	150	244	165	208
30–34	1,161	2,129	1,111	6,412	2,457	2,193	185	163	264	174	225
35–39	1,067	1,982	1,029	6,122	2,272	1,878	155	138	229	137	189
40–44	904	1,689	942	5,105	1,933	1,619	132	119	213	107	174
45–49	758	1,417	815	4,352	1,602	1,444	111	90	203	94	161
50–54	567	1,081	633	3,331	1,320	1,112	72	57	128	6	124
55–59	358	698	400	2,178	978	832	37	27	72	42	63
60–64	212	422	252	1,265	680	483	20	15	37	25	37
65 or older	72	158	109	418	299	208	5	4	8	7	12
Number of sentenced prisoners[d]	1,508,636	1,402,404	453,500	516,900	308,700	123,300	106,232	53,100	22,600	17,800	12,800

Note: Counts based on prisoners with sentences of more than 1 year under the jurisdiction of state or federal correctional authorities. Imprisonment rate is the number of prisoners under state or federal jurisdiction with a sentence of more than 1 year per 100,000 U.S. residents of corresponding sex, age, and race or Hispanic origin. Resident population estimates are from the U.S. Census Bureau for January 1, 2015. Alaska did not submit 2014 data to the National Prisoner Statistics (NPS), so totals include imputed counts for this state. See Methodology.

[a] Includes American Indians and Alaska Natives; Asians, Native Hawaiians, and other Pacific Islanders; and persons of two or more races.

[b] Excludes persons of Hispanic or Latino origin.

[c] Includes persons age 17 or younger.

[d] Race totals are rounded to the nearest 100 to accommodate differences in data collection techniques between jurisdictions.

Sources: Bureau of Justice Statistics, National Prisoner Statistics, 2014; Federal Justice Statistics Program, 2014; National Corrections Reporting Program, 2013; Survey of Inmates in State and Federal Correctional Facilities, 2004; and U.S. Census Bureau, postcensal resident population estimates for January 1, 2015; Carson, E. A. (2015 September). Prisoners in 2014, (NCJ Publication No. 248955). p. 15, Table 10, Washington, DC: U.S. Department of Justice, Bureau of Justice Statistics. Retrieved from http://www.bjs.gov/content/pub/pdf/p14.pdf

(Carson, 2014 September). The rate of imprisonment in the United States remains among the highest in the world—471 per 100,000 U.S. residents (Carson, 2015 September).

To advocate any sentencing approach that may increase the prison population, one should understand the characteristics of those being incarcerated in the United States. Table 1.1 shows that the rate of incarceration varies greatly by race, ethnicity, age, and gender. On December 31, 2014, the incarceration rate for males was 890/100,000, compared to 65/100,000 for females. Black males have the highest incarceration rate (2,724/100,000) of any group broken down by race, ethnicity, and sex. Young black males aged 30–34 have the highest incarceration rate of any other race and gender combination at 6,412/100,000.

Women comprise only about seven percent of the state prison population. The rate of imprisonment among females also varies by race and ethnicity. The rate of imprisonment for black females (109/100,000) is greater than that of Hispanic (64/100,000) or white females (53/100,000). Like males, the age group with the highest rate of imprisonment among females is 30–34 (185/100,000) (Carson, 2015 September). These figures show some great disparities concerning who is imprisoned and suggest that young black males are at particular risk for incarceration in the United States.

The type of crime committed that lands one in prison is also relevant when studying sentencing policies. Table 1.2 breaks down the state prison population (for those offenders sentenced to one year or more) by offense category. The most recent figures show that in state prisons, the largest proportion of offenders has been convicted of a violent offense (53.2%) followed by property offense (19.3%), drug offense (15.7%), public order (11.0%), and other/unspecified (.8%) (Carson, 2015 September).

Table 1.2 Estimated Percent of Sentenced Prisoners under State Jurisdiction, by Offense, Sex, Race, and Hispanic Origin, December 31, 2013

Most Serious Offense	All Inmates[a]	Male	Female	White[b]	Black[b]	Hispanic
Total	100%	100%	100%	100%	100%	100%
Violent	53.2%	54.4%	37.1%	47.8%	56.6%	59.2%
Murder[c]	12.5	12.6	11.2	9.6	13.7	14.2
Manslaughter	1.4	1.3	2.5	1.5	0.8	1.1
Rape/sexual assault	12.5	13.3	2.4	16.7	8.0	13.6
Robbery	13.7	14.0	8.8	8.0	19.9	13.5
Aggravated/simple assault	10.0	10.1	8.5	8.8	10.9	13.0
Other	3.1	3.1	3.7	3.2	3.5	3.7
Property	19.3%	18.6%	28.4%	25.1%	16.4%	13.5%
Burglary	10.5	10.7	7.6	12.4	9.7	8.3
Larceny-theft	3.8	3.4	9.0	5.7	3.5	2.1
Motor vehicle theft	0.8	0.8	0.8	1.1	0.5	1.0
Fraud	2.1	1.6	8.0	3.1	1.5	0.9
Other	2.1	2.0	3.0	2.9	1.3	1.2

(continued)

Table 1.2 Estimated Percent of Sentenced Prisoners under State Jurisdiction,
by Offense, Sex, Race, and Hispanic Origin, December 31, 2013 (continued)

Most Serious Offense	All Inmates[a]	Male	Female	White[b]	Black[b]	Hispanic
Drug	15.7%	15.1%	24.0%	14.5%	16.1%	14.5%
Drug possession	3.6	3.4	6.2	3.8	3.8	4.2
Other[d]	12.1	11.7	17.8	10.7	12.3	10.4
Public order	11.0%	11.2%	9.2%	11.9%	10.3%	12.2%
Weapons	3.8	4.0	1.7	2.4	4.9	5.1
Driving under the influence	1.9	1.9	2.4	2.9	0.7	2.4
Other[e]	5.3	5.3	5.1	6.7	4.7	4.7
Other/unspecified[f]	0.8%	0.8%	1.3%	0.7%	0.4%	0.5%
Total number of sentenced inmates[g]	1,325,305	1,233,724	91,581	468,600	497,000	274,200

Note: Estimates are based on state prisoners with a sentence of more than 1 year under the jurisdiction of state correctional officials. Detail may not sum to total due to rounding and missing offense data. See Methodology.
[a] Includes American Indians and Alaska Natives; Asians, Native Hawaiians, and other Pacific Islanders; and persons of two or more races.
[b] Excludes persons of Hispanic or Latino origin and persons of two or more races.
[c] Includes nonnegligent manslaughter.
[d] Includes trafficking and other drug offenses.
[e] Includes court offenses; commercialized vice, morals, and decency offenses; and liquor law violations and other public-order offenses.
[f] Includes juvenile offenses and other unspecified offense categories.
[g] Race totals are rounded to the nearest 100 to accommodate differences in data collection techniques between jurisdictions.

Sources: Bureau of Justice Statistics, National Prisoner Statistics, 2013; National Corrections Reporting Program, 2013; and Survey of Inmates in State Correctional Facilities, 2004; Carson, E. A. (2015 September). *Prisoners in 2014*, (NCJ Publication No. 248955). p. 16, Table 11, Washington, DC: U.S. Department of Justice, Bureau of Justice Statistics. Retrieved from http://www.bjs.gov/content/pub/pdf/p14.pdf

Table 1.3 shows that for those imprisoned in the federal system, about half were convicted of drug offenses. The category of public order offenses (including both immigration and weapons offenses) comprised the second highest number of offenders. Federal offenders convicted of violent and property offenders comprised a relatively small percentage of federal inmates (Carson, 2015 September).

Table 1.3 Estimated Sentenced Prisoners under Federal Correctional Authority, by
Most Serious Offense, Sex, and Race, September 30, 2014

Most Serious Offense	All Inmates[a]	Male	Female	White[b]	Black[b]	Hispanic
Total[c, d]	192,663	180,140	12,523	51,600	71,300	63,700
Violent	14,100	13,600	600	3,700	7,100	1,300
Homicide[e]	2,800	2,600	200	400	1,700	200

(continued)

Table 1.3 Estimated Sentenced Prisoners under Federal Correctional Authority, by Most Serious Offense, Sex, and Race, September 30, 2014 (continued)

Most Serious Offense	All Inmates[a]	Male	Female	White[b]	Black[b]	Hispanic
Robbery	7,300	7,100	200	2,600	4,000	600
Other violent	4,000	3,900	200	800	1,400	500
Property	11,600	9,300	2,300	5,100	4,200	1,700
Burglary	400	400	0	100	300	0
Fraud	9,000	7,100	1,900	4,000	3,100	1,500
Other property	2,200	1,800	300	1,000	800	300
Drug[f]	96,500	89,100	7,400	20,800	37,400	36,300
Public order	69,100	66,800	2,200	21,300	22,200	24,200
Immigration	17,200	16,700	500	600	300	16,300
Weapons	30,500	30,000	500	7,600	17,700	4,500
Other	21,400	20,200	1,200	13,000	4,300	3,400
Other/unspecified[g]	1,400	1,300	100	700	300	200

Note: Counts are based on sentenced prisoners under federal jurisdiction regardless of sentence length. Detail may not sum to total due to rounding and missing data. See Methodology.

[a] Includes American Indians and Alaska Natives; Asians; Native Hawaiians and other Pacific Islanders; and persons of two or more races.

[b] Excludes persons of Hispanic or Latino origin and persons of two or more races.

[c] Includes all sentenced inmates under federal jurisdiction regardless of sentence length.

[d] Race totals are rounded to the nearest 100 to accommodate differences in data collection techniques between jurisdictions.

[e] Includes murder and negligent and nonnegligent manslaughter.

[f] Includes trafficking, possession, and other drug offenses.

[g] Includes offenses not classified.

Sources: Bureau of Justice Statistics, Federal Justice Statistics Program, 2014; Carson, E. A. (2015 September). *Prisoners in 2014*, (NCJ Publication No. 248955). p. 30, Appendix Table 5, Washington, DC: U.S. Department of Justice, Bureau of Justice Statistics. Retrieved from http://www.bjs.gov/content /pub/pdf/p14.pdf

Many prisons are operating above capacity.[3] This is a problem in state prisons as well as federal facilities run by the Bureau of Prisons (BOP). According to Carson (2015 September), "The year-end 2014 custody populations of the BOP and 18 states exceeded the maximum measure of their prison facilities' capacity. The BOP and 28 states had more prisoners in custody than their minimum number of beds" (p. 11).

Persons under the Sentence of Death

At year-end 2013, 2,979 inmates incarcerated in 35 states and the Federal Bureau of Prisons were under the sentence of death (Snell, 2014, December). This is a very small percentage of the over 1.5 million persons incarcerated in prison in this country. In the states with the death penalty, the designation of a crime as a capital offense is reserved for murder with defined circumstances which vary by state.

Coker v. Georgia (1977) held that the death sentence could not be imposed for rape, because such a punishment was grossly disproportionate to the injury caused to the victim.

This strongly implied that a death sentence was inappropriate except as punishment for murder. In *Kennedy v. Louisiana* (2008), the Supreme Court decided in a 5 to 4 decision that the death penalty is unconstitutional as a punishment for the rape of a child. Federal capital offenses include murder involving a variety of circumstances ("related to the smuggling of aliens," "first-degree murder," "murder by a federal prisoner," etc.) but also still include espionage and treason (Snell, 2014, p. 8).

Capital cases differ in many ways from non-capital cases. The history, court procedures, and Supreme Court decisions relating to the imposition of the death penalty are unique and a proper analysis of sentencing for capital crimes merits an entire book. We therefore concentrate on sentencing for *non-capital* cases in this text.

The Jail Population

There are several differences between prisons and jails. First, those serving short sentences (usually one to two years or less) are typically housed in jails, while those serving longer sentences are housed in prisons. This usually corresponds to how the differentiation between misdemeanors (less serious offenses) and felonies (more serious offenses) is made in the state. Second, the jail population includes those individuals serving shorter sentences as well as those awaiting trial who got no form of pretrial release. In mid-year 2014, approximately 63 percent of jail inmates had not been convicted, but were awaiting court processing, while about 37 percent had been convicted or were convicted but awaiting sentencing in jail (Minton & Zeng, 2015). Third, unlike prisons, which are mostly run by states or the federal system, jails are usually run by counties or cities.[4] In mid-year 2014, there were 744,600 persons confined in jails in the United States. Up until 2008, the jail population had been increasing annually. From June 2008 to mid-year 2014, however, the jail population declined (Minton & Zeng, 2015). The jail incarceration rate was 234 per 100,000 at mid-year 2014.

The Probation and Parole Populations

Most persons under correctional supervision in the United States are supervised in the community on probation or parole or other types of post-release supervision. According to the Bureau of Justice Statistics (Heberman & Bonczar, 2015 January), probation and parole are defined as follows:

> *Probation* is a court-ordered period of correctional supervision in the community, generally as an alternative to incarceration. In some cases, probation can be a combined sentence of incarceration followed by a period of community supervision.
>
> *Parole* is a period of conditional supervised release in the community following a prison term. It includes parolees released through discretionary or mandatory supervised release from prison, those released through other types of post-custody conditional supervision, and those sentenced to a term of supervised release. (p. 2)

Probation is usually a distinct sentencing option often used for less serious or first time offenders — or at least for those offenders who are not chronic serious offenders. To be placed on **parole or other post-release supervision**, however, one must have already served at least a portion of a prison sentence. Both probationers and parolees often have conditions placed on their release that vary in intensity, including curfews, drug testing, home visits, travel restrictions, etc.

At year-end 2013, 4,751,400 people in the United States were under community supervision. Of those, 3,910,600 offenders were on probation while 853,200 were on parole. Approximately 7 out of 10 persons in the correctional population in the United States were supervised in the community, as opposed to being incarcerated. During 2013, the number of adults under community supervision declined for the fifth consecutive year (Heberman & Bonczar, 2015, January).

The adult probation population is less skewed than the prison population in terms of gender, but still predominantly male. As **Table 1.4** shows, in 2013, 75 percent of probationers were male. This contrasts the makeup of the prison population, which is about 93 percent male. White non-Hispanics comprised 54 percent of the probation population, black non-Hispanics made up 30 percent of the probation population, and Hispanics/Latinos accounted for 14 percent of probationers.

Table 1.4 Characteristics of Adults on Probation, 2000, 2012, 2013

Characteristics	2000	2012	2013
Total	100%	100%	100%
Sex			
Male	78%	76%	75%
Female	22	24	25
Race/Hispanic Origin[a]			
White	54%	54%	54%
Black/African American	31	30	30
Hispanic/Latino	13	13	14
American Indian/Alaska Native	1	1	1
Asian/Native Hawaiian/Pacific Islander	1	1	1
Two or more races	...	...	...
Status of Supervision			
Active	76%	72%	69%
Residential/Other treatment program	...	1	1
Financial conditions remaining	...	1	1
Inactive	9	7	6
Absconder	9	10	9
Supervised out of jurisdiction	3	3	2
Warrant status	...	3	9
Other	3	3	3

(continued)

Table 1.4 Characteristics of Adults on Probation, 2000, 2012, 2013 (continued)

Characteristics	2000	2012	2013
Type of Offense			
Felony	52%	53%	55%
Misdemeanor	46	45	43
Other infractions	2	2	2
Most Serious Offense			
Violent	. . . %	19%	19%
Domestic violence	. . .	4	4
Sex offense	. . .	3	3
Other violent offense	. . .	12	12
Property	. . .	28	29
Drug	24	25	25
Public order	24	17	17
DWI/DUI	18	15	14
Other traffic offenses	6	2	2
Other[b]	52	11	10

Note: Detail may not sum to total due to rounding. Counts based on most recent data and may differ from previously published statistics. See Methodology.
Characteristics based on probationers with known type of status.
. . . Not available.
[a] Excludes persons of Hispanic or Latino origin, unless specified.
[b] Includes violent and property offenses in 2000 because those data were not collected separately.

Source: Bureau of Justice Statistics, Annual Probation Survey, 2000, 2012, and 2013; Heberman, E. J. & Bonczar, T. P. (2015, January). *Probation and parole in the United States, 2013,* (NCJ Publication 248029). p. 17, Appendix Table 3, Washington, DC: U.S. Department of Justice, Bureau of Justice Statistics. Retrieved from http://www.bjs.gov/content/pub/pdf/ppus13.pdf

In terms of the type of offense that landed offenders on probation, 55 percent had committed felonies. This might seem quite shocking and even distressing in terms of public safety. When one looks at the most serious offense that put one on probation, however, it's clear that the largest proportion of offenses were property (29 percent) or drug offenses (25 percent). Although cross-tabulations of felony/misdemeanor with offense classification (violent, property, drug, public order, etc.) were not presented, reports and evaluations of probations (and the experience of the author of this text who worked with those on intensive supervision probation and regular probation) show that relatively few probationers are violent felons. The most common offense type of the majority of those convicted of felonies is a property or drug crime.

Sentencing Goals of Corrections

An important question to ask when imposing any criminal sanction is "What purpose should this sentence serve?" Legal scholars and criminologists have identified several sentencing goals of corrections, also referred to as general justifications of punishment. Understanding each goal and the underlying assumptions about crime causation and the appropriateness of punishment or treatment according to each is critical. Before a sentencing scheme is created and implemented, the goal or goals that the designers want to be in the forefront need to be identified and understood. Once the sentencing goal(s) is/are articulated, we can then better grasp how different goals have or have not been met by various sentencing strategies.

In his book, *Doing Justice* (1976), Andrew von Hirsch stated the following:

> Deciding how much to punish is an agonizing process to which conflicting aspirations compete. The best one can do is decide which aspirations, on balance, appear to be the most important—and build one's theory on them. Any such theory will necessarily oversimplify the moral dilemmas the decision-maker faces. Yet a rationale for allocation can bring a sense of priorities into practical decisions about punishment, difficult as these always will be. (p. 59)

We will examine several sentencing goals of corrections—retribution, specific deterrence, general deterrence, incapacitation, and rehabilitation.

So what is "punishment"? In his book, *Punishing Criminals* (1975), noted legal scholar Ernest van den Haag defined punishment as follows:

> "Punishment" is a deprivation, or suffering, imposed by law. Illness, loss, or wrongful imprisonment, although just as painful, are not punishment any more than pain, injury, or death, even when suffered by a fleeing suspect: suffering may be said to be punitive only when it is court-imposed retribution for violating laws. (p. 8)

We differentiate non-utilitarian or "backward-looking" sentencing goals (which have no "utility" or purpose beyond punishment that is "deserved") from utilitarian or "forward-looking" goals of sentencing, which have a utility beyond punishment— meaning some good should come from the imposition of punishment. Retribution is the only non-utilitarian or backward-looking goal. Deterrence, incapacitation, and rehabilitation are each utilitarian or forward-looking goals, and they seek some purpose in delivering the punishment beyond punishment for punishment's sake.

Van den Haag (1975) differentiated punishment from vengeance, stating the following:

> Unlike vengeance, retribution is imposed by courts after a guilty plea, or a trial, in which the accused has been found guilty of committing a crime. Prescribed by the law broken, and proportioned to the gravity of the offense committed, retribution is not inflicted to gratify or compensate anyone who suffered a loss or was harmed by the crime—even if it does so—but to enforce the law and to vindicate the legal order. (p. 11)

Although van den Haag considered multiple sentencing goals or general justifications of punishment, he placed a great deal of focus on retribution. This is the first goal we will consider.

The Non-Utilitarian/Backward-Looking Goal of Retribution

Retribution is considered the only non-utilitarian goal of sentencing because it looks back to the crime that occurred (thus the label "backward-looking") and punishes the act. In other words, retribution is considered "punishment for punishment's sake" and there is no utility or purpose for imposing the criminal sanction except for exacting punishment that is deserved given the harm done to the victim and/or society in general.

Van den Haag (1975) explained:

> Retribution affects the future in much the same way as the payment of debts does. Debts must be paid in the first place because they are owed, because one has promised to pay them. Retribution must be paid because it is owed, because it has been threatened, and a threat is a negative promise. The payment of debts (or of retribution) fulfills an obligation undertaken in the past. Once undertaken, obligations are independent of the current or future usefulness of meeting them. (p. 14)

He explained the idea of a cost of crime as follows: "If we keep in mind that society owes the exaction, it is helpful to conceive of retribution as the price exacted from the offender for his offense, the cost to him" (pp. 17–18).

Two key concepts associated with retribution are **proportionality** and **equity**.

Proportionality (otherwise known as "just deserts" or "commensurate deserts" (von Hirsch, 1976)) means that the severity of the sanction should reflect the seriousness of the crime. More serious crimes should be punished more harshly than less serious crimes. This means, for example, that murderers should be punished more harshly than pickpockets.

The concept of proportionality or "deserts" assumes that there is a consensus about the ranking of seriousness of crimes. We will discuss approaches to determining offense seriousness in Chapter 8. Legislatures have made judgments about offense seriousness by setting different penalties for different offenses. Sentencing commissions in various states, and the federal system, have put enormous time and effort into creating "offense gravity" scores.

Equity means that similar crimes should be punished in a similar manner. For example, all offenders who committed an armed robbery with the same legally relevant characteristics should be given the same (or "equal") punishment. In his book, *An Essay on Crimes and Punishments*, one of the most famous representatives of the Classical school of criminology, Cesare Beccaria (1801), emphasized that the basis of punishment should be the "injury done to society" by the criminal act and not based on the intentions of the criminal (p. 27).[5]

Andrew von Hirsch has been one prominent advocate of the just deserts philosophy. In his book, *Doing Justice* (1976), von Hirsch presented a perspective that resulted from the work of the Committee for the Study of Incarceration, which first met in 1971 to explore the use of imprisonment as a criminal sanction. His book explored what should be done with the criminal offender once he/she has been convicted of a crime. He made the point that the practice of incarceration in the United States has been too widespread and that the experiences of those incarcerated have been exceedingly harsh. He asserted that the state should be able to clearly demonstrate why a particular sentence was handed down and that the burden of proving justification for incarceration should be especially high.

He identified principles that he and the committee believed should guide the punishment of criminal offenders. He emphasized that punishment should reflect the seriousness of the defendant's offense(s) and stated "When the offender is punished commensurately with his offense, the state is entitled to sacrifice his rights to that degree because that is what he deserves" (p. 70). The writings of von Hirsch concluded that the focus should be on **punishing the offense** rather than treating the offender.

Some sentencing reforms which touted retribution as a sentencing goal of corrections have encouraged closely related reforms for corrections. These include limiting the use of incarceration to the most serious crimes and developing community sanctions which would function as alternatives to incarceration for less serious offenders. The focus on sentencing uniformity (i.e., "equity") has been emphasized, as punishment would be based on legally relevant characteristics, such as the severity of the conviction offense. Consequently, judicial discretion should be limited and efforts to standardize sentencing have been promoted.

Scholars have used the terms "punishment," "retribution," and "justice" interchangeably. In his 1975 book, *Punishing Criminals*, legal scholar Ernest van den Haag discussed the notion that punishment may have utility beyond exacting justice. He posed the question, "Do we punish for the sake of utility—to modify future behavior of the convict (and of others)—or do we punish for the sake of justice?" (p. 24). He concluded that there is no need to choose one to the exclusion of the other, stating "No such choice need be made, for although utility and justice often do compete in the criminal justice system, they do not exclude each other" (p. 24).

Utilitarian/Forward-Looking Goals

Utilitarian or "forward-looking" goals of corrections have some purpose beyond punishment for punishment's sake. The imposition of the sentence should bring some good in the future. This may involve the prevention of crime through deterrence, incapacitation, or rehabilitation.

Deterrence

The idea of deterrence is to prevent crime or prevent it from getting worse.

Beccaria (1801) stated, "The end of punishment, therefore, is no other, than to prevent the criminal from doing further injury to society, and to prevent others from committing the like offence" (p. 41). This statement captures the essences of the two types of deterrence—**specific deterrence** (also called individual deterrence) and **general deterrence.**

Specific Deterrence

Specific deterrence applies to individuals who have already committed a crime and received a punishment. When a sanction acts as a specific deterrent, the punishment that the offender received was so unpleasant that the offender does not want to experience the pains of the sanction again and thus does not continue committing crime. In his book, *Punishment and Deterrence* (1974), noted deterrence theorist Johannes Andenaes stated, "By individual prevention we mean the effect of punishment on the punished" (p. 9).

Any sanction could potentially serve as a specific deterrent if the pain of that sanction deters the individual from repeating crime. Overcrowding, physical and sexual abuse, and lack of freedom may be conditions in prison that are experienced by the offender to be so horrific that he or she decides never to commit crime again, because he or she never wants to go through the pains of imprisonment again. Likewise, a sentence to a year of house arrest could serve as an effective specific deterrent. An individual on house arrest may miss the freedom of going out and doing what he or she pleases. The pain of house arrest, which is lack of freedom, would therefore deter the offender from recidivating.

It is also important to understand that sanctions affect different people differently. Andenaes (1974) stated, "The question is not whether punishment has deterrent effects, but rather under what conditions and to what extent the deterrent purpose is effected" (p. 84).

The experience of a short term jail sentence for committing a theft, for example, may be very different for an employed, married, upper class male who owns a home, compared to an unemployed, single, homeless man. That single sanction—short term incarceration—may affect the two men in different ways. For the first man, incarceration would compromise his job and put strains on his marriage. This man is used to living in a spacious home with his wife and has much to lose by being incarcerated. Being incarcerated and the bleak conditions of jail (loss of privacy, loss of control over one's life, overcrowding, fear of assault) may be enough to deter this man from ever committing a crime again. The homeless man, however, may see jail as a way to get three meals a day and a roof over his head. Instead of the sanction of jail serving as a specific deterrent, it might actually encourage this man to commit more thefts (or other crimes) after release because jail is a "step up" from this man's life situation.

General Deterrence

The goal of **general deterrence** suggests that if the (general) public is aware that a certain punishment will follow the commission of a crime, then would-be offenders will be prevented from (or deterred from) committing that crime. Andenaes (1974) described the goal of general deterrence in the following way:

> By general prevention we mean the ability of criminal law and its enforcement to make citizens law abiding. If general prevention were 100 percent effective there would be no crime at all. General prevention may depend on the mere frightening or deterrent effect of punishment—the risk of discovery and punishment outweighing the temptation to commit crime. (p. 7)

A good example of a sanction aimed at promoting general deterrence was the Michigan Felony Firearms Statute—a mandatory sentencing law which went into effect in Michigan in 1977. This law required a two-year sentence to be added on to the base sentence for a felony if that felony was committed with a firearm. This law required that every person in the state of Michigan who was convicted of committing or attempting to commit a violent felony with a gun would get a mandatory two-year prison sentence, above and beyond what he or she would receive for the commission of the felony. Parole was not possible and the sentence could not be suspended. This law was highly publicized—billboards and bumper stickers in the Detroit area read "One With a Gun Gets You Two." The purpose of the law was to decrease gun violence by imposing a strict sanction, thus deterring the general public from committing a violent felony with a gun (Loftin & McDowall, 1981).

For a sanction to have the possibility of being an effective deterrent, it must be known to the general public. The Michigan gun law was unique, in that it was a widely publicized sanction. Unless would-be offenders study state or federal statutes, mandatory sentencing laws, and/or sentencing guidelines, they may not be aware of potential punishments, and these punishments may not serve as effective general deterrents. A mandatory minimum sentence of ten years for armed robbery can only be an effective general deterrent if the public is aware of the sanction.

It is also important to note that whether a sanction serves as a general deterrent varies between persons. Andeneas (1974) asserted, "Citizens are not equally receptive to the general-preventive effects of the penal system" (p. 46). Just like with specific deterrence, in the case of general deterrence, sanctions or the threat or observation of such sanctions have different effects on different people. This may reflect various social positions (what the potential offender has "to lose" if punished) or differing intellectual capabilities or understandings of the sanction.

In *An Essay on Crimes and Punishment* (1801), Cesare Beccaria outlined his perspectives on crime causation and his suggestions of how to devise a fair system of punishment. He viewed man as a rational creature who, when faced with a decision, including the decision of whether to commit a crime, weighs the positive and negative consequences associated with his choice. The individual chooses the alternative that maximizes pleasure and minimizes pain. Deterrence theorists assume that people calculate the costs and benefits of committing crime and choose the option that brings the most benefits with the fewest consequences.

For example, consider a recent college graduate, Jeremy, who has just earned his college degree in criminal justice. Jeremy has grand aspirations of getting a new car, buying a house, and going on a vacation to celebrate his graduation. But of course, these things cost money. Jeremy just got offered a job as a probation officer. His starting salary is $25,000. If Jeremy worked at his job for ten years, and got a modest raise each year, he could expect to earn about $275,000 over ten years. And, of course that's before taxes. So, in reality Jeremy can expect to earn about $185,000 in ten years. But there's another alternative. Jeremy could rob a bank. He could earn $185,000 tax-free in about one-half of an hour—the time it takes to rob the bank. Jeremy estimates that the chance of getting caught is small, however, he realizes that if he's caught that he will likely be convicted and sentenced to prison.

According to deterrence theory, if Jeremy "calculates" that committing a robbery will bring more pleasure than pain, then he will decide to commit the robbery. If he feels the risks of being apprehended are out of his comfort zone and he knows about the horrors of prison life (as he did just get a degree in criminal justice), then he will decide not to rob the bank. In accordance with Beccaria and other deterrence theorists, whatever choice Jeremy makes will be as a result of a rational calculation. He will choose the alternative that he perceives will bring him the greatest amount of pleasure and the least amount of pain.

Beccaria's suggestions about how to prevent crime through sanctioning offenders represent arguments for the criminal sanction to act as both a specific and general deterrent. Beccaria emphasized that sanctions need to be **certain, swift,** and **minimally severe.**

Beccaria (1801) suggested "[c]rimes are more effectually prevented by the *certainty*, than the *severity* of punishment" (p. 94). Andenaes (1974) echoed the importance of certainty of punishment for a sanction to serve as an effective general deterrent. He noted that how efficient the criminal justice system is affects the probability of apprehension and conviction and therefore affects the "calculation" of costs versus benefits when a person considers committing a crime.

Beccaria (1801) highlighted the importance of what he called "immediate punishment" (swiftness of imposition of the sanction) and asserted:

> An immediate punishment is more useful; because the smaller the interval of time between the punishment and the crime, the stronger and more lasting will be the association of the two ideas of *Crime* and *Punishment*; so that they may be considered, one as the cause, and the other as the unavoidable and necessary effect. (pp. 73–74)

A swift punishment would then enhance both general and specific deterrence. The offender and would-be offenders could see that punishment is a real consequence to offending.

According to Beccaria, the severity of the punishment was only to be enough to prevent potential offenders from committing the crime, because they feared the pain associated with the sanction. Beccaria stated, "Such punishments, therefore, and such a mode of inflicting them, ought to be chosen, as will make the strongest and most lasting impressions on the minds of others, with the least torment to the body of the criminal" (pp. 41–42).

He explained the importance of minimizing severity, stating "A punishment to be just, should have only that degree of severity which is sufficient to deter others" (p. 103).

Deterrence theorists seek to ascertain the minimum amount of punishment needed to prevent crime. They seek to increase the certainty and celerity (swiftness) of the imposition of the criminal sanction, while minimizing the severity of the punishment (Beccaria, 1801). What is unknown is how much punishment will deter an individual from committing a crime. Criminologists routinely measure crime rates and recidivism rates—those who *do* offend, not those who *do not* offend. It is difficult to assess whether a sanction and the manner in which it was handed down served as a general or specific deterrent. Regarding general deterrence, Andenaes (1974) stated, "General prevention is more concerned with the psychology of those obedient to the law than with the psychology of criminals" (p. 42). Understanding and predicting human behavior is, indeed, a difficult, if not impossible, objective.

Incapacitation

The goal of incapacitation is to physically separate offenders from society so that they cannot commit more crimes in society while serving their sentence. Incarceration is the most obvious sanction that can serve the goal of incapacitation. Other than the case of prison escapes, inmates cannot reoffend in society while incarcerated.[6] House arrest may also serve the goal of incapacitation to some extent. Convicted offenders are confined in their residences for the vast majority of their sentences and are allowed out of their homes only for a few specific activities (doctor's appointments, church, etc.). Thus, their probability of offending in the community is greatly decreased by their sanction of house arrest.[7]

Incapacitation is a utilitarian goal of corrections because it has a "utility" or purpose beyond punishment for punishment's sake—in this case preventing future crimes by physically separating law breakers from society. In his book, *Thinking About Crime* (1975), James Q. Wilson concluded, "Wicked people exist" and that "nothing avails except to set them apart from innocent people" (p. 235). Separating those who are too dangerous to live in free society by incarcerating them is the essence of the goal of incapacitation.

Critics of so-called mass incarceration have likened the way the United States incarcerates its prisoners to an addiction. In *Addicted to Incarceration* (2009), Travis Pratt suggested that correctional policy makers have an "incarceration addiction." He asserted that like substance abusers who are often in denial about the harm to oneself and others that stems from addiction, policymakers fail to acknowledge the harm done by a widespread reliance on incarceration as punishment for a vast number of offenders. Correctional decision makers may manipulate statistics and provide misinformation to the public to fuel their support of incarcerating more and more people and justify their own policy decisions. Pratt likened the justification of policies that increase incarceration to the rationalizations addicts make that it's "just a drink," with no acknowledgement of the consequences of the addiction.

Cullen and Jonson (2012) highlighted the need, however, to consider **the incapacitation effect of imprisonment**. This involves calculating, through complex statistical procedures, how much crime is prevented by incapacitating people. Cullen and Jonson suggested that imprisonment is being overused as a sanction in this country and encouraged the use of alternatives to incarceration in the community. They acknowledged, however, some positive consequences of incapacitation and concluded, "There is an incapacitation effect, and it is meaningfully large. Prisons prevent crime. Letting people out of prison will increase criminal victimization" (p. 101).

Other researchers have suggested that the increased use of incarceration has a very small effect on crime, and is very expensive. Pratt (2009) provided estimates that to get a 1 percent decrease in crime, one would have to spend between $5.5 billion and $11 billion. Pratt (2009) calculated that each time the prison population is doubled there is a 5–10 percent drop in crime. Putting money into corrections, and specifically into prisons, takes away from other areas, such as education. While researchers may disagree about the impact of incarceration on the crime rate, most would certainly advocate the incarceration of clearly dangerous offenders. We will revisit the monetary and social costs of incarceration in Chapter 10.

Selective Incapacitation

The goal of selective incapacitation is to identify "career criminals" early in their criminal careers and imprison them for long terms, in order to prevent their future criminal behavior and protect society. So, who are "career criminals"? In *Criminal Careers and Career Criminals* (Volume 1, 1986), Blumstein, Cohen, Roth, and Visher identified the elements of career criminality. They drew on criminological research that has shown that a small percentage of criminals are responsible for a large proportion of crime. Career criminals are those offenders who have high rates of criminal activity, who commit serious crimes, and who have long "careers" of active criminality. Selective incapacitation rests on the notion that we can use statistical models to detect which offenders will be career criminals early on and use preventive incapacitation to incarcerate these offenders in order to protect society and potential victims.

Blumstein and colleagues (1986) acknowledged that participation in criminality is not a rare phenomenon and estimated that 25–45 percent of urban males have been arrested for a non-traffic offense by age 18. Most offenders are not career criminals, however. A **high rate of offending** is one characteristic of career criminality. Whereas most active offenders commit only a few crimes per year, a small percentage—the career criminals—commit over 100 crimes per year. Career criminals tend to **commit serious crimes**—meaning violent crimes and serious property offenses, such as burglary. And career criminals have **substantial career lengths** (age at which the offender first commits a crime to the age when he or she commits their last crime), compared to most offenders. For the vast majority of adult offenders committing serious offenses, criminal careers only last about five years. Offenders still committing crimes well into their thirties or forties are unusual, and long career length is another dimension of career criminality.

Wolfgang, Figlio, and Sellin (1972) followed a cohort of people born in 1945 in Philadelphia. They defined "chronic" juvenile offenders as those who had been arrested at least five times by age 18. These individuals comprised only 6 percent of the Philadelphia cohort, yet accounted for 52 percent of all the arrests among the members of the cohort. The chronic offenders began committing delinquent acts at an earlier age than their peers and were committing more serious acts. The finding that a small percentage of offenders were responsible for a large proportion of offending caught the attention of these researchers. Research following Wolfgang and associates' study has included investigations into if, when, and how to identify chronic offenders early in their careers. Scales used to classify whether prisoners are ready to be released that include indicators of career criminality have been utilized by parole boards.

Offender-based policies suggest that if we identify which offenders will be career criminals and extend the imprisonment sentences of these offenders, we will most effectively utilize limited prison space. If we could identify these career criminals early in their careers, we could potentially prevent a large proportion of crimes by incarcerating them. Blumstein and associates, however, forecasted that the crime reduction efforts from selective incapacitation would be modest and would not exceed ten percent.

Blumstein and his associates (1986) also noted that there are some serious ethical issues in predicting future criminality. One concern involves which variables one could consider in building prediction models. Consider the issue of race. If being African American was associated with career criminality, should we then selectively incapacitate based on this extra-legal characteristic? The possibility that the selection process could disproportionately affect minority group members is a serious ethical issue. What about socio-economic status? Or should juvenile record be considered, when in many states, one's juvenile record can be expunged when he or she becomes legally an adult? Many would suggest that predictors that have nothing to do with blameworthiness not be included in prediction models.

Another uncertainty is how accurate any prediction model would be. No prediction model can be perfect and two types of classification errors can occur. "False positives" occur when the model would predict that an offender would become a career criminal, when, in fact, that person would not have continued in crime. If that person was incarcerated for a lengthy period because he or she was predicted to be a habitual offender, their incarceration would not have prevented any crimes, but would rather have been unnecessary and would have robbed that person of their freedom. Alternatively, "false negatives" refer to individuals who were deemed low risk by a statistical model, yet continue to commit frequent and serious offenses for a long period of time. These are people that prediction models miss and whose criminal behavior could have been prevented if they had been incapacitated.

Even before the Blumstein and associates' work, von Hirsch (1976) found what he called "predictive restraint" in the 1970s—incarcerating persons who were predicted by judges and parole boards to re-offend—troublesome because of the inability for decision makers to accurately predict which offenders would indeed re-offend. He considered the practice unjust because it could allow the incarceration of persons who were predicted to re-offend, but in reality would not have (the false positives). These persons were being deprived of their freedom because they were mistakenly predicted (by so-called "experts") to reoffend.

There are also some practical issues that challenge the efficacy of selective incapacitation. One involves a "replacement effect"—that if a career criminal, for example a drug dealer, is put in prison for a lengthy sentence to prevent his future offending, that someone else will just replace him in the drug hierarchy. This would undermine the utility of selective incapacitation in preventing drug offenses.

Reforms such as three strikes laws are, on paper, compatible with the practice of selective incapacitation, but we will assess whether this holds true in practice in later chapters. Locking up serious, repeat offenders who have accrued numerous strikes is thought to protect the public from offenders who are predicted to reoffend if released back into the community. Some states also indicate separate "add-on" enhancements for prior offending within their guidelines (e.g., Ohio). Others make prior record level one of the two criteria (in addition to offense seriousness) in setting presumptive sentencing ranges (e.g., North Carolina and Minnesota, among others).

Rehabilitation

Rehabilitation is perhaps the most obviously utilitarian sentencing goal of corrections. By serving one's sentence, the offender is "treated" according to his or her needs using various approaches that help re-socialize the offender so that he or she is not predisposed to continue offending after the sentence is complete. Treatment is individualized to the offender because it is thought that different factors lead to each offender's criminality.

In his book, *The Decline of the Rehabilitative Ideal* (1981), Francis A. Allen acknowledged the complexity of the term "rehabilitative ideal" and concomitant social policies, but provided the following definition:

> One may begin by saying that the rehabilitative ideal is the notion that a primary purpose of penal treatment is to effect changes in the characters, attitudes, and behavior of convicted offenders, so as to strengthen the social defense against unwanted behavior, but also contribute to the welfare and satisfaction of offenders. (p. 2)

Cullen and Jonson (2012) more recently defined rehabilitation in the following way: "Rehabilitation is a planned correctional intervention that targets for change internal and/or social criminogenic factors with the goal of reducing recidivism and, where possible, of improving other aspects of an offender's life" (p. 149).

The notion that offenders should be rehabilitated, as opposed to merely punished, is compatible with the Positivist school of thought that originated in the 1800s. The Positivist school views an individual's behavior, including criminality, as being determined by factors outside one's control. These factors may be biological, psychological, or social. The sociological approach is dominant in the field of criminology. Those who take this approach might point to an offender growing up in poverty and having substandard educational opportunities as influences (or in a pure Positivist approach—determinants) on his involvement in drug or property crimes in later life. Biological approaches may look at hormonal imbalances, such as high levels of testosterone as playing a role in violent crime. A psychological perspective might consider the effect of a child observing an unhealthy, abusive relationship between his parents on the likelihood of him committing acts of domestic violence as an adult.

What all these perspectives have in common is that unlike the Classical school, which assumes people are rational and *choose* whether to commit crime, the Positivist school rests on the notion that factors beyond one's control influence, determine, or at least predispose one to criminality.[8] In *The Decline of the Rehabilitative Ideal* (1981), Allen, cautioned that the rehabilitative ideal "... does not specify a theory about crime causation" yet he admitted that the rehabilitative ideal is more consistent with determinism than free will.

If involvement in crime is beyond the control of the individual, it does not make sense to punish the offender. Instead, treatment of individual "pathologies," whether they be biological, psychological, or social/structural is the preferred way to respond to crime according to the rehabilitative ideal. A key concept in rehabilitation is to provide individualized treatment to the offender, based on an assessment of what is thought to have caused the individual to become involved in crime. The focus of rehabilitation is on *treating the offender* as opposed to punishing the offense.

A wide variety of treatments come under the umbrella of rehabilitation programs. For those offenders who experienced trauma in early childhood, individual therapy, group therapy, and/or anger management classes may be prescribed. Other offenders suffer from addictions which fueled their crimes of theft and robbery. These offenders may best be treated with 12-step programs, such as Alcoholics Anonymous, Narcotics Anonymous, or Gamblers Anonymous. Sex offenders are often "treated" by participation in very specialized programs which try to address the impulses and desires that fuel sexual offending and help curb these impulses. Other approaches target economic disadvantage and inferior educational opportunities that are disproportionately seen in the United States correctional population. For these offenders, prison programs, such as job skills training and educational support (from basic literacy to GED or even college classes) help make offenders more hirable upon release and encourage pro-social values, such as a positive work ethic. Through serving one's sentence, one is empowered through treatment to return to society with the tools necessary to stay away from crime.

As a utilitarian goal of sentencing, rehabilitation is quite appealing. If, during the time one is serving his or her sentence, he or she can be "rehabilitated" (through whatever methods or programs are deemed appropriate) and empowered to refrain from criminal conduct, sentencing would be quite productive. It would serve to prevent future crimes and serve a purpose beyond punishment for punishment's sake. Questions that have been raised since the inception of rehabilitation programs for offenders include whether they work and under what contingencies and for which offenders various programs are effective. This question will be explored in Chapters 3 and 11 with a discussion of a study by Robert Martinson and a review of results from subsequent studies.

In their book, *Reaffirming Rehabilitation* (1982), Cullen and Gilbert argued the value of rehabilitation, stating "Rehabilitation is the only justification of criminal sanctioning that obligates the state to care for an offender's needs or welfare" (p. 247). Admittedly, rehabilitation promises a payoff to society in the form of offenders transformed into law-abiding, productive citizens who no longer desire to victimize the public.

Both imprisonment and community based correctional supervision sentences can serve the goals of rehabilitation. Day reporting centers, which are considered "intermediate sanctions" grew in popularity in the mid-1990s and early 2000s. This sentence requires offenders, who are also sentenced to either regular probation or intensive supervision probation, to physically show up to a center daily when not at work or in school. Staff at the center review the offender's criminal and personal history and assign him or her a set of programs to participate in, based on what they determine to be the offender's specific needs (see Marciniak, 1999, 2000 for general discussions of day reporting centers). These may include adult basic skills (like writing a check), literacy, parenting skills, anger management, AA, NA, group therapy, and individual therapy, among other treatments.

Regardless of whether the programming takes place within prison walls, at a day reporting center, at various community agencies, or through 12-step programs in the community, the goal of rehabilitation is the same—to help treat offenders based on their individual needs and empower them to become law abiding by the completion of their sentence.

The Compatibility or Incompatibility of Goals of Sentencing and Approaches to Sentencing

The various sentencing goals of corrections rest on some very different assumptions regarding what causes crime and how and why criminals should be punished or treated.

The stated purposes of sentencing reforms (mandatory sentencing, three strikes laws, and sentencing guidelines), however, often incorporate multiple, seemingly incompatible goals of sentencing. We will discuss these issues in depth in Chapter 8 when we examine philosophical challenges to sentencing practices.

In his reflections on the then indeterminate sentencing practices in the federal system, federal judge Marvin Frankel (1973) found problematic Congress's (and states' for that matter) lack of consensus on what the purposes of punishment *should* be. Should the ultimate goal of sentencing be retribution, rehabilitation, deterrence, or incapacitation? In the preface of his book, *Criminal Sentences: Law Without Order* (1973), Frankel posed the question, "If we mean both to punish and rehabilitate, is such a thing possible?" (p. viii).

How can a sanction, like imprisonment, serve both the goals of retribution and rehabilitation, if the assumptions made about crime causation are so different? Retribution rests on the concept that people are rational. People make free will decisions, and because of this, if they choose to commit crime, they deserve to be punished. The goal of rehabilitation is to treat or "cure" offenders and assumes that criminals are suffering from some type of pathology. Because offenders are "sick," they cannot be held strictly responsible for their criminal behavior. According to the rehabilitative ideal, offenders may be "treated" in prison through a variety of programs that help address the underlying causes for their criminal behavior.

The next several chapters trace the history of sentencing practices in the United States. We will discuss what is meant by "reform" and what led to modern sentencing reforms. As we discuss various reforms, one needs to bear in mind the different sentencing goals of corrections. Then one can ascertain if reforms have been successful in meeting their stated goals.

Summary

This chapter introduced many of the main concepts and terms that we will detail in the text. A main point is that someone convicted of the same offense could potentially serve very different sentences in terms of length and how he is ultimately released back into society, depending on where he is sentenced. The fifty states, Washington, DC, and the federal system all have different sentencing processes.

Indeterminate sentencing schemes allow judges wide discretion in handing down sentence type and length. Judges are only constrained by broad statutes. A parole board ultimately decides when an offender will be released from prison. Determinate sentencing refers to sentencing schemes in which the length of the sentence is fixed by the judge at the time of sentencing, with the maximum term being prescribed by the legislature. Commission-based guidelines, mandatory minimum sentences, and three strikes laws are variants of determinate sentencing approaches.

A consideration of the correctional population in the United States is essential to appreciating the effects of sentencing practices. The prison population in the United States has more than quadrupled in the last 35 years. Part of this rise is attributed to harsh sentencing practices. Community-based punishments, however, comprise about seventy percent of the entire correctional population in the United States.

It is also important to understand the various sentencing goals of corrections—retribution, specific deterrence, general deterrence, incapacitation, and rehabilitation. It is integral to the study of sentencing to understand the assumptions made about the offender according to each goal. Some goals are seemingly contradictory, but as we will see in the text, multiple goals are often simultaneously stated within a jurisdiction's declaration of sentencing purposes.

Discussion Questions

1. On a continuum in which 1 is the view that people have complete free will and 100 means people's behavior is completely determined by outside factors (upbringing, socioeconomic status, biological composition), where would you position your view on the causes of criminal behavior? Explain why.
2. What sentencing goal of corrections do you think should guide judges' sentencing decisions?
   a) Does your answer vary by the *type* of crime committed (e.g., violent vs. property, whether the crime is a sex offense, harm to the victim)?
   b) Does your answer vary by the age of the victim (is he or she considered an adult)?
   c) Does your answer vary by the mental capacity of the offender (for example, his or her IQ)?
3. From the knowledge you have gained in your criminal justice classes up to this point in your education, do you favor an indeterminate sentencing approach or a determinate sentencing approach? Explain!
4. What role (if any) do you think prior record should play in determining a sentence for a convicted offender? Give reasons for your response.
5. Which of the four states (Texas, South Carolina, North Carolina, or Ohio) do you feel has the most ideal sentencing practices for forcible rape? Why? Explain your answer.

Notes

1. Note that states use different labels to define the act. The term "forcible rape" is used to describe this crime, as it meets the definition of forcible rape from the Federal Bureau of Investigation's Uniform Crime Report, which is "Penetration, no matter how slight, of the vagina or anus with any body part or object, or oral penetration by a sex organ of another person, without the consent of the victim." https://www.fbi.gov/about-us/cjis/ucr/crime-in-the-u.s/2013/crime-in-the-u.s.-2013/violent-crime/rape

2. Since the state prison population accounts for about 87 percent of the entire prison population in the United States, a smaller percentage decrease in the state prison population (.5%), compared with larger percentage increase in the federal prison population (.8%) still yielded a decrease in the overall prison population from 2009 to 2010 (.3%).

3. According to Carson (2015 September), design capacity is "The number of inmates that planners or architects intended for the facility." Operational capacity is "The number of inmates that can be accommodated based on a facility's staff, existing programs, and services." Rated capacity is "The number of beds or inmates assigned by a rating official to institutions within a jurisdiction." Lowest capacity is "The minimum number of beds across three capacity measures: design capacity, operational capacity, and rated capacity." Highest capacity is "the maximum number of beds reported across the three capacity measures: design capacity, operational capacity, and rated capacity" (p.26).

4. According to Henrichson and Delaney (2012, July 20), "the corrections systems in Connecticut, Delaware, Rhode Island, and Vermont have a unified structure, meaning that jails and prisons are operated by the state rather than county and state jurisdictions, respectively" (p. 8).

5. Note, however, that Beccaria did advocate that criminal attempts deserve punishment, though not as much as completed crimes.

6. Prisoners can, however, offend against fellow inmates and correctional officials within the prison. Physical and sexual assaults, thefts, and other crimes occur within prisons.

7. There have been anecdotal accounts of offenders sentenced to house arrest dealing drugs on their front porches or within the allowed perimeters of movement, however.

8. The "pure Classical" school views man as rational and responsible for all decisions, including the decision to commit crime. This perspective is inherent in the sentencing goals of retribution and general and specific deterrence. The "pure Positivist" school sees behavior as determined and outside of one's control, a view compatible with rehabilitation, which encourages treatment. Most criminologists see behavior as a mesh of the two perspectives. So-called "soft-determinism" sees man as basically rational and responsible for his choices, but acknowledges that social, psychological, and biological factors may predispose or increase the risk of becoming involved in crime.

References

Alarid, L. F., & Reichel, P. L. (2013). *Corrections*. Upper Saddle River, NJ: Pearson Education.

Allen, F. A. (1981). *The decline of the rehabilitative ideal: Penal policy and social purpose*. New Haven: Yale University Press.

Andenaes, J. (1974). *Punishment and deterrence*. Ann Arbor, MI: The University of Michigan Press.

Austin, J., Clark, J., Hardyman, P., & Henry, D. A. (1999). The impact of 'three strikes and you're out'. *Punishment and Society, 1*(2), 131–162.

Beccaria, C., & Voltaire (1801). *An essay on crimes and punishments, translated from the Italian of Beccaria; with commentary, by Voltaire, translated from the French* (Rev. 5th ed). Retrieved from http://hdl.handle.net/2027/njp.32101068978202

Blumstein, A., & Cohen, J. (1973). A theory of the stability of punishment. *Journal of Criminal Law and Criminology, 64*(2), 198–207. Retrieved from http://web.b.ebscohost .com.pitt.idm.oclc.org/ehost/pdfviewer/pdfviewer?vid=15&sid=fb026bc0-f4fb -4130-9c8e-393358206994%40sessionmgr110&hid=109

Blumstein, A., Cohen, J., Roth, J. A., & Visher, C. A. (1986). *Criminal careers and "career criminals"*. (Vol. 1). Washington, DC: National Academy Press.

Bureau of Justice Statistics. (1999). *Correctional populations in the United States, 1996 (Executive Summary)* (NCJ Publication No. 171684). Washington, DC: U.S. Department of Justice. Retrieved from http://bjs.ojp.usdoj.gov/index.cfm?ty=pbdetail&iid=742

Carson, E. A. (2014 September). *Prisoners in 2013*, (NCJ Publication No. NCJ 247282). Washington, DC: U.S. Department of Justice, Bureau of Justice Statistics. Retrieved from http://www.bjs.gov/content/pub/pdf/p13.pdf

Carson, E. A. (2015 September). *Prisoners in 2014*, (NCJ Publication No. 248955). Washington, DC: U.S. Department of Justice, Bureau of Justice Statistics. Retrieved from http://www.bjs.gov/content/pub/pdf/p14.pdf

Coker v. Georgia, 433 U.S. 584 (1977).

Cullen, F. T., & Gilbert, K. E. (1982). *Reaffirming rehabilitation*. Cincinnati, OH: Anderson Publishing.

Cullen, F. T., & Jonson, C. L. (2012). *Correctional theory: Context and consequences*. Thousand Oaks, CA: Sage.

Diroll, D. J. (2011). *H.B. 86 Summary: The 2011 changes to criminal and juvenile law*. Columbus, OH: Ohio Criminal Sentencing Commission. Retrieved from http://www.opd.ohio.gov/Legislation/Le_OhioCrimSentSummary.pdf

Ditton, P. M., & Wilson, D. J. (1999). *Truth in sentencing in state prisons*. Washington, DC: U.S. Department of Justice, Bureau of Justice Statistics.

Frankel, M. E. (1973). *Criminal sentences: Law without order*. New York: Hill and Wang.

Gray, M. (2009, April). A brief history of New York's Rockefeller drug laws. *Time*. Retrieved from http://www.time.com/time/nation/article/0,8599,1888864-2,00.html.

Heberman, E. J., & Bonczar, T. P. (2015, January). *Probation and parole in the United States, 2013*, (NCJ Publication 248029). Washington, DC: U.S. Department of Justice, Bureau of Justice Statistics. Retrieved from http://www.bjs.gov/content/pub/pdf/ppus13.pdf

Henrichson, C., & Delaney, R. (2012). *The price of prisons*. New York: Vera Institute of Justice. Retrieved from http://www.vera.org/sites/default/files/resources/downloads/price-of-prisons-updated-version-021914.pdf

Kennedy v. Louisiana, 554 U.S. 407 (2008).

Loftin, C., & McDowall, D. (1981). "One with a gun gets you two": Mandatory sentencing and firearms violence in Detroit. *Annals of the American Academy of Political and Social Sciences. 455*(1), 150–167.

Marciniak, L. M. (1999). The use of day reporting as an intermediate sanction: A study of offender targeting and compliance. *The Prison Journal. 79*(2), 205–227.

Marciniak, L. M. (2000). The addition of day reporting to intensive supervision probation: A comparison of recidivism rates. *Federal Probation. 64*(91), 34–40.

Martinison, R. (1974). What works? Questions and answers about prison reform. *The Public Interest, 35*, 22–54.

Minton, T. D., & Zeng, Z. (2015, June). *Jail inmates at midyear 2014 — Statistical tables* (NCJ Publication No. 248629). Washington, DC: U.S. Department of Justice, Bureau of Justice Statistics. Retrieved from http://www.bjs.gov/content/pub/pdf/jim14.pdf

North Carolina Sentencing and Policy Advisory Commission. *Structured sentencing training and reference manual: Applies to offenses committed on or after December 1, 2009*. Retrieved from www.nccourts.org/courts/crs/councils/spac/documents/sstrainingmanual_09.pdf

Ohio Rev. Code Ann § 2907.01, Anderson, 2002.

Ohio Code §2907.02, Rape. Retrieved from http://codes.ohio.gov/orc/2907.02

Pratt, T. C. (2009). *Addicted to incarceration: Corrections policy and the politics of misinformation in the United States*. Thousand Oaks, CA: Sage.

Siegel L. J., & Bartollas, C. (2011). *Corrections today*. Belmont, CA: Wadsworth, Cengage Learning.

Siegel, L. J., & Worrall, J. L. (2016). *Introduction to criminal justice* (15th ed.). Boston, MA: Cengage Learning.

Snell, T. L. (2014, September). *Capital punishment, 2013 — Statistical tables* (Revised December 19, 2014) (NCJ Publication No. 248448). Washington, DC: U.S Department of Justice, Bureau of Justice Statistics. Retrieved from http://www.bjs.gov/content/pub/pdf/cp13st.pdf

South Carolina Code of Laws, Title 16 — Crimes and Offenses, "Chapter 1 — Felonies and Misdemeanors; Accessories", Section 16-1-90 "Crimes Classified as Felonies". Retrieved from http://www.scstatehouse.gov/code/title16.php

South Carolina Code of Laws, Title 16 — Crimes and Offenses, "Chapter 3 — Offenses Against the Person". Retrieved from http://www.scstathouse.gov/code/title16.php

South Carolina Code of Laws, Title 24 — Corrections, Jails, Probation, Paroles, and Pardons, "Chapter 13 — Prisoners Generally". Retrieved from http://www.scstatehouse.gov/code/title24.php

Texas Attorney General, *Penal Code of Offenses by Punishment Range: Including updates from the 83rd legislative session*. Retrieved from https://www.texasattorneygeneral.gov/files/cj/penalcode.pdf

Texas Department of Criminal Justice Parole Division & Texas Board of Pardons and Paroles, *Parole in Texas: Answers to common questions* (2012), Austin, TX. Retrieved from https://www.tdcj.state.tx.us/bpp/faq/faq.html

Texas Penal Code, Title 3 "Punishments", Chapter 12 Punishments, Subchapter A. General Provisions). Retrieved from http://www.statutes.legis.state.tx.us/Docs/PE/htm/PE.12.htm

Texas Penal Code, Title 5 "Offenses Against the Person", Chapter 22, "Assaultive Offenses". Retrieved from http://www.statutes.legis.state.tx.us/Docs/PE/htm/PE.22.htm

Tonry, M. (1996). *Sentencing matters*. New York: Oxford University Press.

Van Den Haag, E. (1976). *Punishing criminals: Concerning a very old and painful question*. New York: Basic Books.

Von Hirsch, A. (1976). *Doing justice: The choice of punishments*. New York: Hill and Wang.

Wilson, J. Q. (1975). *Thinking about crime*. New York: Basic Books.

Wolfgang, M. E., Figlio, R. M., & Sellin, T. (1972). *Delinquency in a birth cohort*. Chicago, IL: University of Chicago Press.

Early Sentencing Practices for Serious Crimes — From the Fixed Sentence to Indeterminate Sentencing

Chapter Objectives:

- To learn about the types of punishments used for serious offenses in colonial days up until incarceration was used as a distinct criminal sanction.
- To understand the purposes of early imprisonment systems in the United States and the "fixed" sentence.
- To trace early efforts to promote indeterminate sentencing in other countries.
- To recognize the work of Zebulon Brockway in ushering in indeterminate sentencing in the United States.
- To understand the role of the Progressive Movement and the "medical model" of treating offenders.
- To appreciate the role of rehabilitation in prisons from the Reformatory Era until the late 1960s.

Early Punishments in the Colonies

Corporal Punishments

The earliest forms of punishment in the colonies included harsh corporal/physical punishments. Many of the physical punishments used by colonists to punish lawbreakers were European practices that involved torture, such as whipping, drowning, branding, mutilation, hanging, and burning. In New England, Puritan beliefs held that those who committed crimes made a choice to do so, were sinful and evil, and deserved punishment. The laws were strict and the corporal punishments were severe (Siegel & Bartollas, 2011).

For lesser offenses, lawbreakers could be subjected to the stocks, or forms of informal social control, such as gossip and ridicule, meant to embarrass or shame the offender and deter future criminal involvement. Fines were also used in the colonies to some extent.

In one sense, these punishments could be considered certain. However, there is evidence that social class played some role. Wealthier offenders were more likely to have the option to pay a fine, while poorer offenders were subjected to corporal punishments.

The Death Penalty

The most severe corporal punishment—the death penalty—was used in colonial America as well. In the early 1600s in Jamestown, Virginia, military law pervaded. In 1611, in Jamestown, the *Laws, Moral and Martial* called for the death penalty for offenses such as murder, sodomy, rape, larceny, trading with or attacking Indians, and sacrilege, as well as economic crimes like stealing crops from a garden that one was hired to cultivate (Johnson & Wolfe, 1996).

In 1619 martial law ended in Virginia and criminal law was developed that was very similar to that in England. Offenses punishable by death included murder, burglary, rape, robbery, and forgery. Treason was also punishable by death, which could involve the use of torture. Johnson and Wolfe (1996) noted the following:

> In some cases the punishment involved stretching the traitor on a wheel to break his back, then disemboweling him while he was still living, hanging him until dead, then cutting off and exhibiting his head on a pole. The full sentence, derived from a statute of Henry VIII, was rarely used except when the convicted traitor was an Indian or a black slave (p. 82).

Criminal law in New England in the mid-1600s focused on certainty and was formally written. In 1641, a Massachusetts code entitled the Body of Liberties called for the execution of those convicted of felonies such as murder, sodomy, and kidnapping, as well as offenses such as blasphemy, witchcraft, and insurrection. The Massachusetts Body of Liberties, however, prohibited certain forms of torture.

Banishment

In colonial America, banishment of offenders from settlements to undeveloped wilderness was also used as a distinct criminal sanction. This form of punishment symbolized the sentiments of the law abiding that criminal behavior was not tolerated and the physical removal of an offender from the community was justified. The use of banishment signified the notion that criminals were not welcome to live among the law abiding.

The Use of Jails in the Colonies

In colonial America, imprisonment was not used as a major form of punishment until the early 1800s. Instead, jails were usually used to hold the accused while they were awaiting trial and to detain those offenders determined to be guilty while they awaited the imposition of their sentence. Exceptions involved the use of jails to house debtors and the mentally ill. This practice was also common in Europe.

In debtors' jails, once in jail, the incarcerated individual lacked the means to earn money pay back the jailor. Unless the debtor had persons on the outside willing to help him or her (and if they did, the jailor would demand a fee for delivering the supplies to the incarcerated), the prisoner was responsible for securing food, clothes, and other needed items. Only sometimes was the individual allowed to look for work within the city limits. Given the scarcity of resources, many persons died in debtors' jails. Debtors' jails existed in America until 1840. Jails were also used to house persons with mental illness.

The Influence of Enlightenment Thinkers on American Penology

The philosophical movement that developed in Europe during the 1600s and 1700s deemed the Enlightenment had a profound impact on the sentencing and punishment of criminals in America for years to come. The Enlightenment embraced scientific investigation (as evidenced by Isaac Newton's written work in physics in the late 1600s) and the belief in the perfectibility of man through reason. Enlightenment scholars varied in their specific discipline, yet shared the approach of understanding natural and social phenomena through observation and reason.

In 1764, a decade before the American Revolution, Cesare Beccaria wrote *An Essay on Crimes and Punishment*. This work outlined Beccaria's views on crime causation and his suggestions for penological reform, which were consistent with the ideals of the Enlightenment period. In this writing, Beccaria denounced the Italian methods of torture.

As discussed in Chapter 1, Beccaria suggested that man makes a rational choice in which he weighs the benefits associated with committing the crime with the costs that may follow the commission of the crime. Based on a type of rational calculus, a person decides to commit a crime if the perceived benefits outweigh the expected costs.

Consistent with the assumption that man decides whether to commit a crime based on a rational choice is the notion that punishment can and should serve as a deterrent to criminal behavior. The latter sections of *An Essay on Crimes and Punishment* outlined Beccaria's proposed penological reform, which rested on the concept of deterrence. He focused on the imposition of certain and swift punishments. He also discussed the importance of minimizing the severity of punishment to only that which was necessary to deter crime.

Incarceration as a Distinct Mode of Punishment in America

The Contributions of William Penn

The innovation of using imprisonment (loss of freedom) as a distinct criminal sanction in the American correctional system had its origin in Pennsylvania under the leadership of William Penn, a Quaker and prominent governor of the colony of Pennsylvania.

Penn's views of punishment were similar to Beccaria's and sought to decrease the severity of many punishments (Stohr & Walsh, 2012).

In 1682, legislation was passed in Pennsylvania which in essence rejected English law. This legislation, introduced by William Penn and called the Great Law, drew from his Quaker background and beliefs and limited the use of corporal punishments, including the death penalty, to only the most serious crimes (Stohr & Walsh, 2012). Prior to the Great Law, over 200 offenses could be punished by death (Zupan, 1991). After the legislation was passed, only those convicted of murder could be subject to death by the gallows (Siegel & Bartollas, 2011). Penn's revisions to Pennsylvania's criminal code forbid torture and the capricious use of mutilation and physical punishment and sought to bring alternative punishments to the existing practices of stocks, branding irons, and the gallows. Instead, fines were used for less serious crimes. Hard labor was indicated for many felonies.

Jail time was to be used as the appropriate punishment for most serious crimes. In line with his Quaker influence, the focus of punishment was not violent and involved thoughtful silence on the part of the offender (Stohr & Walsh, 2012). Penn ordered that a new type of institution be built to replace public stocks, gallows, and the branding iron. Each county in Pennsylvania was to build a house of corrections similar to today's jails.

Although his ideas eventually formed the basis for the widespread use of incarceration as punishment in America, at the time he described these changes, not all lawmakers or other contemporaries shared his ideals of punishment reform. After Penn died in 1718, many of the prior practices involving physical punishments were reinstituted in Pennsylvania. The other colonies had not been affected by Penn's codes and continued practices of physical punishments and brutality.

Part of the impetus for the permanent change to utilize incarceration as a distinct sanction for serious offenses came from the post-revolutionary sentiments that blamed problems of criminal behavior, including criminal recidivism, on English laws. A new correctional philosophy in America coincided with ideals found in the Declaration of Independence that stressed an optimistic view of human nature and the belief in each person's perfectibility.

In 1776, the state of Pennsylvania again adopted William Penn's code. In 1787, a group of Quakers led by Benjamin Rush formed the **Philadelphia Society for Alleviating the Miseries of Public Prisons**. The aim of this group was to bring some degree of humane and orderly treatment to the growing penal system. The Philadelphia society sought to have prison serve as an alternative to physical punishment. They believed punishment should prevent crime and should not destroy the offender. The Quakers believed if a person was placed in solitary confinement, that he could consider his crimes, repent, and reform himself. The word **penitentiary** incorporates the idea that criminals need an opportunity for penitence (sorrow or shame for their wrongs) and repentance (willingness to change their ways).

In addition to the ideals of the Quakers, one might argue that the rise of the penitentiary became a reality because of the focus on freedom and on the growth of capitalism at the time. The Declaration of Independence highlighted the country's **freedom from England**. Freedom was valued and the loss of freedom was used as a symbolic punishment. Second, inherent in the capitalist system developing in America, **value** was assigned to everything, including time. It followed that the more severe the offense a person committed, the more time he would have to spend in prison.

The Contributions of Benjamin Rush

Dr. Benjamin Rush (1746–1813) was a medical doctor and signer of the Declaration of Independence. Although his primary career focus was on the practice of medicine, Dr. Rush wrote two papers focused on punishment in America. The first, entitled *An Enquiry into the Effects of Public Punishments Upon Society* was read at the house of Benjamin Franklin for the Society for Promoting Political Enquiries in 1787. In this, Rush protested the 1786 passage of the "wheelbarrow law," which required felons to perform hard labor on the streets of Philadelphia. Rush felt that public punishments, such as the "wheelbarrow law" actually accelerated crime, as opposed to deterring it, and that they robbed the offender of self-respect.

In *An Enquiry into the Effects of Public Punishments Upon Society*, Rush (1787) stated

> . . . all public punishments tend to make bad men worse, and to increase crimes by their influence on society. He contended that public punishments destroy a person by shaming, are of too short duration to exact changes, and that they actually increase criminal propensities because the punished will seek revenge on the community in which he was punished. (p. 5)

Rush proposed not to do away with punishment, but rather to change the "place and manner" of punishment.

He advocated three basic changes. First, Rush advocated the building of an institution in a remote part of the state to house offenders. Second, he believed that punishments be defined and fixed by law, however, Rush also noted (well before Brockway's reforms discussed later in this chapter) that "punishments should always be varied in degree, according to the temper of the criminals, or the progress of their reformation" (p. 11). In this essay, Rush alluded to the integration of labor within the institution and the classification process that is inherent in today's treatment objective for the incarcerated. Third, Rush suggested that the duration of the punishment should be limited, yet that the limitation be secret and that the sense of the unknown (to the criminal) was of extreme importance to reformation. He argued that a criminal would only be released after he was reformed. Rush emphasized the objectives of punishment as physically separating criminals from society through incarceration, reformation of the individual, and preventing crime in society.

Rush (1787) wrote

> Crimes produce a stain, which may be washed out by reformation, and which frequently wears away by time. But public punishments leave fears, which disfigure the whole character; and hence persons, who have suffered them, are ever afterwards viewed with horror or aversion. If crimes are expiated by private discipline, and succeeded by reformation, criminals would probably suffer no more in character from them, than men suffer in their reputation or usefulness from the punishments they have under gone when boys at school. (p. 13)

One tangible result of Rush's paper resulted in the repeal of the "wheelbarrow law." A second consequence of Rush's writing was the coming together of Philadelphians to form the Philadelphia Society for Alleviating the Miseries of Public Prisons in 1787. This organization first met months after *An Enquiry into the Effects of Public Punishments Upon Society* was written and was the predecessor of today's Pennsylvania Prison Society.

The efforts of this group culminated in an act of 1790 that established of a "House of Repentance" within a wing of the three-story stone Walnut Street Jail in Philadelphia. Most scholars consider this designated area within the existing Walnut Street Jail to be the first functioning penitentiary in the United States. A wing of the Walnut Street Jail was reserved for the solitary confinement of what were considered the most hardened and serious offenders. Each cell in the Walnut Street Jail was small and dark (six by eight by nine feet high). Inmates were alone in their cells and no communications were allowed, but they did work in their cells.

Rush's work in penology represented a major change from public and physical punishments to the use of incarceration as a distinct form of sentencing in the United States. Rush emphasized that punishments were necessary, but took issue with the physical punishments being handed down at the time, specifying

> Let it not be supposed, from anything that has been said, that I wish to abolish punishments. Far from it — I wish only to change the **place** and **manner** of inflicting them, so as to render them effectual for the reformation of criminals, and beneficial to society. (p. 10)

Rush's second piece, *Considerations on the Injustice and Impolicy of Punishing Murder by Death* in 1792 outlined his opposition to the death penalty. Later that year, Pennsylvania law retained the capital punishment for only murder in the first degree. Pennsylvania was the first state to legally distinguish between first and second degree murder.

Early Prisons and the Fixed Sentence

The Pennsylvania System — Eastern State Penitentiary

The Philadelphia Society persuaded the legislature to build more institutions and by 1818 the legislature authorized the building of two penitentiaries. In 1826 Western Penitentiary, near Pittsburgh, was built. In 1829, Eastern Penitentiary was built in Philadelphia.

A wealth of information is available on Eastern State Penitentiary, which now serves as a museum open for visitors to tour. Sentences were fixed at Eastern State. The judge would sentence an individual to a certain number of years for his offense.

Eastern State Penitentiary originally had 76 cells and consisted of seven wings, each of which radiated from a central circular area, creating a radial design. The cells were 12 feet long, 8 feet wide, and 10 feet high. Each inmate had an exercise yard adjacent to his cell and the inmate was allowed to get fresh air in the yard one hour per day. At Eastern State Penitentiary, each cell had plumbing and running water, a work bench, tools, and a small area for solitary exercise.

While incarcerated, prisoners were isolated from other prisoners. When they were brought into Eastern State Penitentiary, they were bound with gauze to ensure that they did not see other inmates. It was thought that prisoners would have a contaminating influence on each other. The walls between cells were 18 inches thick, which helped prevent any communication among prisoners in adjacent cells (Siegel & Bartollas, 2011).

Prisoners housed at Eastern were not allowed to talk to each other — total silence was a distinguishing characteristic of the institution. Penitence and repentance were the goals at Eastern. While incarcerated, the prisoners were to reflect on the wrongs they had done, read the Bible, and repent for their crimes. They were allowed to do labor in their cells (DeLisi & Conis, 2013). Similar institutions were built in other states and other countries.

Problems occurred with overcrowding and over time two inmates lived and worked together in a cell originally designed for one inmate. This obviously undermined the goal of solitary confinement. A second story was eventually built in Eastern State Penitentiary to house the growing inmate population. Inmates who did remain in solitary had a horrible psychological ordeal. Eventually the ideals of the Pennsylvania system were not realized. By the 1830s the Pennsylvania system was being replaced by its rival — the Auburn system. The Pennsylvania system was finally ended altogether by 1913 (DeLisi & Conis, 2013).

The New York System — Auburn

The state of New York also instituted changes in their forms of punishment and chose imprisonment as a distinct criminal sanction for serious offenders. In 1796 the legislature limited the death penalty to offenders convicted of first degree murder and treason. Physical punishments were to be replaced with incarceration at Newgate Prison, which was constructed in 1797. When crime rose and prison overcrowding followed, a new prison, Auburn, was built in western New York State in 1816.

The Auburn system was also known as the **congregate** system because most men were kept in individual cells at night, but worked in factory-like shops and ate (face-to-back) in groups (i.e., they congregated) during the day. Inmates moved from one area of the prison to another in a lock-step formation to maintain control. Although they ate and worked in common areas, they were not allowed to talk, and this practice became known as the Auburn Silent System (Siegel & Bartollas, 2011).

Hard work and silence became the foundation of the Auburn system. The Auburn system could house more people with less physical space (they shared common areas to eat and work and were more productive because they used machines), compared to the Pennsylvania system.

Captain Elam Lynds, who enforced the Auburn Silent System during the early years at Auburn, was steadfastly against the notion of individual treatment of offenders. He emphasized that all inmates should be treated the same, and unlike Brockway's reformatory system, discussed later in this chapter, he did not reward positive behavior on the part of inmates. He addressed prisoners by their prison number and obedience was expected. Prisoners were not allowed to receive visitors, and like at Eastern State Penitentiary, their only allowed reading was the Bible.

Some inmates at Auburn were always kept in solitary confinement, because of discipline problems. Suicides and self-mutilations occurred and the practice of full-time solitary confinement was abolished by 1825 (Siegel & Bartollas, 2011).

Comparing the Pennsylvania and Auburn Systems

The Quaker-inspired Pennsylvania method was aimed at producing honest persons, while the New York system sought to mold obedient citizens. The two systems were rivals. Critics of the Pennsylvania system asserted that it was more expensive, labor was unproductive, and that total isolation led to insanity. Critics of the Auburn system felt that contamination would occur when prisoners interacted with each other, that its design increased the inmate's temptation to talk with others, and that more supervision was required, compared to that of the Pennsylvania system.

Both systems isolated the prisoner from society and placed him on a disciplined routine. Advocates of both systems believed that deviance resulted from corruption in the community and that the family and church weren't providing a counter-balance. Eventually the Auburn system predominated and as seen today, inmates interact with each other in common areas within prisons. Both the Pennsylvania and Auburn systems experienced problems with brutality on the part of the guards and both experienced overcrowding. The practice of silence fell apart and as overcrowding increased, men at both institutions and ones that followed were double celled.

Both systems relied on a "fixed" sentence. This practice is what is now known as "determinate" sentencing. When incarceration was first used as a distinct mode of punishment in the United States in the Pennsylvania and Auburn systems, the judge would determine the length of incarceration when he handed down the sentence. The focus was on punishment, although both the Pennsylvania and Auburn systems also tried to reform the offender during his sentence. Parole did not exist. A prisoner would be released only after that time was served in prison (Tonry, 1987).

Early Efforts to Implement Indeterminate Sentencing in Other Countries

In the late 1800s and early 1900s, scholars began to point to an offender's environment as a cause or predisposing factor of criminality. There was a general move away from the Classical school notion that crime is caused by a free will choice and that offenders should receive strict punishment for their offenses via long terms of incarceration. Instead, the predominant reasoning of the Positivist school was that the offender's behavior was determined by factors outside of his or her control. It therefore made more sense to "treat" the pathologies of the individual (whether they be caused by biological, psychological, or social factors), rather than to punish offenders, who according to a determinist perspective, had little or no control over their behavior. The move toward treatments within a correctional setting was ushered in largely by the innovations of Zebulon Brockway, who was a true pioneer of indeterminate sentencing policies in the United States. Indeterminate sentencing schemes assume that there are treatment strategies within prisons that can help "rehabilitate" offenders and that the length of time that one spends in prison should depend on how long it takes to rehabilitate that particular offender.

It is important, therefore, to emphasize that the first type of sentencing reform in the United States was a move from *determinate or fixed sentencing* to *indeterminate sentencing*. The bulk of this text describes the **modern sentencing reform movement**, in which the indeterminate sentencing practices that dominated American corrections from the mid-1930s until the 1970s were replaced by determinate sentencing practices. We will explore the reasons leading up to modern sentencing reforms, such as mandatory sentencing laws and sentencing guidelines. But before we do that, it is important to understand the history of the development of indeterminate sentencing in this country and others.

Zebulon Brockway introduced indeterminate sentencing and penal reforms in the United States in the late 1800s. It is important, however, to note the contributions of earlier innovators in penology from other countries. These include Captain Alexander Maconochie and Sir Walter Crofton (Muraskin, 2010, Silverman, 2001).

Captain Alexander Maconochie and the Mark System

One intrinsic element of indeterminate sentencing in the United States was the mark system. Well before Brockway introduced the mark system at Elmira Reformatory, Alexander Maconochie designed a system of marks while serving as the administrator of the Norfolk Island Penal Colony, which was located off the coast of Australia. During the 1800s convicts from England were being transported to Australia as punishment. The inmates at the penal colony were those who were "doubly convicted"—they were convicted of another crime after being sent to Norfolk Island from Britain (Siegel & Bartollas, 2011).

Maconochie sought to end brutalities that he saw in prisons, as he had been a prisoner of war after being captured by the French (Muraskin, 2010). Although Maconochie asserted that punishment helped deter future criminal behavior, he also believed that the penal system should be a source to help *reform* offenders. According to Maconochie, while serving their sentences, offenders should have opportunities to receive training to become productive citizens upon release and that trained personnel should oversee and guide prisoners (Silverman, 2001). According to Hughes (1986), "Alexander Maconochie wanted to shift the focus of penology from punishment to reform" (p. 498).

Inherent in the focus on reform was a move away from the fixed sentence. Maconochie believed that to achieve reformation an offender's sentence should be "task based" and that sentence length should reflect an offender's work accomplishments and conduct (Silverman, 2001). He advocated indeterminate sentencing.

In 1840, Maconochie developed a **mark system**, which allocated specific points or "marks" that corresponded to the seriousness of the offense. The prisoner would have to earn marks while incarcerated to, in essence, pay off his sentence before he could be freed back to society (Silverman, 2001). Convicts could earn marks or credits for good behavior and hard work. Instead of sentencing someone convicted of burglary to a fixed sentence of seven years, they would instead be sentenced to 6,000 marks. Likewise, 7,000 marks would correspond to ten years, and 10,000 would correspond to life (Hughes, 1986).

Hughes (1986) described the workings of the mark system as follows:

> Hence the length of his sentence was, within limits, up to the convict himself. Marks could be exchanged for either goods or time. The prisoner could buy "luxuries" with his marks from the jail administration — extra food, tobacco, clothing and the like. (p. 500)

The system that Maconochie designed involved several stages. When prisoners first entered the prison, they were assigned to the first stage, the "penal stage," that was the most punitive stage. It involved solitary confinement, rations of bread and water for food, and direction in morals with the goal to have prisoners feel remorse for their crimes. In the second stage, the "associational stage," inmates were allowed to interact with each other and begin earning marks for good behavior, work, and taking part in educational programs. This stage focused on rehabilitating the offender for the future. If the inmate chose not to participate in work or programs, he would not earn marks or make progress toward release. Marks could be added to the offender's sentence while he was in prison if he broke prison rules. Inmates in the third stage earned marks in the context of a group and was called the "social stage."

Maconochie felt that inmates needed to work for the common goal of helping the group. He valued "social responsibility" and believed this set up encouraged this goal. Organized in groups of six inmates, each day the earnings of that group would be divided by six and each inmate would receive one-sixth of the daily group earnings. The last stage would be attained after the prisoner had earned the marks needed to pay off this debt and he received a conditional pardon called a "ticket of leave." This was essentially their ticket to freedom and only a new criminal conviction would land the offender back to prison (Silverman, 2001).

Maconochie's system, when put in practice at the Norfolk Island Prison Colony in 1840, was altered from his intricately designed ideal. It retained the penal stage and the progression toward release using a mark system. He could not release the prisoners who earned marks equal to their sentence, but instead issued an "island ticket of leave" which allowed them to live outside the confines and physical structure of the prison and they could work from themselves on the island (Silverman, 2001).

Maconochie did not initially want to try his system in Norfolk Island. This is because it already had 1,200 twice-convicted prisoners. He was afraid that if they saw "new" prisoners coming in and receiving a seemingly milder sentence than what they had been receiving, that this would create tension between the old and the new convicts. Governor Sir George Gipps instructed Maconochie to keep the old Norfolk residents and the new arrivals as separate as possible. Maconochie defied the orders and applied his system to all inhabitants.

Maconochie instituted profound changes regarding the provisions for the punished. Maconochie requested encyclopedias, magazines on engineering and farming, cookbooks, and books on travel for the Norfolk Island residents. He introduced music as therapy for old and new convicts and even ordered musical instruments. He had two separate churches built on the island—one for Protestants and one for Catholics. He became a "hero" to the convicts. At the same time, there were fewer murders and lower levels of other violence among the convicts, compared to before his arrival on Norfolk Island.

Back in England, however, Maconochie was criticized for being too lenient on the convicted and giving out too many tickets of leave. Governor Gipps visited the island in 1843 and concluded that the critics were wrong and that overall Maconochie's system was working well. During Maconochie's tenure, the prison population fell, so it became questionable whether Norfolk Island could keep supporting itself, given a shrinking labor force.

Despite the fact that Maconochie's plan greatly improved the conditions at this penal colony, there was some negative public sentiment (those in England still firmly felt prison should focus on punishment) and on April 29, 1843, the Colonial Office in England put an end to the mark system and recalled Maconochie from his administrative post.

Sir Walter Crofton and the Irish System

Some of Maconochie's reforms were resurrected by Sir Walter Crofton in 1854, when he began serving as chairman of the board of directors of the Irish prison system and instituted what became known as the "Irish mark system." Like Maconochie, Crofton believed that offenders should be punished for the crimes that they committed, but that they should also be given tools to reform while serving their sentences (Muraskin, 2010).

Crofton designed a four-stage system that allowed inmates to move toward release. It assigned increasing responsibility and privileges to inmates. His system was similar to Maconochie's and also involved prisoners entering at the lowest stage and working their way up the system with a goal of being released from prison. The first stage, the "solitary confinement stage," lasted about 9 months and during this stage, prisoners were incarcerated and subject to silence and solitary confinement when they were not involved in other sanctioned activities, such as work, school, etc. The second stage, the "associational stage" required inmates to be moved to prisons where they could work on public works projects. During this stage that lasted about one year, they had to participate in conduct classes in which they could earn marks that gave them more privileges. Once they earned 108 marks, they could move on to the third stage—the "intermediate stage." This stage of Crofton's plan was unique and has been likened to modern pre-release centers. The inmates had to demonstrate self-control in situations similar to those that they would encounter once freed. They continued training, but under less supervision. Once they finished this stage, prisoners entered the last stage, the "conditional release stage." Inmates' good behavior, positive attitudes, work accomplishments, and other achievements demonstrated in earlier stages earned them conditional release through what Crofton called a "ticket of leave." Individuals in this stage were supervised and had to abide by certain conditions, including not re-offending. This fourth stage is likened to the modern practice of parole (Silverman, 2001).

These two indeterminate sentencing systems served as points of departure for Brockway's innovations at Elmira Reformatory in the state of New York.

Zebulon Reed Brockway — Pioneer of Indeterminate Sentencing in the United States

Zebulon Reed Brockway is best known for the innovations that he instituted at Elmira Reformatory, where he served as the prison's first warden from 1876 to 1881. Brockway introduced indeterminate sentencing, treatment (including educational and vocational training), parole, and a mark system at Elmira. Indeterminate sentencing contrasted with the fixed sentencing practices that had been standard in prisons throughout the nation since prison was first used as a distinct criminal sanction in the early 1800s.

Brockway and the Detroit House of Corrections

What is lesser known, however, is that before he became warden at Elmira, while working in the Detroit House of Corrections and with the Michigan legislature, Brockway rallied for indeterminate sentencing, the treatment of offenders, and a board which oversaw the progress of wards of the state. In 1869, Brockway drafted a bill called the "three years law," which was enacted by the Michigan legislature. This bill targeted female offenders and mandated that girls up to age fifteen be committed to a house of corrections until they turned twenty-one and that girls and women over fifteen years of age who were prostitutes be sentenced to a house of corrections for a three-year term. The law allowed for authorities of the house of corrections (located in Wayne County) to *conditionally release* and re-arrest if necessary, both juvenile and adult female offenders *before* the maximum term expired.

In his book, *Fifty Years of Prison Service: An Autobiography* (1912) Brockway emphasizes that under the "three years law," sentences were no longer unalterable. He detailed cases of young women who were sentenced under this law and focused on the treatment and conditional release that they received prior to the expiration of their mandatory maximum sentence.

The Establishment of a Board of Guardians

In an original draft of a similar but more far-reaching law in 1870, Brockway called for the establishment of a "Board of Guardians," made up of a circuit judge of Wayne County and inspectors at the Detroit House of Corrections to oversee any convicted offender who received imprisonment. He reiterated that the sentence that any offender received would not be fixed or determined by the Board of Guardians before the sentence was served. Instead, he proposed that the Board of Guardians both maintain control over wards in their custody, as well as help them to reform. Brockway referred to this as the original indeterminate sentencing law.

He proposed individualized treatment plans for the wards and suggested a quarterly update on the character of the imprisoned offender, which was to play a role in the decision about when to finally release the individual. The ward also had a right to communicate with the Board of Guardians at least quarterly. Brockway suggested the following:

When it appears to the said Board that there is reasonable probability that any ward possesses a sincere purpose to become a good citizen, and the requisite moral power and self-control to live at liberty without violating the law, and that such ward will become a fair member of society, then they shall issue to such ward an absolute release, but no petition or other power of application for the release of any ward made by any person whatever, and based upon any ground save that herein stated, shall be entertained and considered by the said Board. (p. 131)

National Prison Congress

In 1870, the newly formed National Prison Congress (the predecessor of today's American Correctional Association) met in Cincinnati and called for penal reform. Wardens, politicians, and others were unhappy with the Auburn system. They wanted to set standards in the correctional community. Presenters at the conference discussed what were then quite "progressive" ideas, including providing prisoners with educational and vocational opportunities, as well as religious schooling. Brockway presented a paper at the National Prison Congress in Cincinnati entitled *The Ideal Prison System for a State*. This piece provided a more detailed explanation of the indeterminate sentence and his innovative idea of a reformatory prison system. The participants shared a common sentiment that **reformation** of prisoners should be the dominant goal of corrections. They called for a mark system in which prisoners would be rewarded for good behavior. They also advocated indeterminate sentencing, in contrast to the existing fixed sentences (Siegel & Bartollas, 2011). In this scheme, prisoners would be rewarded for their accomplishments by early release.

By 1875, Brockway was part of a commission that reported to the state of Michigan to revise the criminal laws of the state. The main conclusion of the commission was that time (fixed) sentences be abandoned, in favor of reformatory (indeterminate) sentences for all crimes, except for the most serious offenses.

So, Brockway's contribution to the first wave of "sentencing reform" really began with the "three years law." He detailed his plan of the indeterminate sentence and treatment within prisons at the National Prison Congress in his paper, *The Ideal Prison System for a State*. And the bill before the Michigan legislature in 1870–1871 symbolized the first effort to introduce indeterminate sentencing laws, and therefore profoundly change the prison to become the **reformatory**.

Elmira Reformatory

In May 1876, Brockway was offered the position of superintendent of the then incomplete and unopened Elmira Reformatory. He served as superintendent of Elmira until August 1900. Elmira was located in the south central part of New York State.

In 1876 Judge George R. Bradley designed a bill to establish the reformatory, where inmates would serve an indeterminate sentence. The Indeterminate Sentence Act of 1877 was passed in New York. The bill provided that the duration of an individual's sentence be based on public safety and that the purpose of the reformatory be to form and re-form the characters of those sentenced.

Public safety (by incapacitating dangerous offenders until they were ready to return to society) was also explicitly stated as a goal of imprisonment. Brockway's reforms focused on rehabilitation as a sentencing goal of corrections. Therefore, both reha-bilitation and incapacitation were recognized by Brockway as important goals of imprisonment.

Brockway critiqued both existing models for imprisonment at the time—the Penn-sylvania (Quaker) system and the Auburn (congregate) system. He noted that the soli-tary confinement model that was an original ideal of the Pennsylvania system lacked inmate training that would help prisoners become productive members of society when released. He preferred the Auburn system and noted the productivity of prisoners' labor, but felt that this system was no better than the Pennsylvania system in deterring crime. In Brockway's mind hard labor did not yield penitence, which was an early goal of imprisonment.

Brockway developed a **mark system**, in which prisoners would be rewarded based on work and educational programs. Brockway highlighted how the mark system helped give prisoners incentive to excel at school to receive higher marks. He instituted a pa-role system that was grounded in the notion that the prisoners would be released to the community when they demonstrated that they were ready to return to society, not after fixed period of time. His leadership represented a move away from the "penitentiary" to the "reformatory." The period of 1870–1910 is known in the field of corrections as the "Reformatory Era." Reformatory programs included elementary education for il-literates, library hours, and vocational training. The focus was on teaching prisoners a trade.

Brockway's design and administration at Elmira represented a shift in goals of im-prisonment from those of the Pennsylvania and Auburn models. The physical appear-ance of Elmira was more like that of a college campus, as opposed to a prison. He sought to move from punishment and repentance to reformation and correction of the pris-oner as the desired outcomes of incarceration. He felt that if prisoners believed that the purpose of incarceration was punishment, that this would impede their progress toward reforming.

The inmate population at Elmira during its first few years of operation included both those inmates sentenced to fixed sentences, who were transferred from state prisons such as Auburn and Sing Sing, and those sentenced under indeterminate sentencing. Brock-way found the part of the population which was sentenced under determinate sentenc-ing impeded his goals. As the years went on and the population was composed of only those sentenced via indeterminate sentencing, his goals of reformation were more suc-cessfully attained. Clearly over time, Elmira represented the first prison that instituted the principles of a true reformatory—both in stated purpose and in practice.

Brockway and the Role of the Positivist School

Brockway's beliefs about what caused a man to become involved in crime were con-sistent with those of the Positivist school. He acknowledged the influence that Cesare

Lombroso's writings had on him. Lombroso (1835–1909) was an Italian physician who became known as the founder of the Italian school of Positivist criminology. Lombroso's explanation for crime causation focused on biological factors of the individual, which suggested that crime was inherited. Lombroso performed autopsies of Italian men to compare the physical features of those who had been convicted of crimes with those who had not. He noted that as a group, the criminals had more physical features that were similar to man's ancestor, according to evolutionary theory — apes. These features included sloping foreheads, large ears, lack of facial symmetry, and bumps on one's head. Lombroso also suggested that criminals were less sensitive to pain, lacked morality, were highly impulsive, and more likely to be cruel. He believed criminals were "biological throwbacks," or atavists and were more similar to apes than man. According to Lombroso, criminals were a subhuman type of man.

In his autobiography, Brockway discussed his direct observations of prisoners at Elmira and compared physical features of young men serving time at Elmira with college students living in free society. He noted that the prisoners were shorter, weighed less, had weaker lung capacity, and had weaker chests and backs. He asserted that the physical features of the men in the reformatory more closely resembled those of women in New England colleges than those of college men. He also observed more asymmetries in the faces, eyes, and ears among the reformatory men, which he concluded represented "congenital deficiency" and increased likelihood of disease. His observations of photographs that appeared in year books at the reformatory reiterated his fixation on what he interpreted as evidence that prisoners come from a group of degenerates who were both physically and mentally inferior.

Brockway summarized his observations in the following way: "More closely scanned, the inferiority appears as physical, mental, and moral imperfection, derived, some of it, by inheritance or from early formative circumstances concededly beyond the prisoner's control" (p. 214).

He contended that the sentence to Elmira Reformatory served as a restraint to offenders (to prevent crimes that could otherwise be committed if they were free in the community) and as an opportunity to reform them through training (to encourage law abiding behavior upon release).

Much of his writings came from his direct observations of prisoners at Elmira. He even observed patterns and identified February to June as the time of the year in which prisoners exhibited higher rates of "troublesome behavior" (p. 188). At one point he complained about the increased urbanization, and rise in what he described as "the increased influx of aliens unassimilated to our Americanism" (p. 202). Brockway also described leniency on the part of court practices and laws as contributing to criminality. As he perceived these problems to continue, he maintained an interest in acquiring a better understanding of the causes of crime in order to help prevent it. Brockway did not consider all offenders salvageable and even wrote about such men in a chapter of his autobiography, entitled "Difficult Prisoners."

Although Brockway is considered a prison reformer, some of his practices came under scrutiny. He devoted a considerable portion of his autobiography to describing various committees' inquiries and investigations of the goings-on at Elmira. These included a hook device that was made of a long gas pipe bent at one end to form a handle and at the other end to function as a hook to wrap around a prisoner and pull him to the front of a cell to take away weapons or remove him from the cell. If a prisoner tried to resist, the hook was heated to prevent the prisoner from moving it. In the early 1880s, Brockway also described "paddlings," which were administered solely by the superintendent, Brockway himself.

Consistent with the notion that factors beyond one's control predispose a person to commit crime, was Brockway's contention that there be a move away from punishment as a primary goal of sentencing and toward prevention and reformation. The mark system that Brockway ushered in at Elmira involved assigning prisoners to one of three classes or grades, based on merits and demerits earned in school and work and on the basis of the prisoner's demeanor. The recording of marks helped prison officials determine the offenders' readiness for release into society. Prisoners who excelled in industry (which in the early days at Elmira involved brush making) and in school earned higher marks and this helped them move closer to release.

The opportunities for inmates to be educated at Elmira were vast. Prisoners had a library at Elmira. Brockway believed educational progress was essential to overcoming criminal propensities. Conventional subjects such as reading, writing, literature, mathematics, history, and geography were taught by teachers and professors in the area and local colleges. In addition, an ethics class, entitled "Practical Morality" was begun at Elmira and enrollment reached approximately 500 men. In addition, religious services were held at Elmira with Brockway's stated intent being "to enliven and exalt the mental state" of the prisoners (p. 266).

The Increased Use of Indeterminate Sentencing and the Practice of Parole in the United States

Brockway's reforms were profound and served as a model for widespread changes in sentencing practices and prison operations throughout the nation. States began adopting various indeterminate sentencing laws. Eleven states had incorporated indeterminate sentencing by 1900. This number rose to 31 states by 1915. By 1925, 38 states had indeterminate sentencing laws. In the mid-seventies, all 50 states, the District of Columbia, and the federal system had some form of indeterminate sentencing.

There was some regional variation in the use of indeterminate sentencing. In 1946 over 90 percent of the sentences in Northeast were indeterminate, compared to approximately 22 percent of the sentences handed down in the South. This should be no surprise, given that Brockway's reforms were first instituted at Elmira Reformatory, which was located in the northeastern part of United States (United Nations, 1954). In many states that adopted indeterminate sentencing, there were certain groups of offenders who were ineligible and instead were subject to the fixed sentence. These included those convicted of serious crimes, such as murder, treason, rape, and kidnapping (United Nations, 1954).

The exact length of time that offenders who were sentenced under indeterminate sentencing schemes would serve depended on the decision of the parole board associated with the institution in which they were housed. Whether an inmate would be granted parole was determined in part by the parole board's impression of whether the offender had been rehabilitated. If the offender was deemed "rehabilitated" at the time of the parole hearing, the parole board could make the decision to release that offender after serving only a fraction of the imposed sentence. Parole was first instituted at Elmira Reformatory in 1876. At that time, six months' supervision in the community was standard.

Discretionary parole boards sprang up in most jurisdictions in the United States in the 1920s and 1930s. Since their inception, parole boards have differed in the composition and qualification of their members.

The practice of indeterminate sentencing and parole rested on several assumptions. The first was that the offender needed treatment or rehabilitation. Consistent with the Positivist school of criminology that developed largely in the late 1800s and predominated in the early 1900s, crime was thought to be the result of some individual pathology or sickness or a result of the offender's environment. Based on this reasoning, prisons should offer treatment methods to the individual during the period of incarceration so that after they are released they can return to society "rehabilitated" and not prone to reoffend.

The process of indeterminate sentencing caters to the individual offender. When first introduced, it was assumed that the treatment methods worked, but that offenders might vary in the time it takes for them to be rehabilitated. Some offenders take longer than others, and it was the job of the parole board to decide whether rehabilitation was complete for each individual who came before them. Because some offenders would take longer than others to be rehabilitated, the prison terms of offenders who committed the same crime could, in fact, be very different. Inherent in indeterminate sentencing was the notion that the sentence be catered to the **individual**, not prescribed only by the **offense** that the person committed.

When the practice of parole spread across the country, some changes took place. By the mid-1930s, most parole boards were no longer composed of the warden and a board of managers who were associated with the prison. Instead, separate parole boards were instituted whose members were appointed by the governor of the state (Rothman, 2002). Surprisingly, the qualifications necessary to be a parole board member were unclear in many states (Rideau & Wikberg, 1992). Some have suggested that political party affiliations dictated the composition of the parole board. Criticisms that parole officers were ineffective and that supervision was lax also began soon after the creation of this position in many states (Rothman, 2002). Prison wardens, however, consistently supported the use of parole, because they felt it gave inmates incentive to behave well in prison, and subsequently reduced inmate misbehavior and violence, thus making the job of the warden less stressful.

Variation has existed historically in the specifics regarding parole. The minimum amount of time that a prisoner had to serve before becoming eligible for parole has varied by state. In some states it has been one-third of the sentence, in others, one-fourth of the sentence, and in still others only one-fifth of the sentence. In some states, the fraction depended on the length for the maximum sentence. The Act of 1949 in West Virginia, however, allowed for one to be released after serving any time, if the individual was deemed ready to be released (with the exception of those convicted of offenses carrying a life sentence or those with a second or greater felony conviction) (United Nations, 1954).

The Progressive Movement

Description

The Progressive movement in the United States (1890s to 1920s) embraced social activism and sought to respond to social problems using scientific methods. The Progressives were a group of mostly upper class, white, Anglo-Saxon men in the early 1900s. They viewed urbanization and immigration as threats to society and believed it was their job to remedy social ills. In his book *Conscience and Convenience* (2002), David Rothman detailed the Progressive movement. This movement introduced a variant of the approach used by Brockway, which emphasized the treatment or reformation of the criminal offender. This approach involved *individualizing* treatment to each offender, based on his or her *specific needs*. It stemmed from the belief that different circumstances play a role in predisposing offenders to criminality and because the factors leading to criminality varied, so should the treatment of different offenders. They moved away from a "one size fits all" model for reforming criminals to a **"medical model"** of individualized treatment. The goal was to understand the unique life circumstances of each individual in order to design a program that would help that person desist from criminal activity.

Several different approaches to explaining criminality were suggested by the Progressives and each suggested that the propensity for criminal behavior was beyond the individual's control. Most Progressives focused on either environmental influences or psychological explanations of criminality. Some examined hereditary factors linked to criminality.

During the late 1800s, social sciences were offered at many universities and scholars saw cities as places to study social problems. Sociologists and other social scientists concluded that the poor were "victims" of inferior wages and the Progressives felt that the state had an obligation to balance inequities. Delinquency was explained as a result of the social circumstances of the immigrant, including poverty, bad living conditions, inferior education, and lack of supervision of children and adolescents. The Progressives saw these as solvable problems and initiated efforts to help the poor through housing and other tactics.

A second approach of some Progressives which gained popularity in the 1920s and 1930s identified psychological factors as causes of criminality. They examined the influences of family members and other associates, as well as habits that might predispose one to criminality. A third type of explanation focused on eugenics and suggested hereditary influences on an offender's criminality. Lombroso's "born criminal" concept was used to differentiate offenders and suggest ways to treat the offender (Rothman, 2002).

The Progressive Approach to Criminal Offenders

Regardless of the approach, the Progressives believed that deviance had to be studied on a case-by-case basis. The causes of each offender's criminality had to be assessed individually. Criminality was viewed as treatable in the medical model, whether by interventions taking place in the environment or through psychiatric or psychological treatment. Progressive approaches focused on curing the offender, rather than blaming the offender. Both those who took an environmental approach and those who took a psychiatric/psychological approach focused on the medical model—finding sources of the individual pathology and treating the cause(s).

Given the assumption that the causes of crime are factors outside the individual's control, Progressives sought a penal system that would individualize treatment.

Progressives were unified in their disdain for existing prisons. Rothman (2002) noted:

> Every observer of American prisons and asylums in the closing decades of the nineteenth century recognized that the pride of the one generation had become the shame of another. The institutions that had been intended to exemplify the humanitarian advances of republican government were not merely inadequate to the ideal but were actually an embarrassment and a rebuke. Failure to do good was one thing; a proclivity to do harm quite another—and yet the evidence was incontrovertible that brutality and corruption were endemic to the institutions. (p. 17)

Regardless of their specific approach to explaining the causes of criminality, the Progressives focused on developing treatment programs to address individual pathologies, as opposed to blaming the individual and exacting punishment on him. The consequences of their ideals included the expanded use of **probation** for the treatment of some criminal offenders within the community. For those who were to be incarcerated, the imposition of the **indeterminate sentence** and **parole** were consistent with Progressive ideals. Progressives promoted a shared goal of helping the offender and bettering society. Implicit in their approach was the notion that the state could and should rehabilitate the offender.

Once an offender was found guilty or pleaded guilty, it was the duty of the probation officer to prepare a pre-sentence investigation for each offender. The purpose of this report was, as it is used today, to gather facts about the offender's life, including level of education, family background, neighborhood, home life, and prior record. The probation officer also scheduled mental and physical testing of the individual and integrated all of the findings to produce a recommendation to the judge that was to be beneficial to society and the offender. For those offenders that they deemed appropriate, supervision in the community was accomplished by placing offenders on probation and assigning them a probation officer. By the 1920s, every state had juvenile probation departments and 33 states had adult probation (Rothman, 2002).

Other (more serious) offenders were to serve their sentence in prison. The Progressives opposed fixed or determinate sentences and viewed them as vengeful. They questioned the practice of deriving a formula to determine how much time an offense would carry. This is because they did not feel that one could measure culpability of offenders in an accurate way. How the environment, one's psychological state, or heredity might have predisposed the individual to commit crime was unclear. They also opposed fixed sentences because they could prematurely release a prisoner after he completed his maximum sentence, even if he was seen as a threat to the community upon release.

The Progressive approach to treatment behind bars contrasted that of the previous Jacksonian era (early- to mid-1800s), which focused on a uniform routine for all prisoners (as described in the discussion of Eastern State Penitentiary and Auburn Prison). In contrast, the Progressives followed the medical model, which implied that the treatment (or the "medicine") was necessarily different for each offender. Unlike earlier prisons in the United States, prisons operating with the Progressive influence did away with striped uniforms, the lock-step formation, and rules of silence, and encouraged visitation to normalize the environment, so as to help inmates make a smoother transition back to society.

Progressives and Indeterminate Sentencing

As we will discuss in future chapters, the very flexibility that was afforded the parole board by the state opened the door up to disparate and discriminatory treatment of offenders. At the time, however, the state was seen as benevolent and central to the rehabilitation of criminal offenders. Rothman (2002) stated, "In the end, the question of individual liberty was so easily resolved, actually dismissed, because the Progressives trusted the state to act in the best interest of all" (p. 70).

The response of criminal justice actors to indeterminate sentencing varied. At the 1900 Congress of the National Prison Association, prison wardens showed overwhelming support for indeterminate sentencing and parole. They felt that these practices motivated offenders to behave and cooperate with prison officials, who had the power to either serve on parole boards or make recommendations to an independent parole board. Some judges also supported indeterminate sentencing and parole, despite the fact that some of their decision-making power was moved to the parole board. Others, however, saw indeterminate sentencing as being too easy on the offender. Police forces often expressed frustration with indeterminate sentencing, as they felt that serious offenders could potentially be released too early and would pose a threat to the community. They felt that just because an offender was a model prisoner did not mean that he would not continue offending once released.

Negative public sentiments about parole are as old as the practice itself. As far back as the 1920s and 1930s, there was public outcry about how the practice of parole could allow the premature release of serious and violent criminal offenders. Stories of prematurely releasing dangerous inmates made headlines in newspapers and on television.

Industrial Era/The Big House

The Industrial Prison Era ran from about 1910 to the mid-1930s. During this time, most prisons appeared less as reformatories and more like warehouses and workhouses for prisoners. According to DeLisi and Conis (2013), prisons were crowded, the living conditions were harsh, and inmates were used as free labor. Prisons appeared as factories with profit as their goal. Several governors in the North realized that the labor of prisoners could provide revenue by producing a variety of products, including furniture, metal furnishings, textiles, and crops in prisons which were near farms.

In the North, there were different types of inmate labor systems used, which varied according to the role of private contractors in providing machinery and raw materials and supervising the prisoners. The convict-lease system was popular in the South. In this system the prisoners were literally leased out by the state for a price to a company for their labor. The company was responsible for providing them food, water, shelter, and clothing. Tales of extreme inmate abuse, lack of food and water, and horrific work conditions on plantations in the South were described by two former inmates at Louisiana State Penitentiary, Wilbert Rideau and Ron Wikberg, in their book, *Life Sentences* (1992). Since profit was the goal, these companies provided the minimal (if that) necessities for their "workers."

Note, however, that inmate labor and prison industry are not synonymous. As we discussed in the Pennsylvania system, inmates worked in their cells. It wasn't until 1828 that Auburn and Sing Sing inmates were "paying" for their own confinement by the communal work they did, which helped pay for their incarceration. Prison "industry" began at this point. In 1917, New York adopted a "good time" law, which rewarded good behavior and work (Miller & Grieser, 1986).

According to the American Correctional Association (1986), the stated goals of prisons in the Industrial Era were to promote good work habits among the inmates, to decrease idleness, and to provide repayment to society or victims for the harm done by the crime. During the Industrial Prison Era, work was considered a type of rehabilitation. Inmates were learning trades in prison factories. Education programs were emphasized less and becoming hirable through gaining work experience was underscored as helping prepare inmates for their lives after prison.

Organized labor (notably the textile industry) challenged the use of inmate labor. Helping make prisoners more hirable was not a politically attractive goal either. In 1929, the Hawes-Cooper Act allowed states to enact laws concerning whether prison-made goods could come into their borders. In 1935, the Ashurst-Sumners Act allowed federal prosecution of violations of the Hawes-Cooper Act. In 1940, amendments to the Ashurst-Sumners Act increased the scope of federal enforcement by making any transport of prison-made goods in interstate commerce a federal offense (DeLisi & Conis, 2013). In the early 1900s, about 85 percent of all inmates in the United States worked in prison industries, but by 1940, only 44 percent did (Miller & Grieser (1986).

Spotlight — Ohio State Reformatory

The Ohio State Reformatory is located one mile northeast of Mansfield, Ohio. The cornerstone was laid in 1886 and it opened in 1896. The movie *The Shawshank Redemption* was filmed there in 1993, after the institution was closed in 1990. The Ohio State Reformatory is a good example of an institution that expressed a focus on rehabilitation and the use of discretionary parole release. Today, the institution is open for tours. Next to it is the present Mansfield Correctional Institution, opened in 1990.

In 1866 the Board of State Charities advocated the establishment of a farm where young offenders would be segregated and placed away from older, more hardened offenders who were serving time at the state penitentiary. Between 1886 and 1934 the Ohio State Reformatory operated as an intermediate step between reform schools and penitentiaries. As such it sought to both discipline and reform young men. The average yearly population was 3,500 young men ranging in age from 16 to 30 years old. At the time it was the largest institution of its kind in the United States. The most common crime committed by the men was robbery.

The Ohio State Reformatory is a good example of an institution that emphasized inmate rehabilitation and utilized discretionary parole release.

T.C. Jenkins, Superintendent of the Ohio State Reformatory explained,

> The aim of this institution is to be a "Reformatory" in fact, as well as in name. To accomplish this aim, it must not only penalize but it must furnish the incentive for the individual to direct his activities in a new and worth-while line. (p. 2)

Jenkins stated, "It attempts, also, to rehabilitate the men who leave its doors; to help them find new places for themselves in the social structure outside the high grey wall" (p. 4).

Rehabilitation efforts included **formal schooling** as well as **vocational training**.

Schooling

Superintendent Jenkins pointed out that teaching was very concentrated and that the same learning that required eight years of schooling on the outside was crammed into two years within the institution. Jenkins cited the following example of one young Hungarian student who was in the tenth grade:

> When he came to the institution he could speak only a few words of English yet in twenty-four months he has gone from the first to tenth grade, taking all of the fundamental subjects of reading, writing, spelling, grammar, arithmetic, geography, history, and in addition civics, English, algebra, economy, and fundamentals of agriculture. But he has studied seven hours a day every day in his cell, and had an additional five hours of class room work under supervision six days a week. (p. 15)

In addition to conventional school subjects, there was a separate unit of the school system that involved trades classes. In 1925, these classes included engineering and drafting. Some of these students drew up plans and specifications for dormitories and helped construct the buildings. In 1928, courses in steam engineering, plumbing, steam fitting, and welding were added. These typically involved one hour each day in the classroom followed by seven hours of practical experience in the shops.

Superintendent Jenkins noted that the Director of Education also offered extracurricular activities, including debates in class, as well as short plays and musical programs. He noted, "Every boy and man who leaves the Reformatory may not be a reformed character, but he most certainly is better prepared to fight his battle than before, by reason of a better education and, in many cases, a practical trade" (p. 30).

Vocational Training

The five industries of the Ohio State Reformatory were known as the Manufacturing and Sales Division and included furniture, clothing, shoe, printing, and machine factories. Since November 15, 1912, these factories had operated under the "State-Use System." Before that, the factories were "contract shops," and were operated by private companies, which sold the products on the open market and in competition with free labor. The outlet of the products since then were to state institutions, state departments, city and county institutions and departments, and public schools.

The clothing factory made uniforms for inmates at the institution, officers' uniforms, and clothing for boys at children's homes in Ohio. The printing factory produced catalogs for state colleges and universities. The machine shop manufactured steel institutional beds and hospital beds. The industries both provided employment for the inmate and gave him a chance to develop skills in industries that could help him be more hirable upon release.

The inmates also performed farm work, installed sewage systems, built roads, and made other improvements to the institution. As the years went on, inmates were provided industrial training, including bricklaying, stone cutting, carpentry, painting, and structural work. The inmates also worked on the heating and lighting of the institution. In accordance with the State-Use System, poultry and other farm products of the reformatory were utilized at various state institutions.

Chaplain

Each young man that entered the reformatory was brought to the chaplain for a personal interview. He was asked about his home life, his parents, and his offense. The chaplain's report was reviewed by the superintendent and later by the parole board. The chaplain also acted as an intermediary between the boy and his family. The young men had the opportunity to worship according to their religious beliefs.

Parole

According to Superintendent Jenkins

> In the hands of the Ohio Board of Paroles rests one of the heaviest responsibilities of the entire Welfare Department — that of deciding when a state prisoner is ready to be released from prison and returned to society. (p. 13)

Jenkins described two foci of the Board of Paroles — to protect society and to offer the offender another chance to be rehabilitated in society. Inmates were eligible for parole after serving the minimum sentence if they had demonstrated appropriate conduct. The board would question the offender about his offense, his behavior in prison, his reactions to incarceration, and his attitude toward society in general. The board also had access to the official case documentation, a report on the offender's mental status, and a detailed report of conduct within the prison. In addition, the Bureau of Welfare Examination and Classification, which was a division of the Welfare Department, made reports to the Parole Board as to the psychiatric and psychological welfare of the inmate. Inmates who were paroled were under the supervision of field parole officers for the remaining period of their original sentence.

Sentencing and Corrections Post Depression–Late 1960s

After the Great Depression, we again saw a change in the focus back toward prison rehabilitation. This was the medical model that was originally embraced by the Progressives in the late 1800s to the early 1900s. The focus on education, psychological counseling, and various therapies for inmates regained momentum. The medical model of rehabilitation dominated corrections soon after the Depression and until the late 1960s. Prison industry reemerged in the 1950s and 1960s as a component of rehabilitation. The focus was on preparing the inmate for post release by empowering him with job skills.

A myriad of programs sprang up in the 1950s and 1960s in United States prisons. These included (but weren't limited to) basic education skills training, vocational training, religious training, substance abuse training, and individual and group counseling (Alarid & Reichel, 2013). The focus was on classifying inmates according to their needs (addressing what "caused" their criminality) and developing specific treatment plans.

Indeterminate sentencing was in its heyday. When a prisoner would be released by a parole board was contingent on evidence of his or her progress in assigned programs. Those who were thought to be "rehabilitated" sooner were released sooner, compared to inmates who showed little or no progress. It was assumed that rehabilitation was effective. The flexibility inherent in indeterminate sentencing, which was intricately tied to evidence of rehabilitation, was valued in the period from the 1930s to the late 1960s.

As we will see in Chapter 3, that very flexibility became a source of criticism in the late 1960s and early 1970s. The fairness of the indeterminate sentence and the efficacy of rehabilitation were questioned. Paired with a rising violent crime rate, these criticisms formed the basis of what is considered **modern sentencing reform**, the subject on which the remainder of this book focuses.

Summary

Prisons were not used as a distinct criminal sanction in the United States until the early 1800s. Early prisons, including Eastern State Penitentiary and Auburn Prison, used a "fixed" sentence for offenders which can be likened to "determinate" sentencing practices today. Parole did not exist. A prisoner would be released only after he served his time. While prisons were used to punish, both systems also made efforts to reform the offender during his sentence.

Movements toward indeterminate sentencing began in other countries in the mid-1800s. Alexander Maconochie designed a system of marks at the Norfolk Island Penal Colony in which inmates would make progress towards their release. In 1854 Sir Walter Crofton began serving as chairman of the board of directors of the Irish prison system and instituted what became known as the "Irish mark system."

In the late 1800s, Zebulon Reed Brockway's innovations as warden at Elmira Reformatory in New York State included indeterminate sentencing, treatment (including educational and vocational training), parole, and a mark system. Indeterminate sentencing contrasted the fixed sentencing practices in early prisons in the United States. Brockway's reforms served to prompt widespread changes in sentencing practices and prison operations throughout the nation. By the mid-seventies, all 50 states, the District of Columbia, and the federal system had some form of indeterminate sentencing.

From the late 1800s to the early 1900s, the Progressive Movement in the United States emphasized solving social problems, including crime, using scientific methods. Within prisons, individualized treatment was viewed as an appropriate way to try to reform offenders. The Industrial Prison Era ran from about 1910 to the mid-1930s. During this time, prisons functioned more like warehouses and workhouses for prisoners and less like reformatories. After the Depression, however, there was a move back toward prison rehabilitation. The importance of providing inmates with educational and vocational counseling, as well as various therapies, was prominent in prisons across the country. The refocus on rehabilitation dominated corrections until the late 1960s.

Discussion Questions

1. What might be some problems with the practice of indeterminate sentencing?
2. How did the Positivist school conception of crime causation precipitate the movement from fixed sentencing to indeterminate sentencing?
3. Are your views on crime causation more consistent with the Classical school or the Positivist school? Why?
4. What benefits can a "mark system" bring to inmates? How can it benefit correctional personnel?
5. From your study of corrections and your general knowledge of human behavior, what treatment approach do you think is the most important to "rehabilitating" an offender (education, counseling, job skills training, etc.)?

References

Alarid, L. F., & Reichel, P. L. (2013). *Corrections.* Upper Saddle River, NJ: Pearson Education.

American Correctional Association. (1986). *A study of prison industry: History, components, and goals.* Washington, DC: Government Publishing Office.

Beccaria, C., & Voltaire (1801). *An essay on crimes and punishments, translated from the Italian of Beccaria; with commentary, by Voltaire, translated from the French* (Rev. 5th ed). Retrieved from http://hdl.handle.net/2027/njp.32101068978202

Brockway, Z. R. (1912). *Fifty years of prison service: An autobiography.* New York: Charities Publication Committee. Retrieved from http://coe.csusb.edu/programs/correctionalEd/documents/searchable_Fifty_years_of_prison-service.pdf

DeLisi, M., & Conis, P. J. (2013). *American Corrections: Theory, research, policy, and practice.* Burlington, MA: Jones & Bartlett Learning.

Hughes, R. (1986). *The fatal shore: The epic of Australia's founding.* New York: Alfred A. Knopf.

Jenkins, T. C. (n.d.) *The Ohio state reformatory, Mansfield, Ohio, 1896–1934.*

Johnson, H. A., & Wolfe, N. T. (1996) *History of criminal justice.* Cincinnati, OH: Anderson.

Miller, N., & Grieser, R. C. (1986). The evolution of prison industries. In The American Correctional Association (Ed.), *A study of prison industry: History, components, and goals,* Washington, DC: Government Publishing Office.

Muraskin, R. (2010). *Key correctional issues.* Upper Saddle River, NJ: Prentice Hall.

Rideau, W., & Wikberg, R. (1992). *Life Sentences: Rage and survival behind bars.* New York: Times Books.

Rothman, D. J. (2002). *Conscience and convenience.* Hawthorne, NY: Aldine De Gruyter.

Rush, B. (1787). An enquiry into the effects of public punishments upon criminals and society. In N. K. Teeters (Ed.), (1991). *Two essays: A plan for the punishment of crime by Benjamin Rush, M.D.* (pp. 1–17). Philadelphia, PA: The Pennsylvania Prison Society.

Rush, B. (1792). Considerations on the injustice and impolicy of punishing murder by death. In N. K. Teeters (Ed.), (1991). *Two essays: A plan for the punishment of crime by Benjamin Rush, M.D.* (pp. 18–24). Philadelphia, PA: The Pennsylvania Prison Society.

Siegel, L., & Bartollas, C. (2011). *Corrections today.* Belmont, CA: Wadsworth, Cengage Learning.

Silverman, I. J. (2001). *Corrections—A comprehensive review* (2nd ed.). Wadsworth: Thomson Learning.

Stohr, M. K., & Walsh, A. (2012). *Corrections: The essentials.* Thousand Oaks, CA: Sage.

Tonry, M. (1987). *Sentencing reform impacts.* Washington, DC: National Institute of Justice.

United Nations (1954). *The indeterminate sentence.* New York.

Zupan, L. L. (1991). *Jails: Reform and the new generation philosophy.* Cincinnati, OH: Anderson Publishing Co.

3

MODERN SENTENCING REFORM IN THE UNITED STATES: PRECIPITATING FACTORS AND EARLY APPROACHES

Chapter Objectives:

- To learn about the various factors in the 1960s and 1970s that led to modern sentencing reform.
- To understand the concepts of disparity, discrimination, and discretion associated with indeterminate sentencing schemes.
- To realize that both liberals and conservatives favored a more structured approach to sentencing—but for very different reasons.
- To understand the philosophical critiques of indeterminate sentencing.
- To appreciate the common goals of sentencing reform.
- To get an overview of four approaches to modern sentencing reform.

The Move Toward Modern Sentencing Reform — Precipitating Factors

All 50 states, the District of Columbia, and the federal system had indeterminate sentencing schemes prior to 1975 (Tonry, 1987). Judges had enormous discretion in setting minimum and maximum prison terms when sentencing convicted offenders and were constrained only by broad statutes. The parole board subsequently decided when an inmate would be released, after he or she served a portion of a prison sentence.

Between the mid-seventies and the late-eighties, many states and the federal system initiated some type of **modern sentencing reform**. This broad term encompasses a widespread movement from indeterminate sentencing to determinate sentencing. Variation lied in the particular type(s) of reform proposed. In many states sentencing commissions created sentencing guidelines. Such guidelines essentially collapsed the sentencing decision to be based on two criteria—offense severity and prior record. Another example of sentencing reform was the passage of mandatory sentencing laws, which most often were written to target violent, gun, and drug crimes. Three strikes laws constituted another type of modern sentencing reform and were written to target serious and violent habitual felons. Some states eliminated discretionary parole or adopted parole guidelines as types of sentencing reforms (Tonry, 1987). Regardless of the specific reform(s) enacted by states and the federal system, the goals of reform were consistent and clear: to decrease judicial discretion, to increase sentencing uniformity, to increase predictability, and to decrease sentencing disparity and discrimination.

So, what were some of the reasons behind the development and institution of sentencing reforms? Well, it's important to understand that the impetus for widespread change in sentencing practices came from both liberals and conservatives who both raised critiques of indeterminate sentencing. It is certainly unusual for liberals and conservatives to agree on much about the criminal justice system, but both called for more structured or determinate sentencing schemes. The difference lay in the *reasons* for their dissatisfaction with indeterminate sentencing.

Several forces undermined indeterminate sentencing and led to sentencing reform (Tonry, 1987). We will discuss the following: (1) disparities, discretion, and discrimination inherent in indeterminate sentencing; (2) mounting research that questioned the efficacy of rehabilitation programs; (3) "liberal" critiques of indeterminate sentencing that included a general concern for prisoners' rights; (4) "conservative" critiques of indeterminate sentencing, which coincided in part with decisions of the Warren Court that emphasized the rights of the accused; (5) mounting crime rates; (6) changes in the dominant philosophy about the purposes of punishment; and (7) the economic recession of the 1970s.

Disparity, Discretion, Discrimination, and Indeterminate Sentencing

Both liberals and conservatives pointed to the fact that sentencing disparity was inherent in indeterminate sentencing. Both sides focused on the how indeterminate sentencing could allow defendants in similar cases (according to legally relevant characteristics) to receive vastly different sentences. The decision of whether to parole a prisoner could rest not only on the prisoner's criminal record and behavior in prison, but also on the particular values and/or idiosyncrasies of the parole entity. A common theme was the lack of standards in decision making that determined a convicted offender's sentence.

Unbridled Discretion and Indeterminate Sentencing

The Critiques from Judge Marvin Frankel

Under indeterminate sentencing, the defendant has little sense of how long his or her actual sentence will be. In his book, *Criminal Sentences: Law Without Order* (1973), federal judge Marvin E. Frankel wrote of his general disgust with the practice of indeterminate sentencing for federal offenses, citing both unchecked judicial discretion in handing down a sentence and the broad powers that the parole board had in deciding (without stated standards) when an inmate was to be released.

Frankel pointed to some examples from the federal code in the 1970s, when he wrote the book. Assault on a federal officer could be punishable by a fine and imprisonment for "not more than" ten years. The federal kidnapping statute allowed for "imprisonment for any term of years or for life." Robbing a federally insured bank was punishable by "not more than twenty-five years." He found the phrase "not more than" troublesome and believed this meant that federal trial judges were answerable to no one, except their own consciences. He linked the broad discretion afforded to judges with huge discrepancies in the sentences handed down for those convicted of the same offense.

Frankel concluded:

> This means in a great majority of federal criminal cases that a defendant who comes up for sentencing has no way of knowing or reliably predicting whether he will walk out of the courtroom on probation, or be locked up for a term of years that may consume the rest of his life, or something in between. (p. 6)

Frankel characterized the federal law at the time as lacking "meaningful criteria" for determining sentences. He went on to say that most judges were trained as lawyers and that law curriculum lacks meaningful preparation to address sentencing issues. Frankel also acknowledged the rather homogeneous characteristics of judges—older males who lack extensive contact with criminal defendants. He noted that unlike many criminal defendants, few judges had come from economically disadvantaged backgrounds. He stated, "Whatever few things may be said for them, our procedures for selecting judges do not improve the prospects of sensitive, knowledgeable sentencing" (p. 14).

Referring to mounting research showing sentencing disparity on the part of judges, Frankel commented:

> The evidence is conclusive that judges of widely varying attitudes on sentencing, administering statutes that confer huge measures of discretion, mete out widely divergent sentences where the divergences are explainable only by the variations among the judges, not by material differences in the defendants or their crimes. (p. 21)

Frankel also pointed out potential problems with the presentence investigation report that probation departments compiled to reflect the background of the defendant. He suggested that it may be incomplete or otherwise flawed and the offender's background often plays a significant role in sentencing decisions. Although Frankel observed that judges rarely gave much or any reasoning for imposing sentences, that it was likely that judges considered what should be legally irrelevant characteristics, such as race, religiosity, or their own life experiences with certain types of crimes when deciding on a sentence.

Frankel also found problematic the experiences of prisoners sentenced under indeterminate sentencing schemes. He suggested than when prisoners see disparities in sentencing they have less faith in the criminal justice system as a whole. Frankel suggested that prisoners lacked guidance in how to behave and which prison rules are enforced. He described little communication by parole boards to prisoners about how to obtain parole or for their decisions to grant or deny parole. He suggested that the secrecy of decisions undermined the notion that these decisions are legitimate ones. Instead, Frankel argued that the sentencing practices and correctional system in the 1970s were characterized by a lack of rationality and encouraged arbitrariness and discrimination.

Frankel stated:

> The absurdly broad statutes, the gross inequalities, the unchecked discretion of judges, the absence of reasoned explanations, the haste and the general arbitrariness—all are defects the legal profession is schooled to identify and remedy, not really to foster. The problem has been too little law, not too much. (p. 58)

Critiques from Criminologist Sheldon Glueck

Decades before Judge Frankel's attack on indeterminate sentencing in the federal system, noted criminologist Sheldon Glueck (1936) shared his observations on states' indeterminate sentencing schemes in his book, *Crime and Justice*. Like Frankel, Glueck addressed the fact that the amount of legally relevant information about specific cases that is available to the judge is often limited, that judges didn't take enough time to review the information that they had at their disposal, and that the effect of judges' personal backgrounds, as opposed to the relevant legal characteristics, on their sentencing decisions may be profound. He also noted the lack of judicial training in areas relevant to handing down a meaningful indeterminate sentence. He suggested that those with training in the fields of medicine, psychology, and sociology may be better suited for this task. Like Frankel, Glueck argued 37 years earlier that upon pronouncing a sentence that judges in the states rarely wrote an opinion supporting or justifying the sentence that they chose. They purported to "individualize punishment" but lacked scientific criteria to understand offender criminality which would guide sentencing decisions.

Glueck proposed four suggestions for a more "scientific and just individualization" (p. 225). His first suggestion was to differentiate the sentencing decision from the finding of guilt or not. He asserted that although both the determination of guilt or innocence and sentencing are within the purview of the courts, that the process and goals of each task is different. Judges are trained to follow procedural rules in trial and based on evidence decide whether the defendant is guilty. Determining treatment is a more specialized task—one that requires specific training. His second suggestion involved the establishment of a tribunal, which was to include "a psychiatrist or psychologist, a sociologist or educator and the trial judge" to aid in developing a sentence (p. 226). The third principle discussed by Glueck involved developing a treatment program that was malleable and reflected the offender's progress throughout his or her sentence. The offender's progress report would be given to the tribunal to consider appropriate type and remaining length of treatment. Glueck likened this process to that of a medical doctor who may have to modify treatment of a disease based on how the patient responds to the originally prescribed treatment plan. Glueck's fourth suggestion was to aim to safeguard the offender's rights from arbitrariness by the tribunal. Statutes expressly stating the powers of the tribunal would be ideal and codifying types of offenders and the appropriate treatment for various classes of offenders would promote uniformity. In addition, Glueck suggested that the offender have access to legal counsel and witnesses at the sentencing hearing and access to the reports filed by the tribunal. Another safeguard would involve regular review of the individual's case.

In addition to a concern for the rights of the offender, Glueck also acknowledged the importance of public safety in imposing an indeterminate sentence. He stated:

> To be effective the treatment tribunal would have to be empowered to impose a *wholly indeterminate* sentence, so that manifestly dangerous individuals might be kept under control within institutions and on parole for long periods—if necessary throughout life—while those rapidly rehabilitated might be released, at least experimentally, after relatively short periods of control. (pp. 228–229)

Like the federal system, there often seemed to be no rhyme or reason to how sentences were determined within states. Colorado statutes in the 1960s required someone convicted of first degree murder to serve at least 10 years before becoming eligible for parole, yet someone convicted of a lesser degree of murder was required to serve at least 15 years. Another issue of concern was high maximum sentences. In the 1960s, for offenses in many states, judges could decide on a penalty that ranged from probation to a long prison term of 20 to 25 years in prison. An additional concern was that few sentencing systems distinguished occasional from habitual offenders in setting potential sentences (The President's Commission on Law Enforcement and Administration of Justice, 1967).

California's Adult Authority—An Example of Indeterminate Sentencing

Like the federal system, many states also had indeterminate sentencing statutes that provided enormous discretion to correctional personnel. California's first indeterminate sentencing establishment, under Penal Code § 1168, was passed on May 18, 1917, and was effective on July 27, 1917 (Johnson, 1977). It prohibited the sentencing judge from deciding on an exact sentence length for convicted offenders who were to be imprisoned. Statutes for specific offenses indicated the minimum and maximum sentences and so the sentence that was ultimately served had to lie within these boundaries. The convicted offender, however, was not informed of his or her exact sentence length at the time of sentencing.

Section 1168 of the California Penal Code (West, 1970) read the same from the date of its inception through the 1970s and described the sentencing process as follows:

> Every person convicted of a public offense, for which imprisonment in any reformatory or state prison is now prescribed by law shall, unless such convicted person be placed on probation, a new trial granted, or the imposing of sentence suspended, be sentenced to be imprisoned in a state prison, but the court in imposing the sentence shall not fix the term or duration of the period of imprisonment.

Section 1168a (West, 1970) delineated a similar sentencing process for women in which the duration not be fixed:

> Every female convicted of a public offense, for which imprisonment in any state prison is now prescribed by law shall, unless such convicted female is placed on probation, a new trial granted, or the imposing of sentence suspended, be

sentenced to detention at the California Institution for Women, but the court in imposing the sentence shall not fix the term or duration of the period of detention.

Part D of § 1168 of the California Penal Code (West, 1970) stated:

> The governing authority of the reformatory or prison in which such person may be confined, or any board or commission that may be hereafter given authority so to do, shall determine after the expiration of the minimum term of imprisonment has expired, what length of time, if any, such person shall be confined, unless the sentence be sooner terminated by commutation or pardon by the governor of the state; and if it be determined that such person so sentenced be released before the expiration for the maximum period for which he is sentenced, then such person shall be released at such time as the governing board, commission or other authority may determine.

The "governing authority" in California was originally called the State Board of Prison Directors. In 1941 it was called the Board of Prison Terms. In 1944, it was called the Adult Authority.

An extreme example of a state justice system putting the inmate's fate in the hands of parole authority was the discretion afforded to California's Adult Authority in the 1970s. The Adult Authority decided when to parole an inmate, imposed conditions of parole, and could revoke parole if the offender violated the conditions. During this time in the state of California, 94 percent of prisoners were released through discretionary parole, while 5 percent served the statutorily defined maximum sentence and 1 percent died in prison (Tomlinson, 1973–74).

The California Penal Code § 3020 (West, 1970) stated the powers of the Adult Authority:

> In the case of all persons heretofore or hereafter sentenced under the provisions of Section 1168 of this code, the Adult Authority may determine and redetermine, after the actual commencement of imprisonment, what length of time, if any, such person shall be imprisoned, unless the sentence be sooner terminated by commutation or pardon by the Governor of the State.

Section 3040 (West, 1970) stated, "The Adult Authority shall have the power to allow prisoners imprisoned in the state prisons to go upon parole outside the prison walls and enclosures."

Section 3040, subsection 2, "Purpose" (West, 1970) stated,

> A major purpose of the Indeterminate Sentencing Law § 3020 et seq. is to permit individual treatment of offenders according to the best judgment of the Adult Authority, and the fact that the other prisoners have had their sentences reduced or been granted parole affords no ground for complaint by the petitioner" *Azeria v. California Adult Authority*, (1961) 13 Cal Rptr, 839, 193 C.A. 2d 1.

As a vocal advocate of just deserts philosophy, Andrew von Hirsch (1976) also described the gross inequities in sentence type and length that come with the individualized treatment approach that seeks to rehabilitate offenders. Like Frankel, von Hirsch advocated a presumptive sentence for crimes based on offense seriousness. He also called for reserving incarceration for the most serious offenses, in line with his advocating an approach based on "commensurate deserts."

Questioning the Efficacy of Rehabilitation

The Martinson Report

Another critique of indeterminate sentencing involved the assertion that there was little evidence that rehabilitation programs were effective in reducing offender recidivism. Remember the practice of indeterminate sentencing rests on the notion that prisoners were not to be released until they were deemed by the parole board to have been "rehabilitated."

In the 1970s, scholarly studies evaluating the effect of prison rehabilitation programs on recidivism reported inconsistent findings about the efficacy of rehabilitation in reducing recidivism. Around this time, researchers began to find that prisoners who participated in institutional treatment programs still committed crimes when they were released from prisons.

In 1974, Robert Martinson's article, "What Works: Questions and Answers about Prison Reform" was published in the conservative policy journal, *The Public Interest*. In this work, he reviewed 231 studies published between 1945 and 1967 that evaluated various types of rehabilitation programs. Martinson (1974) listed the following three criteria for a study's inclusion in his review: "A study had to be an evaluation of a treatment method, it had to employ an independent measure of the improvement secured by that method, and it had to use some control group, some untreated individuals with whom the treated ones could be compared" (p. 24).

The studies that he reviewed utilized a variety of outcomes to measure offender improvement, including recidivism rates, vocational success, educational achievement, and personality and attitude changes. He included these in a larger report, but focused his article in *The Public Interest* on how rehabilitation programs affected recidivism. The programs varied in type and Martinson presented separate sections for evaluations of the following types of programs: educational and vocational training, training adult inmates, individual counseling, group counseling, transforming the institutional environment, medical treatment, psychotherapy in community settings, probation or parole compared to prison, intensive supervision, and community treatment. For each section he provided narrative accounts of the programs and summarized the conclusions that the authors made regarding the specific program's effect on recidivism.

His research, which became known as "The Martinson Report," concluded, "**With few and isolated exceptions, the rehabilitative efforts that have been reported so far have had no appreciable effect on recidivism**" (p. 25). His findings ushered in a "nothing works" philosophy regarding rehabilitation programs in the fields of corrections and criminology for about a decade.

His conclusions represented a challenge to the practice of indeterminate sentencing, because indeterminate sentencing schemes call for the release of a prisoner to be based on evidence of rehabilitation. The Martinson Report undermined the idea that individualized/offender-oriented sentencing had positive consequences. Remember, the rehabilitative model encompasses the view that the offender is suffering from some defect that can be corrected. If, as Martinson suggested, rehabilitation does not "work," then the glaring questions that remained were on what basis were people being released and whether they were, in fact, better prepared to live crime-free lives after participating in treatment programs in prison. If rehabilitation programs have little or no effect on recidivism, the question that needed an answer was, "what are we waiting for before we release prisoners back to society?"

The publicity of Martinson's study had a profound impact on the decline in faith in rehabilitation during this time period and therefore it undermined the concept of indeterminate sentencing. Although this may not have had a causative effect on sentencing reform, *The Martinson Report* was well publicized and its implications were consistent with growing sentiments that challenged the practice of indeterminate sentencing.

Later in this chapter we will explore the shift in corrections from emphasizing rehabilitation to focusing on punishment and deterrence. At the end of his article, Martinson pointed to the importance of deterrence, in contrast to rehabilitation, as a guiding goal of sentencing. He asserted that punishment of offenders may accomplish deterrence for would-be offenders. Martinson stated:

> Since we have almost no idea of the deterrent functions that our present system performs or that future strategies might be made to perform, it is possible that there is indeed something that works—that to some extent is working right now in front of our noses, and that might be made to work better—something that deters rather than cures, something that does not so much reform convicted offenders as prevent criminal behavior in the first place. (p. 50)

Other Philosophical Challenges to Rehabilitation

Other criminologists and legal scholars also challenged the practice of basing sentence length on evidence of offender rehabilitation. Judge Marvin Frankel (1973) noted that when imposing an indeterminate sentence the sentencing judge does not know when the offender will be "well" and so the corrections officials who are in charge of treatment decided when he or she would be released.

Frankel criticized the assumption that all offenders are "sick," and therefore he did not believe that all criminals need "therapy" or "rehabilitation." Ernest van den Haag shared this perspective in his book, *Punishing Criminals* (1976). Frankel characterized many criminals as persons who calculate the odds of being caught and punished and chose to commit the crimes. Examples include those convicted of organized crime and counterfeiting, as well as tax evaders. Frankel felt that for such criminals, "treatment" was not meaningful or appropriate.

Frankel also questioned the ability of the criminal justice system to know how to treat those who are deemed "sick" criminals. He stated, "What is disagreeable—and vicious—is to cage prisoners for indeterminate stretches while we set about their assured rehabilitation, not knowing what to do for them or really, whether we can do any useful thing for them" (p. 92).

Frankel questioned the appropriateness of likening the treatment of criminals to a medical model and asserted that when treating other medical illnesses, there is usually an expectation of how long the treatment will take. On the contrary, indeterminate prison sentences do not specify an expected time to "wellness." He perceived a sentence to prison not as a mechanism or venue for rehabilitation (because he found little evidence of effective treatment in prisons), but rather to warehouse offenders.

In his 1976 book, *Doing Justice*, von Hirsch described the notion that the criminal sanction should serve the purpose of rehabilitating the offender as problematic. He disagreed with this practice, stating, "Since this theory looks to offenders' need for treatment rather than to the character of their crimes, it allows different sentences for similar offenses" (p. 12). Instead of basing the sentencing decision on severity of the crime, the sentence (for example prison or not) was determined by whether the offender seemed amenable to prison or community sanctions. Thus, inequities abounded. In addition, von Hirsch pointed to the lack of evidence that rehabilitation actually was effective.

Reitz (1998) summarized the sentiments of the time and noted, "Even for the sophisticated policy makers, who understood that rehabilitation 'occasionally works,' the intellectual and political climate of the 1970s made it difficult to maintain that rehabilitation theory should continue to dictate the framework of *entire* sentencing systems" (p. 544). As we will discuss in the chapters outlining various sentencing reforms, rehabilitation programs began to be considered appropriate only when used as supplements to what was considered deserved punishment, such as imprisonment.

"Liberal" Critiques of Indeterminate Sentencing— A Concern for Prisoners' Rights

So-called liberal criticisms of the practice of indeterminate sentencing centered around a theme that prisoners were at the mercy of corrections officials. Correctional personnel played a role in deciding their release date through communications with parole boards about the inmate's conduct. In addition, the state determined correctional resources and correctional personnel influenced the general living conditions of inmates.

The Practice of Parole

While the specific practices varied widely from one state to another (see Siegel & Bartollas, 2011), offenders could be eligible for parole after serving only a fraction of their sentence. In the early 1980s, inmates at the Louisiana State Penitentiary, for example, were eligible for parole after serving only one-third of the sentence handed down by the judge (Rideau and Wikberg, 1992). The stated task of parole boards across the nation was to determine whether the offender had been rehabilitated. This practice allowed certain offenders to be released earlier than other offenders who had committed the same crime (according to legally relevant characteristics).

In the 1960s and early 1970s, civil rights groups, among others, began to question the benevolence of the government. Many liberal-leaning academics, legal scholars, and activists wondered whether the state and state-run institutions (like prisons) were acting in the best interest of the people. Regarding prisons and the widespread practice of indeterminate sentencing, these groups inquired as to how race affected the actual time an offender would serve in prison before being released via discretionary parole. Was the practice of indeterminate sentencing, in fact, catering to the offender's treatment needs? If so, the race of the offender should have no relation to the parole board's decision of whether to release an offender. Or was the correctional system operating in a discriminatory manner? Were black offenders who had conviction offenses and conduct records in prison similar to those of white offenders being denied parole at a higher rate?

The very flexibility of indeterminate sentencing schemes enabled the potential for parole decisions to be made based on legally irrelevant factors, such as race. Parole board judgments were not subjected to any scrutiny or formal review. There was a possibility that discrimination, not evidence of rehabilitation, was the basis of some parole decisions.

In *Life Sentences: Rage and Survival Behind Bars* (Rideau & Wikberg, 1992), inmate Wilbert Rideau described the parole board process at the Louisiana State Penitentiary from the offender's perspective. He recounted that all five members of the Louisiana parole board had been appointed by the governor and that there were no official qualifications to be eligible to serve on the parole board. He stated that membership on the parole board often reflected the current governor's philosophy. His description of parole proceedings suggested that the process was quite arbitrary and based on the subjective feelings of each member and that the majority vote determined whether an individual was to be released.

Liberals drew from mounting social science literature that showed the extent of disparate and discriminatory sentencing practices. According to Blumstein, Cohen, Martin, and Tonry (1983), "*Disparity* exists when 'like cases' with respect to case attributes—regardless of their legitimacy—are sentenced differently" (p. 8). An example of disparity might involve the differences in sentencing practices of judges within the same jurisdiction. The scholars distinguish disparity from discrimination, "*Discrimination* exists when some case attribute that is objectionable—typically on moral or legal grounds—can be shown to be associated with sentence outcomes after all other relevant variables are adequately controlled" (p. 8). Race, gender, class, and bail status are examples of case characteristics that should not affect sentence outcome. If it is shown that they do, this is evidence of discrimination in sentencing.

Evidence from multiple research studies showed that extralegal characteristics, such as race, affected how long a convicted offender would serve. The majority of studies showed that black defendants were serving longer sentences than white defendants. Studies also showed that longer prison terms were being administered when whites were victimized compared to when blacks were victimized, suggesting that white lives were valued more than black lives.

Some suggested that from the inception of indeterminate sentencing judges and parole boards used vast discretion and this created a prison population that was largely poor and minority. Liberals targeted indeterminate sentencing schemes as facilitating this inequity. For liberals, indeterminate sentencing was a mechanism for instituting racial discrimination within the correctional system.

The President's Commission on Law Enforcement and Administration of Justice report, *The Challenge of Crime in a Free Society* (1967), addressed the fact that parole board members need to pay close attention to the individual elements of each case with which they are presented. They recommended that parole board members should be appointed on the basis of competence and that they should be properly trained. They called for the parole decision to be based on explicit standards.

Prison Violence

In addition to concerns about parole decision making, there was a general concern about prisoners' rights in the 1960s and 1970s that stemmed from the realities of prison overcrowding, violence within prisons, and prison riots.

Inmate-on-Inmate Violence

Wikberg (1992) described an extreme level of inmate-on-inmate violence at the Louisiana State Penitentiary (also known as Angola) in the 1970s:

> By 1973, violence was a brutal, daily reality. Double-bladed hatchets, swords, long steel knives, and Roman-style shields were commonplace. Men slept with steel plates and JC Penney catalogues tied to their chests, even in maximum-security cellblocks, men slept with their doors tied and with blankets tied around their bunks as a means of protection and security. Angola was a lawless jungle, without order or discipline. Fear was the silent ruler of all. From 1972 to 1975, 40 prisoners were stabbed to death and 350 more seriously injured by knife wounds. Gang wars and clique power struggles kept the stretchers rolling; the morbid call, "One on the stretcher!" was soon something to be ignored, generally accepted as a routine factor of doing time. Enslavement among inmates was widespread. By 1975 Angola had become the bloodiest prison in the nation. (p. 41)

Angola was admittedly an extreme example. Although all prisons certainly did not have the level of violence experienced by inmates at Angola, the negative experiences of inmates at other prisons also came to the public's attention during the 1960s and 1970s. A "hands off" doctrine had guided courts regarding the operation of prisons from the Great Depression until the late 1960s. Despite reports of prison riots and violence, there had been little judicial intervention by the courts during this time. It was not until *Robinson v. State of California* (1962) that the Supreme Court applied the Eighth Amendment to complaints levied by state prison inmates. In 1964, in *Cooper v. Pate*, the Supreme

Court decided that because of the Civil Rights Act of 1871, state inmates could bring lawsuits in federal court for grievances. This case symbolically and practically ended the "hands off" era of court nonintervention in the operation of prisons (DeLisi & Conis, 2013).

In 1967 in their report, *The Challenge of Crime in a Free Society* (1967), The President's Commission on Law Enforcement and Administration of Justice, however, still acknowledged problems with the correctional system:

> The correctional apparatus is isolated in the sense that its officials do not have everyday working relationships with officials from the system's other branches, like those that commonly exist between politicians and prosecutors, or prosecutors and judges. It is isolated in the sense that what it does with, to, or for the people under its supervision is seldom governed by any but the most broadly written statutes and is almost never scrutinized by appellate courts. Finally, it is isolated from the public partly by its invisibility and physical remoteness; partly by the inherent lack of drama in most of its activities, but perhaps most importantly by the fact that the correctional apparatus is often used—or misused—by both the criminal justice system and the public as a rug under which disturbing problems and people can be swept. (p. 41)

Social science research also documented the negative consequences of long term incarceration. Clemmer (1940, 1950) described a process of "prisonization," in which inmates were socialized in prison to adopt antisocial values and adopt an oppositional culture. In 1958 Gresham Sykes wrote *The Society of Captives*, in which he described the prison experience as one that embodies the notions of punishment and retribution, as opposed to rehabilitation.

The President's Commission on Law Enforcement and the Administration of Justice (1967) stated the ideal versus the reality of the practice of rehabilitation in prisons at the time as follows:

> Life in many institutions is at best barren and futile, at worst unspeakably brutal and degrading. To be sure, the offenders in such institutions are incapacitated from committing further crimes while serving their sentences, but the conditions in which they live are the poorest possible preparation for their successful reentry into society, and often merely reinforce in them a pattern of manipulation or destructiveness. (p. 159)

The Attica Prison Riot

In the early 1970s the public became more aware of the conditions within prisons. Prison riots, including the Attica prison riot in September 1971, gained national attention as the plight of the prisoner and state response to rioters was televised. Earlier that year, prisoners at Attica had engaged in peaceful protests over the living conditions, including but not limited to poor food, unsatisfactory medical care, little recreation, meaningless job assignments, overcrowding, religious freedom (especially among Muslim inmates), and guard assignments, which led to arbitrary and unclear enforcement of prison rules. Attica's population was overwhelmingly black and Puerto Rican, yet there was only one Puerto Rican correctional officer, and there were zero black officers.

Approximately 1,000 of the Attica prison's approximately 2,200 inmates took control of the prison during the riot. These inmates took 33 staff hostage. Negotiations took place during the first several days of the riot, but broke down over the issue of complete amnesty for inmates involved in the riot. Then-New York governor Nelson Rockefeller (who did not participate in the negotiations in person) called for an armed assault that involved the state police taking back control of the prison, which left 39 people dead, including ten correctional officers. The aftermath of Attica involved an investigation that showed reckless use of firearms by the police. Coverage of the Attica prison riot negotiations and images of the armed assault from outside the prison were televised.

The general concern for prisoners' rights and living conditions was intricately related to the questions of fairness in the process determining sentence length. Why subject offenders to horrific conditions in prison, especially if no good vis-à-vis rehabilitation was accompanying the prison experience? The practice of indeterminate sentencing was under fire by liberals who saw arbitrariness at best and discriminatory and brutal practices at worst regarding the incarceration experience.

The above sentiments urged a need for change in sentencing and were espoused by civil rights groups, civil liberties groups, legal scholars, and criminologists in academia — largely liberal forces. Conservatives also argued for sentencing reform. However, they called for sentencing reform for vastly different reasons.

Conservative Critiques of Indeterminate Sentencing

The Conservative View of Indeterminate Sentencing

Conservatives also pointed to sentencing inequities inherent in indeterminate sentencing schemes, but expressed outrage over the potential that under indeterminate sentencing, an offender could potentially only serve a small fraction of his or her sentence, if deemed "rehabilitated." Instead of focusing on disparity and discrimination as consequences of indeterminate sentencing, conservatives brought to light cases in which *dangerous and violent felons were prematurely released* under indeterminate sentencing.

Conservatives pointed to state statutes which prescribed very wide ranges of years that an offender could serve for a variety of serious crimes. A statute on "the books" in California actually set the range of prison time for a person convicted of murder to between 1 and 99 years. Just how long the convicted offender would actually serve depended on the discretion of the parole board. The notion that a murderer could be released after serving only a year or two in prison struck conservatives as way too lenient.

The Courts and Landmark Supreme Court Decisions

During the 1960s, the Supreme Court, led by Chief Justice Earl Warren, handed down decisions that seemed by many to benefit the accused at the expense of justice and the crime victim. These landmark decisions concerned the actions of criminal justice actors, many of them focusing on the police. Under Chief Justice Warren, the Supreme Court sent a clear message that criminal convictions would be overturned if they were obtained in violation of Constitution amendments. Supreme Court rulings benefitted the defendant with respect to the admissibility of evidence involved the Fourth Amendment, which protects against unreasonable searches and seizures (*Mapp v. Ohio* (1961)), the Fifth Amendment that protects the accused against self-incrimination (*Miranda v. Arizona* (1966)), and the Sixth Amendment, which specifies that a defendant have the assistance of counsel for his defense (*Gideon v. Wainright* (1963)). These decisions fueled perceptions that the criminal justice system was "coddling the criminal."

These decisions clearly impacted the actions of police officers and court actors. They were profound decisions and the public began to perceive that the rights of the accused were more important than imposition of punishments that they felt were just. The perception that a criminal could "get off on a technicality" was rather common. By the 1970s, public opinion polls showed that many Americans felt that the "pendulum had swung too far to the left."

Public reaction to these Supreme Court decisions was consistent with mounting dissatisfaction with indeterminate sentencing and the correctional system in the United States. A barrage of Supreme Court decisions benefitting the accused influenced the general public to question lenient sentencing practices and rehabilitation. There was a call for more determinate sentencing and a criminal justice system that made the offender responsible.

The Role of Victims' Rights Groups

The President's Commission on Law Enforcement and Administration of Justice (1967), stated, "One of the most neglected subjects in the study of crime is its victims: the persons, households, and businesses that bear the brunt of crime in the United States" (p. 38).

The Victims' Rights Movement in the United States developed in the 1960s and 1970s. Social scientists, journalists, government officials, and some members of the criminal justice system made the argument that the victim had become the forgotten person in the criminal justice system. This recognition came as crime rates rose. Victims and their families were distressed by the lack of attention and respect given to the crime victim.

The Victims' Rights Movement began with several different groups trying to bring attention to the plight of the crime victim and advancing remedies to alleviate the suffering brought on both by criminal victimization and by the criminal justice system's often insensitive treatment of victims and their families (Karmen, 2013).

The president's crime commission studied the plight of the crime victim and noted that oftentimes when the offender is incarcerated the victim cannot receive restitution. Their report concluded that legislators, law enforcement officials, and the general public supported some form of state compensation for victims of violent crime. Public support for victim compensation followed society's outrage at brutal predatory violent crimes, which were portrayed by the mass media during the 1960s.

The 1970s brought attention back on to the crime victim and the harm suffered by victims. Concomitant to the focus on helping the victim was making sure the offender would be held responsible for the harm he or she caused the victim. Instead of "treating" the offender, the Victims' Rights Movement focused more on making sure the offender was properly punished.

Mounting Crime Rates and the Law and Order Movement

The Crime Wave of the 1960s and 1970s

The rate of reported violent crimes increased dramatically during the 1960s. In 1960, the Uniform Crime Report (UCR) estimated that the violent crime rate (measured as a composite of Part 1 violent offenses—murder and non-negligent manslaughter, forcible rape, robbery, and aggravated assault per 100,000) was 160.9 per 100,000. By 1965 the rate had risen to 200.2 per 100,000 and by 1969 the violent crime rate was 328.7 per 100,000. In 1960 the rate of murder and non-negligent manslaughter was 5.1 per 100,000, but by 1969, the rate was 7.3 per 100,000 (Uniform Crime Reports, 2012). Property crime also rose during the 1960s.

People were concerned by crime, especially violent crime. Public awareness of the crime situation was widespread. In the 1960s and 1970s, the media was barraging Americans with images of street crimes and political assassinations. In the living rooms of Americans were broadcast mass murders, such as the gruesome killings by the Manson family.

While crime rates were increasing, so were the perceptions that criminals were being treated too leniently by our criminal justice system. Crime became a political issue. Ronald Reagan was elected governor of California in 1966 and Richard Nixon won the presidency in 1968. Both ran on "law and order" campaigns. Nixon vowed to restore safety in America's cities. The law and order movement considered a strong criminal justice system to be the answer to the crime problem. The criticism of the criminal justice system, if any, was that it wasn't harsh enough on criminals.

The law and order movement called for various strategies, including strengthening police forces and ensuring that convicted criminals be punished appropriately for their crimes. Law and order supporters called for harsher criminal sanctions for offenders and suggested that this would deter offenders. Their focus was on protecting law-abiding citizens and they opposed the lenient treatment of criminals that they perceived to be occurring in the United States. It was politically unattractive for a public leader to tout the importance of "treating" the "sick" offender through rehabilitation programs in prisons. As rehabilitation programs went out of fashion in the United States, the practice of indeterminate sentencing, which rests on the practice of rehabilitating the offender until he or she is ready to return to society, was challenged.

Fear of Crime

Ferraro (1995) defined fear of crime as "an emotional reaction of dread or anxiety to crime or symbols that a person associates with crime" (p. xiii). Skogan and Maxfield (1981) noted that early polling organizations such as Gallop and Harris aimed to measure fear of crime by asking respondents about their reactions to crime such as feeling uneasy or being afraid to walk the streets at night. They found by using such measures that fear of crime rose greatly between 1965 and the mid-1970s. The researchers concluded "Other research and our own surveys indicate that people think of crime largely in terms of homicide, robbery, and assaultive violence" (p. 128). During the time that violent crime was rising in the United States, so was fear among its residents.

In their report, *The Challenge of Crime in a Free Society* (1967), the President's Commission on Law Enforcement and Administration of Justice stated, "The most damaging of the effects of violent crime is fear, and that fear must not be belittled." The commission highlighted the fact that most crime is committed by young males and that street crime is largely an urban phenomenon (see also Ferraro, 1995, and Skogan & Maxfield, 1981). The commission found that fear of crime had affected Americans' daily habits and even caused them to move.

During the 1960s and 1970s, Americans witnessed more crimes, especially violent predatory offenses. They were fearful of crime. The general public called for harsher punishments for violent offenses. Indeterminate sentencing seemed to allow for punishments that were too lenient for violent offenders.

Changes in the Dominant Philosophy about the Purposes of Punishment

The criminal justice system was accused by the general public of being too easy on criminals. A common perception about the correctional system in particular was that by only requiring the offender to serve a fraction of the prison sentence handed down (as was the case for most offenders sentenced via indeterminate sentencing), justice was not being served. Many believed that prisoners simply were not serving enough time.

Therefore, not only academics, but politicians and the general public (who elects politicians) questioned the notion of rehabilitation and a sentencing scheme that rests on the assumption that it works. As we noted, however, liberals also had criticisms of indeterminate sentencing, but for very different reasons. It is unusual for liberals and conservatives to agree on anything regarding the criminal justice system. In the case of indeterminate sentencing, however, both agreed that sentencing reform was needed, albeit for different reasons.

Rehabilitation, however, was not replaced by a single sentencing goal of corrections. As early as 1967, the President's Commission on Law Enforcement and Administration of Justice noted multiple goals as appropriate in sentencing:

> There is no decision in the criminal process that is as complicated and difficult as the one made by the sentencing judge. A sentence prescribes punishment,

but it also should be the foundation of an attempt to rehabilitate the offender, to insure that he does not endanger the community, and to deter others from similar crimes in the future. Often, these objectives are mutually inconsistent, and the sentencing judge must choose one at the expense of the others. (p. 141)

Reitz (1998) concisely observed, "The last twenty-five years can be characterized as a period in which no single policy viewpoint has stood squarely behind the operation of U.S. sentencing structures—unless it has been the view that rehabilitation was not the way to go" (pp. 544–545).

The Economic Recession of the 1970s

The reasons we have discussed that led to the move away from indeterminate sentencing to modern sentencing reform are largely philosophical and theoretical in nature. One cannot, however, ignore the nature of the economy in the 1970s as a driving force in the decrease in prison rehabilitation programs, which cost money. The economic recession that occurred between 1973 and 1975 was characterized by both high unemployment and inflation. The term "stagflation" described the economic condition of both continuing inflation (including rising interest rates) and stagnant business activity, coupled with an increasing unemployment rate (U.S. Department of State (2012, August 24)).

In the midst of the recession, law-abiding people were having trouble getting jobs. A question that concerned the general public was why we were helping criminals become more employable with prison educational and vocational programs when law-abiding citizens were struggling to find employment.

Taxpayer money funded prison rehabilitation programs. At this time many United States citizens were struggling to find work and facing economic challenges associated with the recession—like being able to afford to live. Promoting prison rehabilitation programs was far from a popular goal among the general public. Few politicians rallied for these programs that were already facing a barrage of critiques from liberals and conservatives alike. Without support, we saw a decline in rehabilitation programs in prisons. Prisoners had less incentive to participate in rehabilitation programs and the number and variety of prison rehabilitation programs decreased.

The Move to Sentencing Reform

Commonalities of Sentencing Reforms

Siegel and Worrall (2016) stated that determinate sentences, "offer a fixed term of years, the maximum set in law by the legislature, to be served by the offender sentenced to prison for a particular crime" (p. 431). We will differentiate determinate sentencing laws enacted by legislatures from sentencing guidelines created by specially formed commissions. In chapters to follow, we will take a look at mandatory minimum sentencing laws, three strikes laws, and other habitual offender laws. What all of these types of sentencing reforms have in common is that they seek to decrease or eliminate judicial discretion and increase sentencing uniformity.

Determinate sentencing practices establish some sentencing standards. Determinate sentencing practices move the discretion away from judges to other entities. These may include state legislatures, as evidenced in California's determinate sentencing laws. Or jurisdictions may establish a specially formed rule making organization like the Minnesota Sentencing Guidelines Commission.

Tonry (1996) identified four approaches to sentencing reform that began in the 1970s in chronological order. These are (1) changes in parole practices, (2) voluntary/descriptive guidelines, (3) statutory determinate sentencing schemes, and (4) sentencing commissions, which produced sentencing guidelines.

Changes in Parole Practices

Parole Guidelines

The first type of sentencing reform was the establishment of **parole guidelines.** This included efforts to decrease disparity and discrimination in the sentence lengths of prisoners convicted of comparable offenses. Guidelines would establish criteria that would guide the decision of the parole board regarding when and under what circumstances to parole a prisoner.

In *Guidelines for Parole and Sentencing* (1978) Gottfredson, Wilkins, and Hoffman constructed written standards to structure the decision-making work of a parole board while still allowing consideration of relevant individual case characteristics. They aimed to achieve equity in parole decision making—meaning, "similar offenders in similar circumstances, are given similar sentences" (p. 5). They worked with the United States Board of Parole (later called the United States Parole Commission) to devise a parole policy.

At the time Gottfredson and associates began their research, the Parole Commission had nine members who were appointed by the president and approved by the Senate and had the responsibility for making parole decisions for all the prisoners eligible for parole under their jurisdiction. The authors described the broad discretion given to federal judges at the time: "In adult cases, if the offender is imprisoned for a maximum term of more than one year, then the judge may set a minimum term of one-third of that maximum, a lesser minimum term, or no minimum term" (p. 2). They further specified, "The determination of the actual time to be served in prison is made by the parole board within the constraints of the minimum term (if any) and the maximum term (less institutional good time earned)" (p. 2).

Gottfredson and associates sought to design model parole guidelines that would maximize equity while preserving some consideration of individual and case circumstances. They acknowledged up front the need for parole decision-making guidelines to be updated and altered as the criminal justice system and perceptions about sentencing are ever changing.

Their research identified two main factors—**seriousness of the offense** and **prognosis for parole** as the bases of past parole board decisions. These two factors became the basis for the guidelines, with each forming an axis of a grid. One dimension, the prognosis for parole, was represented by the risk that the offender would recidivate or repeat crime once released from parole. The authors constructed an empirically based "Salient Factor Score," which was to be calculated for each offender and measured risk based on objective criteria associated with the offender's case. **Figure 3.1** represents the original eleven-factor Salient Factor Score designed by researchers to use for the parole prognosis axis. The scores were collapsed into four risk categories: (9–11) "very good," (6–8) "good," (4–5) "fair," and (0–3) "poor."

Figure 3.1 Original Salient Factor Score

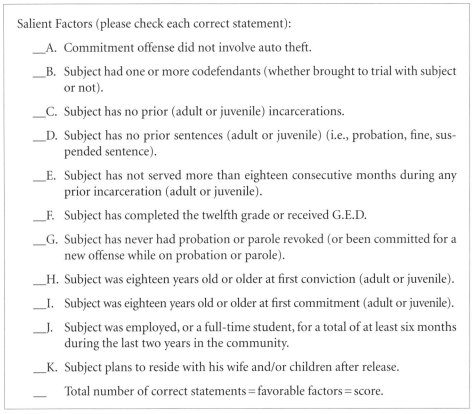

Salient Factors (please check each correct statement):

__A. Commitment offense did not involve auto theft.

__B. Subject had one or more codefendants (whether brought to trial with subject or not).

__C. Subject has no prior (adult or juvenile) incarcerations.

__D. Subject has no prior sentences (adult or juvenile) (i.e., probation, fine, suspended sentence).

__E. Subject has not served more than eighteen consecutive months during any prior incarceration (adult or juvenile).

__F. Subject has completed the twelfth grade or received G.E.D.

__G. Subject has never had probation or parole revoked (or been committed for a new offense while on probation or parole).

__H. Subject was eighteen years old or older at first conviction (adult or juvenile).

__I. Subject was eighteen years old or older at first commitment (adult or juvenile).

__J. Subject was employed, or a full-time student, for a total of at least six months during the last two years in the community.

__K. Subject plans to reside with his wife and/or children after release.

__ Total number of correct statements = favorable factors = score.

Source: "Salient Factor Score (SFS72)," U.S. Board of Parole, 1972, as reprinted in Gottfredson, Wilkins, & Hoffman, *Guidelines for parole and sentencing*, p. 17, Lexington Books, 1978.

The second dimension, seriousness of conviction offense, was constructed from procedures that graded offenses in terms of offense gravity. United States Board of Parole members ranked various offense descriptions in terms of perceived severity. Gottfredson and associates (1978) explained the calculation of the seriousness of offense scale: "For each of a set of offense ratings (offense behavior descriptions) coded by the project, the median time served was calculated. Offense ratings with similar median times served were combined to produce six seriousness level classifications" (p. 17).

Table 3.1 shows the guidelines for the time served before release for adult offenders. The median time was in the form of a range to allow for some discretion. Researchers

Table 3.1 Guidelines for Decision Making (Adult Cases): Average Total Time Served before Release (Including Jail Time)

Offense Characteristics (Seriousness)	Offender Characteristics — Salient (Favorable) Factor Score (Probability of Favorable Parole Outcome)			
Severity	(9–11) Very High	(6–8) High	(4–5) Fair	(0–3) Low
Category A: Low Severity Offenses Minor theft; walkaway; immigration law violations; alcohol law violations	6–10 months	8–12 months	10–14 months	12–16 months
Category B: Low/Moderate Severity Offenses Possess marijuana; possess heavy narcotics, less than or equal $50; theft, unplanned; forgery or counterfeiting, less than $500; burglary, daytime	8–12 months	12–16 months	16–20 months	20–25 months
Category C: Moderate Severity Offenses Vehicle theft; forgery or counterfeiting, greater than $500; sale of marijuana; planned theft; possess heavy narcotics, greater than $50; escape; Mann Act without force; Selective Service	12–16 months	16–20 months	20–24 months	24–30 months
Category D: High Severity Offenses Sell heavy narcotics; burglary, weapon or nighttime; violence, "spur of the moment"; sexual act, force	16–20 months	20–26 months	26–32 months	32–38 months
Category E: Very High Severity Offenses Armed robbery; criminal act with weapon; sexual act, force, injury; assault, serious bodily harm; Mann Act with force	26–36 months	36–45 months	45–55 months	55–65 months
Category F: Highest Severity Offenses Willful homicide; kidnapping; armed robbery, weapon fired or serious injury	Information not available owing to limited number of cases.			

Notes: 1. If an offense behavior can be classified under more than one category, the most serious applicable category is to be used. If an offense behavior involved multiple separate offenses, the seriousness level may be increased.

2. If an offense is not listed, the proper category may be obtained by comparing the seriousness of the offense with those of similar offenses listed.

3. If a continuance is to be recommended, subtract 30 days (one month) to allow for release program division.

Source: "Guidelines for Decision Making (Adult Cases): Average Total Time Served Before Release (Including Jail Time)," U.S. Board of Parole, 1972, as reprinted in Gottfredson, Wilkins, & Hoffman, *Guidelines for parole and sentencing.* pp. 20–21, Lexington Books, 1978.

interacted with board members and incorporated their feedback into the specifications of median ranges. Obviously, not every offense is listed in the table and seriousness level of such offenses was determined by comparing non-listed offenses with those of similar seriousness.

The chart was designed to be used as a tool to guide the parole board's decision in the following manner:

> After scoring the case on the concerns of severity and prognosis, the parole board member or hearing examiner would check the table to see the expected decision. In practice, a range (say twenty to twenty-four months) would be appropriate to allow for some variation within broad severity or risk categories. Should the board member or examiner wish to make a decision outside of the expected range, he would be obligated to specify the factors that make that particular case unique (such as unusually good or poor institutional adjustment, credit for time spent on a sentence of another jurisdiction). At review hearings, the decision to parole or continue would be based primarily on institutional performance (Gottfredson, Wilkens, & Hoffman, p. 16).

The guidelines were used by the United States Board of Parole in 1972 as part of a pilot project and eventually were applied to all federal parole decisions by the end of 1973. States including Oregon, Minnesota, and Washington also established parole guidelines.

Ultimately, it was acknowledged that although this approach aimed to decrease sentencing disparity, that parole boards do not impact the jail population or decisions of the judge to incarcerate versus sentence the offender in the community. The impact of structuring parole decisions on decreasing overall sentencing disparities was therefore limited. Parole guidelines were replaced by sentencing guidelines in the above listed states and in the federal government. Some states, such as Texas, currently have rather structured criteria to guide (but not necessarily to dictate) the parole decision.

The Elimination of Parole Release

It is worth noting another approach to sentencing reform that involved the practice of parole. In 1975, Maine abolished its parole board. Adult offenders who committed crimes after May 1, 1976, are not subject to parole release (Blumstein, Cohen, Martin, & Tonry, 1983).

Recently, Maine has been reconsidering bringing back the state's parole system. In response to the high cost of incarceration (estimated at over $30,000 per inmate per year), and a growing prison population, approximately 70 lawmakers in Maine have signed a bill which would consider reinstating parole release for certain inmates in the state's prisons (Sharon, 2011, May 12). Advocates cite parole as aiding in the offender's reentry, which could lower recidivism rates. Opponents, including Deputy Attorney General Bill Stokes, say it could be unconstitutional because it would violate the Constitution's *ex post facto* laws by subjecting those who have been incarcerated for a long time to a system of parole. Other arguments against the reintroduction of parole include the cost and a concern for the victims and their families, who would appear before the parole board (Sharon, 2011, May 12).

In 1994, Congress authorized billions of dollars to allocate to states to abolish parole release, establish sentencing guidelines, and limit time off a sentence for good behavior (Tonry, 1994–95).

Voluntary/ "Descriptive" Guidelines

The second approach to structuring judicial decision making involved the creation of **"voluntary" or descriptive guidelines**. Such guidelines are termed "voluntary" because there was no statutory mandate to develop them and because there was no mechanism to ensure that judges would follow them. These guidelines were created on either the state level or the judicial district level by judges (Tonry, 1996).

When deriving voluntary guidelines, researchers would calculate average sentences that judges had handed down in the past within a jurisdiction. For example, within a state, the average (mean) sentence for armed robbery would be calculated from each county. Judges in that state were then supposed to impose that average when sentencing all offenders for the crime of armed robbery. The intent was to make sentencing more uniform, even across rather diverse counties or jurisdictions within a single state.

Voluntary guidelines were first set up in Denver in 1976. The research leading to the formation of the guidelines began in July 1974. The sentencing guidelines research work stemmed in part from the guidelines that had been developed by the then United States Board of Parole. The parole guidelines considered two factors — seriousness of the offense and the probability of recidivism (based on a Salient Factor Score) in determining how long an offender would be incarcerated before release. It was thought that the identification of factors that affect sentencing decisions would similarly aid in developing an instrument to guide and standardize judges' sentencing decisions.

Judges in Denver were involved in the development of the guidelines throughout the research, in order to maximize the success and compliance of the venture. At least one judge from each jurisdiction was present at the meetings of the Steering and Policy Committee (Wilkins, Kress, Gottfredson, Calpin, & Gelman, 1978).

According to Wilkins, Kress, Gottfredson, Calpin, and Gelman (1978), researchers working the development of the Denver guidelines assumed that:

> . . . while judges in a particular jurisdiction are making sentencing decisions on a case-by-case or individual level, they are simultaneously and as a byproduct making decisions on a policy level. In other words, the gradual buildup of case-by-case decisions results in the incremental development of a sentencing policy. If an equation can be developed which "predicts" sentencing decisions on the basis of case information, this ability to "predict" decisions may be seen as the identification or description of a latent policy. (p. 10)

To establish guidelines for sentencing, researchers performed statistical analyses to understand the past determinants of sentences decided by judges in Denver. The mathematical models were then applied to another (validation) sample and the voluntary guidelines were developed based on past sentencing practices.

The voluntary/descriptive guidelines were in the form of a matrix. There were separate matrices for three classes of felonies and for each misdemeanor class. Two variables that were shown to account for the largest amount of variation in sentencing, *seriousness of current offense* and *extent of the offender's prior criminal record* were used to create a sentencing matrix, in which each of these factors constituted an axis of the grid. Weights were also assigned to certain aggravating and mitigating factors. The guidelines specified a small range as opposed to an exact number so the judge could consider gravity of a past conviction, for example. Judges were given model sentences for cases according to these criteria (offense severity and offense class) but their compliance was voluntary.

Federal funding for the development of "descriptive" guidelines in Maryland and Florida involved the assessment of how uniform guidelines might apply to very different regions of a single state. In Maryland, for example, some counties are largely urban and border Washington, DC (like Prince Georges County and Montgomery County), while others are quite rural (like Cumberland County).

Evaluations of sentencing guidelines showed that because voluntary guidelines rested only on collegial authority that they **were seldom followed on a statewide scale** (Blumstein, Cohen, Martin, & Tonry, 1983).

Statutory Determinate Sentencing Schemes

The next type of sentencing reform, which emerged in the mid- to late-1970s was statutory determinate sentencing. California's system got great attention, but other states also transitioned from indeterminate sentencing to determinate sentencing schemes. In these states, the **legislature determined the sentences that convicted offenders should serve for a variety of offenses or offense classes.** Upon sentencing the offender would know the maximum amount of time he or she would be serving in prison. Maine was the first state to implement determinate sentencing in 1976, the same year in which it abolished parole. By 1980, California, Indiana, Illinois, Arizona, Alaska, and North Carolina had also adopted some type of determinate sentencing laws (Lipson & Peterson, 1980).

Although we detail differences in the approaches below, these state legislatures established prescribed punishments/sentence lengths or ranges based on the classification of the crime (according to seriousness). The purposes, as with other sentencing reforms, included decreasing judicial discretion, decreasing sentencing disparity and discrimination, and increasing sentencing uniformity. The predominant goals of sentencing were retribution, incapacitation, and deterrence.

California's Determinate Sentencing

Indeterminate Sentencing in California

California used an indeterminate sentencing system for over fifty years. The indeterminate sentencing law was ratified May 18, 1917, and went into effect on July 27, 1917 (Johnson, 1977). The California Penal Code established minimum and maximum terms for each felony. California's original indeterminate sentence law was designed to allow flexibility. Sentence length would reflect how quickly an individual made progress towards rehabilitation. Offenders were to be released when they were deemed ready to return to society.

Notably, soon after the passage of the indeterminate sentencing law, the constitutionality of the law was questioned unsuccessfully in *In re Lee* (1918) 177 Cal. 690, 171 P. 958

(1918). The California court upheld the practice of indeterminate sentencing, making the point that the sentence was legal in terms of the maximum term, thus suggesting it was certain and definite. The discretion given to an administrative body for determining the exact sentence was also upheld by the court. The court cited the practice of indeterminate sentencing in other states. Johnson (1977, p. 137) emphasized the extreme discretion given to the Adult Authority by giving the example of the potential sentence for a person convicted of a felony assault with a deadly weapon, which ranged from six months to life!

The Adult Authority originally had nine members who were appointed by the governor and approved by the Senate. They were to be experienced practitioners or scholars in various fields, including corrections, sociology, law, law enforcement, and education (Johnson, 1977). The Adult Authority had little guidance in the way they conducted their work in reviewing inmates' files and initiating policies for administering indeterminate sentencing laws. As the prison population grew, they employed 29 hearing representatives to help review inmates' files, set prison terms, and make parole decisions for the 40,000 inmates incarcerated in California (Johnson, 1977).

There were several critiques of California's indeterminate sentencing system, including the fact that the offender did not know how long his or her sentence would be, that individuals convicted of the same offense could serve different sentence lengths, and that the Adult Authority had very broad discretion and was subject to limited review. These criticisms were fueled by the question of whether the Adult Authority could rehabilitate offenders.

Chairman's Directive 75/20

This question was answered by the chairman of the Adult Authority, Raymond Procunier, in 1975, when he publicly stated that rehabilitation was not possible within the California system of indeterminate sentencing. He subsequently tried to take a consideration of rehabilitation away from sentencing decisions and introduced Chairman's Directive 75/20. This was an administrative reform that set new procedures for deciding an inmate's release date. It involved the establishment of specific criteria concerning the case to help make more uniform decisions based on offense characteristics. The seriousness of the offense was a primary consideration, so that offenders who committed more serious crimes would serve a larger portion of the maximum sentence. Other considerations included the extent of personal injury to the crime victim, the number of victims, and the extent of damage to property. A base period of confinement was established for each offender, but aggravating and mitigating factors were considered to raise or lower the base sentence. The sentence could be recalculated and lengthened under the directive if the inmate misbehaved in prison (Johnson, 1977).

The Chairman's Directive 75/20 was an attempt to make sentence length more predictable and reflective of seriousness of the crime, as opposed to being based on evidence that the offender was rehabilitated. That exact fact—that the Adult Authority was not going to recognize progress towards rehabilitation in the sentence—served to invalidate the directive. California's indeterminate sentencing law specifically *required* that the offender's sentence be at least partly based on indications of offender rehabilitation and that the inmate was ready to return to society. The California Court of Appeal for the Third District decided this case in *In re Stanley* (1976). Given that the indeterminate sentencing law required a consideration of rehabilitation, but the Adult Authority stated that it was not possible to achieve, this case presented a conclusion that the practice of indeterminate sentencing was untenable.

After Chairman's Directive 75/20 was dismantled and responding to criticisms of indeterminate sentencing, the legislature studied the law and considered several alternative proposals. Senate Bill 42 was passed by the legislature on September 1, 1976, and signed into law by then governor Jerry Brown on September 26, 1976. It abolished the Adult Authority and revived determinate sentencing in California.

Senate Bill 42, The Uniform Determinate Sentencing Law

Senate Bill 42, the Uniform Determinate Sentencing Law (DSL), and the subsequent changes in California's system of criminal justice went into effect on July 1, 1977 (Lipson & Peterson, 1980). This law indicated the length of imprisonment that offenders should serve in state prison for various crimes defined by the state of California. The law was distinguished by the power that the state legislature had in determining sentences.

Lipson and Peterson (1980) described the law as follows:

> Through the law the California legislature not only established general sentencing policy but also limited the variation in sentences, defined the principal bases for such variation, and established the specific lengths of prison terms. For most crimes, judges can still decide not to send convicted felons to prison. However, for those sentenced to prison, judges must calculate the length of prison terms by choosing among a narrow range of statutory options. Similarly, the law severely restricts the power of prison or parole officials to influence the length of prison terms; only by following elaborate due process procedures can they revoke limited amounts of good time. (p. v)

Senate Bill 42 defined the goal of imprisonment to be punishment. The contents of Senate Bill 42 were in stark contrast to the indeterminate sentencing laws that had been in effect for over 50 years. Proportionality (meaning the severity of the punishment was proportionate to the seriousness of the crime) and equity (punishing offenders who committed similar crimes comparably) were emphasized.

Under determinate sentencing in California, five levels of seriousness of offenses were delineated. Within each level is three terms—the lowest being the mitigated term, the middle being the typical or presumptive term, and the highest being the aggravated term. Much of Senate Bill 42 was a list of statutes that defined the terms for each offense. The crime of rape, for example was a level three offense which carried a term of 3 (mitigated), 4, (typical), or 5 (aggravated) years. In contrast, under indeterminate sentencing this crime carried a sentence of 3 months to life (Lipson & Peterson, 1980).

Additional time could be added to one's sentence if "enhancing circumstances" were present in the offense. Sentencing enhancements could be given for past prison terms or for factors involved in the conviction offense, such as being armed with or using a weapon, inflicting great bodily harm on the victim(s), or causing great property loss or damage. The bill also provided that the judge should sentence the offender in the middle range, unless there are aggravating circumstances apart from those that would call for

sentence enhancements, or mitigating factors. Regardless of the term which was chosen, the facts of the case were to be recorded to provide information for any subsequent
appeal (Johnson, 1977).

Senate Bill 42 also detailed the process of granting "good time" credits for inmates
for time served in prison. Under indeterminate sentencing, prisoners complained that
they did not have clear guidelines about their progress toward parole or guidance in
helping them gain release. In contrast, prisoners under determinate sentencing were told
within fourteen days of the beginning of their imprisonment term all the rules within
the prison and were instructed that they could receive a reduction of up to one-third of
their sentence for good time and participation in programs within the prison (Johnson, 1977). Still, even if the inmate did not participate in prison programs and violated
prison rules, he would not have to serve longer than the sentence term pronounced at
sentencing. The exception was if he was convicted of a felony while behind bars, which
would warrant additional time. Every eight months, the prisoner's remaining time to
be served was recalculated based on good time accrued, and the inmate was informed
of the new date of release (Johnson, 1977).

There was some outcry that the terms defined under determinate sentencing were too
lenient, especially when compared to the potential maximum sentences that the offenses
carried under indeterminate sentencing. Regardless of criticism, however, the determinate sentencing law made sentencing more uniform and predictable.

Amendments to the Original Determinate Sentencing Law

The original Determinate Sentencing Law (SB 42) was amended several times. In 1978
it was amended by SB 709 and SB 1057. Increases in the lower, middle, and upper terms
followed SB 709. For rape, the lower, middle, and upper ranges were raised from 3, 4, and
5 years to 3, 6, and 8 years. For arson, the ranges were increased from 2, 3, and 4 years to
2, 4, and 6 years. Sentence enhancements were also permitted. Crime characteristics like
the use of a weapon or great bodily harm to the individual made the offense eligible for
sentence enhancement. In addition, an offender's prior prison terms could justify sentence enhancement. **Table 3.2** compares sentences under the indeterminate sentencing,
under the original DSL term, and under SB 709 (Lipson & Peterson, 1980).

Table 3.2 Prison Terms, under Original DSL and as Amended
by SB 709 (in Years)

Offense	1SL Term (before 7/1/76)	Original DSL Term[a]	Term After SB 709[a]
Murder, second degree	5–life	5, 6, 7	5, 7, 11[b]
Voluntary manslaughter	6 mo–15	2, 3, 4	2, 4, 6
Rape	3–life	3, 4, 5	3, 6, 8
Robbery	5–life	2, 3, 4	2, 3, 5
Arson	2–20	2, 3, 4	2, 4, 6
Burglary, first degree	5–life	2, 3, 4	2, 4, 6
Burglary, second degree	1–15	16 mo, 2, 3	2, 3, 4

(continued)

Table 3.2 Prison Terms, under Original DSL and as Amended
by SB 709 (in Years) (continued)

Offense	1SL Term (before 7/1/76)	Original DSL Term[a]	Term After SB 709[a]
Assault with deadly weapon	6 mo–life	2, 3, 4	2, 3, 4[c]
Vehicle theft	6 mo–10	16 mo, 2, 3	2, 3, 4
Forgery	1–14	2, 3, 4	2, 3, 4
Sale of narcotics	5–life	3, 4, 5	3, 4, 5
Possession of narcotics for sale	5–15	2, 3, 4	2, 3, 4
Possession of narcotics	2–10	16 mo, 2, 3	16 mo, 2, 3

[a] Numbers show lower, middle, and upper prison terms, respectively.
[b] Changed to indeterminate sentence by state initiative.
[c] SB 709 permits great bodily injury enhancement, unavailable under the original DSL.

Source: Lipson, A. J., & Peterson, M. A. (June 1980). *California justice under determinate sentencing: A review and agenda for research* (Research Report No R-2497- CRB). p.5.
Reproduced with permission from RAND Corporation, Santa Monica, CA: Rand. Retrieved from Rand website: http://www.rand.org/pubs/reports/2005/R2497.pdf

Report is available on website http://www.rand.org/pubs/reports/R2497.html

Under California's DSL, the primary purpose of imprisonment shifted from rehabilitation to punishment (Lipson & Peterson, 1980). California's DSL also incorporated several other objectives, including sentencing equity, public protection, sentencing accountability, and procedural fairness. California's DSL focused on proportionality — making the terms of imprisonment in proportion to the seriousness of the offense. Those determining the sentences for the various offenses considered the average sentences that had been handed down in the past. They also examined the penalties for various crimes to help ensure that crimes of equal seriousness would receive similar sentences. While parole release was eliminated, offenders could reduce their sentence by one-third with good time, which was earned if the offender stayed out of trouble during his or her prison term. Murder and some other grave offenses still carry lengthy indeterminate terms.

Consequences of California's Determinate Sentencing Law

Lipson and Peterson's (1980) examination of California's DSL produced several conclusions concerning the impact of DSL on the state of California during the first three years after its implementation. Among them were the following: (1) the rate of prison commitments in the state rose in the three years following the implementation of the law, however, it was noted that the rate began to rise in the early 1970s; (2) prison overcrowding became a significant problem since the law eliminated the use of parole as a mechanism to relieve overcrowding; (3) the use of prison (as opposed to community sanctions) rose and the length of the average prison term rose, which also exacerbated prison overcrowding; and (4) there was evidence of more equity in sentencing for similar offenses.

Proposition 36 — 2000

California's Proposition 36 — the Substance Abuse and Crime Prevention Act — changed how non-violent drug felons, who otherwise would be sent to prison, would be handled by the criminal justice system. In November 2000, 61 percent of California voters voted for this ballot measure that required some categories of non-violent felony drug offenders to participate in drug treatment programs, instead of the prison sentences. It went into effect on July 1, 2001.

Specifically, offenders whose conviction was "non-violent drug possession" received sentences of probation and drug treatment, as opposed to prison. In addition, parolees who violated the conditions of their parole by committing non-violent drug offenses or by committing technical violations (for example testing positive for drugs), were ordered to participate in drug treatment programs, rather than being sent back to prison (Colker, 2004).

Proposition 36 was mired in controversy. Supporters emphasized the role that substance abuse plays in individuals' involvement in crime. For example, drug users may resort to a violent crime, such as robbery, to pay for the drugs to which they are addicted. A measure such as Proposition 36 aimed to address the assumed *cause* of crime — the addiction — and treat, rather than punish the offender. This measure was promoted by the California Campaign for New Drug Policies and had the support of members of the medical community, public health organizations, and those organizations which provide drug treatment (Colker, 2004).

Detractors, however, cited the complex nature of the relationship between substance abuse and crime and maintained that drug crimes, like violent crimes, harm society and deserve punishment. Critics also raised funding issues as potential challenges to the implementation of Proposition 36 (Colker, 2004). In addition, there was some concern that the counties within the state of California could not implement drug treatment uniformly, due to budget issues and services available within different counties, or would simply be unwilling to, as they did not all share the goal of drug treatment (Colker, 2004).

Indiana's Determinate Sentencing Law

On October 1, 1977, a revised version of Indiana's penal code (Indiana Penal Code, Title, 35) which incorporated determinate sentencing went into effect in the state. Clear, Hewitt, and Regoli (1978) characterized the Indiana sentencing law as a comprehensive restructuring of Indiana criminal law. They stated, "Among other changes, the previous set of over 5,000 stated Indiana crimes (with the last major revision in 1905) was consolidated into approximately 200 'new' offenses, with a number of modifications in the elements of the various offenses" (p. 433). They regarded the Indiana statute as a "wholesale criminal code reform."

Table 3.3 shows the sentencing structure of the Indiana Penal Code in 1977 (Clear, Hewitt, & Regoli, 1978). Offenses were categorized as either one of five felony classes (Murder, Class A, Class B, Class C, or Class D) or one of two misdemeanor classes (Class A or Class B). Offenses could be classified in more than one category, depending on case characteristics. For example, serious injury or use or threat of deadly force could move a Class C felony to a Class A felony. For each class of felony, terms of imprisonment are specified. For example, upon conviction of murder, one was to receive 40 years or death. Terms for other classes were as follows: Class A felony — 30 years, Class B felony — 10 years, Class C felony — 5 years, Class D felony — 2 years, Class A misdemeanor — 0–1 year, and Class B misdemeanor — 0–6 months. The Indiana Penal Code also provided sentencing enhancements for aggravation for felony (but not misdemeanor) offenses. Reductions could also be given for mitigating case factors for most categories of felonies (Clear, Hewitt, & Regoli, 1978; von Hirsch, 1980).

Table 3.3 The Sentencing Structure of the Indiana Penal Code, 1977

Class of Offense	Terms of Imprisonment	Enhancement for Aggravation	Reduction for Mitigation
Murder	40 years (or death)	1–20 years	1–10 years
Class A felony	30 years	1–20 years	1–10 years
Class B felony	10 years	1–20 years	1–4 years
Class C felony	5 years	1–3 years	1–3 years
Class D felony	2 years	1–2 years	NA
Class A misdemeanor	0–1 year	NA	NA
Class B misdemeanor	0–6 months	NA	NA

Source: Clear, T. R., Hewitt, J. D., & Regoli, R. M. (1978). Discretion and the determinate sentence: Its distribution, control, and effect on time served. *Crime and Delinquency, 24*, p. 433.

Reproduced with permission by SAGE, Copyright Clearance Center.

The law indicated that a suspended sentence (in which the offender could receive probation as opposed to imprisonment) was only allowable for offenders with a first conviction and whose conviction did not include certain felonies. The code also indicated that the sentencing hearing would follow but be separate from the trial. It was at the sentencing hearing that the prosecutor could present evidence of aggravation or mitigation and issue a recommendation under the constraints of the set terms described above. A "habitual offender" status could also be determined if the convicted offender had two prior unrelated felony convictions, and this would result in a 30-year add-on to the sentence (Clear, Hewitt, & Regoli, 1978). The provisions in the Indiana law appear quite harsh, compared to other sentencing structures when they were passed, and compared the provisions of most states, which have determinate sentencing and/or structured sentencing today.

Clear, Hewitt, and Regoli (1978) asserted that the Indiana sentencing reform had two goals, "first, to place limits on the availability of discretion, and second, to give *more* discretion to the judge and less to correctional administrators" (p. 434). They evaluated Indiana's sentencing code in light of these goals and concluded, "Examining the Indiana Code critically, we conclude that the reformers failed to achieve the first objective and were only partially successful in achieving the second" (p. 435). They maintained that the four entities that can impact criminal sentencing — the legislature, the prosecutor, the judge, and the parole board — all retained considerable discretion after the legislation was passed. They characterized the limits imposed by the legislature as broad and pointed to the large impact that aggravating and mitigating factors could have on sentence length.

Regarding the prosecution, they asserted that the law increased prosecutorial discretion. This could happen for a few reasons. First, the code allowed for flexibility regarding plea bargaining because any offense that carried a sentence that could not be suspended (except murder) could also be charged as an "attempted" offense and "attempted" offenses carry the same penalty as the completed offenses, but could be suspended. The prosecutor could influence the defendant to plead guilty to the attempted offense, for which the elements of proof are less than that of the completed offense. Second, for non-first time offenders who are charged with a less serious offense, or if the prosecutor's case is weak, prosecutors can pressure the defendant to plead guilty to a misdemeanor charge. That way, the prosecutor gets a conviction and the offender gets a suspended sentence, as opposed to prison. In addition, the prosecutor could engage in bargaining with the defendant regarding what aggravating and/or mitigating circumstances he or she would address at the sentencing hearing.

The authors suggested that although one would predict that judges would have less judicial discretion because of legislatively mandated sentences for each class of offense, that the new code may have increased judicial discretion. The judges still retained the discretion to suspend the sentences of first time offenders and sentence them to probation. Judges also could exercise discretion in their acceptance or rejection of aggravating and mitigating factors, which as stated above can drastically alter the so called "determinate" sentence established by the Indiana Penal Code.

Clear, Hewitt, and Regoli also noted that one would expect that the ending of parole release would naturally decrease any discretion concerning sentence length on the part of correctional officers. They, however, pointed to the need for corrections personnel to have incentives to control inmate behavior and stressed that the system of credits for good behavior in prison resurrected the discretion that correctional officials lost due to the elimination of discretionary parole release.

In his analysis of the revised Indiana Penal Code, von Hirsch (1980) reached similar conclusions—that judges retain a great deal of discretion and that the rewarding (and taking away) of good time is less predictable than would be ideal in a determinate sentencing system. Due to uncertainties in sentencing and the duration of a prison sentence, von Hirsch questioned whether the Indiana "revisions" really just constituted a different approach to indeterminate sentencing, rather than representing a legitimate determinate sentencing strategy. His study of the Indiana Code showed that penalties were less certain and more severe—which contradicted the common goals of determinate sentencing practices, which aim for consistency and commensurability. He also suspected that because the legislature wrote the sentencing standards that there may have been influence from the public to make sanctions appear more stringent.

In 2014, Indiana revised its criminal code. While the revisions were extensive, it is beyond the scope of the book to detail all of them. **Table 3.4** shows the new advisory sentencing scheme in Indiana. Note that the Indiana Criminal Code also indicates criminal gang enhancements and firearms enhancements.

Table 3.4 The Sentencing Structure of the Indiana Penal Code, 2014

Level	Length of Imprisonment
Murder	45–65 years (55)
1	20–40 years (30)
2	10–30 years (17.5)
3	3–16 years (9)
4	2–12 years (6)
5	1–6 years (3)
6	0.5–2.5 years (1)

North Carolina's Fair Sentencing Act (FSA)

North Carolina had indeterminate sentencing laws before 1981, which afforded judges wide discretion in the imposition of sentences and the Parole Commission great latitude in deciding the actual time an offender would serve in prison (Freeman, 2009). Studies by the North Carolina Bar Association (NCBA) in the 1970s showed a history of great disparity in sentence length for cases with similar legally relevant characteristics. The Knox Commission (comprised of members of the legislature) was formed by the North Carolina General Assembly in response to the NCBA suggestion to study the criminal justice system in the state and "to develop a coordinated state policy on correctional programs and a clear philosophy for criminal justice sanctions and inmate rehabilitation" (Freeman, p. 3). The Knox Commission concluded that new sentencing laws needed to be enacted and they drafted North Carolina's first determinate sentencing laws, which became known as the Fair Sentencing Act (FSA), and were enacted in 1981 (Freeman).

Several features of the Fair Sentencing Act (FSA) distinguished it from North Carolina's prior indeterminate sentencing approach. First, the FSA did away with discretionary parole release for offenders convicted of most felonies committed on or after the act went into effect. It moved toward determinate sentencing practices in establishing a system in which presumptive sentences were set for felonies, but allowed judges and juries to depart from these sentences if aggravating or mitigating factors were associated with the case. However, the sentence could not exceed the maximum term, as dictated by North Carolina state statute. Under FSA, judges also could decide whether to sentence a convicted offender to incarceration or probation.

Creators of the FSA did not consider the impact it would have on North Carolina's criminal justice system, specifically the prison population. It turned out that the impact was profound and problematic. In the late 1980s, the state of North Carolina was facing possible federal intervention in its prison system because of serious prison overcrowding. According to Freeman (2009), "Between 1985 and 1991, the crime rate rose by almost 56% and the annual rate of prison admissions rose by 74%" (p. 4). Common areas in prisons were used for sleeping areas and some inmates were in bunk beds three high, separated by only 18 inches (Freeman, 2009). The conditions, including the overcrowding, prompted lawsuits alleging cruel and unusual punishment.

Since discretionary parole was eliminated, the number of prisoners would increase, as they were not being released. In response to the increasing prison population, a provision was added to the FSA which allowed prisoners to earn 30 days off their sentence for 30 days of good behavior, in contrast to the prior practice under indeterminate sentencing allowing for 8 days off per 30 days of good behavior. This "good time" provision essentially resulted in prisoners serving only half of their sentence. In response to this practice, judges in turn increased the average prison sentence for many felony offenders, to ensure that they spent what the judge thought to be the appropriate time in prison. Approximately 46 percent of felony sentences in North Carolina were greater than the presumptive sentence in 1986 (Freeman, 2009). This discretion seemed counterproductive to goal of sentencing uniformity suggested by the NCBA.

Acknowledging the problem of prison overcrowding, in 1985 the General Assembly formed a Special Committee on Prisons. They advocated two main short term strategies to deal with the prison population crisis: accelerated parole release and the institution of a prison cap. The Parole Commission released inmates at a high rate in an effort to alleviate overcrowding. Because of this the proportion of the sentence handed down by the judge that was actually served in prison decreased dramatically. Freeman (2009) noted, "From 1986 to 1991, average sentence lengths increased by 27% while average time served declined by 23%" (p. 5).

The Special Committee on Prisons realized that long term solutions to alleviating prison overcrowding were needed. Two approaches to dealing with the rising prison population were advocated by a myriad of commissions and committees in the next few years. The first strategy to alleviating prison overcrowding was **to construct more prisons**. The North Carolina General Assembly approved extensive prison construction, appropriating over $154 million between 1986 and 1990 to construct more prisons. Later, a Governor's Advisory Board on Prisons was created which concluded that the number of prison beds should be increased. The governor and General Assembly compromised and introduced a $200 million bond package to the voters of North Carolina. It was approved by less than one half of one percent of voters (Freeman, 2009).

The second strategy, jumpstarted by Governor (Jim Martin's) crime commission involved a **consideration of existing sentencing practices and community alternatives to imprisonment**. A Sentencing Committee that was formed from the larger Crime Commission provided a comprehensive assessment of sentencing in North Carolina. In 1986 the Sentencing Committee suggested the increased use of community alternatives, decreasing the number and types of misdemeanor crimes that could be given incarceration sentences, developing more local confinement centers, and making sentences more "truthful" (Freeman, 2009).

The Special Committee on Prisons realized that given the expansion of the prison system that the sentencing laws of the state needed to be reassessed. A major concern was "front-end" (meaning who was let into prison) strategies. Given the fact that there were limitations on how large the prison population could get, changes had to be made regarding the decisions involving who should be sent to prison. In February 1988, co-chairs of the Special Committee on Prisons, Rep. Anne Barnes and Sen. David Parnell, suggested that a separate sentencing guidelines commission be established to categorize criminal offenses and establish appropriate punishments for all offenders who committed crimes in the state of North Carolina.

Sentencing Commissions and Presumptive Sentencing Guidelines

In North Carolina and other states, a new administrative agency called the sentencing commission was given the tasks of creating presumptive sentences for various offenses, establishing aggravating and mitigating circumstances, monitoring the sentencing system, providing projections of sentencing provisions on correctional resources (such as prison space), and making any necessary updates to the sentencing system.

Years earlier, federal judge Marvin Frankel had called for such a body in the federal system, which would involve (1) having the legislature state the purposes of punishment, (2) developing a system of weights and measures to offender and crime characteristics for the purposes of determining a sentence, (3) establishing legislative review of sentences, and (4) creating a Commission on Sentencing, which would be a permanent agency to study sentencing, form, and enact rules about sentencing (Frankel, 1973). This agency was to be free of political pressures, so that the passage of sentencing laws would not reflect the whims of elected officials.

While Frankel's contribution to the eventual enactment of the Federal Sentencing Guidelines in 1987 is profound, several states actually adopted systems of sentencing guidelines well before the Federal Sentencing Guidelines were enacted and these state guidelines systems were heavily influenced by Frankel's writings outlining his overwhelmingly negative impression of indeterminate sentencing and his quest and suggestions for reform. By 1996, more than twenty jurisdictions, including the federal system, had sentencing commissions (Reitz, 1998).

In 1994, the American Bar Association (ABA) "Standards for Criminal Justice Sentencing," third edition, described "the intermediate function; guided judicial discretion" in Standard 18-1.3. It stated:

> (a) The legislature should create or empower a governmental agency to transform legislative policy choices into more particularized sentencing provisions that guide sentencing courts. The agency should also be charged with responsibility to collect, evaluate and disseminate information regarding sentences imposed and carried out within the jurisdiction. Guidance of judicial discretion in sentencing and development of an information base about sentencing are the basic appeals of what these Standards describe as "the intermediate function."
>
> (b) The intermediate function should be performed by an agency with state-wide authority. The intermediate function is performed most effectively through a sentencing commission.
>
> (c) If a jurisdiction elects not to create a sentencing commission, the legislature should either undertake the intermediate function itself or designate another

organ of government to do so. If the function is delegated to the judicial branch, it should be made the responsibility of the highest state court or a state-wide judicial conference (pp. 3–4).

The first states to enact legislation establishing sentencing commissions were Minnesota and Pennsylvania—both in 1978. By the late 1980s, Minnesota, Washington, and Pennsylvania had adopted presumptive guidelines that were designed by each state's sentencing commissions. Twenty-one states, the District of Columbia, and the federal system have established sentencing commissions which have produced sentencing guidelines (Kauder & Ostrom, 2006).

Tonry (1996) stated, "After nearly two decades of experimentation, the guideline-setting sentencing commission is the only reform strategy that commands widespread support and continues to be the subject of new legislation" (p. 28). Reitz (1998) stated, "It is fair to say that the commission-based approach has become the most popular vehicle of sentencing reform in the last decade of the twentieth century" (p. 547). We now turn to an in-depth examination of the creation of various state sentencing guidelines and the commissions that created them.

Summary

Between the late 1970s and the 1990s, many states and the federal system moved away from indeterminate sentencing to more structured or determinate sentencing practices. The foci of sentencing reforms were to decrease judicial discretion, to increase sentencing uniformity, to increase predictability in sentences, and to decrease sentencing disparity and discrimination.

Interestingly, the call for more structured sentencing came from both liberals and conservatives, albeit for different reasons. Liberals pointed to the virtually unbridled discretion afforded to judges that resulted in sentencing disparity and discrimination, which adversely affected minorities and the poor, as well as the general concern for the rights of prisoners. Conservatives pointed to the potential of premature release of dangerous offenders that was possible under indeterminate sentencing schemes that relied on discretionary parole boards to decide on when the inmate would be released. These concerns, coupled with research questioning the efficacy of rehabilitation, mounting crime rates, and the economic recession of the 1970s, precipitated sentencing reforms.

Four distinct approaches to sentencing reform ensued. The first involved changes in parole practices. This included the creation of parole guidelines that set criteria to guide parole board members in their decision of whether to release an inmate. Some jurisdictions eliminated discretionary parole release.

The second type of reform was the establishment of "voluntary" or descriptive sentencing guidelines. Average sentences would be calculated for various offenses within a state and judges of the different jurisdictions within the state were asked to sentence offenders of each type of crime to the average sentence to ensure sentencing uniformity within the state. There was no statutory mandate to develop voluntary guidelines and there was no mechanism to ensure that judges would follow them. And research found that judges rarely abided by them.

A third type of sentencing reform was statutory determinate sentencing. The legislature in some states determined the sentences that convicted offenders should serve for a variety of offenses. Upon sentencing the offender would know the maximum amount of time he or she would be serving in prison.

A fourth type of reform is commission-based sentencing guidelines. Unlike voluntary guidelines, a separate entity, a sentencing commission, devised model guidelines for specific offense and prior record combinations. Although there was some variation by state, this new administrative agency had multiple duties. It created presumptive sentences, established aggravating and mitigating circumstances, monitored the sentencing system, provided projections of sentencing provisions on correctional resources (such as prison space), and revised the guidelines as needed.

Discussion Questions

1. What role do you feel the social conditions of the 1960s and 1970s played in the decline of the rehabilitative ideal?
2. Which of the precipitating factors of modern sentencing reform do you feel are still currently influencing sentencing policies in the United States?
3. What relationship (if any) do you think there is between the media's portrayal of prison life (as portrayed on television shows) and the general public's opinion on what should be the dominant goal(s) of sentencing?
4. Do you feel that parole guidelines are an effective way to decrease disparity and discretion in sentence length? Why or why not?
5. Identify several reasons why you think legislatively determinate sentencing strategies declined in popularity, while the formation of sentencing commissions grew.
6. What social factors do you think might be affecting a more punitive approach, with less reliance on rehabilitation, in sentencing today?

References

American Bar Association (1994). *ABA Standards for criminal justice sentencing, Third edition: Sentencing*. Washington, DC: American Bar Association.

Azeria v. California Adult Authority, 13 Cal Rptr, 839, 193 C.A. 2d 1 (1968).

Blumstein, A., Cohen, J., Martin, S. E., & Tonry, M. H. (1983). *Research on sentencing: The search for reform* (Vol. 1). Washington, DC: National Academy Press.

California Penal Code Statutes, ch. 526, § 1, at 665–66.

California Penal Code, § 1168 (West 1970).

California Penal Code, § 1168a (West 1970).

California Penal Code, § 3020 (West 1970).

California Penal Code, § 3040 (West 1970).

Clear, T. R., Hewitt, J. D., & Regoli, R. M. (1978). Discretion and the determinate sentence: Its distribution, control, and effect on time served. *Crime and Delinquency, 24*(4), 428–445.

Clemmer, D. (1940). *The prison community*. New York: Holt, Rinehart, and Winston.

Clemmer, D. (1950). Observations on imprisonment as a source of criminality. *Journal of Criminal Law and Criminology, 41*(3), 311–319.

Colker A. C. (2004, April 1). Health Policy Tracking Service; 2004. Apr 1, [Issue Brief]. Retrieved October 24, 2007, from http://www.ncsl.org/programs/health/capropib .htm

Cooper v. Pate, 378 U.S. 546 (1964).

DeLisi, M., & Conis, P. J. (2013). *American Corrections: Theory, research, policy, and practice*. Burlington, MA: Jones & Bartlett Learning.

Ferraro, K. (1995). *Fear of crime: Interpreting victimization risk*. Albany, NY: State University of New York Press.

Frankel, M. E. (1973). *Criminal sentences: Law without order*. New York: Hill and Wang.

Freeman, L. (2009). *The North Carolina sentencing and policy advisory commission: A history of its creation and its development of structured sentencing*. Retrieved from http://www.nccourts.org/Courts/CRS/?Councils/spac/Documents/commission history aug2009.pdf

Gideon v. Wainwright, 372 U.S. 335 (1963).

Glueck, S. (1936). *Crime and justice*. Boston, MA: Little, Brown, and Company.

Gottfredson, D. M., Wilkins, L. T., & Hoffman, P. B. (1978). *Guidelines for parole and sentencing: A policy control method*. Lexington, MA: Lexington Books.

In re Lee, 177 Cal. 690, 171 P. 958 (1918).

In re Stanley, 54 Cal. App. 3d 238, 248, 126 Cal. Rptr, 524, 531 (1976).

Indiana Penal Code, Title 35 (1977). *Criminal law and procedure, Articles 41–50*. St. Paul, MN: West Publishing.

Johnson, P. (1977). Senate bill 42 — the end of the indeterminate sentence. *Santa Clara Law Review, 17*, 133–162.

Karmen, A. (2013). *Crime victims: An introduction to victimology*. Belmont, CA: Cengage Learning.

Kauder, N. B., & Ostrom, B. J. (2008). *State sentencing guidelines: Profiles and continuum*. National Center for State Courts. Retrieved from http://www.ncsconline.org /csi/PEW-Profiles-v12-online.pdf

Lipson, A. J., & Peterson, M. A. (1980). *California justice under determinate sentencing: A review and agenda for research* (Publication No. R-2497-CRB). Santa Monica, CA: Rand. Retrieved from http://www.rand.org/pubs/reports/2005/R2497.pdf

Mapp v. Ohio, 367 U.S. 643 (1961).

Martinson, R. (1974). What works? Questions and answers about prison reform. *The Public Interest, 35*, 22–54.

Miranda v. Arizona, 384 U.S. 436 (1966).

President's Commission on Law Enforcement and Administration of Justice (1967). *The challenge of crime in a free society*. Washington, DC: Government Printing Office.

Reitz, K. R. (1998). Sentencing. In M. Tonry (Ed.), *The handbook of crime & punishment* (pp. 542–562). New York: Oxford University Press.

Rideau, W., & Wikberg, R. (1992). *Life Sentences: Rage and survival behind bars*. New York: Times Books.

Robinson v. California, 370 U.S. 660 (1962).

Sharon, S. (2011, May 12). Maine lawmaker proposes restoring state's parole system, *The Maine Public Broadcasting Network*. Retrieved from http://www.mpbn.net/News /MPBNNews/tabid/1159/ctl/ViewItem/mid/3762/ItemId/16372/Default.aspx

Siegel, L., & Bartollas, C. (2011). *Corrections today*. Belmont, CA: Wadsworth, Cengage Learning.

Siegel, L. J. & Worrall, J. L. (2016). *Introduction to criminal justice* (15th ed.). Boston, MA: Cengage Learning.

Skogan, W. G., & Maxfield, M.G. (1981). *Coping with crime: Individual and neighborhood reactions*. Beverly Hills, CA: Sage.

Sykes, G. M. (1958). *The society of captives: A study of a maximum-security prison*. Princeton, NJ: Princeton University Press.

Tomlinson, T. (1973–1974). California Department of Corrections and Adult Authority decisionmaking procedures for male felons. *Stanford Law Review, 26,* 1353–1382.

Tonry, M. (1987). *Sentencing reform impacts*. Washington, DC: National Institute of Justice.

Tonry, M. (1994–95). Twenty years of sentencing reform: Steps forward, steps backward. *Judicature, 78,* 169–172.

Tonry, M. (1996). *Sentencing matters*. New York: Oxford University Press.

U.S. Department of State. (2012). *Stagflation in the 1970s*. Retrieved from http:// economics.about.com/od/useconomichistory/a/stagflation.htm

Uniform Crime Reports. (2012). *Estimated crime in the United States—Total*. Retrieved from http://www.ucrdatatool.gov/Search/Crime/State/RunCrimeStatebyState.cfm

Van Den Haag, E. (1976). *Punishing criminals: Concerning a very old and painful question*. New York: Basic Books.

Von Hirsch, A. (1976). *Doing justice: The choice of punishments*. New York: Hill and Wang.

Von Hirsch, A. (1980). The new Indiana sentencing code: Is it indeterminate sentencing? In C. H. Foust & D. R. Webster (Eds.), *An anatomy of criminal justice: A system review* (pp. 143–155). Lexington, MA: Lexington Books.

Wilkins, L. T., Kress, J. M., Gottfredson, D. M., Calpin, J. C., & Gelman, A. M. (1978). *Sentencing guidelines: Structuring judicial discretion—Report on the feasibility study*. Washington, DC: U.S. Department of Justice.

4

Commission-Based Sentencing Guidelines in States

Chapter Objectives:

- To understand common goals of various state sentencing commissions.
- To compare and contrast features of different states' commission-based guidelines, including the goals of the guidelines, the structure of the guidelines, and whether discretionary parole is still used.
- To understand how some judicial discretion remains in guidelines states.
- To study the history and distinguishing features of four states' commissions and resultant guidelines.

Variation in State Sentencing Reforms

We delineated four types of state sentencing reforms in Chapter 3 — changes in parole practices, the creation of voluntary/descriptive guidelines, the establishment of statutory determinate sentencing schemes, and the creation of commission-based prescriptive sentencing guidelines.

It is important to understand that there is no single type of "state sentencing reform." Some states have incorporated more than one type of reform. For example, North Carolina's sentencing commission established both presumptive sentencing guidelines and eliminated discretionary parole release when structured sentencing went into effect in 1994.

The Development of State Sentencing Commissions and Sentencing Guidelines

Overview of Sentencing Commissions

In the late 1970s and early 1980s, several states created sentencing commissions. Tonry (1996) noted, "In American states, the sentencing commission is the only institutional survivor of two decades' experimentation with comprehensive approaches to sentencing reform" (p. 27). The exact role that the administrative agency known as the commission has differed by jurisdiction. The duties of sentencing commissions vary and include (but are not limited to) the following: (1) creating sentencing guidelines, (2) collecting sentencing data from cases and maintaining data clearinghouses, (3) monitoring sentencing policies, (4) performing research on the effect of sentencing reforms on sentencing disparities and the impact of guidelines on the correctional population, (5) working with state legislatures to refine guidelines, and (6) educating those working in the criminal justice system and the general public about the implementation of guidelines. By 1996 more than twenty jurisdictions, including the federal system, had formed sentencing commissions (Reitz, 1998).

One similarity of sentencing commissions across states involves the diversity of membership within the commission. Although the number of members in each sentencing commission varies by size (ranging from nine in Oregon to thirty-one in Ohio), most commissions are composed of a wide variety of individuals representing various components of the criminal justice system. Commission members generally include the chief justice of the state's supreme court, other judges, the attorney general, representatives from the state senate and house of representatives, the commissioner of corrections, representatives from law enforcement, district attorneys, defense attorneys and/or public defenders, academics, a representative from the correctional system (including the parole board), citizens, crime victim(s), and/or victim advocates. Sometimes representatives from the juvenile system also serve on sentencing commissions.

A Sentencing Commission That Did Not Produce Guidelines—Texas

It is important to note that while most states that formed sentencing commissions eventually created sentencing guidelines to structure judicial decision making, not all state sentencing commissions have produced sentencing guidelines. One notable example of a state sentencing commission that was formed to study state sentencing practices but that did not ultimately create guidelines is Texas. This temporary commission ultimately retained indeterminate sentencing but put restrictions on parole release.

The Texas Punishment Standard Commission (PSC) was created by House Bill 92 in 1991 on a temporary basis to study issues regarding sentencing and in order to rewrite the Texas Penal Code (H.B. 92, 72nd Legislature, Second Called Session, 1991 (Article 37.15, Code of Criminal Procedure)). At this time the state of Texas faced increasing costs for a rising prison population, jail overcrowding (often offenders were put in county jails until prison space opened up), the cost of fines owed by the state to counties to compensate them for housing inmates in county jails who were awaiting transfer to state prisons, and a lack of public confidence in the way the state was handling offenders (i.e., early release (Deitch, 1993–1994)).

Among its functions, the commission was to examine criminal penalties prescribed for various offenses, sentencing practices, correctional resources, prison and jail overcrowding, and parole laws. The commission came up with several suggestions, some of which were accepted by the legislature. One change they suggested that ultimately became legislation was that incarceration be used less for less serious offenders.

The commission ranked the severity of felony offenses, adding a fourth degree to the previous three degrees of severity. This became known as the "state jail felony," which is the least severe felony class. Persons convicted of a "state jail felony" are to be confined in a state jail for between 180 days and two years. (Texas Penal Code, Title 3 "Punishments" Sec. 12.35). This new lowest level of felony, the "fourth degree" felony, included many low-level drug offenders and nonviolent property offenders. Legislation establishing the "state jail" felonies deemed such offenders ineligible to receive prison. Instead of imprisonment, these offenders would be sentenced to community based correctional sanctions. Some offenders were deemed unsuitable for community sanctions, however, and those offenders were sentenced to "state jails," which were new regional work facilities.

The PSC also sought to establish "truth-in-sentencing." They realized, however, that this would have deleterious effects on the already immense prison system. The PSC then recommended shorter sentence ranges for each felony category, so that it was reasonable that inmates would serve 80 percent of their sentence. Legislation, however, ultimately rejected this idea and retained Texas's existing (and wide) sentence ranges and use of parole as an early release mechanism.

The PSC also examined the practice in Texas of "jury sentencing," as Texas was (and continues to be) one of the only states in which juries hand down sentences for a range of offenses. They addressed the reality that the enormous range in sentences that could be handed down for a felony conviction (for example 5 to 99 years) could allow widely disparate sentences for the same offense. The PSC considered guidelines, but concluded that the focus on local control was ingrained in the Texas criminal justice system (Deitch, 1993–1994).

Although the PSC considered the imposition of sentencing guidelines in Texas, they ultimately rejected the idea, which would interfere with the local control and jury sentencing — concepts inherent in the Texas system. Indeterminate sentencing was retained. The PSC disbanded on September 1, 1994 (Texas Punishment Standards Commission).

The Creation of States' Commission-Based Sentencing Guidelines

The American Bar Association (ABA) standards for sentencing (1994) suggested that each state should create a sentencing commission whose purpose would be "to develop a more specific set of provisions that guide sentencing courts to presumptive sentences" (American Bar Association 1994, Standard 18-4,1[a]).

Kauder and Ostrom (2008) compiled a summary of the nature of sentencing guidelines for twenty-one jurisdictions that had instituted them in the publication *State Sentencing Guidelines: Profiles and Continuum*, published by the National Center for State

Courts (NCSC). Although we discuss the many differences in sentencing guidelines in the states and the District of Columbia in this chapter, Kauder and Ostrom provided the following succinct series of statements summarizing the similarities:

> Sentencing guidelines provide structure at the criminal sentencing stage by specifically defining offense and offender elements that should be considered in each case. After considering these elements using a grid or worksheet scoring system, the guidelines recommend a sentence or sentencing range. Options usually include some period of incarceration (prison or jail), probation, or an alternative sanction. Goals of guidelines vary, but an underlying theme is that offenders with similar offenses and criminal histories be treated alike. (p. 3)

Comparing and Contrasting Structure and Function of State Sentencing Commissions and Resulting Guidelines

Table 4.1 presents information on the characteristics of state sentencing commissions and Table 4.2 presents information on states' resultant guidelines. Much of the information presented in these tables is reconfigured from the NCSC report by Kauder and Ostrom (2008). Although this publication is used as a point of departure for comparing and contrasting states' commissions and sentencing guidelines, additional characteristics of the commissions and their guidelines are added and updates are presented in these tables. They also include South Carolina, which established broad sentencing guidelines in 2010.[1] As of this publication, 21 states, the District of Columbia, and the federal system have adopted sentencing guidelines.[2] We will discuss the federal guidelines separately in Chapter 5.

It is important to reiterate that the work of sentencing commissions has resulted in some common approaches to structuring judicial decision making. Despite these similarities, state sentencing guidelines vary considerably on many characteristics (Frase, 2005; Kauder & Ostrom, 2008; Kautt & Mueller-Johnson, 2009).

Table 4.1 compares state sentencing commissions on the following criteria: (1) when the commission was established, (2) when the guidelines went into effect, (3) whether the sentencing commission is permanent, (4) the composition of the commission, and (5) other duties of the sentencing commission. Table 4.2 presents data on the commission-based guidelines including: (1) the structure of the guidelines (grid, worksheet, or other approach), (2) whether the guidelines include misdemeanors, (3) whether the guidelines include intermediate punishments, (4) whether there is discretionary parole release, (5) how the guidelines operate (mandatory, voluntary, or somewhere in between), and (6) how appeals are allowed and handled. In addition to the characteristics presented in Tables 4.1 and 4.2, we will also discuss variation in the driving forces behind the creation of the sentencing commission, the stated goal(s) of various commission-based sentencing guidelines, the consideration of juvenile records, and the consideration of aggravating and mitigating factors.

Table 4.1 Comparison of State Sentencing Commissions

State	When was sentencing commission established?	When were guidelines initially instituted?	Is sentencing commission permanent?	Number of Members of State Sentencing Commission	Other Duties of Commission
AL	2000	2006	Yes	16	Education, revise worksheets, data collection and analysis, prepare annual report, make recommendations regarding sentencing
AK	Sentencing commission was active from 1990 to 1993	N/A Commission looked over presumptive sentencing in the 1990s after 1978 reforms	No	N/A	Commission is no longer active
AR	1993	1994	Yes	11	Data collection and production of annual report about compliance with sentencing guidelines, training
DE	1984	1987	Yes	11	Data collection from state or local government entities to carry out commission's functions
DC	1998	2004	Yes	20	Monitor and evaluate guidelines, enhance public's understanding of sentencing policies, propose reforms in the criminal code
KS	1989	1993	Yes	17	Monitor and evaluate the sentencing guidelines, forecast offender populations, education
LA	1987	1992	Yes	23	Review Louisiana sentencing system, make recommendations to governor and the legislature, research on sentencing and correctional practices

(continued)

Table 4.1 Comparison of State Sentencing Commissions (continued)

State	When was sentencing commission established?	When were guidelines initially instituted?	Is sentencing commission permanent?	Number of Members of State Sentencing Commsission	Other Duties of Commission
MD	Maryland State Commission on Criminal Sentencing Policy was created in 1999	A Judicial Committee on Sentencing formed voluntary sentencing guidelines, which went into effect in 1983	Yes	19	Oversight, collect guidelines worksheets, maintain a database, train criminal justice actors who apply the guidelines
MA	1994	1996	Yes	15	Training and support to court practitioners on the use of the sentencing guidelines, conduct research, serve as a clearinghouse for information on sentencing
MI	Originally 1994. In 2014 the Criminal Justice Policy Commission served as a reboot of the previous commission.	1999	No	17	Conduct research on the effectiveness of sentencing guidelines, research intermediate sanctions, ensure resources are available to carry out imposed sentences
MN	1978	1980	Yes	11	Collects data on sentencing practices. Responds to legislative changes, case law, problems that may arise, and to issues raised by various groups, and is responsible for training practitioners
MO	1994	2004	Yes	11	Study sentencing practices in circuit courts and study alternatives to incarceration

NC	Established in 1990, became permanent in 1996	1994	Yes	30	Analyze resource impact of sentencing changes proposed by legislature, make recommendations to the General Assembly, maintain statistical information about correctional population, report on the effectiveness of programs
OH		1990	Yes	31	Study criminal laws of the state, develop sentencing plans, make recommendations to the General Assembly, monitor impact of commission's proposals
OR	Guidelines were initially developed in 1987. In 2011, the Public Safety Commission created a modern sentencing guidelines system.	1989	Yes	9	Monitor implementation of the guidelines and their impact on the state's criminal justice professionals
PA		1978	Yes	11	Collecting and publishing data concerning sentencing processes, establish research and development program to serve as a repository of information on sentencing, make recommendations to the General Assembly
SC		2008	2010	No	NA	Develop and recommend policies for preventing prison overcrowding, annually submit a comprehensive plan for preventing prison and jail overcrowding; research, make recommendations to the General Assembly

(continued)

Table 4.1 Comparison of State Sentencing Commissions (continued)

State	When was sentencing commission established?	When were guidelines initially instituted?	Is sentencing commission permanent?	Number of Members of State Sentencing Commssion	Other Duties of Commission
TN	In 1989 produced advisory guidelines. The Task Force on the Use of Enhancement Factors in Criminal Sentencing was established in 2005 in response to *Blakely v. Washington*	1989	No	NA	The Task Force of 2005 was also charge with the responsibility of monitoring and assessing the impact of the Criminal Sentencing Reform Act of 2005 on Tennessee's criminal justice system.
UT	1993	1995	The commission was created in statute and was renewed every 10 years until recently, when it was made permanent.	27	Publishes guidelines, conducts research, reviews and makes recommendations on legislation, assists the legislature in the review and study of sentencing issues, training and education
VA	1994	1995	Yes	17	Training and education, research on risk assesment, recidivism, and probation violations, assess the fiscal impact of proposed criminal justice legislation

WA	Commission derived from the Sentencing Reform Act (SRA) of 1981	1984	Yes	24	SRA originally mandated that the commission develop and maintan computerized databases of felony dispositions and update sentencing manuals. In 2011, the state legislature transferred such reponsibilities to the Caseload Forecast Council. Now has more of an advisory role.
WI	Several commissions were established and subsequently disbanded. The first was in 1984.	Wisconsin Sentencing Commission was created in 1984 and its guidelines were issued on November 1, 1985. Temporary guidelines were enacted into law in 2001 under Act 109 and became effective on February 1, 2003. The Wisconsin Sentencing Commission replaced these effective July 1, 2005.	No	NA	The Wisconsin Sentencing Commission and its statutory provisions were eliminated in the State's 2007–09 Biennium Budget.

Table 4.2 Comparison of States with Commission-Based Guidelines

State	Guidelines, Grid, or Worksheet Structure	Do guidelines or worksheets include misdemeanors?	Do guidelines include intermediate punishments?	Is there discretionary parole release?	Voluntary or Mandatory Continuum Score (designated by Kauder & Ostrom, 2008)	Is appellate review of the sentence permitted?
AL	Three sets of worksheets — property, drug, and personal. In 2013, the guidelines were made to be presumptive for property and drug offenses. The worksheets are filled out for 27 of the most common felonies committed in the state.	No	No. The worksheets just indicate prison or not. Sentencing to intermediate sanctions is problematic because not all jurisdictions have intermediate sanctions available.	Yes for many, but not all, offenses	3	For offenses where the guidelines are considered presumptive, the state may appeal a departure sentence below the presumptive recommendation and the defendant may appeal a departure sentence above the presumptive recommendation. Appellate review shall be limited to whether the trial court abused its discretion.
AK	Alaska legislature designed statutory presumptive ranges for various classes of offenses — A single grid — 9 offense classes and 3 prior record levels	Yes	No	Some, but not all, offenders are eligible for discretionary parole release. Alaska has very complicated parole eligibility guidelines.	7	The defendant and the state may appeal.

AR	Sentencing Standards Grid has 10 offense classes and 6 criminal history levels	No	Yes, sentencing grid indicates imprisonment in some grid cells as well as community corrections centers and/or alternative sanctions in other grid cells	4	Yes, inmates who, on or after January 1, 1994, commit any Homicide, Sexual Assault in the First Degree, Sexual Assault in the Second Degree, Battery in the First Degree, Domestic Battery in the First Degree, class Y Kidnapping, class Y Rape, Aggravated Robbery, Causing a Catastrophe, Engaging in a Continuing Criminal Enterprise, and Simultaneous Possession of Drugs and Firearms are eligible for discretionary parole	No
DE	12 non-drug felony categories (7 violent and 5 nonviolent) and 5 non-drug misdemeanor categories and 9 drug categories (6 felony and 3 misdemeanor).	Yes	Certain levels on the grid allow for intermediate sanctions.	6	No, except for pre-TIS sentenced offenders— before 1989. All incarceration or full confinement sentences for crimes committed on or after June 30, 1990, are to	No

(continued)

Table 4.2 Comparison of States with Commission-Based Guidelines (continued)

State	Guidelines, Grid, or Worksheet Structure	Do guidelines or worksheets include misdemeanors?	Do guidelines include intermediate punishments?	Is there discretionary parole release?	Voluntary or Mandatory Continuum Score (designated by Kauder & Ostrom, 2008)	Is appellate review of the sentence permitted?
				be served with only limited good time possiblilities. Follows TIS, a minimum of 75% will be served prior to release.		
DC	Master grid — 9 offense and 5 criminal history levels, Drug grid — 4 offense and 5 criminal history levels	No	Some grid cells indicate split sentences or probation sentences (which may include offender services like drug treatment), but they don't explicitly designate intermediate sanctions.	Parole release was abolished and "supervised release" was instituted for felonies committed on or after August 5, 2000. The D.C. Revitalization Act changed parole for D.C. inmates. The power to grant and deny parole for all D.C. inmates convicted of felony crimes was transferred from the D.C. Board of Parole to the U.S. Parole Commission on August 5, 1998.	3	No

| KS | Separate sentencing matrices for nondrug offenses and drug offenses. Each grid has nine criminal history categories. The nondrug offense grid has ten offense severity levels and the drug grid has four severity levels. | No | Yes, the commission lists numerous sentencing options a judge may impose, including prison, drug and alcohol treatments, house arrest, fines, and restitution, among other choices. | As of July 1, 1993, a guidelines system was enacted and Kansas has postrelease supervison, the length of which is determined at the time of sentencing. For those offenders sentenced before the guidlines system, under the indeterminate release structure, the Prisoner Review Board determines when an incarcerated inmate will be released. | 10 | If a sentence is within the presumptive sentencing range provided for the crime on the proper grid, or the product of a plea agreement, it is generally not appealable. A departure sentence may be appealed by the defendant or the state, and appellate review for a departure sentence is limited to whether the court's findings of fact and reasons justifying departure are supported by evidence on the record and constitute substantial and compelling reasons for departure. |

(continued)

Table 4.2 Comparison of States with Commission-Based Guidelines (continued)

State	Guidelines, Grid, or Worksheet Structure	Do guidelines or worksheets include misdemeanors?	Do guidelines include intermediate punishments?	Is there discretionary parole release?	Voluntary or Mandatory Continuum Score (designated by Kauder & Ostrom, 2008)	Is appellate review of the sentence permitted?
LA	When the guidelines were in effect, 9 offense and 7 criminal history score levels. Guidelines were essentially not used after 1994. Now offense penalties are determined by legislative statutes, which often indicate wide ranges.	No	Original guidelines did, and current commission mentions substance abuse programs and other alternative treatment methods	For some non-violent crimes	5 originally, currently N/A	Defendant can appeal setnence, and the court must give reasons for giving a particular sentence to facilitate appellate review.
MD	Separate sentencing matrices for offenses against the person (15 offense and 8 prior record levels), drug offenses (7 offense and 8 prior record levels) and property offenses (6 offense and 8 prior record levels).	Crimes that carry no possible penalty of incarceration are excluded from guidelines.	No	Yes. The Maryland Parole Commission is charged with determining, on a case-by-case basis, whether inmates serving sentences of six months or more in state or local facilities are suitable for release into the community under certain conditions or supervision.	7	Defendants may not appeal sentencing departures.

MA	Single grid, 9 offense seriousness levels and 5 criminal history levels	Yes	Yes—Certain grid cells indicate that intermediate punishments can or should be used, as well as provide four levels of intermediate punishments that can be chosen from.	Yes	7	The defendant and the commonwealth have limited rights to appeal a sentence.
MI	9 grids (correspond to 2nd degree manslaughter, Class A, B, C. D, E, F, G, and H felonies)	No	Yes—There are three dispositional "cell" types in the sentencing grids—"prison" cells where imprisonment is required, "straddle" cells where judges may sentence either to prison or to intermediate sanctions, and "intermediate sanction" cells that preclude state imprisonment.	Yes, but eligibility has changed over the years. Truth in Sentencing is a 1998 state law which eliminates disciplinary credits, good time, and corrections centers for certain offenders and requires offenders to serve the entire minimum sentence in prison prior to being considered for parole. TIS took effect for enumerated assaultive offenses committed on or after 12/15/98 and for all offenses committed on or after 12/15/00.	8*	If the judge imposes a minimum sentence that is longer or more severe than the appropriate sentence range, the court shall advise the defendant on the record and in writing that he or she may appeal the sentence as provided by law on grounds that it is longer or more severe than the appropriate sentence range.

*It should be noted, however, that as of July 31, 2015, the Michigan Supreme Court ruled that state's guidelines unconstitutional and so were all minimum sentences produced as a result of the guidelines. The ruling was based on the guidelines causing judges to find facts that were not presented to the jury during the trial, and such facts would impact the sentence as a result. The guidelines are now advisory rather than mandatory.

(continued)

Table 4.2 Comparison of States with Commission-Based Guidelines (continued)

State	Guidelines, Grid, or Worksheet Structure	Do guidelines or worksheets include misdemeanors?	Do guidelines include intermediate punishments?	Is there discretionary parole release?	Voluntary or Mandatory Continuum Score (designated by Kauder & Ostrom, 2008)	Is appellate review of the sentence permitted?
MN	Felony grid — 11 offense severity levels and 7 prior record levels, separate sex offender grid — 8 offense severity levels and 7 prior record levels	No	When a sentence is "stayed" the court places the offender on probation and may impose up to one year of conditional confinement in a local facility (jail or workhouse). Other conditions such as fines, restitution, community work service, treatment, house arrest, etc. may also be imposed on the offender.	The sentence pronounced is fixed and there is no parole board to grant early release from prison. When a prison sentence is pronounced by the court it consists of two parts: a term of imprisonment equal to two-thirds of the total executed sentence and a supervised release term equal to the remaining one-third.	11	If the court does depart, the judge must state the reasons for departure and either the prosecution or the defense may appeal the pronounced sentence.

MO	Voluntary guidelines—called "recommended sentences"—20 offense grids, each with 3 severity and 5 prior record levels (5 offense types—violent, sex, and child abuse, non-violent, drug, and DWI)—For each type, 4 grids corresponding to Class A, B, C, and D felonies within the type. Recommended sentences within each grid based on severity level and prior record.	No	Yes, most recent statute directs the commission to study alternative sentences and lists many different types.	Yes — For most offenses. Exceptions include offenders with special sentencing conditions (i.e., mandatory minimum sentencing), and those convicted of dangerous felonies.	2	A defendant may not appeal a sentence departure.
NC	Felony grid—10 offense and six prior record levels, misdemeanor grid—4 offense and three prior record levels	Yes, separate grid	Yes	No, but post release supervision of 6 months to 3 years to begin when offender is within 9 months of maximum sentence	12	Both the defendant and the state may appeal if the sentence results from an incorrect finding of the defendant's prior record level or contains a sentence disposition or

(continued)

Table 4.2 Comparison of States with Commission-Based Guidelines (continued)

State	Guidelines, Grid, or Worksheet Structure	Do guidelines or worksheets include misdemeanors?	Do guidelines include intermediate punishments?	Is there discretionary parole release?	Voluntary or Mandatory Continuum Score (designated by Kauder & Ostrom, 2008)	Is appellate review of the sentence permitted?
						sentence length not authorized by the structured sentencing law. The defense may appeal whether a sentence imposed outside the presumptive range (within the aggravated range) is supported by the evidence. The state may appeal whether a finding of "extraordinary mitigation" is supported by the evidence or is sufficient as a matter of law to support the dispositional deviation.

OH	Sentencing ranges of basic prison terms are indicated for five levels of felonies; repeat violent offender enhancements ranging from 1–10 years are added to prison terms for 1st and 2nd degree offenses.	No	Yes, suggests a presumptive of community sanctions for less serious felonies	Only for offenders sentenced before guidelines. Post release control applies to crimes that were committed on or after July 1, 1996, and offenders who were sentenced under Senate Bill 2 to a definite prison term. For some offenders, the ORC mandates post-release control. For others, the ORC specifies that post release control is discretionary by the Parole Board.	1	Yes
OR	Felony Grid—11 offense and 9 prior record levels.	No	Yes. Structured sanctions are key to guidelines.	Not for those sentenced on or after 11/1/1989. Prisoners can earn up to 20% off their sentence. They must serve a post-prison supervision term. There is discretionary parole release for offenders in Oregon prisons	10	The defendant or the state may appeal.

(continued)

Table 4.2 Comparison of States with Commission-Based Guidelines (continued)

State	Guidelines, Grid, or Worksheet Structure	Do guidelines or worksheets include misdemeanors?	Do guidelines include intermediate punishments?	Is there discretionary parole release?	Voluntary or Mandatory Continuum Score (designated by Kauder & Ostrom, 2008)	Is appellate review of the sentence permitted?
				who committed their crimes prior to November 1, 1989; for aggravated murderers and murderers eligible for parole and for those convicted by the courts as dangerous offenders, regardless of crime date.		
PA	Basic Sentencing Matrix for most felonies and misdemeanors with 14 offense gravity scores and 8 prior record levels, in additon, three separate matrices—two for Deadly Weapon Enhancement and one for Youth/School Enhancement Matrix for applicable cases.	Yes, same grid	Yes	Pennsylvania has both state and county level parole systems. If the sentence was 24 months or longer, it is a state sentence and the Parole Board makes the decision whether to grant parole and determines the conditions of parole. If the sentence is less than 24 months, it is a county sentence and the sentencing judge makes the decision.	9	Yes—defense can appeal if judge departed from guidelines, if sentence imposed is deemed "unreasonable." State can also appeal.

SC	Sets maximum sentences for 4 classes of felonies: Class A yields 30 years or less. Class B yields 25 years or less. Class C yields 20 years or less. Class D felony yields 15 years or less. Misdemeanors: Class A, three years or less; Class B misdemeanor, two years or less; and Class C misdemeanor, one year or less.	No	No	Yes for most offenses. South Carolina law defines a no-parole offense as a Class A, B, or C felony, or any crime that is exempt from classification but punishable by a maximum term of 20 years or more. Under S.C. Code § 24-13-150, Early release, a person convicted of a no-parole offense is not eligible for parole and cannot be released until they have served at least 85% of their sentence.	Note that South Carolina Guidelines were passed after Kauder and Ostrom's work, so they did not provide a score, however, South Carolina describes their guidelines as "voluntary."	Yes, a criminal defendant may appeal to the state appellate courts from a criminal conviction or sentence asserting that error was committed during trial, which requires that the case be remanded to the trial court or requires that the conviction or sentence be vacated or reversed. They may not appeal a departure since guidelines are advisory.
TN	Single grid — 5 felony classes and 5 defendant type categories	No	No	Yes	3	A defendant may not appeal a departure from the sentencing guidelines. A defendant may appeal an excessive sentence but must rebut the presumption that the trial court's sentence was correct.

(continued)

Table 4.2 Comparison of States with Commission-Based Guidelines (continued)

State	Guidelines, Grid, or Worksheet Structure	Do guidelines or worksheets include misdemeanors?	Do guidelines include intermediate punishments?	Is there discretionary parole release?	Voluntary or Mandatory Continuum Score (designated by Kauder & Ostrom, 2008)	Is appellate review of the sentence permitted?
UT	Felony grid, 12 offense and 5 criminal history levels; sex offender grid, 10 offense and 3 criminal history levels	The only misdemeanors considered in the guidelines are class A misdemeanor sex offenses in the sex offender matrix.	The guidelines designate certain grid cells to receive intermediate sanctions.	Yes—the constitution of the state of Utah creates the Board of Pardons and Parole, and delegates the power and authority of the state to the board to determine whether, and under what conditions, persons committed to prison may be released, supervised, or returned to custody.	6	A defendant may not appeal a sentence departure.
VA	Sixteen felony offense and criminal history worksheets, as well as worksheets for sentencing revocation and probation violators	No	Yes	On January 1, 1995, discretionary parole release was abolished and good time was eliminated. The Virginia Parole Board reviews all eligible offenders. If (1) The offender committed the crime prior to January 1, 1995,	6	No

WA	Felony grid — 16 seriousness levels and 10 prior record scores, "Anticipatories" grid — 16 seriousness levels and 10 offender scores, Drug sentencing grid — 3 seriousness levels and 3 offender scores, and Drug Sentencing Grid — Solicitations — 3 seriousness levels and 3 offender scores	No	Sentencing ranges are expressed in terms of total confinement. For certain offenders, a court can convert terms of total confinement to partial confinement or to community service.			
			Eliminated parole release to ensure that offenders who commit similar crimes and have similar criminal histories receive equivalent sentences. Exceptions include felony offenders who committed crimes before July 1, 1984, and went to prison and a select group of sex offenders who have committed offenses after August 31, 2001.	10	(2) The offender has multiple misdemeanors committed prior to July 1, 2008, and (3) The offender was sentenced to indeterminate sentences under the Youthful Offender Act.	Exceptional sentences may be appealed by the offender or by the state.

(continued)

Table 4.2 Comparison of States with Commission-Based Guidelines (continued)

State	Guidelines, Grid, or Worksheet Structure	Do guidelines or worksheets include misdemeanors?	Do guidelines include intermediate punishments?	Is there discretionary parole release?	Voluntary or Mandatory Continuum Score (designated by Kauder & Ostrom, 2008)	Is appellate review of the sentence permitted?
WI	Separate worksheets for 11 offense categories. Each worksheet is divided into four sections: offense severity; risk factors, the specific offense chart, and other factors that may warrant adjustment of sentence.	No	On worksheets, there is the possibility that the offender may be eligible for a boot camp or a substance abuse program.	No. Under TIS laws, any person who commits a felony offense on or after Dec. 31, 1999 and is sentenced to at least one year in prison will not be eligible for parole. Expected to serve entire sentence with some exceptions for early release. The Wisconsin Parole Commission is the final authority for granting discretionary parole for sentences handed down for crimes committed before Dec. 31, 1999.	1	A defendant may not appeal a sentence departure.

Sentencing Commissions—Temporary or Permanent?

Most sentencing commissions produced sentencing guidelines that are still utilized today. In most states, the responsibilities of the sentencing commission to develop and revise guidelines have remained and some have expanded their duties. Commissions that are permanent include those in Alabama, Arkansas, Delaware, District of Columbia, Kansas, Louisiana, Maryland, Massachusetts, Minnesota, Missouri, North Carolina, Ohio, Oregon, Pennsylvania, Utah, and Virginia.

In the state of Washington, certain duties originally afforded to the sentencing commission have been transferred to other entities. The Sentencing Reform Act (SRA), which established sentencing guidelines for offenders who committed crimes on or after July 1, 1994, also mandated that the "Sentencing Guidelines Commission develop and maintain computerized databases of adult felony and juvenile dispositions, produce annual updates to adult and juvenile sentencing manuals, and conduct research related to adult and juvenile sentencing." In addition, the commission has traditionally assessed the prison and jail impact of proposed sentencing policy changes as part of the state's "fiscal note process" (State of Washington Caseload Forecast Council, 2011).

In 2011, the legislature passed a bill (ESSB 5891) that transferred the responsibility for the sentencing databases, the sentencing manuals, and research to be performed on sentencing practices, including policy impacts, from the commission to the Caseload Forecast Council. The council assumed these duties on August 24, 2011. Court clerks now submit copies of judgment and sentencing forms in all adult felony convictions to the Caseload Forecast Council (State of Washington Caseload Forecast Council, 2011).

In Louisiana, the function of the commission has transformed. The Louisiana Sentencing Commission was initially established in 1987 and created sentencing guidelines. In practice, however, judges essentially stopped considering them (although they were not formally repealed) in 1994 when truth-in-sentencing went into effect. Legislatively defined statutes establish ranges for individual offenses and the judge hands down a determinate sentence (a specific number of years) in that range. Offenders convicted of violent and serious offenses must serve 85 percent of this time. Other offenders may earn two days' credit for one day served and work toward "good time release." A small percentage of non-violent offenders may be released via discretionary parole after serving one-third of their sentence.

The Louisiana Sentencing Commission, however, was reinvigorated in 2008. It is now an active commission (despite the fact that members volunteer service on the commission, which has no budget) that has refocused its purposes in a state with the highest incarceration rate in the country. It has been statutorily mandated to "conduct a comprehensive review of Louisiana's current sentencing structure, sentencing practices, probation and parole supervision, and the use of alternatives to incarceration" (R.S. 15:321, http://www.lcle.la.gov/sentencing_commission/20120315 _LSC_overview.pdf).

In other states (for example, Alaska, Michigan, South Carolina, Tennessee, and Wisconsin) the sentencing commission disbanded after it developed presumptive sentencing approaches and/or guidelines. In Wisconsin, for example, several sentencing commissions have come and gone. The Wisconsin Sentencing Commission replaced these effective July 1, 2005. Neither the commission nor any other agency will continue to collect and analyze sentencing guidelines worksheets.

Another interesting situation involves the Oregon Sentencing Guidelines, which were initially implemented in 1989. The guidelines initially covered most felony offenses. Since the guidelines' inception, however, Oregon has passed Measure 11, a mandatory sentencing law that requires harsher sanctions for serious violent felonies (which will be discussed in depth in Chapter 6, which deals with mandatory sentencing). The Oregon Criminal Justice Commission newsletter (Winter 2011) pointed out that many of the crimes that send the most people to prison in the state of Oregon are now sentenced according to Measure 11, and not the original guidelines.

The Goals of State Sentencing Guidelines

The stated purpose of each state's guidelines is routinely espoused by the state's sentencing commission. While no two states' written purposes are identical, there are several consistent themes in the articulation of the purposes of sentencing across states. Commissions routinely embrace the goals of making sentences more uniform and fair. Many note the importance of equity and proportionality in sentencing. Most explicitly state a goal of decreasing sentencing disparity and discrimination through their sentencing process. Newly formed commissions have often stated the importance of reviewing extant sentencing laws and practices. Ensuring public safety is an often stated purpose of commissions. Some commissions state the goal of ensuring "truth-in-sentencing."

Some address the issue of prison overcrowding within their states and identify the goal of reserving prisons space for the most serious, violent, and/or repeat offenders. A number of commissions explicitly call for the use of intermediate sanctions to serve as alternatives to incarceration for otherwise prison-bound offenders who are not violent or repeat offenders. The call for intermediate sanctions is justified in order to reduce prison overcrowding and also to use the least restrictive sanction necessary to prevent future crime. Many acknowledge that sentencing guidelines help to structure judicial decision making, but that judges still retain some discretion in sentencing to account for important and legally relevant offense and offender characteristics (i.e., aggravating and mitigating factors).

When discussing sentencing goals of corrections, commissions routinely list multiple (and some would argue inherently incompatible) goals. These include the non-utilitarian goal of retribution as well as utilitarian goals including general deterrence, specific deterrence, incapacitation, and rehabilitation.

There are many different concepts espoused in sentencing goals across jurisdictions. No two states have identical purposes or goals. The variation in sentencing goals guides the sometimes subtle and sometimes substantive differences in the structure of different states' guidelines.

Design—The Two Dimensional Grid, Sentencing Worksheets, and Other Approaches

Two Dimensional Sentencing Grid

Most commission-based sentencing guidelines are based on a two dimensional sentencing matrix or grid (these terms will be used interchangeably in this chapter). One axis of the grid reflects the severity of the conviction offense (which is graded into seriousness levels as determined by the jurisdiction's sentencing commission) and the other represents the extent and gravity of prior record (which is also calculated and put into categories by the particular sentencing commission). Offenders fall into a grid cell based on the intersection of these two criteria. Each grid cell indicates the type or types of sentences one can receive (i.e., prison, intermediate sanction, or probation) and the length of sentence. Within the grid cell a presumptive sentence or narrow range of years or months is indicated. Sentencing grids structure sentencing by essentially collapsing the criteria that largely determine the presumptive sentence into two elements—offense severity and prior record.

The type of sentence that an offender can receive (i.e., prison, intermediate sanction, or community punishment) is easily identified by the position of the grid cell assignment within the matrix. On most sentencing matrices, disposition type is indicated by where the grid cell lies in relation to a dark dispositional line or by coloring or shading of grid cells. For those matrices with dispositional lines, cells on one side of the line (above or below—depending on the ordering of seriousness on the axis representing offense seriousness) are given prison sentences and for those cells on the other side of the line, intermediate sanctions or other community based sanctions are indicated. This is what is known as the "in/out" line, referring to whether the offender is to be put "in prison" or not. Minnesota's sentencing commission, which was the first to create a sentencing matrix, drew this line to separate grid cells to be given "executed" prison sentences from those which could receive "stayed" prison sentences, which translated into community based sentences. **Figure 4.1** shows the current Minnesota Sentencing Guidelines Grid (Minnesota Sentencing Guidelines Commission (2015, August 1)).

Number of Grids

Some states' guidelines commissions, like Minnesota's, have produced a single sentencing grid. Most often such states have created a grid for only felony, not misdemeanor, offenses. Other states have multiple grids. In these states separate grids are created for different types of offenses. In North Carolina, for example, the sentencing commission created one grid for felony offenses and a separate grid for misdemeanor offenses. The differences obviously include seriousness of offense and the penalties, but they also vary in how prior record is calculated.

Other states have separate grids for different offense types. Minnesota, the first state to implement prescriptive guidelines (in 1978), added a separate grid for sex offenders in 2006. Alabama has separate grids for drug, property, and person crimes. Kansas has different grids for drug and non-drug offenses. Missouri has twenty offense grids, each with three severity and five prior record levels.

Figure 4.1 Minnesota Sentencing Guidelines Grid

4.A. Sentencing Guidelines Grid

Presumptive sentence lengths are in months. Italicized numbers within the grid denote the discretionary range within which a court may sentence without the sentence being deemed a departure. Offenders with stayed felony sentences may be subject to local confinement.

SEVERITY LEVEL OF CONVICTION OFFENSE (Example offenses listed in italics)		CRIMINAL HISTORY SCORE						
		0	1	2	3	4	5	6 or more
Murder, 2nd Degree (intentional murder; drive-by-shootings)	11	306 *261-367*	326 *278-391*	346 *295-415*	366 *312-439*	386 *329-463*	406 *346-480[2]*	426 *363-480[2]*
Murder, 3rd Degree Murder, 2nd Degree (unintentional murder)	10	150 *128-180*	165 *141-198*	180 *153-216*	195 *166-234*	210 *179-252*	225 *192-270*	240 *204-288*
Assault, 1st Degree Controlled Substance Crime, 1st Degree	9	86 *74-103*	98 *84-117*	110 *94-132*	122 *104-146*	134 *114-160*	146 *125-175*	158 *135-189*
Aggravated Robbery, 1st Degree; Controlled Substance Crime, 2nd Degree	8	48 *41-57*	58 *50-69*	68 *58-81*	78 *67-93*	88 *75-105*	98 *84-117*	108 *92-129*
Felony DWI; Financial Exploitation of a Vulnerable Adult	7	36	42	48	54 *46-64*	60 *51-72*	66 *57-79*	72 *62-84[2,3]*
Controlled Substance Crime, 3rd Degree	6	21	27	33	39 *34-46*	45 *39-54*	51 *44-61*	57 *49-68*
Residential Burglary; Simple Robbery	5	18	23	28	33 *29-39*	38 *33-45*	43 *37-51*	48 *41-57*
Nonresidential Burglary	4	12[1]	15	18	21	24 *21-28*	27 *23-32*	30 *26-36*
Theft Crimes (Over $5,000)	3	12[1]	13	15	17	19 *17-22*	21 *18-25*	23 *20-27*
Theft Crimes ($5,000 or less) Check Forgery ($251-$2,500)	2	12[1]	12[1]	13	15	17	19	21 *18-25*
Sale of Simulated Controlled Substance	1	12[1]	12[1]	12[1]	13	15	17	19 *17-22*

[1] 12[1]=One year and one day

Presumptive commitment to state imprisonment. First-degree murder has a mandatory life sentence and is excluded from the Guidelines under Minn. Stat. § 609.185. See section 2.E. for policies regarding those sentences controlled by law.

Presumptive stayed sentence; at the discretion of the court, up to one year of confinement and other non-jail sanctions can be imposed as conditions of probation. However, certain offenses in the shaded area of the Grid always carry a presumptive commitment to state prison. See sections 2.C and 2.E.

[2] Minn. Stat. § 244.09 requires that the Guidelines provide a range for sentences that are presumptive commitment to state imprisonment of 15% lower and 20% higher than the fixed duration displayed, provided that the minimum sentence is not less than one year and one day and the maximum sentence is not more than the statutory maximum. See section 2.C.1-2.

[3] The stat. max. for Financial Exploitation of Vulnerable Adult is 240 months; the standard range of 20% higher than the fixed duration applies at CHS 6 or more. (The range is 62-86.)

Source: Minnesota Sentencing Guidelines Commission, *Minnesota sentencing guidelines and commentary, August 1, 2015.* p. 73, Figure 4A. Retrieved from http://mn.gov/sentencing-guidelines/assets /2015%20Minnesota%20Sentencing%20Guidelines%20and%20Commentary_tcm30-46700.pdf

Pennsylvania is unique in that its Basic Sentencing Matrix covers felonies and misdemeanors, but has separate grids if the offense involved the possession or use of a deadly weapon in the commission of a crime and another grid if the offense violated crimes involving youth or crimes which happened in the proximity of a school.

Calculation of Seriousness Levels of Current Offense and Prior Criminal History

The way prior record level is calculated in different states also varies. In North Carolina, prior record level is calculated by adding prior convictions (weighted by seriousness), adding a point if all the elements of the present offense are included in any prior offense, and adding a point "if the offender is on supervised or unsupervised probation, parole, or post-release supervision, serving an active sentence in jail or prison, or is on escape from a correctional institution while serving a sentence of imprisonment at the time the present offense was committed" (North Carolina Sentencing and Policy Advisory Commission, *Structured sentencing training and reference manual: Applies to offenses committed on or after December 1, 2009*, p. 11).

Washington considers five criteria when calculating the offender (prior criminal history) score. The number of points an offender receives depends on five factors: "(1) the number of prior criminal convictions or juvenile dispositions; (2) the relationship between any prior offense(s) and the current offense of conviction; (3) the presence of other current convictions; (4) the offender's community custody status at the time the crime was committed; and (5) the length of the offender's crime-free behavior between offenses" (State of Washington Caseload Forecast Council (2011)).

Variation also exists in the number of levels of offense severity and prior record level. Most states have ten or twelve levels of offense severity, and six to eight prior record levels.

Worksheets

Another approach to structuring sentencing relies on scoring worksheets. Alabama, Delaware, Virginia, and Wisconsin have opted to structure sentencing not by the creation of a grid, but by the design of offense-specific worksheets. Alabama has 27 offense and criminal history worksheets.

In Delaware there are twelve non-drug felony categories (seven violent and five nonviolent) and five non-drug misdemeanor categories, as well as nine drug categories (six felony and three misdemeanor). For each category, a statutory range and a presumptive sentence are indicated. Wisconsin has worksheets for eleven offense categories. Virginia has separate worksheets for sixteen felony offenses. The Virginia Criminal Sentencing Commission website provides worksheets used to calculate sentences for sixteen felony offenses in lieu of creating a general felony grid (Virginia Criminal Sentencing Commission, 2012a).

In Virginia, worksheets are filled out for each conviction and the Sentencing Guidelines Cover Sheet presents the offender information, a list of convictions, method of adjudication, the recommended sentence based on the relevant sentencing guidelines worksheet(s), a nonviolent risk assessment (only for those persons convicted of drug, fraud, and/or larceny crimes), the type and length of sentence which was handed down, and any reason(s) for departure.

Figure 4.2 Virginia Sentencing Worksheet for Rape

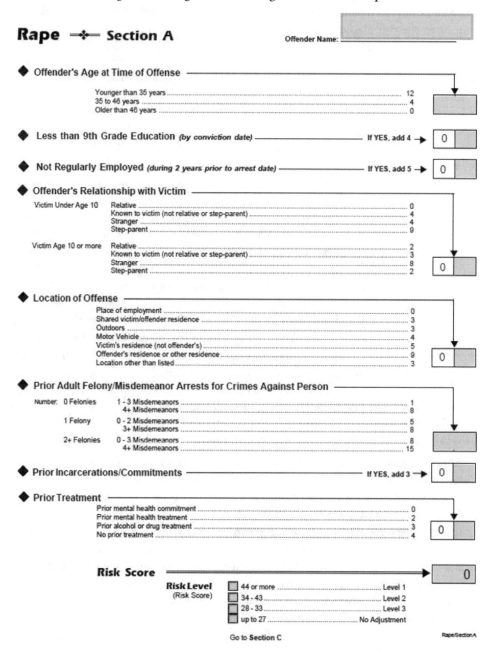

Rape ✦ Section C

Offender Name: _____

There is no Section B for this offense.

◆ **Primary Offense** — — — — — — — — — — — — —

— Prior Record Classification —
Category I | Category II | Other

A. Attempted or conspired forcible rape, forcible sodomy or object sexual penetration
  1 count .... 60 .... 30 15

B. Forcible rape or object sexual penetration, victim under age 13
  1 - 2 counts .... 312 .... 208 117
  3 counts .... 882 .... 588 331

C. Forcible sodomy, victim under age 13
  1 - 2 counts .... 354 .... 236 133
  3 counts .... 882 .... 588 331

D. Forcible rape or object sexual penetration, victim age 13 or older
  1 count .... 402 .... 288 151
  2 counts .... 882 .... 588 331

E. Forcible sodomy, victim age 13 or older
  1 count .... 324 .... 216 122
  2 counts .... 882 .... 588 331

Score
▼

◆ **Primary Offense Additional Counts** Assign points to each count of the primary not scored above and total the points ——

Maximum Penalty: 10 5
(years) Life 18

`0`

◆ **Additional Offenses** Assign points to each additional offense (including counts) and total the points ——

Maximum Penalty: Less than 2 0
(years) 2, 3 1
  4, 5 2
  10 5
  20 9
  30 14
  40 or more 18

`0`

◆ **Weapon Used, Brandished, Feigned or Threatened** — — — — — If YES, add 39 → `0`

◆ **Victim Injury** — — — — — — — — — — — — — — —

  Threatened or emotional 3
  Physical 20
  Serious physical 76

`0`

◆ **Prior Felony Sexual Assault Convictions/Adjudications** — — — — —

Number 1 13
of Counts: 2 26
  3 or more 39

`0`

Total Score ══════════════════════ `0`

See Rape Section C Recommendation Table for guidelines sentence range.

If necessary, on the cover sheet also enter the adjusted high end of the guidelines sentence range based on Risk Level: ☐1 ☐2 ☐3 or ☐n/a

Rape/Section C

[Clear Form] [Go to Cover]

Source: Virginia Criminal Sentencing Commission. (2012b). *Worksheets*. Retrieved from http://www.vcsc.virginia.gov/worksheets_2015/Rape_.pdf

The worksheet specific to the crime of rape is presented in **Figure 4.2**. This worksheet assigns points to various aspects of the crime to reach a final score, which is used to determine the sentence. It counts prior adult felonies and misdemeanors and weighs multiple prior felonies heavily. It adds points for prior incarcerations or commitments. Regarding the offense, it weighs completed rapes more heavily than attempts and increases the number of points if the victim was under the age of 13. Points are added for additional offenses and if a weapon was used. Victim injury also affects the score. The highest number of points is added if the victim suffered *serious* physical injury, followed by physical injury, and then emotional injury.

Hybrid Approaches

Some states use both worksheets and sentencing matrices to structure judicial decision making. In most states' sentencing matrices, level of **severity of offense** either comes from a list of offenses that are graded in terms of seriousness (for example, North Carolina, Minnesota, and Pennsylvania) or from a worksheet form that considers both seriousness grade plus additional factors (for example, Maryland). Most states use worksheets which consider various criteria (but always at least consider number and seriousness of adult priors) to calculate **prior record**. These criteria are calculated and assigned levels on a sentencing grid. For many states (Minnesota, Pennsylvania, North Carolina), this grid forms the basis of the sentence. For Maryland, the grid assignment is identified in a sentencing matrix (**Figure 4.3**) and then added to the "Maryland Sentencing Guidelines Worksheet" (**Figure 4.4**), which the judge completes at sentencing (Maryland State Commission on Criminal Sentencing Policy (2015)).

Other Approaches

Some states have introduced other approaches to structuring judicial decision making. Ohio is one of those states. Ohio's commission-based guidelines differ from most other states' guidelines, in that they do not use a grid or a worksheet structure. Instead, felonies are classified into one of five levels. Ranges of prison time or community sanctions are indicated for each level. The amount of post-release time is also predicated on the level of offense. The guidelines also provide sentence enhancements for repeat violent offenders. Ohio is one of the guidelines states that we will detail later in this chapter.

South Carolina is another state that differs in its creation of sentencing "guidelines." In 2010, South Carolina adopted a voluntary guidelines system, which established maximum imprisonment terms for four categories of felonies. Under the "guidelines," a Class A felony yields 30 years or fewer, a Class B felony yields 25 years or fewer, a Class C felony yields 20 years or fewer, and a Class D felony yields 15 years or fewer. Clearly these "guidelines" still allow for wide judicial discretion.

The Consideration of Juvenile Record

The vast majority of states with sentencing guidelines consider at least some measure of prior juvenile adjudication when determining a recommended sentence. Exactly how juvenile record affects sentencing under guidelines and worksheet structures varies by state, however.

Juvenile adjudications are used in the calculation of prior record in some states. Each state, however, delineates under what circumstances juvenile adjudications are counted. In Pennsylvania, Minnesota, and Kansas, prior juvenile adjudications add points to the prior record score. In Maryland, findings of delinquency and juvenile commitments are assigned point values in the calculation of offender score (prior record). In the District of Columbia, juvenile adjudications generally count if the amount of time between the date of disposition and the commission of the current offense for which the offender is being sentenced is 5 years or less. In Alabama, juvenile adjudications are factored into

Figure 4.3 Maryland Sentencing Matrix for Offenses Against Persons

Offense Score	Offender Score							
	0	1	2	3	4	5	6	7 or more
1	P	P	P-3M	3M-1Y	3M-18M	3M-2Y	6M-2Y	1Y-3Y
2	P-6M	P-1Y	P-18M	3M-2Y	6M-3Y	1Y-5Y	18M-5Y	3Y-8Y
3	P-2Y	P-2Y	6M-3Y	1Y-5Y	2Y-5Y	3Y-7Y	4Y-8Y	5Y-10Y
4	P-3Y	6M-4Y	1Y-5Y	2Y-5Y	3Y-7Y	4Y-8Y	5Y-10Y	5Y-12Y
5	3M-4Y	6M-5Y	1Y-6Y	2Y-7Y	3Y-8Y	4Y-10Y	6Y-12Y	8Y-15Y
6	1Y-6Y	2Y-7Y	3Y-8Y	4Y-9Y	5Y-10Y	7Y-12Y	8Y-13Y	10Y-20Y
7	3Y-8Y	4Y-9Y	5Y-10Y	6Y-12Y	7Y-13Y	9Y-14Y	10Y-15Y	12Y-20Y
8	4Y-9Y	5Y-10Y	5Y-12Y	7Y-13Y	8Y-15Y	10Y-18Y	12Y-20Y	15Y-25Y
9	5Y-10Y	7Y-13Y	8Y-15Y	10Y-15Y	12Y-18Y	15-25Y	18Y-30Y	20Y-30Y
10	10Y-18Y	10Y-21Y	12Y-25Y	15Y-25Y	15Y-30Y	18Y-30Y	20Y-35Y	20Y-L
11	12Y-20Y	15Y-25Y	18Y-25Y	20Y-30Y	20Y-30Y	25Y-35Y	25Y-40Y	25Y-L
12	15Y-25Y	18Y-25Y	18Y-30Y	20Y-35Y	20Y-35Y	25Y-40Y	25Y-L	25Y-L
13	20Y-30Y	25Y-35Y	25Y-40Y	25Y-L	25Y-L	30Y-L	L	L
14	20Y-L	25Y-L	28Y-L	30Y-L	L	L	L	L
15	25Y-L	30Y-L	35Y-L	L	L	L	L	L

P=Probation, M=Months, Y=Years, L=Life

Source: Reproduced with permission from the *Maryland sentencing guidelines manual, Version 7.1*, Effective February 1, 2015 with updated June 1, 2015. p. 31, Table 8-1. Sentencing Matrix for Offenses Against Persons, Maryland State Commission on Criminal Sentencing Policy, College Park, MD. Retrieved from http://www.msccsp.org/Files/Guidelines/MSGM/guidelinesmanual.pdf

Figure 4.4 Maryland Sentencing Guidelines Worksheet

MARYLAND SENTENCING GUIDELINES WORKSHEET

OFFENDER NAME - Last, First, Middle | SID# | SEX __M__F | BIRTHDATE | JURISDICTION

PSI __Yes __No | DATE OF OFFENSE | DATE OF SENTENCING

AT THIS SENTENCING, NUMBER OF: CONVICTED OFFENSES [ ] CRIMINAL EVENTS [ ]

WORKSHEET #_____ OF

CRIMINAL EVENT #_____.

DISPOSITION TYPE
- __ ABA plea agreement
- __ Non-ABA plea agreement
- __ Plea, no agreement
- __ Court trial
- __ Jury trial
- __ Reconsideration
- __ Review

REPRESENTATION
- __ Private
- __ Public Defender
- __ Court Appointed
- __ Self

ETHNICITY
Hispanic/Latino Origin __Yes __No

Victim Court Costs Imposed __Yes __No

RACE
- __ Black
- __ White
- __ Native Hawaiian/Pacific Islander
- __ American Indian/Alaskan Native
- __ Unidentifiable
- __ Asian
- __ Other

CONVICTED OFFENSE TITLE	I-VII	CJIS CODE	MD CODE, ART, & SECTION	STAT. MAX	MAND. MIN	CASE #/DOCKET #
1st Convicted Offense		—				
2nd Convicted Offense		—				
3rd Convicted Offense		—				

OFFENSE SCORE(S) – Offense Against a Person Only

1st Off	2nd Off	3rd Off		A. Seriousness Category
1	1	1	=	V – VII
3	3	3	=	IV
5	5	5	=	III
8	8	8	=	II
10	10	10	=	I

1st Off	2nd Off	3rd Off		B. Victim Injury
0	0	0	=	No Injury
1	1	1	=	Injury, Non-Permanent
2	2	2	=	Permanent Injury or Death

1st Off	2nd Off	3rd Off		C. Weapon Presence
0	0	0	=	No Weapon
1	1	1	=	Weapon Other Than Firearm
2	2	2	=	Firearm or Explosive

1st Off	2nd Off	3rd Off		D. Special Victim Vulnerability
0	0	0	=	No
1	1	1	=	Yes

_____ _____ _____ OFFENSE SCORE(S)

OFFENDER SCORE

A. Relationship to CJS When Instant Offense Occurred
- 0 = None or Pending Cases
- 1 = Court or Other Criminal Justice Supervision

B. Juvenile Delinquency
- 0 = 23 years or older **or** crime-free for 5 years **or** no more than 1 finding of a delinquent act
- 1 = Under 23 years old **and:** 2 or more findings of a delinquent act **or** 1 commitment
- 2 = Under 23 years **and** committed 2 or more times

C. Prior Adult Criminal Record
- 0 = None 3 = Moderate
- 1 = Minor 5 = Major

D. Prior Adult Parole/Prob Violation
- 0 = No 1 = Yes

_____ OFFENDER SCORE

GUIDELINES RANGE

1st Con. Off. _____ TO _____

2nd Con. Off. _____ TO _____

3rd Con. Off. _____ TO _____

Overall Guidelines Range (Multiple Counts Only) _____ TO _____

50% of Sentence Announced for COVs __Yes __No

ACTUAL SENTENCE - Imposed, Suspended, Time Served, Probation, Restitution, Fine, Corrections Options Programs (Drug Treatment Court, Home Detention, Etc.)

1st Convicted Offense

For Theft, Fraud, and Related Crimes, please indicate: ☐Economic loss $_____; ☐Unknown Amount
Subsequent Offender Filed __Yes __No Restitution Requested __Yes __No
Subsequent Offender Proven __Yes __No Restitution Proven __Yes __No

2nd Convicted Offense

For Theft, Fraud, and Related Crimes, please indicate: ☐Economic loss $_____; ☐Unknown Amount
Subsequent Offender Filed __Yes __No Restitution Requested __Yes __No
Subsequent Offender Proven __Yes __No Restitution Proven __Yes __No

3rd Convicted Offense

For Theft, Fraud, and Related Crimes, please indicate: ☐Economic loss $_____; ☐Unknown Amount
Subsequent Offender Filed __Yes __No Restitution Requested __Yes __No
Subsequent Offender Proven __Yes __No Restitution Proven __Yes __No

Was the offender sentenced to a Corrections Options program under Commission criteria?
Drug Court __Yes __No Other __Yes __No

Additional Information or Institutional/Parole Recommendation

Parole Notification __Yes __No

Worksheet Completed By

Title

Sentencing Judge (Please Print)

Sentencing Judge's Signature

VICTIM INFORMATION

Victim	__ **Yes**	__ **No**
Victim Non-participation	__ **Yes**	__ **No**
Victim Notification Form	__ Yes	__ No
Victim Notified Plea	__ Yes	__ No
Victim Notified Date	__ Yes	__ No
Victim Present	__ Yes	__ No
Written VIS	__ Yes	__ No
Oral VIS	__ Yes	__ No
No Contact Requested	__ Yes	__ No
No Contact Ordered	__ Yes	__ No

SENTENCE DEPARTURE INFORMATION

If the actual sentence departs from the guidelines range, please indicate the Court's reason(s) using the numerical code(s) on the list of common departure factors in the manual, if applicable.

[ ] [ ] [ ]

Departure Code 9 or 18 (Please Explain):

COPIES: White – Judge; Blue – Sentencing Commission; Green – Attach to Commitment or Probation Order; Yellow – File; Pink – Prosecution; Gold – Defense 4/2013 (1.8)

Source: Reproduced with permission from the *Maryland sentencing guidelines manual, Version 7.1,* Effective February 1, 2015, with updated June 1, 2015. p. 9, Maryland Sentencing Guidelines Worksheet, Maryland State Commission on Criminal Sentencing Policy, College Park, MD. Retrieved from http://www.msccsp.org/Files/Guidelines/MSGM/guidelinesmanual.pdf

the worksheet that determinates whether an offender will serve prison but not the worksheet that determines sentence length. In Delaware, prior juvenile adjudications are considered for those offenses adjudicated at age 14 or older.

The Consideration of Aggravating and Mitigating Factors

Calculated within the Guidelines or Considered as Reasons for Departure?

Commission-based sentencing guidelines systems typically allow for the consideration of aggravating and mitigating circumstances. Aggravating factors are those case characteristics which make the offense more serious or offender characteristics that make the offender more culpable. The exact factors that are considered aggravating circumstances vary in type and number by state. Examples of aggravating circumstances include the offender playing a dominant role with co-offenders, offenses committed while the individual was under correctional supervision, the commission of a crime against an especially vulnerable victim (very young or very old), and a crime that results in serious and long term injuries to the victim. Factors such as these could augment the sentence severity (type and/or length). Conversely, case or offender attributes that could be considered as mitigating factors, which would decrease sentence severity, might include victim provocation (for example, if the ultimate "victim" threw the first punch), if the offender was under duress at the time of the offense (but that did not constitute a legal defense), or if the offender played a minor role in the offense.

A good example of aggravating and mitigating factors appears in the North Carolina Sentencing and Policy Advisory Commission's lists of twenty statutorily prescribed aggravating factors and twenty-one mitigating factors in the North Carolina *Structured Sentencing Training and Reference Manual* (2009). **Figure 4.5** and **Figure 4.6** list these factors.

Figure 4.5 List of Aggravating Factors in North Carolina

1. The defendant induced others to participate in the commission of the offense or occupied a position of leadership or dominance of other participants.
2. The defendant joined with more than one other person in committing the offense and was not charged with committing a conspiracy.
2a. **(For offenses committed on or after December 1, 1997)** The offense was committed for the benefit of, or at the direction of, any criminal street gang, with the specific intent to promote, further, or assist in any criminal conduct by gang members, and the defendant was not charged with committing a conspiracy. A "criminal street gang" means any ongoing organization, association, or group of three or more persons, whether formal or informal, having as one of its primary activities the commission of felony or violent misdemeanor offenses, or delinquent acts that would be felonies or violent misdemeanors if committed by an adult, and having a common name or common identifying sign, colors, or symbols.

(continued)

Figure 4.5 List of Aggravating Factors in North Carolina (continued)

3. The offense was committed for the purpose of avoiding or preventing a lawful arrest or effecting an escape from custody.
4. The defendant was hired or paid to commit the offense.
5. The offense was committed to disrupt or hinder the lawful exercise of any governmental function or the enforcement of laws.
6. (**Added "serious injury" for offenses committed on or after December 1, 1997; added "social worker" for offenses committed on or after December 1, 2005**) The offense was committed against or proximately caused serious injury to a present or former law enforcement officer, employee of the Department of Correction, jailer, fireman, emergency medical technician, ambulance attendant, social worker, justice or judge, clerk or assistant or deputy clerk of court, magistrate, prosecutor, juror, or witness against the defendant, while engaged in the performance of that person's official duties or because of the exercise of that person's official duties.
6a. (**Offenses committed on or after December 1, 2007; added "search and rescue animal" for offenses committed on or after December 1, 2009**) The offense was committed against or proximately caused serious harm as defined in G.S. 14-163.1 or death to a law enforcement agency animal, an assistance animal, or a search and rescue animal as defined in G.S. 14-163.1, while engaged in the performance of the animal's official duties.
7. The offense was especially heinous, atrocious, or cruel.
8. The defendant knowingly created a great risk of death to more than one person by means of a weapon or device which would normally be hazardous to the lives of more than one person.
9. The defendant held public office at the time of the offense and the offense related to the conduct of the office.
10. The defendant was armed with or used a deadly weapon at the time of the crime.
11. The victim was very young, or very old, or mentally or physically infirm, or handicapped.
12. The defendant committed the offense while in pretrial release on another charge.
12a. (**Offenses committed on or after December 1, 2008**) The defendant has, during the 10-year period prior to the commission of the offense for which the defendant is being sentenced, been found by a court of the State to be in willful violation of the conditions of probation imposed pursuant to a suspended sentence or been found by the Post-Release Supervision and Parole Commission to be in willful violation of a condition of parole or post-release supervision imposed to release from incarceration.
13. The defendant involved a person under the age of 16 in the commission of the crime.
14. The offense involved an attempted or actual taking of property of great monetary value or damage causing great monetary loss, or the offense involved an unusually large quantity of contraband.
15. The defendant took advantage of a position of trust or confidence, including a domestic relationship, to commit the offense.

(continued)

Figure 4.5 List of Aggravating Factors in North Carolina (continued)

16. The offense involved the sale or delivery of a controlled substance to a minor.
16a. (**For offenses committed on or after December 1, 2004**) The offense is the manufacture of methamphetamine and was committed where a person under the age of 18 lives, was present, or was otherwise endangered by exposure to the drug, its ingredients, its by-products, or its waste.
16b. (**For offenses committed on or after January 15, 2006**) The offense is the manufacture of methamphetamine and was committed in a dwelling that is one of four or more continuous dwellings.
17. The offense for which the defendant stands convicted was committed against a victim because of the victim's race, color, religion, nationality, or county of origin.
18. The defendant does not support the defendant's family.
18a. The defendant has previously been adjudicated delinquent for an offense that would be a Class A, B1, B2, C, D, or E felony if committed by an adult.
19. The serious injury inflicted upon the victim is permanent and debilitating.
20. Any other aggravating factor reasonably related to the purposes of sentencing. (**Effective June 24, 2004**—This factor must be alleged in the indictment or other charging instrument.)

Source: North Carolina Sentencing and Policy Advisory Commission. (2009). *Structured sentencing training and reference manual: Applies to offenses committed on or after December 1, 2009.* pp. 21–22, Table 3: Aggravating Factors. Retrieved from http://www.nccourts.org/Courts/CRS/Councils/spac/Documents/sstrainingmanual_09.pdf

Figure 4.6 List of Mitigating Factors in North Carolina

1. The defendant committed the offense under duress, coercion, threat, or compulsion that was insufficient to constitute a defense but significantly reduced the defendant's culpability.
2. The defendant was a passive participant or played a minor role in the commission of the offense.
3. The defendant was suffering from a physical condition that was insufficient to constitute a defense but significantly reduces the defendant's culpability for the offense.
4. The defendant's age, immaturity, or limited mental capacity at the time of commission of the offense significantly reduced the defendant's culpability for the offense.
5. The defendant has made substantial or full restitution to the victim.
6. The victim was more than 16 years of age and was a voluntary participant in the defendant's conduct or consented to it.
7. The defendant aided in the apprehension of another felon or testified truthfully on behalf of the prosecution in another prosecution of a felony.

(continued)

Figure 4.6 List of Mitigating Factors in North Carolina (continued)

8.   The defendant acted under strong provocation, or the relationship between the defendant and the victim was otherwise extenuating.
9.   The defendant could not reasonably foresee that the defendant's conduct would cause or threaten serious bodily harm or fear, or the defendant exercised caution to avoid such consequences.
10. The defendant reasonably believed that the defendant's conduct was legal.
11. Prior to arrest or at an early stage of the criminal process, the defendant voluntarily acknowledged wrongdoing in connection with the offense to a law enforcement officer.
12. The defendant has been a person of good character or has a good reputation in the community in which the defendant lives.
13. The defendant is a minor and has reliable supervision available.
14. The defendant has been honorably discharged from the United States armed services.
15. The defendant has accepted responsibility for the defendant's criminal conduct.
16. The defendant has entered and is currently involved in or has successfully completed a drug treatment program or an alcohol treatment program subsequent to arrest and prior to trial.
17. The defendant supports the defendant's family.
18. The defendant has a support system in the community.
19. The defendant has a positive employment history or is gainfully employed.
20. The defendant has a good treatment prognosis, and a workable treatment plan is available.
21. Any other mitigating factor reasonably related to the purposes of sentencing.

Source: North Carolina Sentencing and Policy Advisory Commission. (2009). *Structured sentencing training and reference manual: Applies to offenses committed on or after December 1, 2009.* p. 23, Table 4: Mitigating Factors. Retrieved from http://www.nccourts.org/Courts/CRS/Councils/spac/Documents /sstrainingmanual_09.pdf

In North Carolina, the court can decide to impose a sentence outside the presumptive range and instead sentence within the aggravated range if aggravating factors are present and/or if aggravating factors outweigh mitigating factors. Likewise, the court can decide to sentence within the mitigated range if mitigating circumstances are present and/or the mitigating factors outweigh the aggravating factors. Other states have such lists.

Differences between states also exist concerning the way aggravating and mitigating circumstances can affect the sentence. The variations lie with which factors are considered, how they are considered, and at what point in the state's sentencing process they factor in.

For some states, such as North Carolina, the presence of aggravating and mitigating factors determines the range (presumptive, aggravating, or mitigating) from which an offender will be sentenced. In other jurisdictions, aggravating and mitigating factors may serve as reasons for departure from a presumptive range in a grid cell. The guidelines for the District of Columbia are in the form of a two dimensional matrix. In each grid cell, however, there is only one set of numbers that represent the presumptive range. According to these guidelines, the judge may sentence outside that range if he or she cites an aggravating or mitigating factor that is listed in the Voluntary Sentencing Guidelines Manual (District of Columbia Sentencing and Criminal Code Revision Commission, 2014, June 30). Minnesota is another state in which aggravating and mitigating factors may justify judicial departures from the presumptive sentence represented within a grid cell.

Before June 2004, the state had the burden of proving *by a preponderance of evidence* that an aggravating factor was present in the case. After June 24, 2004, the state must prove *beyond a reasonable doubt* that an aggravating circumstance exists. The jury in the case must decide whether an aggravating factor is present, or the offender may admit to the existence of an aggravating factor in the context of a plea bargain. This change resulted from *Blakely v. Washington* (2004), a Supreme Court case involving sentencing guidelines that we will discuss in depth in Chapter 7. What is important to know now is that the Supreme Court concluded under the Sixth Amendment that any fact, other than a prior conviction, that is used to increase the sentence from the presumptive range must be admitted by the defendant or proven beyond a reasonable doubt. The offender has the responsibility of proving beyond a preponderance of evidence that a mitigating factor exists.

Some Controversial Aggravating and Mitigating Factors

State sentencing guidelines and worksheets may consider a variety of factors that can impact sentencing. There are some controversies about the designation of certain offense and offender characteristics as "aggravating" or "mitigating." Notice that some of the factors that impact sentencing involve what most would consider to be extra-legal factors. We will discuss a few.

In North Carolina, for example, a statutorily defined mitigating factor is "The defendant has been honorably discharged from the United States armed services." Other things being equal, a judge may sentence an offender in the mitigated range if this factor is presented by the defendant. Having taught in coastal North Carolina in the proximity of several military bases, the author of this text has had many students who have served in the military. There was disagreement when asked in class as to whether students felt an honorable discharge should be considered a mitigating factor in criminal sentencing. Some argued that having an honorable discharge and having given service to the country should give an offender a "break." Others argued that it is not difficult to receive an honorable discharge and that this shouldn't impact sentencing decisions. Still others (both those with and without a military background) believed that those in the military should be held to a *higher* standard of behavior, compared to persons with no military service.

Another ambiguous factor considered in North Carolina's sentencing calculations involves whether the defendant supports his/her family. If he/she does, it's considered a mitigating factor. If he/she does not, it's considered an aggravating factor. One may question the relevance of this clearly extra-legal factor (and one that does not have anything to do with the crime committed or offender culpability) to the sentence. One can argue that the offender who supports his/her family exhibits pro-social traits and responsibility and should be granted some leniency. One could also, however, take issue with this factor because not all defendants have a family that they could or could not support. Other case characteristics being equal, why should a defendant who committed arson be sentenced in a mitigated range because he supports his family, while another arsonist, who is unmarried with no children, be sentenced in the presumptive range?

In Virginia's worksheet for offenders convicted of rape, *age* plays an interesting role in the calculation of total points that are allocated to the offender for sentencing. A higher number of points corresponds to harsher sentencing. Younger offenders (under 35) are given 12 points, those 35 to 45 are given 4 points, and those over 40 are given no points. The allocating of more points for younger offenders apparently reflects career criminality research that suggests that as most offenders get older, they "age out of crime." According to this logic, younger offenders have a higher risk of reoffending and are given harsher sentences that would keep them incapacitated during their crime-prone years, in accordance with a selective incapacitation rationale. Age, however, is considered by most to be an extra-legal factor.

Virginia also adds points for other extra-legal factors, such as education level (adds 4 points if offender has less than an eighth grade education and if the offender is not regularly employed). Professor Michael Tonry (2004) has taken issue with Virginia's scoring these characteristics as aggravating factors. He noted, for example,

> Punishing people because they are unemployed may injure those already disadvantaged by lack of marketable skills, mental disabilities, or high unemployment rates. Giving greater punitive weights to offenders' ages than to their past criminality violates basic and widely shared culpability notions. (p. 154)

State sentencing commissions share the common goal in structuring judicial decision making to make sentences more uniform and predictable. The factors that each state sentencing commission considers in calculating prior record, however, vary. Likewise, the designation of which factors may increase or decrease the presumptive sentence or sentencing range (i.e., aggravating and mitigating circumstances) also vary. These variations reiterate the fact that there is no one model for structuring sentencing on the state level.

Off-Grid or Off-Worksheet Crimes

While state sentencing guidelines present grids for most felony offenses (and in some states, misdemeanor offenses too), certain crimes are routinely excluded from the grids. These include homicide offenses, which often carry sentences of mandatory life imprisonment or the death penalty, regardless of prior record. For example, in Kansas, the crimes of capital murder, murder in the first degree, treason, terrorism, the illegal use of weapons of mass destruction, and several sex offenses involving young victims are sentenced to imprisonment for life. Other offenses considered "no grid" in Kansas also include felony DUI, felony domestic battery, and animal cruelty. For these offenses, the offense specific statute dictates the sentence that can be imposed.

Other crimes that are routinely sentenced off of a state's sentencing grid or work-sheet form include those offenses that carry mandatory minimum sentences. Although there is variation by state, mandatory minimum sentences are given most often for violent offenses, firearms offenses, and drug trafficking offenses. Mandatory minimum sentencing is discussed in Chapter 6.

The Retention of Some Judicial Discretion within Sentencing Guidelines

While states vary with respect to their guidelines or worksheet design, it is important to understand that judges retain some discretion. This discretion may involve (1) whether the judge sentences the offender to a presumptive sentence or whether he or she departs from the sentence (meaning imprisonment versus community punishment), (2) type of sentence—some guidelines include grid cells that allow a judge to choose between a sentence of incarceration, an intermediate punishment, and/or a community based sanction, and (3) the exact sentence—often a narrow range is indicated and the judge can decide on a number within that range.

The Relationship between the Sentencing Commission and Its Legislature

There have been notable differences in the relationship between a state's sentencing commission and its legislature. Some of the first sentencing commissions established (like in Utah and Washington) experienced pressures from legislatures to increase the penalties within the guidelines (Orland & Reitz, 1993). This coincided with the call for effective crime control by the legislatures and their constituents alike. Other state sentencing commissions seemed to operate relatively independently despite political pressures. Commissions in Tennessee and Washington found it difficult to operate independently because of statutes that required that the legislature approve all of the guidelines and amendments proposed. In other states like Pennsylvania, the amendments proposed by their commissions were effective unless the legislature opposed them. In this case, Pennsylvania's commission operated without as much political pressure (Orland & Reitz, 1993).

Sentencing Guidelines, Parole, and Good Time

Many sentencing guidelines states incorporate a more determinate sentencing structure, in which the amount of time one will spend in prison is known at the time of sentencing. Sentencing guidelines largely dictate how much time in prison a judge can actually impose. In some states with guidelines, discretionary parole release is eliminated for offenders sentenced on or after the date in which the guidelines were enacted. Instead of parole release, prisoners may earn a limited time off their sentences for good behavior. Terms differ by state and include "good time" and "earned time." The amount of time that can be taken off is typically limited to no more than 15 percent of the minimum sentence, in accordance with the original federal truth-in-sentencing mandate.

On January 1, 1995, the state of Virginia abolished discretionary parole release from prison, as well as the system of giving inmates credits for good behavior. This was to enforce Virginia's truth-in-sentencing laws, which required persons convicted of a felony to serve at least 85 percent of the sentence pronounced by the judge at the time of sentencing. One responsibility of Virginia's sentencing commission was to give judges recommendations for sentencing for felony cases consistent with truth-in-sentencing (Virginia Criminal Sentencing Commission, 2012b).

Some states which have enacted sentencing guidelines, however, have retained discretionary parole release for *at least some offenders*. Some states have discretionary parole release for those sentenced before truth-in-sentencing and/or their sentencing guidelines went into effect. States that have retained discretionary parole release, for at least some offenders, since guidelines were instituted include Alabama, Alaska, Arkansas, Louisiana, Maryland, Massachusetts, Missouri, Pennsylvania, South Carolina, Tennessee, and Utah.[3]

Voluntary, Presumptive, or Somewhere in Between?

One key source of variation is how much judges are expected to conform their decisions to their state's sentencing guidelines. The NCSC (Kauder & Ostrom, 2008) placed each state on a continuum of how "mandatory" the guidelines are. On one end of the continuum are states that have purely voluntary guidelines (Ohio and Wisconsin) and on the other end are the few states that direct judges to abide strictly by the guidelines (Minnesota and North Carolina) (Kauder & Ostrom, 2008). The numerical ratings vary from "1" for purely voluntary guidelines to "12" for the most mandatory guidelines. The rating for each guidelines state is displayed in **Table 4.2**.

Even states which have guidelines that are considered "voluntary" vary regarding judicial compliance. Louisiana judges largely ignore the voluntary guidelines and their discretion is limited only by the ranges indicated by statutorily defined sentences. In contrast, there has been a high degree of compliance with the District of Columbia's voluntary guidelines since they were enacted in 2004. In 2013, compliance with the guidelines was about 90 percent (The District of Columbia Sentencing and Criminal Code Revision Commission, 2014, April 25).

Appeals of Sentence

Table 4.2 shows the trend that states with more voluntary guidelines are less likely to permit the defendant to appeal the sentence. In states with more mandatory sentencing guidelines, the sentences are appealable by the defendant and/or the state. The exact mechanisms for appeal vary by state.

One example is Pennsylvania, a presumptive guidelines state. The appeals process for a sentencing departure are clearly delineated. If a sentence lies outside the guidelines, it may be scrutinized by an appeals court to determine if the sentence was "unreasonable."

In its review of the sentence, the appellate court would ascertain the following (Pennsylvania Commission on Sentencing, (§303.1)—Case Law):

(1)   The nature and circumstance of the offense and the history and characteristics of the defendant;
(2)   The opportunity of the sentencing court to observe the defendant, including any presentence investigation;
(3)   The findings upon which the sentence was based; and
(4)   The guidelines promulgated by the commission. (p. 2)

Both the state and the defense can appeal the sentence and argue that the judge's departure from the guidelines was "unreasonable." In line with the *Apprendi* case (to be discussed in Chapter 7) the maximum sentence is the statutory limit, not the maximum sentence recommended by the sentencing guidelines (Pennsylvania Commission on Sentencing (§303.1)—Case Law, 2008, p.5).

An In-Depth Look at Commission-Based Guidelines in Four States

We will now take an in-depth look at commission-based sentencing in four states—Minnesota, Pennsylvania, North Carolina, and Ohio. These states were chosen for a detailed examination, as they represent variation on the "more voluntary/more mandatory" continuum as characterized by Kauder and Ostrom (2008). North Carolina is classified as "12" and their guidelines are the most mandatory in practice, compared to other states. Minnesota is considered an "11." Pennsylvania is considered a "9." Ohio is considered a "1"—the most voluntary. These states were also chosen because many research studies on outcomes of sentencing guidelines (which we will review in Chapter 9) have come out of these states.

The Minnesota Sentencing Guidelines

Several characteristics of Minnesota's felony sentencing guidelines made this system unique, groundbreaking, and one that would serve as a model for many other states. These include the creation of a two-dimensional sentencing matrix based on offense severity and prior criminal history and the role of the sentencing commission in the creation of the grid. The Minnesota Commission, like those of other state commissions which later developed sentencing guidelines, identified several simultaneous goals in establishing Minnesota's guidelines. These included creating a presumptive sentencing system that would increase sentencing uniformity and proportionality, providing truth-in-sentencing, and coordinating sentencing policies with available correctional resources (Dailey, 1993–1994).

History/Background of the Guidelines

Minnesota's Sentencing Guidelines Commission was created by the legislature in 1978 to establish sentencing standards for felony offenders (Minnesota Laws 1978, ch. 723, Minn. State. Ch. 244 et sec). On May 1, 1980, Minnesota enacted the first felony sentencing guidelines in the country, which applied to persons sentenced to felonies committed on or after that date. The commission became a permanent policymaking body within the state.

Before the guidelines were established, Minnesota had an indeterminate sentencing system. As we discussed generally in Chapter 3, criticisms of indeterminate sentencing were lodged by both conservatives and liberals. Minnesota was no different. Regardless of *why* they were not satisfied with indeterminate sentencing, both sides supported a sentencing system that was more determinate and one which eliminated discretionary parole release (Daily, 1993–1994).

The Minnesota Guidelines Commission was given certain directives by the legislature. They were to establish:

1) The circumstances under which imprisonment of an offender is proper; and
2) A presumptive fixed sentence for offenders for whom imprisonment is proper, based on each appropriate combination of reasonable offense and offender characteristics. (Minnesota Sentencing Guidelines Commission, 1980, January 1)

The commission was also to bear in mind the existing sentencing and releasing practices in the state, as well as considering existing correctional resources like prison and jail space. In devising the guidelines, the commission conducted research on judicial sentencing practices, including the sentence lengths handed down judges within the state, as well as releasing practices of the then active Minnesota Corrections Board (MCB).

The commission identified factors that were associated with the judicial decision of whether to imprison the offender. Prior criminal history was the most important factor in the decision of whether to incarcerate (with the number of prior felony convictions being the dominant factor concerning criminal history). The second most important factor was the severity of the current offense. These two factors were also found by the commission to be the most important in the MCB's decisions concerning when to release prisoners. Because offense severity and prior convictions were strong predictors of disposition and duration of prison sentences, these two factors became the basis for Minnesota's sentencing guidelines.

Discretionary parole release was eliminated and participation in rehabilitation programs within prisons became voluntary. Time off of an offender's sentence (up to a one-third reduction) could be earned by good behavior. Time earned could also be taken away if the offender had disciplinary infractions. If the offender earned time off his or her sentence, he or she would be put on a type of mandatory parole release, termed, "The Supervised Release Term" upon release from prison (Frase, 1994; Minnesota Sentencing Guidelines Commission, 2011).

Structuring the Guidelines—A "Modified Just Deserts" Model
Offense Severity and Criminal History

Minnesota's guidelines were the first in the nation to set presumptive sentences for offenses based on their position on a two dimensional rectangular grid. **Figure 4.1** shows the present Sentencing Guidelines Grid.[4]

The vertical axis on the left of the grid represents severity levels of the conviction offense. Offenses in Minnesota's criminal code are graded on the basis of seriousness.

Like the present grid, the original grid classified crimes against a person as more serious than property crimes. The original grid had ten categories represented, ranging from the least serious felonies (Level I) on the top to the most serious felonies (Level X) on the bottom. Today's grid has eleven categories of offenses which decrease in severity as one moves down the grid. The upper horizontal axis represents "criminal history score" and is graded into seven categories. One's score on the criminal history index reflects the number of prior felony convictions (including juvenile adjudications), prior misdemeanors, and the "custody status" at the time of the conviction (meaning whether the offender was on probation or parole at the time the current offense was committed) (Minnesota Sentencing Guidelines Commission, 1980).

An offender's placement into a grid cell, based on the intersection of these two criteria, determines the possible sentence type and length. Within each cell for which imprisonment is indicated is a number and/or a range of numbers representing the sentence length in months. The original ranges established by the commission were rather narrow (plus or minus five to eight percent around the presumptive sentence). The commission decided not to use broader ranges and stated, "The Commission felt that broad ranges would increase the disparate treatment of similar cases and, in a sense would allow disparity to continue in practice while defining it away in theory" (Minnesota Sentencing Guidelines Commission, 1980, p. 12).

The Dispositional Line

Where a grid cell appears in relation to the dark line delineated on the grid indicates the type of disposition to be handed down. The solid darkened step-shaped "line" separates those grid cells for which offenders should receive imprisonment from those that allow a "stayed" sentence (in which the incarceration sentence would be stayed by means of a stay of execution, in which case the offender would be supervised in the community and subject to conditions set by the judge). According to the Minnesota Sentencing Guidelines Commission (1980):

> If the judge decided to grant a stayed sentence by means of a stay of imposition, no prison sentence is pronounced, and the imposition of sentence is stayed to some future date. The judge then establishes such conditions of the stayed sentence as the judge deems appropriate. We provide presumptive prison sentences for stayed sentences to cover situations wherein the stay is later revoked and the sentence imposed and to assure that those who are imprisoned following revocation of a stayed sentence do not serve longer prison sentences than those with longer criminal histories (at any given level of offense severity) for whom the guidelines recommended imprisonment. (p. 12)

The present Minnesota Sentencing Guidelines Grid indicates those cells falling above and/or to the right of the dark line to receive a sentence of imprisonment. Offenders falling below or to the left of the line are to receive a "stayed" sentence. The shape of the "in/out" (meaning whether the sentence would be served in or out of prison) line illustrates the emphasis put on incarcerating the most serious and repeat offenders, while sentencing less serious offenders and those with little or no prior record to alternatives to state prison.[5]

The Meaning behind Labeling the Guidelines "Modified Just Deserts"

The Minnesota sentencing guidelines grid has been labeled a **"modified just deserts"** scheme. In comparison, under a "pure" just deserts model, the sentence would be based *only on the seriousness of the conviction offense.* The sentencing goal of retribution or "just deserts" seeks to punish the offense, and would not incorporate previous criminal acts that the offender committed in the sentencing of the current offense. The Minnesota guidelines, by design, assign longer prison sentences to offenders (with equal offense severity) with longer and/or more serious prior records. Because the calculation of the offender's sentence is essentially collapsed into two measurable criteria—both the severity of the offense *and* the offender's criminal history—the Minnesota guidelines follow a "modified" just deserts approach to determining sentencing (Minnesota Sentencing Guidelines Commission, 1982; von Hirsch, 1982; Moore & Miethe, 1986).

Despite the labeling of the original Minnesota Sentencing Guidelines matrix as "modified just deserts," elements of other sentencing goals, such as rehabilitation and incapacitation, are inherent in the design and implementation of the guidelines. Frase (1994) noted that the statute enabling the guidelines allowed for contemplation of the needs of the offender regarding treatment and a consideration of the safety of the community/offender dangerousness in the decision of whether to assign a sentence to prison or not.

The Establishment of Prescriptive Sentences

Another distinguishing characteristic of the original Minnesota guidelines is that the guidelines were constructed to be prescriptive, as opposed to advisory. After the guidelines went into effect in 1980, judges have been required by law to abide by them when sentencing offenders. Departures from the disposition and/or the duration in the presumptive range in months in the assigned cell must be justified in writing by the judge.

Lists of acceptable and unacceptable reasons for departure are integrated into the sentencing laws. Examples of acceptable reasons for an upward departure would be if "the victim was treated with particular cruelty for which the individual offender should be held responsible" and "the victim was particularly vulnerable due to age, infirmity, or reduced physical or mental capacity, which was known or should have been known to the offender." Mitigating factors included "the victim was an aggressor in the incident" and "the offender played a minor or passive role in the crime or participated under circumstances of coercion or duress" (Minnesota Sentencing Guidelines Commission, 1980, p. 31). Extralegal characteristics (race, gender, employment history and status, and social factors) were listed as unacceptable reasons for departure from the guidelines. Any other departure from the guidelines required "substantial and compelling" reasons, which would have to be explicitly stated in writing from the judge. Both the prosecution and the defense can appeal the sentence, regardless of whether it involved a departure (Minnesota Sentencing Guidelines Commission, 1980; Frase, 1994).

Revisions and Clarifications to the Original Minnesota Guidelines

Some changes to the original Minnesota Sentencing Guidelines have been enacted by the legislature in recent years. The following are some of the most notable changes: First, statutes have been passed that formally allow criminal justice personnel (judges and correctional officers) to assess the offender's treatment amenability as well as offender dangerousness in sentencing decisions. Second, the legislature has passed mandatory minimum sentences for certain offenses. Third, in 1989 the guidelines statute that established the guidelines was amended to indicate that the primary consideration in crafting the guidelines should be **public safety**. Fourth, a separate sex offender grid was adopted by the commission and went into effect for offenses committed on or after August 1, 2006.

The Pennsylvania Sentencing Guidelines

The Pennsylvania Sentencing Guidelines are similar to the Minnesota guidelines, as they structure sentences based on the two same criteria—seriousness of the current offense and extent and gravity of prior record. Pennsylvania's system of sentencing dictates that, "The court shall consider the sentencing guidelines in determining the appropriate sentence for offenders convicted of, or pleading guilty or nolo contendere to, felonies and misdemeanors" (Pennsylvania Commission on Sentencing, 2012, Title 204. Judicial System General Provisions, Part VIII Criminal Sentencing, Chapter 303, §303.1(a)).

"In every case in which a court of record imposes a sentence for a felony or misdemeanor, the court shall make as a part of the record, and disclose in open court at the time of sentencing, a statement of the reason or reasons for the sentence imposed. In every case where a court of record imposes a sentence outside the sentencing guidelines, the reason or reasons for the deviation from the guidelines shall be recorded on the Guideline Sentence Form, a copy of which shall be electronically transmitted to the Pennsylvania Commission on Sentencing in the manner described in §303.1(e)" (Pennsylvania Commission on Sentencing. (2012). Title 204. Judicial System General Provisions, Part VIII Criminal Sentencing, Chapter 303, §303.1(d)). In contrast with Minnesota, Pennsylvania has retained discretionary parole release.

History/Background of the Guidelines

In Pennsylvania, there were some interesting precursor reforms that led to the eventual establishment of their sentencing commission. In 1975, the Pennsylvania legislature changed the sentencing codes to allow councils of judges to jointly sentence defendants. This practice, however, was struck down by the Supreme Court of Pennsylvania as the code was deemed unconstitutional. The legislature sought out another approach to reforming sentencing in 1976, when the Senate passed and the House almost passed a mandatory sentencing bill that required minimum incarceration sentences be imposed for repeat offenders and which added a year onto the sentence if the crime was committed with a firearm. An impact study showed that the bill was cost prohibitive in terms of providing more prison space (Kramer & Kempinen, 1993–1994).

In response to efforts to impose these mandatory sentencing laws in the state, the Pennsylvania Joint Council for Criminal Justice formed a task force to look at sentencing practices in the state. The Joint Council and the General Assembly organized a statewide sentencing conference in February 1977. They opposed the mandatory penalties described above because they could potentially treat very different offenders the same and because the mandatory sentences could be circumvented by plea bargaining (this process, labeled the "hydraulic effect" will be discussed in Chapter 9), and that mandatory sentencing would increase the prison population. Instead, legislators attending the conference introduced legislation in late 1977 that would create a sentencing commission to develop sentencing guidelines. The bill was enacted in November 1978. Both the House and Senate voted to create the Pennsylvania Commission on Sentencing (Act 319) (Kramer & Kempinen, 1993–1994).

The purpose of this commission was to create sentencing guidelines to structure judicial decision making and reduce sentencing disparity. The guidelines were to decrease the practice of judge shopping by lawyers who sought lenient sentences for their clients and to increase sentence uniformity throughout the state of Pennsylvania. The act directed the commission to propose sentencing guidelines that would formally consider the gravity of the current offense, as well as prior felony convictions, and the use of a deadly weapon. In addition, aggravating and mitigating factors surrounding the crime were to be considered.

The commission created a grading of offenses on a ten-point scale based on the gravity of the offense. Offenses which involved physical harm to the victim(s) were graded as most serious. In addition, the commission divided some broadly defined crimes (like burglary) into subcategories to maximize fairness. They enhanced penalties for offenses committed with a firearm. The commission also devised weights for prior record, considering both seriousness and frequency. They decided to include juvenile record. After the Basic Sentencing Matrix was established, the commission set sentence lengths. The legislation did not require that correctional capacity be considered when the commission was established. The initial lengths suggested by the commission put more emphasis on the conviction offense than on prior record.

The initial set of guidelines was rejected by the legislature. They were perceived as restricting judges too much and providing sentences that were overly lenient. The commission then revised the guidelines by widening sentence ranges within grid cells and by indicating more punitive sanctions. The guidelines were enacted on July 22, 1982, and applied to felonies and misdemeanors committed on or after that date. Compared to the past, the Pennsylvania Sentencing Guidelines recommended harsher sentences for violent offenders. For serious property crimes they called for more certain, but shorter incarceration sentences. For the least serious felonies and most misdemeanors, the commission left the discretion of whether to incarcerate to the sentencing judge.

Revisions to the guidelines were made once in 1983 and twice in 1986. On October 7, 1987, however, the Pennsylvania Supreme Court invalidated all of the previous guidelines because of a procedural error that happened in 1981 when the Pennsylvania legislature rejected the guidelines originally proposed by the Pennsylvania Commission on Sentencing. Reformulated guidelines were accepted unanimously by the General Assembly and went into effect on April 25, 1988 (Pennsylvania Commission on Sentencing (2012), Title 204. Judicial System General Provisions, Part VIII Criminal Sentencing, Chapter 303, §303.1(c) (2)). Since then, revised guidelines have been instituted in 1991 (twice), 1994, 1997, 2005, 2008, and 2012. Amendments to the guidelines went into effect in 2013, 2014, and 2015.

Structuring the Guidelines

The Basic Sentencing Matrix

Figure 4.7 shows the Pennsylvania Basic Sentencing Matrix. Felonies and misdemeanors found in Pennsylvania's crimes code are graded according to seriousness and

Figure 4.7 Pennsylvania Sentencing Matrix

Pennsylvania Commission on Sentencing

§303.16(a). Basic Sentencing Matrix.   **7th Edition Amendment 3 (09/25/2015)**

Level	OGS	Example Offenses	Prior Record Score								
			0	1	2	3	4	5	RFEL	REVOC	AGG/MIT
LEVEL 5 State Incar	14	Murder 3 Inchoate Murder (SBI) Rape (victim <13 yrs)	72-SL	84-SL	96-SL	120-SL	168-SL	192-SL	204-SL	SL	-/-12
	13	Inchoate Murder (No SBI) Weapons Mass Destr-Use PWID Cocaine (>1,000 g)	60-78	66-84	72-90	78-96	84-102	96-114	108-126	240	+/- 12
	12	Rape-Forcible Compulsion IDSI-Forcible Compulsion Robbery-Inflicts SBI	48-66	54-72	60-78	66-84	72-90	84-102	96-114	120	+/- 12
	11	Agg Assault-Cause SBI Voluntary Manslaughter Sexual Assault PWID Cocaine (100-1,000 g)	36-54 BC	42-60	48-66	54-72	60-78	72-90	84-102	120	+/- 12
	10	Kidnapping Agg Indecent Assault F2 Arson-Person in Building Hom by Vehicle-DUI & Work Zone PWID Cocaine(50-<100 g)	22-36 BC	30-42 BC	36-48 BC	42-54	48-60	60-72	72-84	120	+/- 12
	9	Sexual Exploitation of Children Robbery-Commit/Threat F1/F2 Burglary-Home/Person Present Arson-No Person in Building	12-24 BC	18-30 BC	24-36 BC	30-42 BC	36-48 BC	48-60	60-72	120	+/- 12
LEVEL 4 State Incar/ RIP trade	8 (F1)	Agg Assault -Cause BI w/DW Theft (Firearm) Identity theft (3rd/+ & Vic>=60 yrs) Hom by Veh-DUI or Work Zone Theft (>$100,000) PWID Cocaine (10-<50 g)	9-16 BC	12-18 BC	15-21 BC	18-24 BC	21-27 BC	27-33 BC	40-52	NA	+/- 9
LEVEL 3 State/ Cnty Incar RIP trade	7 (F2)	Robbery-Inflicts/Threatens BI Burglary-Home/No Person Present Statutory Sexual Assault Theft (>$50,000-$100,000) Identity Theft (3rd/subq) PWID Cocaine (5-<10 g)	6-14 BC	9-16 BC	12-18 BC	15-21 BC	18-24 BC	24-30 BC	35-45 BC	NA	+/- 6
	6	Agg Assault-Cause Fear of SBI Homicide by Vehicle Burglary-Not a Home/Person Prsnt Theft (>$25,000-$50,000) Arson-Endanger Property PWID Cocaine (2<5 g)	3-12 BC	6-14 BC	9-16 BC	12-18 BC	15-21 BC	21-27 BC	27-40 BC	NA	+/- 6
LEVEL 2 Cnty Incar RIP RS	5 (F3)	Burglary F2 Theft (>$2000-$25,000) Bribery PWID Marij (1-<10 lbs)	RS-9	1-12 BC	3-14 BC	6-16 BC	9-16 BC	12-18 BC	24-36 BC	NA	+/- 3
	4	Indecent Assault M2 Forgery (Money, Stocks) Weapon on School Property Crim Trespass F2	RS-3	RS-9	RS-<12	3-14 BC	6-16 BC	9-16 BC	21-30 BC	NA	+/- 3
	3 (M1)	Simple Assault-Attempt/Cause BI Theft ($200-$2000) Carrying Explosives Simple Possession	RS-1	RS-6	RS-9	RS-<12	3-14 BC	6-16 BC	12-18 BC	NA	+/- 3
LEVEL 1 RS	2 (M2)	Theft ($50-<$200) Retail Theft (1st/2nd Offense) Bad Checks ($500-<$1,000)	RS	RS-2	RS-3	RS-4	RS-6	1-9	6- <12	NA	+/- 3
	1 (M3)	Most Misd. 3's;Theft (<$50) DUI (M) Poss Small Amount Marij	RS	RS-1	RS-2	RS-3	RS-4	RS-6	3-6	NA	+/- 3

1. Designated areas of the matrix indicate restrictive intermediate punishments may be imposed as a substitute for incarceration.
2. When restrictive intermediate punishments are appropriate, the duration of the restrictive intermediate punishment programs are recommended not to exceed the guideline ranges.
3. When the range is RS through a number of months (e.g. RS-6), RIP may be appropriate.
4. All numbers in sentence recommendations suggest months of minimum confinement pursuant to 42 Pa.C.S. 9755(b) and 9756(b).
5. Statutory classification (e.g., F1, F2, etc.) in brackets reflect the omnibus OGS assignment for the given grade.

Key:

BC	=	boot camp	RIP	=	restrictive intermediate punishments
CNTY	=	county	RS	=	restorative sanctions
INCAR	=	incarceration	SBI	=	serious bodily injury
PWID	=	possession with intent to deliver	SL	=	statutory limit (longest minimum sentence)
REVOC	=	repeat violent offender category	~	=	no recommendation (aggravated sentence would exceed statutory limit)
RFEL	=	repeat felony 1 and felony 2 offender category	<; >	=	less than; greater than

Source: Pennsylvania Commission on Sentencing. *Basic sentencing matrix.* Retrieved from http://pcs .la.psu.edu/guidelines/sentencing/sentencing-guidelines-and-implementation-manuals/7th-edition -amendment-3-sentencing-guidelines-9-25-2015/303.16-a-basic-sentencing-matrix-color/view

assigned an Offense Gravity Score (OGS). These scores range from 1 for third degree misdemeanors to 14 for the most serious felonies (including third degree murder and rape of a child). First and second degree murder are excluded from the Basic Sentencing Matrix. In Pennsylvania, murder of the first degree and murder of a law enforcement officer of the first degree carry a mandatory minimum sentence of death or life imprisonment. Murder of the second degree, murder of a law enforcement officer of the second degree, first degree murder of an unborn child, and second degree murder of an unborn child carry a mandatory minimum sentence of life imprisonment.

Like in the Minnesota guidelines, prior criminal record is the second major factor that affects sentence in the Pennsylvania guidelines. The convicted offender is assigned a Prior Record Score (PRS). Point based prior record levels range from zero (indicating no prior record) to five (indicating serious and/or numerous prior offenses). Offenders with longer and/or more serious prior records are given harsher sentences.

Prior convictions and adjudications are scored to reflect their seriousness. The most serious priors, such as murder, are considered "four point offenses." Other less serious offenses are graded in decreasing severity as "three point offenses" (which include other felony 1 offenses), "two point offenses" (which include most felony 2 offenses), and "one point offenses" (typically misdemeanor 1 offenses). The points for all priors are added up to create the Prior Record Score (PRS).

In addition to the calculated prior record scores within the Basic Sentencing Matrix are columns for two particular types of prior records, which involve those persons deemed repeat offenders. To the right of the highest prior record level score are columns for sentencing repeat felony 1 and felony 2 offenders (RFEL) and for repeat violent offenders (REVOC). The sentence or range indicated for these two categories is greater than the highest prior record score on the grid (5). An offender is classified as a REVOC if his or her current conviction has an OGS of 9 or higher and has two or more prior convictions or adjudications for 4 point offenses. The RFEL classification is for all individuals, regardless of OGS, who have prior convictions or adjudications for felony 1 or felony 2 offenses and have a total of six or more in the prior record level calculation, but do not fall into the repeat violent category (Pennsylvania Commission on Sentencing, 2012, Title 204. Judicial System General Provisions, Part VIII Criminal Sentencing, Chapter 303, §303.4).

The convicted offender is placed in a grid cell, based the intersection of his or her OGS and PRS and each cell indicates a norm sentence (Pennsylvania Commission on Sentencing, 2012, Title 204. Judicial System General Provisions, Part VIII Criminal Sentencing, Chapter 303, §303.9). For those who are to receive incarceration sentences, the grid cell within which one falls indicates a range of minimum number of months of incarceration according to Pa C.S. 9755(b) and 9756(b). The establishment of "norms" within each grid cell assumes that the legally relevant characteristics of persons convicted of an offense with the specified offense class and the same prior record would appropriately receive similar sentences.

Variation of Dominant Sentencing Goals by Sentencing Level

Offense gravity scores are divided up into five categories which indicate the type of sentence that can be imposed. The sentencing goals that are emphasized vary with sentencing level.

Level 5 (State Incarceration) includes grid cells with offenders who have an OGS ranging from 9 to 14 with any PRS or offenders with an OGS of 7 or 8 who are classified as RFEL a repeat felony 1 and felony 2 offender category. Offenders who fall in Level 5 are violent offenders and those who have committed major drug offenses. Level 5 indicates a sentence of incarceration. According to the Pennsylvania Commission on Sentencing, (2008b), §303.11 (b) (5), "The primary purposes of the sentencing options at this level are punishment commensurate with the seriousness of the criminal behavior and incapacitation to protect the public." The minimum number of months to be served behind bars is twelve, for an offender with an OGS of 9 with no priors. As Figure 4.7 shows, most of the minimum sentences to be served, as indicated by the numbers in these cells are long imprisonment terms.

Level 4 (State Incarceration/RIP) is comprised of various combinations of offense scores and prior record levels, and include offenders with an OGS as high as 8 with a prior record level of 1 and offenders with an OGS of 3 and a prior level designation of RFEL as well as cases in between (in terms of OGS and PRS). The primary goals of sentencing Level 4 offenders are "punishment and incapacitation" (§303.11(b)(4)). Offenders falling in these grid cells are to be given state incarceration, but they may be allowed to serve their sentence in a county facility. Some offenders in Level 4 who have a mandatory minimum sentence of 30 months or less may receive a restrictive intermediate punishment (RIP) — county or state intermediate punishment. Restrictive intermediate punishments are developed by county intermediate punishment boards and emphasize strict supervision of the offender. This flexibility of sentencing to incarceration or restrictive intermediate punishment is designed to allow non-violent offenders with substance abuse issues to obtain drug and/or alcohol treatment, but still be under a considerable level of surveillance.

Level 3 (State/County Incarceration/RIP) includes combinations including offenders with an OGS of 8 with no prior record to offenders with and OGS of 1 — third degree misdemeanors whose prior record level is RFEL. Offenders falling in these grid cells may receive state or county incarceration or restrictive intermediate punishments. As indicated by the range of minimum sentences in these cells, if the incarceration sentence is chosen, the lower limit of incarceration is less than twelve months. The foci of sentencing these offenders is "retribution and control over the offender" (§303.11(b) (3)). If the offender is eligible, treatment may be recommended for drug dependent offenders, instead of incarceration.

Level 2 (County Incarceration/RIP/RS)) includes offenders with an OGS as high as 5 with no prior record and those with an OGS of 1 with a PRS of 5 and cases involving OGS and PRS combinations in between. These are mostly non-violent offenders and those with multiple, but less serious priors. Level 2 offenders may receive a variety of several possible sanctions — total confinement in a county facility (less than twelve months), partial confinement in a county facility, county intermediate punishment, or restorative sanctions (RS). Treatment is emphasized for drug dependent offenders. The stated purposes of sentencing at this level are "control over the offender and restitution to victims" (§303.11(b)(2)).

Level 1 (RS) includes offenders with OGS of 1 or 2 with a PRS of zero. Individuals falling into these grid cells are to be given restorative sanctions (RS). According to

§303.11b(1), "The primary purpose of this level is to provide the minimal control necessary to fulfill court-ordered obligations." According to §303.9 (f), these RS sanctions "... suggest[] the use of the least restrictive, non-confinement sentencing alternatives including probation, fine, and restitution."

Aggravating and Mitigating Circumstances

The Basic Sentencing Matrix includes a column which allows for a consideration of aggravating and mitigating factors. The number of months that the sentence can be increased or decreased is listed in the last column of the Basic Sentencing Matrix. For example, the minimum incarceration sentence can be increased or decreased by 12 months for persons convicted of an offense with an offense gravity score of 14. For someone convicted of an offense with an OGS of 5, their sentence could be increased or decreased by 3 months. While aggravating and mitigating factors can be formally considered in the Pennsylvania guidelines, note that the addition of months to a sentence for aggravating factors (or subtraction in months for mitigating factors) is limited. If the judge decides to sentence in the aggravating or mitigating ranges, he or she is required to provide a detailed written statement of why the sentence was imposed outside of the standard or "norm" range of minimums. These reasons are to be recorded on the Guidelines Sentence Form and a copy of this form is electronically sent to the Pennsylvania Commission on Sentencing.

Separate Matrices for Crimes Involving Weapons and Children

According to §303.10(a), Deadly Weapon Enhancement Sentence Recommendation, offenders who are determined by the court to have *possessed* a deadly weapon in the commission of their crime are placed on a separate grid — the DWE/Possessed Matrix (§303.17a). Those who the court determined to have *used* a deadly weapon are sentenced under the DWE/Used Matrix (§303.17b). **Figure 4.8** shows the deadly weapons enhancement grid for possession and **Figure 4.9** shows the deadly weapons enhancement grid for use. The same grid cells (OGS and PRS combinations) that indicate imprisonment in the Basic Sentencing Matrix are prescribed longer minimum sentences in these enhanced matrices.

According to §303.10(b) The Youth/School Enhancement is applied in the following way: "When the court determines that the offender either distributed a controlled substance to a person or persons under the age of 18 in violation of 35 P.S. or manufactured, delivered, or possessed with intent to deliver a controlled substance within 1000 feet of the real property on which is located a public or private elementary or secondary school, the court shall consider the range of sentences described in §303.9(c)." Sentence enhancements are also indicated under §303.9 (c), Youth/School Enhancement Sentence Recommendation. **Figure 4.10** shows this grid.

Figure 4.8 Pennsylvania Deadly Weapon Enhancement/Possessed Matrix

Pennsylvania Commission on Sentencing   **7th Edition Amendment 3 (09/25/2015)**

§303.17(a). Deadly Weapon Enhancement/Possessed Matrix

Level	OGS	Deadly Weapon	Prior Record Score								
			0	1	2	3	4	5	RFEL	REVOC	AGG/MIT
Level 5	14	Possessed	81-SL	93-SL	105-SL	129-SL	177-SL	201-SL	213-SL	240	-/- 12
	13	Possessed	69-87	75-93	81-99	87-105	93-111	105-123	117-135	240	+/-12
	12	Possessed	57-75	63-81	69-87	75-93	81-99	93-111	105-123	120	+/-12
	11	Possessed	45-63	51-69	57-75	63-81	69-87	81-99	93-111	120	+/-12
	10	Possessed	31-45	39-51	45-57	51-63	57-69	69-81	81-93	120	+/-12
	9	Possessed	21-33	27-39	33-45	39-51	45-57	57-69	69-81	120	+/-12
Level 4	8	Possessed	15-22	18-24	21-27	24-30	27-33	33-39	46-58	NA	+/-9
	7	Possessed	12-20	15-22	18-24	21-27	24-30	30-36	41-51	NA	+/-6
	6	Possessed	9-18	12-20	15-22	18-24	21-27	27-33	33-46	NA	+/-6
Level 3	5	Possessed	6-15	7-18	9-20	12-22	15-22	18-24	30-42	NA	+/-3
	4	Possessed	3-6	3-12	3-<15	6-17	9-19	12-19	24-33	NA	+/-3
	3	Possessed	3-4	3-9	3-12	3-<15	6-17	9-19	15-21	NA	+/-3
	2	Possessed	3-3	3-5	3-6	3-7	3-9	4-12	9-<15	NA	+/-3
	1	Possessed	3-3	3-4	3-5	3-6	3-7	3-9	6-9	NA	+/-3

1. Level 3 and Level 4 indicate restrictive intermediate punishments may be substituted for incarceration.

2. When county intermediate punishment is appropriate, the duration of the restrictive intermediate punishment program(s) shall not exceed the guideline ranges.

3. The mitigated recommendation is never less than three months (§303.10(a)).

4. All numbers in sentence recommendations suggest months of minimum confinement pursuant to 42 Pa.C.S. §9755(b) and §9756(b).

5. If the standard range includes the statutory limit, there is no aggravated recommendation.

6. If any recommendation is longer than the statutory limit, see §303.9(g).

Source: Pennsylvania Commission on Sentencing. *Deadly weapon enhancement/possessed matrix.* Retrieved from http://pcs.la.psu.edu/guidelines/sentencing/sentencing-guidelines-and-implementation-manuals/7th-edition-amendment-3-sentencing-guidelines-9-25-2015/303.17-a-deadly-weapon-enhancement-possessed/view

Other Duties of the Pennsylvania Commission on Sentencing

In addition to creating sentencing guidelines, the Pennsylvania Commission on Sentencing is also given many additional powers and duties. These include collecting and publishing data concerning sentencing processes in the state and the establishment of a research and development program within the commission to serve as a repository of information on sentencing, resentencing, and parole practices in Pennsylvania. The Pennsylvania Commission on Sentencing can also make recommendations to the General Assembly to modify extant sentencing, parole, and/or correctional statutes in accordance with their goal of maintaining "effective, humane and rational sentencing policy" (42 Pa.C.S.A §2153, Powers and Duties, 2008). The commission reports on their activities annually to the General Assembly, the Administrative Office of Pennsylvania Courts, and the governor. The Pennsylvania Sentencing Guidelines have been the subject of numerous evaluation studies, which will be discussed in Chapter 9.

Figure 4.9 Pennsylvania Deadly Weapon Enhancement/Used Matrix

Pennsylvania Commission on Sentencing   **7th Edition Amendment 3 (09/25/2015)**

§303.17(b). Deadly Weapon Enhancement/Used Matrix

Level	OGS	Deadly Weapon	Prior Record Score								
			0	1	2	3	4	5	RFEL	REVOC	AGG/MIT
Level 5	14	Used	90-SL	102-SL	114-SL	138-SL	186-SL	210-SL	222-SL	SL	~/- 12
	13	Used	78-96	84-102	90-108	96-114	102-120	114-132	126-144	240	+/-12
	12	Used	66-84	72-90	78-96	84-102	90-108	102-120	114-132	120	+/-12
	11	Used	54-72	60-78	66-84	72-90	78-96	90-108	102-120	120	+/-12
	10	Used	40-54	48-60	54-66	60-72	66-78	78-90	90-102	120	+/-12
	9	Used	30-42	36-48	42-54	48-60	54-66	66-78	78-90	120	+/-12
Level 4	8	Used	21-28	24-30	27-33	30-36	33-39	39-45	52-64	NA	+/-9
	7	Used	18-26	21-28	24-30	27-33	30-36	36-42	47-57	NA	+/-6
	6	Used	15-24	18-26	21-28	24-30	27-33	33-39	39-52	NA	+/-6
	5	Used	12-21	13-24	15-26	18-28	21-28	24-30	36-48	NA	+/-3
Level 3	4	Used	6-9	6-15	6-<18	9-20	12-22	15-22	27-36	NA	+/-3
	3	Used	6-7	6-12	6-15	6-<18	9-20	12-22	18-24	NA	+/-3
	2	Used	6-6	6-8	6-9	6-10	6-12	7-15	12-<18	NA	+/-3
	1	Used	6-6	6-7	6-8	6-9	6-10	6-12	9-12	NA	+/-3

1. Level 3 and Level 4 indicate restrictive intermediate punishments may be substituted for incarceration.

2. When county intermediate punishment is appropriate, the duration of the restrictive intermediate punishment program shall not exceed the guideline ranges.

3. The mitigated recommendation is never less than six months (§303.10(a)).

4. All numbers in sentence recommendations suggest months of minimum confinement pursuant to 42 Pa.C.S. §9755(b) and §9756(b).

5. If the standard range includes the statutory limit, there is no aggravated recommendation.

6. If any recommendation is longer than the statutory limit, see §303.9(g).

Source: Pennsylvania Commission on Sentencing. *Deadly weapon enhancement/used matrix.* Retrieved from http://pcs.la.psu.edu/guidelines/sentencing/sentencing-guidelines-and-implementation-manuals /7th-edition-amendment-3-sentencing-guidelines-9-25-2015/303.17-b-deadly-weapon-enhance ment-used/view

The North Carolina Sentencing Guidelines

History/Background of the Guidelines

The road to implementing structured sentencing guidelines in North Carolina was long and full of many twists and turns. In a movement towards more determinate sentencing practices, two major sentencing reforms were passed by the North Carolina General Assembly—The Fair Sentencing Act in 1981 and the 1994 North Carolina Structured Sentencing Act. Today a recent revision of the 1994 Structured Sentencing Act determines sentencing for most felony and misdemeanor offenders in the state of North Carolina. A major impetus for transitioning from indeterminate sentencing to structured sentencing was the practical and serious problem of prison overcrowding in the state in the 1980s and 1990s.

Figure 4.10 Pennsylvania Youth/School Enhancement Grid

Pennsylvania Commission on Sentencing   **7th Edition Amendment 3 (09/25/2015)**

§303.18(c). Youth and School Enhancement Matrix

| Level | OGS | Prior Record Score | | | | | | | | Agg/Mit |
		0	1	2	3	4	5	RFEL	REVOC	
5	14	NA	NA	NA	NA	NA	NA	NA	NA	~/-12
	13	78 - 114	84 - 120	90 - 126	96 - 132	102 - 138	114 - 150	126 - 162	240	+/-12
	12	NA	NA	NA	NA	NA	NA	NA	NA	+/-12
	11	54 - 90	60 - 96	66 - 102	72 - 108	78 - 114	90 - 120	102 - 120	120	+/-12
	10	40 - 72	48 - 78	54 - 84	60 - 90	66 - 96	78 - 108	90 - 120	120	+/-12
	9	30 - 60	36 - 66	42 - 72	48 - 78	54 - 84	66 - 96	78 - 108	120	+/-12
4	8	27 - 52	30 - 54	33 - 57	36 - 60	39 - 63	45 - 69	58 - 88	NA	+/-9
	7	24 - 50	27 - 52	30 - 54	33 - 57	36 - 60	42 - 66	53 - 81	NA	+/-6
	6	21 - 48	24 - 50	27 - 52	30 - 54	33 - 57	39 - 63	45 - 76	NA	+/-6
	5	18 - 45	19 - 48	21 - 50	24 - 52	27 - 52	30 - 54	42 - 72	NA	+/-3
	4	18 -39	18 - 45	18 - <48	21 - 50	24 - 52	27 -52	39 -66	NA	+/-3
	3	18 - 37	18 - 42	18 - 45	18 - <48	21 - 50	24 - 52	30 - 54	NA	+/-3

1. This enhancement may only be applied to violations of 35 P.S. §780-113(a)(14) and (a)(30).

2. Level 4 indicates restrictive intermediate punishments may be substituted for incarceration.

3. When county intermediate punishment is appropriate, the duration of the restrictive intermediate punishment program shall not exceed the guideline ranges.

4. The mitigated recommendation is never less than eighteen months (§303.10(b)).

5. All numbers in sentence recommendations suggest months of minimum confinement pursuant to 42 Pa.C.S. §9755(b) and §9756(b).

6. If the standard range includes the statutory limit, there is no aggravated recommendation.

7. If any recommendation is longer than the statutory limit, see §303.9(g).

Source: Pennsylvania Commission on Sentencing. *Basic sentencing matrix with youth/school enhancement: Youth enhancement.* Retrieved from http://pcs.la.psu.edu/guidelines/sentencing/sentencing -guidelines-and-implementation-manuals/7th-edition-amendment-3-sentencing-guidelines-9-25 -2015/303.18-c-youth-and-school-enhancement/view

In Chapter 3 we described The Fair Sentencing Act (FSA). While it was designed to promote determinate sentencing, it had some deleterious consequences, including extreme prison overcrowding. A subsequent provision to the FSA allowed prisoners to earn 30 days off their sentence for 30 days of good behavior. As judges became aware of this they augmented sentences for felony offenders to ensure that offenders were serving what was considered just sentences.

The North Carolina Commission on Sentencing—Description and Scope of Authority

The Special Committee on Prisons realized that given the expansion of the prison system, the sentencing laws of the state needed to be reassessed. A major concern was front-end strategies (meaning who was let in the "front door" to prison). In February

1988, co-chairs of the Special Committee on Prisons, Rep. Anne Barnes and Sen. David Parnell, suggested that the committee examine North Carolina's criminal justice system to find long term solutions to its problems. Among their suggestions was that a **separate sentencing guidelines commission be established.**

The commission's major purposes would be to categorize criminal offenses that had previously been broadly defined and establish appropriate penalties for all offenders who committed crimes in the state of North Carolina. The need for sentencing uniformity was recognized. The Special Committee on Prisons also realized that criminal justice policies must take into account available correctional resources and identified the increased use of alternative sanctions as an avenue to reduce overall correctional expenditures. The committee stressed the importance of having the proposed commission include representatives from various actors in the criminal justice system.

In July 1990, upon the recommendation of the Special Committee on Prisons, the General Assembly created the North Carolina Sentencing and Policy Advisory Commission. The legislation delineated the tasks of the Sentencing Commission as follows: "1) classify offenses based on severity; 2) recommend sentencing structures for judges; 3) recommend a comprehensive community corrections plan; and 4) develop a correctional population simulation model to project the impact of its recommendations" (Freeman, 2009, p. 9).

A central issue that had to be resolved within the commission was what purpose(s) sentencing should serve. They identified the goals of retribution, incapacitation, deterrence, and rehabilitation. They sought to balance these purposes within the structured sentencing system that they proposed in a way that would reflect the type of offense and the offender's prior record. Retribution and incapacitation were the predominant goals in sentencing repeat violent offenders, while rehabilitation was emphasized for non-violent and first time offenders. The commission concluded that protecting the general public from repeat violent offenders through certain and lengthy incarceration was of paramount importance.

Structuring the Guidelines

The commission developed structured sentencing in North Carolina by systematically considering four elements that would dictate presumptive guidelines. These involved **classifying offenses** (according to seriousness), **assessing prior record level** (based on type, extent, and gravity of prior offenses), **assigning dispositions** (prison, intermediate sanctions, or community sanctions), and **setting sentence lengths.** A subcommittee was established for each of these four stages—Offense Structures Subcommittee, Defendant Structures Subcommittee, Dispositional Subcommittee, and Durational Subcommittee. In addition, a Community Corrections Subcommittee was formed with the purpose of devising a major plan to incorporate and expand community corrections within the state.

The Creation of the Felony Punishment Chart—The Work of Subcommittees

Like the sentencing commissions in Minnesota and Pennsylvania, North Carolina's commission created a two-axis matrix to structure judicial decision making. They created separate matrices for felonies and misdemeanors. The initial work described below documents how felony sentences were structured.

The **Offense Structure Subcommittee** had the task of creating an offense classification system, in which all existing crimes defined by the state would be given a seriousness score. The focus was on characterizing the harm that resulted from the defendant's behavior. They considered the harms of personal injury, personal property loss, public order violations, and affronts to public morality from minor to serious. They grouped offenses on the basis of harm into ten categories.

A second subcommittee, the **Defendant Structures Subcommittee**, had the duty of deciding what relevant information about the defendant's prior record should be considered in sentencing. They considered the broad issues of defendant culpability and risk of recidivism. After reviewing other states' considerations of prior record in their sentence grids, they concluded that the extent and gravity of prior convictions, as well as the offender's status in the criminal justice system at the time of the commission of the offense (for example, if he or she was in prison or on probation at the time) should factor into the calculation of prior record level.

Figure 4.11 shows the current worksheet used to calculate prior record (North Carolina Sentencing and Policy Advisory Commission, 2009, p. 14). Initially the prior record score ranged from Level I (no points/priors) to Level 6 (serious prior offenses and/ or many prior offenses). In 2009, an amendment altered the categorization of levels, but kept the number the same. It clumped together persons with no prior record with those who only had one prior point into Prior Record Level I. This meant persons with only a misdemeanor prior would be assigned to Prior Record Level I. Then it changed the ranges for Prior Record Levels II–V so that each level indicated a four-point incremental change.

Figure 4.12 shows the current Felony Punishment Chart. Once Offense Class and Prior Record Level are calculated, the offender falls into a grid cell. The conviction of a Class A felony (murder in the first degree or "unlawful use of a nuclear, biological, or chemical weapon of mass destruction") mandates death or life without parole. For all other offenses, the contents of the grid cells indicate disposition or dispositional options and sentence length in a presumptive, aggravated, and mitigated range.

The **Dispositional Subcommittee** decided what type of sentence should be imposed and the length of minimum sentence for each grid cell. Three letters correspond to disposition types on the Felony Punishment Chart—"A" indicates active prison sentences, "I" denotes intermediate sanctions like intensive supervision probation and day reporting centers, and "C" represents community based punishments (including supervised or unsupervised probation, restitution, and fines). Note that in some grid cells more than one disposition is possible. For these cells, the judge has the discretion to impose one of two or three possibilities. For example, the felony punishment chart indicates "I/A" as the disposition for an offender falling into the grid cell with offense class "F" and prior record level "III." This means that the judge may suspend a prison sentence and instead sentence the individual to an intermediate punishment.

The **Community Corrections Subcommittee** played an important role in the development of a wide range of community based sanctions. This is one of the most notable features of North Carolina structured sentencing—the emphasis on the development

Figure 4.11 Prior Record Worksheet for Felonies Committed in North Carolina

I. SCORING PRIOR RECORD/FELONY SENTENCING

NUMBER	TYPE	FACTORS	POINTS
	Prior Felony Class A Conviction	x 10	
	Prior Felony Class B1 Conviction	x 9	
	Prior Felony Class B2 or C or D Conviction	x 6	
	Prior Felony Class E or F or G Conviction	x 4	
	Prior Felony Class H or I Conviction	x 2	
	Prior Misdemeanor Class A1 or 1 Conviction*, Prior Impaired Driving Conviction, or Prior Impaired Driving in a Commercial Vehicle Conviction	x 1	
		SUBTOTAL	
	If all the elements of the present offense are included in any prior offense, whether or not the prior offense was used in determining prior record level.	+ 1	
	If the offense was committed: (a) while on supervised or unsupervised probation, parole, or post-release supervision; or (b) while serving a sentence of imprisonment; or (c) while on escape.	+ 1	
		TOTAL	

Class 1 misdemeanor offenses under Chapter 20 are not assigned any points except for misdemeanor death by vehicle [G.S. 20-141.4(a2)]

II. CLASSIFYING PRIOR RECORD LEVEL

POINTS	LEVEL
0 – 1	I
2 – 5	II
6 – 9	III
10 – 13	IV
14 – 17	V
18+	VI

PRIOR RECORD LEVEL _____

Source: North Carolina Sentencing and Policy Advisory Commission. (2009). *Structured sentencing training and reference manual: Applies to offenses committed on or after December 1, 2009.* p. 14, Table 2. Retrieved from http://www.nccourts.org/Courts/CRS/Councils/spac/Documents/sstrainingmanual_09 .pdf

of community based sanctions to serve as alternatives to incarceration. According to Freeman (2009):

> The five major tasks of the Community Corrections Subcommittee included: 1) recommending a state organizational structure for community corrections programs; 2) identifying programs that should be in a continuum of community

Figure 4.12 North Carolina Felony Punishment Chart

*** Effective for Offenses Committed on or after 12/1/09 ***

FELONY PUNISHMENT CHART
PRIOR RECORD LEVEL

OFFENSE CLASS		I 0-1 Pt	II 2-5 Pts	III 6-9 Pts	IV 10-13 Pts	V 14-17 Pts	VI 18+ Pts	
A		Death or Life Without Parole						
B1		A 240 - 300 192 - 240 144 - 192	A 276 - 345 221 - 276 166 - 221	A 317 -397 254 - 317 190 - 254	A 365 - 456 292 - 365 219 - 292	A Life Without Parole 336 - 420 252 - 336	A Life Without Parole 386 - 483 290 - 386	DISPOSITION Aggravated Range PRESUMPTIVE RANGE Mitigated Range
B2		A 157 - 196 125 - 157 94 - 125	A 180 - 225 144 - 180 108 - 144	A 207 - 258 165 - 207 124 - 165	A 238 - 297 190 - 238 143 - 190	A 273 - 342 219 - 273 164 - 219	A 314 - 393 251 - 314 189 - 251	
C		A 73 – 92 58 - 73 44 - 58	A 83 - 104 67 - 83 50 - 67	A 96 - 120 77 - 96 58 - 77	A 110 - 138 88 - 110 66 - 88	A 127 - 159 101 - 127 76 - 101	A 146 - 182 117 - 146 87 - 117	
D		A 64 - 80 51 - 64 38 - 51	A 73 - 92 59 - 73 44 - 59	A 84 - 105 67 - 84 51 - 67	A 97 - 121 78 - 97 58 - 78	A 111 - 139 89 - 111 67 - 89	A 128 - 160 103 - 128 77 - 103	
E		I/A 25 - 31 20 - 25 15 - 20	I/A 29 - 36 23 - 29 17 - 23	A 33 - 41 26 - 33 20 - 26	A 38 - 48 30 - 38 23 - 30	A 44 - 55 35 - 44 26 - 35	A 50 - 63 40 - 50 30 - 40	
F		I/A 16 - 20 13 - 16 10 - 13	I/A 19 - 23 15 - 19 11 - 15	I/A 21 - 27 17 - 21 13 - 17	A 25 - 31 20 - 25 15 - 20	A 28 - 36 23 - 28 17 - 23	A 33 - 41 26 - 33 20 - 26	
G		I/A 13 - 16 10 - 13 8 - 10	I/A 14 - 18 12 - 14 9 - 12	I/A 17 - 21 13 - 17 10 - 13	I/A 19 - 24 15 - 19 11 - 15	A 22 - 27 17 - 22 13 - 17	A 25 - 31 20 - 25 15 - 20	
H		C/I/A 6 - 8 5 - 6 4 - 5	I/A 8 - 10 6 - 8 4 - 6	I/A 10 - 12 8 - 10 6 - 8	I/A 11 - 14 9 - 11 7 - 9	I/A 15 - 19 12 - 15 9 - 12	A 20 - 25 16 - 20 12 - 16	
I		C 6 - 8 4 - 6 3 - 4	C/I 6 - 8 4 - 6 3 - 4	I 6 - 8 5 - 6 4 - 5	I/A 8 - 10 6 - 8 4 - 6	I/A 9 - 11 7 - 9 5 - 7	I/A 10 - 12 8 - 10 6 - 8	

A – Active Punishment   I – Intermediate Punishment   C – Community Punishment
Numbers shown are in months and represent the range of minimum sentences

Revised: 08-31-09

Source: North Carolina Sentencing and Policy Advisory Commission. (2009). *Structured sentencing training and reference manual: Applies to offenses committed on or after December 1, 2009.* p. 4, Figure A. Retrieved from http://www.nccourts.org/Courts/CRS/Councils/spac/Documents/sstrainingmanual_09.pdf

sanctions; 3) developing a state-local funding mechanism of community corrections programs; 4) identifying categories of offenders eligible for community corrections programs; and 5) analyzing the rate of recidivism for offenders in these programs. (p. 15)

Representatives from various community corrections programs in the state briefed the Community Corrections Subcommittee about their programs and the subcommittee came up with grading of the programs based on their structure and level of supervision. The focus of this committee was to reserve prison for the most serious and repeat offenders, while sentencing previously otherwise prison-bound offenders who were convicted of a less serious offense and had fewer priors to community and intermediate sanctions. The committee added a new sanction—the Day Reporting Center as an intermediate sanction to be used as an alternative to prison.

A notable function of the Community Corrections Subcommittee was to initiate a state-local partnership and devise funding for it. They sought ways to fashion local, community based programs that would allow the necessary flexibility to work in the context of their specific needs, but also be accountable to the state. They devised a State-County Criminal Justice Partnership Act (Chapter 534 of the 1993 Session Laws), which was adopted by the entire North Carolina Sentencing Commission and presented to the General Assembly. The legislation outlined the ways counties in North Carolina would obtain funding from the state to put into action new types of correctional programs. The emphasis was on integrating intermediate punishments into the specific county's sanction possibilities for offenders who would otherwise have gone to prison.[6]

An additional function of the Community Corrections Subcommittee was to devise a misdemeanor sentencing grid. In accordance with the goal of reserving incarceration for the more serious offenses, active sentences were specified for only misdemeanants convicted of the most serious misdemeanors and who had long prior records.

The **Durational Subcommittee** worked to establish sentence lengths for each grid cell and to decide the minimum percentage of time that the offender must serve. It aimed to provide "truthful" sentencing, but they also acknowledged the need for some good time (which they labeled "earned time") to let the Department of Corrections retain some incentive for good inmate behavior. They decided that within each cell there would be a presumptive minimum sentence range. The longest presumptive minimum range is about 20–25 percent higher than the shortest presumptive minimum range. After the judge decided the number of months within the minimum range, a second table indicated a corresponding maximum number of months. Inmates would have to serve no less than the minimum sentence. Throughout the process of deciding sentence lengths, the subcommittee considered the impact that sentence lengths would have on prison resources. In addition to setting minimum sentence lengths, the Durational Subcommittee also integrated a consideration of aggravating and mitigating circumstances into the minimum sentence ranges, considered post-release supervision, and set prison terms separate from the Felony Punishment Chart for drug trafficking offenses.

As Figure 4.12 shows, there is a middle, upper, and lower set of ranges within each cell. These correspond to presumptive, aggravating, and mitigating ranges. A "typical" case would be sentenced in the presumptive (middle) range. Minimums for cases with aggravating factors, or cases in which aggravating factors outweigh mitigating factors, would be chosen from the top range within the cell. For cases where mitigating factors were present, the minimum sentence would be chosen from the lower range. Judges retain some discretion by choosing a number of months within the narrow ranges.

North Carolina eliminated discretionary parole release with the passage of structured sentencing in 1994. Once the commission's proposal went to the General Assembly, the requirement of "post-release supervision" was added and is in place today. Post-release supervision is mandatory parole release and requires that the offender be released and supervised in the community for a period of six months to three years. Incarcerated offenders are released from prison and put on post-release supervision nine months before the expiration of their maximum sentence, less earned time credits. In no case will the offender serve less than the minimum sentence handed down by the judge.

The North Carolina Sentencing Commission Today

The North Carolina Sentencing Commission became permanent in 1996. According to Freeman (2009):

> The Commission's continuing statutory duties include: (1) analyzing the re-
> source impact of any proposed legislation which creates a new offense, changes
> the classification of an existing offense, or changes the punishment or disposi-
> tion for a particular classification, (2) making recommendations to the Gen-
> eral Assembly regarding the proposed legislation's consistency with Structured
> Sentencing, (3) maintaining statistical data related to sentencing, corrections,
> and juvenile justice, (4) reporting on the effectiveness of community correc-
> tions and prison treatment programs, based on recidivism rates, other outcome
> measures, and program costs, and (5) reporting on juvenile recidivism and on
> the effectiveness of programs that receive grant funding from the state's Juve-
> nile Crime Prevention Councils. (p. 25)

Through the years, like the Minnesota and Pennsylvania guidelines, the North Carolina guidelines have been periodically revised. Updates generally involve reclassification of crimes and duration of punishments within the grid cells and are represented in revised training manuals that are available to the public.

The Ohio Sentencing Guidelines

History/Background of the Guidelines

Historically, Ohio's Criminal Code had been consistent with the Model Penal Code and utilized indeterminate sentencing. Judges chose a minimum term of incarceration from statutorily defined ranges for four felony levels. The offender would be eligible for parole after serving the minimum term (less good time) and the parole board would decide if the offender should be released at that time (Woolredge, Rauschenberg, Griffin, & Pratt, 2002).

In 1983 the Ohio legislature enacted Senate Bill 199, which created three new "aggravated felony" ranges and three new "repeat aggravated felony" ranges. These indicated mandatory prison sentences for serious offenses. In addition, the act also created two non-mandatory determinate prison sentence ranges for non-violent and low-level felony offenders and a mandatory sentence of three years for those offenders who had a gun in the commission of a felony. Thus, twelve new ranges for prison sentences were established (Woolredge, Rauschenberg, Griffin, & Pratt, 2002).

The Ohio General Assembly created a permanent Sentencing Commission in 1990 by statute. This followed the recommendation of a committee studying prison overcrowding in the state. The chief justice serves as chair. The Supreme Court of Ohio (https://www.supremecourt.ohio.gov/Boards/Sentencing/) describes the current responsibilities of the commission as follows:

> It is responsible for conducting a review of Ohio's sentencing statutes and sentencing patterns, and making recommendations regarding necessary statutory changes. The Commission consists of 31 members, 10 of whom are judges appointed by the Chief Justice.

This statement is similar to that of other sentencing commissions, however, Ohio's guidelines structure differs from those of other states, which rely on sentencing grids and worksheets. The path taken by the Ohio Sentencing Commission, which culminated in a five felony level guideline structure, explains why the differences came about.

The tasks that the Ohio Sentencing Commission would perform when it first began its work centered around four concerns: (1) the skyrocketing Ohio prison population and the cost of incarceration, (2) the complexity in the sentencing laws (regarding the number of felony ranges and the wording in crime classifications), (3) concerns over racial disparity and discrimination, and (4) the lack of judicial discretion (judges felt their hands were tied in pronouncing mandatory sentencing, were dismayed over the power of the Parole Authority to determine time served, and took issue with practices of furlough and shock parole) (Woolredge, Rauschenberg, Griffin, & Pratt, 2002).

In discussions leading up to the crafting of Ohio's sentencing guidelines, commission members identified multiple goals of reforming sentencing in Ohio. These included "getting tough" on criminals and bearing in mind public safety issues, decreasing disparate and discriminatory treatment of offenders, working toward "truth-in-sentencing" (so that the offender will serve a large proportion of his/her sentence), retaining appropriate judicial discretion, and utilizing both incarceration as well as community sanctions, while keeping in mind correctional resources (Woolredge, Rauschenberg, Griffin, & Pratt, 2002).

Members identified some concerns with using a two-axis grid that the federal system and several states had established. They noted that some scholars and criminal justice practitioners had criticized sentencing grids as being too inflexible and not allowing the judge to take into account relevant individual characteristics concerning the nature of the crime and characteristics of the offender (Woolredge, Rauschenberg, Griffin, & Pratt, 2002). They also studied evaluations of strict sentencing reforms that showed when restrictions were made on judicial discretion that discretion moved to the prosecutors.

Structuring the Guidelines

The commission wanted to establish more flexible presumptive guidelines that decreased sentencing disparities and incorporated truth-in-sentencing. The result of their work was the creation of guidelines for felony offenses. **Figure 4.13** shows the current felony sentencing table (Ohio Criminal Sentencing Commission, 2015).

Figure 4.13 Ohio Felony Sentencing Table

FELONY SENTENCING TABLE - APRIL 2015							
Felony Level	Sentencing Guidance [§2929.13(B) through (E)]	Prison Terms [§2929.14(A)]	Maximum Fine [§2929.18(A)(2) and (3)]	Repeat Violent Offender Enhancement [§2929.14(B)(2)]	Is Post-Release Control (PRC) Required? [§2967.28(B) and (C)]	PRC Period [§2967.28(B)]
F-1	Presumption for prison (also applies to "in favor" drug offenses)	3, 4, 5, 6, 7, 8, 9, 10, or 11 years	$20,000	1, 2, 3, 4, 5, 6, 7, 8, 9, or 10 years	Yes	5 years
F-2		2, 3, 4, 5, 6, 7, or 8 years	$15,000			
F-3	No guidance, other than PURPOSES AND PRINCIPLES (Also applies to "Div.(C)" drug offenses)	9, 12, 18, 24, 30, or 36 months or 12, 18, 24, 30, 36, 42, 48, 54, or 60 months[b]	$10,000	For F-2 involving attempted serious harm or for involuntary manslaughter: 1, 2, 3, 4, 5, 6, 7, 8, 9, or 10 years; otherwise none	Yes, if sex or violent offense; otherwise optional	If sex offense, 5 years
F-4	Mandatory 1- year community control for non-violent, no prior felony, etc.[c]	6, 7, 8, 9, 10, 11, 12, 13, 14, 15, 16, 17, or 18 months	$5,000	None	Yes, if sex offense; otherwise optional	Otherwise, up to 3 years
F-5	Otherwise: If any of 11 factors and not amenable to other sanction(s), guidance for prison.[c] If none of 11 factors, guidance against prison (Also applies to "Div.(B)" drug offenses)	6, 7, 8, 9, 10, 11, or 12 months	$2,500			

SENTENCING TABLE NOTES

Exceptions: Indeterminate sentences *for aggravated murder, murder, human trafficking, and certain sex offenses and crimes with sexual motivation.*

 Drug Offenses – *Note penalties track degree of offense, but the sentencing guidance may be different than for other offenses at that felony level.*

Repeat Violent Offenders are [§2967.01((C)]: *Being sentenced for aggravated murder, murder, a violent F-1 or F-2 that is an offense of violence, or an attempt to commit any of these offenses if the attempt is an F-1 or F-2, with a prior conviction for one or more of the same offenses or their equivalents.*

Post-Release Control [§2967.28(D)(5)]: *The board or court shall review the releasee's behavior and may reduce the duration. The reduction for offenses described in division (B)(1) shall not be a period less than the length of the stated prison term originally imposed, and in no case shall the board or court permit the releasee to leave the state without permission of the court or the*

releasee's parole or probation officer.

[a] **Maximum Fines:** *Cover conventional and day fines. There are exceptions in drug trafficking cases* [§2929.18(B)(4) through (7)]. *And some offenses call for a superfine of up to $1 million* [§2929.32]. *For the fine, if the offender is an organization, see* [§2929.31].

In addition to any other fine that is or may be imposed under this section, the court imposing sentence upon an offender for a felony that is a sexually oriented offense or a child-victim oriented offense, as those terms are defined in [§2950.01], *may impose a fine of not less than $50, nor more than $500.* [§2929.18(B)(9)]

[b] **Higher F-3s:** *The longer-sentence range applies to aggravated vehicular homicides and assaults, sexual battery, GSI, sex with minor, and robbery or burglary with 2 or more separate aggravated or non- aggravated robberies or burglaries (See* [§2929.14(A)(3)(a)]).

[c] **F-4s & F-5s:** *See Certain F-4s & F-5s* [§2929.13(B)(1)(a) through (c)] *and Other F-4s, F-5s, or "Div. B" Drug Offenses* [§2929.13(B)(2) and (3)].

Source: Ohio Criminal Sentencing Commission. (2015). *Felony sentencing quick reference guide.* (p. 5). Retrieved from https://www.sconet.state.oh.us/Boards/Sentencing/resources/summaries/felonyQuick Ref.pdf

Under Ohio's Senate Bill 2 (SB 2), felonies were divided into five categories (down from twelve), with first degree felonies being the most serious and fifth degree felonies being the least serious. Each level indicated a range of sentence lengths. The guidelines also provided increments at each level (one year increments are indicated for first, second, and third degree felonies, while one month increments are given for fourth and fifth degree felonies). For each level, the guidelines indicate a maximum amount of post-release supervision to be administered by the Ohio Adult Parole Authority. The table also presents a range of sentence enhancements from 1–10 years for repeat violent offenders sentenced for first, second, and third degree felonies.

There was a presumption that the judge would hand down prison sentences for first and second degree felonies, but not fourth or fifth degree felonies under SB 2. Judges were also presumed to hand down sentences toward the minimum for first offenses. Defendants could appeal if the judge imprisoned an offender contrary to the above guidelines. Similarly, the prosecution could appeal the sentence if the judge imposed a non-prison sentence that carried a presumptive term of imprisonment.

The commission recommended to the General Assembly that the guidelines be adopted in the state of Ohio on July 1, 1993. Senate Bill 2 (SB 2) resulted from the commission's recommendation and was passed by the legislature in June,1995 and signed into law in August 1995 (Woolredge, Rauschenberg, Griffin, & Pratt, 2002). Senate Bill 2 became effective on July 1, 1996. Senate Bill 2 represented the most major sentencing reform in Ohio in decades. Diroll (n.d.) has claimed "S.B. 2 likely is the nation's most *honest* truth-in-sentencing law."

In 2011, House Bill 86 (HB 86) made some revisions to the SB 2. Diroll (2011) detailed these changes that went into effect on September 30, 2011. They include (but are not limited to) the following:

> 1) Whereas, SB 2 steered fourth and fifth degree felons from prison terms, House Bill 86 *prohibits* imprisonment sentences for certain fourth and fifth degree felons.
>
> 2) House Bill 86 also increased the maximum term for a first degree felony from ten to eleven years.
>
> 3) Three provisions of SB 2 regarding presumptions of imprisonment and the use of consecutive sentences were changed in response to *State v. Foster* (2006). This decision reflected the reasoning of two United States Supreme Court cases that we will examine in Chapter 7, *Apprendi v. New Jersey* (2000) and *Blakely v. Washington* (2004). These decisions basically stated that any factor that increases the sentence handed down by the judge must be proven beyond a reasonable doubt by a jury or through the defendant pleading guilty, otherwise it violated provisions in the Sixth Amendment.
>
> 4) House Bill 86 explicitly describes the purposes of sentencing felony offenders in Ohio (Ohio Revised Code §2929.11) as follows:
>
> (A) A court that sentences an offender for a felony shall be guided by the overriding purposes of felony sentencing. The overriding purposes of felony sentencing are to protect the public from future crime by the offender and others and to punish the offender *using the minimum sanctions that the court determines accomplish those purposes without imposing an unnecessary burden on state or local government resources.* To achieve those purposes, the sentencing court shall consider the need for incapacitating the offender, deterring the offender and others from future crime, rehabilitating the offender, and making restitution to the victim of the offense, the public, or both. (Amended by 129th General Assembly File No. 29, HB 86, § 1, eff. 9/30/2011, 1996 (http://codes.ohio.gov/orc/2929.11) (emphasis added)).

5) House Bill 86 eliminated the difference between crack and powder cocaine and established one table for trafficking and one table for possession. Each sets levels based on amounts of cocaine.

6) The bill designed new sentencing options that allow for early releases for some offenders. One option, "risk reduction sentencing," is based on risk reduction programs that were developed by the Department of Rehabilitation and Correction (DRC).

6) Earned credit possibilities were expanded. Under SB 2, "earned credit" could earn a maximum of one day a month for participating in specific programs, including educational programs, vocational training, and substance abuse treatment. HB 86 also permitted "earned credit" for these programs, but explicitly removed sex offender treatment from the list.[7]

7) House Bill 86 requires the DRC to use a risk assessment tool to assess the likelihood of recidivism at various stages of criminal justice processing, including sentencing, in correctional settings, and post release.

8) House Bill 86 requires the DRC to write a reentry plan, which is individualized to the inmate.

The range in possible prison sentence length for felonies is greater in Ohio, compared to the presumptive sentencing guidelines ranges in states like North Carolina or Minnesota. In Ohio, the sentencing range for a first degree felony is 3 to 11 years, meaning that there could be an eight-year difference in the possible sentence for two offenders convicted of the same crime. In a presumptive guidelines state like North Carolina, the range in the possible sentence handed down by a judge for two offenders who committed the same crime would be months, not years.

Summary

Throughout this chapter we have examined similarities and differences in sentencing commissions and the guidelines that they have produced. Texas is a state that formed a sentencing commission that ultimately decided not to create sentencing guidelines, but rather retained indeterminate sentencing. States which have adopted commission-based guidelines share goals of increasing sentencing uniformity, ensuring fairness to the defendant, punishing proportionately, decreasing sentencing discrimination, and ensuring safety to the general public.

How different states go about working towards these goals varies in the context of the specific sentencing systems and procedures developed by their commissions. The structure of the guidelines differ—some states use a sentencing grid, while others use worksheets. Some states include misdemeanors in their guidelines or have separate guidelines for felonies and misdemeanors, while others don't have guidelines for misdemeanors. The way the guidelines operate (mandatory, voluntary, or somewhere in between) also varies by state. The way aggravating and mitigating circumstances are factored into the sentence is different in different states. Some commissions consider juvenile record in prior record calculation while others ignore juvenile record. Some sentencing commissions have explicitly considered how the guidelines would impact correctional resources, while others have not. Some have retained discretionary parole release after the guidelines were enacted, while others eliminated it in efforts to comply with "truth-in-sentencing." Clearly, there is no one formula for attaining the common goals espoused in different states.

An in-depth look at commission-based guidelines in Minnesota, Pennsylvania, North Carolina, and Ohio was presented. Comparisons and contrasts in the calculation of the sentence and the factors described above were presented for these states.

Discussion Questions

1. What are some positives and negatives of adopting voluntary, as opposed to more mandatory, sentencing guidelines? Reflect on this question from the lens of the prosecution, the defense, the offender, the victim, and the judge.
2. What are some avenues by which judges can retain discretion in the context of presumptive sentencing guidelines systems?
3. Do you think that a guidelines system can concurrently serve the goals of retribution/just deserts, incapacitation, general deterrence, specific deterrence, and rehabilitation? Why or why not?
4. Of the four states we showcased in the chapter, which state's sentencing guidelines do you feel are the fairest to the defendant? Why?
5. Do you think concerns of the prison population should serve as a guiding force in the development of sentencing guidelines within a state? If so, do you think that undermines the commonly stated purpose of "just deserts"?
6. What are some critiques of structuring judicial decision making via commission-based sentencing guidelines?

Notes

1. South Carolina's "guidelines" indicate maximum sentences for different felony classes and do not follow a grid or worksheet approach. They are included in the table because this sentencing approach came out of the work of a sentencing commission.

2. The term "state sentencing guidelines" will be used in this chapter to describe the twenty-one states plus the District of Columbia which have sentencing guidelines. Although the District of Columbia is obviously not a state, it will be grouped in this term to avoid overly cumbersome wording throughout the chapter.

3. The situation in Alabama is notable. The *Initial Voluntary Sentencing Standards & Worksheets* (Alabama Sentencing Commission, 2006), describes the sentencing reforms initiated by the Alabama Sentencing Commission, which were approved by the legislature under Act 2006-312. Under the "Statement of Purpose," this document states that traditional parole and good time credits for convicted felons would be abolished and that "truth-in-sentencing" would be adopted. Alabama's prison overcrowding, however, prompted the Alabama Sentencing Commission to consider how the state's sentencing practices were impacting prison overcrowding. A Vera Institute of Justice study showed that

between 1979 and 2000, the incarceration rate in the state rose 326 percent. While the voluntary guidelines went into effect on October 1, 2006, the implementation of "truth-in-sentencing" standards were to be delayed until October 1, 2009, (Alabama Sentencing Commission, 2006) due to the problem of prison overcrowding in Alabama, which was at crisis levels at the time.

The Alabama Sentencing Commission (2012) has stated that their prisons are currently operating at 190 percent of capacity. They acknowledge that the state of California, which has also operated at a high level of overcrowding, was ordered by the Supreme Court to reduce its prison population. Current continued prison overcrowding and projections that truth-in-sentencing would exacerbate crowding in the future led to a bill in 2011 that pushed the adoption of truth-in-sentencing back until 2020.

This explains the state's continued reliance on "back door" strategies to relieve overcrowding. Two such strategies — both good time and discretionary parole release — are used to reduce prison overcrowding in the state. The amount of good time an inmate can accrue while serving his or her sentence in Alabama is considerable. The Correctional Incentive Time Act, referred to as the Good Time Law, automatically reduces the proportion of time an offender will serve in prison. Except for certain excluded offenders (including those serving over 15 years, those convicted of a Class A felony or a sex offense involving a child, those serving a confinement portion of a split sentence, and those serving mandatory enhancements), all defendants will receive good time and the judge has no discretion in allocating good time. In other words, good time credits are afforded to each inmate as provided by statute, but can be forfeited if the inmate exhibits bad conduct or violates a prison rule. Most offenders (those not convicted of child sexual abuse or assault in which a victim suffered permanent physical damage) are afforded generous good time. For example, an offender sentenced to 4 years would be released on good time (absent disciplinary infractions) after 1 year and 4 months. An inmate sentenced to 15 years would be released after 4 years, 7 months, and 22 days.

4. The current Minnesota Sentencing Guidelines have eleven offense seriousness categories and that the ordering is reversed, compared to the original guidelines. In the original guidelines, the most serious offenses (level X) appeared on the bottom and offense seriousness decreased as one moved up the vertical axis to the lowest offense seriousness level (level I) at the top. There are still seven categories representing criminal history, which are ordered the same as the original matrix.

5. The original grid indicated that those cells falling above or to the left of the dark line (which were less serious offenses and/or those with a lower criminal history score) could receive a "stayed" sentence. Offenders in the grid cells falling below or to the right of the dark line (which involved combinations of a higher severity level of the conviction offense and a higher criminal history score) were to be sentenced to imprisonment.

6. The author of this text was a member of one of North Carolina's County Criminal Justice Partnership Advisory Boards beginning in 1994. The membership of the board was diverse and included the county manager, the county sheriff, a judge, a prosecutor, a representative from adult probation, a victim's advocate, and some at-large members among others. A representative from the state came to some meetings and explained the guidelines and the opportunity the group had in shaping alternative sanctions in the county. The decision making about which offenders to target (for example first time offenders, and/or probation violators) and what alternative sanction to explore (in our case the group decided on opening a Day Reporting Center) was truly in the hands of the committee. Such advisory boards were formed throughout the state in the mid-1990s and resulted in the development of a variety of intermediate punishment programs.

7. In addition, under HB 86, DRC could award between 1 to 5 days per month of programming to be added toward the completion of his prison sentence. Some exceptions do exist, including those serving mandatory prison terms, life or death sentences, or sexually oriented offenses committed on or after September 30, 2011. Generally, offenders convicted of more serious offenses and those sentenced before September 30, 2011, could earn one day per month. Offenders convicted of serious offenses after September 30, 2011, and those serving time for less serious offenses (third, fourth, or fifth degree felonies) could earn up to five days per month. HB 86 states that no inmate can earn credits that are greater than eight percent of his/her sentence. In other words, all prisoners must serve at least 92 percent of the sentence handed down by the judge, in the spirit of "truth-in-sentencing."

References

Alabama Sentencing Commission. (2006). *Initial voluntary sentencing standards & worksheets: Approved by the legislature—Act 2006-312.* Retrieved from http://sentencing commission.alacourt.gov/Publications/ASC%202006%20WorkshopManual.pdf

Alabama Sentencing Commission. (2012). *Sentencing reference manual for circuit and district judges.* Retrieved from http://sentencingcommission.alacourt.gov/Publications /Judges%20Reference%20Manual_July2012.pdf

American Bar Association (1994). *ABA Standards for criminal justice sentencing, Third edition: Sentencing.* Washington, DC: American Bar Association.

Apprendi v. New Jersey, 530 U.S. 466 (2000).

Blakely v. Washington, 542 U.S. 296 (2004).

Daily, D. L. (1993–1994). Minnesota: Sentencing guidelines in a politically volatile environment. *Federal Sentencing Reporter, 6*(3), 144–146.

Deitch, M. (1993–1994). Giving guidance the boot: The Texas experience with sentencing reform. *Federal Sentencing Reporter, 6*(3), 138–143.

Diroll, D. J. (2011, September 26). *H.B. 86 Summary: The 2011 changes to criminal and juvenile law.* Columbus, OH: Ohio Criminal Sentencing Commission. Retrieved from http://www.supremecourt.ohio.gov/Boards/Sentencing/resources/summaries /HB86Summary.pdf

Diroll, D. (n.d.). *Thoughts on applying S.B. 2 to "Old Law" inmates.* Columbus, OH: Ohio Criminal Sentencing Commission. Retrieved from http://www.supremecourt.ohio .gov/Boards/Sentencing/resources/Publications/SB2.pdf

District of Columbia Sentencing and Criminal Code Revision Commission. (2014, April 25). *2013 annual report.* Washington, DC. Retrieved from http://scdc.dc.gov /sites/default/files/dc/sites/scdc/publication/attachments/Annual_Report2013.pdf

District of Columbia Sentencing and Criminal Code Revision Commission. (2014, June 30). *Voluntary sentencing guidelines manual, June 30, 2014.* Retrieved from http:// scdc.dc.gov/sites/default/files/dc/sites/scdc/publication/attachments/2014%20Vol untary%20Sentencing%20Guidelines%20Manual%20_0.pdf

Frase, R. S. (1994). Purposes of punishment under the Minnesota sentencing guidelines. *Criminal Justice Ethics, 13*(1), 11–20.

Frase, R. S. (2005). State sentencing guidelines: Diversity, consensus, and unresolved policy issues. *Columbia Law Review, 105*(4), 1190–1232.

Freeman, L. (2009). *The North Carolina sentencing and policy advisory commission: A history of its creation and its development of structured sentencing.* Retrieved from http://www.nccourts.org/Courts/CRS/Councils/spac/Documents/commission _history_aug2009.pdf

Kauder, N. B., & Ostrom, B. J. (2008). *State sentencing guidelines: Profiles and continuum.* National Center for State Courts. Retrieved from http://www.ncsc.org/~/media /Microsites/Files/CSI/State_Sentencing_Guidelines.ashx

Kautt, P. M., & Mueller-Johnson, K. (2009). Cross-jurisdictional disposition variability under sentencing guidelines: The example of equivalent sex offenses. *Criminal Justice Review, 34*(3), 350–381.

Kramer, J. H., & Kempinen, C. (1993–1994). History of Pennsylvania sentencing reform. *Federal Sentencing Reporter, 6*(3), 152–157.

Maryland State Commission on Criminal Sentencing Policy. (2015). *Maryland sentencing guidelines manual, version 7.1, effective February 1, 2015 with updated June 1, 2015 offense table (Appendix A)*. Retrieved from http://www.msccsp.org/Files/Guidelines /MSGM/guidelinesmanual.pdf

Minnesota Sentencing Guidelines Commission. (1980). *Report to the legislature*. St. Paul, MN: Minnesota Sentencing Guidelines Commission.

Minnesota Sentencing Guidelines Commission. (1982). *Preliminary report on the development and impact of the Minnesota Sentencing Guidelines*. St. Paul, MN: Minnesota Sentencing Guidelines Commission.

Minnesota Sentencing Guidelines Commission. (2011). *Minnesota felony sentencing enhancements highlights from 1987 to 2011*. Retrieved from http://www.msgc.state.mn .us/data_reports/2010/MN%20Sentencing%20Guidelines%20Comm%20MN%20 Sentencing%20Enhancements-1987%20to%202011.pdf

Minnesota Sentencing Guidelines Commission. (2011). *MSGC report to the legislature, January, 2011*. St. Paul, MN: Minnesota Guidelines Commission.

Minnesota Sentencing Guidelines Commission (2015, August). *Minnesota sentencing guidelines and commentary, August 1, 2015*. Retrieved from http://mn.gov/sentencing -guidelines/assets/2015%20Minnesota%20Sentencing%20Guidelines%20and%20 Commentary_tcm30-46700.pdf

Missouri Sentencing Advisory Commission. (2011). *Recommended sentencing user guide, 2010–2011*. Retrieved from http://www.mosac.mo.gov/file.jsp?id=45394

Missouri Sentencing Advisory Commission. (n.d.). *MOSAC-Purposes and goals*. Retrieved from http://www.mosac.mo.gov/page.jsp?id=45401

Moore, C. A., & Miethe, T. D. (1986). Regulated and unregulated sentencing decisions: An analysis of first-year practices under Minnesota's felony sentencing guidelines. *Law & Society Review, 20*(2), 253–277.

North Carolina Sentencing and Policy Advisory Commission. (2009). *Structured sentencing training and reference manual: Applies to offenses committed on or after December 1, 2009*. Retrieved from http://www.nccourts.org/Courts/CRS/Councils/spac /Documents/sstrainingmanual_09.pdf

Ohio Criminal Sentencing Commission. (2015). *Felony sentencing quick reference guide*. Retrieved from https://www.sconet.state.oh.us/Boards/Sentencing/resources/sum maries/felonyQuickRef.pdf

Oregon Criminal Justice Commission. (2011). *Newsletter—Winter 2011*.

Orland, L., & Reitz, K. R. (1993). Epilogue: A gathering of state sentencing commissions. *University of Colorado Law Review, 64*, 837–847.

Pennsylvania Commission on Sentencing. (2008). *Complete case law: 6th edition, revised guidelines*. Retrieved from http://pcs.la.psu.edu/guidelines/sentencing/sentencing -guidelines-and-implementation-manuals/6th-edition-revised/complete-case-law -6th-edition-revised-guidelines-large-file/view

Pennsylvania Commission on Sentencing. (2012). *Sentencing guidelines implementation manual. 7th edition, Effective December 28, 2012*. Retrieved from http://pcs.la.psu.edu

/guidelines/sentencing/sentencing-guidelines-and-implementation-manuals/7th
-edition/GL7th-edition-sentencing-guidelines-manual/view

Pennsylvania Commission on Sentencing. (2012). Title 204. Judicial System General
Provisions

Part VIII Criminal Sentencing, Chapter 303. Sentencing Guidelines. Retrieved from
http://pcs.la.psu.edu/guidelines/sentencing/sentencing-guidelines-and-implemen
tation-manuals/7th-edition-amendment-3-sentencing-guidelines-9-25-2015/title
-204.-judicial-system-general-provisions.-part-viii-criminal-sentencing.-chapter
-303.-sentencing-guidelines-amendment-3-guideline-text/view

Reitz, K. R. (1998). *Sentencing.* In M. Tonry (Ed.), *The handbook of crime & punishment*
(pp. 542–562). New York: Oxford University Press.

South Carolina Sentencing Reform Oversight Committee. (2011). *State expenditure savings report.* Retrieved from http://www.ncsl.org/Documents/cj/SCSROCreport.pdf

State of Washington Caseload Forecast Council. (2011). *2011 Washington state adult
sentencing guidelines manual.* Retrieved from http://www.cfc.wa.gov/Publication
Sentencing/SentencingManual/Adult_Sentencing_Manual_2011.pdf

Texas Penal Code, Title 3 Punishments: Chapter 12 Punishments, Subchapter A. General Provisions. Retrieved from http://www.statutes.legis.state.tx.us/Docs/PE/htm/PE
.12.htm

Texas Punishment Standards Commission: An Inventory of Punishment Standards
Commission Records at the Texas State Archives, 1983, 1986–1993, undated, bulk
1989–1993. Retrieved from http://www.lib.utexas.edu/taro/tslac/50081/tsl-50081
.html

Tonry, M. (1996). *Sentencing matters.* New York: Oxford University Press.

Tonry, M. (2004). *Thinking about crime: Sense and sensibility in American penal culture.*
New York: Oxford University Press.

Virginia Criminal Sentencing Commission. (2012a). *Worksheets.* Retrieved from http://
www.vcsc.virginia.gov/worksheets_2015/Rape_.pdf

Virginia Criminal Sentencing Commission. (2012b). *2012 Annual report.* Retrieved from
http://www.vcsc.virginia.gov/2012VCSCAnnualReport.pdf

Von Hirsch, A. (1982). Constructing guidelines for sentencing: The critical choices for
the Minnesota sentencing guidelines commission. *Hamline Law Review, 5,* 164–215.

Woolredge, J., Rauschenberg, F., Griffin, T., & Pratt, T. (2002). *The impact of Ohio's Senate Bill 2 on sentencing disparities: Project report submitted to the National Institute of
Justice.* Retrieved from http://www.uc.edu/content/dam/uc/ccjr/docs/reports/project
_reports/SB2_final_report.pdf

5

Sentencing in the Federal System

Chapter Objectives:

- To gain a historical perspective of various efforts at federal sentencing reform.
- To understand the purposes of the Sentencing Reform Act of 1984 and the establishment of the United States Sentencing Commission.
- To appreciate how accurate guideline application is the starting point of a three-step process to federal sentencing post *United States v. Booker*.
- To identify the objectives of the Federal Sentencing Guidelines.
- To learn, in order, the multiple steps used to determine a sentence for federal offenders.
- To consider the complexity of the process of federal sentencing, including a consideration of departures and variances.
- To examine the federal response to drug offenders, including the Anti-Drug Abuse Act of 1986 and the Fair Sentencing Act of 2010.

Introduction

At the 2015 Annual Seminar on the Federal Sentencing Guidelines in New Orleans, Louisiana, the Honorable Ricardo H. Hinojosa, chief district judge of the United States District Court, Southern District of Texas, reflected on the easiest and hardest parts of his job. He said that the easiest part of the job is not hard to guess. It is when he gets to administer the oath to individuals who decide to become our fellow Americans. He noted that that experience is by far the one thing that happens in the courtroom that makes everyone leave happy. He stated that those persons have honored us by the decision to become our fellow citizens. They're happy because they've become Americans.

The most difficult part of being a judge, according to Judge Hinojosa, is sentencing. He admitted he didn't think that would be the hardest part of the job when he took it. He had initially wondered ". . . when someone committed an offense that they would be punished and use guidelines to decide, and how hard could that be? Well as you all know it is a very important decision. It is important not only for the defendant but others in general" (Hinojosa, 2015, September 16).

In this chapter, we will describe the history leading up to the Federal Sentencing Guidelines. We will also detail the intricate process of sentencing under the federal guidelines. In addition, we will describe federal mandatory minimum sentences for drug offenders.

The Structure of Federal Courts

Trial courts in the federal system are called **district courts**. They have jurisdiction over the vast majority of federal cases — both criminal and civil. There are 94 judicial districts. There is at least one district court in each state, the District of Columbia, and Puerto Rico. There are 13 courts of appeals, referred to as **circuit courts**. Circuit court offices are usually located in large cities. Each circuit court hears appeals from the district courts within its circuit. As appellate courts, they do not retry cases, but rather review substantive and procedural issues that have to do with people's constitutional rights. The **United States Supreme Court** is the highest appellate court in the United States, comprised of nine members appointed for a life term. Considered "the court of last resort," the Supreme Court hears cases that were tried in federal or state courts. The Supreme Court decides which cases it will hear. The cases usually involve interpretations of the Constitution and federal laws. If deemed appropriate, the Supreme Court will hear a case and the decision becomes precedent and must be abided by in all lower courts (United States Courts, n.d.; Siegel & Worall, 2016).

Siegel and Worrall (2016) have characterized the Supreme Court as follows:

> The Supreme Court is unique in several ways. First, it is the only court established by constitutional mandate instead of federal legislation. Second, it decides basic social and political issues of grave consequences and importance to the nation. Third, the justices shape the future meaning of the U.S. Constitution. Their decisions identify the rights and liberties of citizens throughout the United States. (p. 338)

Through much of this chapter, we will examine how the Federal Sentencing Guidelines are applied by district court judges. We will also explain how Supreme Court decisions have dictated how the federal guidelines are to be applied. Chapter 7 will provide an overview of more significant court decisions involving sentencing laws and procedures.

Early Efforts to Structure Judicial Decision Making

Before the Federal Sentencing Guidelines went into effect on November 1, 1987, there were some attempts to help make the decisions of federal judges more uniform. One involved the formation of sentencing institutes by Congress in the late 1950s. Another entailed the adoption of sentencing councils in the 1960s by a few judges in various federal districts.

Sentencing Institutes

Congress passed a law in 1958 that called for the convening of sentencing institutes. Federal judges had proposed the idea, which came from a concern over sentencing disparities by federal courts in different parts of the country, between districts, and within the same districts. Sentencing institutes brought together several groups of individuals, including judges, United States attorneys, criminologists, psychiatrists, and penologists.

The goal was to promote sentencing uniformity by having these individuals consider and share views on the goals of sentencing, sentencing policies, and the criteria which should be used for sentencing federal offenders. It was suggested that sentencing institutes would help to establish consistency while maintaining judicial independence. The subjects covered would include the sentencing of particular crimes (for example, auto theft or selective-service violations), information on sentencing alternatives, and occasionally on reforming the law.

Copies of presentence reports were examined by the participants and the discussion that ensued often showed great variation in judges' opinions about what the proper sentence should be. While they served as an opportunity for judges to get together and consider various sentencing options, the sentencing institutes had little concrete impact on focusing judicial philosophies or on reforming the actual sentencing process to increase uniformity or decrease the consideration of extra-legal case characteristics in sentencing (Frankel, 1973).

Sentencing Councils

In his 1973 book, *Criminal Sentences: Law Without Order*, Frankel suggested that a more effective approach to promote more uniform sentencing occurred when judges formed sentencing councils in the 1960s. He described how judges in the United States District Court for the Eastern District of Michigan held weekly meetings about sentencing concerns. After these judges described their activities to other judges in the field, judges in several other federal districts also adopted sentencing councils.

The work of these councils involved the judge presiding over a particular case sharing the presentence report with two other judges, who would also study the report and suggest a sentence for the defendant. The three judges would meet (many times with a probation officer also present) and share their observations of the case and the judge might then revise his sentence.[1] The judge's final decision made at the sentencing hearing could then incorporate the perspectives of more than one decision maker. Frankel concluded that judges ultimately tended to integrate the perspectives of the other judges and choose less "extreme" sentences, and overall judges tended to choose a more lenient sentence compared to what the judge who was assigned to the case was leaning towards prior to the sentencing council meeting.

Frankel admitted that the practice did not become widespread. There was no accountability for the judges to impose a "negotiated" sentence. And obviously, this practice was time consuming. Some judges even criticized sentencing councils as undermining the "independence" of sentencing judges. Others found it problematic to the defendant that he or she did not have the ability to confront all of the "decision makers" in the sentencing process—meaning those other judges at the sentencing councils who consulted with the sentencing judge. Frankel concluded, however, that the sentencing council approach was superior to that of a single judge deciding a defendant's fate with what Frankel considered to be effectively unbridled discretion.

Noted criminologist Sheldon Glueck (1936) also proposed that sentencing should incorporate multiple decision makers. He proposed a panel of three—a judge, a psychiatrist or psychologist, and a sociologist or educator. He reiterated that no single judge would or could be versed in all the issues relevant in the sentencing decision, such as the offender's mental state. This approach, however, was never adopted by any jurisdiction.

As discussed in Chapter 4, federal judge Marvin Frankel's ideas about structuring judicial decision making were first implemented in the state of Minnesota in 1980 through the passage of the state's sentencing guidelines. A few years later, Frankel's ideas came to fruition in the federal system. The establishment of the Federal Sentencing Guidelines culminated after several years and multiple attempts involving proposed bills to structure federal sentencing.

The Formation of the United States Sentencing Commission

Authority

The current United States Sentencing Commission *Guidelines Manual*, effective November 1, 2015 (United States Sentencing Commission, 2015 USSC *Guidelines Manual*, "Chapter One—Introduction, Authority, and General Application Principles," Part A— Introduction and Authority) describes the history and purposes of the Federal Sentencing Guidelines. It also highlights the revisions and modifications made to the guidelines since they first became effective on November 1, 1987. According to this document:

> The United States Sentencing Commission ("Commission") is an independent agency in the judicial branch composed of seven voting and two non-voting, ex-officio members. Its principal purpose is to establish sentencing policies and practices for the federal criminal justice system that will assure the ends of justice by promulgating detailed guidelines prescribing the appropriate sentences for offenders convicted of federal offenses.
> The guidelines and policy statements promulgated by the Commission are issued pursuant to Section 994(a) of Title 28, United States Code. (p. 1)

The members of the United States Sentencing Commission (USSC) are appointed by the president and confirmed by the Senate. They serve a six-year term. The commission must include three federal judges. No more than four can belong to the same political party. The Attorney General and the chair of the United States Parole Commission serve as the ex-officio members (United States Sentencing Commission. *Introduction to the Federal Sentencing Guidelines*, "Part 1—Overview of the United States Sentencing Commission," [Video]).

Background of the United States Sentencing Commission and the Federal Sentencing Guidelines

Issues that influenced Congress to create the United States Sentencing Commission and subsequently, the Federal Sentencing Guidelines, included disparities in sentencing "similarly situated" defendants (in terms of legally relevant characteristics), the importance of certainty in punishment, and crime control. The federal system had indeterminate sentencing, parole procedures that could reduce the offender's prison sentence up to one third of that pronounced by the judge, and good time credits which could reduce the offender's prison sentence up to an additional third. Congress was concerned that judges could sentence anywhere within broad statutory penalties (for example, zero years to life imprisonment) and that the reasons for their sentences were unknown. Another issue was that this sentencing system had limited due process rights (United States Sentencing Commission. *Introduction to the Federal Sentencing Guidelines*, "Part 1 — Overview of the United States Sentencing Commission," [Video]).

Congress researched and deliberated issues surrounding federal sentencing. They concluded the following: "1) the previously unfettered discretion accorded federal trial judges needed to be structured, 2) the administration of punishment needed to be more certain, and 3) specific offenders, for example white collar and violent repeat offenders, needed to be targeted for more serious penalties" (United States Sentencing Commission. *Introduction to the Federal Sentencing Guidelines*, "Part 1 — Overview of the United States Sentencing Commission," [Video]).

Congress created and passed in a bipartisan fashion the **Comprehensive Crime Control Act of 1984**. This act represented the first major revision of the U.S. Criminal Code since the early 1900s. President Ronald Reagan signed it into law.

The Sentencing Reform Act of 1984 changed federal sentencing practices in significant ways. It instituted a determinate sentencing scheme and abolished parole for federal offenders. It established supervised release, which was a term of supervision for all offenders convicted of felonies and Class A misdemeanors (See 18 USC § 3559(a) and § 3583(b)&(e)(3)) after release from federal prison to help reintegrate the offender back into society. This is an example of the practice of mandatory parole release that we discussed in earlier chapters. The act also limited good time to no more than 54 days per year for offenders serving a prison sentence over one year. Those ineligible for good time are those offenders serving a life sentence or sentences of one year or less (See 18 USC § 3624(b)(1)). Due process provisions were also expanded (United States Sentencing Commission. *Introduction to the Federal Sentencing Guidelines*, "Part 1 — Overview of the United States Sentencing Commission," [Video]).

The Sentencing Reform Act of 1984 gave the United States Sentencing Commission (USSC) the authority to create sentencing guidelines for federal offenses. The commission submitted the initial sentencing guidelines to Congress on April 13, 1987. The guidelines went into effect on November 1, 1987. Criminal offenders who committed their crime(s) on or after this date were to be sentenced under the new United States Sentencing Guidelines. In 1989 the guidelines were upheld in *Mistretta v. United States*, 488 U.S. 361 (1989).

Sentencing Guidelines Are Now Advisory, Not Mandatory

The Federal Sentencing Guidelines were designed "to provide federal judges with fair and consistent sentencing ranges to consult at sentencing" (United States Sentencing Commission. *Introduction to the Federal Sentencing Guidelines*, "Part 2 — Overview of the Federal Sentencing Guidelines," [Video]). The purpose of applying the Federal Sentencing Guidelines is to arrive at a sentencing range that applies to a particular offender. Like the sentencing grids fashioned in many states, this range is based on the intersection of two major criteria — seriousness of the instant criminal offense (left, vertical axis) and length and severity of prior criminal record (upper, horizontal axis). Numerical proxies for each appear on each axis of the Sentencing Table.

The role that the guidelines play in sentencing criminal defendants has changed since they were first put into effect on November 1, 1987. Since *United States v. Booker* (543 U.S. 220, 2005), the **Federal Sentencing Guidelines are now advisory, not mandatory.** In this Supreme Court case, which will be discussed at length in Chapter 7, it was decided that the defendant's right to a jury trial, under the Sixth Amendment, means that other than prior criminal convictions, only information that was admitted by a defendant or proven beyond a reasonable doubt to a jury can be used to calculate the sentence for a defendant. This applies to cases in which the defendant has pleaded guilty as well as those in which the defendant is found guilty by a court of law.

Accurate guideline application is now considered to be the starting point in the sentencing process. While not bound to apply the guidelines, district courts must consult the guidelines and take them into account when sentencing. In other words, correct guideline application is the required starting point in sentencing (Hinojosa & Dorhoffer, 2015, September 16). Sentences are to be based on factors identified in 18 U.S.C. § 3553(a)(1)–(7). These factors must be considered by (1) the district court when imposing the sentence and (2) the appellate courts when they are reviewing "reasonableness" of a sentence. The code states, "The court is to impose a sentence *sufficient but not greater than necessary* to comply with the 'purposes of sentencing.'" These include

(1) Nature & circumstances of offense; history & characteristics of the defendant
(2) "Purposes of sentencing" — punishment, deterrence, incapacitation, and rehabilitation
(3) Kinds of sentences available
(4) The sentencing guidelines
(5) The guideline policy statements
(6) Avoiding unwarranted sentencing disparities
(7) Need to provide restitution

At the 2015 Annual National Seminar on the Federal Sentencing Guidelines, Judge Hinojosa and Judge Dorhoffer (2015, September 16) presented a three-step approach to federal sentencing following the *United States v. Booker* (543 U.S. 220 (2005)) decision:

1. Correctly apply and consider the sentencing guidelines, including the guideline range and other aspects of the sentence called for by the guidelines. See §1B1.1(a)
2. Consider the guidelines' policy statements, including those addressing departures, that might warrant consideration in imposing sentence (see §1B1.1(b)
3. Consider §3553(a) taken as a whole (see §1B1.1(c)), and determine if the appropriate sentence is
   - One within the advisory guideline system:
     - a sentence within the guideline range, or
     - a "*departure*"
   OR
   - One outside the advisory guideline system:
     - a "*variance*"

The main purposes of the United States Sentencing Commission are (1) to establish sentencing policies and practices for the federal courts, including guidelines to be consulted regarding the appropriate form and severity of punishment for offenders convicted of federal crimes (this includes amending practices when deemed appropriate); (2) to advise and assist Congress and the executive branch in the development of effective and efficient crime policy; (3) to collect, analyze, research, and distribute a broad array of information on federal crime and sentencing issues; and (4) to serve as an informational and educational resource for Congress, the executive branch, the courts, criminal justice practitioners, the academic community, and the public (United States Sentencing Commission. *Introduction to the Federal Sentencing Guidelines*, "Part 1 — Overview of the United States Sentencing Commission," [Video]).

The commission has the task of monitoring the implementation of guidelines. Ongoing responsibilities include understanding and objectively evaluating effects of the guidelines on the criminal justice system. It is to propose to Congress revisions to the guidelines and suggest changes in criminal statutes and sentencing procedures. The commission is to carry out research and education programs concerning sentencing issues.

The commission's staff is composed of approximately 100 employees in five offices — general counsel, education and sentencing practice, research and data, legislative and public affairs, and administration. The duties of the sentencing commission and the directives regarding the creation of the guidelines and the commission are detailed in 28 U.S.C. 991–998.

Each year, the commission can propose amendments to the guidelines between the beginning of the regular congressional session and May 1. Amendments take effect 180 days after they are submitted — on November 1, unless a law is passed negating them.

The original guidelines resulted from extensive work and careful consideration of information garnered from multiple sources including research, hearings, and public input. The commission characterizes the guidelines process, however, as evolutionary. It acknowledges that research and practical application of the guidelines will result in periodic revisions which will be submitted to Congress. The USSC is a permanent agency. The Federal Sentencing Guidelines apply to over 90 percent of all felony and Class A misdemeanors.

The Complexity of Federal Sentencing Guidelines

The Federal Sentencing Guidelines are more complex than any state guidelines system. The 2015 USSC *Guidelines Manual* is 591 pages long and contains eight chapters. The first six chapters are the ones relevant for the determination of the guideline ranges for individual offenders. Chapter 7 of the manual describes sentencing procedures for violations of probation and supervised release. Chapter 8 details the sentencing of organizations.

The manual provides step-by-step instructions for determining the sentence range for a criminal offender and follows chapters in chronological order. It also includes the Sentencing Table. In addition, there are three appendices, an index to the *Guidelines Manual*, and a list of departure provisions.

The United States Sentencing Commission holds regular three-day training seminars for those working within the federal system. Participants include federal judges, federal prosecutors, federal defense attorneys, and federal probation officers. They are also open to researchers—the author of this text has attended these meetings. Subjects of specific sessions have included an introduction to the sentencing guidelines, ethics, drug offenses, fraud and theft offenses, criminal history, role in the offense and adjustments, restitution and victims' rights issues, grouping of multiple counts, child pornography and sex offenses, relevant conduct, immigration offenses, and firearms offenses.

While the guidelines aim to make sentencing more honest, uniform, and proportional, one could argue that the sheer complexity of the guidelines might hinder these goals. The guidelines indicate 43 offense levels and six criminal history categories, set sentencing ranges according to the offender's position on this sentencing grid, yet provide avenues for departure that some would argue open the door to disparity and discrimination. Comprehending the guidelines is anything but simple. The guidelines were crafted to be evolutionary, meaning that updates and revisions have been anticipated since their inception. Those involved in the federal system must be fully informed of any and all amendments to facilitate the accurate imposition of federal sentences.

One chapter cannot cover all of the text and the intricacies of sentencing in the federal system. What we will try to do is introduce the reader to the history, structure, and function of the guidelines. We will also illustrate the steps taken to apply the guidelines to a criminal offender's case.

The Creation of the Federal Sentencing Guidelines

Objectives of the Guidelines

According to the USSC (United States Sentencing Commission (2015, November 1), 2015 USSC *Guidelines Manual*, "Chapter One—Introduction, Authority, and General Application Principles"), the basic objective of the Federal Sentencing Reform Act of 1984 was "... to enhance the ability of the criminal justice system to combat crime through an effective, fair sentencing system" (p. 2).

Congress identified three objectives of the Sentencing Reform Act of 1984 that would guide the work of the commission when crafting the guidelines. The first emphasized **honest sentencing**. This meant that the sentence handed down by the judge would represent the amount of time that the offender would actually serve in prison, with only slight modifications for good behavior. The second objective delineated by Congress was to **increase sentencing uniformity**. Offenders who committed similar crimes and offenders with comparable legally relevant characteristics should serve similar sentences. Third, Congress emphasized the importance of **proportionality**—that the severity of the sanction should reflect the seriousness of the offense.

The commission asserts that the elimination of parole release for federal offenders enhances honesty in sentencing. It acknowledges, however, a certain strain between the goals of uniformity and proportionality. Uniformity could be realized in a simple way by having only a limited number of offense categories and sentencing all offenders within each level with the same sanction. While uniformity would be maximized, this approach would lump all offenders convicted of an offense, such as robbery, in the same seriousness level. Offenses that meet the legal definition of robbery, however, vary. The commission acknowledged that some robberies are committed with a weapon while others are not, that some result in injury while others do not, and that the amount of money taken varies enormously between crimes that share the label "robbery." The opposite approach—to classify every robbery according to a myriad of factors which would account for every possible particular robbery scenario, however, would prove to be unwieldy.

The act indicated that a sentence for a crime should be made from within the guidelines range. If a case was deemed atypical, however, the court would be allowed to depart from the prescribed guidelines range. An appellate court could review a sentence that was handed down within the guidelines to determine whether the guidelines were applied correctly. An appellate court could also review the "reasonableness of the departure" if the sentencing court departed from the guidelines range (United States Sentencing Commission, 2015, November 1).

The commission developed resultant guidelines in an effort to greatly reduce disparities in sentencing similar crimes, but which also considered what is deemed to be relevant individual case characteristics. The number of offense levels (43) is significantly greater than any state commission-based guidelines system that we discussed in Chapter 4. The number of criminal history categories (6), however, is similar to the number in most states.

Sentencing Goals of Corrections — The Federal System

As discussed in Chapter 4, states' sentencing commissions commonly declare multiple goals of sentencing as relevant to the development and implementation of their guidelines systems. While "crime control" is a basic objective of sentencing, how that is realized—by focusing on just deserts or deterrence or incapacitation or rehabilitation, is subject to opinion. When developing the Federal Sentencing Guidelines, the USSC heard from advocates of various sentencing goals.

The commission states that the resultant guidelines did not emanate from a choice to emphasize one overriding goal of punishment, however. Like many states' guidelines discussed in Chapter 4, the Federal Sentencing Guidelines were to be fashioned to promote several justifications of punishment including deterrence, incapacitation, just punishment, and rehabilitation.

The Use of Empirical Data from Past Sentencing Practices as a Point of Departure

The commission examined empirical data on past sentencing practices as a point of departure in the formation of the guidelines. This included a consideration of pre-guidelines data including presentence investigation reports, various elements of different crimes that were detailed in substantive criminal statutes, and the guidelines used by the United States Parole Commission about when to release an offender from prison. According to the commission (United States Sentencing Commission, 2015, November 1):

> This empirical approach helped the Commission resolve its practical problem by defining a list of relevant distinctions that, although of considerable length, was short enough to create a manageable set of guidelines. Existing categories are relatively broad and omit distinctions that some may believe important, yet they include most of the major distinctions that statutes and data suggest made a significant difference in sentencing decisions. Relevant distinctions not reflected in the guidelines probably will occur rarely and sentencing courts may take such unusual cases into account by departing from the guidelines. (p. 4)

While the commission researched past federal sentencing practices, they did not automatically designate identical pre-guidelines offense classes or average sentences in the creation of the Federal Sentencing Guidelines. One reason they could not do so was that a year before the federal guidelines went into effect, the Anti-Drug Abuse Act of 1986 (which we will discuss in some depth later in this chapter) enacted more severe penalties and some mandatory minimum sentences for certain drug offenses. Another reason involved an analysis of the data that revealed sentencing disparities between economic crimes and other crimes which were considered equal with respect to seriousness. The data showed that economic crimes were given significantly lighter sentences and the commission did not want to continue disparate sentencing practices for crimes similar in offense severity. The goals of the USSC involved developing truthful sentencing that promoted sentencing uniformity, equity, and proportionality.

Real Offense vs. Charge Offense Sentencing

The Federal Sentencing Guidelines have differed from any states' guidelines system we have examined in that they considered what is labeled "real offense sentencing" as opposed to "charge offense sentencing" in the design of the guidelines. "Real offense sentencing" is based ". . . upon the actual conduct in which the defendant engaged regardless of the charges for which he was indicted or convicted" (United States Sentencing Commission, 2015, November 1, p. 5). Charge offense sentencing, on the other hand, is based on "the conduct that constitutes the elements of the offense for which the defendant was charged and of which he was convicted" (United States Sentencing Commission, 2015, November 1, p. 5). All of the state sentencing guidelines follow "charge offense sentencing." They provide sentence guidelines only for the crimes that the offender was found guilty of by a court of law or those to which the offender has plead guilty.

The USSC first considered a real offense approach, noting that the pre-guidelines system took this approach to some extent. The sentencing court considered all of the conduct related to the offense in the presentence report and the parole commission did the same in parole hearings. The USSC, however, decided against this approach, citing the complexity and time that it would take to calculate harms done and in determining which relevant case characteristics should enter into the sentencing decisions in addition to the conviction offense(s). The original guidelines that were submitted to Congress in April 1987 were more in line with a system of charge offense sentencing.

Determination of Type of Sentence

The enabling statute to the guidelines directs the guidelines to "reflect the general appropriateness of imposing a sentence other than imprisonment in cases in which the defendant is a first offender who has not been convicted of a crime of violence or an otherwise serious offense . . . 28 U.S.C. §994(j)" (United States Sentencing Commission, 2015, November 1, p. 8).

The commission noted that before the guidelines the federal courts had sentenced offenders convicted of economic crimes disproportionately to probation, as opposed to prison, and that they viewed these crimes as serious. These offenses include embezzlement, tax evasion, antitrust offenses, and insider trading. When devising the guidelines the commission classified these crimes in a way that would assign at least a short imprisonment term, as opposed to just probation.

The Development of Sentencing Ranges

The commission devised sentence ranges for each offense by calculating the pre-guidelines average sentences within each category. Pursuant to the act, the commission was to consider past processes in federal sentencing and develop new practices including the creation of categories of offense behavior and the characteristics of the offender. One duty of the commission was to establish guidelines ranges for sentences for each combination of offense class and offender characteristics category. When the punishment was imprisonment, the range was to be narrow, meaning that the maximum of the range could not exceed the minimum range by more than 25 percent or six months.

In line with pre-guidelines practices, which often resulted in lesser sentences for defendants who plead guilty, the federal guidelines allow the court to impose lighter sentences for defendants who "accept responsibility" for their offenses. Likewise, those who provide "substantial assistance" may receive a downward departure (see the *Sentencing Departures* section of this chapter).

The commission acknowledged the impact that the sentencing ranges it set would have on the prison population. Certain legislation, including the Anti-Drug Abuse Act of 1986 and the part of the Sentencing Reform Act of 1984 that dealt with career offenders, was expected to yield guidelines that would produce an increase the prison population.

Application of the Guidelines

The Sentencing Table

Figure 5.1 Federal Sentencing Table, Effective November 1, 2015

SENTENCING TABLE
(in months of imprisonment)

			Criminal History Category (Criminal History Points)			
Offense Level	I (0 or 1)	II (2 or 3)	III (4, 5, 6)	IV (7, 8, 9)	V (10, 11, 12)	VI (13 or more)
1	0-6	0-6	0-6	0-6	0-6	0-6
2	0-6	0-6	0-6	0-6	0-6	1-7
3	0-6	0-6	0-6	0-6	2-8	3-9
4	0-6	0-6	0-6	2-8	4-10	6-12
5	0-6	0-6	1-7	4-10	6-12	9-15
6	0-6	1-7	2-8	6-12	9-15	12-18
7	0-6	2-8	4-10	8-14	12-18	15-21
8	0-6	4-10	6-12	10-16	15-21	18-24
9	4-10	6-12	8-14	12-18	18-24	21-27
10	6-12	8-14	10-16	15-21	21-27	24-30
11	8-14	10-16	12-18	18-24	24-30	27-33
12	10-16	12-18	15-21	21-27	27-33	30-37
13	12-18	15-21	18-24	24-30	30-37	33-41
14	15-21	18-24	21-27	27-33	33-41	37-46
15	18-24	21-27	24-30	30-37	37-46	41-51
16	21-27	24-30	27-33	33-41	41-51	46-57
17	24-30	27-33	30-37	37-46	46-57	51-63
18	27-33	30-37	33-41	41-51	51-63	57-71
19	30-37	33-41	37-46	46-57	57-71	63-78
20	33-41	37-46	41-51	51-63	63-78	70-87
21	37-46	41-51	46-57	57-71	70-87	77-96
22	41-51	46-57	51-63	63-78	77-96	84-105
23	46-57	51-63	57-71	70-87	84-105	92-115
24	51-63	57-71	63-78	77-96	92-115	100-125
25	57-71	63-78	70-87	84-105	100-125	110-137
26	63-78	70-87	78-97	92-115	110-137	120-150
27	70-87	78-97	87-108	100-125	120-150	130-162
28	78-97	87-108	97-121	110-137	130-162	140-175
29	87-108	97-121	108-135	121-151	140-175	151-188
30	97-121	108-135	121-151	135-168	151-188	168-210
31	108-135	121-151	135-168	151-188	168-210	188-235
32	121-151	135-168	151-188	168-210	188-235	210-262
33	135-168	151-188	168-210	188-235	210-262	235-293
34	151-188	168-210	188-235	210-262	235-293	262-327
35	168-210	188-235	210-262	235-293	262-327	292-365
36	188-235	210-262	235-293	262-327	292-365	324-405
37	210-262	235-293	262-327	292-365	324-405	360-life
38	235-293	262-327	292-365	324-405	360-life	360-life
39	262-327	292-365	324-405	360-life	360-life	360-life
40	292-365	324-405	360-life	360-life	360-life	360-life
41	324-405	360-life	360-life	360-life	360-life	360-life
42	360-life	360-life	360-life	360-life	360-life	360-life
43	life	life	life	life	life	life

Zone A (offense levels 1–8), Zone B (offense levels 9–11), Zone C (offense levels 12–13), Zone D (offense levels 14–43)

Source: United States Sentencing Commission. (2015). *United States Sentencing Commission Guidelines Manual.* p. 404, Sentencing Table. Retrieved from http://www.ussc.gov/sites/default/files/pdf/guidelines-manual/2015/GLMFull.pdf

Figure 5.1 is the Sentencing Table for federal offenses. There are 43 offense levels and six criminal history categories. There is some overlap in the ranges at different offense levels. For example, for an Offense Level of 26 and a Criminal History Category I, the guidelines range is 63–78 months. For one level lower (25) the guidelines range is 57–71 and for one level higher the guidelines range is 70–87.

The commission explains the assignment of levels in the following way (United States Sentencing Commission (2015, November 1):

> Each level in the table prescribes ranges that overlap with the ranges in the preceding and succeeding levels. By overlapping the ranges, the table should discourage unnecessary litigation. Both prosecution and defense will realize that the difference between one level and another will not necessarily make a difference in the sentence that the court imposes. Thus, little purpose will be served in protracted litigation trying to determine, for example, whether $10,000 or $11,000 was obtained as a result of a fraud. At the same time, the levels work to increase a sentence proportionately. A change of six levels roughly doubles the sentence irrespective of the level at which on starts. The guidelines, in keeping with the statutory requirement that the maximum of any range cannot exceed the minimum by more than the greater of 25 percent or six months (28 U.S.C. §994(b)(2)), permit courts to exercise the greatest permissible range of sentencing discretion. The table overlaps offense levels meaningfully, works proportionately, and at the same time preserves the maximum degree of allowable discretion for the court within each level. (p. 11)

The Steps to Calculating a Sentence

Chapter 1 of the *Guidelines Manual* includes the "Introduction to the Guidelines" that first appeared in 1987 and explains the history of the development of the Federal Sentencing Guidelines and instructions, definitions, and application principles to be used with the guidelines.

A revised manual has been produced by the commission each year beginning in 1987. This is because the guidelines are amended each year. When going through the process of determining a sentence, one is to use the *Guidelines Manual* that is in effect at the time of sentencing. An exception would be the case of an *ex post facto* issue. In this event, the *Guidelines Manual* in effect at the time the offense was committed should be used (United States Sentencing Commission. *Introduction to the Federal Sentencing Guidelines*, "Part 3—Basic Guideline Structure and Initial Application Decisions" [Video]).

Figure 5.2 lists the steps the court should take in imposing the sentence (United States Sentencing Commission, 2015, November 1, p. 16). The steps are portrayed in chronological order and detailed in chapters two through five of the manual. We will highlight the main components of each step and illustrate the process, assuming that the sentencing involves a single count. The handling of sentencing for multiple counts is more complex and the interested reader can access the relevant procedures in the *Guidelines Manual*.

Figure 5.2 General Application Principles

§1B1.1. <u>Application Instructions</u>

    (a)   The court shall determine the kinds of sentence and the guideline range as set forth in the guidelines (<u>see</u> 18 U.S.C. § 3553(a)(4)) by applying the provisions of this manual in the following order, except as specifically directed:

        (1)   Determine, pursuant to §1B1.2 (Applicable Guidelines), the offense guideline section from Chapter Two (Offense Conduct) applicable to the offense of conviction. <u>See</u> §1B1.2.

        (2)   Determine the base offense level and apply any appropriate specific offense characteristics, cross references, and special instructions contained in the particular guideline in Chapter Two in the order listed.

        (3)   Apply the adjustments as appropriate related to victim, role, and obstruction of justice from Parts A, B, and C of Chapter Three.

        (4)   If there are multiple counts of conviction, repeat steps (1) through (3) for each count. Apply Part D of Chapter Three to group the various counts and adjust the offense level accordingly.

        (5)   Apply the adjustment as appropriate for the defendant's acceptance of responsibility from Part E of Chapter Three.

        (6)   Determine the defendant's criminal history category as specified in Part A of Chapter Four. Determine from Part B of Chapter Four any other applicable adjustments.

        (7)   Determine the guideline range in Part A of Chapter Five that corresponds to the offense level and criminal history category determined above.

        (8)   For the particular guideline range, determine from Parts B through G of Chapter Five the sentencing requirements and options related to probation, imprisonment, supervision conditions, fines, and restitution.

    (b)   The court shall then consider Parts H and K of Chapter Five, Specific Offender Characteristics and Departures, and any other policy statements or commentary in the guidelines that might warrant consideration in imposing sentence. <u>See</u> 18 U.S.C. § 3553(a)(5).

    (c)   The court shall then consider the applicable factors in 18 U.S.C. § 3553(a) taken as a whole. <u>See</u> 18 U.S.C. § 3553(a).

Source: United States Sentencing Commission. (2015). *United States Sentencing Commission Guidelines Manual*. p. 16, Part B—General Application Principles. Retrieved from http://www.ussc.gov/sites/default/files/pdf/guidelines-manual/2015/GLMFull.pdf

Step one involves **determining the offense guidelines section in Chapter 2** (Offense Conduct) that is to be applied to the conviction offense pursuant to §1B1.2 (Applicable Guidelines). Statutes are listed in the manual's Appendix A—Statutory Index. A list of statutes of conviction appears on the left and on the right are corresponding applicable guideline(s) for each. **Figure 5.3** shows a section of Appendix A.

Figure 5.3 Offense Guideline Section Applicable to the Statute of Conviction

INDEX

Statute	Guideline	Statute	Guideline
2 U.S.C. § 192	2J1.1, 2J1.5	7 U.S.C. § 13(e)	2B1.4
2 U.S.C. § 390	2J1.1, 2J1.5	7 U.S.C. § 23	2B1.1
7 U.S.C. § 6	2B1.1	7 U.S.C. § 87b	2N2.1
7 U.S.C. § 6b(A)	2B1.1	7 U.S.C. § 87f(e)	2J1.1, 2J1.5
7 U.S.C. § 6b(B)	2B1.1	7 U.S.C. § 136	2Q1.2
7 U.S.C. § 6b(C)	2B1.1	7 U.S.C. § 136j	2Q1.2
7 U.S.C. § 6c	2B1.1	7 U.S.C. § 136k	2Q1.2
7 U.S.C. § 6h	2B1.1	7 U.S.C. § 136l	2Q1.2
7 U.S.C. § 6o	2B1.1	7 U.S.C. § 149	2N2.1
7 U.S.C. § 13(a)(1)	2B1.1	7 U.S.C. § 150bb	2N2.1
7 U.S.C. § 13(a)(2)	2B1.1	7 U.S.C. § 150gg	2N2.1
7 U.S.C. § 13(a)(3)	2B1.1	7 U.S.C. § 154	2N2.1
7 U.S.C. § 13(a)(4)	2B1.1	7 U.S.C. § 156	2N2.1
7 U.S.C. § 13(c)	2C1.3	7 U.S.C. § 157	2N2.1
7 U.S.C. § 13(d)	2B1.4	7 U.S.C. § 158	2N2.1

Source: United States Sentencing Commission. (2015). *United States Sentencing Commission Guidelines Manual.* p. 543, Appendix A —Statutory Index. Retrieved from http://www.ussc.gov/sites/default /files/pdf/guidelines-manual/2015/GLMFull.pdf

For most statutes of conviction, there is a single guideline corresponding to that stat-ute of conviction. It is also possible that a single statute, however, has more than one guideline associated with it. For example, for statute 18 U.S.C. 2113(a) there are four guidelines that correspond to it—USSG §2B1.1 (the larceny, embezzlement, fraud, and forgery guideline), USSG §2B2.1 (the burglary guideline), USSG §2B3.1 (the robbery guideline), and USSG §2B3.2 (the extortion by force or threat of injury or serious damage guideline). In this example the statute describes a *range of criminal conduct*. In this case the court selects the appropriate Chapter 2 guideline by looking at the count to which the offender was convicted. If the count of description describes robbery, for example, then USSG §2B3.1, the robbery guideline, should apply.

Figure 5.4 portrays the structure of a sentencing guideline (United States Sentenc-ing Commission, 2015, November 1, p. 35).

Figure 5.4 Structure of a Federal Guideline

§1B1.6.   Structure of the Guidelines

The guidelines are presented in numbered chapters divided into alphabetical parts. The parts are divided into subparts and individual guidelines. Each guideline is identified by three numbers and a letter corresponding to the chapter, part, subpart and individual guideline.

The first number is the chapter, the letter represents the part of the chapter, the second number is the subpart, and the final number is the guideline. Section 2B1.1, for example, is the first guideline in the first subpart in Part B of Chapter Two. Or, §3A1.2 is the second guideline in the first subpart in Part A of Chapter Three. Policy statements are similarly identified.

To illustrate:

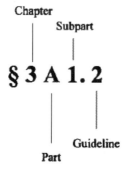

Historical Note: Effective November 1, 1987.

Source: United States Sentencing Commission. (2015). *United States Sentencing Commission Guide-lines Manual.* p. 35, Structure of the Guidelines. Retrieved from http://www.ussc.gov/sites/default/files/pdf/guidelines-manual/2015/GLMFull.pdf

Several statutory provisions may indicate that the same guideline be applied. For example, first degree murder, which is assigned USSG §2A1.1, is defined by multiple statutes including 18 U.S.C. §§1111, 1841(a)(2)(C), 1992(a)(7), 2113(e), 2118(c)(2), 2199, 2282A, 2291, 2332b(a)(1), 2340A, and 21 U.S. C. §848(e).

Each guideline is detailed in "Chapter 2—Offense Conduct." Chapter 2 is divided into 18 parts—Part A—Offenses against the Person; Part B—Basic Economic Crimes; Part C—Offenses Involving Public Officials and Violations of Federal Election Campaign Laws; Part D—Offenses Involving Drugs and Narco-Terrorism; Part E—Offenses Involving Criminal Enterprises and Racketeering; Part G—Offenses Involving Commercial Sex Acts, Sexual Exploitation of Minors, and Obscenity; Part H—Offenses Involving Individual Rights; Part J—Offenses Involving the Administration of Justice; Part K—Offenses Involving Public Safety; Part L—Offenses Involving Immigration, Naturalization, and Passports; Part M—Offenses Involving National Defense and Weapons of Mass Destruction; Part N—Offenses Involving Food, Drugs, Agricultural Products, Consumer Products, and Odometer Laws; Part P—Offenses Involving Prisons and Correctional Facilities; Part Q—Offenses Involving the Environment; Part R—Antitrust Offenses; Part S—Money Laundering and Monetary Transaction Reporting; Part T—Offenses Involving Taxation; and Part X—Other Offenses.[2]

For each part, categories of offenses are listed. For example, Part A covers offenses against the person. Categories of offenses against the person include "homicide," "assault," "kidnapping, abduction, or unlawful restraint," and "air piracy and offenses against mass transportation systems." Individual offenses are listed under the major categories. Section I of Part A, "Homicide," includes the following offenses with the corresponding guideline in parentheses: first degree murder (USSG §2A1.1), second degree murder (USSG §2A1.2), voluntary manslaughter (USSG §2A1.3), involuntary manslaughter (USSG §2A1.4), and conspiracy or solicitation to commit murder (USSG §2A1.5). Part X offenses include conspiracies, attempts and solicitations, aiding and abetting, accessory after the fact, and Class A Misdemeanors.

Figure 5.5 shows the breakdown of primary offense types of 75,836 federal offenses sentenced in fiscal year 2014. Drug offenses accounted for the largest percentage (31.7%), followed by immigration offenses (29.3%), with firearms a distant third (10.5%) (United States Sentencing Commission (n.d.).

Step two describes how to **determine the base offense level. For each Chapter 2 guideline, the numerical base offense level on the federal sentencing grid is specified.** In addition, for each guideline, the following may be indicated: (1) any specific offense characteristics which are factors that may provide increases or decreases to the base offense level, (2) cross references, which may direct the court to apply another guideline section if a particular factor is present in the defendant's conduct in the instant offense of conviction, and (3) special instructions guiding the court on the application of a particular guideline (United States Sentencing Commission. *Introduction to the Federal Sentencing Guidelines*, "Part 3—Basic Guideline Structure and Initial Application Decisions" [Video]).

The base offense level for USSG §2A1.1, which corresponds to first degree murder, is 43. This is the highest level, which indicates the longest sentence, a life sentence. The base offense level for USSG §2A1.2, second degree murder, is 38. It carries a sentence of anywhere from 235 months to life, depending on criminal history. The base offense level for USSG §2A1.3, voluntary manslaughter, is 29. It carries a sentence of 87 months to

Figure 5.5 Pie Chart of Federal Offenses, FY 2014

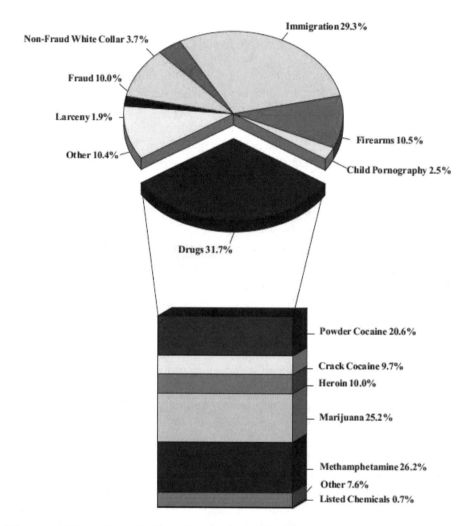

OFFENDERS IN EACH PRIMARY OFFENSE CATEGORY[1]
Fiscal Year 2014

[1] The Drug category includes the following offense types: trafficking, use of a communication facility, and simple possession. The Non-Fraud White Collar category includes the following offense types: embezzlement, forgery/counterfeiting, bribery, money laundering, and tax. Descriptions of variables used in this figure are provided in Appendix A.

SOURCE: U.S. Sentencing Commission, 2014 Datafile, USSCFY14

Source: United States Sentencing Commission. (n.d). *Interactive sourcebook of federal sentencing statistics.* Table A. Retrieved from http://www.ussc.gov/sites/default/files/pdf/research-and-publications /annual-reports-and-sourcebooks/2014/FigureA.pdf

188 months, depending on criminal history. USSG §2A1.4, which applies to involuntary manslaughter, indicates some contingencies when assigning the base offense level, based on the nature of the offense. It assigns a 12 if the offense involved criminal negligence, but this is raised to 18 "if the offense involved reckless conduct" and 22 "if the offense involved the reckless operation of a means of transportation" (United States Sentencing Commission, 2015, November 1, p. 49). USSG §2A1.5, conspiracy to commit murder, indicates a base level of 33, but can be increased by 4 levels, "if the offense involved the offer or the receipt of anything of pecuniary value for undertaking the murder" (United States Sentencing Commission, 2015, November 1, p. 50).[3]

Step three directs the application of **adjustments related to the victim, role, and obstruction of justice**, which appear in Parts A, B, and C respectively, of Chapter 3. An increase in the base offense level is indicated for certain **victim characteristics** (specified in Part A). These include if the offense was a hate crime, if the victim was considered vulnerable (with respect to age, or physical or mental condition), if the victim was a current or former government employee, if the victim was restrained during the course of the offense, if the felony offense involved terrorism, or if the defendant was convicted of a serious human rights offense.

Part B specifies adjustments to the base offense level based on the **defendant's role in the offense**. It indicates increases if the defendant played an aggravating role (for example, an organizer or leader), if the defendant abused public or private trust or used special skill in trying to conceal the offense, if the defendant used a minor to commit the crime, or if the defendant used body armor in drug trafficking crimes or crimes of violence. Decreases are indicated if the defendant played a minor role in the offense.

Part C of Chapter 3 details instances involving **obstruction of justice** that would augment the base offense level. These include if the defendant obstructed or attempted to obstruct the administration of justice in the stages of investigation, prosecution, and/or sentencing of the conviction offense, if he or she created a substantial risk of death or serious bodily injury while fleeing from law enforcement, or if the defendant committed the offense while on release.

Step four indicates the process for **determining a single offense level for a crime that involves multiple counts of conviction**. Steps 1 through 3 are to be repeated for each count to determine the sentence. The most serious offense is used as the starting point in the calculations and additional counts determine the amount by which the offense level is to be increased.

There is some discretion as to whether multiple-count indictments will result in raising the guideline range. The *Guidelines Manual* (United States Sentencing Commission, 2015, November 1), describes this issue:

> Some offenses that may be charged in multiple-count indictments are so closely intertwined with other offenses that conviction for them ordinarily would not warrant increasing the guideline range. For example, embezzling money from a bank and falsifying the related records, although legally distinct offenses, represent essentially the same type of wrongful conduct with the same ultimate harm, so that it would be more appropriate to treat them as a single offense for purposes of sentencing. Other offenses, such as an assault causing bodily

injury to a teller during a bank robbery, are so closely related to the more serious offense that it would be appropriate to treat them as part of the more serious offense, leaving the sentence enhancement to result from application of a
specific offense characteristic. (p. 362)

Generally,

> Convictions on multiple counts do not result in a sentence enhancement unless
> they represent additional conduct that is not otherwise accounted for by the
> guidelines. In essence, counts that are grouped together are treated as consti-
> tuting a single offense for purposes of the guidelines. (United States Sentenc-
> ing Commission (2015, November 1, p. 362)

The commission notes that guidelines for certain offenses, like theft, fraud, and drug
offenses, have provisions that address repetitive or ongoing behavior. In contrast, guidelines for offenses like assault and robbery focus on single episodes of criminal behavior.

Step 5 addresses **adjustments that can be made if the defendant accepts responsibility.** Part E of Chapter 3 describes acceptance of responsibility as actions by the defendant that helped authorities in the investigation or prosecution of his or her misconduct
by notifying them in a timely way of the intent to plead guilty. The plea spares the government and court efforts of preparing for trial. Acceptance of responsibility decreases
offense level by 2 points if the offense level is less than 16 and 1 point if it is 16 or higher.
In addition to admitting to the conduct which comprises the conviction offense, acceptance of responsibility may also involve other actions by the defendant, including but
not limited to the following: voluntarily terminating criminal conduct or associations,
voluntary payment of restitution before adjudication, promptly surrendering to authorities after the commission of the offense, and involvement in rehabilitation efforts after
the offense was committed.

Step 6 involves the **determination of the offender's criminal history** and is covered
in "Chapter 4—Criminal History and Criminal Livelihood." The commission states
that past criminality is relevant to sentencing for several reasons. First, it increases the
defendant's culpability, thus making the repeat offender deserving of a more severe punishment, compared to a first-time offender. Second, the commission emphasizes the
general deterrent effect of punishing repeat offenders more severely than first-time
offenders. Third, the commission addresses the importance of incapacitation in discussing the need to protect the public from further criminal victimization by repeat
criminals.

Figure 5.6 shows how points are added to calculate the criminal history category. The
highest number of points (three) is assigned for each prior sentence of imprisonment
of more than one year and one month. If the sentence was imposed more than fifteen
years before the commission of the current offense, it is not counted, unless the defendant's incarceration continued into the fifteen-year period. A sentence imposed for an
offense committed by the offender before his or her eighteenth birthday is counted if
the offense was considered an adult conviction (as opposed to a juvenile adjudication).
Two points are added for any other prior sentence of imprisonment of at least 60 days,

Figure 5.6 Calculation of Criminal History for Federal Offenders

§4A1.1. **Criminal History Category**

The total points from subsections (a) through (e) determine the criminal history category in the Sentencing Table in Chapter Five, Part A.

(a) Add **3** points for each prior sentence of imprisonment exceeding one year and one month.

(b) Add **2** points for each prior sentence of imprisonment of at least sixty days not counted in (a).

(c) Add **1** point for each prior sentence not counted in (a) or (b), up to a total of **4** points for this subsection.

(d) Add **2** points if the defendant committed the instant offense while under any criminal justice sentence, including probation, parole, supervised release, imprisonment, work release, or escape status.

(e) Add **1** point for each prior sentence resulting from a conviction of a crime of violence that did not receive any points under (a), (b), or (c) above because such sentence was treated as a single sentence, up to a total of **3** points for this subsection.

Source: United States Sentencing Commission. (2015). *United States Sentencing Commission Guidelines Manual.* p. 377, Criminal History Category. Retrieved from http://www.ussc.gov/sites/default/files/pdf/guidelines-manual/2015/GLMFull.pdf

unless that offense occurred more than ten years before the current conviction (or more than five years for those who committed the offense prior to age 18). One point is added to all other offenses, committed within ten years of prior sentence imposition (or five years for those who committed the offense prior to age 18) not to exceed four points.

More detailed instructions concerning other circumstances of criminal history (including the counting of non-felony offenses and foreign convictions) are detailed in Chapter 4 of the *Guidelines Manual.* Like many states' systems, two points are added if the offense was committed while the defendant was serving another sentence (probation, parole, imprisonment, etc.). The cumulative criminal history points are divided up into six criminal history categories, which appear in **Figure 5.1**—I (0–1 points), II (2 or 3 points), III (4, 5, or 6 points), IV (7, 8, or 9 points), V (10, 11, or 12 points), or VI (13 or more points).

Chapter 4 also contains directives in sentencing career offenders and in instances in which criminals are shown to have made their criminal activity a "livelihood." The criminal history is considered Level VI for all offenders designated as career criminals. The offense level is determined by a table based on the statutory maximum. This table for career criminals indicates higher offense levels and therefore harsher sentences, compared to offenders not deemed "career criminals." An offender deemed an "armed career criminal" is a career criminal who used or possessed a firearm or ammunition in connection with a crime of violence or controlled substance. Such offenders are given an enhanced offense level. Those deemed "repeat and dangerous sex offender[s] against minors" are also subject to enhanced offense levels. An offense level no less than 13 is given to offenders who committed an offense "as a part of a pattern of criminal conduct engaged in as a livelihood."

Step seven determines the **guideline range**. The Sentencing Table, portrayed in **Figure 5.1**, shows a range of months of imprisonment for each numerical intersection of Offense Level (1–43) and Criminal History Category (I–VI).

Step eight involves the **determination of the sentencing type**. Grid placements in Zone A of the Sentencing Table qualify for a sentence of up to six months, a fine, or probation. Placements in Zone B may be sentenced to three possibilities. They may receive probation but must be sentenced also to a condition that substitutes intermittent confinement, community confinement, or home detention for imprisonment. Or these offenders may be sentenced to at least one month of imprisonment *plus* supervised release with a condition that substitutes community confinement or home detention for imprisonment. Otherwise Zone B offenders get a straight imprisonment sentence. Probation terms range from one to five years for offense levels of 6 or higher and less than three years for other cases. In Zone C, the sentence may be served in prison, or by a term of imprisonment that has a term of community confinement or home detention, as long as one-half of the minimum term is served in prison. Zone D requires imprisonment.

A term of supervised release generally follows a sentence of imprisonment of more than one year or when required by statute. The length of supervised release is related to the offense classification. Sex offenders and other offenders who are considered at risk for injuring others can be put on supervised release for life. Restitution is indicated in cases with an identifiable victim. Fine levels are displayed in a fine table and determined by offense level. Forfeitures are imposed based on relevant statutes.

Statutorily authorized minimums and maximums supersede applicable guidelines ranges. According to Judge Hinojosa and Judge Dorhoffer (2015, September 16), in accordance with the Guidelines section 5G1.1, the statutes "trump" the guidelines. They stated, "[r]egardless of what sentence the guidelines may call for, the sentence imposed must fall within the restrictions set by statute (e.g., statutory maximums and mandatory minimums)." The commission (United States Sentencing Commission, 2015, November 1) provides some concrete examples as follows:

> For example, if the applicable guidelines range is 51–63 months and the maximum sentence authorized by statute for the offense of conviction is 48 months, the sentence required by the guidelines under subsection (a) is 48 months; a sentence of less than 48 months would be a guideline departure. If the applicable guideline range is 41–51 months and there is a statutorily required minimum sentence of 60 months, the sentence required by the guidelines under subsection (b) is 60 months; a sentence of more than 60 months would be a guideline departure. If the applicable guideline range is 51–63 months and the maximum sentence authorized by statute for the offense of conviction is 60

months, the guideline range is restricted to 51–60 months under subsection
(c). (p. 444)

The importance of understanding any discrepancies between guidelines ranges and
statutes has been key in Supreme Court cases, such as the *United States v. Booker* (543 U.S.
220 (2005)) decision that we will present in Chapter 7.

After these steps are followed, the court is then to consider specific offender characteristics before the imposition of the sentence. Part H describes which offender characteristics can or cannot influence the sentencing decision.

The commission reaffirms the directive of the Sentencing Reform Act of 1984—"that
the guidelines and relevant policy statements are 'entirely neutral' regarding five characteristics—race, sex, national origin, creed, and socioeconomic status" (United States
Sentencing Commission, 2015, November 1, p. 453). The commission also addresses the
relevance of eleven specific offender characteristics on the sentence, including (1) age;
(2) educational and vocational skills; (3) mental and emotional conditions; (4) physical conditions, including drug or alcohol dependence or abuse or a gambling addiction;
(5) employment record; (6) family ties and responsibilities; (7) role in the offense; (8)
criminal history; (9) dependence upon criminal activity for a livelihood; (10) military,
civic, charitable, or public service; employment-related contributions; record of prior
good works; and (11) lack of guidance as a youth and similar circumstances (United
States Sentencing Commission, 2015, November 1, pp. 453–458). Five of those characteristics (education, vocational skills, employment record, family ties and responsibilities, and community ties) are deemed by the act to be generally inappropriate to the
decision of whether and/or how long to incarcerate an individual.

The commission emphasizes the goal of reducing unwarranted sentencing disparities in the discussion of specific offender characteristics and states (United States Sentencing Commission, 2015, November 1) the following:

> Generally, the most appropriate use of specific offender characteristics is to
> consider them not as a reason for a sentence outside the applicable guideline
> range but for other reasons, such as in determining the sentence within the
> applicable guideline range, the type of sentence (e.g., probation or impris-
> onment) within the sentencing options available for the applicable zone on
> the Sentencing Table, and various other aspects of an appropriate sentence.
> (p. 453)

The commission cites the Supreme Court case *Gall v. United States* (552 U.S. 38, 49
(2007))—that reiterated that the guideline range, based on two factors—defendant's
criminal conduct and his or her criminal history—should serve as "the appropriate starting point and the initial benchmark" in determining the sentence. The commission, does, however, note that like other provisions in the lengthy manual, those
dealing with how appropriate it is to consider specific offender characteristics is "evolutionary" in nature. Modifications and revisions are expected in response to the
practice of carrying out the federal guidelines and from research findings concerning
the guidelines.

Sentencing Departures

The last section of Chapter 5 is Part K—Departures.

Sentencing departures from the federal guidelines are permitted by statute only when the court finds "an aggravating or mitigating circumstance of a kind, or to a degree, not adequately taken into consideration by the sentencing commission in formulating the guidelines that should result in a sentence different from that described" (18 U.S.C. §3553(b)).

According to the commission, (United States Sentencing Commission, 2015, November 1)

> The Commission intends the sentencing courts to treat each guideline as carving out a "heartland," a set of typical cases embodying the conduct that each guideline describes. When a court finds an atypical case, one to which a particular guideline linguistically applies but where conduct significantly differs from the norm, the court may consider whether a departure is warranted. (p. 6)

The commission identifies two reasons for its policy regarding departures. They acknowledge that one set of guidelines could not practically anticipate every possible scenario or combination of factors that would merit a sentencing departure. As stated earlier, the federal guidelines are considered evolutionary—they were written and may be periodically revised by the United States Sentencing Commission. As a permanent body, the USSC collects and analyses sentencing data, including departure data. These data help the commission monitor court practices, such as guidelines departures. The USSC studies the reasons for departures and reflects as to whether the departures were warranted. Subsequent adjustments to the guidelines are made over time that may incorporate scenarios that hadn't been anticipated earlier.

The other issue relevant to sentencing departures concerns the expectation on the part of the commission that despite the courts' ability to depart from the guidelines, that they will not do so often. This is because the data from the sentencing practices of the federal courts before the guidelines were enacted showed which factors had been most important in sentencing decisions. These relevant case characteristics were figured into the development of the federal guidelines for the myriad of federal offenses for which the commission formed guidelines. If a factor in a subsequent case was deemed important but did not appear in the federal guidelines because it hadn't been anticipated, such an unusual scenario would be considered an acceptable basis for departure.

Part K—Departures details two categories of departures—"**substantial assistance to authorities**" (USSG §5K1.1) and "**other grounds for departure**" (USSG §5K2.0). The policy statement for substantial assistance to authorities states (United States Sentencing Commission, 2015, November 1):

> Upon motion of the government stating that the defendant has provided substantial assistance in the investigation or prosecution of another person who has committed an offense, the court may depart from the guidelines.

(a) The appropriate reduction shall be determined by the court for reasons stated that may include, but are not limited to, the consideration of the following:

    (1) the court's evaluation of the significance and usefulness of the defendant's assistance, taking into consideration the government's evaluation of the assistance rendered;

    (2) the truthfulness, completeness, and reliability of any information or testimony provided by the defendant;

    (3) the nature and extent of the defendant's assistance

    (4) any injury suffered, or any danger or risk of injury to the defendant or his family resulting from his assistance;

    (5) the timeliness of the defendant's assistance. (p. 461)

Substantial assistance by the defendant can yield a sentence lower than that of a statutorily required minimum sentence. The judge can exercise some discretion and the commission indicates that the latitude given to the sentencing judge is based on the above listed factors. The judge must state reasons for any sentence reduction. This reduction is separate from the consideration of reduction based on acceptance of responsibility. The refusal to assist, however, cannot be considered an aggravating factor (USSG §5K1.2).

The policy statement for **other grounds for departure** (United States Sentencing Commission, 2015, November 1, p. 451) delineates two other types of departures, limitations on departures, and prohibited departures. Upward departures in general and downward departures in criminal cases other than child crimes and sexual offenses comprise one type of departure. The second involves downward departures in child crimes and sexual offenses. For both, circumstances "of a kind, or to a degree, not adequately taken into consideration by the sentencing commission in formulating the guidelines" and that, in order to be consistent with the objectives set forth in the United States code should result in a sentence different from that which the guidelines dictate.

Twenty-four circumstances are identified.[4,5] Some factors which could lead to upward departures involve the **nature of the harm to the victim** and include death, physical injury, extreme psychological injury, abduction or unlawful restraint, and property damage or loss. Other circumstances that could lead to an upward departure involve **criminal purpose** and include if the defendant committed the offense in order to facilitate or conceal the commission of another offense, if semiautomatic firearms capable of accepting large capacity magazines were used, and if it involved violent street gangs. The **victim's conduct** may serve as a reason for a downward departure if it is decided that the victim provoked the offense behavior in some way. Other **mitigating factors involving the defendant** include coercion and duress and diminished capacity.

Departures based on race, sex, national origin, creed, religion, and socio-economic status are prohibited. Some other characteristics, such as the defendant's acceptance of responsibility and their aggravating or mitigating role in the offense, are prohibited as a reason for departure, since these circumstances are factored in under "Chapter 3 — Adjustments." Written reasons for the above described departures are required.

Sentencing Variances

At the beginning of this chapter, we showed the three steps to be taken in the sentencing process since the *Booker* decision. Although the courts are not required to apply the guidelines in sentencing offenders, they are to take them into account in sentencing. *Gall v. United States*, 552 U.S. 38, 49 (2007), specified that the federal sentencing guidelines should be "the starting point and initial benchmark."

After this first step results in calculating a sentencing guidelines range, the district court is to consult the *Guidelines Manual* to determine whether the case warrants a departure as step two. According to the USSC (2012, March) and as detailed in *Irizarry v. United States*, 553 U.S. 708, 714 (2008), "'departure' is a term of art under the Guidelines and refers only to non-Guidelines sentences imposed under the framework set out in the Guidelines" (p. 36).

The third step requires the sentencing court to examine the factors contained in 18 U.S.C. § 3553(a). **Only after departures (as detailed above) have been considered is a *variance* possible**. According to the USSC (2012, March),

> A "variance"—"a sentence outside the guideline range other than as provided for in the *Guidelines Manual*—is considered only after departures have been considered. Courts have held that variances are not subject to the guideline analysis for departures—in some cases, a circumstance prohibited for departure may be considered as a basis for a variance." See, e.g., *United States v. Chase*, 560 F.3d 828 (8th Cir. 2009) (holding that "departure precedent does not bind district courts with respect to variance decisions, it is merely persuasive authority"). Variances are also not subject to the notice requirements applicable to departures (see discussion above). A court may grant a departure and a variance in the same sentence (e.g., a departure for substantial assistance and a variance for the defendant's history and characteristics). (p. 36)

The USSC (2012, March) produced the report, *Selected Departure and Variance Decisions*. One can access this report from the USSC website and read about cases in which the sentencing court "varied from the applicable guideline range based on § 3553(a) factors." One source for variance, for example, is Section 3553(a)(1): "The nature and circumstances of the offense and the history and characteristics of the defendant." This can include situations that involve defendant's criminal history, characteristics of the defendant, defendant's health problems, family circumstances, or the nature of the offense. Another example involves Section 3553(a)(2):

> The need for the sentence imposed to reflect the seriousness of the offense, to promote respect for the law, and to provide just punishment for the offense; to afford adequate deterrence to criminal conduct; to protect the public from further crimes of the defendant; and to provide the defendant with needed educational or vocational training, medical care, or other correctional treatment in the most effective manner. Variances may reflect the need to protect the public from further crimes, the need to provide just punishment for the offense, and the need to reflect the seriousness of the offense.

Chapter 6 covers "Sentencing Procedures, Plea Agreements, and Crime Victims' Rights." A United States Probation Officer (USPO) is in charge of conducting a presentence investigation (PSI) and submitting a presentence report (PSR) to the court before the sentence is handed down. The defendant, the defendant's attorney, and an attorney for the government are given the report no less than 35 days before sentencing. They must state in writing any objections they have with the report within 14 days. The burden of proof rests with the party seeking an adjustment. Objections may involve "material information, sentencing guideline ranges, and policy statements contained in or omitted from the report" (United States Sentencing Commission, 2015, November 1, p. 480). The USPO may be able to resolve disputes and submit an amended PSR to the parties and the judge. If he or she cannot resolve the dispute, the court then hears from each side and makes a decision about the issue(s) in question.

The commission (United States Sentencing Commission, 2015) emphasizes that plea agreements ideally "(1) promote the statutory purposes of sentencing prescribed in 18 U.S.C § 3553(a); and (2) do not perpetuate unwarranted sentencing disparity" (p. 483). Both the prosecution and defense must disclose the plea agreement in court. The court is expected to impose a sentence that is within the applicable guidelines range. Otherwise, the court needs to explicitly describe justifications for not sentencing within the applicable range.

Violations of Probation and Supervised Release

Chapter 7 describes policy statements regarding "Violations of Probation and Supervised Release." The commission chose to issue policy statements regarding these areas, as opposed to guidelines. This is consistent with an "evolutionary" approach, which would allow criminal justice actors (federal judges, probation officers, etc.) to react to and inform policy about the real workings of probation and supervised release.

The commission notes that judges may no longer suspend prison sentences and impose probation, as they had been able to before the guidelines went into effect November 1, 1987. This is because the Sentencing Reform Act identified probation as a distinct criminal sanction for those crimes that lie in Zone A of the Sentencing Table. Supervised release represents an "add-on" to the sentence, after the prison term has been served.

Revocations of either probation or supervised release may occur if the offender commits a new crimes or violates conditions of supervision. If the offender commits a new crime that is serious, the court will revoke probation or supervised release and the offender will be imprisoned for a term according to criminal history category when the defendant was originally sentenced.

How Much Do Judges Adhere to the Federal Sentencing Guidelines?

Table 5.1 shows the position of sentences in relation to the guidelines range for 74,126 cases in fiscal year 2014. It shows that 46.0 percent of the sentences are *within the guideline range*. Only 2.2 percent of sentences handed down are *above the guideline range*.

Table 5.1 Federal Sentences Imposed Relative to Guideline Range, FY 2014

NATIONAL COMPARISON OF SENTENCE IMPOSED AND POSITION RELATIVE TO THE GUIDLINE RANGE[1] Fiscal Year 2014		
	N	%
TOTAL CASES	74,126	100.0
CASES SENTENCED WITHIN GUIDELINE RANGE	34,117	46.0
CASES SENTENCED ABOVE GUIDELINE RANGE	1,645	2.2
DEPARTURE ABOVE GUIDELINE RANGE	466	0.6
Upward Departure from Guideline Range[2]	343	0.5
Upward Departure with *Booker* /18 U.S.C § 3553[3]	123	0.2
OTHERWISE ABOVE GUIDELINE RANGE	1,179	1.6
Above Guideline Range with *Booker* /18 U.S.C. § 3553[4]	1,104	1.5
All Remaining Cases above Guideline Range[5]	75	0.1
GOVERNMENT SPONSORED BELOW RANGE[6]	22,494	30.3
§5K1.1 Substantial Assistance Departure	9,482	12.8
§5K3.1 Early Disposition Program Departure	6,944	9.4
Other Government Sponsored below Range	6,068	8.2
NON-GOVERNMENT SPONSORED BELOW RANGE	15,870	21.4
DEPARTURE BELOW GUIDELINE RANGE	2,564	3.5
Downward Departure from Guideline Range[2]	1,757	2.4
Downward Departure with *Booker* /18 U.S.C. § 3553[3]	807	1.1
OTHERWISE BELOW GUIDELINE RANGE	13,306	18.0
Below Guideline Range with *Booker* /18 U.S.C. § 3553[4]	12,894	17.4
All Remaining Cases below Guideline Range[5]	412	0.6

[1] This table reflects the 75,836 cases sentenced in Fiscal Year 2014. Of these, 1,710 cases were excluded because information was missing from the submitted documents that prevented the comparison of the sentence and the guideline range. Descriptions of variables used in this table are provided in Appendix A.

[2] All cases with departures in which the court did not indicate as a reason either United States v. Booker, 18 U.S.C. § 3553, or a factor or reason specifically prohibited in the provisions, policy statements, or commentary of the Guideline Manual.

[3] All cases sentenced outside of the guideline range in which the court indicated both a departure (see footnote 2) and a reference to either United States v. Booker, 18 U.S.C. § 3553, or related factors as a reason for sentencing outside of the guideline system.

[4] All cases sentenced outside of the guideline range in which no departure was indicated and in which the court cited United States v. Booker, 18 U.S.C. § 3553, or related factors as one of the reasons for sentencing outside of the guideline system.

[5] All cases sentenced outside of the guideline range that could not be classified into any of the three previous outside of the range categories. This category includes cases in which no reason was provided for a sentence outside of the guideline range.

[6] Cases in which a reason for the sentence indicated that the prosecution initiated, proposed, or stipulated to a sentence outside of the guideline range, either pursuant to a plea agreement or as part of a non-plea negotiation with the defendant.

Source: U.S. Sentencing Commission, 2014 Datafile, USSCFY14.

Source: United States Sentencing Commission. (n.d.). *Interactive Sourcebook of Federal Sentencing Statistics.* Table N. Retrieved from http://www.ussc.gov/sites/default/files/pdf/research-and-publications/annual-reports-and-sourcebooks/2014/FigureA.pdf

Approximately 52 percent of cases were sentenced *below the guidelines range*. A little over 30 percent of cases were government sponsored below range. These include cases involving the government making a 5K1.1 motion which is then granted by the court. This is a "substantial assistance" motion. The second category of government sponsored departures below range may result from either an early disposition program (which often involve immigration cases and are common in the Texas and New Mexico borders) covered by §5K3.1. The category "Other below" includes some USSG §5K2 departures which we detailed above. About 21.4 percent of below range sentences were non-government sponsored below range. These include sentencing when the judge goes outside the *Guidelines Manual*. This is referred to as a "variance," which is consistent with 18 USCS §3553(a).

The Reputation of Federal Sentencing Guidelines

In his book *Sentencing Matters*, Tonry (1996) asserted, "The U.S. commission's guidelines are easily the most disliked sentencing reform initiative in the United States in this century" (p. 25). Tonry critically reflected on the crafting of the federal guidelines and noted,

> Because the federal commission had the prior experiences of the states to draw on, ample resources, and the capacity to recruit staff from throughout the country, all of the auguries would have predicted that the U.S. Sentencing Commission would build on the state experiences and produce the most successful guidelines system to date. The commission managed to defy that prediction. (p. 11)

At a law review symposium in 1993, representatives from twelve state sentencing commissions met to discuss the establishment of state guidelines. A common sentiment at the meeting was that their states had tried to distance themselves from any association with the Federal Sentencing Guidelines. When beginning work on their state's sentencing reforms, commissions in several states opposed using the federal guidelines as a design for their own sentencing policies (Orland & Reitz, 1993). North Carolina even opted for the phrase "structured sentencing," as opposed to "sentencing guidelines."

Not everyone is pessimistic about the federal system's guidelines, however. At the 2015 Annual Seminar on the Federal Sentencing Guidelines in New Orleans, Louisiana, Judge Hinojosa, emphasized how the guidelines maximize transparency and due process. He discussed a case in which he was questioning a defense attorney, during which a young man raised his hand. This young man turned out to be the defendant's 19-year-old son. Judge Hinojosa said that the young man answered his question much better than the defense attorney and did a great job for his dad. Judge Hinojosa noted that the defendant's son was able to clarify this point through an open discussion. Judge Hinojosa pointed to the fact that the guidelines have actually brought this transparency and due process into the system.

Judge Hinojosa stated,

> I hope that we never return to the system that we had before the guidelines. There's always room for improvement with regards to the guidelines, or any system. But the idea of going back to total discretion and less transparency and less due process, and less clarity as to what the factors are that the courts consider, to me would be a serious mistake. And so, therefore, I think the guidelines system is a good one. I think it's important. (Hinojosa, 2015, September 16)

Have the Goals of Federal Sentencing Reform Been Realized?

Increasing sentencing uniformity through the Federal Sentencing Guidelines has been a stated goal of the USSC since its inception. The achievement of this goal would mean that factors other than those deemed legally relevant would not affect sentencing. Sentencing studies have examined the effects of a variety of extra-legal variables, including characteristics of the offender and judge, as well as how characteristics of the judicial district and circuit may impact sentencing practices. We will examine relevant studies concerning sentencing practices of states and the federal system in Chapter 9.

Within each grid cell, a sentencing range is indicated. Despite this structuring of sentences in the federal guidelines, there still remains room for some judicial and prosecutorial discretion to serve as avenues to disparate and/or discriminatory sentencing practices.

Lingering Avenues to Sentencing Disparity

Post-guidelines sentencing disparities in the federal system could potentially result from several different situations. The first involves the possibility that sentencing disparities may be manifested as differences in the sentence length within the assigned range the grid cell into which one falls. For example, the possible sentence for an individual convicted of an offense with a base offense level of 25 with a criminal history level of II ranges from 63 to 78 months. The judge has discretion as to where within the range he or she can impose the sentence. One could argue that if, for example, the vast majority of African American offenders are sentenced in the upper end of the range, while most white offenders are sentenced in the lower end of the range, sentencing discrimination is still occurring.

A second way that disparity and/or discrimination may persist involves sentencing departures and variances. Whether the same characteristic is deemed a departure (or variance) may vary by case. Although USSG §5K1.1 delineates what is meant by "substantial assistance," federal prosecutors may vary in their interpretation and this difference may constitute an avenue to disparity. If the extent to which defendants assist in the apprehension of another offender is similar, but some are deemed to have provided "substantial assistance" and others are not, then this factor would lower the sentences of the former, but not the latter offenders. In addition, the USSC has noted in its March 2012 report, *Selected Departure and Variance Decisions* that a single factor may not be grounds for a departure, but it could be grounds for a variance. In this report, the commission presented overviews of cases with some seemingly contradictory decisions involving the acceptability of various case and offender characteristics in the sentencing process.

The discretion afforded to the prosecutor in charging decisions is a third way in which sentencing disparities can ensue. As detailed above, the first step in the sentencing process is to determine the offense level of the offense of conviction. If the prosecutor exercises discretion to charge an individual with a crime that carries a lower offense level, this will automatically "give the offender a break." If the prosecution's charging decisions are linked with legally irrelevant characteristics, disparity and discrimination would still be occurring within the federal system.

Current Issues of Interest to the United States Sentencing Commission

As discussed earlier in the chapter, the Federal Sentencing Guidelines were crafted to be evolutionary in the sense that the commission continually studies the guidelines, collects and analyzes data on sentencing practices and their consequences, and suggests revisions to Congress. The commission sends recommendations to Congress on May 1 of each year. Unless there is disagreement with the proposed amendments and revisions, these changes go into effect on November 1 of that year.

The USSC recently identified several issues on which it is currently focusing. At the 2015 Annual Seminar on the Federal Sentencing Guidelines in New Orleans, Louisiana, the Honorable Rachel Barkow, commissioner, identified several current areas that the commission will focus on in the next year (2015, September 17). One involves the issue of statutory and guideline recidivist provisions. The USSC is proposing new amendments to the guidelines that integrate the commission's ongoing study of recidivists.

A second focus involves the continued study of immigration guidelines. In April 2015, the commission finished a study and released a report from FY 2013. At the 2015 annual meeting, Commissioner Barkow noted several findings of the report. On average, illegal reentry offenders had been deported more than three times before their most recent illegal reentry offense. Nearly 40 percent of illegal reentry offenders had been deported and previously convicted and sentenced for prior illegal entry or reentry convictions. Over 90 percent of illegal reentry offenders had at least one prior conviction for a non-traffic offense. On average offenders had been convicted more than four times prior to the reentry offense. Fewer than 5 percent of illegal reentry offenders had no prior convictions. The USSC will look at immigration guidelines and whether related criminal history rules should be reviewed. This is a perfect example of how research informs policy recommendations from the USSC.

A third area of interest identified by Commissioner Barkow was mandatory minimums, including those for drug trafficking offenders. Issues include the use of safety valves (which we will discuss in the next chapter) and as well as the Fair Sentencing Act (which we discuss in this chapter) and retroactivity. The USSC's recommendations on these issues are informed in part by the commission's recidivism study, which found that offenders released early did not reoffend any more than those who served their entire sentence.

The Federal Response to Drug Offenses

A consideration of federal drug laws through the years is a crucial part of a comprehensive examination of federal sentencing reform. The way that federal laws have disparately punished powder cocaine offenders, as compared to crack cocaine offenders, has come under much scrutiny. It is important to reflect on the actions of Congress and several presidents and understand the history of federal sentencing in the context of "the war on drugs."

Chapter 6 focuses on mandatory minimum sentencing and strikes laws. It describes more comprehensively the history and goals of various federal and state mandatory minimum laws. A consideration of the Federal Sentencing Guidelines in the present chapter, however, would be incomplete if it excluded a discussion of more recent federal sentencing policy for drug offenses, how the laws intersect with the federal sentencing guidelines, and the USSC's response to such policies. The end of this chapter also highlights the 2010 Fair Sentencing Act, signed into law by President Obama.

Spotlight — Basketball Star Len Bias Dies of a Cocaine Overdose

The shocking death of Len Bias from a cocaine overdose made national headlines in 1986. Bias was a 22-year-old African American star basketball player at the University of Maryland and on his way to the NBA. Shortly before his death, Bias had been drafted by the Boston Celtics, an accomplishment that made him proclaim that his dream had been realized. He had also agreed to a money-spinning endorsement with Reebok. Len Bias was predicted by many to be an outstanding star in the NBA.

On the night of June 18, 1986, Bias returned to the University of Maryland from a trip to Boston which involved media interviews about his future with the Celtics. He spent the night with his friends. Early in the morning of June 19, he began having seizures on the floor of his suite in Washington Hall and became unconscious. A friend called 911 and told the operator, "This is Len Bias. You have to get him back to life. There's no way he can die." Bias was rushed to Leland Hospital in Riverdale, Maryland, by paramedics. After doctors spent two hours trying to revive him, at 8:51 am June 19, 1986 Leonard Bias was pronounced dead. When informed about Bias's death, Larry Bird, a legendary player on the Celtics team, said the news was "one of the cruelest things I've even heard."

The cause of Bias's death was diagnosed by autopsy to be "cocaine intoxication." According to the autopsy report the cocaine had "interrupted the normal electrical control of his heartbeat, resulting in the sudden onset of cardiac arrest." A healthy young student athlete with a promising career lost his life to cocaine.

ESPN writer Michael Weinreb asserted in his article, "The Day Innocence Died," that "Len Bias's death can be classified as the most socially influential moment in the history of modern sports." Some would argue that if this tragedy happened today, the public might be less surprised and automatically assume that the cause of death was drugs, as today there is more public awareness of cocaine abuse and people are a little more jaded.

When the news of Bias's death came out the morning of June 19, 1986, utter shock was the reaction by the University of Maryland community, local and national media, and the general public. Later in the day, sources were informing the media that traces of cocaine were found in Bias's system and by the evening that information was being broadcast. The mere thought that a healthy young man in the prime of life could die from cocaine was shocking and terrifying to those following the story.

As time went on, sources suggested that this was not Bias's first time using cocaine. An associate of Bias claimed that Bias introduced him to cocaine. A state medical examiner asserted that Bias probably wasn't a first-time user of cocaine. Weinreb wrote, "As the news congealed, as police discovered several grams of cocaine under the seat of Bias's leased sports car, as the autopsy was issued, as it became clear cocaine was the cause of Bias's demise, as denial turned to anger, we began to widen the scope of our outrage."

Soon after Len Bias's death, media began addressing the health risks of cocaine and drugs more and drug abuse became a greater political concern. The danger of drugs was not an entirely new issue, however. President Nixon had declared drug abuse as "public enemy number one in the United States" on June 17, 1971. He created the Special Action Office for Drug Abuse Prevention. Interestingly, only during the Nixon era did the war on drugs allocate the largest amount of money on treatment, as opposed to enforcement. In 1973, the Drug Enforcement Administration (DEA) was established. In 1984, Nancy Reagan introduced the "Just Say No" campaign, which largely focused on white, middle-class youth (PBS).

By the mid-eighties, the use of crack cocaine — a potent form of cocaine that could be smoked, spread over New York City. It was cheap and addictive and used widely in inner cities. Whereas the typical image of a powder cocaine user was a young, upper-class, white person, the profile of a crack cocaine user was poor, black, and from the inner city.

Some early reports that Bias used crack cocaine have been challenged, and overwhelming evidence suggests that Bias used powder cocaine. Bias's death, however, seemed to prompt knee-jerk reactions that greatly increased penalties for crack cocaine offenses. The awareness of the country's "vulnerability" to drug offenses prompted then Democratic speaker of the House of Representatives, Thomas "Tip" O'Neil (who came from Boston and worked in the DC area mere miles from the Maryland border) and Republicans to rigorously rally for policies that would get tough on drug offenses.

The result was the passage by Congress of the **Anti-Drug Abuse Act of 1986**, which had bipartisan support. It appropriated $1.7 billion to the fight against drugs. This act, described in detail below, targeted crack cocaine offenses and established tough mandatory minimum penalties.

The cocaine overdose death of Len Bias is significant to our nation in many ways. It shocked the nation and heightened public awareness to the pervasiveness of cocaine use. In a convoluted way, it moved the focus of the drug problem to the danger and spread of crack cocaine through poor minority communities. It set the stage for aggressive law enforcement that targeted poor black neighborhoods. It also served as a catalyst for major legislation, which would affect how drug offenses would be prosecuted in the federal system and impact the federal prison population for years to come. The practical targets of this law were young African American males who used crack cocaine. The social and economic costs of mass incarceration to young black men was great, as it affected the communities from which they came for years to come.

Anti-Drug Abuse Act of 1986

In the early to mid-eighties, the number of arrests for heroin and cocaine offenses skyrocketed (Dorsey & Middleton, n.d.). The Office of Drug Abuse Policy characterized cocaine as a dangerous drug. It estimated that over four million Americans were using cocaine in 1984 and that half of the users were between the ages of 18 and 25 (United States Office of Drug Abuse Policy, 1984). The Office of Drug Abuse Policy also observed that because of lower prices, cocaine use in 1983 was apparently spreading from the affluent to poorer people.

The Anti-Drug Abuse Act of 1986 was a 193-page bill that addressed various aspects of a war on drugs. The stated purpose of the Anti-Drug Abuse Act of 1986 was:

> To strengthen Federal efforts to encourage foreign cooperation in eradicating illicit drug crops and in halting international drug traffic, to improve enforcement of Federal drug laws and enhance interdiction of illicit drug shipments, to provide strong Federal leadership in establishing effective drug abuse prevention and education programs, to expand Federal support for drug abuse treatment and rehabilitation efforts, and for other purposes.

There were fifteen titles of the act and multiple subtitles under each. **Title 1 of the Act, "Anti-Drug Enforcement,"** included twenty-one subtitles. We will discuss several of these and direct the interested reader to the original document for a detailed description of each (Pub. L. 99–570, Oct 27, 1986). **Subtitle A — Narcotics Penalties and Enforcement Act of 1986** delineated penalties for controlled substances. The most striking element of the Narcotics Penalties and Enforcement Act was to be the most infamous — the 100:1 ratio of quantity for powder-to-crack offenses that would set in motion the same mandatory prison sentences.

It mandated no less than a **ten-year prison sentence** (and up to a life sentence) for a trafficking offense ("manufacture, distribute, or dispense, or possess with intent to manufacture, distribute, or dispense") that involved *50 grams or more of crack cocaine or 5,000 grams or more of powder cocaine*. If **death or serious bodily injury** occurred as a result of the use of the substance the sentence was to be **no less than 20 years and no more than life**. Similarly, it provided for a **five-year mandatory minimum prison sentence** (and up to 40 years) for drug trafficking offenses that involved *five grams of* *crack cocaine.* The same sentence would be given to drug traffickers whose offense involved *500 grams of powder cocaine.* If **death or serious bodily injury** resulted from the use of the substance, the sentence could range from **20 years to life.** Since the law required 100 times more powder cocaine than crack cocaine to result in the same mandatory minimum penalty, the structure became known as the "100:1 drug quantity ratio." The sentences for crack cocaine offenses were on average three to eight times longer than those for an analogous quantity of powder cocaine (Stone, 2007–2008).

Concerns about sentencing disparities which involved race followed soon after the passage of the Anti-Drug Abuse Act of 1986. Users of powder cocaine were more likely to be young, white, and upper-class, while crack cocaine users were typically poor, black, and from the inner city. Even though crack weighs more than powder cocaine, the penalty structure seemed discriminatory to many. A significantly lower quantity of crack, compared to powder cocaine, triggered the same penalty. The USSC was an early critic of this policy, as were groups including the Sentencing Project and Families Against Mandatory Minimums (FAMM), which we will describe in Chapter 8. Within a decade, the commission recommended changing the discrepancy but in 1995 their proposal to do so was overridden by Congress.

Subtitle C—Juvenile Drug Trafficking Act of 1986 set enhanced penalties to drug offenses that involved juveniles. It addressed offenders who hired or otherwise induced in some way, person(s) under eighteen to be involved in drug operations or to help avoid detection or apprehension of such offenses. Penalties for drug offenses were doubled if they involved juveniles in these ways. Prison terms handed down were twice those otherwise authorized and fines were also increased up to twice compared to those that didn't involve juveniles. Drug offenders with prior convictions who involved juveniles were given up to three times the penalties. Subtitle C indicated that sentences of imprisonment were not to be suspended and that a probation sentence would not be given to drug offenders whose criminal acts that involved juveniles.

Subtitle I—the Career Criminals Amendment Act of 1986 amended the section of Title 18, the United States Code that identified offenses that would count toward the designation of an offender as a "career criminal." It expanded the predicate offenses for armed career criminal penalties to include serious drug offenders. Instead of stating "robbery or burglary, or both," the new version stated "for a violent felony or a serious drug offense, or both."

Anti-Drug Abuse Act of 1988

Congress delineated additional ways that powder cocaine and crack cocaine offenses were to be treated differently in the Anti-Drug Abuse Act of 1988. The 1988 act set a mandatory minimum penalty for simple possession of crack cocaine. Persons in **possession of five grams or more of crack cocaine** would receive a *mandatory minimum sentence of five years in prison* for first-time offenders. This contrasted the penalty for simple possession of any quantity of any other controlled substance (except flunitrazepan) for a first-time offender—a maximum of one year in prison (and considered a misdemeanor). This meant that pursuant to the 1988 act, an offender who simply possessed five grams of crack cocaine would be sentenced to a five-year mandatory minimum penalty—the same punishment that a trafficker of other drugs would receive.

Revisions to Penalties for Crack Cocaine Offenses

Some of the most significant changes in the federal guidelines have involved changes to the penalties for crack cocaine. For years, critics raised concerns about the disparities in sentencing for offenses involving powder cocaine and crack cocaine. Given the differences between sanctions that were correlated with the form of cocaine (which is associated with race), the federal drug laws were deemed racially discriminatory by legal scholars, special interest groups (like FAMM), and some members of the general public. Federal sentencing of crack cocaine offenders seemed to undermine the goals of sentencing reform, which included increasing sentencing uniformity and decreasing disparate practices based on legally irrelevant factors.

Amendments 706 and 713

In 2007, the United States Sentencing Commission reexamined the cocaine sentencing policy. They focused on both the five-year mandatory minimum prison sentence for trafficking offenses involving five grams or more of crack cocaine or 500 grams of powder cocaine, as well as the ten-year mandatory minimum prison sentence for offenses involving 50 grams of crack cocaine or 5,000 grams of powder cocaine. Many entities assisted the USSC in considering cocaine sentencing policies. The commission heard expert testimony from the executive branch, the federal judiciary, defense attorneys, state and local law enforcement officials, medical and treatment professionals, social scientists, academics, and community members in 2006 and 2007. They analyzed sentencing data concerning cocaine offenses, examined studies about the pharmacological effects of cocaine and information about cocaine dependency, and looked at various states' laws regarding cocaine. The commission felt strongly that the 100:1 drug quantity ratio undermined the purposes of the Sentencing Reform Act, which included the reduction in disparate and discriminatory sentencing practices.

The commission issued a report summarizing its findings and suggestions. The commission concluded the following (United States Sentencing Commission, 2007, May):

(1) The current quantity-based penalties overstate the relative harmfulness of crack cocaine compared to powder cocaine.

(2) The current quantity-based penalties sweep too broadly and apply most often to lower level offenders.

(3) The current quantity-based penalties overstate the seriousness of most crack cocaine offenses and fail to provide adequate proportionality.

(4) The current severity of crack cocaine penalties mostly impacts minorities. (p. 8)

The commission emphasized its belief that the 100:1 drug quantity ratio was not consistent with the goals of the 1984 Sentencing Reform Act. It made the following three suggestions (United States Sentencing Commission, 2007, May):

(1) Increase the five-year and ten-year statutory mandatory minimum threshold quantities for crack cocaine offenses to focus the penalties more closely on serious and major traffickers as described generally in the legislative history of the 1986 Act.

(2) Repeal the mandatory minimum penalty provision for simple possession of crack cocaine under 21 U.S.C. § 844.

(3) Reject addressing the 100-to-1 drug quantity ratio by decreasing the five-year and ten-year statutory mandatory minimum threshold quantities for powder cocaine offenses, as there is no evidence to justify such an increase in quantity-based penalties for powder cocaine offenses. (p. 8)

The commission felt that these issues were so important and urgent, that on April 27, 2007, it promulgated an amendment to the USSG §2D1.1 of the United States Sentencing Guidelines. The United States Sentencing Commission put forth an amendment to the guidelines which indicated a reduction for base levels for crack cocaine offenses, among other provisions that addressed crack cocaine possession.

Amendment 706, which became effective November 1, 2007, provided a **downward adjustment by two levels for the crack cocaine offenses per quantity**. For example, before this amendment, a person convicted of a drug offense that involved five grams of cocaine would be assigned a base level of 26, which indicated a 63–78-month prison sentence if he or she had a Criminal History Category 1. This guideline range exceeded the five-year (60 month) statutory minimum by at least three months. After the amendment, the base offense level for an offense involving five grams of cocaine with a Criminal History Category 1 was changed to 24, with a range from 51 to 63 months. This range included the five-year (60 month) statutory minimum. Similarly, before the amendment, a base offense level of 32 (with a guideline range of 121 to 151 months) was indicated for a crack cocaine offense involving 50 grams or more of crack cocaine with a Criminal History Category 1. This guideline range exceeded the ten-year statutory minimum for such offenses by at least one month. After the amendment, an offender committing the same offense with a Criminal History Category 1 would be assigned a base level of 30, with a corresponding guidelines range of 97–121 months, which included the associated ten-year (120 month) statutory minimum.

Crack cocaine levels other than those dictated by mandatory minimums were also adjusted downward by two base levels. In addition, the amendment set into place a procedure to determine a combined base level for an offense that involved both crack cocaine and other controlled substances. Although this amendment did not change the 100:1 crack-to-powder ratio, the commission considered Amendment 706 to be an "interim measure" to alleviate some problems that they identified in crack cocaine sentencing.

Amendment 713 subsequently amended USSG §1B1.10, "Reduction in Term of Imprisonment as a Result of Amended Guideline Range," to include Amendment 706, and became effective March 3, 2008. The reduction in level would be applied with the consideration of public safety. A prison impact model suggested that the modifications to the Drug Quantity Table would affect about 70 percent of crack cocaine offenders who were sentenced to a term of imprisonment according to USSG §2D1.1. They projected that the average sentence of crack cocaine offenses would decrease from 121 months to 106 months.

The Fair Sentencing Act of 2010 and Amendments 748, 750, and 759

In 2010 both the House and the Senate passed legislation to reduce the sentencing disparity involving crack and powder cocaine. On August 3, 2010, President Barack Obama signed the Fair Sentencing Act (FSA), Pub. L. 111–220. The two most notable changes of the act were the reduction the weight disparity for powder cocaine to crack cocaine from a 100:1 ratio to an 18:1 ratio and the elimination of the statutory five-year mandatory minimum penalty for simple possession of crack cocaine.

Congress voted to promulgate Amendment 748 on October 15, 2010, and it became effective November 1, 2010, implementing the emergency directive of Section 8 of the Fair Sentencing Act of 2010.

One significant part of Amendment 748 was the revision of the Drug Quantity Table in USSG §2D1.1 (Unlawful Manufacturing, Importing, Exporting, or Trafficking (Including Possession with Intent to Commit These Offenses); Attempt or Conspiracy) in accordance with Section 2 of the Fair Sentencing Act. This section lowered the statutory penalties for manufacturing and trafficking crack cocaine by increasing the quantity that would trigger a mandatory minimum term of imprisonment. It increased the amount of crack cocaine needed to set off the five-year mandatory minimum prison sentence for possession of crack cocaine from 5 grams to 28 grams. Similarly, it increased the amount needed to trigger a 10-year mandatory minimum prison term from 50 grams to 280 grams. In accordance with the act, offenses involving 28 grams were given a base level of 26 and those involving 280 grams were assigned a base level of 32. They also adjusted the base level of offenses involving other quantities, so that, "the relationship between the statutory penalties for crack cocaine offenses and the statutory penalties for offenses involving other drugs is consistently and proportionally reflected throughout the Drug Quantity Table" (United States Sentencing Commission, 2011, November 1, p. 382).

In addition, the amendment revised USSG §2D2.1 (Unlawful Possession; Attempt or Conspiracy) in response to Section 3 of the Fair Sentencing Act. This section eliminates the mandatory minimum prison sentence of five years for simple possession of over five grams of cocaine. The statutory penalty for simple possession of crack cocaine was changed to that which is similar to other controlled substances — a maximum term of one year for a first-time offender.

Amendment 748 also provided a method to determine a single offense level in cases that involve crack cocaine and one or more other controlled substances. It set an equivalency of 1 gram of crack cocaine to equal 3,571 grams of marijuana. The commission (2011, November 1) offered the following example: "For example, the threshold quantities at base offense level 26 are 100,000 grams of marihuana and 28 grams of crack cocaine; 100,000 grams divided by 28 is 3,571 grams" (p. 382).

Amendment 748 also revised offense level adjustments specified in USSG §2D1.1 in various circumstances including but not limited to the following: provides an offense level decrease for cases in which the defendant was a "minimal participant," provides an offense level increase for defendants whose offense involved violence, provides an offense level increase if the defendant bribed or tried to bribe a law enforcement officer to facilitate the crime, provides an offense level increase if the defendant maintained a premises for manufacturing or distributing a controlled substance, and provides an offense level increase if the defendant played an aggravating role in the offense (if the case involved additional factors).

Effective November 1, 2011, Amendment 750 re-promulgated Amendment 748 as permanent. Also effective on the same day was Amendment 759, which amended USSG §1B1.10 (Reduction in Term of Imprisonment as a Result of Amended Guideline Range (Policy Statement)) to include Amendment 750.

Retroactivity of the Fair Sentencing Act

Once the Fair Sentencing Act was passed in 2010, efforts to make it retroactive ensued. On June 1, 2011, in a hearing held by the USSC, former Attorney General Eric Holder pronounced the Fair Sentencing Act as "a historic step forward" but rallied for retroactive application of lesser penalties for some crack cocaine offenders. He stated, "Although the Fair Sentencing Act is being successfully implemented nationwide, achieving its central goals of promoting public safety and public trust—and ensuring a fair and effective criminal justice system—requires the retroactive application of its guideline amendment."

On June 30, 2011, the USSC voted unanimously to provide retroactive effect to its proposed amendment to the Federal Sentencing Guidelines, which would carry out the measures put forth by the Fair Sentencing Act of 2010. They proposed that the retroactivity would become effective November 1, 2011, the day the amendment that they proposed to be permanent would become law. This vote represented the commission's recognition of the unfairness of past federal policies involving cocaine offenses and a proposed remedy for this injustice. Practically, this would mean that federal cocaine offenders who met certain criteria could have the length of their sentenced reduced in accordance with the Fair Sentencing Act of 2010 (United States Sentencing Commission, 2011, June 30).

This proposal was challenged by some. The issue of retroactivity was ultimately decided by the Supreme Court. On June 24, 2012, the U.S. Supreme Court ruled that the Fair Sentencing Act of 2010 would apply not only to offenders who committed related crimes on or after November 1, 2011 (the date the FSA went into effect) but also to persons whose offenses occurred before the law was passed but who were sentenced afterwards. This meant that the 18:1 ratio, for example, would apply to those who committed relevant offenses before the enactment of the FSA, but who were sentenced after its 2010 passage. The ruling was narrow and relates to those offenders whose sentences were pending and does not make retroactive the length of all prison sentences for every offender serving time for a crack cocaine offense (Burke, 2012, June 21).

Research on the Fair Sentencing Act

The USSC's *Report to Congress: Impact of the Fair Sentencing Act of 2010* (2015, August) presented data on the prosecution and sentencing of crack and powder cocaine offenders. It highlighted four observations. The first is that there has been a steep reduction in the number of crack cocaine offenders prosecuted annually since the Fair Sentencing Act was passed. The number, however, is still sizable.

Figure 5.7 Number of Powder Cocaine and Crack Cocaine Trafficking Offenders, Fiscal Years 1992–2014

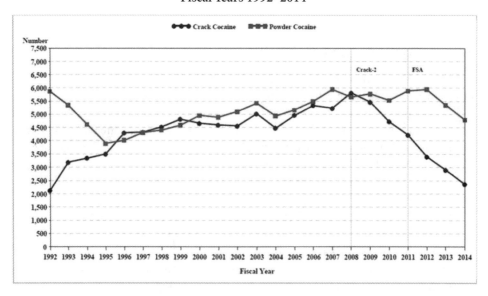

Source: United States Sentencing Commission: *Report to Congress: Fair Sentencing Act of 2010*. p. 11, Figure 1A. Retrieved from http://www.ussc.gov/sites/default/files/pdf/news/congressional-testimony -and-reports/drug-topics/201507_RtC_Fair-Sentencing-Act.pdf

Figure 5.7 shows that in 2014, about half as many crack cocaine offenders were sentenced in the federal system, compared to those sentenced in 2010. The reduction began in 2008, pre-FSA. The second point of the report is that the crack cocaine offenders who have been prosecuted since the FSA are overall not more serious offenders, compared to those prosecuted before the FSA. The majority are still street level dealers, not high level suppliers or organizers/leaders. A third major finding is that the rates of crack cocaine offenders who cooperate with law enforcement has not changed despite the penalty changes. A fourth point is that the average crack cocaine sentences have become closer to the powder cocaine sentences since the FSA. **Figure 5.8** shows the difference in months of those sentenced for crack cocaine compared to powder cocaine has decreased since the FSA.

Figure 5.8 Average Sentence Imposed for Crack Cocaine and Powder Cocaine
Trafficking Offenders, Fiscal Years 2005–2013

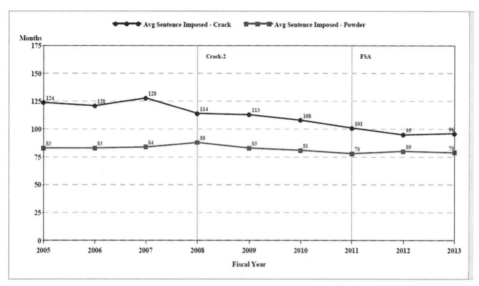

Source: United States Sentencing Commission, *Report to Congress: Fair Sentencing Act of 2010.* p. 23, Figure 14A. Retrieved from http://www.ussc.gov/sites/default/files/pdf/news/congressional-testimony -and-reports/drug-topics/201507_RtC_Fair-Sentencing-Act.pdf

Summary

Early efforts to promote sentencing uniformity in the federal system included sentencing institutes and sentencing councils. Neither approach gained much momentum or lasted. The Sentencing Reform Act of 1984 profoundly changed the federal sentencing practices. It instituted a determinate sentencing scheme and abolished parole for federal offenders. The act also decreased the amount of good time that offenders could accrue. The United States Sentencing Commission was created to devise sentences for federal offenders.

The Federal Sentencing Guidelines shared similar goals with many state guidelines systems—to promote equity and fairness in sentencing, to decrease judicial discretion, and to reduce sentencing disparities. Like many states' guidelines systems, the federal guidelines use offense severity and prior record as two axes of a grid that indicates sentencing ranges. The federal guidelines are much more complex than any state guidelines system, however. Multiple steps are required to determine a sentence for those convicted of federal offenses. There are many ways to adjust guidelines sentences, including sentencing departures and variances. Some would argue that these avenues operate in a way that preserves sentencing disparities.

The federal stance on drug offenders is especially notable when studying federal sentencing. Disparities in sentencing crack cocaine offenders and powder cocaine offenders were codified in the 1986 and 1988 Anti-Drug Abuse Acts. Subsequently, however,

federal guidelines and mandatory minimums have been reduced for many drug trafficking offenses. The Fair Sentencing Act of 2010 reduced the disparity in sentencing
crack cocaine and powder cocaine drug trafficking offenders.

Discussion Questions

1. What reasons led to the formation of the United States Sentencing Commission and the formation of the federal guidelines? How do they compare
   to those which precipitated sentencing reform in the states we discussed?
2. Describe some similarities and differences in the federal guidelines with the
   state guidelines systems that we detailed in Chapter 4.
3. Do you think that the United States Sentencing Commission should have
   identified one major sentencing goal in their crafting of the guidelines? Why
   or why not?
4. Do you think the sentencing goal of rehabilitation is devalued in the application of federal guidelines?
5. How do you think that the *Booker* decision (which deems the federal guidelines advisory, not mandatory) will affect the rates of sentencing departures
   in federal cases in years to come?
6. The Federal Sentencing Guidelines have been criticized as too complex. What
   are the positives and negatives of having such a complex system that guides
   sentencing in the federal system?
7. Should the components of the Fair Sentencing Act that address crack cocaine offenses be retroactive to *all* crack cocaine traffickers and users? Why
   or why not?
8. Do the Federal Sentencing Guidelines encourage or discourage plea
   bargaining?

Notes

1. Frankel only uses the term "his" when discussing sentencing councils. It is assumed that only
male judges participated in them during the 1960s. If women judges did participate, the term " his or
her" would be more appropriate.

2. Part F was deleted on November 1, 2001. The heading, Part F — Offenses Involving Fraud or
Deceit, was deleted after §§2F1.1 and 2F1.2 were deleted.

3. For each Chapter 2 guideline there is a section entitled "Commentary." This section has additional instructions and information about the application of a particular guideline. This discussion
includes statutory provisions (lists of the statute(s) for which the guideline is usually applied), application notes (definitions, application instructions, and sometimes departure factors that the court
needs to consider in the application of the guideline and the sentencing of the defendant), background
(factors considered in the creation of the guideline), and/or historical notes, which provide a list of
amendments and the year in which the amendments were made to that particular guideline. Historical notes function as the legislative history of a particular Chapter 2 guideline (United States Sentencing Commission. *Introduction to the Federal Sentencing Guidelines*, "Part 3 — Basic Guideline Structure
and Initial Application Decisions" [Video]).

4. Terrorism (USSG §5K2.15—"If the defendant committed the offense in furtherance of a terroristic action, the court may increase the sentence above the authorized guideline range") was deleted effective November 1, 1995. Appendix C (p. 450) explains that the Violent Crime Control and Law Enforcement Act of 1994 instructed the commission "to provide an appropriate enhancement for any felony that involves or is intended to promote terrorism." Amendment 526 addresses this directive by adding a Chapter 3 enhancement at USSG §3A1.4 (International Terrorism) in place of the upward departure provision at USSG §K21.15 (Terrorism) (United States Sentencing Commission (November 1, 2003), Appendix C (Volume I)—Amendments to the *Guidelines Manual*, p. 450.

5. Post-Sentencing Rehabilitative Efforts (USSG §5K2.19) was deleted effective November 1, 2012. It had specified "Post-sentencing rehabilitative efforts, even if exceptional, undertaken by a defendant after imposition of a term of imprisonment for the instant offense are not an appropriate basis for a downward departure when resentencing the defendant for that offense." Amendment 768 draws from the Supreme Court decision in *Pepper v. United States*, 131 S. Ct. 1229 (2011) and states "when a defendant's sentence has been set aside on appeal, a district court at resentencing may consider evidence of the defendant's postsentencing rehabilitation." (United States Sentencing Commission (November 1, 2012), Supplement to Appendix C—Amendments to the *Guidelines Manual*, pp. 20–21).

References

Anti-Drug Abuse Act of 1986, 21, U.S.C. §841 (b) (1) (1986).

Anti-Drug Abuse Act of 1988, H.R. 5210, Pub.L. 100–690 (100th Congress) (1988).

Burke, L. B. (2012, June 21). Retroactivity: Supreme court rules on crack cocaine sentences. *Politic365*. Retrieved from http://politic365.com/2012/06/21/supreme-court-rules-some-crack-cocaine-sentences-are-retroactive

Dorsey, T. L., & Middleton, P. (n.d.). *Drugs and crime facts* (NCJ Publication No. 165148). Washington, DC: U.S. Department of Justice, Bureau of Justice Statistics. Retrieved from http://www.bjs.gov/content/pub/pdf/dcf.pdf

Fair Sentencing Act of 2010, Public Law 111–220 (2010).

Frankel, M. E. (1973). *Criminal sentences: Law without order*. New York: Hill and Wang.

Gall v. United States, 552 U.S. 38 (2007).

Glueck, S. (1936). *Crime and justice*. Boston: Little, Brown, and company.

Hinojosa, R. (2015, September 16). *Introduction to the guidelines*.: Initial comments. Presented at the 2015 Annual National Seminar on the Federal Sentencing Guidelines. New Orleans, LA.

Hinojosa, R. & Dorhoffer, A. (2015, September 16). *Introduction to the guidelines*. Presented at the 2015 Annual National Seminar on the Federal Sentencing Guidelines. New Orleans, LA.

Irizarry v. United States, 553 U.S. 708, 714 (2008).

Mistretta v. United States, 488 U.S. 361 (1989).

Orland, L., & Reitz, K. R. (1993). Epilogue: A gathering of state sentencing commissions. *Colorado Law Review, 64*, 837–847.

PBS, *Thirty years of America's drug war: A chronology*. Retrieved from http://www.pbs.org/wgbh/pages/frontline/shows/drugs/cron

Siegel, L. J., & Worrall, J. L. (2016). *Introduction to criminal justice* (15th ed.). Boston, MA: Cengage Learning.

Stone, S. A. (2007–2008). Federal drug sentencing—What was Congress smoking? The uncertain distinction between "cocaine" and "cocaine base" in the Anti-Drug Abuse Act of 1986. *Western New England Law Review, 30,* 296–349.

Tonry, M. (1996). *Sentencing matters.* New York: Oxford University Press.

United States Courts. *Federal courts' structure.* Retrieved from http://www.uscourts.gov /FederalCourts/UnderstandingtheFederalCourts/FederalCourtsStructure.aspx

United States Office of Drug Abuse Policy. (1984). *1984 National strategy for prevention of drug abuse and drug trafficking.* Washington, DC: Office of Policy Development.

United States Sentencing Commission. *Introduction to the federal sentencing guidelines, Part 1—Overview of the United States Sentencing Commission* [Video]. Available from http://www.ussc.gov/Videos/Federal_Sentencing_Guidelines_Intro.cfm

United States Sentencing Commission. *Introduction to the federal sentencing guidelines, Part 2—Overview of the Federal Sentencing Guideline* [Video]. Available from http:// www.ussc.gov/Videos/Federal_Sentencing_Guidelines_Intro.cfm

United States Sentencing Commission. *Introduction to the federal sentencing guidelines, Part 3—Basic guidelines structure and initial application decisions* [Video]. Available from http://www.ussc.gov/Videos/Federal_Sentencing_Guidelines_Intro.cfm

United States Sentencing Commission. (2007, May). *Report to the Congress: Cocaine and federal sentencing policy.* Retrieved from http://www.ussc.gov/sites/default/files/pdf /news/congressional-testimony-and-reports/drug-topics/200705_RtC_Cocaine _Sentencing_Policy.pdf

United States Sentencing Commission. (2011, June 30). *News Release: U.S. sentencing commission votes unanimously to apply Fair Sentencing Act of 2010 amendment to the federal sentencing guidelines retroactively.* Retrieved from http://www.ussc.gov/Legislative _and_Public_Affairs/Newsroom/Press_Releases/20110630_Press_Release.pdf

United States Sentencing Commission. (2011, November 1). *Appendix C (Volume III)— Amendments to the guidelines manual.* Retrieved from http://www.ussc.gov/sites /default/files/pdf/guidelines-manual/2015/Appendix_C_Vol_III.pdf

United States Sentencing Commission. (2012). *Selected departure and variance decisions.* Retrieved from http://www.ussc.gov/Legal/Primers/Primer_Departure_and_Variance .pdf

United States Sentencing Commission (2015, August). *Report to the Congress: Impact of the Fair Sentencing Act of 2010.* Retrieved from http://www.ussc.gov/sites/default/files /pdf/news/congressional-testimony-and-reports/drug-topics/201507_RtC_Fair -Sentencing-Act.pdf

United States Sentencing Commission. (2015, November 1). *United States Sentencing Commission guidelines manual.* Retrieved from http://www.ussc.gov/sites/default/files /pdf/guidelines-manual/2015/GLMFull.pdf

United States Sentencing Commission. (n.d.). *Interactive Sourcebook of Federal Sentencing Statistics.* Table A. Retrieved from http://www.ussc.gov/sites/default/files/pdf/research -and-publications/annual-reports-and-sourcebooks/2014/FigureA.pdf

United States v. Booker, 543 U.S. 220 (2005).

United States v. Mistretta, 488 U.S. 361 (1989).

Weinreb, M. (n.d.). *The day innocence died. ESPN.* Retrieved from http://espn.go.com /espn/eticket/story?page=bias

6

MANDATORY MINIMUM SENTENCING AND THREE STRIKES LAWS

Chapter Objectives:

- To understand the background and purposes of mandatory minimum sentencing laws.
- To gain knowledge about the history of the federal response to drug offenders.
- To get an overview of the Rockefeller Drug Laws and Michigan's 650 Lifer Law.
- To learn about federal and select states' mandatory minimum sentencing laws for firearms offenses.
- To comprehend federal mandatory minimum statutes and guidelines for child pornography offenses.
- To study the background and purposes of three strikes laws.
- To compare and contrast Washington's and California's three strikes laws.

Like sentencing guidelines, mandatory minimum sentencing laws and three strikes laws share the goal of increasing sentencing uniformity. Sentencing guidelines and worksheet systems aim to *decrease* judicial discretion. Mandatory minimum sentencing laws aim to *eliminate* judicial discretion. Three strikes laws aim to drastically curtail judicial discretion, although a little bit remains in some jurisdictions.

Mandatory minimum sentencing laws typically target certain offenses. They most commonly involve drug offenses, firearms offenses, and certain violent crimes. In the federal system, many child pornography offenses are subject to mandatory minimum sentencing. The sanction is usually a lengthy prison term or life imprisonment.

Most strikes laws are "three strikes" laws. These laws indicate automatic and lengthy prison sentences for offenders who have accrued convictions for three serious and/or violent offenses. Three strikes laws rest on the notion that certain offenders are "habitual offenders." The approach is to incarcerate offenders for life or very long prison sentences in order to prevent these habitual offenders from returning to society prematurely and reoffending.

We will first discuss the history of mandatory minimum sentencing laws and give examples of these laws through the years. We will do the same for three strikes laws. In Chapter 8 we will discuss ethical issues and social movements and organizations that have challenged these laws. In Chapter 9 we will present detailed evaluation research on the effectiveness of various sentencing reforms, including mandatory minimum and three strikes laws.

What Are Mandatory Minimum Sentencing Laws?

Although we will focus on the mandatory sentencing laws imposed since widespread modern sentencing reform began in the 1980s, mandatory sentencing laws are not an entirely modern phenomenon. Since the early republic, there have been mandatory penalties, such as death for offenses considered serious, like murder and treason. Congress introduced mandatory minimum penalties at the time it first enacted penal laws during the late eighteenth century. Congress defined a set of federal offenses when the 1790 Crimes Act was passed. This act articulated 23 federal crimes, seven of which carried a mandatory death penalty: treason, murder, three offenses relating to piracy, forgery of a public security of the United States, and the rescue of a person convicted of a capital crime. Thirteen of the crimes in the 1790 Crimes Act resulted in sentences of imprisonment that carried a statutory maximum of up to one year (three offenses), three years (seven offenses), or seven years (three offenses) (United States Sentencing Commission, October, 2011a).

One stated goal of mandatory minimum sentencing laws is to send a message to would-be offenders that serious crimes will not be tolerated. Mandatory minimum sentencing laws have been enacted both in states which have adopted some type of structured sentencing, as well as those which continue to rely on indeterminate sentencing.

Federal Mandatory Minimum Sentences for Drug Offenders

Round One of Mandatory Minimum Sentencing for Federal Drug Offenders

The 1951 Boggs Act

The first federal law that established mandatory minimum sentences for drug offenders was the Boggs Act. Passed by Congress in 1951, the Boggs Act (named for its sponsor, Representative Hale Boggs (D-LA)) imposed lengthy sentences for drug offenders. The mandatory sentences applied to drug crimes, regardless of whether they involved simple possession or drug trafficking. The mandatory penalty for a first offense was 2 to 5 years of imprisonment. A second offense carried a sentence of 5 to 10 years, and a third or subsequent offense meant a sentence of 10 to 15 years. The sentencing scheme did not differentiate drug users from drug traffickers.

Much of the momentum for the Boggs Act came from the commissioner for the Federal Bureau of Narcotics, Harry Anslinger. Anslinger blamed rising rates of addiction and violence by juveniles on judges who he perceived as being too soft on crime. He rallied for lengthy terms of incarceration for drug offenders, as opposed to treatment for drug abusers. Anslinger characterized drug addicts as contagious and recommended that they be physically separated from society. Accordingly, Anslinger pushed for Congress to pass long mandatory minimum incarceration sentences for illegal drug offenders (Gill, n.d.).

The Narcotics Control Act of 1956

Four years after the Boggs Act was passed, a Senate subcommittee, which was headed by Senator Price Daniel (D-TX) began to study the sale and trafficking of illegal narcotics. This committee also deemed drug addiction "contagious" and recommended that drug addicts be separated from society. As a result of Daniel's committee's conclusions and public concern over the drug problem in the United States, the **Narcotics Control Act of 1956** was passed. Provisions of the act included increasing the mandatory minimum sentence for a first-time drug offender convicted of a trafficking offense from two to five years to a five-year minimum. Convicted drug traffickers would receive a mandatory minimum ten-year sentence for subsequent offenses.

Despite the enactment of a series of harsh penalties for drug offenders, there was no evidence that mandatory sentencing decreased drug use or drug related offenses in the United States. The decade of the sixties was characterized by an increase in the use of illegal drugs and more acceptance of the use of recreational drugs. Federal sentencing laws did not seem to prevent the drug problem in the 1960s and 1970s (Gill, n.d.).

The Movement Away from Federal Mandatory Minimums—Re-establishment of Judicial Discretion in Federal Drug Cases

Presidential Commissions Study Drug Abuse, Drug Crimes, and Mandatory Minimums

When John F. Kennedy became president in 1963, policy makers sought to initiate a more effective approach to curb the drug problem. A **President's Advisory Commission on Narcotics and Drug Abuse** (also known as the Prettyman Commission) was established to study the problem of illegal drug addiction and the (in)effectiveness of the laws that had been passed to control it.

Instead of increasing sanctions against drug offenders, this commission suggested that rehabilitating drug abusers should be of paramount importance. If incarceration was deemed appropriate for serious drug offenders, rehabilitation, as opposed to retribution, was promoted. In 1963, President Kennedy commuted the sentences of some drug offenders who had received lengthy sentences under the Narcotics Control Act of 1956. This move was symbolic of a change in approach toward drug offenders

A recommendation of the President's Commission on Law Enforcement and the Administration of Justice (established in 1966) was for the courts and correctional agents to be able to exercise discretion when administering sentences to drug offenders. Discretion would allow these criminal justice actors to take into account relevant offender and case characteristics in sentencing (Gill, n.d.). The recommendation clearly contradicted the very core of mandatory minimum sentencing that eliminates judicial discretion.

The Comprehensive Drug Abuse Prevention and Control Act of 1970

When Richard M. Nixon became president in 1969, he too expressed concern over the problem of drug addiction. Nixon recognized that the issue affected not only poor people living in inner cities, but also more affluent people living in the suburbs. It became clear that mandatory minimum sentencing for drug offenders was not the solution to the problem of drug abuse and drug crimes. President Nixon identified public education about the drug problem and rehabilitation of drug offenders as the appropriate avenues to combat the issue of drug use and trafficking.

Pursuant to Congressional testimony that challenged the effectiveness of mandatory minimum sentencing laws in combatting the drug problem, the **Comprehensive Drug Abuse Prevention and Control Act of 1970** was passed. The federal tactics to address the drug problem changed substantively. Notable was the elimination of all of the mandatory minimum sentencing schemes for drug offenses, except for one. The only one that was retained involved drug offenders who earned significant profits from major drug operations, which were considered "continuing criminal enterprises."

Instead of facing a mandatory minimum sentence of two to five years, first-time drug offenders convicted of simple possession of a controlled substance without intent to distribute were classified as misdemeanants. Misdemeanor penalties included fines and probation. Judges could examine the specific offender and offense characteristics and exercise their discretion when sentencing persons convicted of simple possession. Under the act, those offenders who were convicted of manufacturing and/or trafficking offenses could receive sentences of *up to* 15 years for the first offense, *up to* 30 years for the second or subsequent offenses, and *up to* 30 years for selling drugs to minors. The foci of the act included treatment of drug abusers, empowering law enforcement to curb drug trafficking and manufacture, and redesigning the sentences for drug offenders in a more balanced way (Gill, n.d.).

There was bipartisan support for the act that established some very different policies than the Boggs Act. It took a twofold approach — punishing drug traffickers and treating drug abusers. Both Democrats and Republicans hailed the act, which afforded discretion to judges in the sentencing stage of federal criminal case processing. They reflected on past mandatory minimum sentencing laws as undermining respect for the law and the administration of justice and noted that prior drug laws hindered enforcement and had little deterrent effect on drug crimes.

The timing of the passage of Comprehensive Drug Abuse Prevention and Control Act of 1970 was interesting. It was sent by Congress to the president on October 14, 1970, and Nixon signed it into law on October 27, just days before midterm congressional elections. Although it might seem counterintuitive, repealing almost all mandatory laws was not contradictory to a pro-law enforcement campaign. Nixon ran a "law and order" campaign and focused much attention on combatting rising crime rates. The many proponents of the act did not lose support in the elections. In fact, every senator that voted for the 1970 act was reelected, except for one who lost for an unrelated reason. Similarly, the vast majority of House candidates were reelected (Gill, n.d.).

Round Two of Mandatory Minimum Sentencing for Federal Drug Offenders

The Anti-Drug Abuse Act of 1986 and the Anti-Drug Abuse Act of 1988

Chapter 5 detailed the Anti-Drug Abuse Act of 1986 and the Anti-Drug Abuse Act of 1988. These acts set in place harsh mandatory minimum prison sentences for cocaine trafficking and possession offenses. The Anti-Drug Abuse Act of 1986 established the famous 100:1 ratio of powder cocaine to crack cocaine amounts that would trigger identical penalties. It mandated a minimum of ten years in prison (and up to a life sentence) for a trafficking offense that involved 50 grams or more of crack cocaine or 5,000 grams or more of powder cocaine. Similarly, it set a mandatory prison sentence of five years for drug trafficking offenses that involved five grams of crack cocaine. The same sentence would be given to drug traffickers whose offense involved 500 grams of powder cocaine. The Anti-Drug Abuse Act of 1988 Act set a mandatory minimum penalty for simple possession of five grams or more of crack cocaine.

The decision-making process that led to the second round of mandatory minimum sentencing for drug offenders did not result from a series of congressional hearings involving experts in the field of substance abuse or from personnel in the areas of policing, courts, or corrections. Instead, it was based on a knee-jerk reaction to the cocaine overdose death of rising basketball star Len Bias (as detailed in Chapter 5). Within a week of Bias's death, the House Judiciary Committee designed and passed new mandatory minimum penalties for drug offenses. The 1988 mandatory minimum sentencing laws that subjected those convicted of simple possession of crack symbolized a significant concern with crack cocaine and its users.

Sentencing below a Mandatory Minimum — Two Strategies

There are two possible ways to sentence a federal drug offender below a mandatory minimum. They include if the defendant provides substantial assistance to the prosecution and through the use of so-called "safety valves."

Substantial Assistance

We discussed the effect of **substantial assistance** on guideline application for federal offenses in Chapter 5. Section 5K1.1 permits a sentence *below* the minimum of the guideline range. Section 18 USC § 3553(e) permits a sentence *below* a mandatory minimum. Each requires a government motion (*Wade v. U.S.*, 504 U.S. 181 (1992)). A separate government motion under 18 USC § 3553(e) is required to go below a mandatory minimum (*Melendez v. U.S.*, 518 U.S. 120 (1996)). The court ultimately decides if a sentence reduction based on "substantial assistance in the investigation or prosecution of another person who has committed an offense" will be granted.

The Creation of Safety Valves

For the years following the 1986 and 1988 acts, the prison population increased dramatically, as did the proportion of the prison population sentenced for drug offenses.

In response, Congress created so called **"safety valves"** in the mid-nineties to relieve prison overcrowding and lessen the punishment of offenders who were considered by many to have received overly harsh terms of imprisonment. Safety valves allowed judges to use discretion and sentence some non-violent drug offenders with little or no criminal record below the sentence indicated by the mandatory minimum statutes.

The United States Sentencing Commission has identified five criteria, all of which must be met for an offender to be considered for a reduction in a mandatory minimum sentence via a "safety valve." They are:

1) Defendant does not have more than 1 Criminal History Point
2) <u>Defendant</u> did not use violence/threats of violence or possess a firearm or other dangerous weapon in connection with the offense
3) <u>Offense</u> did not result in death or serious bodily injury
4) Defendant was not an organizer/leader/manager/supervisor in the offense; was not engaged in a CCE (continuing criminal enterprise)
5) That not later than the time of the sentencing hearing, the defendant has truthfully provided to the Government all information and evidence the defendant has concerning the offense that was part of the same course of conduct or common scheme or plan. (Hinojosa & Dorhoffer, 2015, September 16).

This last item involves ascertaining whether the defendant provided to the government all information. The defendant is expected to do more than merely accept responsibility, but not as much as he or she would be expected to do such that the court would consider it to be substantial assistance. As long as this information is presented before the sentencing hearing, potential recipients of a safety valve would have to provide relevant information to the court.

According to the United States Sentencing Commission (October, 2011b),

> In fiscal year 2010, more than half (54%, n=8,619) of drug offenders convicted of an offense carrying a mandatory minimum penalty received relief from the mandatory minimum penalty. Approximately one quarter (26.1%, n=4,136) of the drug offenders received relief through operation of the safety valve alone. Drug offenders who did not qualify for the safety valve but who provided substantial assistance to the government accounted for 19.3 percent (n=3,062) of all drug offenders convicted of an offense carrying a mandatory minimum penalty. An additional 9.0 percent (n=1,421) of drug offenders received relief from the mandatory minimum penalty by qualifying for application of both the safety valve and substantial assistance provisions. (p. 158)

Congress to Focus on Mandatory Minimum Sentencing Issues

Recently Congress has showed renewed interest in sentencing issues. In March 2013, Senator Patrick Leahy (D-VT), joined by Senator Rand Paul (R-KY) introduced a measure, the Justice Safety Valve Act of 2013, to allow judges more flexibility in sentencing in cases for which mandatory sentencing is deemed, according to Leahy, to be "unnecessary and counterproductive." This would allow judges to hand down sentences **below the mandatory minimum to all offenders convicted of all federal crimes**, not just offenders convicted of select drug offenses. The Justice Safety Valve Act of 2013 will be detailed in the final chapter.

Former Attorney General Eric Holder and the USSC Call for Reduction in Mandatory Minimum Drug Sentences

Eric Holder's August 2013 Speech

At a speech to the American Bar Association in San Francisco on August 12, 2013, then-Attorney General Eric Holder announced that the Justice Department would stop pursuing mandatory minimum sentences for some non-violent, low-level drug offenders. Holder critiqued the criminal justice system's current approach to the "war on drugs." Holder issued new guidelines to federal prosecutors that would decrease the number of people charged with crimes carrying mandatory minimum sentences.

During this speech, Holder brought attention to racial disparities in sentencing practices that result in disproportionate representation of minorities in the prison population. He asserted that when people of color are processed in the criminal justice system that they "often face harsher punishments than their peers." He called this disparity "unacceptable," "shameful," and "unworthy of the legal tradition of the United States."

Holder also noted that almost half of the 219,000 federal inmates were imprisoned for drug-related crimes and that many of these persons suffer from substance abuse problems. Holder stated that mass incarceration, which has resulted in overcrowding in federal, state, and local facilities is "both ineffective and unsustainable." In addition to economic costs, Holder recognized the social costs of widespread incarceration.

He described an approach, effective immediately, to decrease prosecutions for drug offenders who have no ties to major organizations, gangs, or cartels. He explained that such offenders would no longer be charged with crimes that "impose draconian mandatory minimum sentences." These offenders will instead be charged with crimes that carry sentences that better reflect their conduct. Holder said he requested to federal prosecutors that they establish locally tailored guidelines that will help them decide whether federal charges should be pursued. This strategy aims to better differentiate violent offenders and drug kingpins from lower level drug offenders. He also called for anti-violence strategies in crime-ridden areas.

In addition to fewer prosecutions, Holder called for a decrease in mandatory minimum prison sentences, which would save money. He named his strategy the **"Smart On Crime" Initiative**, which resulted from a Justice Department review that he began earlier in 2013. Holder highlighted the need to understand what types of drug treatment and community programs could serve as alternatives to incarceration. Holder also emphasized the appropriateness of "compassionate release" from prison of incarcerated persons who don't pose a safety risk to the public (Merica & Perez, 2013, August 12; Fox News, 2013, August 12).

2014 United States Sentencing Commission Votes to Reduce Some Drug Sentences

In January 2014, Holder encouraged the Senate Judiciary Committee to pass a far-reaching reform of mandatory minimums. In April 30, 2014, the USSC voted unanimously to amend the guidelines for most drug trafficking offenders. The base offense levels were lowered by two levels in the Drug Quantity Table across drug types in guideline §2D1.1, which encompasses drug trafficking cases. This meant that from that point forward the sentences for drug offenders would be lowered. This amendment is referred to as the "drugs minus two" or the "2014 drug guidelines amendment" (United States Sentencing Commission, n.d.).

On July 18, 2014, the United States Sentencing Commission voted unanimously to reduce the sentences of approximately 40,000 inmates who were already serving prison terms for drug offenses. This meant that a reduction of the sentencing guidelines levels applicable to most federal drug trafficking offenses would be reduced retroactively. We will detail the consequences of this move in Chapter 11.

Patterns in the Federal Response to Drug Offenders

The federal approach to sentencing drug offenders can be likened to a pendulum. When it swings all the way to one side, the strategy is to vigorously enforce mandatory minimum sentences, focus on punishment, ignore individual characteristics associated with the case, and to send a "get tough on crime" message that incorporates zero tolerance. When the pendulum swings all the way to the other side, there is a backing off of mandatory minimums in favor of allowing judges to decide what sentences are best suited for particular offenders. This approach rests on the concept of many drug offenders as drug abusers who are in need of treatment. In this approach, judges can exercise discretion as to the type of sentence to impose (incarceration or community-based) based on individual offender and offense characteristics.

Former Attorney General Holder's August 2013 speech in front of the American Bar Association suggested backing off of a "one size fits all" strategy in combatting the drug problem. It symbolized a more individualized approach to sentencing drug offenders that aims to punish major drug traffickers while lessening sanctions for lower level, less dangerous drug offenders. It may very well indicate that a more "middle ground" approach will characterize how the federal system will deal with drug offenders in the future.

State Sentencing Laws Targeting Drug Offenders

Many states have also established mandatory minimum sentencing laws for drug offenders. Oftentimes mandatory minimum sentencing laws have been enacted in addition to the implementation of sentencing guidelines.

North Carolina's Current Mandatory Minimum Sentences for Drug Trafficking Offenders

North Carolina, for example, has established a separate grid for offenders convicted of drug trafficking offenses. **Figure 6.1** shows the lengthy minimum and maximum sentences for drug trafficking offenses for Class C felonies through Class H felonies (North Carolina Sentencing and Policy Advisory Commission, 2009). An active prison sentence is mandated for all felony drug trafficking offenses. Except in the case of substantial assistance, the indicated ranges of prison terms must be followed. For each offense level, the minimum prison sentence mandated for drug trafficking offenses exceeds that for a non-drug trafficking offense of the same class with the highest prior record level.

Figure 6.1 Mandatory Minimum Penalties for Drug Trafficking Offenders in the State of North Carolina

Minimum and Maximum Sentences for Drug Trafficking *G.S. 90–95(h)*

Unless the court finds that the offender provided substantial assistance in the identification, arrest or conviction of any accomplices, accessories, co-conspirators or principals, the offender convicted for drug trafficking must receive the following minimum and maximum sentence regardless of the prior record level.

> Class C Drug Trafficking: Minimum 225 months; maximum 279 months.
> Class D Drug Trafficking: Minimum 175 months; maximum 219 months.
> Class E Drug Trafficking: Minimum 90 months; maximum 117 months.
> Class F Drug Trafficking: Minimum 70 months; maximum 84 months.
> Class G Drug Trafficking: Minimum 35 months; maximum 42 months.
> Class H Drug Trafficking: Minimum 25 months; maximum 30 months.

If the court finds "substantial assistance," the court may impose any lesser minimum and corresponding maximum sentence, or suspend the sentence and enter any sentence within the court's discretion.

Example: *An offender is convicted of selling 50 grams of cocaine (a Class G felony). Since this is a drug trafficking offense under G.G 90–95(h), the minimum sentence is mandated by statute to be 35 months, and the maximum sentence is mandated by statute to be 42 months. For this offense, there is no requirement to determine the prior record level or to refer to the Felony Punishment Chart. If the court finds "substantial assistance," however, the court could suspend the sentence or could impose a shorter minimum and maximum sentence (for example, a minimum of 12 months and a maximum of 15 months).*

Source: North Carolina Sentencing and Policy Advisory Commission. (2009). *Structured sentencing training and reference manual: Applies to offenses committed on or after December 1, 2009.* p. 33. Retrieved from http://www.nccourts.org/Courts/CRS/Councils/spac/Documents/sstrainingmanual_09.pdf

For example, an offender convicted of a second degree rape (offense class C) with the highest prior record level (VI) who is sentenced in the highest part of the aggravated range, would get a minimum of 182 months in prison and a corresponding maximum of 228 months. Someone convicted of a class C drug trafficking offense would receive a mandatory minimum of 225 months and a maximum of 279 months.

Rockefeller Drug Laws

Background

Approximately 40 years ago, then-New York governor Nelson Rockefeller initiated a set of sweeping laws aimed at combatting the drug problem of the 1960s and 1970s. These laws, called the Rockefeller Drug Laws, symbolized a new approach to combatting drugs on the state level — through strict mandatory minimum prison sentences.

Before Rockefeller introduced these laws, he had supported rehabilitation programs as well as job training and housing for low-level offenders, including drug offenders (Mann, 2013, February 14). During the 1960s, New York, in fact, had a reputation for addressing drug addiction as a medical problem as opposed to a crime problem (Mann, 2013, January 24).

By the 1970s, however, heroin use exploded, especially in cities. Some deemed it a heroin epidemic and the American public was demanding that something be done about it. There was much attention paid to the narcotics epidemic and it was a subject in the films *The French Connection* and *Panic in Needle Park*. From 1972 to 1973 there were 1,600 homicides in New York City alone. This was a four time increase over the preceeding one-year period. Other violent crimes, including muggings, rose and many community leaders considered drugs to be a major source of the crime problem (Mann, 2013, January 24).

Nixon's War on Drugs

In an address to Congress, President Nixon (Nixon, 1971) deemed the drug problem a "national emergency" and asked Congress to amend the 1972 budget with an additional $155 million to control drug abuse. Nixon characterized the enforcement provisions of the Comprehensive Drug Abuse Prevention and Control Act of 1970 as falling short of meaningfully impacting drug abuse in the nation. Although Nixon identified reducing supply as one important approach, he also recognized the importance of reducing demand and stated, "We must rehabilitate the drug user if we are to eliminate drug abuse and all the antisocial activities that flow from drug abuse" (Nixon, 1971). He vowed to appropriate more funds to the cost of rehabilitating drug abusers.

Nixon established the Special Action Office of Drug Abuse Prevention, which would act as a central authority on the federal level for drug abuse prevention, education, rehabilitation, and research. This body would concentrate on demand and study of effective prevention of drug use and treatment of drug abusers. Nixon asked Congress for $105 million more to be added to the 1972 budget to be specifically used for treatment and rehabilitation of persons addicted to drugs. Nixon asked Congress to amend the Narcotic Addict Rehabilitation Act of 1966 to broaden the authority under the act to use methadone maintenance programs.

Rockefeller's Approach

Nixon's message promoted goals of offender rehabilitation that involved flexibility on the part of the judge. Governor Rockefeller, however, seemed to react to his state's drug problem in a diametrically opposite way. What was his solution? He introduced mandatory minimum prison sentences that *eliminated* judicial discretion and created laws that punished both traffickers and users.

Rockefeller's dramatic approach to dealing with drug offenders occurred in 1972. In a meeting with aides that year, Rockefeller announced that he wanted to establish a zero-tolerance policy in dealing with drug offenders. He believed at that time that more progressive approaches to dealing with drug addiction were not working. Rockefeller concluded that life sentences should be imposed for "drug pushing" and that there should be no parole or probation for these offenders (Mann, 2013, February 14). Rockefeller introduced his crusade to get tough on drug offenders in New York in a January 1973 State of the State speech in which he called for mandatory prison sentences of 15 years to life for both drug dealers and addicts. This included persons who possessed small amounts of marijuana, cocaine, or heroin. He stated "I have one goal and one objective and that is to stop the pushing of drugs and to protect the innocent victim" (Mann, 2013, February 14).

Rockefeller's tough stand on drug offenses received initial support from the general population in New York State. On May 8, 1973, Rockefeller signed into law the statutes concerning the possession and sale of narcotics drugs in the New York State Penal Code, termed the "Rockefeller Drug Laws." The legislature that passed these laws assumed that strict mandatory sentences for drug possession and drug trafficking crimes would deter would-be drug offenders (Herman, 1999–2000).

These laws introduced a major change to the sentencing scheme. Before the Rockefeller Drug Laws, felonies were classified as A, B, C, D, and E. The Rockefeller Drug Laws created three new subcategories that delineated drug offenses: A-I, A-II, and A-III. **Figure 6.2** shows the classifications of felonies and examples of non-drug offenses in the same categories for A-I, B, C, D, and E felonies as well as Class A misdemeanors.

Note that Class A-II and A-III felonies were drug offenses with no non-drug analogs. While the laws set threshold amounts of various types of drugs that would constitute A-I, A-II, and A-III felonies, we will focus most on those classifications and penalties for narcotics offenses (National Institute of Law Enforcement and Criminal Justice, 1978).

The sale of any amount under 1/8th of an ounce of a narcotic drug was classified as an A-III felony. The sale of between 1/8th of an ounce and up to one ounce of a narcotic drug was an A-II felony. The sale of one ounce or greater of a narcotic drug was classified as an A-I felony. This figure shows that the assignment of an A-I drug felony is considered as serious a crime as murder in the first or second degree (Laws of New York, 1973, §220.39, §220.41, §220.43; National Institute of Law Enforcement and Criminal Justice, 1978).

The 1973 drug laws also classified drug possession offenses according to the A-I, A-II, and A-III offense categorizations. Criminal possession of up to one ounce of narcotics was a Class A-III felony. Criminal possession of more than one ounce to less than two ounces of narcotics was a Class A-II penalty. Criminal possession of two or more ounces of narcotics was a Class A-I felony (Laws of New York, 1973, §220.16, §220.18, §220.21). The Rockefeller Drug Laws also established different weights of other types

Figure 6.2 Crime Classification and Selected Examples under New York
State Penal Law

TABLE A-1
CRIME CLASSIFICATION AND SELECTED EXAMPLES
UNDER NEW YORK STATE PENAL LAW

Classification	Drug Crime Example	Non-Drug Crime Example
A-I Felony	Sale of 1 oz. of heroin	Murder 1° and 2°
A-II Felony	Sale of between 1/8 oz. and 1 oz. of heroin	None
A-III Felony	Sale of less than 1/8 oz. of heroin	None
B Felony	Second offender, class C drug crime	Rape 1°, Robbery 1°
C Felony	Possession of ½ oz. of methamphetamine	Assault 1°, Burglary 2°
D Felony	Sale of any amount of any controlled substance	Grand Larceny 2°, Forgery 2°
E Felony	None	Perjury 2°, Criminal Contempt 1°
A Misdemeanor	Possession of any amount of any controlled substance	Unauthorized Use of Vehicle
B Misdemeanor	None	Menacing

Source: National Institute of Law Enforcement and Criminal Justice. (1978). *The nation's toughest drug law: Evaluating the New York experience.* p. 33. Retrieved from https://www.ncjrs.gov/pdffiles1 /Digitization/47795NCJRS.pdf

Reprinted with permission of the Association of the Bar of the City of New York

of drugs (including but not limited to methamphetamines, LSD, and marijuana) that would result in classifications of A-I, A-II, and A-II felonies.[1]

Figure 6.3 shows the minimum and maximum indeterminate sentence ranges under the New York State Penal Law as of June 1977. Judges could sentence persons convicted of Class A-I felonies within the minimum range of 15–25 years with a maximum life sentence. Those convicted of Class A-II felonies could be sentenced in the minimum range of 6–8 1/3 years to a maximum term up to life. Offenders convicted of Class A-III felonies could receive a minimum sentence from a range of 1–8 1/3 years to a maximum sentence of life. Alternatives to a state prison sentence (i.e., probation or another community based sentence) could not be used to sentence any offender convicted of a Class A-I, A-II, or A-III felony offense (National Institute of Law Enforcement and Criminal Justice, 1978). All Class A drug offenders were to be put on mandatory lifetime parole supervi-

Figure 6.3 First Offender Penalties for Classes of Crime under New York State Penal Law (as of June 1977)

FIRST OFFENDER PENALTIES FOR CLASSES OF CRIME UNDER NEW YORK STATE PENAL LAW
(*as of June 1977*)

Classification	INDETERMINATE SENTENCE TO STATE PRISON		Alternatives to a State Prison Sentence[a]
	Minimum	Maximum	
A-I Felony	15–25 yrs.	Life	None[b]
A-II Felony	6–8 1/3 yrs.	Life	None
A-III Felony	1–8 1/3 yrs.	Life	None[c]
B Felony	1–8 1/3 yrs.	3–25 yrs.	None
C Felony	1–5 yrs.	3–15 yrs.	Probation (5 yrs.), conditional discharge, unconditional discharge[d, e, f, g]
D Felony	1–2 1/3 yrs.	3–7 yrs.	Probation (5 yrs.), local jail (1 yr.), intermittent imprisonment (1 yr.), conditional discharge, unconditional discharge[e, f, g]
E Felony	1–1 1/3 yrs.	3–4 yrs.	Probation (5 yrs.), local jail (1 yr.), intermittent imprisonment, conditional discharge, unconditional discharge[e, f, g]
A Misdemeanor	None	None	Local jail (1 yr.), intermittent imprisonment, probation (3 yrs.), conditional discharge, unconditional discharge[f, g, h]
B Misdemeanor	None	None	Local jail (3 months), intermittent imprisonment, probation (1 yr.), conditional discharge, unconditional discharge[f, g]

[a] Excluding fines

[b] Murder in the first degree (of a police officer under particular circumstances) is a class A-I felony that carries a mandatory death sentence.

[c] But informants who aid in the investigation or prosecution of a drug felony may be sentenced to lifetime probation.

[d] Defendants indicted for class A-III felonies who plead guilty to a class C felony as authorized by the 1976 amendment to the law, may receive a local jail sentence of up to one year instead of an indeterminate sentence to state imprisonment.

[e] No alternative is available for defendants convicted of certain specified class C and class D felonies. Conditional discharge and unconditional discharge are not available to defendants convicted of drug felonies.

[f] Offenders who are adjudicated Youthful Offenders may not receive a state prison sentence with a maximum of more than four years.

(continued)

Figure 6.3 First Offender Penalties for Classes of Crime under New York State Penal Law (as of June 1977) (continued)

[g] Offenders who have been found to be narcotics addicts under the procedures set forth in the New York State Mental Hygiene Law must receive either a probation sentence requiring treatment for their addiction or a sentence to either state prison or local jail.

[h] Offenders who are adjudicated Youthful Offenders in a local criminal court and who have not previously been so adjudicated or convicted of a crime may not receive a definite sentence of more than six months.

Source: National Institute of Law Enforcement and Criminal Justice. (1978). *The nation's toughest drug law: Evaluating the New York experience.* p. 34. Retrieved from https://www.ncjrs.gov /pdffiles1/Digitization/47795NCJRS.pdf

Reprinted with permission of the Association of the Bar of the City of New York.

sion. The only exceptions to these mandatory penalties involved youthful offenders and some informants. These offenders could receive a sentence of lifetime probation without imprisonment (National Institute of Law Enforcement and Criminal Justice, 1978).

Anyone indicted on a Class A-III offense could not plead guilty to a lesser offense. Those charged with Class A-I or A-II offenses could plead to no less than a Class A-III offense. As a result, an offender who was indicted on selling as little as less than 1/8th of an ounce of heroin, for example, would have to serve at least one year in prison. In 1976, the limitation on plea bargaining for Class A-III offenses was eliminated.

Criminal sanctions for drug felonies less than Class A-I were increased as well. After the Rockefeller Drug Laws were passed, fewer drug offenses were punishable as misdemeanors. Misdemeanors could result in punishment of up to one year in jail. Felonies were punishable by one or more years in prison.

Figure 6.4 shows how various drug offenses were reclassified under the Rockefeller Drug Laws. For example, sale of less than 1/8th of an ounce of heroin was previously clas-

Figure 6.4 Reclassification of Selected Drug Crimes under the 1973 Law

RECLASSIFICATION OF SELECTED DRUG CRIMES UNDER THE 1973 LAW

Crime	Old Law Classification	New Law Classification
Sale of 1 oz. heroin	C Felony	A-I Felony
Sale of 1/8 oz.-1 oz. heroin	C Felony	A-II Felony
Sale of less than 1/8 oz. heroin	C Felony	A-III Felony
Sale of 5 mg. LSD	D Felony	A-II Felony
Possession of 5.25 mg. LSD	A Misdemeanor	A-III Felony
Possession of 2 oz. methamphetamine	A Misdemeanor	C Felony

Source: National Institute of Law Enforcement and Criminal Justice. (1978). *The nation's toughest drug law: Evaluating the New York experience.* p. 35. Retrieved from https://www.ncjrs.gov /pdffiles1/Digitization/47795NCJRS.pdf

Reprinted with permission of the Association of the Bar of the City of New York.

sified as a Class C felony offense. Under the 1973 laws, this was changed to an A-III felony that mandated imprisonment. Convictions for any of these three subcategories could result in a maximum of life imprisonment and each subcategory designated a mandatory minimum (National Institute of Law Enforcement and Criminal Justice, 1978).

Criticisms of Rockefeller Drug Laws

As soon as the Rockefeller Drug Laws were introduced, criticisms of these mandatory minimum penalties for drug offenses were raised. Specialists in drug treatment scoffed at the idea of punishing those who suffered from drug addiction. Legal experts called the sentences "draconian." It was argued that there was no justice in sentencing low level offenders the same as drug kingpins. Herman (1999–2000) suggested that the focus in assigning penalties should not reflect *potential harm* simply based on weights of drugs which were assigned a certain class depending on their chemical properties, but rather on *actual harm* done in the specific drug offense. In questioning the proportionality of the Rockefeller Drug Laws, Herman (1999–2000) posited, "One way to frame this question is to ask whether an individual distributing two ounces of heroin is in fact as culpable as murdering someone" (p. 783).

Others critiqued the way the laws were enforced. Evidence suggested that these laws were being disproportionately applied to offenders coming from poor black and Hispanic neighborhoods. This negatively impacted both families in those neighborhoods and race relations in general.

Reforms to the Rockefeller Drug Laws

By the 2000s, polls showed that the public favored more judicial discretion and the opportunity to send some drug addicts to rehabilitation programs rather than prison (New York Times, n.d.). As a result of both ideological concerns and practical ones — the state of New York was suffering from budget problems — then Governor Pataki placed some changes in a 2003 budget bill that would reduce the length of prison sentences. Those convicted of class A1 mandatory sentences could earn "merit" time to decrease their sentence lengths. Between 2003 and 2005, eligibility for merit time was extended in several ways for such offenders if they exhibited good behavior, and/or participated in work or treatment programs. Parole eligibility was also moved up for those offenders convicted of A1 drug crimes who had already served ten years of 15-to-life sentences. Another measure in the 2003 budget bill increased the number of offenders who could qualify for the Department of Correctional Services' (DOCS) "earned eligibility" program (Greene & Mauer, 2010).

More reforms to the Rockefeller Drug Laws followed the 2004 legislative session, which would significantly alter some of the most severe components of the mandatory sentencing provisions. Sentences for drug offenders were changed from indeterminate to determinate. Also, the threshold amounts needed to trigger the most severe mandatory minimums were increased. The A-III felony classification was eliminated. Offender charged with A-I and A-II offenses no longer had to plead guilty to an A-III felony. The indeterminate sentence of 15-to-life for Class A-I crimes was changed to a determinate sentence in which the judge would decide in a range of eight to 20 years. There were no longer life sentences for any drug offense (Mancuso, 2009–2010). Hundreds of A-I offenders who were serving a 15-to-life sentence at the time could petition a judge to be resentenced under the new law. In contrast, resentencing was not available to offenders convicted of A-II drug offenses (Greene & Mauer, 2010).

In 2005, legislators passed another round of reforms to the Rockefeller Drug Laws. An additional "merit time" provision was extended to those drug offenders convicted under class A-II. These offenders were also then given the right to petition the judge for resentencing. These reforms also gave judges more discretion in resentencing by widening the range for determinate sentencing (Greene & Mauer, 2010, Mancuso, 2009–2010).

David Paterson, a Democrat, was elected governor of New York in 2008. Democrats also won leadership in the state Senate that year. Paterson continued, with support from the state Senate, to initiate additional revisions to the Rockefeller Drug Laws that had begun under Republican Governor Pataki. In the late 2000s, many still felt the laws in the state of New York were too harsh. In the late 2000s, almost 12,000 persons were imprisoned for drug offenses. In 2008, over 5,000 people in the state of New York were incarcerated for nonviolent drug offenses (Smith, 2009).

The New York State Assembly organized joint hearings concerning more reforms to the Rockefeller Drug Laws in fall 2008. The theme involved taking an approach that focused on health and drug issues, and experts in the field of drugs and advocates for change testified in support of this change in focus. On April 7, 2009, Governor Paterson signed reforms into law. According to Greene and Mauer (2010) the key elements of the 2009 drug law reforms included the following: increased judicial discretion to place drug offenders into treatment, to divert those who commit non-drug crimes because of substance dependence, and opportunities to re-sentence persons who were given indeterminate sentences prior to 2005 who were still serving time.

Michigan's 650 Lifer Law

Not long after the Rockefeller Drug Laws went into effect, the state of Michigan passed the 650 Lifer Law, which would come to be known as the strictest narcotics law in the nation. The following *Spotlight* section describes the 650 Lifer Law through the story of JeDonna Young, one of the first persons sentenced under this law.

Spotlight — JeDonna Young Sentenced under Michigan's 650 Lifer Law

In October of 1978 at the age of 25, JeDonna Young was arrested and charged with possession of over 650 grams of heroin with intent to deliver. Under Michigan's 650 Lifer Law, Young was sentenced to life imprisonment without parole. This mandatory minimum sentencing law was written to put away major drug dealers.

JeDonna Young, however, did not fit the profile of a major drug dealer. This was Young's first conviction (and first arrest) for a crime she claimed she did not know she was committing.

At the time of the arrest, Young was dating 52-year-old James Gulley, a man who showered Young with gifts, including a new Cadillac. Young said she did not know then that Gulley made his money to pay for such gifts by selling drugs. On the day of her arrest, Gulley asked Young to drive him around to do errands. Before they left he asked her to put some packages in the car for him and she complied. JeDonna Young swore she did not know that one of the packages was three pounds of heroin. Police, who had been suspicious of Gulley for some time, watched Young put the packages in the car. They followed the car and pulled her over. They ordered Young and Gulley out of the car and asked Young whose package was in the car. They then put Young and Gulley in separate cars and according to Young that was when "the nightmare began" (CBS, February 11, 2009).

The Michigan criminal justice system prosecuted Young under the 650 Lifer Law, which was designed to imprison for life major drug traffickers who possessed, delivered, or intended to deliver over 650 grams (approximately one and one-half pounds) of narcotics. This mandatory minimum sentencing law would not allow judges to alter the sentence, even in light of the fact that Young had no prior convictions. Compared to federal mandatory minimums for drug offenses, Michigan's 650 Lifer Law was stricter.

Over two hundred people were convicted and sentenced to life without parole under the 650 Lifer Law. Over 85 percent of those offenders convicted under the law had no prior incarceration record and seven teenagers were convicted to life without parole under the law (CBS, February 11, 2009). Pratt (1997, March 3) noted that the bill enacted by Michigan lawmakers was added to a public health bill without public hearings or any impact analysis and that judges were not consulted prior to the passage of the 650 Lifer Law.

During the same time period that Michigan laws mandated lengthy sentences for nonviolent drug offenders, Michigan's corrections budget skyrocketed. Between the mid-1970s and mid-1990s, the corrections budget increased 1,428 percent from $65 million to $1.27 billion. From the mid-1980s to the mid-1990s, the percent of Michigan's general fund allocated for prison spending more than doubled (Pratt, 1997, March 3).

In the same month that Young was arrested, Tim Allen Dick, who would later become known as Tim Allen, the actor who starred in the situation comedy, *Home Improvement*, was also arrested for the possession of over 650 grams of cocaine. Tim Allen, however, was prosecuted under the federal system and was given a sentence of only two and one-half years in prison, after he cooperated with federal prosecutors in exchange for a reduced sentence (CBS, 2009; Pratt, 1997). Young clearly fared worse, after being charged under Michigan's new mandatory minimum sentencing law.

Young's case highlighted the major critique of mandatory sentencing laws—that they completely eliminate judicial discretion for those sentenced under them. In the case *Young v. Miller* (1989), the Sixth Circuit Court established that JeDonna Young was not a partner in James Gulley's drug trafficking business and had no prior criminal record. In regards to the imposition of the 650 Lifer Law in Young's case, the court stated, "In this case, we believe that the tiger trap may have sprung upon a sick kitten. We are not at all convinced that petitioner Young is the type of 'kingpin' drug dealer the Michigan legislature has targeted for its harshest punishment" (Pratt, 1997, March 3). The court, however, decided to deny her appeal, stating that heroin dealing in any amount was too serious an offense (CBS, 2009). This case highlighted how the "one size fits all" approach of mandatory minimums can result in sentences that are grossly disproportionate to the harm inflicted by the convicted offender.

In 1998, state legislators voted to permit parole release for offenders after serving 17–20 years who were sentenced under Michigan's 650 Lifer Law. JeDonna Young appeared in front of the parole board and became the first offender sentenced under the 650 Lifer Law to be released. She earned a bachelor's degree while in prison and also served as a paralegal and advisor to other incarcerated women. Since being released, she has earned her master's degree in social work, served as Families Against Mandatory Minimums' (FAMM) Midwest Coordinator, and is currently FAMM's Detroit Coordinator. (http://famm.org/facesofFAMM/SuccessStories/JeDonnaYoung .aspx).

Federal and State Drug Laws — Complementary or Contradictory?

Overlapping Jurisdiction

Oftentimes charges for drug offenses may be filed by either federal or state authorities. In these situations, acts such as drug trafficking violate both state and federal laws. It is up to state and local authorities to decide who will pursue the case.

Spotlight — Medical Marijuana — A Look at the Differences between California State Law and Federal Law

An interesting situation exists in California, where the acts of growing and dispensing medical marijuana are legal according to state law, but both acts violate federal drug laws. In his investigative series on CNN, *Inside Man*, Morgan Spurlock showcased the issue of contradictory federal and state laws in California in his episode entitled "Medical Marijuana."

California legalized medical marijuana in 1996, after which dispensaries were established throughout the state. While these dispensaries are licensed and legal under California state law, they exist illegally, according to federal law. It is legal in the state of California for a person who has been issued a medical marijuana card to grow up to 24 plants. This would, however, violate federal law. Unlike dispensaries, growers are not licensed and have no legal protection.

Throughout the program, Spurlock showcased the Harborside Health Center, the largest dispensary of medical marijuana in the state of California. This facility is also considered by federal authorities to be the largest illegal drug distribution center in the country. According to federal authorities, the Harborside Health Center is a criminal organization. Spurlock chronicled the legal challenges to the facility.

He also profiled the case of Matt Davies, an MBA-educated man who grew marijuana that he sold in his California dispensary. Davies faced up to 40 years in federal prison for acts (growing and dispensing marijuana for medical use) that are legal in the state of California. Davies ultimately plead guilty and was sentenced to a mandatory five years in federal prison.

Conflict between state and federal law clearly exists regarding the sale and dispensing of medical marijuana in California and the federal response has been puzzling. Spurlock reported that in 2008, then candidate-Obama denounced the Bush administration's federal raid on medical marijuana facilities. He indicated that he would not use Justice Department resources to try to circumvent state laws on medical marijuana. Memos put forth under the Obama administration suggested that users and growers in states where medical marijuana was legal would not be targeted by federal authorities. A 2011 Justice Department memo suggested that patients using prescribed medical marijuana would be free from federal prosecution for using and growing, but that industrial growers would not be overlooked.

By April 2012, well into Barack Obama's presidency, there had been approximately 200 dispensary raids resulting in 60 federal indictments. This figure represents more raids during just four years of the Obama administration than the total number of raids during the entire eight years of George W. Bush's administration (Spurlock, 2013, June 23).

In 2010, former Attorney General Eric Holder warned California voters that he would vigorously enforce federal law if marijuana was legalized in the state. Several years later, however, a major turn in this practice was symbolized by Holder's failure to warn voters similarly when measures to legalize marijuana in Colorado, Washington, and Oregon were on the ballot (Nadelmann, 2014, September).

Currently, four states—Colorado, Washington, Oregon, and Alaska—have legalized marijuana for recreational use. Twenty-three states and the District of Columbia currently have laws legalizing marijuana in some form (medical and/or recreational). It now seems far-fetched to imagine federal system officials vigorously enforcing all extant federal laws regarding possession of small amounts of marijuana.

Federal Mandatory Minimum Sentencing for Firearms Offenders

There are two major federal mandatory minimum sentencing provisions relating to firearms offenses. The first, contained in section 924(c) of title 18, United States Code (U.S.C.) defines the offense of using or carrying a firearm during and in relation to, or possessing a firearm in furtherance of, a crime of violence or a drug trafficking crime. According to the United States Sentencing Commission (2011c):

> The statute prescribes a mandatory minimum penalty of at least five years of imprisonment for committing the offense, with increasingly longer mandatory minimum penalties based on how the firearm was used (seven years if the firearm was brandished and ten years if the firearm was discharged) and the type of firearm involved (ten years if the firearm was a short-barreled rifle, a

short-barreled shotgun, or a semiautomatic assault weapon and 30 years if the firearm was a machine gun, a destructive device, or was equipped with a silencer or muffler). (pp. 269–270)

Section 924(c) also dictates that the mandatory minimums designated for these firearms violations are imposed in addition to the punishment for the underlying crime of violence or drug trafficking and that the mandatory minimums are also to be served consecutively (as opposed to concurrently) to the underlying crime. The section establishes longer mandatory minimum sentences (usually 25 years of imprisonment) for each "second or subsequent conviction" of a section 924(c) offense (United States Sentencing Commission, 2011c, p. 270).

The second federal provision related to firearms is the Armed Career Criminal Act, described in 18 U.S.C. §924(e). It requires a mandatory minimum sentence of 15 years for a defendant who has violated 18 U.S.C. §922(g) and who has at least three prior convictions for either violent felonies or serious drug offenses. According to the United States Sentencing Commission (October, 2011c), Section 922(g)

> makes it unlawful for certain prohibited persons, including convicted felons, fugitives from justice, persons dishonorably discharged from the armed forces, and aliens who are illegally or unlawfully in the United States, to possess a firearm or ammunition that is in or affecting commerce, to ship or transport a firearm or ammunition in interstate or foreign commerce, or to receive any firearm or ammunition which has been shipped or transported in interstate or foreign commerce (p.271). This section enhances the sentence for committing an offense under 18 U.S.C. §922(g) and, therefore, §924(e) doesn't establish a separate criminal offense.

State Mandatory Minimum Sentencing for Firearms Offenses

Many states have established mandatory minimum sentences for firearms offenses. We will look at two of the earliest — Massachusetts' Bartley-Fox Amendment and Michigan's Felony Firearms Statute.

Massachusetts' Bartley-Fox Amendment

In July 1974, the Bartley-Fox Amendment was adopted in Massachusetts. This law required a mandatory one-year prison term for offenders who were convicted of the unlicensed carrying of firearms. It amended an existing law that prohibited carrying of a firearm without a required permit. The amendment was named after its sponsors, David Bartley, who was then Speaker of the Massachusetts House and John Fox, a retired judge. The law specifically prohibited courts from circumventing the imposition of the mandatory penalty by informally disposing of eligible cases. One year of incarceration was to be imposed for anyone (regardless of criminal record) who violated the law, the sentence was to be served without the possibility of parole or furlough, and the imprisonment sentence could not be suspended.

The existing gun laws in Massachusetts at the time the Bartley-Fox Amendment was put into place were already relatively stringent, compared to other states. Starting in 1906, a Massachusetts statute required persons carrying a loaded pistol or revolver to have a license. In 1968, the requirement to have a permit was extended to the ownership or possession of any gun. At the time the amendment was proposed, the laws pertaining to ownership, possession, and carrying of firearms delineated two requirements involving identification and licensing. To *own or possess a handgun* or *to own, possess, or carry a long gun*, citizens had to obtain a "firearm identification (FID) card." To *carry a handgun*, a citizen was required to get a separate license from a local authority if the individual was deemed to be "a suitable person" who has "good reason to fear injury" or has "any other proper purpose" (Beha, 1977, p. 102).[2] In order for a citizen to *purchase* a handgun, the individual was required to have a license to carry or a special permit and an FID card. The requirements for purchase, which were enacted in 1926, are what have characterized Massachusetts as restrictive relative to other states.

The punishment system prior to Bartley-Fox had only differentiated between improper ownership or possession of any firearm and the improper carrying of a handgun. Beginning in 1968 the penalty imposed for improper ownership or possession of any firearm was a maximum of one year of imprisonment or a $500 fine. The punishment for improper carrying of a handgun ranged from at least six months in jail to a maximum of up to five years in state prison. The statute, however, included a clause that allowed the court to sentence a defendant without a previous felony conviction to a maximum fine of fifty dollars or to imprisonment of no greater than two and one half years. Repeat offenders were punished more harshly and could not have their imprisonment sentences suspended or be eligible for parole or time off for good behavior. Beha (1977) characterized Massachusetts' penalty structures for these firearms violation laws as having "something of a mandatory flavor" (p. 103) even before Bartley-Fox.

The Bartley-Fox Amendment did not change the punishment structure of *improper ownership or possession offenses*. Four revisions to the penalties for *carrying offenses*, however, were enacted. First, separate provisions for firearms were made compared to those for other dangerous weapons. Second, the minimum incarceration sentence that would be imposed for illegally carrying a firearm was increased from six months to one year. Third, the carrying offense now included the carrying of a long gun without having an FID card. This contrasted with earlier law, in which illegal carrying of a long gun was not distinguished from illegal possession and the maximum penalty was one year of incarceration. Fourth, the statute imposed strict provisions for all persons who were charged under the law. Included was the requirement that those convicted under the law had to serve the mandatory minimum sentence of one year. In other words, every defendant convicted under the law (all offenders whose cases were neither dismissed nor who were acquitted) had to serve a minimum of one year of imprisonment. The law also indicated that prosecutions were not to be disposed of informally (Beha, 1977).

The statute did not disallow plea bargaining of a charge involving carrying, however. A defendant's plea to another charge could result in a dismissal of a carrying charge. Carrying cases could also be dismissed by the prosecution.

There were multiple purposes of the law. Bartley-Fox was, in part, designed to decrease gun-related crime. It was also meant to decrease illegal carrying of firearms. Pierce and Bowers (1981) suggested that the law's target group was made primarily those who carry guns but who have no criminal intent. They labeled these offenders, "casual carriers."

Before the Bartley-Fox Amendment went into effect, the law was highly publicized. As we discussed in Chapter 1, to be an effective deterrent a sanction must be known to the general public. Through an intense media campaign, the message was spread that the law would be carried out in a swift and certain manner. The media campaign which highlighted the penalties for carrying a gun without a license began two months before the law's imposition. The consequences of the law were stated as, "If you are caught with a gun, you will go to prison for a year and nobody can get you out" (Pierce and Bowers, 1981). The law went into effect on April 1, 1975.

Michigan Felony Firearms Statute

Another example of a mandatory sentencing law was the Michigan Felony Firearms Statute, which went into effect January 1, 1977. This law required a two-year sentence to be added on to the base sentence for a felony if that felony was committed with a firearm. For example, a robbery could be committed with various weapons (gun, knife, baseball bat, etc.). A person who committed a robbery *with a firearm would get two years automatically added on to his or her sentence* for the robbery offense.

The statute also emphasized a policy that the Wayne County (Detroit) prosecuting attorney could not drop charges involving cases in which a firearm was used in the crime for the exchange of a guilty plea. The law also prohibited sentencing offenders who committed a felony with a firearm from receiving probation, parole, or a suspended sentence (Loftin & McDowall, 1981).

This law was crafted in 1976, when Detroit's already serious crime problem had gotten worse. Violent crime rates soared in 1976. A purpose of this law was for the mandatory two- year add-on sentence to serve as a deterrent for would-be offenders who would otherwise commit felonies involving firearms. The Michigan law was widely publicized. A Citizens Committee to Deter Crime supported and publicized the law by distributing bumper stickers and posting billboards in Detroit that read "One With a Gun Gets You Two." The Wayne County Prosecuting Attorney, William Cahalan, also publicly supported the law (Loftin & McDowall, 1981). Some argued that the popularity of the law stemmed from the fact that it did not target a hot topic like illegal gun possession charges, but rather concentrated on criminals who committed felonies with firearms.

Federal Mandatory Minimum Sentencing for Child Pornography Crimes

History of Statutes and Sentencing Guidelines Covering Child Pornography Offenses

Congressional action regarding the distribution and receipt of child pornography began with the passage of the Protection of Children Against Sexual Exploitation Act of 1977. Pursuant to this act, the production and the *commercial* distribution and receipt of child pornography was prohibited. The act set into law a ten-year statutory maximum for first-time traffickers and a 15-year statutory maximum and a two-year mandatory minimum prison sentence for subsequent offenses. The Child Protection Act of 1984 established penalties for producers and traffickers of child pornography as well as for those who committed the offenses for non-pecuniary purposes (meaning regardless of whether the material was sold). Congress passed the Child Sexual Abuse and Pornography Act of 1986 and the Child Abuse Victims' Rights Act of 1986, which acknowledged the detrimental effects of child pornography offenses on innocent victims. It increased the mandatory minimum sentence for repeat child pornography offenders from two to five years in prison. The Crime Control Act of 1990 outlawed simple possession of child pornography (United States Sentencing Commission, 2012a).

When the United States Sentencing Commission first set guidelines for specific offenses in 1987, they set sentencing ranges for offenders convicted of 18 U.S.C. §2251 (production of child pornography) and 18 U.S.C. §2252 (transport, distribution, and receipt of child pornography). In 1987, guidelines were not established for simple possession because simple possession of child pornography was not a federal crime at the time. The last time the United States Sentencing Commission made notable changes in the sentencing guidelines for child pornography crimes was in 2004, a year after the PROTECT Act was enacted.

The 2003 Protect Act

Harsh federal mandatory minimum sentences for a variety of child sex offenses and child pornography crimes were established in the 2003 when the PROTECT Act was passed. This law set in place mandatory minimum statutes for a variety of child sex and child pornography crimes. It established a five-year mandatory minimum for receipt, transportation, and distribution offenses and raised the statutory mandatory minimum for production offenses from ten to fifteen years. It also raised the statutory maximum penalties for production, as well as non-production offenses.

Congress passed the Child Protection Act of 2012, which raised the statutory maximum prison sentence from ten to twenty years for those convicted of possession of child pornography that depicted a prepubescent child or a minor under the age of twelve.

Under the PROTECT Act, Congress took a unique step in actually amending extant sentencing guidelines by increasing the number and types of sentencing enhancements that could be used in child pornography offense guidelines. At the time of the PROTECT

Act, the guidelines were still mandatory (as opposed to being advisory now, pursuant to *United States v. Booker* (2005) which will be described in Chapter 7) and Congress limited the sentencing judge's ability to depart below the guideline ranges for child pornography crimes.

Current Federal Child Pornography Statutes and Guidelines

Figure 6.5 shows the federal statutory penalty ranges for four categories of offenses involving child pornography.

Figure 6.5 Federal Child Pornography Statutory Penalty Ranges

Production			Receipt/Distribution/ Transportation		Possession		Obscenity	
No Prior Sex Conviction	Prior Sex Conviction	> 1 Prior Sex Conviction	No Prior Sex Conviction	Prior Sex Conviction	No Prior Sex Conviction	Prior Sex Conviction	18 U.S.C. § 1466A	18 U.S.C. §§ 1461 *et seq.*
15 to 30 years	25 to 50 years	35 years to life	5 to 20 Years	15 to 40 years	0 to 10 years or 0 to 20 years (depending on age of victim)	10 to 20 years	Mirrors penalties in CP statutes	0 to 5 years or 0 to 10 years (varies by statute)

Source: United States Sentencing Commission. (2012). *Report to Congress: Federal child pornography offenses, Executive summary*. p. v., Table 1. Retrieved from http://www.ussc.gov/Legislative_and_Public _Affairs/Congressional_Testimony_and_Reports/Sex_Offense_Topics/201212_Federal_Child _Pornography_Offenses/Executive_Summary.pdf

Production offenses yield the most lengthy mandatory imprisonment ranges. Offenders convicted of a production offense must serve at least 15 years in prison. Those convicted of production offenses with multiple priors can be sentenced up to life in prison. **Non-production offenses** include four categories — receipt, distribution, transportation, and possession. **Receipt/Distribution/Transportation (R/T/D) offenses** carry a mandatory minimum sentence range of 5 to 20 years if the offender has no prior sex convictions. Those with any prior sex convictions must serve a prison sentence from the range of 15 to 40 years. Those convicted of **possession** with no prior sex conviction are sentenced to zero to 10 years or zero to 20 years (depending on the age of the victim). Offenders convicted of possession with a prior sex conviction must serve 10 to 20 years in prison (United States Sentencing Commission, December, 2012a).

As we discussed in Chapter 5, the Federal Sentencing Guidelines have been put in place to serve as guides to federal judges in an effort to make sentencing federal offenders a more uniform practice. The Federal Sentencing Guidelines §2G2.1 establish guidelines for production offenses, while §2G2.2 covers non-production offenses.

Because approximately 90 percent of federal child pornography prosecutions are for non-production offenses, we will focus on the guidelines and statutes that apply to non-production offenses. We reiterate the USSC statement that "the statutes trump the guidelines." Therefore, the recommended guideline cannot be outside the range of minimum and maximum sentence prescribed by statute. It is relevant to look at the federal guidelines regarding child pornography offenses to ascertain typical base offense levels assigned to various non-production offenses and what kind of offense and offender characteristics can raise or lower the offense level. We can then see if the sentences are at the low end or high end of the statutory mandatory ranges.

Section 2G2.2 presents the guidelines for non-production offenses. These offenses are broken down into simple possession (with a base offense level of 18) and R/T/D offenses, which have a base level of 22. The base level for offenders convicted of a receipt crime who did *not* intend to traffic or distribute the child pornography is reduced by 2. Therefore, there are three base level starting points in sentencing for non-production offenders—conviction for possession (18), conviction of receipt *without* intent to distribute (20), and receipt *with* intent to distribute, as well as those convicted of distribution or transportation (22).

Section 2G2.2 also presents six sentencing enhancements that can be applied to any of these non-production offenses: (1) age (**add 2 levels** if the minor was prepubescent or had not turned 12), (2) if material involved portrayed sadistic or masochistic conduct or other depictions of violence (**add 4 levels**), (3) number of images (**add 2 levels** for at least 10 images, **add 3 levels** for 150–299 images, **add 4 levels** for 300–599 images, and **add 5 levels** for 600 or more images), (4) if the offense involved use of a computer (**add 2 levels**), (5) if offense involved distribution under any of a variety of circumstances (**add the greatest addition of 5 to 7 levels**), and (6) if defendant engaged in a pattern of activity involving the sexual abuse or exploitation of a minor (**add 5 levels**).

Departures and variances may result from any of the following: psychosexual evaluations, risk of engaging in conduct sex offenses (low or high risk), length of time looking at child pornography and collecting behavior (e.g., cataloguing images), material in images (e.g., babies in images), age of victims and age of the defendant, military service, computer sophistication (or lack thereof), findings of forensic experts, rehabilitation (e.g., successful sex offender treatment), and physical condition of defendant (United States Sentencing Commission, 2015, September 17).

The USSC has recognized that sentences for child pornography offenders must be within the range indicated by statute. In establishing base offense levels, the commission took an approach in **setting the base levels below the mandatory minimums**. The USSC relied on specific offense characteristics detailed in the previous paragraph and Chapter 3 adjustments (detailed in Chapter 5) to reach the mandatory minimums required by statute. One or more sentencing enhancements were applied in most non-production cases. Four of the six enhancements detailed above now apply to most non-production offenders. According to the United States Sentencing Commission (2012a), "In fiscal year 2010, §2G2.2(b)(2) (images depicting pre-pubescent minors) applied in 96.1 percent of cases, §2G2.2(b)(4) (sado-masochistic images) applied in 74.2 percent of cases; §2G2.2(b)(6) (use of computer) applied in 96.2 percent of cases; and §2G2.2(b)(7) (images table) applied to 96.9 percent of cases" (p. xi).

So, for example, the base offense level for an R/T/D offender with no prior sex convictions is 22, which indicates a sentence range of 41–51 months on the guideline matrix. This is below the statutory penalty range of 5 to 20 years for an R/T/D offense. However, because most offenders will be assigned sentencing enhancements, their sentences will not just meet, but exceed the statutory minimum of 60 months (5 years). With respect to possession convictions, there is no mandatory minimum prison sentence. The base offense level for such offenses (18) committed by offenders without a prior sex conviction indicates a sentencing range of 27–33 months, around 2 ½ years. Typically, the guidelines range calculated from the base offense level plus sentencing enhancements ends up towards the statutory maximum sentence.

After the PROTECT Act of 2003 was enacted, guideline penalty ranges, average imprisonment length, and average terms of supervised release increased. The 2004 fiscal year was the last fiscal year that the federal guidelines were mandatory, as opposed to their status today as advisory, and also the first full fiscal year after the PROTECT Act was enacted. In 2004, the average guideline minimum for non-production child pornography offenses was 50.1 months in prison and the average sentence imposed was 53.7 months. In the 2010 fiscal year, the average guideline minimum for non-production offenses was 117.5 months in prison and the average sentence imposed was 95.0 months (United States Sentencing Commission, December 2012a, p. x).

Prison Lengths for Child Pornography Offenders

Figure 6.6 Sentence Length in Months for Federal Non-Production
Child Pornography Offenses

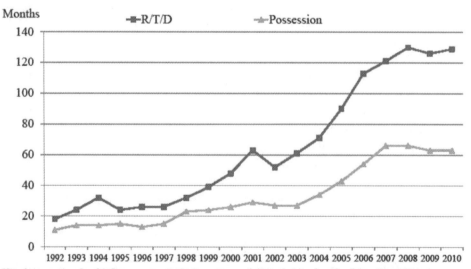

**Non-Production Sentences Over Time
Fiscal Years 1992-2010**

Note: Average sentence length is shown as average total prison sentence excluding probation and months of alternative confinement.
SOURCE: U.S. Sentencing Commission, 1992-2010 Datafile, USSCFY92-10 and FY10 Child Pornography Plea Agreement Special Coding Project.

Source: United States Sentencing Commission. (2012). *Report to Congress: Federal child pornography offense, Chapter 6, Analysis of sentencing data in cases in which offenders were sentenced under the non-production sentencing guidelines.* p. 132, Figure 6-4. Retrieved from http://www.ussc.gov/Legislative_and _Public_Affairs/Congressional_Testimony_and_Reports/Sex_Offense_Topics/201212_Federal _Child_Pornography_Offenses/Chapter_06.pdf

Figure 6.6 shows that the average length of imprisonment rose substantially from fiscal year (FY) 1992 to FY 2010 for both possession and R/T/D offenses. For possession offenses, the average prison sentence increased from 11 months in FY 1992 to 34 months in FY 2004 to 63 months in FY 2010. For R/T/D offenses, the average prison sentence in FY 1992 was 18 months, in FY 2004 was 71 months, and by 2010 was 129 months. (United States Sentencing Commission, December, 2012b).

United States Sentencing Commission Undertakes Study of Sentencing Practices for Child Pornography Offense

Child sex offenses and child pornography offenses deeply disturb mainstream society and produce immeasurable harm to victims. These crimes exploit, devalue, and damage children physically and psychologically. Approximately half of child pornography in the United States shows the sexual victimization of a child under six years of age and about one-quarter portray such abuse of a child two or younger. In addition to the harm to a child when these crimes are committed is the re-victimization of the child each and every time the image is shared or distributed, often through the internet. Research by the USSC showed that of the 1,654 non-production child pornography cases in fiscal year 2010, almost two-thirds of offenders distributed child pornography to others. The most common mechanism was a P2P file sharing program (United States Sentencing Commission, December, 2012a, p. viii).

Despite the harm inflicted on victims of child pornography, some have argued that the mandatory minimum sentences are disproportionate to the nature of some of these offenses. In his presentation *Viewers of Child Pornography: A Psychiatric Perspective*, delivered at the 2015 USSC National Annual Seminar, Dr. Fred Berlin of Johns Hopkins University labelled some child pornography offenders, "naively curious." He discussed how easy it is to view child pornography on the internet. He suggested that people who would never have looked at it might get pop-ups of adult pornography and discover that simply by pushing a button on their mouse child pornography is quite easy to receive.

Dr. Berlin asserted that this material might involve more of a fantasy that intrigues some people and that they are unaware that it will have real life consequences. He noted that some men who are aroused by rape scenarios would never in fact rape a woman. He also suggested that just because someone has a fantasy interest or is aroused by looking at child pornography does not necessarily mean they have any real-life interest in having sex with a child.

Dr. Berlin presented some cases of persons convicted of child pornography offenses. One involved a 30-year-old male who was a physician. This man had a history of being in foster care due to parental neglect. He was sexually abused and exposed to pornography as a child. Several months before arrest this man "discovered" child pornography. He didn't know he was being investigated. His behavior involved a file sharing network. He never produced materials or paid money for materials. He never had discussions with children. Berlin characterized him as a "man of good character." The man thought that because he privately viewed material that was already out there that it wouldn't cause harm. About 1 month prior to his arrest, the doctor became disgusted with himself and stopped. He received a substantial federal sentence.

The United States Sentencing Commission undertook a comprehensive study of the practice of sentencing child pornography offenses and produced the *Report to Congress: Federal Child Pornography Offenses* in December 2012. This report included a summary of the mandatory penalties and federal guidelines for child pornography offenses, a review of data about actual sentencing practices, and information from clinicians who study child sex offending. The report issued recommendations to Congress regarding the sentencing structure for child pornography offenses.

The commission has noted that while the percentage of federal cases that involve child pornography offenses is still relatively small (2.5 percent) that the percent of the federal caseload that involves child pornography offenses has increased dramatically during the past twenty years. According to the commission (2012b), "In fiscal year 1992, non-production cases accounted for 0.2 percent of 36,498 total federal criminal cases. By fiscal year 2010, such cases accounted for 2.0 percent of all 83,946 federal cases" (p. 126).

The report re-examined federal guidelines and the mandatory minimums established since the PROTECT Act of 2003 and the *United States v. Booker* (2005) case that decided that the guidelines should be considered *advisory* as opposed to *mandatory*. The commission reported that the rate of sentences for non-production offenses imposed *within* the guidelines ranges decreased from 83.2 percent in fiscal year 2004 to 32.7 percent in fiscal year 2011. The rate of below range sentences has increased and this rate was 62.8 percent in fiscal year 2011. According to the USSC, the continued decrease in the rate of sentences imposed within the applicable guideline ranges over the years has happened at the same time we have seen an increase in the average minimums of the ranges. The commission suggested that this might reflect the belief of court personnel that the current sentencing scheme for non-production offenses is overly harsh for some offenders.

The USSC has suggested that the guidelines be re-examined, as they fail to differentiate in a meaningful way the levels of seriousness of various offenses. The commission explained that the increases in the guideline minimums reflected an increase of the incidence of underlying conduct and case characteristics that trigger sentencing enhancements. These case characteristics were initially deemed to serve as sentencing enhancements. As aggravating circumstances in sentencing, these factors were to differentiate some cases as more serious. Today, however, case characteristics such as use of a computer and a large number of images are typical in non-production cases and fail to distinguish levels of seriousness or harm to victim. Changes in computer technology, regarding speed and capacity and features such as file sharing in the last decade, have contributed to the increase in the proportion of non-production child pornography offenders who are assigned the relevant sentencing enhancements. The USSC has concluded that the non-production guidelines in place today are outdated and in need of revision.

Another interesting finding of the commission was that over one-half of the §2G2.2 offenders were convicted of only possession, even though presentence investigation reports and/or plea agreements suggested that over 90 percent of child pornography offenders had committed R/T/D offenses (United States Sentencing Commission, December 2012a, p. xiii). Possession does not carry a mandatory minimum prison sentence (if the offender has no prior sex conviction) and R/T/D offenses do. This contributes to further evidence that court personnel perceive the penalty structure for some R/T/D offenses as overly harsh and that this perception results in charging them with only possession. This undercharging serves to circumvent the statutory mandatory minimums for offenders who receive, transport, or deliver child pornography.

The stance that current federal guidelines no longer effectively distinguish offenders based on their dangerousness and level of culpability is shared by the Department of Justice, the federal defender community, and the Criminal Law Committee of the Judicial Conference of the United States Courts. The commission has targeted what it has termed "disproportionate enhancements related to offenders' collecting behavior" and the failure of current guidelines to meaningfully distinguish offenders who are or are not involved in child pornography communities and which offenders are sexually dangerous. The commission has characterized the current guidelines as resulting in overly harsh sentences for some offenders, overly lenient penalties for other offenders, and inconsistent application of guidelines which have a goal of increasing sentencing uniformity.

The commission recommends revising the guidelines to better account for "the full range of an offender's collecting behavior, the degree of his involvement in a child pornography community, and any history of sexually dangerous behavior" (United States Sentencing Commission, 2012a, p. xxi). The commission encourages the consideration of social science research to aid in understanding sexual dangerousness.

The commission also calls for revisions in the structure of the federal statutes. It calls for a statutory structure that better aligns sentences for receipt and possession which would reduce current sentencing disparities. The commission recommends that if Congress were to align penalties for receipt and possession that the statutory minimum should be less than five years. In addition, the commission suggests that Congress update the penalty structure for offenses involving distribution to one that differentiates older and newer technologies used by offenders who distribute child pornography (The United States Sentencing Commission, 2012a).

A Broad Mandatory Minimum Sentencing Law — Oregon's Measure 11

While many mandatory sentencing laws focus on specific offenses (firearms, drugs, or child pornography) or target repeat offenders, Oregon's Measure 11, which went into effect on April 1, 1995, represented a broader effort to eliminate judicial discretion for a wide range of offenses. In 1994, Oregon residents voted to pass Measure 11, which mandated long prison terms for 16 specific violent and/or sexual offenses.[3] This mandatory sentencing law was passed after Oregon had already established more general sentencing guidelines for a wide range of offenses.

Measure 11 eliminated judicial discretion for persons who were convicted of any of the 16 offenses and set lengthy prison terms, based on the seriousness of the crime. The minimum prison term for those sentenced under Measure 11 (whose crimes were committed on or after April 1, 1995) ranged from 70 months for assault in the second degree to 300 months for murder. Prior record was irrelevant. Although they were not the drafters of Oregon's Measure 11 mandatory sentencing provisions, Crime Victims United (CVU), a prominent victim's rights group in Oregon, supported this legislation, noting its emphasis on punishing the most serious violent offenders through sentences commensurate to the harm done by the offender (Merritt, Fain, & Turner, 2006).

Revisions have been made to Measure 11. Six additional offenses were added to the list of Measure 11 offenses. A "Measure 11 exceptions" statute (ORS 137.712) allowed an offender who would have been sentenced under Measure 11, to be sentenced to fewer months than Measure 11 dictated, if the case met certain conditions.

The Status of Mandatory Sentencing in the United States

State Mandatory Minimum Sentencing Provisions

Table 6.1 Overview of Mandatory Minimum Sentencing

This list of examples of mandatory sentencing laws in each state is not an exhaustive list of every single mandatory minimum in each state. Rather, it presents examples of the mandatory minimums in various jurisdictions. For states that have revised mandatory minimums, a summary of the most recent revision concludes the state entry.

Sentencing laws, including mandatory minimums, are subject to revisions. The interested reader is encouraged to check out the most recent revisions to mandatory minimums in each state.

Alabama There are multiple mandatory minimum sentences in the state. For drug trafficking, there is a mandatory 3-year, 5-year, 15-year, 25-year, or life sentence without parole based on the quantity of drugs involved. There is also a 5-year minimum for offenses committed near schools or housing projects.

Alaska The state does not have mandatory minimums sentences except in the case of first-degree murder with certain circumstances that can subject an offender to a mandatory 99-year sentence.

Arizona Arizona categorizes its felony crimes as dangerous or non-dangerous. Depending on the class of the felony, there is a minimum sentence indicated. The only class of felony not covered by the statutory minimums are Class One felonies. First and second degree murder are the only Class One felonies in the state. First degree murder has a mandatory sentence of life without parole or death.

Arkansas A person convicted of a capital offense shall be punished by death by lethal injection or by life imprisonment without parole. Any person who commits a

(continued)

Table 6.1 Overview of Mandatory Minimum Sentencing (continued)

felony offense involving homicide, assault or battery, or domestic battering or assault on a family member or household member may be subject to an enhanced sentence of an additional term of imprisonment of not less than one year if the offense is committed in the presence of a child. Possession of marijuana yields mandatory minimum sentences as follows: 10 to less than 25 pounds—3 years, 25 to less than 100 pounds—5 years, 100 to less than 500 pounds—6 years. Delivery of marijuana yields mandatory minimum sentences as follows: 4 ounces to 25 pounds—3 years, 25 pounds to 100 pounds—5 years, 100 to 500 pounds—6 years. Trafficking of marijuana over 500 pounds is 10 years.

Arkansas enacted a prison reform bill in March 2011 that reduced minimum penalties for possession of drugs and reduced some of the harsher mandatory terms for distribution of drugs.

California In addition to California's three strikes law, California has other sentencing enhancements for prior crimes. A current conviction for a "serious" felony gets a 5-year enhancement if the defendant has a prior serious felony conviction. A 3-year enhancement applies to "violent" felonies if the defendant served time in prison for a prior violent felony. A 1-year enhancement applies to any felony if the defendant served time in prison for any felony. A person convicted of certain sex crimes on a list will receive a 5-year enhancement for each prior conviction of those certain sex crimes. If the defendant previously went to prison for a crime on the list, the court imposes a 10-year enhancement for each prior prison term. Convictions for narcotic offenses get a 3-year enhancement for each prior drug-crime conviction. There are sentence enhancements for the use and discharge of a firearm that results in serious injury or death for violent felonies. These enhancements are 10-, 20-, and 25-years-to-life, respectively.

Colorado First degree murder is life imprisonment or the death penalty. There are various mandatory minimums for drug crimes in the state, specifically for Level One drug felonies, which require a minimum of 8 years. Any offender convicted of a crime of violence must be sentenced to a prison term which is at least at the midpoint in the presumptive range. There are no mandatory minimums for firearms, however, a firearm may aggravate the sentence imposed.

In 2013, the Colorado legislature extensively amended the existing offenses and penalties relating to marijuana offenses and drug offenses in general. Under the new law, all of the offenses previously listed as felonies, misdemeanors, or petty offenses, are now designated as "drug felonies," "drug misdemeanors," and "drug petty offenses," with what, in general, amounts to a slightly lesser degree of punishment compared to the punitive scheme applicable to other felonies. Drug felonies are classified in C.R.S. section 18-1.3-401.5(2)(a) and (b) and apply to offenses committed on or after October 31, 2013.

(continued)

Table 6.1 Overview of Mandatory Minimum Sentencing (continued)

Connecticut Any person who commits any class A, B, or C felony and in the commission of such felony uses, or is armed with and threatens the use of, or displays, or represents by his words or conduct that he possesses any firearm, as defined in section 53a-3, except an assault weapon, as defined in section 53-202a, shall be imprisoned for a term of five years, which shall not be suspended or reduced and shall be in addition and consecutive to any term of imprisonment imposed for conviction of such felony. Capital murder is life without the possibility of parole. Multiple mandatory minimums exist for several violent crimes, including 10-year mandatory minimum for manslaughter in the first degree with a firearm, 10-year mandatory minimum for a robbery in the first degree if armed with a deadly weapon, assault in the first degree if deadly weapon is used to cause serious physical injury or 20-year mandatory minimum if the victim is under age 10 or a witness.

In 2001, Connecticut legislators gave courts some leeway to relax mandatory minimum sentencing laws for sale or possession of drugs if there is "good cause," even if the offense occurred within a drug-free school zone.

Delaware Any person who is convicted of first degree murder shall be punished by death or by imprisonment for the remainder of the person's natural life without benefit of probation or parole or any other reduction. Serious sex offenders or pedophile offenders convicted will receive no less than 25-years-to-life if the defendant has previously been convicted of certain sex offenses or if the victim of the instant offense is less than 14 years of age. For trafficking in controlled substances, Delaware has sentences of 2 years, 4 years, and 8 years for the following drugs based on the amount one has: marijuana, cocaine, opiates, methamphetamine, amphetamine, PCP, LSD, designer drugs, and Ecstasy. If the defendant has a prior conviction for distribution, trafficking, or distributing to a minor, then the sentence: for manufacture with intent to deliver is 3 years, manufacture with intent to deliver heroin is 5 years, distributing a non-narcotic to a minor is 7 years, and distributing a narcotic to a minor is 10 years. Possession of a firearm during the commission of a felony for the first or second conviction has a 3-year add-on for the first and second conviction, and this increases to a 5-year add-on for a third conviction.

In 2011, Delaware enacted a new law that eliminated mandatory minimum sentences for some first-time drug offenders and reduced minimum prison sentences for drug felonies. The new law also reduced the size of drug-free school zones from 1,000 feet to 300 feet, to restore the original intent of the law. In 2001, Delaware legislators reduced the mandatory minimum prison terms for trafficking cocaine from three years to two years, and increased the quantity of drugs needed to trigger that penalty.

District of Columbia First degree murder of a police officer is life without opportunity for release. First degree murder is 30 years. Most of the mandatory minimums involve violent and/or firearms offenses. For example, it is illegal to possess a firearm

(*continued*)

Table 6.1 Overview of Mandatory Minimum Sentencing (continued)

or imitation firearm during a crime of violence. The penalty is a mandatory minimum sentence of 5 years without probation or parole for the first offense and 10 years for the second and subsequent offenses. Armed carjacking carries a mandatory minimum of 15 years. Carjacking carries a mandatory minimum of 7 years. The unlawful possession of a firearm by a person with a conviction of a crime of violence is 3 years. The unlawful possession of a firearm by a person with a conviction that carries a sentence of a year or more is 1 year.

Bill 10-617, the District of Columbia Nonviolent Offenses Mandatory-Minimum Sentences Amendment Act of 1994 repealed all mandatory minimum sentences for non-violent drug offenders in the District of Columbia.

Florida Florida has passed many mandatory minimum sentences. Mandatory minimums for drug crimes are 3 years, 7 years, or 15 years depending on the quantity of the drugs. In some cases the mandatory minimum is 25 years for extreme quantities of certain drugs such as heroin. There are multiple firearms mandatory minimum sentences, and the minimum length depends on the type of firearm, whether it was simply possessed or discharged, and the type of offense it was party to. Violation for lewd or lascivious molestation of a child under age 12 by an adult over the age of 18 has a mandatory sentence of 25 years in prison followed by probation or life in prison, and for second and subsequent offenses, there is a mandatory life sentence.

On January 28, 2016, a unanimous Florida Senate removed the crime of aggravated assault from the list of gun-related crimes that require a mandatory 20-year prison sentence under a law known as 10-20-Life. In 2014, Florida eliminated mandatory minimum sentences for certain low-level drug offenses, reduced the mandatory sentences for other drug offenses by up to fifty percent, and increased the drug weights needed to trigger some of those offenses.

Georgia Georgia law identifies seven felonies, known as the "seven deadly sins," that require mandatory minimum sentences, including kidnapping, armed robbery, rape, aggravated child molestation, aggravated sodomy, and aggravated sexual battery. These offenses result in 10 years without possibility of parole. The seventh offense, murder, requires life imprisonment without possibility of parole for at least 25 years. A second conviction of any of these offenses mandates life without parole. The penalty is 25 years mandatory for sexual offenses like rape and sexual battery, as well as for kidnapping if the victim is under 14. There are several mandatory minimum sentences for drug trafficking, and the sentence length depends on the quantity of drugs that were allegedly trafficked. For cocaine, the sentence is 10 years for 28–200 grams, 15 years for 200–400 grams, and 25 years for over 400 grams. Possession of a firearm during the commission of a felony results in a 5-year consecutive sentence added on to the underlying felony charge. For second and subsequent convictions it is a 10-year sentence that cannot be altered by the judge.

(continued)

Table 6.1 Overview of Mandatory Minimum Sentencing (continued)

In 2013, Georgia enacted a drug "safety valve" law that allows judges to sentence below the mandatory minimum for certain non-violent first-time felonies. In 2012, Georgia reduced mandatory minimums for certain possession offenses.

Hawaii First degree murder has a mandatory sentence of life without parole. Second degree murder has a mandatory sentence of life with parole eligibility. There are varying minimums for violent crimes committed on those over 60, blind, paraplegic, or under 8 years of age. The minimums depend on the crime committed against one of the aforementioned groups and are added on to the underlying sentence depending on the felony class. There are multiple sentence enhancements for offenses that involve a firearm. These enhancements apply to second degree murder and Class A, B, and C felonies, and the length depends on the crime's classifications and type of firearm.

Idaho There are several mandatory minimum sentencing laws for drugs. Trafficking of heroin from 2 to 7 grams is 3 years, 7 to 28 grams is 10 years, and 28 grams and over is 15 years. Possession with intent to distribute marijuana carries 1-, 3-, or 5-year mandatory minimums, depending on quantity. Sale or delivery of marijuana carries 1-, 3-, or 5-year mandatory minimums, depending on quantity. First degree murder carries a sentence of life in prison unless the jury recommends the death penalty. There is an extended term sentence available for violent crimes with certain circumstances, and it is a 20-year add-on to the original sentence for the crime. There is a 15-year sentencing enhancement that applies to defendants who displayed, used, threatened, or attempted to use a firearm or other deadly weapon while committing or attempting to commit the crime.

Illinois The Class X is the most serious felony other than first-degree murder and carries a mandatory minimum of 6–30 years. For marijuana possession, there are 1-, 2-, 3-, and 4-year mandatory minimums, depending on the amount. For marijuana trafficking, there are 1-, 2-, 3-, 4-, and 6-year mandatory minimums, depending on the amount. Bringing 2,500 grams or more of marijuana into the state of Illinois brings a mandatory minimum sentence of twice the minimum sentence for the sale or manufacture of the same weight of marijuana. There are sentence enhancements for offenses committed with a firearm. Use of a firearm is a 15-year add-on, discharge of a firearm is a 20-year add-on, and discharge that results in serious injury or death is a 25-year-to-life add-on.

Indiana First degree murder with aggravating circumstances is life in prison unless there is a death sentence. All other sentences can be suspended except for minimum for murder (45 years) and Level 1 (20 years)—may only suspend that part of sentence in excess of the minimum sentence. There are no mandatory minimums for Level 2 and 3 drug offenses, even with a prior felony. State can seek a sentencing enhancement of between 5 and 20 years if a person uses a firearm to commit a felony

(continued)

Table 6.1 Overview of Mandatory Minimum Sentencing (continued)

under I.C. 35–42 that resulted in death or serious bodily injury, kidnapping, or criminal confinement as a level 2 or 3 felony. Criminal gang enhancement means the court must impose an additional fixed term of imprisonment equal to the longest sentence imposed for the underlying felonies (or equal to the sentence for the underlying felony if there is only 1 underlying felony) and cannot be suspended. Firearms enhancement may be a fixed term of imprisonment for 5 to 20 years for an offense against a person that results in death or serious bodily injury. There is a firearms enhancement for dealing offenses too.

Indiana revamped its Criminal Code in 2014, establishing new sentence ranges for various levels of crimes. Most drug laws are now completely suspendable. Penalties were lowered significantly for possession offenses. In 2001, Indiana eliminated its mandatory 20-year prison sentence for drug offenders arrested with 3 grams or more of cocaine, giving courts authority to sentence drug offenders who sell drugs to support their drug dependency to treatment instead of prison.

Iowa Iowa has one of the toughest sentences of any state with its "life without parole" sentence for sexual abuse in the first degree, a Class A felony. That is a "mandatory minimum" sentence. Selling any amount of marijuana to a someone younger than 18 years old is a felony, and is punishable with a 5-year mandatory minimum prison sentence (and up to 25 years). Cultivation or distribution to a minor within 1,000 feet of a park, elementary or middle school, or school bus is a 10-year enhancement. A person who has been convicted for a first violation for conspiring to manufacture or deliver amphetamine or methamphetamine to a minor shall not be eligible for parole until the person has served a minimum term of confinement of ten years.

Kansas Capital murder is death or life without the possibility of parole. Kansas' version of Jessica's Law directs if a defendant is 18 or older and commits aggravated trafficking with a victim under 14, rape, aggravated indecent liberties with a child, aggravated criminal sodomy, promoting prostitution, sexual exploitation of a child, or an attempt/conspiracy to commit any of the aforementioned offenses, the mandatory sentence for a first conviction is 25 years before parole eligibility. Sentencing enhancements include 6-month add-on to the sentence for possessing a firearm during the commission of a drug felony and 18-month add-on if the firearm was discharged during the commission of a drug felony. Sale or distribution of marijuana within 1,000 feet of a school zone is a mandatory 4-year sentence.

Kentucky For violent offenses, the state requires 85% of the sentence to be served before parole eligibility. Any enhancements to sentences come in the form of upgrading the felony class to give the offense a longer sentence than it would normally receive.

Louisiana Since the 1970s, Louisiana has had very harsh mandatory minimum sentencing laws. Possessing 400 grams or more of a Schedule I narcotic drug incurs a minimum prison sentence of 15 (and up to 30) years. Possession of marijuana

(continued)

Table 6.1 Overview of Mandatory Minimum Sentencing (continued)

yields mandatory minimums, dependent on the amount—60 to less than 2,000 pounds is 2 years, 2,000 pounds to less than 10,000 pounds is 5 years, 10,000 pounds or more is 25 years. Distribution of any amount and distribution of marijuana to a minor is 5 years. For violent offenses, the state requires that 85% of the sentence be served prior to being eligible for parole.

In May 2012, Act 160 gave prosecutors discretion to waive mandatory minimum prison terms for non-violent, non-sex offenses. In 2012, Act 401 allowed offenders who have been sentenced to life without parole for certain non-violent offenses to be eligible for parole after serving a definitive number of years in prison. In 2001, Act 403 repealed mandatory minimum sentences for simple drug possession and many other non-violent offenses and cut in half minimum sentences for drug trafficking. The state also restored the possibility of parole, probation, or suspension of sentence for a wide range of non-violent crimes.

Maine Maine has relatively few mandatory minimum sentences. For felony crimes that involves the use of a firearm against a person, and for drug trafficking crimes, the mandatory minimum prison terms depend on the class of crime. Maine's mandatory minimum prison sentences for gun or drug felonies are as follows: a Class A crime is 4 years, Class B crime is 2 years, Class C crime is 1 year.

In 2003, Maine passed legislation commonly known as a safety valve provision that allows courts to hand down a sentence other than a mandatory minimum term of imprisonment based upon the presence of specific individual characteristics. These include if the mandatory minimum would result in substantial injustice to the defendant, if imposing another sentence would not adversely affect public safety, or if it would not fail to deter others from committing trafficking or cultivation of scheduled drugs. The defendant must also be an appropriate candidate for an intensive supervision program and have some prospect of being rehabilitated.

Maryland Use of assault weapon or magazine with a capacity of more than 10 rounds in the commission of a felony or crime of violence, first offense is a 5-year mandatory minimum. Possess, use, wear, carry, or transport a firearm in a drug offense, first offense is 5-year mandatory minimum. Unlawful use of firearm in commission of felony or crime of violence, first offense is 5-year mandatory minimum. Rape, first degree, adult offender with victim younger than 13 years old is 25-year mandatory minimum. Rape, second degree, adult offender with victim younger than 13 years old is 15-year mandatory minimum. Drug distribution—drug kingpin is 20-year mandatory minimum. Manufacture, distribute, dispense, or possess certain Schedule I or II controlled dangerous substances, large amounts as specified in CR, §5-612, is 5-year mandatory minimum.

In May 2015, Maryland enacted a "safety valve" law that lets judges below the mandatory minimum for drug offenses if the mandatory sentence would be excessive and public safety is not at risk.

(*continued*)

Table 6.1 Overview of Mandatory Minimum Sentencing (continued)

Massachusetts Massachusetts has many mandatory minimums for drug offenses. Trafficking marijuana 50 to 100 pounds is 1 year, 100 to 2,000 pounds is 2 years, 2,000 to 10,000 pounds is 3 ½ years, 10,000 pounds or more is 8 years. School zone offense is 2 years. Using minors to sell drugs is 5 years. Trafficking certain Class A drugs (e.g., heroin): 18 to 36 grams is 3 ½ years, 36 to 100 grams is 5 years, 100 to 200 grams is 8 years, 200 or more grams is 12 years.

On August 2, 2012, Governor Deval Patrick signed into law the sentencing bill, An Act Relative to Sentencing and Improving Law Enforcement Tools. Mandatory minimum sentences for many drug offenses were reduced. The quantity of drugs needed to trigger certain low-level trafficking offenses was increased. School zone laws were reformed. In 2010, the Massachusetts legislature eased restrictions on drug offenders serving mandatory minimum sentences at county Houses of Correction. They can now be eligible for parole after serving half of their sentences, unless the drug offense involved violence, a weapon, or children, or if the drug offender "directed the activities of another" during the offense.

Michigan The most notorious mandatory minimum was Michigan's 650 Lifer Law, which was passed in 1978 and mandated life-without-parole sentences for anyone convicted of possession of 650 grams or more of cocaine or heroin.

In 1998, Governor John Engler signed modifications of the "650 Lifer Law" that eliminated life without parole, and provided parole eligibility to people serving sentences under the law. In 2003, the Michigan legislature repealed almost all mandatory minimums and implemented new sentencing guidelines. It should be noted, however, that as of July 31, 2015, the Michigan Supreme Court ruled that state's guidelines unconstitutional and so were all minimum sentences produced as a result of the guidelines. The ruling was based on the guidelines causing judges to find facts that were not presented to the jury during the trial, and such facts would impact the sentence as a result. The guidelines are now advisory rather than mandatory.

Minnesota First degree murder is life without parole. Firearms offenses include a 5-year minimum for possession of a firearm by a convicted felon, use of a firearm in a designated offense is 3 years that extends to 5 years with subsequent offenses, and a 1 year and 1 day minimum for using a dangerous weapon other than a firearm, which increases to 3 years for repeat offenders. First degree sex offenses have a 144-month minimum sentence, and second degree sex offenses have a 90-month minimum.

In 2009, the Minnesota legislature changed its laws so that courts could impose sentences for certain low-level drug felonies outside of mandatory minimums. Minnesota has one-, three-, and five-year consecutive mandatory minimum sentences for using or displaying a gun or dangerous weapon while committing certain offenses, including many violent offenses (murder, assault, robbery, sex offenses) and drug crimes. Courts may sentence some of these offenders below the manda-

(continued)

Table 6.1 Overview of Mandatory Minimum Sentencing (continued)

tory minimums (or give them probation instead of prison time) whenever the court finds "substantial and compelling reasons to do so."

Mississippi Displaying or using a firearm in a felony is a 5-year add-on. A convicted felon using a firearm in a felony is a 10-year add-on. Possession of marijuana depends on quantity: 250 to 500 grams is 2 years, 500 grams to 1 kilogram is 4 years, 1 to 5 kilograms is 6 years, 5 kilograms or more is 10 years. Committing a felony or other crime for the furtherance of a gang is a 1-year sentence enhancement.

In 2014, HB 585 was passed, which requires those convicted of a violent offense to serve at least 50 percent of their sentence, while anyone convicted of a non-violent offense will serve at least 25 percent before being eligible for parole. The measure also allows judges greater flexibility to impose alternate sentences, including sending convicted drug users to treatment instead of jail.

Missouri First degree murder is death or life without parole. In 1994, Missouri passed the Truth-in-Sentencing Act, designed to lessen the disparity between court sentences and actual time served in prison. The mandate ensured that an offender guilty of a Class A felony — including assault, arson, robbery, murder, forcible rape of a child, and some drug crimes — must serve at least 85 percent of his or her sentence before facing a parole board. Life without parole, on the other hand, denies an offender the chance of ever facing the board. Missouri has quite a few mandatory minimum sentences for drug crimes.

In May 2012, Missouri reduced its crack-powder cocaine disparity by increasing the amount of crack cocaine that triggers a mandatory minimum sentence. The new crack-powder disparity decreased from 75:1 to 18:1.

Montana Montana has 2-year mandatory minimums for aggravated assault, robbery, kidnapping, sexual assault, criminal distribution of dangerous drugs, and aggravated promotion of prostitution. Distribution of any amount of marijuana, with or without compensation, is punishable by a mandatory minimum of 1 year and a maximum sentence of life imprisonment and/or a fine up to $50,000.

Among other crimes, Montana has mandatory minimums for aggravated assault, many sex offenses, robbery, kidnapping, and drug crimes. In these cases, Montana's safety valve allows courts to give sentences below the mandatory minimum if the offender was a minor, had a significantly impaired mental capacity, committed the crime under unusual or substantial duress, was an accomplice who played a minor role, or when the crime did not involve a weapon or serious injury to the victim.

Nebraska Class IA felony is life imprisonment. Class IC felony is a mandatory minimum of 5 years imprisonment. Class ID felony is a mandatory minimum of 3 years imprisonment. So if a violent, drug, or firearms crime is a Class IC felony, the defendant would receive a mandatory 5-year sentence. Sale or manufacture of any amount of marijuana is a mandatory 1-year imprisonment sentence. Sale of mari-

(continued)

Table 6.1 Overview of Mandatory Minimum Sentencing (continued)

juana to a minor within 1,000 feet of a school or between 100–1,000 feet of other designated areas is a mandatory 1-year imprisonment sentence.

As of April 2015, a bill is underway to eliminate these mandatory minimums and reword the habitual offender statute to only apply to violent offenses instead of all felonies.

Nevada There are numerous mandatory minimum sentences for drug crimes, some with severe sentences and some with very minor minimum sentences. Possession of 1 ounce or less of marijuana—fourth offense is 1 year. Sale or delivery of less than 100 pounds of marijuana—first or second offense is 1 year, subsequent offenses is 3 years.

In 2007, the legislature in Nevada repealed mandatory sentencing enhancements and expanded "good time" eligibility for certain offenses.

New Hampshire First degree murder is life without parole or death. Life imprisonment for murder in the second degree. Manufacturing, delivering, selling, and/or using a controlled drug on or within 1,000 feet of a school is 1 year. Being convicted as a drug enterprise leader carries a 25-year sentence.

New Jersey New Jersey strictly enforces mandatory minimum penalties in its drug laws. A law enacted by the 1986 Congress addressed specific crimes in which the judge is forced to deliver fixed sentences regardless of mitigating factors. The judge shall not sentence an individual to less time than the minimum. Those who are serving mandatory minimum sentences are also ineligible to parole. The Mandatory minimum is determined by the type of drug, weight of the mixture, and prior convictions.

In 2010, New Jersey passed a law allowing judges some discretion when sentencing defendants convicted of drug-free "school zone" violations.

New Mexico First degree murder has a mandatory life sentence that can include parole after 30 years or no parole. Intentional abuse of a child under 12 that results in the child's death is a life sentence. Criminal sexual contact of a minor is a 3-year sentence. Aggravated criminal sexual penetration in the first degree is life imprisonment (eligible for parole in 30 years). Criminal penetration in the second degree of a child between the ages of 13–18 is 3 years. Criminal sexual contact of a minor in the second degree is 3 years. Use of a firearm during the commission of a noncapital felony is 1 year.

A proposed mandatory-minimum sentencing measure would bar judges from suspending or deferring more than 15 percent of a sentence for voluntary manslaughter, first degree kidnapping, assault on an officer, or drive-by shooting convictions.

New York New York's Rockefeller Drug Laws, enacted in 1973, mandated long prison sentences for many drug offenders. These laws are detailed in the text. For example, the penalty for selling two ounces of heroin, morphine, opium, cocaine, or

(continued)

Table 6.1 Overview of Mandatory Minimum Sentencing (continued)

cannabis was a minimum of 15 years to life in prison, and a maximum of 25 years to life in prison. The state legislature enacted significant changes to those laws over time. An offender who possesses a gun while committing certain violent offenses will get a 5-year add-on prison sentence.

The most recent reforms to the state's drug laws came in April 2009. At that time, mandatory prison sentences for some drug offenses were eliminated and minimum sentence lengths were reduced for others. The reforms expanded treatment options. Judges now have much discretion in imposing sentences based on the individual and case characteristics. New York law now gives the court discretion to ignore the 5-year add-on for the use of a firearm in the commission of certain violent offenses.

North Carolina North Carolina sets harsh mandatory minimum sentences for drug trafficking offenses. Unless the court finds that the offender provided substantial assistance, the offender must serve the following minimums for drug trafficking offenses: 225 months for a Class C (for example, 28 or more grams of heroin), 175 months for a Class D (for example, 400 or more grams of cocaine), 90 months for a Class E (for example, sell or deliver a controlled substance within 1,000 feet of a school), 70 months for a Class F, and 35 months for a Class G.

North Dakota North Dakota state has mandatory minimum sentences for some offenses. Mandatory minimums regarding drugs mostly apply to repeat offenses. For example, there is a 5-year minimum for a second conviction for selling heroin.

In 2001, North Dakota lawmakers repealed a one-year mandatory minimum sentence for first-time drug offenders

Ohio For possession of automatic or muffled firearm during the commission of a felony, there is a 6-year minimum. There is a 3-year minimum if a firearm is displayed, brandished, or otherwise indicated during a felony. There is a 1-year minimum for possession of a firearm during a felony, even if the weapon was not brandished or used.

In 2011, Ohio enacted legislation that repeals mandatory minimum sentences for some drug offenders. It requires first-time non-violent offenders to be sent to alternative treatment programs instead of prison. It also permits shorter sentences for low-level drug trafficking and possession offenses.

Oklahoma Oklahoma has had many mandatory minimum sentencing laws. These have included 5 years for robbery by 2 or more persons, 3 years for theft of horse, cow, or hog, 2 years for second offense for shoplifting (less than $500), 5 years for Schedule I or II non-marijuana drug distribution, and 2 years for marijuana distribution. Use of a firearm during a felony is 2 years. Discharging a firearm during the commission of a felony is 10 years. Pointing a firearm for the purpose of threatening is 1 year. Use or possession of restricted bullets is 2 years. Discharging a firearm into a public place or building is 2 years.

(continued)

Table 6.1 Overview of Mandatory Minimum Sentencing (continued)

In 2015, Oklahoma's Governor Fallin signed into law reforms that will allow judges some discretion from the state's many mandatory sentences. The states' Justice Safety Valve Act, HB 1518, will allow judges to give shorter sentences or divert some offenders to mental health or drug treatment if the convictions were for many non-violent crimes.

Oregon Measure 11, passed by Oregon voters in November 1994 applies long mandatory minimum sentences to 21 violent and serious offenses committed on or after April 1, 1995. There is no possibility of any sentence reduction for good behavior. These offenses include, but aren't limited to, murder, attempted murder, attempted aggravated murder, manslaughter, felony assaults, kidnapping offenses, rape and sodomy offenses, sexual penetration, sexual abuse, robbery offenses, arson, compelling prostitution, and use of child in a display of sex act. Measure 73 was approved in November 2012 by statewide ballot. The initiative set a 25-year mandatory minimum prison sentence for repeat offenders of any four felony sex crimes.

Oregon's safety valve lets judges sentence below the statutory minimums for several crimes including kidnapping, second degree manslaughter, some second degree sex offenses, and repeat property offenders. The court considers the offense and decides if "a substantial and compelling reason under the rules of the Oregon Criminal Justice Commission justifies the lesser sentence."

Pennsylvania Pursuant to *Commonwealth v. Newman* (2012), Pennsylvania has a moratorium on mandatory minimum sentences.

The Supreme Court of Pennsylvania issued an opinion on June 15, 2015, that found unconstitutional the state's Drug Free School Zones Act, which set mandatory minimum sentences for selling drugs near schools. The court's reasoning applies to nearly all of the state's drug- and gun-related mandatory minimum sentencing laws and will therefore invalidate those mandatory sentencing laws, too. The case is *Commonwealth of Pennsylvania v. Hopkins* (2015).

Rhode Island First degree murder is life in prison. Committing a crime of violence while armed with a firearm, explosive, etc. is 3 years for a first offense, 10 years for a second, and 15 years for a third. Using a firearm to commit a crime of violence is 10 years for a first offense, 20 years for a second offense, and life for a third offense. Possession of a firearm by a convicted felon is 2 years.

The state no longer has any mandatory minimum sentences for drug offenses, after repealing the sentences in 2009, over the governor's veto. Previously, drug offenders received 10- and 20-year sentences, even for possession offenses, along with $10,000 and $25,000 fines.

South Carolina Murder has a mandatory death, life without parole, or 30-year sentence. Most drug sentences in the state are indeterminate, and those sentences that include a minimum often apply to a second or third offense. For example, trafficking

(continued)

Table 6.1 Overview of Mandatory Minimum Sentencing (continued)

10 to 100 pounds of marijuana for a third offense is 25 years. Trafficking 200 to 400 grams of cocaine is 25 years.

In 2010, South Carolina removed the 10-year mandatory minimum sentence for school zone violations, allowed the possibility of probation for certain second and third drug possession convictions, and eliminated mandatory minimum sentences for first convictions of simple drug possession.

South Dakota First degree murder is death or life imprisonment with no possibility of a lighter sentence. Sale of marijuana within 1000 feet of a school or 500 feet of other designated area is 5 years. Committing or attempting to commit a felony while armed with a firearm is 5 years added on to the sentence for the underlying crime, and it increases to 10 years for a second and subsequent convictions.

Tennessee Most offenses are sentenced based on the class of felony committed, and in the appropriate range for that felony class. The court also takes aggravating and mitigating factors into consideration when sentencing, so the exact sentence is left to the judge's discretion. First degree murder is the only crime in the state with a mandatory sentence, which in this instance is given by the jury. The sentence can be life without parole, life with parole, or death. The mandatory sentence given to habitual violent offenders may also apply if the defendant fits the category.

Texas The overwhelming majority of crimes in Texas have no mandatory minimum sentences. Most sentences are based on the degree of felony and the discretion of the court. Capital murder is death or life without parole. There are many mandatory minimums for a variety of drug offenses. For example, possession of 5 to 50 lbs is 2 years, 50 to 2,000 lbs is 2 years, over 2,000 lbs is 5 years. Sale of 5 to 50 lbs is 2 years, 50 to 2,000 lbs is 5 years, over 2,000 lbs is 10 years. Sale to minor is 2 years.

Utah If the current conviction is for one or more of the following three sex offenses that qualify as "Jessica's Law," the required mandatory sentence is imprisonment of 25-years-to-life without the possibility of the court suspending or reducing the sentence: rape of a child, object rape of a child, sodomy on a child.

Vermont Vermont's lawmakers designate crimes as felonies and fix sentences on a crime-by-crime basis. For most crimes they state maximum terms of imprisonment (for example, "up to five years"). The punishment for murder in the first degree shall be imprisonment for a minimum term of not less than 35 years and a maximum term of life, or life without the possibility of parole.

Virginia Virginia has many mandatory minimum sentences in its criminal code, covering a wide range of offenses. Examples include, but are not limited to: Assault with a firearm is 3 years for a first offense, and 5 for a second or subsequent. Selling schedule I/II drugs to a minor is 5 years. Marijuana in the Continuing Criminal

(continued)

Table 6.1 Overview of Mandatory Minimum Sentencing (continued)

Enterprises (CCE) statute is 20 years for 100 to 250 kilograms, and 40 to life if over 250 kilograms. Reproducing, transmitting, or selling child pornography is 5 years. Object sexual penetration, forcible sexual sodomy, or rape with victim under 13 that is part of burglary or kidnapping is 25 years.

A safety valve exists for drug cases that is similar to the federal safety valve. To impose a sentence below the statutory mandatory minimum, a Virginia court must find that (1) the defendant does not have a prior conviction for certain felony offenses; (2) the defendant did not use violence or credible threats of violence or possess a firearm or other dangerous weapon; (3) the offense did not result in death or serious bodily injury to any person; (4) the defendant was not an organizer, leader, manager, or supervisor of others in the offense; and (5) the defendant tells prosecutors all he knows about the offense (VA CODE ANN. sec 18.2-248 (2012).

Washington Any person convicted of aggravated murder in the first degree shall be sentenced to life imprisonment without possibility of parole or release. Anyone convicted of first degree murder will be sentenced to 20-year mandatory minimum. There are sentence enhancements that a defendant can be subject to for possessing/using a deadly weapon at the time of the offense in question. For a Class C felony, the enhancement is 6 months for the use of a deadly weapon or 18 months for the use of a firearm. For a Class B felony, it's 1 year or 3 years, and for a Class A felony 2 years or 5 years. If there was a previous offense with a weapons enhancement, then the current enhancement is doubled.

West Virginia First degree murder is life imprisonment. There are mandatory minimums for certain drug offenses. For example, there is a two-year mandatory minimum for sale/distribution to a minor or if sale/delivery occurs within 1,000 feet of a school.

Wisconsin Most crimes in Wisconsin are based on the classification of the particular felony in question. First degree murder is punished by life imprisonment. Wisconsin has mandatory minimums for some child sex offenses. For example, having sex or sexual contact with a person under 13 that causes great bodily harm carries a 25-year mandatory prison sentence. Repeat serious sex offenses and repeat serious violent crimes are also subject to a minimum of 3 1/2 years imprisonment with no possibility of probation.

A bill was proposed as of June 2015 in which convicted felons would face a mandatory minimum of three years in prison for possession of a firearm. If a felon uses a gun to commit a violent felony, he or she would face a mandatory minimum of five years in prison plus the three years for possession. Felons who commit less severe violent felonies with a gun would face a mandatory minimum of three years for possession plus a minimum of 1 1/2 years to 3 years depending on the crime. The bill has not been passed as of this writing.

(continued)

Table 6.1 Overview of Mandatory Minimum Sentencing (continued)

Wyoming In Wyoming, lawmakers set punishment on a crime-by-crime basis for felonies. Mandatory minimums are rarely imposed. First degree murder is life or death. Intent to distribute marijuana is a felony but does not carry a mandatory minimum sentence. However, if that felony is committed within 500 feet of school property or on a bus, the defendant, if found guilty, will be sentenced to a minimum of two years in prison.

All fifty states passed some type of mandatory sentencing law at one time. **Table 6.1** provides examples of mandatory sentencing laws that have been passed in each state and Washington, D.C. It highlights select mandatory minimums for felonies in four main categories—drug, violent, firearms, and sex crimes. Although most states have mandatory minimums for DUI offenses, these are not included in the table. Many states have mandatory minimums for first degree murder that are life without parole or death, although some states just establish a minimum number of years one must serve. Note that this table presents examples of mandatory minimum sentences within each jurisdiction and is not exhaustive of all the mandatory minimums within the state. Also note it does not list all sentences for repeat or habitual offenders, even though some laws establish harsh mandatory minimum sentences for second, third, and subsequent offenses.

State Safety Valve Provisions

Table 6.1 also indicates revisions to mandatory minimum sentencing within a state. So-called "safety valves" for federal drug offenders were discussed earlier in the chapter. Several states have implemented safety valves, which have resulted in the scaling back of mandatory penalties within their jurisdiction for drug and other offenses otherwise sentenced under mandatory minimums. These include Connecticut, Georgia, Maine, Minnesota, Montana, New York, Oregon, Rhode Island, and Virginia. Judges are allowed to exercise some discretion in the types and/or lengths of sentences subsequent to the passage of safety valves in these states. These types of revisions to mandatory sentencing laws have been implemented in part because of the growing prison populations in some states and the high cost of incarceration.

Maine, for example, passed legislation in 2003 which was known as a safety valve provision that let courts impose a sentence other than the mandatory minimum based on individual circumstances in the case. These include if the court finds substantial evidence that (a) the imposition of a mandatory minimum prison sentence will result in substantial injustice to the defendant; (b) imposing a sentence other than the mandatory minimum prison sentence will not have an adverse effect on public safety; and (c) imposing a sentence other than a mandatory minimum sentence will not fail to deter others from committing aggravated trafficking, furnishing or cultivation of scheduled drugs. In addition, the court must find that the defendant is a good candidate for an intensive supervision program in which he or she would otherwise be ineligible to participate if a mandatory minimum prison sentence was imposed or that the defendant's background, attitude, and prospects for rehabilitation, and the nature of the victim and offense indicate that imposing a mandatory minimum prison sentence would fail to fulfill the general purposes of sentencing (Maine Revised Statutes).

In 2009, in response to a skyrocketing prison population Rhode Island legislators voted to repeal all the mandatory minimum sentences for non-violent drug offenses. Prior to this vote, mandatory minimum sentences for non-violent drug offenses were very harsh. Even simple possession carried between a 10- and 20-year mandatory minimum imprisonment sentence.

Pennsylvania's Moratorium on Mandatory Minimums

Of note is the state of mandatory sentencing in Pennsylvania. The Pennsylvania Superior Court decision in the case *Commonwealth v. Newman* (2012) stemmed largely from the United States Supreme Court ruling in *Alleyne v. United States* (2013), which held that mandatory minimum sentences and any other sentence that increases the punishment for a crime, is unconstitutional if the element that increases the punishment or warrants the mandatory sentence is not presented to the jury and proven beyond a reasonable doubt. If there is no such presentation of elements of the crime that enhance the punishment or warrant a mandatory sentence, then there is a violation of the Sixth Amendment right to a trial by a fair and impartial jury.

This case came about when police executed a search warrant at the apartment of James Newman and found crack cocaine, drug paraphernalia, and a handgun. Newman and his codefendants were arrested and brought to trial. Newman himself was convicted of two counts of possession with intent to deliver, two counts of simple possession, one count of possession of drug paraphernalia, one count of dealing in proceeds of unlawful activities, one count of possessing an instrument of crime, and five counts of criminal conspiracy. Prior to sentencing, the Commonwealth filed a notice to seek a mandatory sentence under Pennsylvania law, section 9712.1, which enhances the minimum sentence where a firearm is found on a drug dealer, an accomplice, or in the vicinity of the contraband. The mandatory sentence specified is five years, and Newman was sentenced to five to fifteen years in June of 2012. In August of 2014, the Superior Court vacated the judgement and remanded the case for sentencing, citing the *Alleyne* decision.

This ruling effectively put a moratorium on mandatory minimum sentencing in Pennsylvania. However, the ruling only really affected crime involving drugs, firearms, and sexual abuse since those are the only crimes with mandatory sentences in the Commonwealth. The Supreme Court of Pennsylvania issued an opinion on June 15, 2015, that found unconstitutional the state's Drug Free School Zones Act, which set mandatory minimum sentences for selling drugs near schools. The court's reasoning applies to nearly all of the state's drug- and gun-related mandatory minimum sentencing laws and will therefore invalidate those mandatory sentencing laws, too. The case was *Commonwealth of Pennsylvania v. Hopkins* (2015).

Three Strikes Laws

Background

Three strikes laws impose lengthy (often life) prison terms for offenders who have accrued three convictions for serious and/or violent crimes. Although the particulars vary by jurisdiction, the premise of such laws is that offenders who have repeatedly committed and been convicted of three serious crimes or "strikes" are "out," like in the game of baseball. These have alternatively been called "three strikes and you're in" (prison for life) laws.

Three strikes laws were introduced shortly after career criminal research (discussed in Chapter 1) was widely disseminated in the late 1980s. Career criminal research showed that a small percentage of offenders are responsible for a disproportionate amount of crime. Career criminals are those offenders who have committed a large number of offenses, have committed serious offenses, and who have lengthy criminal careers (often marked by an early age of onset into delinquency and criminality and a late age of desistance).

Purposes

Three strikes laws seek to punish serious repeat, "career criminals," also known as "habitual offenders" with lengthy prison sentences. The imposition of long prison sentences for these offenders is purported to serve multiple objectives. The first concerns the issue of just punishment. Many would argue that an offender convicted of rape who has multiple prior serious convictions is more blameworthy than an offender convicted of rape who has no criminal history. Thus, it is argued that justice is served when repeat offenders are punished more harshly than first-time offenders.

Another argument for three strikes laws is that a habitual offender will probably offend again and will probably commit additional serious and/or violent crimes. It is in society's best interest to incarcerate that offender. By physically separating him or her from society, future criminal behavior is prevented. This reasoning suggests that there will be fewer victims if a dangerous repeat offender is incapacitated in prison.

Deterrence—both general and specific—has also been cited by advocates of three strikes laws. If the laws are properly implemented, the general public should be deterred from ever committing serious felonies, as they will know that they will be punished severely upon conviction of multiple offenses (general deterrence). Three strikes advocates also see the potential of such laws to serve as a specific deterrent to offenders who have already been convicted of one or two serious and/or violent offenses. These offenders should be deterred from committing future crimes, which would count as "strikes" and land them in prison for life. In addition, there is the practical issue that money is saved by invoking strike laws, in that it decreases the number of times a habitual offender is processed by the criminal justice system (see Greenwood, Rydell, Abrahamse, Caulkins, Chiesa, Model, & Klein, 1996).

The Popularity of Three Strikes Laws

From 1993 to 1995, twenty-two states, many of which already had some provisions for punishing habitual offenders more harshly, enacted three strikes laws (Mentor, 2002). By 2003, over half of states had enacted some form of three strikes laws. The federal government introduced three strikes laws as part of the Violent Crime Control and Law Enforcement Act of 1994.

Just as differences exist in various state and federal sentencing guidelines and in mandatory minimum sentences in different jurisdictions, there is variation in three strikes laws by jurisdiction. Differences include what types of offenses constitute a "strike," how many strikes set in motion mandatory penalties, and what the mandatory penalty is for accruing so many strikes. In addition, as we will discuss in Chapter 9, the effects of three strikes laws — including how they are implemented, cost, and the impact of the prison population, vary by jurisdiction.

Like other sentencing reforms, three strikes laws were enacted in response to the public perception that the criminal justice system was "too soft" on repeat serious and/or violent offenders. Looking back, some criminologists characterize the enactment of three strikes laws as a kneejerk reaction to a complicated social problem. The creation of sentencing guidelines garnered support from both liberals (who were concerned with sentencing disparity and discrimination inherent in indeterminate sentencing) as well as conservatives (who thought that indeterminate sentencing allowed for the premature release of dangerous offenders). In contrast, three strikes laws have been supported largely by conservatives who believe them to be a necessary way to punish repeat offenders and give the message to would-be criminals that crime does not pay.

Habitual Offender Laws

Laws which target habitual offenders for increased penalties are not new. Such laws were in place in many jurisdictions before the era of modern sentencing reform. In colonial America, statutes called for harsher sanctions for offenders with prior criminal history. In the early to mid-1900s, habitual offender laws allowed some discretion on the part of the judge. In 1926, New York State sentenced third time offenders to life imprisonment. By 1949, forty-eight states had enacted mandatory penalties for habitual offenders. Most of these states allowed judges to retain some discretion regarding whether the "mandatory" punishment was appropriate or if a lesser sentence was warranted (Mentor, 2002).

In several guidelines states, persons convicted of repeat violent and/or serious crimes were often placed in a separate column on the guidelines axis which delineated prior criminal history. Being designated a habitual offender meant that the offender would be sentenced from this column, which indicated longer sentences of incarceration compared to those offenders with fewer serious priors.

In contrast, three strikes laws eliminate judicial discretion in situations in which the defendant has accrued three offenses that are considered "strikes" in that jurisdiction. While many states have had habitual offender laws "on the books" for years, it was not until the early 1990s that states and the federal government enacted so-called three strikes laws. We will highlight federal three strikes laws and those of two states—Washington, the first state to pass three strikes legislation, and California, the state which many have argued has the toughest three strikes legislation in the country.

The Federal "Three Strikes" Law

Part of the Violent Crime Control and Law Enforcement Act of 1994 contained provisions for a three strikes law for federal offenders. The federal "three strikes" law mandates a punishment of life imprisonment for defendants convicted in federal court of a serious violent felony if they had two or more prior convictions. The offender's prior convictions could have been in federal court or any of the states' courts.

One of the prior convictions has to be for a serious violent felony. Qualifying offenses include murder, manslaughter, a sex offense, kidnapping, robbery, or any offense that has elements involving "force or a significant risk of force" and that is punishable by a prison sentence of at least ten years. The other prior could be for a serious drug offense. To invoke sentencing under the federal "three strikes" law, the prosecutor must file a notice with a trial court before the trial or plea agreement. This notice must indicate which prior convictions will be used when seeking enhanced sentencing under the "three strikes" law provisions.

Washington's Three Strikes Law

Washington's Prior Habitual Offender Statutes

Prior to the passage of its three strikes law, Washington State already had two provisions for sentencing habitual offenders through its Habitual Criminal Statute. This statute required that all persons who were convicted of a felony and who had a prior felony conviction or two misdemeanor convictions would be labeled a habitual offender and imprisoned for a minimum of ten years. Another component of the statute indicated that anyone convicted of either a third felony or a fourth misdemeanor or gross misdemeanor involving fraud would receive a life sentence (LaCourse, 1997).

In practice, however, judges in Washington decided whether and how to apply this law. The Habitual Criminal Statute could be overridden by the prosecution or the parole board. Like many states with habitual offender statutes, Washington's law designated habitual offender status as a separate conviction. In addition to a conviction for robbery, for example, an offender who met the criteria defining habitual offender status would also be convicted of being a habitual offender and face additional punishment. Prosecutors could exercise discretion as to whether to charge a defendant as a habitual offender in addition to the instant offense of robbery. Dropping the charge of habitual offender for a plea of guilty represented a plea bargaining tool.

When indeterminate sentencing had been in place, judges were allowed to suspend a life sentence indicated by the old Habitual Offender Statute and hand down a lighter sentence. Another loophole under indeterminate sentencing involved the parole board granting parole to habitual offenders if the members deemed it appropriate. Given the multiple ways to get around imposing Washington's habitual offender statute, LaCourse (1997) deemed the old law "nearly worthless."

Passage of the Nation's First Three Strikes Law

In 1993, Washington became the first state to enact a three strikes law. Washington's three strikes law mandated a life sentence without parole for persons convicted of three serious felonies. Those sentenced under the law were not eligible for furloughs or time off for good behavior. The only possible avenue for release was if the offender was granted a pardon or clemency by the governor. The three strikes law was written to trump any maximum sentence that had been set for offenses prior to its passage.

If an offender was convicted of a third offense that was deemed a strike by law, the judge had to sentence him or her to a life sentence in prison without the possibility of parole. Individual or case characteristics could play no role in sentencing. Judicial discretion was completely eliminated at the stage of sentencing of a three strikes case.

Washington's three strikes law targets serious and/or violent habitual offenders. The research that led to the drafting of Washington's three strikes legislation was initiated in 1991 at the Washington Institute for Policy Studies as a summer project. The focus of the project was to examine existing sentencing procedures for repeat habitual offenders and make recommendations for improvement (LaCourse, 1997).

In 1993 an initiative for the law was passed by Washington voters. Over 76 percent of voters cast their approval of the three strikes law. The Washington three strikes law required that the offender be convicted as an adult (as opposed to being adjudicated delinquent in the separate juvenile justice system) for a serious felony on three separate occasions. The qualifying crimes included murder or manslaughter, rape, robbery, serious assault, and child molestation. A provision in the law allowed some serious felony crimes (excluding Class A felonies or sex offenses) to be not counted if the offender had spent a period of five or ten years living in the community with no convictions during that time frame (LaCourse, 1997).

At the time the three strikes law was passed, Washington State had a determinate sentencing system that used a sentencing grid that based a sentence on the current offense severity and the criminal history of the offender. The Washington sentencing guidelines aimed, like most reforms, to decrease disparity and promote sentencing uniformity.

A criticism of the Washington State sentencing grid was that it was too lenient in punishing career criminals and that because of this, public safety was jeopardized. In his article, *Three Strikes, You're Out: A Review*, LaCourse (1997) provided the following three examples: A first degree child molester with two previous sex offenses would receive a sentence of nine years and six months. A first degree robber with two prior violent offenses could get a recommended sentence of five years. A first degree rapist with two prior violent sex offense convictions would receive a recommended sentence of fourteen years and two months. In contrast, under Washington's three strikes law, in each of these scenarios, the offender would be sentenced to life in prison without parole.

Between December 1993 and December 1996, 83 criminals had been sentenced under Washington's three strikes law. The breakdown by third strike offense was 45 percent robbers, 20 percent sex offenders, 10 percent murderers, 6 percent kidnappers, 5 percent armed/violent burglars, and one arsonist (LaCourse, 1997). As of January 2013, twenty years after the three strikes law was passed, approximately 330 persons were serving sentences of life without parole under the law (*Seattle Times*, 2013, January 23).

Spotlight — Washington Governor Grants Clemency for Three Strikes Offender

Steven Dozier became the first lifer sentenced under Washington's three strikes law to be released from prison. Governor Chris Gregoire granted Dozier clemency in May 2009. When released from the Monroe Correctional Complex, Dozier had served fifteen years behind bars. What distinguishes Steven Dozier's case is not only that he was the first three strikes offender to be granted clemency, but his story and the crimes that led him to be sentenced under Washington's three strikes law.

Shortly after Steven Dozier graduated from high school, he began abusing drugs, including cocaine. In 1986, at age 25, Steven Dozier punched a woman during a purse snatching. He committed similar crimes — hitting and punching women during purse snatchings over the next eight years. He committed these crimes to support his cocaine habit. Just prior to his last conviction for grabbing a 69-year-old woman's purse and pushing her down in February 1994, Washington passed its three strikes law. Dozier was sentenced to life imprisonment without the possibility of parole for this "third strike" (Murphy, 2009, August 11; Sullivan, 2009, June 10).

Regardless of the fact that Dozier did not cause major injury to his victims nor did he use a weapon, most would argue that Dozier's acts were heinous. Some, however, have questioned whether the commission of second degree robbery (the offense for which he was convicted on his third strike) should be counted as a strike, especially considering convictions for more serious offenses, including murder, rape, and kidnapping also qualify as "strike" offenses.

The way that Dozier passed his time in prison distinguished him from other inmates. He worked at jobs within the institution, participated in drug and alcohol counseling programs, and joined the "Concerned Lifers," a group of incarcerated men serving life sentences who gather to discuss social issues.

While Dozier pointed to prayer and luck as the reasons he was eventually released, he had several supporters who fought for him to be released. Just who was behind this movement to give Dozier a second chance? A mix of some surprising supporters, including King County Prosecutor Dan Satterberg, King County Council Member Larry Gossett, and conservative radio talk show host John Carlson. Both Gossett and Carlson spoke in front of the state Clemency and Pardons Board at Dozier's hearing. The board voted 4-0 to recommend clemency. Larry Evans, a legislative aide to Larry Gossett, met Dozier approximately five years earlier during Evans' involvement in Seattle's Village of Hope, which is an organization that works closely with black men who are incarcerated. According to Evans, "Steven is an extraordinary individual . . . There's no question in my mind about his sincerity. I think one of those things that separate Steven from a lot of people is Steven has done so much introspection. He has become grounded" (Sullivan, 2009).

Shortly after release, Dozier began reaching out to politicians, community centers, and school district offices, asking them if he could have an opportunity to tell his story to at-risk children. Dozier has demonstrated a keen interest in preventing children from falling into a life of crime.

Dozier got a job at a janitorial company where his wife worked shortly after release. He later took a position at the Sea of Stars Foundation, which helps at-risk youth. Reflecting on his past, Dozier told a reporter, "I picked myself off the ground and I started looking at myself. What had led me down this road? Drugs were a big contributing factor. Drugs and laziness. So I said, 'I'm not going to do drugs again'" (Murphy, 2009, August 11).

While there has been an outpouring of support for Dozier, not everyone was happy that Governor Gregoire granted him clemency. Mary Bedford, who was the victim of the 1994 attack, informed the prosecutor's office that she did not want him to be granted clemency. The Seattle police detective who was assigned to the 1994 case characterized Dozier as a sociopath who should not have been freed. Detective Mike Ciesynski said that during his 30-year career he had rarely interacted with a more dangerous person. Adamant about his view, Ciesynski stated, "They're putting people's lives at risk by having someone like Steven Dozier released." He continued, "They could have found murderers with less of a chance to re-offend" (Sullivan, 2009).

California's Strikes Laws

Spotlight—The Murder of Polly Klaas

One major impetus for the drafting of legislation for sentencing habitual offenders in the state of California was a widely publicized tragedy—the kidnapping and murder of 12-year-old Polly Klaas on October 1, 1993, in Petaluma, California. During a sleep-over party at Klaas's house, a knife-wielding man entered Polly's bedroom, tied several girls up, and then abducted Polly. A statewide and national search for Polly ended in the discovery of her body on December 3, 1993 (Polly's abduction, http://www.pollyklaas.org/about/pollys-story.html). The man who murdered Polly Klaas was Richard Allen Davis, a repeat offender with a long criminal career. He had convictions for burglary by age 20 and by age 26 was convicted of kidnapping one woman, assaulting two others, and receiving stolen property. Although Davis was tried, convicted, and sentenced for these offenses in 1976 (at age 22) to one-to-25 years for the kidnapping and two-to-life for the assaults, he was paroled after only serving six years in prison. After being released from prison, he committed a robbery that upon conviction landed him a sixteen-year prison sentence but was released only eight years later in 1993—the year Polly was kidnapped. Davis had a record of brutal attacks on women, yet was repeatedly released from prison before completing his entire sentence. Davis was convicted of kidnapping and murder and currently sits on California's death row.

Polly Klaas's story and those like them precipitated widespread public support for three strikes laws. The public was strongly united in wanting to prevent the premature release of dangerous violent and habitual criminals.

Elements of California's Original Strikes Laws

While Washington was the first state to enact three strikes laws, California's strikes laws have justifiably earned the reputation of the most severe strike laws in the United

States. The most publicized component of California's original strikes law was that upon conviction of a third felony (with two prior convictions of "strikeable offenses," meaning serious felonies) an indeterminate life sentence would be handed down in which the offender would not eligible for parole for at least 25 years. A conviction for a third strike meant 25 years to life in prison. The third "strike," however, could be *any* felony, including a violent, drug, property, or public order offense.

This meant that if the offender accrued three strikes, the sentencing judge was required to sentence the offender to a lengthy prison term. The purpose of the law was to punish repeat serious and/or violent offenders harshly with lengthy prison sentences. The judge's discretion to impose probation, suspend the sentence, or divert the offender from the criminal justice system was eliminated. Simply put, those sentenced under California's strike laws had to serve a long time in a California state prison (Greenwood, et al., 1996).

Two very similar versions of the California strike law existed. The California legislature passed the California Penal Code §667(b)–(i) and it was signed into law by the governor on March 7, 1994. A second version, found under Penal Code §1170.2, known as Proposition 184, was voted into law by the general public on November 8, 1994, by a margin of 72 percent to 28 percent (Shichor & Sechrest, 1996). Some argue that the legislative action was expedited because under California law, voter initiated legislation is harder to amend, requiring a vote from the electorate or a two-thirds majority vote of each legislative house (Austin, Clark, Hardyman, & Henry, 1999). The notable differences in the otherwise essentially identical bills was that the version crafted by legislature explicitly stated that convictions in other states and juvenile adjudications could count as strikes.

Two components of the original laws in California distinguish their strikes laws as uniquely punitive. The first involves what types of offenses can be considered a *third strike*. California's law permitted the conviction of *any felony offense* to constitute a third strike if the offender has accrued a first and second conviction for what are considered "strikeable" offenses. Most of the offenses deemed strikeable in California are those considered strikes in other states, and include murder, rape, aggravated assault, robbery, and kidnapping. Additional offenses, such as convictions for mayhem and drug sales to minors, are also considered strikes in California.

The second feature that represents considerable focus on the punishment of repeat offenders in California's strikes laws involves the prescribed sanctions for *second* strikes. The California law also contains a two strike provision, which mandates that an offender, upon conviction of *any* felony, who has one conviction for a strikeable offense will receive a prison sentence *double* of that of an offender convicted of the same offense, but who does not have a prior conviction for a strikeable offense (Austin, Clark, Hardyman, & Henry, 1999). It made certain that these augmented sentences would be served in prison, as opposed to jail or in the community, and required that sentences be served consecutively, as opposed to concurrently, for multiple counts. It also decreased the amount of "good time" that a prisoner could earn from a maximum of 50 percent of the sentence to 20 percent (Greenwood, et al., 1996).

In 1996, in *People v. Superior Court (Romero)*, the State Supreme Court of California ruled that a court may decide to dismiss prior serious or violent felony convictions under the three strikes law. This decision has allowed judges to ignore a prior conviction in the interest of justice in the process of deciding whether to designate a defendant as a three strikes offender. The decision to dismiss an action in furtherance of justice could spare an offender the mandatory 25-years-to-life sentence otherwise mandated by California's three strikes law.

In practice, prosecutors also can shape whether the case is a three strikes case by exercising their discretion in how certain prior offenses will be counted. They can make this decision when they initially file charges for the current offense.

Changes to California's 1994 "Three Strikes" Law
Proposition 36 — 2012

On November 6, 2012, Proposition 36, a ballot measure that revised some of the strict provisions of California's three strikes law, was voted in by Californians. A little over 69 percent of voters favored measures that would reduce the number of offenders who would be eligible to receive a sentence of 25 years to life. The law now imposes a life sentence for a third strike *only if the third felony conviction is considered "serious or violent" or if the individual convicted of a third felony that is considered "non-serious or non-violent" had a previous conviction for murder, rape, or sexual assault on a child.* In addition, Proposition 36 is retroactive, so that offenders who had been sentenced to life imprisonment for a third "strike" that was a non-serious or non-violent offense can be resentenced, as long as a judge does not deem that person as posing an unreasonable risk to public safety.

Precipitating Factors

The Three Strikes Project was initiated to examine what many to believe to be disproportionately harsh sentences imposed on offenders sentenced under California's three strikes laws. The Three Strikes Project is directed by Lecturer in Law Michael Romano and Professor Larry Marshall of Stanford University, who co-founded the organization in 2006 (http://www.law.stanford.edu/profile/michael-romano).

The Three Strikes Project has represented persons sentenced under California's three strikes law whose third "strike" was for a nonviolent crime. Such offenders comprise approximately 4,000 of the 9,000 offenders who have been convicted under the law (Stanford Law School). According to Romano,

> These are not serial rapists we happen to get off the street because we caught them stealing a radio from a parked car ... These people are generally homeless drug addicts. Have they committed crimes? Absolutely. Do they deserve to be punished? Absolutely. But we think that a life sentence for these crimes is unjust, it's disproportionate, it's not what the voters wanted, it doesn't improve public safety at all. (Donald, 2013, June 6)

Offenses that have been counted as third strikes and led to the imposition of life sentences have included "stealing a dollar in loose change from a parked car, possessing less than a gram of narcotics, and attempting to break in to a soup kitchen" (Stanford Law School). Under California's original three strikes law, other offenses on the books that could count as a strike include many low-level felonies like shoplifting a pair of work gloves from a department store or passing a bad check (Staples, 2012, November 24).

Research has shown that the recipients of three strikes sentences of 25 years to life are disproportionately minorities and the mentally ill (Donald, 2013, June 6; Staples, 2012, November 24). The Three Strikes Project estimated that almost forty percent of three strike lifers in California prisons are mentally ill.

Even before Proposition 36, Stanford University law students had helped to overturn the life sentences of 26 individuals sentenced under the three strikes law. For some cases they showed that the defendants' counsel was insufficient. In some of these cases the Three Strikes Project workers showed that the defense failed to provide evidence of the mental illness of their client. Michael Romano commented on the imposition of the three strikes law, suggesting,

> In my experience, every person who has been sentenced to life in prison for a nonserious, nonviolent crime like petty theft suffers from some kind of mental illness or impairment — from organic brain disorders, to schizophrenia, to mental retardation, to severe P.T.S.D. (Staples, 2012, November 24)

The Three Strikes Project in collaboration with the NAACP Legal Defense Fund was instrumental in changing the law. They aimed to balance fair and proportionate sentencing with the recognition that there need to be appropriate exceptions while still maintaining the safety of the general public. As of June 6, 2013, approximately 500 inmates have been released from California prisons due to the retroactive provisions of Proposition 36 (Donald, 2013, June 6).

Summary

Mandatory minimum sentencing laws, which most often target violent, drug, and firearms offenses, eliminate judicial discretion. Regardless of individual characteristics, everyone who is convicted of a crime carrying a mandatory minimum must receive the stated mandatory penalty. Mandatory minimums were designed to send a message to would-be offenders that they will be punished if they break the law.

Harsh mandatory minimum sentences for federal drug offenders were passed in the 1980s in response to the perceived crack cocaine epidemic. Harsh mandatory minimums for a variety of child sex offenses and child pornography crimes were established in the 2003 when the PROTECT Act was passed. States also passed mandatory minimum sentencing laws. New York's Rockefeller Drug Laws, which went into effect in the 1970s, were so severe that some drug offenders received sentences equivalent to those of murderers. Michigan's 650 Lifer Law put drug traffickers away for life.

Three strikes laws impose lengthy (often life) prison terms for offenders who have accrued three convictions for serious and/or violent crimes. They were crafted to incapacitate career criminals who posed a clear threat to public safety.

California's original three strikes laws, which went into effect in 1994, were deemed the harshest in the nation, as they required a 25-years-to-life sentence if an offender accrued three strikes. The third strike could be *any* felony. In November 2012, Proposition 36 passed, which required that for an offense to be considered a third strike that it had to be serious or violent.

In 1996, in *People v. Superior Court (Romero)*, the State Supreme Court of California ruled that a judge could have the discretion to dismiss prior serious or violent felony convictions under the three strikes law.

Both mandatory minimum and three strikes laws aim to send a "get tough on crime" message to would-be offenders.

Discussion Questions

1. How has society's view of drug offenders affected the federal approach to sentencing of these offenders? Have there been time periods when the perception that drug offenders are suffering from substance abuse problems has impacted the response to drug crimes?

2. How do you think the Michigan Felony Firearms Statute impacted the number of violent crimes committed with firearms? Keep in mind the factors that are key to a sanction serving as an effective deterrent.

3. How do you think the Bartley-Fox Amendment affected (a) the discretion of police officers and prosecutors, (b) the number of carrying offenses, and (c) gun-related crimes, including assaults, robberies, and homicides? Draw on your knowledge of deterrence.

4. How might the following sentencing goals of corrections be met by three strikes laws?
   a. Retribution
   b. Incapacitation
   c. General Deterrence
   d. Specific Deterrence

5. What assumptions about child pornography offenders do you think have influenced the provisions of the PROTECT Act? For example, can they be deterred by strict sanctions? Are they "sick" and in need of rehabilitation programs?

6. Compare and contrast three strikes laws in California and Washington, in terms of the following:
   a. The numbers and types of offenses for which an offender can accrue strikes
   b. The ability of prosecutors and/or the courts to circumvent the law
   c. The discretion afforded to the sentencing judge

Notes

1. A more comprehensive table listing the class of sale and possession offenses for a variety of drug offenses and the minimum and maximum sentencing ranges is available in Table A-4 in the Executive Summary, *The Nation's Toughest Drug Law: Evaluating the New York Experience*, National Institute of Law Enforcement and Criminal Justice, 1978.

2. Pursuant to Mass. Gen Laws Ann. Ch. 140, § 131 (1974), "A person may not obtain a license to carry a handgun or a license to possess and carry a machine gun if he is an alien, has been convicted

of a felony, or the unlawful use, possession, or sale of narcotics or harmful drugs, is a minor under eighteen, or is a minor over eighteen without the written consent of his parent or guardian."

3. These included murder, manslaughter in the first degree, manslaughter in the second degree, assault in the first degree, assault in the second degree, kidnapping in the first degree, kidnapping in the second degree, rape in the first degree, rape in the second degree, sodomy in the first degree, sodomy in the second degree, unlawful sexual penetration in the first degree, unlawful sexual penetration in the second degree, sexual abuse in the first degree, robbery in the first degree, and robbery in the second degree.

References

Alleyne v. United States, 570 U.S. _____, (2013). No. 11-9335 Supreme Court of the United States, 133 S. Ct. 2151; 186 L. Ed. 2d 314; 2013 U.S. LEXIS 4543; 81 U.S.L.W. 4444; 24 Fla. L. Weekly Fed. S 310 (2013).

Austin, J., Clark, J., Hardyman, P., & Henry, D. A. (1999). The impact of 'three strikes and you're out'. *Punishment & Society, 1*(2), 131–162.

Beha, J. A. (1977). "And nobody can get you out": The impact of a mandatory prison sentence of the illegal carrying of a firearm on the use of firearms and on the administration of criminal justice in Boston — Part I. *Boston University Law Review, 57,* 96–146.

Berlin, F. S. (2015, September 17). *Viewers of child pornography: A psychiatric perspective.* Presented at the 2015 Annual National Seminar on the Federal Sentencing Guidelines. New Orleans, LA.

CBS. (2009, February 11). Rethinking the 'Lifer law'. [60 minutes II]. Retrieved from http://www.cbsnews.com/2100-500164_162-49670.html

Commonwealth of Pennsylvania v. Newman, 2014 PA Super 178 No. 1980 EDA (2012).

Donald, B. (2013). Stanford Law's Three Strikes Project works for fair implementation of new statute. *Stanford Report.* Retrieved from http://news.stanford.edu/news/2013/june/three-strikes-project-060613.html

Fox News. (2013, August 12). Holder calls for scaled-back use of mandatory minimum drug sentences. Retrieved from http://www.foxnews.com/politics/2013/08/12/holder-to-call-for-changes-in-drug-sentencing-guidelines/

Gill, M. M. Correcting course: Lessons from the 1970 repeal of mandatory minimums. Retrieved from http://famm.org/Repository/Files/8189_FAMM_BoggsAct_final.pdf

Greene, J., & Mauer, M. (2010). Downscaling prisons: Lessons from four states. *The Sentencing Project.* Retrieved from http://www.sentencingproject.org/doc/publications/publications/inc_DownscalingPrisons2010.pdf

Greenwood, P., Rydell, C. P., Abrahamse, A. F., Caulkins, J. P., Chiesa, J., Model, K. E., & Klein, S. P. (1996). Implementing the law. In D. Shichor & D. Sechrest (Eds.), *Three strikes and you're out, Vengeance as public policy.* Thousand Oaks, CA: Sage.

Herman, S. (1999–2000). Measuring culpability by measuring drugs? Three reasons to reevaluate the Rockefeller drug laws. *Albany Law Review, 63,* 777–798.

Hinojosa, R. & Dorhoffer, A. (2015, September 16). *Introduction to the guidelines.* Presented at the 2015 Annual National Seminar on the Federal Sentencing Guidelines. New Orleans, LA.

LaCourse, R. D. (1997). Three strikes, you're out: A review. *Washington Policy Center.* Retrieved from http://www.washingtonpolicy.org/publications/brief/three-strikes -youre-out-review

Loftin, C., & McDowall, D. (1981). "One with a gun gets you two": Mandatory sentencing and firearms violence in Detroit. *Annals of the American Academy of Political and Social Sciences, 455,* 150–167.

Maine Revised Statutes Title 17-A Section 1151. Retrieved from http://legislature.maine .gov/legis/statutes/17-A/title17-Ach47sec0.html

Mancuso, P. A. (2009–2010). Resentencing after the "fall" of Rockefeller: The failure of the Drug Law Reform Acts of 2004 and 2005 to remedy the injustices of New York's Rockefeller Drug Laws and the compromise of 2009. *Albany Law Review, 73,* 1535–1581.

Mann, B. (2013, January 24). *How the Rockefeller drug laws changed America. North Country Public Radio.* Retrieved from http://www.northcountrypublicradio.org/news /story/21316/20130124/how-the-rockefeller-drug-laws-changed-america

Mann, B. (2013, February 14). The drug laws that changed how we punish. *NPR.* Retrieved from http://www.npr.org/2013/02/14/171822608/the-drug-laws-that-changed -how-we-punish

Melendez v. United States, 518 U.S. 120 (1996).

Mentor, K. W. (2002). Habitual felon laws. In D. Levinson (Ed.), *Encyclopedia of crime and punishment.* Thousand Oaks, CA: Sage. doi: 10.4135/9781412950664

Merica, D. & Perez, E. (2013, August 12). Eric Holder seeks to cut mandatory minimum drug sentences. *CNN.* Retrieved from http://www.cnn.com/2013/08/12/politics /holder-mandatory-minimums

Merritt, N., Fain, T., & Turner, S. (2006). Oregon's get tough sentencing reform: A lesson in justice system adaptation. *Criminology and Public Policy, 5*(1), 5–36.

Murphy, K. (2009, August 11). Washington state revisits three-strikes law. *The Los Angeles Times.* Retrieved from http://articles.latimes.com/2009/aug/11/nation/na-three -strikes11

Nadelmann, E. (2014, September). Eric Holder was great on drugs. *Politico Magazine.* Retrieved from http://www.politico.com/magazine/story/2014/09/eric-holder-was -great-on-drugs-111354.html#.VHFl9k0tCUk

National Institute of Law Enforcement and Criminal Justice. (1978). *The nation's toughest drug law: Evaluating the New York experience.* Retrieved from https://www.ncjrs .gov/pdffiles1/Digitization/47795NCJRS.pdf

New York Times. (n.d.). *Rockefeller drug laws.* Retrieved from http://topics.nytimes.com /topics/reference/timestopics/subjects/d/drug_abuse_and_traffic/rockefeller_drug _laws/index.html

Nixon, R. M. (1971). *Special message to the Congress on drug abuse prevention and control.* Retrieved from The American Presidency Project website: http://www.presidency .ucsb.edu/ws/?pid=3048

North Carolina Sentencing and Policy Advisory Commission. (2009). *Structured sentencing training and reference manual: Applies to offenses committed on or after December 1, 2009.* Retrieved from http://www.nccourts.org/Courts/CRS/Councils/spac /Documents/sstrainingmanual_09.pdf

Pierce, G. L., & Bowers, W. J. (1981). The Bartley-Fox gun law's short-term impact on crime in Boston. *Annals of the American Academy of Political and Social Science*, 455, 120–137.

People v. Superior Court (Romero), 13 Cal. 4th 497, 917 P. 2 D 628, 53 Cal. RPTR. 2D (1996).

Pratt, M. (1997, March 3). 650-lifer punishment is a crime. *Mackinac Center, Viewpoint on Public Issues*. Retrieved from http://www.mackinac.org/article.aspx?ID=35

Seattle Times. (2013, January 23). Editorial: Time to reform state's 'three strikes' law [Editorial]. *The Seattle Times*. Retrieved from http://seattletimes.com/html/editorials/2020198986_editthreestrikesclemencyxml.html

Shichor, D., & Sechrest, D. K. (1996). *Three strikes and you're out: Vengeance as public policy.* Thousand Oaks, CA: Sage.

Smith, P. (2009). Feature: New York Assembly passes Rockefeller Drug Law reform bill — Fight moves to Senate. Retrieved from Stop the Drug War website: http://stopthedrugwar.org/chronicle/2009/mar/06/feature_new_york_assembly_passes

Spurlock, M. (2013). Medical marijuana [Television documentary series episode]. In M. Spurlock, *Inside Man*. Atlanta, GA: CNN.

Stanford Law School. *Three Strikes Project: Overview*. Retrieved from http://www.law.stanford.edu/organizations/programs-and-centers/stanford-three-strikes-project

Staples, B. (2012, November 24). California horror stories and the 3-strikes law. *The New York Times Sunday Review, Editorial*. Retrieved from http://www.nytimes.com/2012/11/25/opinion/sunday/california-horror-stories-and-the-3-strikes-law.html?_r=0

Sullivan, J. (2009, June 10). Freed 3-strikes offender is being watched closely by supporters, critics. *Seattle Times*. Retrieved from http://seattletimes.com/html/politics/2009325750_threestrikes11m.html

United States Sentencing Commission. (2011a). *Report to the Congress: Mandatory minimum penalties in the federal criminal justice system. Chapter 2, History of mandatory minimum penalties and statutory relief mechanisms*. Retrieved from http://www.ussc.gov/Legislative_and_Public_Affairs/Congressional_Testimony_and_Reports/Mandatory_Minimum_Penalties/20111031_RtC_PDF/Chapter_02.pdf

United States Sentencing Commission. (2011b). *Report to the Congress: Mandatory minimum penalties in the federal criminal justice system. Chapter 8, The use of mandatory minimum penalties for drug offenders*. Retrieved from http://www.ussc.gov/Legislative_and_Public_Affairs/Congressional_Testimony_and_Reports/Mandatory_Minimum_Penalties/20111031_RtC_PDF/Chapter_06.pdf

United States Sentencing Commission. (2011c). *Report to the Congress: Mandatory minimum penalties in the federal criminal justice system. Chapter 9, Mandatory minimum penalties for firearms offenses*. Retrieved from http://www.ussc.gov/Legislative_and_Public_Affairs/Congressional_Testimony_and_Reports/Mandatory_Minimum_Penalties/20111031_RtC_PDF/Chapter_09.pdf

United States Sentencing Commission. (2012a). *Report to Congress: Federal child pornography offenses, Executive summary*. Retrieved from http://www.ussc.gov/Legislative_and_Public_Affairs/Congressional_Testimony_and_Reports/Sex_Offense_Topics/201212_Federal_Child_Pornography_Offenses/Executive_Summary.pdf

United States Sentencing Commission. (2012b). *Report to Congress: Federal child pornography offense, Chapter 6, Analysis of sentencing data in cases in which offenders were sentenced under the non-production sentencing guidelines.* Retrieved from http://www.ussc.gov/Legislative_and_Public_Affairs/Congressional_Testimony_and_Reports/Sex_Offense_Topics/201212_Federal_Child_Pornography_Offenses/Chapter_06.pdf

United States Sentencing Commission. (2014). *U.S. Sentencing Commission unanimously votes to allow delayed retroactive reduction in drug trafficking sentences.* News Release. Retrieved from http://www.ussc.gov/sites/default/files/pdf/news/press-releases-and-news-advisories/press-releases/20140718_press_release.pdf

United States Sentencing Commission. (2015, September 17). *Child pornography offenses.* United States Sentencing Commission Annual Seminar, New Orleans, LA.

United States Sentencing Commission. (n.d.). *Frequently asked questions: Retroactive application of the 2014 drug guidelines amendment.* Retrieved from http://www.ussc.gov/sites/default/files/pdf/amendment-process/materials-on-2014-drug-guidelines-amendment/20140724_FAQ.pdf

United States v. Booker, 543 U.S. 220 (2005).

Wade v. United States, 504 U.S. 181 (1992).

7

Legal Scrutiny of
Sentencing Practices

Chapter Objectives:

- To get an overview of the role that proportionality review has played in cases involving sentencing laws.
- To understand how the Supreme Court has considered the Eighth Amendment prohibition against cruel and unusual punishment in proportionality review.
- To differentiate the role of proportionality review in capital and non-capital cases.
- To learn that the constitutionality of the Federal Sentencing Guidelines was upheld by the Supreme Court in *Mistretta v. United States*.
- To detail the landmark Supreme Court cases *Blakely v. Washington* and *United States v. Booker* and appreciate the relevance of the Sixth Amendment right to a jury trial in these cases.
- To understand how the *Booker* decision changed the application of the federal guidelines from mandatory to advisory.
- To appreciate how *Booker* and subsequent decisions have used a reasonableness standard in assessing sentence appeals.

Introduction

Throughout United States history, sentencing practices have come under judicial scrutiny. Some of the state and federal sentencing reforms that we introduced in the earlier chapters have been challenged by the courts. In some cases, courts have upheld reforms. In others, sentencing reforms and the way they have been implemented have been deemed unconstitutional. In this chapter, we will outline significant cases that courts have ruled on involving sentencing issues.

Court Cases Involving Proportionality Review in Sentencing

Proportionality Review — Federal System
Weems v. United States (1910)

Before we examine court decisions involving various sentencing reforms in different jurisdictions, it is important to understand some early court opinions involving sentencing that predate modern sentencing reforms. A common challenge to sentencing practices has involved the Eighth Amendment's clause that protects citizens against "cruel and unusual punishment." Through the years the question of whether sentences are too harsh or disproportionate to the crime committed has been repeatedly raised.

Zeigler and Del Carmen (1996) identified *Weems v. United States* (217 U.S. 349 (1910)) as the first case in which the Supreme Court made a decision based on the issue of whether the punishment fit the crime. The concept of proportionality was introduced in Chapter 1. Proportionality means that the severity of the sanction should be in proportion to the seriousness of the offense. For example, murderers should be punished more harshly than robbers and robbers should be punished more severely than pickpockets.

Weems was a federal case, in which the defendant was a public official who was convicted of public document falsification and subsequently sentenced to a term of 15 years of imprisonment which required hard labor, during which he was shackled at the ankle and waist. His sentence also indicated that he was to be subjected to lifelong surveillance, would lose his right to vote, his ability to acquire honors, and his eligibility to receive retirement pay.

The central question in this Supreme Court case was the legality of a statute of the Penal Code of the Philippine Islands and the sentence handed down to Mr. Weems. The Eighth Amendment protection against cruel and unusual punishment was scrutinized. This guarantee was stated in the Bill of Rights of the Philippine Islands at the time of the offense. This case may at first glance seem irrelevant to the United States criminal justice system and sentencing, however, at the time of the case the Philippine Islands were a territory of the United States.

The Court acknowledged the legislature's power to define crimes and designate appropriate punishments. It also emphasized that it is the duty of the judiciary to decide whether the legislature has violated provisions of the Constitution in this process. The Court asserted that if this was the case that the power of the judiciary is considered to be superior to that of the legislature.

At the time this case reached the Supreme Court, there was no clear precedent dictating how the term "cruel and unusual punishment" should be interpreted in a consideration of the appropriateness of a harsh sentence. The Court based the decision on examining how similar cases were punished in other jurisdictions in the United States and how more serious crimes had been punished within the same jurisdiction. The Court cited the concept of proportionality, stating ". . . it is a precept of justice that punishment for crime should be graduated and proportioned to the offense" (*Weems v. United States* (1910), p. 367).

The Court concluded that then prisoner Weems' punishment was not proportionate to the offense he committed. The sentence was determined to be cruel and unusual and therefore in violation the Bill of Rights. The fault was in the law, not in the sentence. The judgment was reversed and the case was dismissed.

Zeigler and Del Carmen (1996) asserted, "The decision can be read as the first pronouncement by the Supreme Court on the basic conflict between legislative enactment of punishment measures and judicial interpretation of their constitutionality" (p. 6). It could be argued that the *Weems* decision laid the groundwork for challenges to reforms such as three strikes laws and mandatory sentencing practices.

Proportionality Review—States

Robinson v. California (1962)

Proportionality review was first applied to states over fifty years after the *Weems* decision in *Robinson v. California* (370 U.S. 660 (1962)). This case centered on two issues that came under judicial scrutiny. The first was whether the status of being addicted should be criminalized, and the second concerned proportionality in sentencing.

The defendant, Mr. Robinson, was sentenced to 90 days in jail by a trial court for being addicted to narcotics. This "offense" violated a section of California's Health & Safety Code. The decision was upheld by the Appellate Department of the Superior Court of California in Los Angeles County.

The Supreme Court reviewed the case and examined records from the incident, including testimony from a police officer. The officer remarked that the appellant had "scar tissue and discoloration on the inside" of his right arm and "what appeared to be numerous needle marks and a scab which was approximately three inches below the crook of the elbow" on the appellant's left arm (*Robinson v. California* (1962, p. 661)). This officer assumed that these physical features resulted from injections by hypodermic needles. The police officer also stated that the defendant said he had occasionally used narcotics. At the time of his arrest, Mr. Robinson was not engaged in any illegal conduct.

The Court likened addiction to an illness and stated:

> It is unlikely that any State at this moment in history would attempt to make it a criminal offense for a person to be mentally ill, or a leper, or to be afflicted with a venereal disease. A State might determine that the general health and welfare require that the victims of these and other human afflictions be dealt with by compulsory treatment, involving quarantine, confinement, or sequestration. But, in the light of contemporary human knowledge, a law which made a criminal offense of such a disease would doubtless be universally thought to be an infliction of cruel and unusual punishment in violation of the Eighth and Fourteenth Amendments. (p. 666)

The Supreme Court decided that the law which criminalized the state of being addicted to narcotics, regardless of possession or use of such substances, was unconstitutional as it violated the Eighth Amendment for inflicting cruel and unusual punishment. The Court reasoned that the imprisonment sentence handed down to Mr. Robinson for being addicted to narcotics, as opposed to possessing or selling the substance, was disproportionate. The sentence was nullified.

Proportionality Issues Involving Sentencing Enhancements for Habitual Offenders

Graham v. West Virginia (1912)

In *Graham v. West Virginia* (224 U.S. 616 (1912)) the Supreme Court decided that a West Virginia statute that provided for sentencing enhancements for repeat offenders was constitutional. This case involved not only the issue of imposing sentence enhancements to repeat offenders but also addressed the issue of determining the identity of an individual who was convicted of an offense under a different name.

Mr. Graham was convicted of grand larceny under a different name. Although the defendant was a twice convicted felon at the time of sentencing, the trial court was not aware of his true identity (and that he had two prior convictions). He was sentenced to a relatively short prison sentence, which was considered reasonable for someone with no criminal record.

The statute in question allowed a prisoner who had been convicted and sentenced to prison whose identity was questioned to be tried on information. If his identity was proven, the statute indicated that the finding of one prior conviction would yield an additional five years in prison. If it was determined that the individual had two prior convictions, he would be sentenced to life. Pursuant to the West Virginia statute, because the grand larceny was Mr. Graham's third conviction, he was handed down a life sentence. Mr. Graham appealed this sentence enhancement, arguing that the protection against double jeopardy under the Fifth Amendment and the Eighth Amendment protection from cruel and unusual punishment were violated.

The Supreme Court held that the trial court decision was constitutional. A person who has been previously convicted of a crime is not denied due process nor is he put in double jeopardy by having the question of his identity determined separately at a later date. The Court recognized that throughout the history of the United States increased punishment for repeat offenders is not a second punishment for earlier crimes. Rather, repeat criminal behavior aggravates one's guilt and justifies harsher punishment for subsequent offenses. The Court decided in this case, sentencing enhancement for repeat convictions does not constitute cruel and unusual punishment.

Rummel v. Estelle (1980)

The case *Rummel v. Estelle* (445 U.S. 263 (1980)) considered the constitutionality of a sentencing enhancement for repeat felons under Texas law. In 1973, Mr. William James Rummel was convicted of obtaining $120.75 by false pretenses. He had two prior convictions—credit card fraud (in which he tried to get $80.00 worth of merchandise) and passing a forged check for $28.36. Each of the three offenses Rummel was convicted of was considered a felony under Texas law. A Texas recidivist statute mandated that a third conviction would send a repeat offender to prison for life. Pursuant to the law, Mr. Rummel was sentenced to a mandatory life sentence upon his third felony conviction (*Rummel v. Estelle*, 1980, p. 264–266).

In 1976, while serving his sentence, Mr. Rummel initiated procedures to obtain a **writ of *habeas corpus*** in the United States District Court for the Western District of Texas in which he argued that his life sentence was "grossly disproportionate" to his three criminal convictions that led to the sentence. *Habeas corpus* translates roughly to "You should have the body" and is a legal recourse in which a person is in essence claiming he or she is being unlawfully detained or imprisoned, usually through a prison official. Mr. Rummel argued that his sentence to life in prison therefore violated the ban on cruel and unusual punishment under the Eighth and Fourteenth Amendments.

Mr. Rummel did not challenge the Texas recidivist statute in general, but argued that it should not have been applied to his case, given the nature of his criminal history (all non-violent offenses). Both the district court, as well as the United States Court of Appeals for the Fifth Circuit, did not find the sentence to be unconstitutional.

In a 5 to 4 decision the Supreme Court affirmed the lower courts' denial of a writ of *habeas corpus*. The Supreme Court identified three issues in the decision. First, the Court stated that sentencing policies emanated from the legislature, not the judiciary. Second, because Mr. Rummel was eligible for discretionary parole release, there was a possibility that he would not have to serve the entire sentence handed down by the trial court. Mr. Rummel was, in fact, eligible for parole after serving twelve years in prison. Third, the Court noted that because Mr. Rummel was convicted of two offenses that were considered felonies under Texas law that he failed to demonstrate conduct that was socially appropriate. The sentencing enhancement indicated by the "recidivist statute" and applied in sentencing Mr. Rummel was deemed constitutional and did not amount to "cruel and unusual punishment."

Hutto v. Davis (1982)

In 1982, the Supreme Court cited the *Rummel* decision in *Hutto v. Davis* (454 U.S. 370 (1982)) when the majority reiterated the argument that the establishment of sentence length is the responsibility of a state's legislature, not the duty of its courts.

On October 26, 1973, Mr. Davis's house was raided and officers found nine ounces of marijuana as well as various drug paraphernalia in his dwelling. A few days prior to the raid officers had tape recorded a conversation that Mr. Davis had with a police informant to whom he "sold" marijuana and other controlled substances. He was convicted of possession with intent to distribute and the distribution of marijuana. The jury handed down a fine of $10,000 and sentenced him to two twenty-year prison terms to be served consecutively. When Mr. Davis was convicted, Virginia law allowed fines of up to $25,000 and prison terms of 5 to 40 years of *each* offense (*Hutto v. Davis*, p. 371).

Mr. Davis initiated a *habeas corpus* action in the United States District Court of the Western District of Virginia in which he maintained that the 40-year prison sentence he received constituted cruel and unusual punishment because it was grossly disproportionate to his offense. The district court granted Mr. Davis a writ of *habeas corpus*. The United States Court of Appeals for the Fourth Circuit affirmed this. Upon appeal from the state the Supreme Court remanded the case back to the circuit court, directing the circuit court to reconsider the case given the recent and relevant *Rummel* (1980) decision.

The central issue was the stance taken by the Supreme Court in *Rummel* that argued that federal courts should be reluctant to review prison terms that have been legislatively mandated and that proportionality challenges should be rare. The Fourth Circuit Court decided again that Mr. Davis's sentence constituted cruel and unusual punishment, characterizing it as grossly disproportionate to the offense committed. It contended that Mr. Davis's sentence was an example of a "rare" instance in which the issue of the proportionality of a legislatively determined sentence merited review by the judiciary.

The Supreme Court ultimately reversed the decision of the Fourth Circuit Court in a 6 to 3 decision and dismissed inmate Davis's petition for a writ of *habeas corpus*. The Court emphasized that federal courts should be reluctant to judge whether a legislatively mandated term of imprisonment constitutes cruel and unusual punishment. The majority maintained that successful challenges to the proportionality of sentences should be rare. In an obvious reference to *Rummel v. Estelle*, the opinion for the majority stated that the precedents of the Supreme Court are to be followed by lower federal courts (*Hutto v. Davis*, p. 374).

Proportionality and the Death Penalty

The focus of this text is on sentencing offenders who have committed non-capital crimes. A review of Supreme Court cases that have provided opinions about proportionality involving a defendant who was convicted of a capital crime is relevant, however, because some of the Court's holdings have informed subsequent Court decisions on cases involving non-capital offenses—at least to some extent.

Furman v. Georgia (1972)

In a 5 to 4 decision, the Supreme Court ruled in *Furman v. Georgia* (408 U.S. 238 (1972)), that the death penalty constituted cruel and unusual punishment.[1] William Furman was an African American man given a death sentence following a conviction for a murder in the commission of a robbery. In Georgia, the law allowed the judge to impose capital punishment at his or her personal discretion. Furman was sentenced to death.

Why did the Supreme Court deem the death penalty to be cruel and unusual punishment? Various reasons for the decision were espoused by different justices. Only two justices (Brennan and Marshall) argued that it was *per se* **cruel and unusual**—that imposing the death penalty on a person who killed or raped was in and of itself cruel and unusual punishment. These justices argued that the imposition of the death penalty for someone who killed was incompatible with evolving standards of decency in a contemporary society. Justices Douglas, Stewart, and White argued it was cruel and unusual because it was being ***administered in an* arbitrary and capricious way**. Only a few of the many people convicted of heinous crimes were sentenced to death. Most were given imprisonment instead. Justices Douglas, Stewart, and White argued that courts had so much discretion that they could impose capital punishment on only a select group of people—which were commonly the poor and racial minorities. They argued that the state statutes in question were unconstitutional because they offered judges and juries *no standards or guidelines* to consider in deciding between life and death. Justice Stewart likened receiving the punishment of death to being "struck by lightning" because it was so rare and unpredictable. The state and federal death penalty statutes were too arbitrary, capricious, and discriminatory to withstand Eighth Amendment scrutiny.

The dissenting judges (Burger, Blackmun, Powell, and Rehnquist) suggested that in a democracy, issues such as capital punishment should be decided by the legislative branch of government—the people's representatives, and not by the courts. They also cited how capital punishment has been recognized under Anglo-American legal convention as an appropriate punishment for serious crimes.

In the *Furman* decision, the Court called for states to establish consistency in the process of determining if an offender convicted of a capital crime would be sentenced to death or life without parole. One avenue by which states could enact new capital punishment laws involved the establishment of a two-stage procedure or bifurcated trial. A trial at which the question of culpability could be determined would be followed by an additional proceeding for those found guilty. In the second stage evidence could be presented to make the decision for death or life more informed and procedurally sound. Following *Furman v. Georgia*, many states passed laws designed to maintain the death penalty by trying to remove the arbitrary aspects of the proceedings. Some states came up with checklists of case circumstances to be considered when a jury was deciding death versus life imprisonment to remove the concern that the death penalty was administered in an arbitrary and capricious manner.

Gregg v. Georgia (1976)

Georgia created such a checklist of aggravating factors to guide jurors' decisions as to whether to impose a life sentence or the death penalty. In 1976, the Supreme Court ruled on the constitutionality of five state death penalty statutes, one of which was Georgia's. In *Gregg v. Georgia* (428 U.S. 153 (1976)) the Court created a detailed analysis of proportionality into the assessment of whether the death penalty constituted cruel and unusual punishment. This examination was required in capital cases. In a 7 to 2 decision, the Court ruled that (1) the death penalty isn't in and of itself cruel and unusual and (2) a two-part proceeding—one for the determination of innocence or guilt and the other for determining the sentence—is constitutional and meets the objections noted in *Furman v. Georgia*.

A jury found Mr. Troy Gregg guilty of two counts of armed robbery and two counts of murder. At sentencing, the judge instructed the jury to consider aggravating and mitigating circumstances in the case when deliberating whether to impose life imprisonment or death. The Georgia statute required the jury to find at least one "aggravating circumstance" out of ten to give the death penalty. In this case, the jury found beyond a reasonable doubt two such factors: (1) the offender was engaged in the commission of two other capital felonies (in this case the armed robberies of the victims) and (2) the offender committed the offense of murder for the purposes of receiving money and other financial gains (in this case the victims' money and automobile). The jury then returned a sentence of death.

The development of checklists of aggravating and mitigating factors that a jury must consider in a life or death decision was accepted as substantiation that this decision was structured, guided, and no longer arbitrary. The scrutiny of criminal cases involved an assessment of proportionality. Georgia served as a model for many other states.

The Supreme Court maintained that the Eighth Amendment has been interpreted in a flexible and dynamic manner and in accordance with "evolving standards of decency." The Court noted that legislative measures adopted by people's chosen representatives weighed heavily in the assessment of contemporary standards of decency. Support for the death penalty was evidenced by the fact that at least 35 states enacted new statutes providing for the death penalty in the four years following the *Furman* decision (pp. 179–183).

Coker v. Georgia (1977)

In *Coker v. Georgia* (433 U.S. 584 (1977)), the Supreme Court decided that the death penalty was grossly disproportionate and excessive punishment for the crime of rape. Imposing the death penalty for the rape of an adult woman was deemed cruel and unusual punishment and therefore in violation of the Eighth Amendment.

Mr. Ehrlich Anthony Coker was a repeat violent offender serving time for rape, murder, and kidnapping. He was serving three life terms, two 20-year terms, and one 8-year term of imprisonment which were to run consecutively at the time of the offense. Approximately one year into serving these terms, Coker escaped from prison and during the commission of other offenses including armed robbery, raped a 16-year-old woman in front of her husband and then abducted her from her home and inflicted serious bodily harm on her.[2]

Following Coker's conviction for these offenses, the jury sentenced him to death for the rape count. Georgia's death penalty statutes permitted the imposition of the death penalty for rape if the evidence showed aggravating factors to be associated with the case. The jury found two aggravating circumstances were present — the rape was committed by a person who had previously been convicted of a capital felony and the rape was committed during the commission of another capital felony or aggravated battery. The Supreme Court of Georgia affirmed the conviction and the sentence.

In a 7 to 2 decision, the Supreme Court held that the sentence of death was grossly disproportionate and excessive punishment for the crime of rape and thus violated the Eighth Amendment. The Court looked at trends of state legislatures to pass or repeal sentences of death for persons convicted of rape. It also noted the fact that since 1973, Georgia juries did not sentence defendants convicted of rape of an adult to death in 90 percent of cases. The Court stated that although rape was a crime deserving of serious punishment, the punishment should not be the same as for an offender who killed another human being.

Enmund v. Florida (1982)

In *Enmund v. Florida* (458 U.S. 782 (1982)) the Supreme Court considered several sentencing issues including proportionality in deciding whether the imposition of the death penalty for a getaway driver in a robbery turned double murder violated the Eighth Amendment's clause barring cruel and unusual punishment.

Mr. Earl Enmund was found guilty of two counts of first degree murder and one count of robbery. In a separate sentencing hearing, a jury recommended that he and co-defendant Sampson Armstrong be sentenced to death. The trial judge imposed the death penalty.

According to Florida law, Enmund was considered a "constructive aider and abettor" and thus was considered a principal in the first degree murder of a couple. As such he was eligible to receive the death penalty. Enmund challenged the sentence, arguing that he did not take part in the murders and did not intend or expect lethal force to be used to carry out the robbery. The Florida Supreme Court affirmed the conviction and his death sentence.

In a 5 to 4 decision, the Supreme Court decided that the sentence of death for Enmund constituted cruel and unusual punishment as it violated the Eighth and Fourteenth Amendments. In explaining the decision the Court identified issues including proportionality and whether the sentence could possibly serve the goals of retribution and deterrence.

The Court reflected on *Weems v. United States*, which introduced limits on sentence length and severity, and *Coker v. Georgia*, which introduced limits on the type of crime that could receive the death penalty. The Court recognized that when executed, the death penalty is irrevocable and although it acknowledged that robbery is a serious crime it did not consider it a crime for which the only adequate response was the death penalty.

The Court also examined Enmund's conduct and emphasized that the focus in sentencing should be on the defendant's culpability and not on the culpability of those who actually robbed and murdered the victims. There was no record suggesting that Enmund planned or participated in the murders. The Court noted that at the time the crime was committed, very few states deemed the death penalty an appropriate punishment for a defendant who was involved in a robbery in which a murder was ultimately committed, but who did not take or try to take a life or intend lethal force to be used.

Kennedy v. Louisiana (2008)

In a 5 to 4 decision, the Supreme Court ruled in *Kennedy v. Louisiana* (554 U.S. 407 (2008)), that the imposition of the death penalty on someone convicted of child rape violated the Eighth Amendment's protection against cruel and unusual punishment. Many have interpreted this to mean that the death penalty is only to be reserved for those convicted of first degree murder. The Court concluded that regardless of the heinous nature of child rape, that a sentence of death is disproportionate to the severity of the offense.

Mr. Patrick Kennedy was convicted of brutally raping his then 8-year-old stepdaughter. The victim endured extensive injuries. Emergency surgery was required. An expert in pediatric forensic medicine testified in Kennedy's trial that the victim's injuries were the most severe he had seen from a sexual assault in his four years of practice.

Kennedy was charged with and convicted of aggravated rape of a child and the state sought the death penalty. The Supreme Court of Louisiana rejected the petitioner's argument that the death penalty for the rape of a child under 12 years was disproportionate and upheld the constitutionality of the Louisiana statute under the Eighth Amendment.

The United States Supreme Court, however, reached an opposite conclusion and concluded that the death penalty in this case was disproportionate punishment to the crime for which the defendant was convicted. The Court held that the Eighth Amendment barred the state of Louisiana from handing down the death sentence to the defendant who raped, but did not kill or intend to kill a child.

The Court pointed to the concept that standards concerning whether a punishment was excessive were to reflect current norms, not those recognized when the Eighth Amendment was adopted in 1791. The Court reviewed the history of the death penalty for crimes of child rape and examined various state statutes at the time of the offense, as well as current enactments and also scrutinized the number of executions since 1964.[3] The Court concluded that there was a national consensus against imposing the death penalty for the crime of child rape. The majority concluded in its independent judgment that the death penalty was not proportional punishment for the crime of child rape.

The Court termed its opinion as consistent with two sentencing goals of punishment — retribution and deterrence. With respect to retribution, the Court looked at whether the death penalty balances the wrong done to the victim in non-homicide cases. It concluded that there was little evidence that the hurt inflicted on a victim of child rape is lessened when the law permits the perpetrator's death, especially given the length of testimony required on the part of the victim in a capital case (and given the notion that a child may not be of a mature age to make a choice to testify). Regarding deterrence, the Court concluded that the death penalty may not result in more effective enforcement of the law. The reasoning was that if the death penalty is a potential sanction the child rape victim may fear negative consequences for the perpetrator and actually be less likely to report, especially if the perpetrator is a family member.[4] In addition, the Court reasoned that by making the punishment for child rape and murder equivalent, a state may remove a strong incentive for the rapist not to kill the victim.[5]

Roper v. Simmons (2005)

In *Roper v. Simmons* (543 U.S. 551 (2005)), the Supreme Court ruled that imposing a death sentence for a juvenile who committed murder while he was under 18 years of age was in violation of the Eighth Amendment.

In 1993, at age 17, Christopher Simmons planned and committed a capital murder. Simmons confessed to the murder and agreed to perform a videotaped reenactment at the crime scene. In accordance with Missouri's criminal justice system, Simmons was tried as an adult for burglary, kidnapping, stealing, and murder in the first degree. A jury found Simmons guilty of murder.

The state sought the death penalty and presented several aggravating factors in the case. Simmons' attorneys presented mitigating factors, including that Simmons had no prior convictions and no previous charges filed against him and that his mother and a neighbor plead for his life. The trial judge instructed jurors that they could consider Simmons' age as a mitigating factor. The jury recommended the death penalty after concluding that the state had proven each of the aggravating factors. The trial judge agreed and Simmons was sentenced to death.

After sentencing, Simmons obtained new counsel who moved in the trial court to set aside the conviction and sentence. It was argued that Simmons had received ineffective counsel at trial. The trial court did not find any constitutional violation by reason of ineffective assistance of counsel and denied a motion for post-conviction relief. The Missouri Supreme Court affirmed. After these proceedings, however, the Supreme Court had held in *Atkins v. Virginia* (536 U.S. 304 (2002)) that the Eighth and Fourteenth Amendments prohibited the execution of a mentally retarded person. Simmons filed a new petition for state post-conviction relief, arguing that the reasoning in the *Atkins* decision meant that the Constitution prohibited the execution of a juvenile who was under the age of 18 when the crime was committed. The Missouri Supreme Court agreed. It set aside the death sentence for Simmons and resentenced him to life imprisonment without the possibility of parole. The state appealed.

In their deliberations of *Roper v. Simmons*, the Supreme Court reviewed legislation in various jurisdictions in the United States to assess a consensus concerning juvenile capital punishment. Thirty states had prohibited the juvenile death penalty—12 had rejected the death penalty altogether and 18 maintained it, but by express provision or judicial interpretation, had excluded it from its reach. In the 20 states that lacked a formal prohibition on executing juveniles, the death penalty was infrequently handed down to juveniles.

The Court reasoned that death penalty sentencing involves an assessment of both the circumstances of the crime and the characteristics of the offender. The justices concluded that American society considered juveniles as categorically less culpable than the average criminal. While the Court focused on whether sentencing a juvenile to death was in accordance to the United States Constitution, it also considered international opinion, which was clearly against the juvenile death penalty.

The Court held in a 5 to 4 decision that the Eighth Amendment forbids the imposition of the death penalty on offenders under the age of 18. Because the death penalty is the most severe punishment, special consideration of issues including the identification of categories of offenders who may or may not be eligible to receive a sentence of death is deemed appropriate. The Court decided in *Roper* that age at the time of the offense is one such category.

Summary of Supreme Court Decisions Involving Proportionality and the Death Penalty

Through its review of these cases, the Supreme Court has established some approaches to delineating whether there has been gross proportionality in the sentencing of capital offenses. In *Roper v. Simmons* (2005) when deciding whether a capital sentence constituted "cruel and unusual punishment," the Court deliberated as to whether sentencing an offender to death for a crime committed while he was a juvenile contradicted, "the evolving standards of decency that mark the progress of a maturing society."

In this and other capital cases the Court has considered the following data: (1) how many states impose the death penalty for specific offenses (for example, rape of an adult or rape of a child and felony murder) or offenders (juveniles), (2) how frequently states that statutorily authorize the death penalty for certain offenses and offenders actually impose capital punishment for these cases, and (3) an analysis of a "broader social and professional consensus" against the death penalty from which a conclusion is based on official positions of professional and religious organizations or polls of the United States or "world community." In addition, the Court has considered whether the death penalty serves commonly recognized goal(s) of sentencing and whether the class of offender is at elevated risk for being wrongly convicted (Fong Sheketoff, 2010). Such factors have influenced the decision of whether the death penalty is considered disproportionate and therefore deemed "cruel and unusual" punishment.

The Development of a Three-Factor Proportionality Test— *Solem v. Helm* (1983)

The 5 to 4 decision in *Solem v. Helm* (463 U.S. 277 (1983)) represented a change in the Supreme Court's response to proportionality concerns about sentence length indicated by a recidivist statute. This was a non-capital case. Since *Weems*, the Court was hesitant to assess whether sentence lengths for non-capital cases that were set by state legislatures were disproportionate, as evidenced by the decisions in *Graham v. West Virginia* (1912), *Rummel v. Estelle* (1980), and *Hutto v. Davis* (1982).

In 1979, Mr. Helm was convicted of writing a check from a fictitious account. This was his seventh non-violent felony conviction. If this had been his first offense, the maximum punishment under South Dakota law would have been imprisonment for five years and a $5,000 fine. The state's recidivist statute, however, indicated a sentence of life imprisonment without the possibility of parole. The South Dakota Supreme Court affirmed the sentence.

Mr. Helm applied for commutation of his sentence, which was denied. He then pursued *habeas corpus* relief in the federal district court, arguing that the punishment was cruel and unusual punishment but was denied at this level. Subsequently, the United States Court of Appeals for the Eighth Circuit granted Mr. Helm's request for *habeas corpus* relief. Then the petitioner, Mr. Solem, who was warden of the South Dakota State Penitentiary where Mr. Helm was imprisoned, appealed this decision.

The Supreme Court agreed to *habeas corpus* relief on the grounds that the sentence constituted "cruel and unusual" punishment and overturned the sentence. The Court found the sentence of life without parole to be disproportionate to the offense. This decision seemed at odds with decisions of *Rummel* and *Hutto*, wherein the explanations of these Supreme Court rulings stressed the reluctance of the Court to judge states' legislatively mandated sentence lengths even when they appeared excessive.

The Court noted that the concept of proportionality had historically guided courts in England and through common law and that it was implicit in the Eighth Amendment (*Solem v. Helm*, pp. 284–286). Also underscored were the cases of *Weems v. United States*, *Robinson v. California*, and *Enmund v. Florida*, in which the Court explicitly referenced the issue of proportionality in the review of the punishment in relation to the offenses committed in these cases.

In an unprecedented move, the Court also crafted rules that all courts would have to consider in determining whether a sentence is proportional to a specific crime. The following three issues were to be assessed:

  i. The gravity of the offense and the harshness of the penalty;
 ii. The sentences imposed on other criminals in the same jurisdiction, that is, whether more serious crimes are subject to the same penalty or to less serious penalties; and
iii. The sentences imposed for commission of the same crime in other jurisdictions (pp. 290–292).

The Court applied these rules to Helm's case and noted first that the crime that Mr. Helm committed that constituted his seventh conviction was not considered serious by society in general as it lacked force or threat of force. Second, the Court noted that Mr. Helm's sentence was the most severe the state could have imposed on any criminal for any crime, as capital punishment was not authorized in South Dakota. Third, the Court compared the sentence for the same crime to that in other jurisdictions and found that in only one state could Mr. Helm have received a life sentence without parole. The Court did not strike down state statutes that indicated lengthy sentences for habitual offenders. Rather it allowed for exceptions to such statutes if they are judged to be disproportionate to the crime committed and therefore deemed "cruel and unusual."

One might expect all subsequent cases involving proportionality challenges to be decided by using the three-factor proportionality test. As we will learn, however, the Court has not always strictly adhered to the standard produced in *Solem v. Helm*.

Mandatory Minimum Sentence Laws and the Issue of Proportionality

Harmelin v. Michigan (1991)

The Supreme Court considered the issue of proportionality of a mandatory minimum sentence in *Harmelin v. Michigan* (501 U.S. 957 (1991)). In Chapter 6 we examined Michigan's 650 Lifer Law, which established a mandatory sentence of life without parole for persons convicted of possessing, delivering, or intending to deliver over 650 grams (approximately one and one-half pounds) of narcotics.

Mr. Harmelin was convicted of possessing over 650 grams of cocaine and sentenced to life without parole under Michigan's 650 Lifer Law. Mr. Harmelin appealed, arguing that the sentence was disproportionate to the crime he committed and that it constituted "cruel and unusual" punishment. He argued that his offense was a nonviolent, "victimless" crime. Harmelin also brought up the fact that because he was sentenced under a mandatory sentencing law that the sentencing judge could not take into account his particular circumstances — that he had no prior felony convictions. The Court of Appeals of Michigan affirmed Mr. Harmelin's sentence.

The Supreme Court decided in a 5 to 4 decision that Michigan's mandatory sentencing law that resulted in sentencing Mr. Harmelin to life imprisonment without the possibility of parole for possession of 672 grams of cocaine did not constitute cruel and unusual punishment. While Mr. Harmelin's mandatory punishment was arguably severe, the Court did not find it to be unusual because mandatory sentences have been employed throughout the nation's history. The Court stated that a sentence that otherwise would not have been considered "cruel and unusual" would not be deemed such just because it was made mandatory.

The Court decided that the Eighth Amendment did not require proportionality analysis for non-capital cases. This argument may seem to contradict the proportionality criteria we just discussed that were established by *Solem v. Helm*, and indeed it did. In *Harmelin v. Michigan* the Court rejected its prior decision of *Solem v. Helm*. The Court's prior conclusion that disproportionate punishments constituted "cruel and unusual" punishments was negated. The reasoning was while mandatory punishments may be severe or cruel, they are not unusual when considering the Constitution. The Court highlighted the use of mandatory penalties throughout history.

Arguments Concerning Proportionality Review in Non-capital Cases

It is important to understand that this case generated multiple arguments about the appropriateness of proportionality review in non-capital cases. We will briefly outline positions of some justices, which illustrate notable and substantive differences in the interpretation of whether and how the Eighth Amendment requires proportionality in non-capital cases.

Justice Scalia joined by Chief Justice Rehnquist stated that there is no *guarantee* of proportionality in the Eighth Amendment. It was argued that a punishment was considered "cruel and unusual" if were outside the judge's power to impose, making the term "cruel and unusual" synonymous with "cruel and illegal." According to this reasoning a disproportionate punishment did not make it "cruel and usual."

Scalia emphasized that sentence lengths are to be established by the legislature and opined that the three factor test established in *Solem v. Helm* should be overturned.[6] Scalia contended that the first two criteria established in *Solem*—a consideration of the gravity of the offense and the sentences imposed for similarly serious offenses in some jurisdictions—lacked objectivity. It was stated that various statutes have been enacted in different times and places and that there has been considerable variation regarding what offenses are deemed serious. The third criterion—how sentences are imposed by other states for the same offense—was characterized as irrelevant to the Eighth Amendment (pp. 962–994).

Justice Kennedy, joined by Justice O'Connor and Justice Souter, concluded that decisions regarding proportionality in non-capital cases have lacked clarity and consistency. He asserted that the Eighth Amendment's clause regarding cruel and unusual punishment calls for a narrow proportionality principle in non-capital cases. He identified several principles that help capture the essence of appropriate proportionality review. First, he identified the legislature as the appropriate body for fixing of the lengths of prison sentences for specific offenses, not the courts. Second, he acknowledged multiple sentencing goals (retribution, deterrence, incapacitation, and rehabilitation) but argued that the Eighth Amendment does not delineate which should guide sentencing and suggested that it is in the states' purview to decide which goal(s) should guide sentencing in their jurisdictions. Third, Kennedy noted that because of the first two principles there is bound to be variation in the lengths of sentences within jurisdictions and between different jurisdictions and just because sentences are different doesn't mean they are irrational or inappropriate, considering variation in local attitudes and perceptions of what are appropriate terms for certain crimes. This suggested eliminating the intrajurisdictional and inter-jurisdictional comparisons called for in *Solem*. Fourth, although some proportionality challenges have been successful in cases involving capital offenses, proportionality review by federal courts concerning sentence length for non-capital crimes have lacked objective standards and resulted in few successful challenges. Finally, Kennedy declared that the Eighth Amendment does not require strict proportionality between the offense and the sentence, but only bars sentences that are considered grossly disproportionate to the offense (pp. 996–1001). He asserted that an analysis outlined in *Solem v. Helm* was appropriate in rare cases in which one could infer gross disproportionality. The majority did not view Harmelin's case as such.[7]

In the dissent, Justice White maintained that a proportionality principle *was* inherent in the Eighth Amendment. Justice White, joined by Justice Blackmun and Justice Stevens, cited the part of the Eighth Amendment that forbids "excessive fines." He contended that, like a proscription of excessiveness of fines in relation to the severity of the offense, a similar intention would bar sentences in which imprisonment was considered to be excessive. Justice White argued that Harmelin's sentence was excessive and it was the kind of sentence that is barred according to the Eighth Amendment. White approved of the criteria established in *Solem*.

Three Strikes Laws and the Issue of Proportionality

Ewing v. California (2003)

Twelve years after *Harmelin*, the Supreme Court revisited the appropriateness of proportionality review in *Ewing v. California* (538 U.S. 11 (2003)).

On March 12, 2000, Mr. Gary Albert Ewing, who was on parole from a nine-year prison term, walked into a pro shop of the El Segundo Golf Course in Los Angeles County, put three golf clubs in his pants leg and exited the premises. After an employee saw Ewing limping and became suspicious, he called the police and police apprehended Ewing in the parking lot.

Mr. Ewing had an extensive criminal record. In October and November of 1993 he committed three burglaries and one robbery at a Long Beach, California, apartment complex over a five-week period. A jury found Ewing guilty of first degree robbery and three counts of residential burglary. He was sentenced to nine years and eight months in prison, but was paroled in 1999.

Ewing stole the golf clubs merely ten months after he was released from prison and paroled. He was convicted of one count of felony grand theft of personal property in excess of $400. The prosecutor formally alleged and the trial court found that he had four serious or violent felonies—the three burglaries and the robbery in the apartment complex. In accordance with California's three strikes law, Ewing was sentenced to 25 years to life.

During his sentencing hearing, Ewing requested that the court reduce the conviction of one count of felony theft to that of a misdemeanor, so that he that his latest conviction wouldn't invoke California's three strikes law. California law designated the theft as a "wobbler" offense because the prosecutor could charge the offense as a felony or a misdemeanor. He also asked the trial court to dismiss some of his priors to avoid the three strikes sentence. As discussed in Chapter 6, in the case of *People v. Superior Court (Romero)* (1996), the State Supreme Court of California ruled that the court may decide to dismiss prior serious or violent felony convictions under the three strikes law. This decision has allowed judges to ignore a prior conviction in the interest of justice in the process of deciding whether to designate a defendant as a three strikes offender. The trial court judge ultimately decided that the grand theft should remain a felony and that the four prior strikes for the three burglaries and the robbery in Long Beach should stand. He was subsequently sentenced to 25 years to life.

Arguing that his sentence was grossly disproportionate to his offense, thus violating the Eighth Amendment, Ewing appealed to the California Court of Appeal, which affirmed his sentence. Drawing on *Rummel v. Estelle* (1980), this court rejected Ewing's claim. The appellate court maintained that enhanced sentences under recidivist statutes, such as California's three strikes law, serve a "legitimate" goal of deterring and incapacitating repeat offenders. The Supreme Court of California denied Ewing's petition for review.

In a 5 to 4 decision, the United States Supreme Court affirmed the decision by the California Court of Appeal. Justice O'Connor, joined by Chief Justice Rehnquist and Justice Kennedy, concluded that Ewing's sentence was not grossly disproportionate. The Court cited a "narrow proportionality principle" that is applicable to non-capital sentences. The Supreme Court acknowledged that state legislatures enact three strikes laws, making deliberate policy choices that repeat offenders who have engaged in serious and/or violent offenses and whose conduct has not been deterred by more conventional punishment approaches should be isolated from society in an effort to promote public safety. There is a tradition of deference to state legislatures in making policy decisions, and, therefore, nothing in the Eighth Amendment bars California from deciding to incapacitate criminals with a serious and/or violent criminal history to lengthy sentences. Recidivism is recognized as a legitimate reason for sentence enhancement. The legislature, not the judiciary, is the appropriate venue for criticism of such a policy choice.

Regarding Mr. Ewing's sentence, Justice O'Connor, joined by Justice Rehnquist and Justice Kennedy, maintained that even if one just looked at his latest conviction, grand larceny, it could be argued that such an offense should not be taken lightly. It was argued that the so-called "wobbler" offense appropriately remained a felony. Likewise, an examination of Ewing's lengthy criminal history in sentencing was justified. Ignoring the gravity of his current offense and his prior convictions would have been at odds with the legislature's establishment of the three strikes law. The state's interest in deterrence and incapacitation justified the sanction of Ewing, a serious repeat offender. Like in *Rummel v. Estelle*, it did not violate the Eighth Amendment to sentence a repeat offender to life in prison with the possibility of parole.

Lockyer v. Andrade (2003)

The Supreme Court considered the issue of proportionality concerning California's three strikes law again in *Lockyer v. Andrade* (538 U.S. 63 (2003)). In this case the offender had no prior violent felony convictions. He, however, had a string of other convictions. Some of the convictions counted as strikes according to California law.

On November 4, 1995, Mr. Leandro Andrade stole five videotapes valued at $84.70 from a Kmart store in Ontario, California, and was caught by security employees. On November 18, 1995, he went into a different Kmart store in Montclair, California, and stole four videotapes, which were worth $68.84, and was detained by security staff after he tried to exit the store without paying for them. He was arrested for both crimes.

Mr. Andrade had a lengthy criminal history, which included serving prison terms for various state and federal offenses. Two residential burglary convictions counted as the first and second strikes. At the time of the offense, California law designated petty theft as a "wobbler" offense. In Andrade's case, the prosecutor decided to charge each count of theft as a felony. A jury found Mr. Andrade guilty of two counts of petty theft and found that he had been convicted of two prior strikeable offenses (the residential burglaries). In accordance with California's three strikes law, the trial court sentenced Mr. Andrade to two consecutive terms of 25 years to life (one for each offense).

Mr. Andrade appealed his sentence to the California Court of Appeals, which affirmed his sentence and rejected Mr. Andrade's claim that his sentence violated the Eighth Amendment's clause barring cruel and unusual punishment. The case went to the Supreme Court.

Although the same claim was made in *Andrade* as in *Ewing v. California*, the procedural posture differed. In *Ewing*, the Supreme Court was reviewing the decisions from the California state court system and basically determined whether a three strikes sentences constituted cruel and unusual punishment. If the defendant had won, he would have been re-sentenced. In contrast, Andrade argued that his punishment was grossly disproportionate and violated the Eighth Amendment. This case involved a *habeas corpus* petition.

The petitioner, Attorney General of California Bill Lockyer, argued that the inmate's sentence under California's three strikes law was not contrary to established federal law. According to the Antiterrorism and Effective Death Penalty Act, the Supreme Court could not grant *habeas corpus* relief unless it concluded that the California State Courts upheld Mr. Andrade's sentence in a way that was "contrary to, or involved an unreasonable application of, clearly established Federal law, as determined by the Supreme Court of the United States." In its deliberations, the Court sought to ascertain the meaning of "clearly established." It reviewed the decisions discussed above that dealt with the issue of proportionality—*Rummel v. Estelle* (1980), *Solem v. Helm* (1983), and *Harmelin v. Michigan* (1991).

In a 5 to 4 decision the Supreme Court upheld the sentence. The Court concluded that its decisions in these prior cases did *not* establish a clear or consistent path for courts to follow in deciding whether a particular sentence length violated the Eighth Amendment. It noted that the applicability and appropriateness of proportionality analysis was questioned since the *Harmelin v. Michigan* decision. The Court acknowledged the importance it had put on deciding "gross proportionality" in past cases. It, however, admitted that the Court had lacked *clarity* in determining what factors indicate gross disproportionality and that the precise contours of proportionality have been unclear and only applicable in "exceeding rare" and "extreme" cases, as indicated by *Harmelin v. Michigan* (1991).

Justice O'Conner delivered the opinion of the Court, and was joined by Justices Rehnquist, Scalia, Kennedy, and Thomas. The Court held that the affirmance of the sentence by the California Court of Appeals did not contradict the governing legal principles set forth in prior cases. Regarding the length of sentencing, the availability of parole for the inmate, the severity of the underlying offense, and the consequences on recidivism, Andrade's sentence involved a consideration of factors identified in *Rummel v. Estelle* and *Solem v. Helm*. The Court acknowledged the governing legal principle that allocates broad discretion to legislatures to set sentences that fit the scope of proportionality and that the precise contours of proportionality were unclear. It was not objectively unreasonable, therefore, for the California Court of Appeal to have reached the decision that the contours allowed for the defendant's sentence to be affirmed.

Proportionality and Sentencing Juvenile Offenders to Life Imprisonment

An examination of cases in which the defendant is a juvenile (but tried in criminal court) provides some information on how the Supreme Court has ruled with respect to proportionality in cases in which offenders are considered less culpable.

Graham v. Florida (2010)

In *Graham v. Florida* (560 U.S. 48 (2010)), the Supreme Court decided that a sentence of **life without parole for a juvenile offender convicted of a non-homicide offense was unconstitutional**. This decision followed the landmark case *Roper v. Simmons* (2005), which had abolished the death penalty for juvenile offenders. While the focus of this text is on adult offenders who have committed non-capital offenses, this case is relevant to understanding the Court's recent decision regarding proportionality in sentencing.

In July 2003, at the age of 16, Mr. Terrance Graham committed armed burglary and attempted robbery. Florida law allowed the prosecutor to decide whether to charge 16- and 17- year-olds charged with felonies as either adults or juveniles. The prosecutor decided to charge Terrance Graham as an adult for armed burglary with assault or battery (a first degree felony, which carried a maximum penalty of life imprisonment without the possibility of parole) and attempted robbery (a second degree felony, which carried a maximum sentence of 15 years in prison). Graham pleaded guilty to these crimes and wrote a letter to the court in which he stated that he was finished getting into trouble and that he decided to turn his life around. He was sentenced to two 3-year terms of probation to be served concurrently. In the plea agreement the Florida trial court withheld adjudication of guilt for both charges.

Within six months, Terrance Graham was arrested again. The state of Florida made the case that on December 2, 2004, 34 days short of his 18th birthday, Graham took part in a home invasion robbery with two 20-year-old men. The trial court found that Graham had violated probation by committing a home invasion, possessing a firearm, and associating with people engaged in criminal activity. He was found guilty of the armed burglary and attempted armed robbery that first led to his sentence of probation. Before delivering the sentence, the trial court judge addressed Mr. Graham and made the point that he was given a chance to get on track, that he reoffended within a short period of time, and that he demonstrated an escalating pattern of criminal conduct. The judge asserted that it was then appropriate to consider community safety. Graham was sentenced to the maximum sentence for each offense, which meant a sentence of life without parole. Because Florida had abolished its parole system, Graham's only possible avenue for release was executive clemency from the governor.

Graham unsuccessfully filed a motion in the trial court which challenged his sentence under the Eighth Amendment's clause barring cruel and unusual punishment. Subsequently, the First District Court of Appeal of Florida affirmed the sentence. This appellate court noted the seriousness of Graham's criminal conduct, which included violence, that he was not a young adolescent, and concluded that he was not capable of being rehabilitated. It characterized Graham's original sentence to probation for a felony as "unheard of," brought up the letter Graham had written in which he vowed not to reoffend, and pointed to a strong family structure that Graham had to support him. The Florida Supreme Court denied review.

In a 6 to 3 decision the Supreme Court reversed and remanded.[8] Justice Kennedy delivered the opinion of the Court and was joined by Justices Stevens, Ginsburg, Breyer, and Sotomayor. Justice Kennedy identified the central issue in this case as whether the Constitution permits a juvenile offender to be sentenced to life imprisonment without the possibility of parole for a non-homicide crime.

The Court's opinion addressed several issues. The Court noted that defendants who do not kill or intend to kill or foresee that a life will be taken are less deserving of the severe punishment that is considered appropriate for murderers. Also, juveniles have less culpability than adults. Juveniles lack maturity, have an underdeveloped sense of responsibility, and are more vulnerable to negative influences and peer pressures. As such, juveniles are less deserving of the most severe punishment. A key point made by the Court was that a defendant who committed a non-homicide crime need not be *guaranteed* a release from a life sentence, but should have some realistic opportunity to be released prior to the serving the entire life sentence. Another point dealt with the fact that sentencing a juvenile who did not commit a homicide to a sentence of life without parole was very rare and a national consensus had developed against such a term. The Court also stated that it could not be conclusively determined at the time of sentencing that Graham would pose a danger to society for the remainder of his life. The Court made the point that a sentence of life without parole inappropriately denied the juvenile offender an opportunity to show growth, maturity, and rehabilitation. It concluded that the Eighth Amendment forbids states from judging or predicting that juveniles will never be fit to reenter society.

Miller v. Alabama (2012)

Recently, the Supreme Court ruled on the constitutionality of **mandatory life without parole sentences for juvenile offenders convicted of homicide** in *Miller v. Alabama* (576 U.S., ___ (2012)). The Court scrutinized two cases in which both the Arkansas Supreme Court and the Alabama Court of Appeals had held that such mandatory sentences laws did not violate the Eighth Amendment protection against cruel and unusual punishment.

After an evening of drinking and drug use, 14-year-old Evan Miller and a friend of his beat Miller's neighbor and set fire to his trailer. The victim died. Although Evan Miller was initially charged as a juvenile, his case was moved to an adult (criminal) court and he was charged with murder in the course of arson. Miller was found guilty by a jury. The Court of Criminal Appeals of Alabama affirmed the sentence after concluding that Miller's sentence was not overly harsh in comparison to the crime of which he was convicted and that the mandatory sentence of life without the possibility of parole was permissible under the Eighth Amendment.

At the age of 14, Kuntrell Jackson accompanied two other juvenile males to a video store with the intention to commit a robbery. On the way to the store, Jackson learned that one of the boys was carrying a shotgun. Although Jackson was outside during most of the robbery, after he entered the store, one of his co-conspirators shot and killed the store clerk. Jackson was charged as an adult with capital felony murder and aggravated robbery. A jury convicted him of both offenses. The trial court handed down a statutorily mandated sentence of life imprisonment without the possibility of parole. The Supreme Court of Arkansas denied *habeas corpus* relief after Jackson argued that a mandatory sentence of life without parole for a 14-year-old violated the Eighth Amendment, and the court affirmed the sentence.

The Supreme Court reversed and remanded. In a 5 to 4 decision, the Court concluded that the Eighth Amendment forbade a sentence of mandatory imprisonment without the possibility of parole for persons who were juveniles at the time in which the offense was committed, even if that offense is murder.

In *Miller*, the Court concluded that imposing a mandatory life without parole sentence for a juvenile made it impossible to consider the offender's age and age-related issues such as immaturity, impulsivity, and the inability to fully appreciate risks and consequences associated with one's behavior. It also prevented taking into consideration family factors and a minor's home environment, from which the juvenile could not usually extricate himself regardless of the brutality or dysfunction of that environment. The Court also noted that the mandatory life without parole sentence failed to consider the circumstances of the homicide, including the juvenile's role in the offense and how peer pressure affected him. Children are also considered different than adults as their character is not as "well formed" as an adult's and their traits may be "less fixed," and so a juvenile's actions may not be evidence of irretrievable depravity.

In essence, the Supreme Court decided in *Miller* that a judge or jury must have the opportunity to consider mitigating circumstances before imposing the harshest penalty for juveniles. Requiring all juveniles convicted of homicide to receive a sentence of life without the possibility of parole violates the principle of proportionality and therefore violates the Eighth Amendment's ban on cruel and unusual punishment.

Making Sense of Supreme Court Decisions Concerning Proportionality Review of Sentences for Non-Capital Offenses

How can we summarize the opinion of the Supreme Court on the appropriateness of proportionality review for non-capital cases? What patterns (if any) have been established that may guide one's understanding of the Court's position on the proper place of proportionality review with regard to the establishment of modern sentencing reforms such as mandatory minimum sentencing and three strikes laws? The answers to these questions are far from straightforward. Table 7.1 provides an overview of instances when the Supreme Court has considered proportionality in capital and non-capital cases.

Table 7.1 Overview of the Consideration of Proportionality in Non-Capital and Capital Cases by the Supreme Court

Case	Vote	Summary
Proportionality Review—Non-Capital Cases		
Weems v. United States (1910)	5–2	Allowed proportionality review—federal judgement reversed, case dismissed
Graham v. West Virginia (1912)[a]	n.a.	Upheld sentencing enhancement for repeat offender
Robinson v. California (1962)	6–2	Frankfurter took no part in consideration. Allowed proportionality review—state decided law criminalizing "state of being addicted" unconstitutional
Rummel v. Estelle (1980)	5–4	Upheld sentencing enhancement for repeat felons
Hutto v. Davis (1982)	6–3	Upheld sentencing law that mandated imprisonment; majority maintained that challenges to the proportionality of sentences should be rare
Solem v. Helm (1983)	5–4	Constructed proportionality test—found recidivist statute unconstitutional, disproportionate to crime
Harmelin v. Michigan (1991)	5–4	Upheld mandatory minimum law—didn't deem proportionality review appropriate
Ewing v. California (2003)	5–4	CA's three strikes law not disproportionate; not unconstitutional; deference to state legislature
Lockyer v. Andrade (2003)	5–4	Affirmed sentence; not grossly disproportionate
Graham v. Florida (2010)	6–3	Life without parole sentence for juvenile convicted of non-homicide offense unconstitutional; proportionality among factors considered

(continued)

Table 7.1 Overview of the Consideration of Proportionality in Non-Capital and
Capital Cases by the Supreme Court (continued)

Case	Vote	Summary
Miller v. Alabama (2012)	5–4	Mandatory life without parole for juvenile convicted of homicide unconstitutional; proportionality among other factors considered
Proportionality Review — Capital Cases		
Furman v. Georgia (1972)	5–4	Death penalty was cruel and unusual as applied
Gregg v. Georgia (1976)	7–2	Upheld death penalty — new statute used checklist of factors in deciding life or death
Coker v. Georgia (1977)	7–2	Death penalty disproportionate punishment for rape of adult
Enmund v. Florida (1982)	5–4	Death penalty disproportionate for getaway driver in murder
Kennedy v. Louisiana (2008)	5–4	Death penalty disproportionate for rape of a child
Roper v. Simmons (2005)	5–4	Death penalty disproportionate for persons under 18 convicted of murder

[a] Author unable to locate vote for this case. Voting breakdowns do not seem to have been consistently kept in earlier times.

As detailed above, the Supreme Court's opinion as to whether and in what capacity the Eighth Amendment requires proportionality review for non-capital cases, in which the issue is sentence length, seems rather inconsistent. Since the early 1900s the Supreme Court has invalidated non-capital sentences in only five cases — *Weems v. United States* (1910), *Robinson v. California* (1962), *Solem v. Helm* (1983), *Graham v. Florida* (2010), and *Miller v. Alabama* (2012). In a sizable number of cases, however, the Supreme Court has upheld sentencing laws established by the legislature. These cases include *Graham v. West Virginia* (1912) (which involved an early habitual offender statute), *Rummel v. Estelle* (1980) (which examined a sentencing enhancement for repeat felons under Texas law), *Hutto v. Davis* (1982) (which involved a lengthy prison term and large fine for possession with intent to distribute and the distribution of marijuana), *Harmelin v. Michigan* (1991) (which considered Michigan's mandatory 650 Lifer Law), *Ewing v. California* (2003), and *Lockyer v. Andrade* (2003) (the latter two dealt with California's three strikes laws).

Differences in the resulting Supreme Court decisions on these cases may be partly attributable to legally relevant differences in the cases. Variation in the decisions of these cases may also have to do with who was seated on the Court at the time of the decision. Most Supreme Court cases concerning proportionality in sentencing for non-capital offenses have been decided by a narrow margin. Some seemingly contradictory decisions may be, at least in part, explained by the fact that justices that voted in one case had not been on the Supreme Court when earlier cases were decided.

One example of this involves *Harmelin v. Michigan* (1991), for which Justice Scalia wrote a majority opinion. In his opinion, Justice Scalia wrote that a disproportionate punishment did not make it "cruel and usual" and asserted that the three-factor test established in *Solem v. Helm* (1983) should be overturned. Justice Scalia was not a Supreme Court Justice at the time *Solem v. Helm* was decided. Justice Scalia was appointed to the Supreme Court by President Reagan and has been described as the intellectual anchor of the Court's conservative wing.

Even the majority decision often incorporated multiple opinions regarding the legal reasoning that led to a particular justice's vote. Likewise, the minority opinion was usually expressed by more than one justice, and described different avenues to reaching that decision. The Court decisions involve lengthy legal proceedings that include multiple written interpretations of whether and to what extent the Eighth Amendment's prohibition against cruel and unusual punishment requires a test or analysis of proportionality for non-capital offenses.

Takeaways — What We Can (and Can't) Conclude about the Supreme Court's Opinion on the Appropriateness of Proportionality Review

The Supreme Court has considered various cases in which the issue of the appropriateness of proportionality analysis for non-capital cases has been central and arrived at different decisions and reasons for those decisions. With this huge caveat, we can identify several prominent issues that have been cited by the Court regarding proportionality and sentencing. We will discuss these issues, noting analyses and reflections that legal scholars have made about the Court's position on proportionality.

First, death penalty cases are considered substantively "different" from non-death penalty cases. Proportionality has been established as relevant to the decision of whether to sentence an offender to life or death (*Gregg v. Georgia* (1977)). In more recent cases that have examined whether death is an appropriate sentence for crimes other than murder (rape of an adult in *Coker v. Georgia* and rape of a child in *Kennedy v. Louisiana*) the focus has been on whether the sentence is *proportionate* to the harm done to the victim.

Second, for non-capital cases, there is variation in legal opinions about whether proportionality analysis should play a role, and if so, whether and how "gross proportionality" can be established. The divergent legal reasoning stems from various interpretations of the Eighth Amendment's ban on cruel and unusual punishment. While some argue that the Eighth Amendment bans certain *modes* of punishment and not sentence lengths, others assert that a ban on grossly disproportionate sentence *lengths* is also implicit in the Eighth Amendment. Those who adhere to latter position characterize the discrepancy in the Supreme Court's review of capital and non-capital offenses as unwarranted (see Fong Sheketoff, 2010).

Proportionality analysis has been performed by state courts for non-capital cases involving severe sentences such as life without the possibility of parole, life with the possibility of parole, and effective life sentences. Most state constitutions contain provisions barring cruel and unusual punishment and many of these have been interpreted to incorporate a guarantee of proportionate punishment (Fong Sheketoff, 2010). Some argue that such analysis is an appropriate task for the Supreme Court when considering the issue of "gross proportionality" of non-capital sentences.

A third issue that has been repeatedly deliberated regards the appropriateness of the legislature in crafting sentence lengths for non-capital offenses. Some arguments claim that the judiciary should have little or no role in passing judgment on legislatively enacted sentencing laws. The other side sees the duty of the judiciary to determine whether sentencing laws enacted by the state legislature are, in fact, "cruel and unusual," and thus in violation of the Eighth Amendment.

This leads to a fourth issue about which courts have deliberated—that of "gross disproportionality." Generally, courts have acknowledged that grossly disproportionate punishments are in the purview of the courts. Just what constitutes "gross disproportionality," however, has been the subject of numerous written opinions of various justices of the Supreme Court. In *Lockyer v. Andrade*, Justice Souter, joined by Justices Stevens, Ginsberg, and Breyer, argued that the conviction offense that triggered three strikes sentencing (a sentence of 25 years to life for stealing videotapes) is just the kind of sentence that the Eighth Amendment was created to bar. In this case the majority opinion, however, held that the sentence did not constitute cruel and unusual punishment.

The fifth issue regards the proposal (by those who deem it appropriate for the judiciary to review proportionality) to construct objective measures of proportionality. The three-principled test established in *Solem v. Helm* has not been consistently applied to all subsequent cases in which proportionality review was an issue. The substantive issue that remains is if the judiciary is to perform some "objective" proportionality analysis, how should such analysis be performed? If such analysis is considered appropriate, should proportionality be measured differently in different states, reflecting different local standards, customs, and morals? Another question is who would perform such analyses? Most lawyers and judges have been educated in the study of law through law school, and are not trained social scientists. Who would present social science research to judges and Supreme Court justices? Would they understand the proper methodology needed to properly assess proportionality "objectively" (if that is even possible)?

A related concern is whether an inquiry as to whether a specific sentence is "disproportionate" is subjective (as the Court has repeatedly opined). The argument is that it would be difficult to determine exact proportionality with regard to sentence lengths. Opinions on what is or is not proportionate may depend on the individual judge. Whether and how proportionality analysis can be objective is an issue the courts have not resolved.

A sixth issue involves whether the defendant's sentence provided for some opportunity for sentence reductions. This seems to have played a role in the Court's decision regarding proportionality. In *Rummel v. Estelle*, the Court considered the possibility that Rummel may not have had to serve his entire life sentence. His sentence was upheld. In *Harmelin v. Michigan*, Harmelin's sentence under Michigan's 650 Lifer Law was upheld. The Court pointed to clemency and the possibility that the legislature could retroactively change Harmelin's sentence as avenues for the offender to serve a shorter sentence.

In *Graham v. Florida*, which reversed the defendant Graham's sentence, the defendant was given a sentence of life without the possibility of parole. Since Florida had abolished its parole system, Mr. Graham had no opportunity to be released from prison earlier.

The seventh issue is the consideration of whether and how the Constitution is progressive. Could a punishment not deemed cruel and unusual 200 years ago be deemed cruel and unusual by today's standards? The Court has made reference to "evolving standards of decency" in cases that have scrutinized the imposition of the death penalty for certain crimes (like child rape in *Kennedy v. Louisiana*) and certain classes of offenders (including juvenile offenders in *Roper v. Simmons*). This reference has not been consistently brought up by the Court in the review of non-death penalty cases regarding proportionality.

Some legal scholars have asserted that the decisions involving proportionality "clearly" show one thing or another. A review of cases suggests that the only clarity regarding the Court's opinion on the appropriateness of proportionality review is the observation that Court decisions seem to depend to some degree on specific offense and offender characteristics as well as who is serving on the Supreme Court at the time.

The Constitutionality of Federal Sentencing Guidelines

In *Mistretta v. United States* (488 U.S. 361 (1989)), the constitutionality of the Federal Sentencing Guidelines was challenged. The defendant, John Mistretta, who was indicted in the United District Court for the Western District of Missouri on three counts regarding a cocaine sale, moved to have the sentencing guidelines set forth by the United States Sentencing Commission ruled invalid under the Constitution.

His argument was that the sentencing guidelines that he was to be sentenced under were unconstitutional because (1) the commission which promulgated the guidelines was constituted in violation of the principle of separation of powers and (2) Congress had delegated excessive (legislative) authority to the commission to structure the guidelines.

After the district court upheld the validity of the Federal Sentencing Guidelines, Mistretta plead guilty to conspiracy to sell cocaine in return for a removal of the other two counts. He received a sentence of 18 months' imprisonment in accordance with federal guidelines. Mistretta filed an appeal with the United States Court of Appeals for the Eighth Circuit. Subsequently, he and the prosecution petitioned the Supreme Court for certiorari before judgment. The Court granted the writ of certiorari to consider the constitutionality of the federal guidelines.

As discussed in Chapter 5, the federal system had historically operated under an indeterminate sentencing system, in which statutes afforded federal judges considerable discretion as to sentence type (incarceration, probation, and/or fine) and sentence length. Pursuant to concerns over disparate and discriminatory treatment of federal offenders, Congress passed the Sentencing Reform Act of 1984. Under this act, discretionary parole release was eliminated and the United States Sentencing Commission was created as an independent body of the judicial branch.

The USSC was given the power to designate determinate sentences for persons convicted of most federal offenses based on specific offender and offense factors. The act made the Sentencing Commission's guidelines binding on the courts, but allowed judges some discretion to depart from a guideline if the judge found that aggravating or mitigating circumstances existed that were appropriate to sentencing but were not considered when the guidelines were created. The court was also required to provide reasons for the sentence. Limited appellate review was provided for in the act by the defendant if the sentence was above the guidelines range, by the government if the sentence was below the range, and by either side if the guideline was incorrectly applied.

In an 8 to 1 decision, the Court decided in *Mistretta* that the act was constitutional and affirmed the trial court's decision involving Mistretta's sentence.

Court Cases Involving the Sixth Amendment Right to Trial by Jury

Legal Scrutiny of Constitutional Protections

The Sixth Amendment guarantees the right to a jury trial and applies to states through the due process clause of the Fourteenth Amendment. The burden of proof to find a defendant guilty is "beyond a reasonable doubt." This applies both to jury trials and bench trials (those that are decided by a judge, not a jury).

Historically, at the sentencing stage, state and federal judges have been permitted to individualize punishments by considering various relevant offender and case characteristics. The prosecution is responsible for bringing aggravating circumstances to the judge's attention, while the defense presents mitigating factors. The judge then bases his or her conclusions about which sentencing factor(s) exist on the standard of proof known as "preponderance of evidence." Historically this lower burden of proof—"preponderance of evidence"—has been needed to establish the existence of these factors, compared to the standard of proof needed to establish guilt in a trial, which is "beyond a reasonable doubt."

Sentencing reforms have restructured, restricted, or eliminated (in the case of mandatory minimum sentencing) judicial discretion. With these reforms have come cases which have sparked legal debates that have been ultimately decided by the Supreme Court. One such debate involves the interpretation of how offenses and offense characteristics are defined. For example, does possessing a firearm in the commission of a violent felony constitute an element of the crime or is it just considered a factor to be considered at sentencing after the offender has been found guilty of a base offense?

When an act is considered an element of the crime then the defendant has a right to a jury trial and it is the burden of the prosecution to prove that the element exists beyond a reasonable doubt. If the act is considered a sentencing element, then the existence of such circumstances has been determined by a judge who would incorporate "preponderance of evidence" as the burden of proof. For years, judges have exercised discretion and individualized sentences based on offender and offense characteristics, using "preponderance of evidence" as the level of proof.

The Supreme Court cases we will discuss involve determining the constitutionality of various sentencing practices and reforms that interact with the Sixth Amendment. We will examine them in chronological order. These cases will lead up to the landmark cases *Blakely v. Washington* (2004) and *United States v. Booker* (2005).

We will now turn to some of the cases heard by the Supreme Court, outline the relevant legal issues, and form some conclusions as we dissect the intricacies of these cases. A series of Supreme Court decisions involved ascertaining the requirements necessary to prove elements of a criminal offense "beyond a reasonable doubt" for crimes that were sentenced under various sentencing enhancements, including those specified by sentencing guidelines. State and federal guidelines oftentimes provided for sentencing enhancements for certain crime characteristics (such as brandishing a firearm during the commission of a felony).

Sentencing Factors, Offense Factors, and the Sixth Amendment

McMillan v. Pennsylvania (1986)

In *McMillan v. Pennsylvania* (477 U.S. 79 (1986)) the Supreme Court considered the constitutionality of a mandatory five-year prison sentence under Pennsylvania's Mandatory Minimum Sentencing Act (42 Pa. Cons. Stat. §9712). The act, adopted in 1982, mandated a minimum five-year sentence for defendants convicted of certain felonies if they visibly possessed a firearm during the offense. The act provided that the visible possession shall not be an element of the crime. Under the act, if the sentencing judge found by a **preponderance of evidence** that the person visibly possessed a firearm during the commission of the offense, then the judge was mandated to sentence the defendant to five years in prison. At the sentencing hearing, the judge could consider evidence introduced at trial, as well as that offered by the defendant or the Commonwealth of Pennsylvania. The act took away judicial discretion that would allow the judge to sentence the defendant convicted of the underlying felony to a sentence less than five years.

In each of four consolidated cases, the trial judge held that §9712 violated the Sixth Amendment and the due process clause of the Fourteenth Amendment. In each case, the petitioner was convicted of one of the act's enumerated offenses, yet the judge imposed a sentence less than five years' imprisonment. The Pennsylvania Supreme Court consolidated the commonwealth's appeals, vacated the petitioners' sentences, and remanded for sentencing pursuant to the act. The Pennsylvania Supreme Court held that the act was consistent with due process and rejected the petitioners' argument that visible possession of a firearm was an element of the crimes for which they were sentenced. In accordance with this conclusion was the decision that visible possession of a firearm did not have to be proven beyond a reasonable doubt.

The Supreme Court's deliberations focused on two central issues. The first was whether a judge, after hearing from the prosecution and defense, could impose the mandatory sentence based on "preponderance of evidence," or whether visibly possessing a firearm had to be proven "beyond a reasonable doubt." Integral to this decision was a second issue—whether to characterize "visibly possessed a firearm" as an element of the offense or sentencing factor.

In a 5 to 4 decision the Court affirmed the decision of the Pennsylvania Supreme Court. The majority held that the act did not violate the due process clause of the Fourteenth Amendment and that due process does not require the state to prove visible possession of a firearm beyond reasonable doubt. It noted that visible possession of a firearm could be treated as a sentencing consideration and not as an element of the offense.

Apprendi v. New Jersey (2000)

Apprendi v. New Jersey (530 U.S. 466 (2000)) was a landmark Supreme Court decision involving the Sixth Amendment right to a jury trial. In a 5 to 4 decision, the Court **prohibited judges from increasing sentences over and above the statutorily established maximum sentence** due to an offense factor that would otherwise increase the sentence **unless that factor was proven beyond a reasonable doubt by a jury trial.**

The case involved Mr. Charles Apprendi, Jr., who fired several bullets into the house of an African American family that had recently moved into his neighborhood. He was arrested several hours later and admitted in a statement that he later retracted that he didn't want the family moving into the neighborhood because they were black. Although a New Jersey grand jury returned a 23-count indictment charging Apprendi with shootings on four different dates, as well as unlawful possession of various weapons, Apprendi agreed to a plea bargain that reduced the number of charges. Part of the plea deal stipulated that he would plead guilty to two counts of possessing a firearm for an unlawful purpose in the second degree, one count of unlawful possession of an anti-personnel bomb in the third degree, and that the sentence of the third degree offense would run concurrently (at the same time) with the other sentences. In addition, the plea deal stipulated that the prosecution would reserve the right to seek a sentencing enhancement in accordance with New Jersey's "hate crime" statute that could add years of imprisonment to the sentence if a trial judge found **with preponderance of evidence** that a defendant committed a crime with the purpose to intimidate a person or group on the basis of specified characteristics including race, but which had not been referred to in the indictment.

The trial judge accepted Apprendi's three guilty pleas. New Jersey law indicated 5 to 10 years of imprisonment for a second degree offense. The prosecutor subsequently filed a motion to enhance the sentence on the basis that the crime was a hate crime, based on race. The judge heard police testimony that suggested that Apprendi's offense was racially motivated and testimony from Apprendi and a psychologist that contended that the offense resulted from intoxication. The trial judge decided, by a preponderance of evidence, that the shooting was racially motivated. The New Jersey statute increased the maximum penalty of the defendant's weapon possession offense from 10 to 20 years if the trial court found by preponderance of evidence that the defendant committed a "hate crime." Apprendi was sentenced to a 12-year sentence on one firearms count and shorter consecutive sentences on the other counts.

Apprendi appealed to the Appellate Division of the New Jersey Superior Court, arguing that the finding of racial bias had to be proven beyond a reasonable doubt by a jury. This court affirmed the sentencing enhancement, reasoning that racial motivation was a "sentencing factor" not an "element" of the offense and therefore did not have to be proven beyond a reasonable doubt. The court decided that the state legislature's decision to make hate crime enhancement a sentencing factor was within the state's power, that the hate crime statute did not create a presumption of guilt, and that despite the fact that the hate crime statute exposed criminal defendants to increased punishment, this factor in and of itself did not render the statute unconstitutional. The New Jersey Supreme Court agreed with the appellate court's conclusion and affirmed Apprendi's sentence. Apprendi then appealed to the Supreme Court.

In a 5 to 4 decision, the Supreme Court reversed and remanded. The Court stated that "Other than the fact of a prior conviction, any fact that increases the penalty for a crime beyond the prescribed statutory maximum must be submitted to a jury, and proved beyond a reasonable doubt."[9] Since the New Jersey Hate Crime Statute did not specify this requirement, the 12-year sentence imposed in accordance to the New Jersey statute was not permissible because it exceeded the ten-year statutory maximum for the offense for which the offender was convicted.

The Court concluded that the designation of the offense as a "hate crime" did not merely establish it as a sentencing factor. The hate crime designation, rather, in practice constituted a core criminal offense "element." Justice Thomas, joined by Justice Scalia, maintained that "the Constitution requires a broader rule than the Court adopts . . . If a fact is by law the basis for imposing or increasing punishment—for establishing or increasing entitlement—it is an element." Therefore, that element must be proven beyond a reasonable doubt.

In a foreshadowing of subsequent Court decisions, the dissenters (Justice O'Connor, Chief Justice Rehnquist, Justice Kennedy, and Justice Breyer) pointed to the implications the ruling would have on state determinate sentencing schemes, including sentencing guidelines.

Harris v. United States (2002)

In *Harris v. United States* (536 U.S. 545 (2002)), the Supreme Court reviewed Sixth Amendment issues regarding Mr. William Joseph Harris's conviction for federal drug and firearms offenses. Harris was convicted of selling illegal narcotics out of his pawnshop with an unconcealed pistol at his side, violating statutes including 18 U.S.C. §924(c)(1)(a). This statute provided, in part, that a person who used or carried a firearm during and in relation to a drug trafficking offense would, in addition to the punishment for the crime, "(i) be sentenced to a term of imprisonment of not less than 5 years; (ii) if the firearm [was] brandished, be sentenced to a term of imprisonment of not less than 7 years; and (iii) if the firearm [was] discharged, be sentenced to a term of imprisonment of not less than ten years."

With respect to §924(c)(1)(a), the indictment charged Harris with knowingly **carrying** a firearm during and in relation to a drug trafficking crime, but did not allege brandishing. At a bench trial in the United States District Court for the Middle District of

North Carolina, the judge found Harris to be guilty as charged. At a subsequent sentencing hearing, the district court overruled Harris' objections that the statute should be interpreted to mean that **brandishing** ought to be considered an element of a separate offense for which he had not been accused or tried. At sentencing this court also found, by preponderance of evidence, that Harris had brandished the weapon. He was sentenced to 7 years in prison. The U.S. Court of Appeals for the Fourth Circuit affirmed.

In a 5 to 4 decision, the Supreme Court affirmed. In sections of the opinion of Justice Kennedy, joined by Chief Justice Rehnquist, and Justices O'Connor, Scalia, and Breyer, which formed the opinion of the Court, the following was held: (1) In interpreting the statute, the Court concluded that Congress intended §924(c)(1)(a) to define a single offense for which brandishing and discharging were to be considered sentencing factors to be found by a judge, as opposed to meaning §924(c)(1)(a)(ii) defined a separate offense of which brandishing would be an element and (2) that given this interpretation of statute §924(c)(1)(a), the Constitution allowed a judge to find the facts that resulted in imposing the mandatory minimum sentence for brandishing a firearm because (a) the factor of brandishing did not have to be alleged in an indictment, submitted to a jury, or proven beyond a reasonable doubt and (b) given the present case, the district court's basing a two-year increase in the defendant's minimum sentence on the finding of brandishing did not violate the Fifth or Sixth Amendments.

The other part of the opinion of Kennedy, joined by Rehnquist, O'Connor, and Scalia, reflected on the holding of *McMillan v. Pennsylvania* as not inconsistent with *Apprendi v. New Jersey*. These two cases were deemed fundamentally different. It was concluded that any fact that extended the defendant's sentence beyond the maximum authorized by the jury's verdict would have been considered an element of an aggravated crime and thus would have to be determined by a jury (as concluded in *Apprendi v. New Jersey*) as indicated by the Bill of Rights. However, this is not the case in the situation in which a fact that would increase the mandatory minimum but not extend the sentence beyond the statutory maximum (*McMillan v. Pennsylvania* (1986)). In this case, the jury's verdict authorized the judge to impose the minimum with or without the finding. Such is likened to facts that judges have traditionally considered in exercising their discretion in deciding on a sentence within a range authorized by a jury's verdict (which do not have to be alleged in the indictment, submitted to a jury, or proved beyond a reasonable doubt).

Court Cases Involving Presumptive Sentencing, Sentencing Guidelines, and the Sixth Amendment Right to Trial by Jury

The scope and legality of presumptive sentencing guidelines has been decided by two Supreme Court cases—one involving a state's sentencing guidelines (*Blakely v. Washington* (2004)) and the other involving federal sentencing guidelines (*United States v. Booker* (2005)). The decision in both strongly implies that any factor that can increase the sentence must be proven by the standard "beyond a reasonable doubt."

Blakely v. Washington (2004)

The Case

Mr. Ralph Blakely had an extensive and serious criminal history, involving assault, shoplifting, and other offenses. After Blakely's wife of 23 years filed for divorce, Blakely kidnapped her from her home in a rural area in Washington State. Blakely held a knife against his wife and forced her into a wooden box in the back of his truck and crossed state lines into Montana. During the kidnapping, he ordered the couple's son, who was only thirteen years old at the time, to follow his truck in another car and he told the son that he would shoot his mother with a shotgun if he refused. While in route to Montana, Blakely's son changed course and drove to Moses Lake, Washington, where he informed the police and FBI agents of the situation. They arrested Blakely in Montana.

Although Blakely was initially charged with first degree kidnapping, he plead guilty to second degree kidnapping involving domestic violence and the use of a firearm. At the time of his sentencing, Washington law allowed for a maximum sentence of 10 years in prison for second degree kidnapping (a class B felony). The facts that he admitted in the plea corresponded to a maximum prison term of 53 months, as dictated by Washington's mandatory sentencing guidelines, however. The sentencing guidelines also allowed the judge to impose a lengthier term than the prescribed maximum if there were "substantial and compelling" reasons associated with the case and the judge articulated these findings for the record. After reviewing the case, the judge decided that Blakely acted with "deliberate cruelty" and sentenced him to a prison term of 90 months.

Blakely appealed, arguing that in line with *Apprendi v. New Jersey*, (530 U.S. 466 (2000)), his Sixth Amendment rights were violated. Specifically, it was argued that all the facts that were legally relevant to his sentence be determined by a jury, or that he admit to them in the course of his guilty plea. In Blakely's case, the maximum sentence was enhanced by the judge's perception that Blakely acted with "deliberate cruelty" and this was not established when he pleaded guilty to second degree kidnapping. This characteristic of his crime (deliberate cruelty) that led the judge to sentence him to a longer term was not determined beyond a reasonable doubt by a jury.

The Washington Court of Appeals upheld the sentence and the Washington State Supreme Court denied review of the case. The Supreme Court decided to hear the case in 2003 and decided it in June 2004.

The Decision

In a 5 to 4 decision the Supreme Court reversed and remanded. It held that the judge's imposition of the 90-month sentence violated the defendant's right to a jury trial guaranteed by the Sixth Amendment. The majority reasoned that the purported facts that supported the conclusion that Blakely's offense involved deliberate cruelty had not been admitted by him or established by a jury. Washington State law would not allow a sentence of 90 months based solely on his guilty plea of second degree kidnapping and use of a firearm. As stated by the Court in *Apprendi*, other than the fact of a prior conviction, any fact that increased the penalty for a crime beyond the prescribed statutory maximum had to be submitted to a jury, and proved beyond a reasonable doubt. The judge's authority to sentence had to be derived wholly from a jury's verdict (or guilty plea).

The Supreme Court applied the decision in *Apprendi v. New Jersey*. In essence, not only does the accused have a right to a jury trial to determine whether he or she is guilty, but once found guilty, the convicted offender also has the right to have all of the elements of the crime that affect the type and length of sentencing be heard and determined to be factual by a jury. Because Mr. Blakely did not admit "deliberate cruelty" in his guilty plea nor was the "deliberate cruelty" presented to and established by a jury, this case characteristic could not be used to increase the statutory maximum sentence.

The profound nature of the decision in this Supreme Court case was described by Justice Sandra Day O'Connor as a "Number 10 earthquake." In a dissenting opinion, Justice O'Connor argued that the guidelines system did not challenge the defendant's right to a jury trial and that the guidelines provided more predictability and uniformity in sentencing. Dissents by Justice O'Connor, Justice Kennedy and Justice Breyer argued the ruling would diminish legislatures' ability to set uniform sentencing guidelines. Justice O'Connor anticipated that the consequences of applying the *Apprendi* decision to sentencing guidelines would necessitate the presentation of relevant sentencing factors in the indictment and require a jury to decide that these legally relevant factors existed beyond a reasonable doubt. This could lead to bifurcated proceedings in which guilt beyond a reasonable doubt is determined by a jury in one stage and factors that were legally relevant to the sentencing decision be determined by the same burden of proof at the sentencing stage. In her written opinion, Justice O'Connor explored the possible ramifications of the *Blakely* decision stating, "The adverse impact of the majority's holding on sentencing reform efforts across the country will be far reaching and disastrous."

In his explanation of the majority opinion, Justice Scalia did not foresee *Blakely v. Washington* (2004) as a symbolic end to determinate sentencing. He reinforced the decision that determinate sentencing, including sentencing guidelines, be implemented in a way that does not violate a defendant's Sixth Amendment right to a jury trial.

Although this case examined Washington State's sentencing guidelines, the decision in *Blakely v. Washington* (2004) prompted many to wonder what impact this case would have on the Federal Sentencing Guidelines. Six weeks later, the Supreme Court answered this question when the Court decided to hear two cases, *United States v. Booker* (2005) and *United States v. Fanfan* (2004), both of which questioned the constitutionality of Federal Sentencing Guidelines.

The Supreme Court Rules on the Federal Sentencing Guidelines

United States v. Booker (2005)

The Court's decision in *United States v. Booker* (543 U.S. 220 (2005)) resulted in a profound change in the way federal guidelines are to be utilized by federal judges. It dictated a move from the *mandatory* application of federal guidelines in sentencing federal offenders to deeming the guidelines *advisory* in the practice of sentencing federal offenders. Since the *Booker* decision, the Federal Sentencing Guidelines now serve as the starting point of a three- pronged process in sentencing detailed by the USSC in Chapter 5.

The Supreme Court considered two similar cases— *United States v. Booker* and *United States v. Fanfan*—in its proceedings. Both cases involved augmenting the punishment for cocaine distribution offenses. The sentence of the first defendant, Mr. Freddie Booker, followed the imposition of the Federal Sentencing Guidelines and was reversed by the United States Court of Appeals for the Seventh Circuit. In the case of Mr. Duncan Fanfan, the government appealed his sentence to the United States Court of Appeals for the First Circuit.

Mr. Freddie Booker was charged with possession with intent to distribute at least 50 grams of cocaine base (crack). The jury heard evidence that he had 92.5 grams in a duffel bag and found him guilty of violating the law under a federal criminal statute that prescribed a minimum sentence of 10 years in prison to a maximum of life.

The Federal Sentencing Guidelines authorized a sentence following a jury verdict in Booker's case of 210–262 months in prison (17.5 years–21.8 years). Mr. Freddie Booker's original sentence was increased under the Federal Sentencing Guidelines by more than eight years after the trial judge determined that defendant Booker possessed a greater quantity of cocaine than found by the jury. At a post-trial sentencing hearing, the judge found additional facts by a preponderance of evidence. The judge determined that Booker had possessed an additional 566 grams of crack and that he was guilty of obstructing justice. These findings mandated a sentence of between 360 months (30 years) and life.

Instead of a sentence of 21.8 years, the judge handed down a sentence of 30 years. The Seventh Circuit held that the application of the guidelines contradicted the *Apprendi v. New Jersey* decision. In light of *Blakely v. Washington*, the Court held that the sentence violated the Sixth Amendment and directed the district court either to sentence Mr. Booker within the sentencing range supported by the jury's finding or to hold a separate sentencing hearing before a jury.

This decision was made regardless of the fact that Booker's violation of the relevant federal statute could have resulted in a life sentence. Booker was sentenced in accordance with the federal guidelines. Because of this, adding time to his sentence based on the trial judge's finding of additional facts was deemed unconstitutional.

Mr. Duncan Fanfan was also charged with violating a federal drug statute. He was convicted in a federal district court by a jury of conspiracy to distribute and to possess with intent to distribute at least 500 grams of cocaine. The maximum authorized sentence based on the guidelines was 78 months in prison (6.5 years).

At the sentencing hearing (which was held a few days following the *Blakely* decision), the judge found, by preponderance of evidence, additional case facts. These included that Fanfan was responsible for 2.5 kilograms of cocaine powder and 261.6 grams of crack. The judge also concluded that Fanfan had been an organizer, leader, manager, or supervisor in the criminal activity.

Under the Federal Sentencing Guidelines, a sentence of between 188 to 235 months (15.6 to 19.6 years) was indicated. The judge, however, declined to impose a sentence in the augmented range, citing the *Blakely v. Washington* decision, and sentenced Fanfan in the range "based solely on the guilty verdict in the case." He did not augment the sentence based on drug quantity or role in the offense. After a motion to correct Fanfan's sentence was rejected, the government filed a notice of appeal in the United States Court of Appeals for the First Circuit and subsequently a petition for a writ of certiorari, which was granted by the Supreme Court.

The Supreme Court held that the decision in *Blakely*, which recognized the Sixth Amendment guarantee to the right to a jury trial, should be applied to the Federal Sentencing Guidelines. The sentence of Mr. Booker, accordingly, was decided to have violated the Sixth Amendment. The Court reaffirmed the holding in *Apprendi* concerning sentences that were increased beyond the maximum based on facts that were established by a jury trial or guilty plea.

The Court decided that the remedy was to (1) deem two provisions of the Sentencing Reform Act of 1984 unconstitutional — 18 U.S.C. § 3553(b)(1), which made the guidelines mandatory, and 18 USCS §3742(e), which depended on the guidelines being mandatory, (2) to sever these provisions, and (3) to excise them.

In accordance with these decisions, **the Federal Sentencing Guidelines were to be considered advisory, not mandatory**. The above holdings applied to cases which were pending direct review and included Mr. Booker and Mr. Fanfan's cases. Regarding Booker's case, the Supreme Court affirmed the decision of the United States Court of Appeals for the Seventh Circuit and remanded. In Fanfan's case, the Court vacated and remanded for resentencing under the procedures outlined by the Court.

In practice, district courts were subsequently required to take the guidelines ranges 18 U.S.C. § 3553(a)(4) into account but were also permitted to tailor the sentence with respect to statutory concerns too. The district courts were to still consider the relevant USSC's policy statements that aimed to avoid unwanted disparities in sentencing. Sentencing courts, however, **were no longer mandated to follow the sentencing ranges dictated by the guidelines in sentencing**.

Reviews of sentences were to be subjected to an "unreasonableness" standard. This involved a standard of review appropriate for appellate courts that was not different than that already used by such courts in the previous two decades that considered departures from the guidelines' basic sentencing ranges as indicated by the sentencing grid. Reviews were to involve analysis of statutory language, consideration of the structure of the statute, and sound administration of justice.

Guidance from 18 U.S.C. §3553(a) was to continue. Thus, in appellate review, the following factors were to be considered:

(1) Nature and circumstances of offense; history and characteristics of the defendant
(2) "Purposes of sentencing" — punishment, deterrence, incapacitation, and rehabilitation
(3) Kinds of sentences available
(4) The sentencing guidelines
(5) The guideline policy statements
(6) Avoiding unwarranted sentencing disparities
(7) Need to provide restitution

The majority opinion also identified the role of the United States Sentencing Commission in collecting and studying decisions made by appellate courts. One purpose of this information is to modify guidelines as deemed necessary in light of the information drawn from the data. This process was in accordance with the guidelines being considered evolutionary with the goal to develop better sentencing practices which promote sentencing uniformity.

Rita v. United States (2007)

In *Rita v. United States* (551 U.S. 338 (2007)), the Supreme Court considered whether there could be a presumption of reasonableness for a sentence which fell into the range calculated by the USSC manual. The Supreme Court recognized the Federal Sentencing Guidelines as **an appropriate staring point** in determining a sentence for a federal offense.

Mr. Victor A. Rita was convicted of offenses related to providing false testimony to a grand jury regarding the purchase of a machinegun parts kit. The guidelines range indicated a sentence of 33 to 41 months' imprisonment, which was recommended by the presentence report. At the sentencing hearing, Rita argued that he was a vulnerable defendant because he had been involved in government criminal justice work and there could be retribution against him in prison, that his sentence should be lowered because of his military experience, and that he was in poor physical condition. The government did not ask for his sentence to be augmented, but maintained that Rita's perjury had interfered with the government's case and that as a former government criminal justice employee, he should have known better. The sentencing judge failed to find that the sentencing guidelines range was inappropriate and sentenced him to 33 months of imprisonment.

Rita asserted that his sentence was improperly subjected to a presumption of reasonableness in the course of appellate court review just because it was within the penalty range calculated under the guidelines. He also argued that the sentencing court did not adequately explain its reasons for not lowering his sentence. The defendant appealed the judgment of the United States of Appeals for the Fourth Circuit, which affirmed the defendant's sentence.

The Supreme Court held that it was proper for the lower appellate court to apply a presumption of reasonableness to the defendant's within-guidelines sentence, because the presumption of reasonableness was not binding, did not indicate strong judicial deference, and merely recognized that a sentencing court's discretionary sentence, which was also in accord with the advisory guidelines, was probably reasonable. The Court also concluded that the sentencing court's statement of reasons for the sentence, although brief, sufficiently indicated that the defendant's circumstances and arguments for a lesser sentence were considered but were deemed inadequate to warrant leniency outside the guidelines. The judgment by the appellate court which affirmed the defendant's sentence was affirmed.

The Supreme Court pointed out that the Federal Sentencing Guidelines are a product of careful study based on extensive empirical evidence drawn from reviewing thousands of individual sentencing decisions. It noted the basic purposes of the USSC—"to provide certainty and fairness in sentencing, to avoid unwarranted disparities, to maintain sufficient flexibility to permit individualized sentencing when warranted by mitigating or aggravating factors not taken into account in the establishment of general sentencing practices, and to reflect to the extent practicable sentencing-relevant advancement in the knowledge of human behavior."

The Court held that while the guidelines were no longer mandatory post-*Booker*, the guidelines should be the **starting point and the initial benchmark in sentencing.** The judge is then to allow both parties to argue for whatever sentence they believe is appropriate. The judge would also then consider all of the 18 U.S.C. § 3553(a) factors to determine whether they support the sentence requested by a party. The judge should not presume the guidelines range is reasonable, but rather make an individualized assessment based on the facts presented. If he or she decides that a sentence outside the guidelines range is appropriate, the judge should consider the extent of deviation and ensure that the justification is sufficiently compelling to support the degree of variance. The Court suggested that a major departure be supported by more substantial justification, compared to a minor one. After the judge decides on a sentence, he or she must provide adequate explanation for the chosen sentence to allow for a meaningful appellate review and to promote the perception of fair sentencing.

A court of appeals may apply a presumption of reasonableness to a district court sentence that is within the guidelines. That presumption, however, is not binding. The guidelines are therefore recognized as an appropriate starting point in the sentencing process. Sentences are to be based on the factors at 18 U.S.C § 3553(a)(1)–(7). Sentences may be reviewed for "reasonableness" by appellate courts.

Gall v. United States (2007)

One notable case that considered the appropriate procedures to be followed in appellate review of federal sentences was *Gall v. United States* (552 U.S. 38 (2007)). The manner in which sentences from district courts could be scrutinized by appeals courts with regard to reasonableness was laid out. If a sentencing decision in a district court was procedurally sound, the appellate court was to review the substantive reasonableness of the sentence imposed under a "deferential abuse-of-discretion" standard. **The decision in this case indicated that the Supreme Court wanted less appellate review.**

While in college, Mr. Brian Michael Gall had joined an ongoing enterprise which involved distribution of the controlled substance commonly known as ecstasy. After seven months, however, he withdrew from the conspiracy and stopped involvement in all drug activity. He worked consistently after graduation from college.

Three and one-half years after he had withdrawn from drug offending, Gall pled guilty to his participation. In accordance with the Federal Sentencing Guidelines, a presentence report recommended that he be sentenced to between 30 and 37 months of *imprisonment*. The district court, however, sentenced him to 36 months of *probation*. The court reasoned that this lesser sentence was appropriate because it reflected the seriousness of the offense and that imprisonment was not necessary since the defendant had voluntarily withdrawn from the conspiracy, his post-offense conduct suggested that he would not return to crime, and because he was not a danger to society.

Upon appeal from the government, the Eighth Circuit reversed on the ground that the sentence was outside the range indicated by Federal Sentencing Guidelines, and characterized the difference between the sentence of probation and the bottom of the guidelines range (30 months) to be "extraordinary." As such, the appellate court reasoned that the variance should be supported by extraordinary circumstances, but argued that the sentence was not supported by extraordinary circumstances. It referenced a test for justifying a sentence outside the guidelines range that used the percentage of a departure as a standard, and in this case it was argued that the sentence was a marked variance. As such, the appellate court reasoned that "proportional" justification was required but was not provided in Gall's case.

The Supreme Court agreed that it was appropriate for the appeals court to consider the degree of variance and consider the extent of the deviation from the guidelines, but held that the Eighth Circuit court **erred in requiring "extraordinary" circumstances** to justify the variance. The Court decided that the appeals ruling that required "proportional" justification was not consistent with the *Booker* decision. The Court rejected the use of a rigid mathematical formula that uses the percentage of a departure as the standard for determining the strength of justification needed for a specific sentence.

The decision guided appellate courts in establishing appropriate procedures in assessing sentencing decisions of lower courts. The Court cited the *Rita* decision, that although the guidelines are considered advisory, the correct calculation of guidelines should still serve as a starting point and initial benchmark in sentencing. The appellate court should first ensure that the district court did not commit a significant procedural error, like making mistakes in the calculation of the proper guideline range. The consideration of §3553(a) factors in relation to the sentence was the next step. The sentencing judge is to perform an individualized assessment based on the facts present.

In the event that the district judge decides on a sentence that is outside the guidelines, he or she should consider the extent of deviation and make sure that the justification is compelling enough to support the degree of variance. The judge must explain the chosen sentence to allow for meaningful appellate review and promote the perception of fair sentencing. The **"deferential abuse-of-discretion"** standard had guided appellate review in the past and was cited as an appropriate approach. The Court concluded that the court of appeals in Gall's case had not given due deference to the district court's reasoned and reasonable decision in sentencing Gall, as the district court did indeed justify the sentence of probation based on 18 U.S.C §3553(a) factors. The Court pointed out that although prison sentences are viewed as more severe than probation sentences, probationers are subject to multiple conditions.

The Supreme Court held that the appellate court should take into account the totality of circumstances in sentencing, including the variation from the guidelines range. If the sentence is within the guidelines, the appellate court may, but is not required to, apply a presumption of reasonableness. Similarly, if the sentence is outside the guidelines range, the appellate court is not to presume that the sentence is unreasonable. Although the appellate court can consider the extent of deviance, it should also take into account the 18 U.S.C. §3553 (a) factors to justify the extent of variance. Just because the appellate court might reasonably have concluded that a different sentence was appropriate does not mean that the appellate court is sufficiently justified to reverse the sentence imposed by the district court.

Kimbrough v. United States (2007)

In *United States v. Kimbrough* (552 U.S. 85 (2007)), the Court affirmed the below guidelines sentence by a district court of a crack cocaine offender. The Court again cited that the Federal Sentencing Guidelines were to be advisory, not mandatory. The Court referred to the appropriateness of review for reasonableness but pointed to the fact that the guidelines were subject to revisions that would decrease sentencing disparities, such as those for crack versus powder cocaine.

Goals of Sentencing — Can Rehabilitation Impact Sentence Length?

Tapia v. United States (2011)

In *Tapia v. United States* (131 S. Ct 2382 (2011)) the Supreme Court considered whether in light of the Federal Sentencing Reform Act of 1984 and the resultant Federal Sentencing Guidelines the sentencing goal of rehabilitation could factor into a judge's decision about the length of a prison term. Ms. Tapia was convicted by a federal district court of inter alia, smuggling unauthorized aliens into the United States. The guidelines indicated a sentence of imprisonment of between 41 and 51 months. Ms. Tapia was sentenced to 51 months so that she could qualify for and complete the U.S. Bureau of Prison's Residential Drug Abuse Program.

Even though Ms. Tapia's sentence was within the stated guidelines range, in a unanimous decision, the Court decided that a consideration of rehabilitation, which resulted in handing down the maximum sentence, was not permitted. The Sentencing Reform Act of 1984 directs the federal judge to impose at least one of several sanctions — imprisonment (usually followed by supervised release), probation, or a fine. The factors to be considered in whether to impose imprisonment are detailed in 18 U.S.C.S. §3582(a). This section identifies four sentencing goals — retribution, deterrence, incapacitation, and rehabilitation. It emphasizes that **imprisonment is not an appropriate way to promote rehabilitation.**[10] In contrast, courts can consider whether the offender could benefit from training and treatment programs in deciding whether to impose probation or supervised release.

This ruling meant that the other sentencing goals — retribution, deterrence, and incapacitation — should guide the decision about the sentence length of imprisonment. The Court concluded that Congress intended that all sentencing officials would work to carry out the same directive and reject imprisonment as a means of promoting rehabilitation. The case was remanded.

The Sixth Amendment Right to a Jury Trial and California's Determinate Sentencing Law — *Cunningham v. California* (2007)

In *Cunningham v. California* (549 U.S. 270 (2007)), the Supreme Court again considered a defendant's right to a jury trial, but this time, instead of sentencing guidelines, the subject of scrutiny was California's Determinate Sentencing Law (DSL). As detailed in Chapter 3, under Senate Bill 42 (the DSL), the legislature established fixed prison terms for various levels of crime which reflected offense seriousness. In addition, the legislature assigned within each level of offense three sets of numbers, which corresponded to whether the case should be sentenced to a low (mitigated), middle (presumptive), or high (aggravated) term. Over time the original DSL was revised and the low, medium, and high terms were raised for various sentencing levels. The major identified goal in sentencing under the DSL was uniform and proportionate punishment, in contrast to California's prior indeterminate sentencing, which had the goal of rehabilitation.

Mr. John Cunningham was convicted of continuous sexual abuse of a child under the age of 14. Under California's DSL, the mitigated sentence was 6 years, the presumptive sentence was 12 years, and the aggravated term was 16 years. The DSL required the trial court to impose the middle term unless there was evidence of aggravating or mitigating circumstances. The court found, by preponderance of evidence, that six aggravating circumstances existed, including the particular vulnerability of the victim and Cunningham's violent conduct, which indicated a serious danger to the community. It also established one mitigating circumstance — that the defendant had no prior criminal record. The judge concluded that the aggravating factors outweighed the mitigating factors and sentenced Cunningham to 16 years in prison. The defendant appealed to the California Court of Appeal, First Appellate District, which affirmed his sentence. Subsequent state court review was denied.

In a 6 to 3 decision the Supreme Court decided that California's Determinate Sentencing Law violated the Sixth Amendment right to a jury trial as applied through the Fourteenth Amendment of the Constitution because it exposed the defendant to a sentence that was in excess of the statutory maximum (which was in this case the presumptive 12-year term) based on facts established by a preponderance of evidence. In line with the decisions detailed in *Blakely* and *Booker*, the middle term should be considered the statutory maximum. This was because this was the maximum sentence that could be imposed based on the jury's verdict alone. A concern for reasonableness identified by California's system was considered as ancillary to the defendant's Sixth Amendment right.

When the trial court judge in *Cunningham* relied on the burden of proof of "preponderance of evidence," as indicated by the DSL, the rule of *Apprendi* was violated. The aggravating circumstances that led to a sentence in the upper term had to be proven beyond a reasonable doubt. The court of appeals judgment was reversed as to the sentence and the case was remanded for further proceedings.

The Sixth Amendment Right to Trial by Jury and Mandatory Minimums — *Alleyne v. United States* (2013)

Allen Ryan Alleyne and two accomplices robbed a convenience store manager during a nightly deposit at his bank. Alleyne was indicted for robbery and possessing a firearm. He was convicted of using or carrying a firearm in relation to a crime of violence under 18 U.S.C.S §924(c) (1)(A). Conviction of this firearms offense carried with it a mandatory minimum five-year prison sentence, which was to be increased to seven years if the firearm was brandished. He was subsequently convicted of both counts and given a 130-month sentence. The sentence was based on a finding that he brandished the firearm, however, a jury did not find this to be proven beyond a reasonable doubt. A district court overruled defendant's sentencing objection on the basis of *Harris v. United States*, discussed earlier in this chapter. The U.S. Court of Appeals for the Fourth Circuit affirmed.

The Supreme Court held that because the finding of brandishing increased the penalty to which defendant was subjected, that **it was an element of the offense**, which had to be found by the jury beyond a reasonable doubt. Because the Court could not point to any basis to distinguish facts that raised the maximum sentence from those that increased the minimum sentence, the Court concluded that the *Harris* decision was inconsistent with *Apprendi*. Accordingly, the Supreme Court overruled *Harris*.

Summary

The Supreme Court has decided about the constitutionality of various sentencing practices, including modern sentencing reforms. Many of these decisions have been made with narrow margins (often 5 to 4 decisions). In some cases, more recent decisions seem to contradict earlier ones.

The issue of proportionality of sentencing laws has been considered by the Supreme Court in various capital and non-capital cases. In some decisions the Supreme Court has acknowledged the appropriateness of proportionality review, while in others it has deferred to the legislature in determining proportionate punishment.

The Court has more often deemed proportionality review appropriate in capital cases. In deciding whether a capital sentence constituted "cruel and unusual punishment," the Court has considered whether a sentence of death for a particular case contradicted "the evolving standards of decency that mark the progress of a maturing society." The Court has also examined the following: (1) how many states impose the death penalty for specific offenses, (2) how frequently states that statutorily authorize the death penalty for certain offenses and offenders actually impose capital punishment for these cases, and (3) an analysis of a "broader social and professional consensus" against the death penalty based on official positions of professional organizations or polls of the United States or "world community."

In non-capital cases the Supreme Court's opinion as to whether and in what capacity the Eighth Amendment requires proportionality review, in which the issue is sentence length, seems rather inconsistent. Whether and how "gross proportionality" can be measured is unclear. The role of the legislature in assigning sentence lengths for non-capital offenses has been debated and seemingly inconsistent decisions have resulted. One concern of the Court in imposing harsh sentences, such as mandatory minimum sentences, has been whether the defendant's sentence may be reduced in the future (for example, by clemency).

The Supreme Court upheld the constitutionality of the Federal Sentencing Guidelines in *Mistretta v. United States*.

Several court cases have centered around the right to trial by jury, as guaranteed by the Sixth Amendment. In *Blakely v. Washington*, the Supreme Court considered a sentence under Washington's sentencing guidelines and adhered to the *Apprendi* decision. The Court decided that other than the fact of a prior conviction, any fact that increased the penalty for a crime beyond the prescribed statutory maximum had to be submitted to a jury, and proven beyond a reasonable doubt. In *United States v. Booker*, the Supreme Court held that the decision in *Blakely* should be applied to the Federal Sentencing Guidelines. The Court's decision in *United States v. Booker* also resulted in changing the way federal guidelines are to be applied by federal judges to federal offenders from *mandatory* to *advisory*. In *Rita v. United States*, the Supreme Court recognized the Federal Sentencing Guidelines as an appropriate staring point in determining a sentence for a federal offense. In *Gall v. United States*, the Court maintained that if a sentencing decision in a district court was procedurally sound, the appellate court was to review the substantive reasonableness of the sentence imposed under a "deferential abuse-of-discretion" standard. This decision indicated that the Supreme Court wanted less appellate review.

Discussion Questions

1. Do you think that the Eighth Amendment's prohibition against cruel and unusual punishment dictates a court's consideration of proportionality for:
    a. Capital cases?
    b. Non-capital cases?
    c. Sentence type (e.g., imprisonment versus probation)?
    d. Sentence length (of a sentence of imprisonment)?
2. The Supreme Court cases we have reviewed deem juvenile offenders less culpable than adults. Should lessened culpability affect issues surrounding proportionality? Why or why not?
3. Now that the Federal Sentencing Guidelines are considered advisory and not mandatory, do you believe sentencing post-*Booker* will result in increased sentencing disparity? If so, might that undermine the goal of sentencing uniformity?
4. In reviewing relevant cases, what factors do you feel have led the Supreme Court to consider proportionality review to be appropriate? What factors do you feel have led the Supreme Court to consider proportionality review to be inappropriate?

Notes

1. By invalidating all existing state death penalty statutes, *Furman* also served to remove over 600 persons from death row.

2. Interestingly, the "woman" was considered an adult at age 16, while in subsequent cases to be discussed, a defendant is considered a "juvenile" if he or she was under the age of 18 at the time the offense was committed.

3. At the time *Kennedy v. Louisiana* was decided, 36 states and the federal government imposed capital punishment, but only 6 authorized it for child rape.

4. One is left to wonder, however, if a victim is a "child" (in the case of *Kennedy v. Louisiana* the child was eight years old), if it is reasonable to assume that he or she would be aware of the sanctions indicated by state statutes and/or be able to meaningfully evaluate what the potential implications of the death sentence versus life imprisonment would be.

5. An obvious question unanswered by the Court is how often child rapists engage in rational choice when perpetrating an unimaginable, dehumanizing, and brutal offense, which may be more spontaneous than planned, as a result of weighing benefits and risks.

6. *Solem v. Helm* was decided before Justice Scalia was appointed to the Supreme Court.

7. Five justices concluded that Mr. Harmelin's sentence did not constitute cruel and unusual punishment. Six justices, however, thought that some type of proportionality analysis was appropriate. Three of these judges favored an analysis that deferred much of the judgment to the legislature, while three favored a proportionality analysis that would have likely struck down Michigan's 650 Lifer Law.

8. In February 2012, Terrance Jamar Graham was resentenced by the original trial judge to a sentence of 25 years in prison.

9. Or admitted by a defendant (as in the case of a plea agreement).

10. The idea that imprisonment is not compatible with rehabilitation reflects ideological and practical concerns about rehabilitation (discussed in Chapter 3) that preceded modern sentencing reforms.

References

Alleyne v. United States, 570 U.S. _____, (2013). No. 11-9335 Supreme Court of the United States, 133 S. Ct. 2151; 186 L. Ed. 2d 314; 2013 U.S. LEXIS 4543; 81 U.S.L.W. 4444; 24 Fla. L. Weekly Fed. S 310 (2013).

Apprendi v. New Jersey, 530 U.S. 466 (2000).

Atkins v. Virginia, 536 U.S. 304 (2002).

Blakely v. Washington, 542 U.S. 296 (2004).

Coker v. Georgia, 433 U.S. 584 (1977).

Cunningham v. California, 549 U.S. 270 (2007).

Enmund v. Florida, 458 U.S. 782 (1982).

Ewing v. California, 538 U.S. 11 (2003).

Fong Sheketoff, J. (2010). State innovations in noncapital proportionality doctrine. *New York University Law Review, 85*, 2209–2240.

Furman v. Georgia, 408 U.S. 238 (1972).

Gall v. United States, 552 U.S. 38 (2007).

Graham v Florida, 560 U.S. 48 (2010).

Graham v. West Virginia, 224 U.S. 616 (1912).

Gregg v. Georgia, 428 U.S. 153 (1976).

Harmelin v. Michigan, 501 U.S. 957 (1991).

Harris v. United States, 536 U.S. 545 (2002).

Hutto v. Davis, 454 U.S. 370 (1982).

Kennedy v. Louisiana, 554 U.S. 407 (2008).

Lockyer v. Andrade, 538 U. S. 63 (2003).

McMillan et al. v. Pennsylvania, 477 U.S. 79 (1986).

Miller v. Alabama, 557 U. S. _____ (2012), 132 S. Ct. 2455 (2012).

Mistretta v. United States, 488 U.S. 361(1989).

People v. Superior Court (Romero), 13 Cal. 4th 497, 917 P. 2 D 628, 53 Cal. RPTR. 2D 789 (1996).

Rita v. United States, 551 U.S. 338 (2007).

Robinson v. California, 370 U.S. 660 (1962).

Roper v. Simmons, 543 U.S. 551 (2005).

Rummel v. Estelle, 445 U.S. 263 (1980).

Solem v. Helm, 463 U.S. 277 (1983).

Tapia v. United States, 564 U.S. _____, (2011), 131 S. Ct 2382 (2011).

United States v. Booker, 543 U.S. 220 (2005).

United States v. Kimbrough, 552 U.S. 85 (2007).

Weems v. United States, 217 U.S. 349 (1910).

Zeigler, F. A., & Del Carmen, R. V. (1996). Constitutional issues arising from "Three strikes and you're out" legislation. In D. Shichor & D. Sechrest (Eds.), *Three strikes and you're out: Vengeance as public policy* (pp. 3–23). Thousand Oaks, CA: Sage.

8

Philosophical Issues and Ethical Challenges of Sentencing Reforms

Chapter Objectives:

- To identify the multiple goals of various sentencing reforms.
- To assess whether various sentencing goals of corrections are compatible with each other.
- To understand how sentencing goals of corrections are expressed in commission-based guidelines, mandatory minimums, and three strikes laws.
- To consider an alternative goal of "reforms"—the warehousing of offenders.
- To look at social movements and organizations that have formed in response to mandatory minimum sentencing and three strikes laws.
- To present interviews of those working in the criminal justice system.

Sentencing Goals of Corrections and Sentencing Reform

We have discussed the history and provided examples of various sentencing reforms, including commission-based guidelines, mandatory minimum sentencing, and three strikes laws. Now it's time to revisit the sentencing goals of corrections first introduced in Chapter 1. We are now equipped to ascertain how various sentencing goals of corrections are expressed in the three main types of modern sentencing reforms.

Stated Goals of Sentencing Reforms—A Mix

When identifying the stated goals of corrections of different sentencing reforms, one is struck by the fact that the crafters of such reforms often cite multiple goals. Many commission-based guidelines approaches, mandatory minimum sentencing laws, and three strikes laws explicitly or implicitly state the goals of retribution, general deterrence, specific deterrence *and* incapacitation. Some state guideline systems also include rehabilitation as a goal of sentencing, at least for some offenders (usually those convicted of non-violent offenses with few priors).

Indeed, the American Bar Association (ABA) *Standards for Criminal Justice: Sentencing,* Third Edition, describes Standard 18-2.1 "Multiple purposes; consequential and retributive approaches," under a section outlining societal purposes of sentencing. The standard states:

(a) The legislature should consider at least five different societal purposes in designing a sentencing system:

(i) To foster respect for the law and to deter criminal conduct.
(ii) To incapacitate offenders.
(iii) To punish offenders.
(iv) To provide restitution or reparation to victims of crimes.
(v) To rehabilitate offenders.

(b) Determination of the societal purposes for sentencing is a primary element of the legislative function. The legislature may be aided by the agency performing the intermediate function.

State legislatures rarely pick a single "societal purpose." Within guidelines systems, commissions often cite multiple goals to be achieved through the imposition of a sentence.

The Compatibility and Incompatibility of Sentencing Goals of Corrections — Can Reforms Serve Multiple Purposes?

Many of these goals, although they are often simultaneously expressed by sentencing commissions or by law, seem inherently incompatible with each other. For example, can a sentencing reform serve the goal of retribution, which is a non-utilitarian or backward-looking goal, and also serve the goal of incapacitation, which is a forward-looking or utilitarian goal of sentencing? Or are these aims of sentencing contradictory? Let's look at a couple of examples.

Retribution and Incapacitation

Retribution seeks to look back at the offense committed and punish that offense based on the concepts of proportionality and equity. According to Cullen and Jonson (2012), just deserts or retribution justifications of punishment aim to balance the scales of justice. They argued that according to such philosophy, "Offenders are punished for the mere sake of punishment. They have harmed, so in turn they suffer harm. This act of retribution — of inflicting harm — is what achieves justice, plain and simple" (p. 38).

There is no "utility" or purpose in punishing, except because it is deserved — the offender harmed an individual and/or society and deserves commensurate punishment. Andrew von Hirsch (1976) submitted the following with respect to just deserts:

We think that the commensurate-deserts principle should have priority over other objectives in decisions about how much to punish. The disposition of convicted offenders should be commensurate with the seriousness of their offenses, even if greater or less severity would promote other goals. For the principle, we have argued, is a requirement for justice, whereas deterrence, incapacitation, and rehabilitation are essentially strategies for controlling crime. (p. 75)

In contrast, incapacitation is a "forward-looking" goal, as it aims to protect the public from further crime while the offender is serving his or her sentence (usually by being incarcerated) because he or she is physically separated from society. Judges' decisions about how long to sentence an offender to prison are often aided by some prediction of how long that offender will be dangerous to society (i.e., likely to reoffend). There is a utility in handing down a sentence that goes beyond "punishment for punishment's sake." The purpose is preventing future crime in an effort to protect society.

Consider a case of a 50-year-old offender who commits a murder. Most people who commit murder do not commit another murder once they are released from prison. On average, offenders 40 or older have lower recidivism rates within three years of release, compared to younger offenders (Durose, Cooper, & Snyder, 2014).

Now imagine that there is a prediction instrument criminologists develop that is 100 percent accurate and that we could predict how long the offender's criminal career would last. Now we know from our discussion of career criminal research in Chapter 1 that in reality prediction instruments fall far short of 100 percent accurate prediction. But, let's just imagine for a minute that the instrument predicted the probability of repeating a murder or any other crime to be extremely unlikely.

If one based the decision of how long to sentence a 50-year-old for murder solely on the goal of incapacitation, one might sentence that person to a short sentence—let's say 3 years. After predicting whether the offender would repeat the crime and pose a threat to society, one might conclude that the probability is low and that that person is not a career criminal. A short sentence for an offender convicted of murder may then meet the goal of incapacitation.

To most readers, however, a 3-year sentence for the crime of murder sounds absurd. Murder is considered by most to be the most serious offense a person can commit. If the goal is retribution then someone convicted of murder, the most serious offense, should receive a sentence proportional to the harm done to the victim. Pure retributivists would argue that offenders convicted of murder should receive the most severe sanctions—a lengthy prison sentence, life without parole, or the death penalty. That is because most people's opinions about what is "fair" punishment takes into account the seriousness of the offense committed. Consequently, most people feel that murderers should receive "just" punishment that is proportionate to the harm done.

On the other hand, consider the case of a 24-year-old person convicted of a felony larceny, who has ten priors for larceny theft over $2,500. The recidivism rates for persons convicted of a felony larceny are relatively high. Durose, Cooper, and Snyder (2014, p. 8) estimated that the recidivism rate (as measured by re-arrest) for persons sentenced to prison whose most serious conviction offense was "larceny or motor vehicle theft" was 77.6 percent within three years and 84.1 percent within five years of release from prison. These three- and five-year recidivism figures were higher for this category of conviction offense, compared to any other property, violent, drug, or public order offense.

And the recidivism rate for persons aged 24 and under is 78.2 percent, a rate higher than for any other age group (Durose, Cooper, & Snyder, 2014, p 3).

If a judge's sentencing decision were based solely on the goal of incapacitation, which incorporates the idea of separating the offender from society so he or she doesn't repeat the crime while incarcerated, he or she may sentence this young repeat felony larceny offender to a lengthy sentence, let's say 15 years in prison. This sentence is imposed to allow the offender to be incapacitated while he "ages out" of crime. Separating that offender from society may indeed prevent that person from committing another felony larceny and protect the general public. However, few people would believe that that sentence is fair, because it is not commensurate, or in proportion to, the seriousness of the offense. A long sentence may serve the goal of incapacitation, but not serve the goal of retribution and vice-versa.

Retribution and Rehabilitation

The two sentencing goals of corrections that are the most strikingly incompatible are retribution and rehabilitation. According to retribution, all offenders who have committed the same offense, according to legally relevant characteristics, should pay the same "price" for having committed that offense. And the punishment should be *commensurate to the seriousness of the offense*. There is no individualization of punishment based on the concern of what "caused" the individual to offend. There is no effort to "cure" him or her so that he or she does not repeat the crime. Punishment is for punishment's sake.

Rehabilitation, on the other hand, is a utilitarian or forward-looking goal. Some good should come out of imposing a criminal sanction. Whether through imprisonment or some form of community supervision, the offender should be re-socialized so that he or she does not want to repeat offending.

When rehabilitation guides sentencing, the ideal is that the offender will be empowered to live a crime-free life after the sentence is completed. According to Seiter (2014), rehabilitation is ". . . a programmed effort to alter the attitudes and behaviors of inmates and improve their likelihood of becoming law-abiding citizens" (p. 30). The empowerment to do so may result from offender participation in programs that aim to address *why* he or she committed crime(s) in the first place. These may be educational or vocational training programs, if it is thought that the offender turned to crime because he or she lacked legitimate opportunities to make money. Anger management or counseling programs may be indicated for inmates whose crimes are thought to stem from psychological or developmental issues. Substance abuse programs may be prescribed for those whose drug habits fueled their offending. Treatments are to be *individualized to the offender*.

A pure retributivist approach indicates the same punishment for all offenders who commit the same crime, because that is what is deserved. According to this perspective, all men convicted of rape of a child should receive the same sentence, for example, 20 years in prison. One could argue that this sentence serves the goal of retribution because it is severe and in proportion to the harm done to the victim. It also provides equity, because every man convicted of child rape receives the same sentence. Individual characteristics of the offender, such as history of being sexually abused as a child, should play no role in determining the ultimate sentence for the offense.

In contrast, if the goal of sentencing a person convicted of child rape to prison is rehabilitation, then the sentence lengths for all offenders convicted of this horrific act could be very different. How long a person would serve in prison would depend on evidence that he has been rehabilitated. And mental health professionals' assessments of what caused the offender to commit the crime and the methods for rehabilitating him could be different for each man. Just how long it takes one man to be "rehabilitated" would also vary. If a man participates in intensive therapy and deemed ready to re-enter society, his sentence may be two years. Another man may take longer and thus have to serve 20 years before being considered ready to re-enter society at the point he is considered rehabilitated. This sentencing approach, which leaves the length of the sentence up to the parole board, is in direct contrast to the goal of retribution that focuses on punishing the *offense* (and punishing equally), not treating the *offender* and addressing his specific needs.

Can a single sentencing strategy (whether it be sentencing guidelines, mandatory minimums, or three strikes laws) serve all the sentencing goals of corrections? The answer is decidedly "no." The assumptions about human behavior, crime causation, and why we should punish or treat the offender inherent in the goals are at the very least incompatible and in some cases completely contradictory.

We will examine the multiple sentencing goals of corrections—retribution, general deterrence, specific deterrence, incapacitation, and rehabilitation—that have been stated in conjunction with various sentencing reforms. We will detail each goal and how it may (or may not) be promoted by each of the three types of modern sentencing reforms on which we have focused in the text—commission-based sentencing guidelines, mandatory minimums, and three strikes laws.

Revisiting the Sentencing Goals of Corrections— How Are Various Sentencing Goals of Corrections Reflected in Sentencing Reforms?

Retribution and Sentencing Reforms

The Key Elements of Retribution

Three prominent concepts integral to retribution are *proportionality*, *equity*, and *punishment of the offense*. *Proportionality* means that the severity of the punishment should be in proportion to the seriousness of the offense. *Equity* means that all "equal" crimes, in terms of legally relevant characteristics, be assigned the same punishment. The punishment should reflect the nature and severity of the *offense committed* and not be based on characteristics of the offender.

The Issues of Proportionality and Determining Offense Seriousness

Is the goal of retribution promoted by various sentencing reforms? The answer depends upon which type of reform one is examining. One main question is whether the sentencing approach purports to establish proportionality in sentencing.

The dictate of proportionality has been examined by criminologists and legal scholars. One key issue that has to be addressed before one can ascertain if punishment is proportional to the crime committed is to **understand how offense seriousness is determined**. Only after we gain insight into how seriousness of crimes is determined can we determine if punishment is in fact proportional to the seriousness of the offense.

Is there an absolute standard by which offense seriousness is calculated for all criminal incidents? The answer is no. There is variation between states as to how particular offenses are graded. One source of variation stems from the different opinions of the people put in charge of determining offense seriousness. The grading of offenses and the determination of what types of punishments these offenses carry may come from the legislature or from sentencing commissions. Practitioners have drawn in part from criminological research to help them grade the seriousness of offenses and to determine what the proper punishment should be.

Ways to Measure Offense Seriousness

Criminological research has examined how the general public and criminal justice personnel rank the seriousness of a variety of offenses. Generally speaking, violent crimes have been considered more serious, compared to property crimes. Research, however, has shown that the meaningfulness of ranking types of crimes (serious, property, drug, etc.) is limited. Rather, one must consider the characteristics of the crime (harm done to victims, whether a weapon was used, amount of money stolen, etc.) in order to meaningfully assess crime seriousness of a particular offense.

The following *Spotlight* section details efforts to measure crime seriousness and the results of such research.

Spotlight — Measuring the Seriousness of Crime

Thurston Sellin and Marvin Wolfgang are considered to be the pioneers in research on crime seriousness. Their research which, culminated in the 1964 book *The Measurement of Delinquency*, reported seriousness rankings for 141 offense descriptions given to samples of judges, police officers, and college students in Philadelphia. Sellin and Wolfgang took a subgroup of 15 offenses and attached details of each offense (such as the extent of personal injury or money damage) and asked research subjects to provide a scale score from 1 (least serious) to 11 (most serious) for each detailed offense.

The findings showed that respondents assigned the seriousness of Part 1 (Index) offenses measured by the FBI's Uniform Crime Report in the following order from most serious to least serious: criminal homicide, forcible rape, aggravated assault, robbery, auto theft, burglary, and larceny of 50 dollars or more. For Part 2 (non-Index offenses) the respondents on average rated other assaults as the most serious, followed by sex offenses, and larceny under 50 dollars. Offenses including disorderly conduct, traffic violation, trespassing, and malicious mischief were considered the least serious. They found that there was agreement among judges, police, and college students with respect to the relative ordering of offenses and the scale scores assigned to the offenses (Sellin & Wolfgang, 1964).

Sellin and Wolfgang (1964) noted that broad categories of crime, such as "rape" or "robbery," don't capture the uniqueness of each crime that meets the legal definition of the term. Robberies, for example, may differ by the number of victims, injury to the victim(s), weapon used, the amount of money stolen, etc. Each crime incident is unique. This observation necessitates an approach to understanding the perceptions of seriousness of crime by providing the rater with a detailed description of the crime.

Applying that logic today, simply having people rate broad categories of crime fails to integrate the particularities of each criminal incident. While robbery is generally considered more serious than larceny, an attempted robbery committed without injury to the victim in which no money was taken may be considered less serious than a credit card scam in which there are thousands of victims and losses in the millions.

Some criminologists raised the question of whether Sellin and Wolfgang's results could be generalized to the population as a whole. Subsequent studies on crime seriousness, which drew from different samples of the general public and criminal justice professionals, however, showed similarities in crime rankings (Rossi, Waite, Bose, & Berk, 1974; Figlio, 1975; Roth, 1978). There appeared to be a norm in ratings of relative seriousness of a variety of offenses.

Wolfgang and associates developed the National Survey of Crime Severity in 1977 that signified the largest survey of perceptions of crime seriousness (Wolfgang, Figlio, Tracy, Singer, 1985). It supplemented the National Crime Survey and was administered to 60,000 persons 18 and older. The results using a national sample also suggested that there was a great deal of consensus in scoring seriousness of crime by various subgroups of the population.[1]

It should be noted, however, that some criminologists have characterized research that reports people's appraisals of crime seriousness and resulting rankings as suffering some weaknesses and/or uncertainties in methodology (Cullen, Link, Travis, & Wozniak, 1985; Lynch & Danner, 1993; Miethe, 1982) and some have questioned the notion that there exists a "norm" in perceptions of crime seriousness. Hawkins (1980) asked samples of undergraduates what level of punishment they thought should be administered to offenders involved in 25 criminal acts. He found that while overall, respondents tended to agree that certain crimes deserved more punishment, that there were some differences between black and white respondents, and that blacks tended to be more punitive than whites.

Lynch and Danner (1993) critiqued studies that provided respondents with scenarios and asked them to rate seriousness of the described offense. They argued that this approach yielded oversimplified perceptions of offense seriousness and led to measurement error and distorted scales. They instead employed the Hedonic Price Index approach, which utilized a rating scale in which actual crime victims rated the relative severity of crimes for which they had been victims. The researchers asked respondents who had reported a victimization in the last twelve months to report how upsetting the victimization experience was for them. They also identified certain characteristics of the crime (such as victim-offender relationship and whether there were multiple victims) that affected perceptions of seriousness that were not usually included in the scenario approach. They suggested that their method could complement the mainstream scenario approach in understanding the importance of various offense attributes on the perception of offense seriousness.

Other approaches to measuring crime seriousness have been used. One approach is to calculate the costs of crime to victims and society. Estimates based on jury awards and the costs of crime to society have been used to quantify offense seriousness. Cohen (1988) identified three costs of crime to victims. The first is direct "out of pocket" monetary losses, such as value of lost or stolen property, lost wages due to missed work, and medical costs (including psychological counseling). The second is pain and suffering caused by physical or mental injury, in which estimates are informed by jury awards for accident victims. The third is risk of death (calculated by multiplying the probability of being killed by the criminal for each type of crime by a statistical "value-of-life" estimate of $2 million). Miller, Cohen, and Wiersema (1996) used a similar approach. They calculated monetary value of pain and suffering by applying jury awards for injuries resulting from individual crimes but weighted the costs by the probability that a victim would sustain various types of injuries which were linked with the specific crime.

Both studies showed similar results regarding crime seriousness ranking, compared with the results from studies employing Sellin and Wolfgang's scenario approach. Cohen's study, however, found differences between survey and monetary approaches in perceptions of violent and nonviolent crimes. Monetary estimates suggest that violent crimes (compared to property crimes) are more costly than survey responses suggest.

A more recent approach estimating the "cost of crime" involved measuring the public's willingness to pay for crime control programs (Cohen, Rust, Steen, & Tidd, 2004). These estimates were higher than other research estimating the cost of crime and Cohen and colleagues suggested that their method of estimation also captured people's perceptions of the social costs of crime.

A Consideration of the Seriousness of White Collar Crimes

While most people think of crime in terms of street crimes, there has been an increased public awareness of white collar crimes and their impact on victims. In the 1970s, several studies showed that on average, people tended to attach similar seriousness levels for white collar crimes and so-called "victimless" crimes and that such crimes were viewed as relatively non-serious (Geis, 1973; Rossi, White, Bose, & Berk, 1974). Later research suggested that this conclusion may have been too simplistic and did not take into consideration the varieties of white collar offenses (Cullen, Link, & Polanzi, 1982; Schrager & Short, 1980; Wolfgang, Figlio, Tracy, & Singer, 1985).

Once the level of harm produced by various white collar offenses was taken into consideration, people scored select white collar offenses as serious (Cullen, Clark, Mathers, & Cullen, 1983). Cullen, Clark, Link, Mathers, Niedospial and Sheahan (1985) showed that in some situations, specific white collar crimes (such as manufacturing unsafe products and selling contaminated food) were thought to be more serious than street crimes such as armed robbery and arson.

Examining a national sample, Wolfgang and colleagues found that the average severity score was higher for the scenario, "A factory knowingly gets rid of its waste in a way that pollutes the water supply of a city. As a result, 20 people die," compared to the scenario, "A woman stabs her husband. As a result, he dies" (Wolfgang, Figlio, Tracy, & Singer, 1985). Using a sample of assistant district attorneys, Roth (1978) found that with the exception of tax evasion, prosecutors considered white collar crimes to be much more serious compared with larcenies of the same dollar amount.

Using a national random probability sample, Leeper Piquero, Carmichael, and Piquero (2008) examined public perception of seriousness of various white collar and street crimes. They found that in the majority of comparisons, white collar crimes were perceived to be more serious than street crimes. For example, when asked to decide which crime was more serious—"a person steals a handbag containing $100 from someone on the street" with "a bank teller embezzles $100 from his employer," approximately 27 percent of the sample answered the former, about 54 percent answered the latter, and approximately 18 percent viewed the crimes as equally serious.

Remember that in the 1980s the United States Sentencing Commission explicitly called for increasing the use of incarceration for white collar offenders. Sentencing commissions are amenable to changes, and these changes may stem in part from public perceptions of crime seriousness.

Public Ratings of Crime Seriousness and Sentencing Schemes

Some have argued that the public's rankings of crime seriousness should impact the actions of the criminal justice system (Rossi, Waite, Bose, & Bell, 1974; Wolfgang, Figlio, Tracy, & Singer, 1985). Roth (1978) suggested that prosecutors may use information about crime seriousness to inform decisions on how to prioritize caseloads. It might follow that today's sentencing commissions should assign offense seriousness scores to offenses in a way that reflects public opinion. Ramchand and colleagues (2009) suggested, "Ideally, that is, sentencing guidelines reflect the public's perceptions of crime severity, and the public's perceptions track closely with the real burdens different crimes impose on victims and society" (p. 133).

Noted criminologist Frank Cullen and colleagues, however, cautioned against using existing research on the rating of seriousness of crimes in establishing sentencing policies (Cullen, Link, Travis & Wozniak, 1985). They noted that while there seems to be consensus on ranking the seriousness of certain crimes, that these rankings in and of themselves cannot capture all the information that is of importance to assigning a proportionate punishment.

For example, there is a general consensus that rape is a more serious offense than an aggravated assault. But *how* much more punishment does a man convicted of rape deserve, compared to a man convicted of an aggravated assault? It seems to depend on who you ask.

Blumstein and Cohen (1980) examined public attitudes about sentence length for various crimes. They found public consensus about the *relative* sentences of various offenses, but disagreement about the *absolute* magnitude of the sentences. In other words, people tended to agree with the ordering of sentence lengths for various offenses. There was disagreement, however, with what was considered an appropriate sentence for the offenses. The researchers noted, "The differences in scale among the groups, however, suggest that there are significant differences in the population over just how much punishment is 'just' for any particular offense" (p. 252).

Gauging public perceptions of crime seriousness is complicated. Two different sentencing commissions may draw on different studies and if they base their ranking on one study over another, there will be variation between commissions in how crimes are ranked in terms of offense seriousness. The composition of the sentencing commission or appointed subcommittees, therefore, may also affect the assignment of a punishment or range of punishments for each crime level indicated on a sentencing grid. And just how much more crimes in one offense level should be punished (in terms of type and length of sentence) compared to another level may be influenced by who is serving on the commission.

Changing Perceptions of Offense Seriousness over Time

It is important to acknowledge that perceptions of crime seriousness may change over time. Commission-based guidelines may be updated, three strikes laws may be revised, and mandatory minimum sentences may be abolished because over time changes have been deemed necessary by lawmakers, sentencing commissions, sentencing advocacy groups, and/or the general public. "New" offenses, such as those linked with terrorism, have been added to sentencing structures over time, as well.

Like other aspects of guidelines, offense seriousness grading can be modified. This meshes with the idea that the guidelines are "evolving"—a point made by the USSC when crafting the Federal Sentencing Guidelines. Most sentencing commissions have developed guidelines that can be updated and modified. The "evolutionary" nature of guidelines permits flexibility in changing offense gravity scores, as well as prescribed punishments. Some of these changes have been influenced by public concerns.

North Carolina's sentencing guidelines provide some concrete examples of how guidelines have been changed over the years in response to public concerns. In 1994, the original North Carolina Sentencing Commission designated several child abuse offenses as Class E offenses. These included "Child abuse inflicting serious injury," "Child abuse (prostitution)," and "Child abuse (sex act)." In 2013, each act was assigned a more serious offense class—class D. One incentive for increasing the offense seriousness grades of these offenses was public pressure.

Public perceptions of crime severity may be subject to short term shifts in attitudes that reflect concern about specific offenses (like the crack cocaine in the 1980s). They may also evolve and change over time as the base of knowledge about the deleterious effects of certain crimes are brought to light. For example, the concept of "white collar crime" is relatively new in the field. Public exposure to the negative consequences has been portrayed in media over the years. This may have influenced changes in public perception of the severity of various white collar offenses over the last 50 years.

The official stance of the USSC, as well as former Attorney General Eric Holder's position on drug offenses, led to changes in the Federal Sentencing Guidelines for certain drug offenses. Recent amendments to the guidelines have indicated a decrease in the base level of the guidelines for certain cocaine offenses. Some federal mandatory minimums for cocaine offenses have been lifted. These changes followed the USSC recommendations, as well as the impact of groups such as Families Against Mandatory Minimums (a group we will discuss later in this chapter).

Are Sentencing Guidelines Compatible with the Goal of Retribution?

Commission-based guidelines grids were first introduced in Minnesota in 1980 and have been labeled "modified" just deserts schemes (Minnesota Sentencing Guidelines Commission, 1982; von Hirsch, 1982; Moore & Miethe, 1986). The grid cell approach to sentencing is considered "modified," as opposed to "pure" just deserts because prior record as well as offense seriousness affect sentence (Minnesota Sentencing Guidelines Commission, 1982; Moore & Miethe, 1986; von Hirsch, 1982).

To assess whether guidelines approach the essence of just deserts/retribution as a sentencing goal of corrections, we should concentrate only the axis that represents offense seriousness and the punishment(s) indicated for various levels of offense seriousness. We need to answer the question, "Do commission-based guidelines systems assign punishments that are in proportion to offense severity?" Now ... how can we go about answering that question? It's more complicated than one might think.

In general, guideline grids indicate harsher punishments for crimes that are deemed more serious, which is consistent with the concept of proportionality integral to the goal of retribution. However, in most guidelines schemes, because prior record plays a role, someone convicted of a more serious crime will not always serve a harsher sentence compared to someone convicted of a less serious offense who has a lengthy prior record.

A purported goal of most commission-based sentencing guidelines is to decrease sentencing disparities and increase sentencing uniformity. This should maximize equity. Sentencing guidelines indicate small ranges of possible sentences within each grid cell. This reduces judicial discretion. This enhances equitable sentencing for similarly situated offenders. State and federal guidelines systems do, however, allow for a consideration of aggravating and mitigating factors that can affect the sentence handed down. So while guidelines are set to decrease sentencing disparity and judicial discretion, a little bit of each remains.

Are Mandatory Minimums Compatible with the Goal of Retribution?

Mandatory minimum sentencing is an approach designed to maximize equity in sentencing. All offenders convicted of an offense carrying a mandatory sentence, as delineated by the legislature, are to receive the exact same sentence. Individual characteristics of the offender are completely ignored. Judicial discretion is **eliminated**. As written, mandatory minimum sentences ensure equal punishment for all who break the applicable law.[2]

When assessing whether mandatory minimums are compatible with the goal of retribution, the key issue is whether the punishment is in proportion to the harm done to the victim or society in general. This is a topic of much debate. As we learned in Chapter 6, mandatory minimum sentences have been designed to target certain offenses, namely drug offenses, firearms offenses, and child pornography offenses, as well as some violent crimes. The question is whether the prescribed punishments for these offenses, which normally involve lengthy prison terms, *are in proportion to* the harm done to the victim.

One approach to assessing whether mandatory minimum sentences are proportionate punishment is to compare the sentence lengths of various mandatory minimum statutes with those for serious offenses that are not subject to mandatory minimums.

Table 8.1 Mean Sentence Length and Time Served for First Releases from Prison from National Corrections Reporting Program, 2009

Most Serious Offense	Maximum Sentence Length (Mean)[a, b, c]	Mean Time Served[d]
All Offenses	60 mos.	28 mos.
Violent Offenses	81 mos.	50 mos.
Homicide	159	116
Murder/non-negligent manslaughter	209	158
Murder	232	172
Non-negligent manslaughter	151	110
Negligent manslaughter	94	52
Unspecified homicide	138	73
Kidnapping	77	56
Rape	132	92
Other sexual assault	82	51
Robbery	91	53
Assault	56	30
Other violent	50	24
Property Offenses	51 mos.	20 mos.
Burglary	61	25
Larceny	43	17
Motor vehicle theft	39	18
Arson	76	35
Fraud	46	17
Stolen property	48	18
Other property	42	15
Drug Offenses	58 mos.	20 mos.
Possession	49	16
Trafficking	68	23
Other/unspecified	51	23
Public Order Offenses	45 mos.	21 mos.
Weapons	47	24

(*continued*)

Table 8.1 Mean Sentence Length and Time Served for First Releases from Prison
from National Corrections Reporting Program, 2009 (continued)

Most Serious Offense	Maximum Sentence Length (Mean)[a, b, c]	Mean Time Served[d]
Driving while intoxicated	43	15
Other public order	46	23
Other Offenses	79 mos.	30 mos.

[a] N=264,025. The sample is restricted to those for whom information on maximum sentence length was available for first releases from state prison. [b] Sentence length refers to the maximum sentence that an offender may be required to serve for the most serious offense. [c] Excludes sentences of life without parole, life plus additional years, life, and death. [d] N=265,700

Adapted from Bonczar, T. National Corrections Reporting Program, (2009). Table 9 (ncrp0908. csv)—First releases from state prison, 2009: Sentence length, and percent of sentence served in prison, by offense. Date of version: 5/5/11 by the Bureau of Justice Statistics. Retrieved from http://www.bjs.gov/index.cfm?ty=pbdetail&iid=2045

Table 8.1 shows the mean prison sentences and the mean time an offender actually served before first release for offenders who were sentenced under state prison systems. The mean maximum prison sentence handed down for all offenses was 60 months or five years. In contrast, the mean time that was actually served was 28 months (2.33 years). Those convicted of homicide were given a maximum sentence of 159 months (13.25 years) on average and served a mean prison term of 116 months (9.67 years). Rape offenders received the second longest mean maximum sentence length (132 months/11 years) and mean time served (92 months/7.67 years).

To get an idea of whether mandatory minimums are compatible with retribution, and specifically with the goal of proportionality, an examination of sentence lengths dictated by various mandatory minimum laws is useful. If we provided a complete analysis of all mandatory minimum sentencing laws, we would have enough information to write an entire book. For now, let's compare the lengths of one state and one federal mandatory sentencing statute with the numbers in Table 8.1. A cursory examination of two mandatory minimum laws should stimulate thinking about whether such laws are proportionate to the harm inflicting on individual victims and society as a whole.

North Carolina Mandatory Minimums for Drug Trafficking Offenses

As discussed in Chapter 6, North Carolina has a separate mandatory minimum sentencing table for drug trafficking offenses. **Table 8.2** shows the minimum and maximum sentences for drug trafficking offenses in the state of North Carolina (North Carolina Sentencing and Policy Advisory Commission, 2009). For each offense class, the prison sentence for a drug trafficking offense in North Carolina is significantly longer than for the same class offense that is a non-drug trafficking offense. The difference is most pronounced for Class C and D offenses.

Table 8.2 Comparison of Minimum and Maximum Sentences for Drug and Non-Drug Trafficking Offenses in the Same Offense Class in North Carolina

Felony Offense Class	Drug Trafficking Offense		Non-Drug Trafficking Offense	
	Minimum[a]	Maximum[b]	Minimum	Maximum
C	225 mos.	279 mos.	44 mos.	228 mos.
D	175	219	38	201
E	90	117	15	85
F	70	84	10	59
G	35	42	8	47
H	25	30	4	39

Note: The judge can exercise discretion as to whether some Class E and Class F Non-Trafficking Offenses could receive either an Active Sentence (prison or jail) or an Intermediate Sanction (i.e., intensive supervision probation or day reporting center). The judge can exercise discretion as to whether some Class G and Class H Non-Trafficking Offenses could receive an Active Sentence, an Intermediate Sentence, or a Community Sentence (such as unsupervised probation). For each Offense Class, judges can exercise this discretion for offenders with a lower prior record level, which allows offenders to receive a non-incarceration sentence. The numbers shown are the months if an Active Sentence is chosen.

[a] Minimum sentence for an individual sentenced who has the lowest prior record level and who is sentenced to the lowest number of months in the mitigated range.

[b] Maximum sentence for an individual sentenced who has the highest prior record level and who is sentenced to the highest number of months in the aggravated range.

Under North Carolina law, unless there is evidence of substantial assistance, those convicted of a Class C drug trafficking felony, for example, "trafficking in opium or heroin (28 grams or more)" must receive a minimum of 225 months (18.75 years) and a maximum of 279 months (23.25 years) in prison. This range of minimums and maximums is considerably greater than that for Class C non-drug trafficking offenses. Non-drug trafficking Class C offenses include "second degree rape," "assault with a deadly weapon with intent to kill inflicting serious injury," "patient abuse and neglect, intentional conduct proximately causes death," and "human trafficking (victim is minor)."

According to this chart, the lowest minimum sentence for an offender convicted of a non-drug trafficking Class C felony with the lowest prior record level and who is sentenced in the mitigated range is 44 months (3.66 years). The longest maximum sentence for those sentenced in the maximum range with the highest prior record level is 228 months (19 years).

North Carolina's mandatory minimums for drug trafficking offenses also appear extremely high when compared to the mean prison sentence handed down for all drug trafficking offenses which are processed by state courts. Table 8.1 shows that the mean maximum prison sentence handed down to offenders convicted of trafficking offenses was 68 months (5.67 years) and the mean time served was 23 months (1.92 years). While Table 8.1 groups all drug trafficking offenses together (regardless of amount and type of drug), these figures provide a stark contrast between sentences imposed and served for drug trafficking in North Carolina and in the nation as a whole. The mean time served for all drug trafficking offenses across the country (23 months) is slightly lower than the minimum mandatory sentence for Class H (the *least* serious) drug trafficking offenses in North Carolina (25 months) and much lower than the mandatory minimum for Class C drug trafficking offenses (225 months).

Clearly drug trafficking offenders in North Carolina face extremely harsh mandatory minimum sentences, compared to serious violent non-drug trafficking offenses within the state. Drug traffickers also receive comparatively harsh sentences compared to the mean maximum sentences handed down and served for drug trafficking across the nation. North Carolina's mandatory minimums for drug trafficking offenses clearly challenge the goal of proportionate sentencing.

Federal Child Pornography Laws

In Chapter 6, we discussed the 2003 PROTECT Act, part of which provided harsh mandatory minimum sentences for child pornography offenses. These offenses are placed into one of three groups—"possession," "receipt/distribution/transportation" (R/T/D), and "production." Persons who are convicted of possession and have a prior sex conviction face a mandatory minimum sentence of 10 years in prison and a maximum of 20 years. First-time offenders convicted of R/T/D offenses must receive a mandatory minimum sentence of 5 years (and a corresponding 20-year maximum sentence). Recidivist offenders convicted of R/T/D face a 15-year mandatory minimum and 40-year maximum sentence. Production offenses are punished the harshest. First offenders face a 15-year mandatory minimum and 20-year maximum. Recidivists convicted of a production offense will get a mandatory minimum sentence of 25 years and a 50-year maximum (United States Sentencing Commission, 2012).

Sex crimes with children as victims are morally abhorrent to most people. Most federal child pornography offenses are non-production offenses. Federal mandatory minimums for non-production offenses, except for possession for a first-time offender, however, are harsher than punishments for many violent offenses. Possession and receipt/distribution/transportation offenses have become easier to commit compared to 30 years ago with technology such as file sharing.

Proportionality is difficult to gauge in any crime, and especially so for those offenses in which a child has been sexually exploited. However, the lack of violence in non-production child pornography offenses lead some to question the severe punishments for these crimes. Some argue that these mandatory sentences are disproportionately harsh and thus mandatory minimums do not meet the goal of proportionality that is integral to the goal of retribution.

Are Three Strikes Laws Compatible with the Goal of Retribution?

Now let's turn to questions about proportionality and equity with respect to three strikes laws. In the next chapter we will examine whether *in practice* three strikes laws promote equity in sentencing. But for now, let's consider the "ideals" of three strikes laws. In other words, were they crafted to serve the goal of retribution?

Three strikes laws have been written to "get tough on crime." The impetus of passing these laws was public knowledge and outrage about serious recidivists—rapists, murderers, and child abductors, who were prematurely released from prison only to reoffend. On the surface, three strikes laws seem to have been written to punish harshly persons convicted of serious crimes.

However, remember that according to the goal of retribution, one should punish the current offense proportionately, without regard to prior criminal behavior. Likewise, a pure retributivist would argue that punishment is handed down for the sake of punishment. There is no "utility" in punishing, such as the prevention of future crimes.

A main purpose of three strikes laws, however, is to *prevent* future crime by locking up persons who have displayed a pattern of serious and/or violent criminal behavior. Three strikes laws were written to lock up "career criminals." These laws were written to selectively incapacitate hardened, serious, and violent offenders with the goal of *preventing* future crime.

Because three strikes laws seek to prevent future crime, and take into account behavior preceding the current conviction offense, these laws don't meet the tenets of retribution.

Another reason that three strikes laws don't meet the goal of retribution involves states that count a third strike as "any" felony—violent or not. Stealing golf clubs was considered an offense that counted as a third strike, triggering a 25-years-to-life sentence under California's original three strikes law. Few could argue that this theft offense, in and of itself, would merit a 25-years-to-life sentence.

Deterrence and Sentencing Reforms

The Key Elements of Deterrence

As discussed in Chapter 1, there are two types of deterrence—**general** and **specific**. According to Paternoster and Piquero (1995), general deterrence occurs "when persons refrain from offending, offend less frequently, or commit less serious crimes" (p. 252). The rationale of general deterrence is that if people are aware that y punishment will be imposed if x crime is committed, and they wish to avoid y punishment, then they won't commit x offense. General deterrence assumes offenders are rational creatures.

Noted legal scholar Ernest van den Haag (1982) described the goal of **general deterrence**, asserting that "Criminal laws prohibit some acts and try to deter from them by conditional threats which specify the punishments of persons who were not deterred. Sufficiently frequent imposition of these punishments by courts of law makes the threats credible" (p. 769).[3]

Specific deterrence is a goal that applies to persons who have already committed an offense. For a sanction to serve as a **specific deterrent**, an individual must have committed an offense that carries a sentence. That sanction serves as a specific deterrent if the offender finds the experience of the sanction to be so unpleasant that he or she never wants to experience the pains associated with that sanction again, and consequently chooses never to commit that offense (or any that would elicit that sanction) again. Paternoster and Piquero (1995) stated that specific deterrence has occurred "when punished offenders cease offending, commit less serious offenses, or offend at a lower rate because of the fear of some future sanction" (p. 251).

Traditionally, the notion of specific deterrence has been associated with persons who have already offended, while general deterrence has been associated with persons who have not yet committed crimes. This assumption suggests that people are affected by one or the other, but not both. Stafford and Warr (1993) and Paternoster and Piquero (1995) reconceptualized deterrence theory by suggesting that people may be subject to both general and specific deterrence at the same time. They argued that while specific deterrence may stem from one's *direct* or personal experience with punishment, general deterrence may occur subsequent to a person's *indirect* experience with punishment — termed "vicarious" experiences, meaning how the person sees others be punished.

These scholars also pointed out that one's experience with punishment is not the only part of the deterrence process. In addition to experiences of punishment, perceptions of the risk of committing crimes also comes from experience with punishment *avoidance*. How one has avoided punishment or "gotten away" with offending or seen others get away with crime also affects one's likelihood of committing crimes. Paternoster and Piquero argued that the relative influence of each varies for each individual. Persons with little or no personal experience committing crimes will be more affected by vicarious experiences — the extent to which they have seen (or not seen) others punished for offenses.

In 1764, Cesare Beccaria wrote *An Essay on Crimes and Punishment*, in which he called for major changes in the ways in which society should deal with crime and criminals. He criticized the criminal justice system in Europe during the eighteenth century as being overly harsh and cruel and one that afforded preferential treatment based on hereditary privilege. Beccaria argued that the legal system should be impartial and that sanctions be applied equally to all who violate the law.[4]

Beccaria believed that punishment should have some utility or purpose beyond punishment for punishment's sake. Deterrence is a utilitarian or forward-looking goal of sentencing. It seeks to prevent future crime by imposing sanctions.

Beccaria identified several important facets that make a punishment an effective deterrent — **certainty, swiftness**, and **level of severity**. Beccaria emphasized that certainty was more important than severity. With respect to severity, Beccaria advised that the punishment be only harsh enough to deter the crime and not overly severe. He also emphasized that the punishment be imposed soon after the crime has been committed. In addition to certainty, swiftness, and minimal severity, deterrence theorists have noted that the punishment must be **known to offenders** and would-be offenders in the general public. In other words, a sanction for a crime can't be effective if people don't know what it is.

A Note about Swiftness

Before we examine how three types of sentencing reforms — commission-based sentencing guidelines, mandatory minimums, and three strikes laws — may be certain, minimally severe, and known to the public, let's consider the general issue of swiftness (or lack thereof) of sentencing in the United States. An integral component of any effective deterrent is that it is carried out in a swift manner. Regardless of the whether the individual is sentenced under an indeterminate sentencing scheme, commission-based sentencing guidelines, mandatory minimums, or three strikes laws, we need to ascertain whether the time that elapses from when the offender committed the crime to when he or she is sentenced is swift.

In the case of specific deterrence, is the offender sentenced shortly after he or she commits the crime? Does the offender see the punishment as a proximate consequence of the commission of the offense? In the case of general deterrence, does the general public have the perception that crime is punished in a timely manner?

We can construct an answer this question with available courts data. There are a few research issues to consider first, however. It is not known whether the time it takes to sentence an offender varies systematically by the type of sentencing practice. We don't know if mandatory minimums are handed down more swiftly than sentences emanating from sentencing guidelines, for example.

What is known are aggregate figures on how long (on average) it takes to process a criminal case from the time one is arrested until the time one is convicted. The National Judicial Reporting Program (NJRP) collects data from state courts nationwide about the sentences that felons receive. In the most recent report, Rosenmerkel, Durose, and Farole (2009, revised 2010) looked at data from a nationally representative sample of state courts in 300 counties. They examined offenses that the states' penal codes identified as felonies. This meant a potential punishment of a year or more in prison.

Table 8.3 Time between Arrest and Sentencing for Persons Convicted of a Felony in State Courts, by Offense, 2006

Most Serious Conviction	Median Time (in Days)	Following arrest, cumulative percent sentenced within:			
		1 month	3 months	6 months	1 year
All Offenses	265	4%	14%	33%	67%
Violent Offenses	295	2%	9%	26%	62%
Murder/Nonnegligent manslaughter	505	1	3	8	31
Sexual assault[a]	348	1	5	19	54
Robbery	282	1	7	25	65
Aggravated assault	279	2	10	29	65
Other Violent[b]	244	4	14	35	72
Property Offenses	237	3%	15%	38%	70%
Burglary	234	3	15	39	71
Larceny	220	5	18	41	71
Fraud/Forgery[c]	261	2	12	33	66
Drug Offenses	271	6%	15%	32%	66%
Possession	257	9	20	35	68
Trafficking	282	3	12	30	64
Weapon Offenses	253	4%	15%	34%	69%
Other Specified Offenses[d]	253	3%	14%	34%	69%

Note: Data on time to dispose of felonies were reported for 33% of convicted felons.
[a] Includes rape.
[b] Includes offenses such as negligent manslaughter and kidnapping.
[c] Includes embezzlement.
[d] Comprises nonviolent offenses such as vandalism and receiving stolen property.

Source: Rosenmerkel, S., Durose, M., & Farole, D., Jr. (2009). *Felony sentences in state courts, 2006— Statistical tables.* p. 29, Figure 4.5. Washington, DC: U.S. Department of Justice, Bureau of Justice Statistics. Retrieved from http://www.bjs.gov/content/pub/pdf/fssc06st.pdf

Table 8.3 shows the median time between arrest and sentencing for offenders convicted of a felony in state courts in 2006. It shows that the median time between arrest and sentencing for **all offenses** is 265 days. The cumulative percent who are sentenced within 1 month is 4 percent, within 3 months is 14 percent, within 6 months is 33 percent, and within 1 year is 67 percent. The category with the longest median time between arrest and sentencing was violent offenses (295 days), followed by drug offenses (271 days), weapons offenses (253 months), and property offenses (237 days) (Rosenmerkel, Durose, & Farole, 2009, revised 2010).

These figures may not be a surprise to those familiar with how clogged court systems are throughout the United States. Sentencing is not carried out swiftly after arrest. One could argue that because of this, the deterrent capacity of punishment (which for many felonies means imprisonment) is undermined.

Also, these figures show time from arrest to sentencing. The time after which one *commits a crime* until he or she is *arrested* may vary and may be substantial, however. These figures may actually **underestimate** the length of time from commission of a crime to sentencing. Either way, it's hard to argue that sentences are handed down swiftly across various jurisdictions in the United States.

Are Sentencing Guidelines Compatible with the Goal of General Deterrence?

Are Sentencing Guidelines Crafted to Promote Certainty of Punishment?

Sentencing commissions that created guidelines schemes in the 1980s and beyond sought, in part, to increase sentencing uniformity and decrease judicial discretion. In other words, a commonality in the crafting of sentencing guidelines among commissions was to **increase the certainty of punishment** for similarly situated offenders (in terms of offense seriousness and prior record). By providing model sentences or ranges of sentences for similar offenders, there would be more predictable punishments.

Jurisdictions with commission-based guidelines, however, vary with regard to how stringently they adhere to their guidelines. As discussed in Chapter 5, the federal guidelines are now utilized as a "starting point" in determining sentences for federal offenders. They are advisory, rather than mandatory, in practice. States vary with regard to what degree judges are to follow the guidelines. Many states, however, require that a judge provide written reasons why they didn't follow the guidelines if they sentence above or below what the guidelines dictate for a specific offender, which encourages accountability and, some would argue, enhances certainty.

Another way in which sentencing guidelines increase the certainty of punishment involves what percentage of prison time the sentenced offender must serve. Many states that have adopted guidelines systems have adopted some type of truth-in-sentencing, also referred to as "honest sentencing." Truth-in-sentencing approaches mean that the actual time that the offender must serve in prison is determined at sentencing, less a small amount that may be subtracted for good behavior while incarcerated.

Commission-based guidelines systems in various states and the federal system have **increased the certainty** of punishment for certain crimes, compared to jurisdictions that rely on indeterminate sentencing and discretionary parole boards. Some judicial discretion remains in all jurisdictions with guidelines systems, however. Other factors, such as aggravating and mitigating circumstances, may also be considered by the judge. These factors may affect where within the range the judge will impose the sentence. Also, some guidelines systems allow the judge to decide sentence type. Most guidelines systems aim to produce more uniform, predictable sentencing for offenders similarly situated on the grid. As such, commission-based guidelines *increase* certainty, but still allow some variation by offender and case characteristics in addition to grid cell placement.

Are Sentencing Guidelines Crafted to Minimize Severity?

Sentencing commissions assign possible sanctions to each grid cell in a manner so that more serious sanctions and longer sentence lengths are indicated for serious offenders with more extensive criminal histories. While there is variation in jurisdictions with guidelines systems about where the "in/out" line (meaning incarceration or not) is drawn, sentencing commissions craft the possible sentences so that offenders are not subject to overly severe sentences. Sentences are indicated in a way that is supposed to complement the grading of seriousness of offenses. Some sentencing commissions explicitly state that incarceration only be used for the most serious, repeat offenders.

Is the General Public Aware of Sentencing Guidelines?

State and federal sentencing guidelines are public information. Anyone can look up how offenses are graded, how prior record level is calculated, view the sentencing grid or worksheet calculations, take into account whether aggravating or mitigating circumstances play a role in the case, and form a good approximation of what the sentence could be. Is it likely, however, that the general public will do this? Are the guidelines (albeit accessible to the public) user friendly? The answer to both questions is decidedly "no."

We have presented the many cumbersome steps associated with calculating sentences in various jurisdictions—both state and federal. It does not seem reasonable to assume that most offenders base their decision of whether to commit crime on a precise calculation of what possible sanction(s) he or she might face.[5] Therefore, while the general public may anticipate the sentence he or she might receive for a given crime using publicly available information, such a process is labor intensive, cumbersome, and unlikely. The complicated nature of guidelines may undermine their deterrent capacity.

Are Mandatory Minimums Compatible with the Goal of General Deterrence?

Are Mandatory Minimums Crafted to Promote Certainty of Punishment?

The stated purpose of many mandatory minimum sentences is to make **certain** that all offenders convicted of a crime that carries a mandatory minimum sentence will be given the exact same punishment. Mandatory minimums are written to maximize certainty of punishment moreso than any other type of sentencing reform. Even if the judge believes the mandatory minimum sentence is disproportionately harsh relative to the circumstances of the crime, he or she must, by law, impose that sentence. Judicial discretion is eliminated and certainty is maximized.

Are Mandatory Minimums Crafted to Minimize Severity?

Obviously not. Most mandatory minimum sentences dictate lengthy prison terms. As discussed above, many would argue that mandatory minimum sentences are disproportionately harsh. Such sentences almost always take away the possibility of alternative or community based sentences.

One could make the case that instead of minimizing severity that mandatory minimum sentencing laws actually maximize severity by mandating long prison terms. Classical school proponents and contemporary criminologists would argue that increasing the severity of the punishment beyond what is needed to deter crime is both ineffective and unnecessary.

Is the General Public Aware of Mandatory Minimums?

The answer to this question depends on the law and how well publicized it is. Michigan's Felony Firearms Statute was well publicized. In major cities, including Detroit, billboards read "One with a gun gets you two"—meaning a violent felony committed with a firearm would land an offender a two-year add-on sentence of imprisonment (in addition to the base sentence) compared to if that offense was committed with another weapon. The message was clear to would-be offenders.

Like sentencing guidelines, the details of mandatory minimum sentencing laws are public information. Anyone can look up the components of mandatory minimums in any jurisdiction of the United States. Laws are not secret in this country—anyone can do an internet search to see what types of offenses carry what type of mandatory minimum sentencing. But can we assume that would-be offenders do this? Most likely not.

Are most mandatory minimums that a jurisdiction carries known to the general public? No. The mandatory minimum sentences for federal child pornography offenses, for example, are not common knowledge among the general public in the United States. Arguably, then, many mandatory minimum sentencing laws don't serve as effective general deterrents.

Are Three Strikes Laws Compatible with the Goal of General Deterrence?

Are Three Strikes Laws Crafted to Promote Certainty of Punishment?

Three strikes laws were written to put away for lengthy terms of imprisonment, habitual offenders convicted of violent and/or serious felonies, thus maximizing the certainty of punishment. If an offender accrues three convictions for what the jurisdiction deems strikeable offenses, then he or she is sentenced to a long prison term, usually 25 years to life. On paper, three strikes laws show the general public that if they are convicted of three strikeable offenses that they will face a certain punishment under a three strikes law. While we will explore whether these laws are carried out uniformly to subgroups of the offender population in Chapter 9, they were originally written to increase the certainty of punishment for serious, violent, and repeat offenders who meet criteria of the law in the specified jurisdiction.

We must recall, however, that California, whose three strikes law was been deemed the harshest in the country, has provided some avenues for discretion in the application of the law. As discussed in Chapter 6, the decision in *People v. Superior Court (Romero)* (1996) provided an avenue for the court to dismiss prior serious or violent felony convictions (which otherwise would count as strikes) when deciding whether to consider an offender a three strikes offender. The discretion afforded to California judges decreases the certainty that everyone who on paper has accrued three strikeable convictions will be given the same punishment — 25 years to life.

Are Three Strikes Laws Crafted to Minimize Severity?

Clearly, three strikes laws are not crafted to minimize severity. Offenders sentenced under these laws face severe punishment. Lawmakers sought to establish very harsh sentences for three strikes offenders, in part to show the general public that they were getting tough on crime. Politicians suggested that would-be criminals would "think twice" before committing a third offense that could land them in prison for life.

It is unknown how much punishment in reality would deter would-be offenders from committing a third serious and/or violent offense. It is indeed difficult to predict human behavior and how an offender or offenders on average would (or whether they would) weigh the pleasure and pain associated with the commission of three "strikeable" offenses. Three strikes laws do not appear to be compatible with Beccaria's suggestion that punishment be only severe enough to deter the criminal.

Is the General Public Aware of Three Strikes Laws?

Like with other sentencing reforms, people can look up the elements of the three strikes laws that apply to their state or they can look up federal three strikes laws on the United States Sentencing Commission website. Also, when three strikes laws are up for vote by the general public, people become aware of them and their basic components. In California, for example, voters became aware of proposed revisions to California's three strikes law when a majority voted to pass Proposition 36 in November 2012.

Specific Deterrence and Sentencing Reforms

Are Sentencing Guidelines Compatible with the Goal of Specific Deterrence?

A few questions are relevant to sentencing and the concept of **specific deterrence**. One is whether and what kind of punishments deter the individual who has already committed crime from committing more crimes or more serious crimes. Another question is how much the goal of specific deterrence is promoted by various sentencing reforms. While the former is best left to empirical research, we will examine the latter presently.

Are Sentencing Guidelines Crafted to Promote Certainty of Punishment?

The Alabama Sentencing Commission (2013, October 1) lists the purposes of sentencing, which include "(1) Secure the public safety of the state by providing a **swift** and **sure** response to the commission of crime" (emphasis added) (p. 1). These guidelines explicitly identify elements of deterrence in their purpose.

As noted in our discussion of general deterrence, sentencing guidelines were crafted to increase uniformity of sentencing and decrease judicial discretion, therefore decreasing sentencing disparities and discrimination. The step-by-step calculations of sentences outlined in commission-based guidelines demonstrate what a limited role factors outside of those delineated by the commissions can take in determining the sentence. In this respect, certainty is increased, compared to indeterminate sentencing approaches.

Specific deterrence suggests that the unpleasant *experience* of the punishment can prevent one from committing more crimes. Whether one is deterred by the sanction handed down in accordance with the guidelines may depend on the sanction type and the individual offender's reaction to that punishment.

Are Sentencing Guidelines Crafted to Minimize Severity?

Commission-based guidelines vary by the way they classify offenses and establish who goes to prison and who gets community punishment. No guidelines system within the United States, however, indicates imprisonment for all offenders. Offenders convicted of more serious offenses who have more extensive prior records are punished more harshly with prison. Less serious offenses are punished with intermediate sanctions, community punishment, fines, and/or restitution. One could argue that in many cases guidelines minimize severity.

Are Mandatory Minimums Compatible with the Goal of Specific Deterrence?

Are Mandatory Minimums Crafted to Promote Certainty of Punishment?

If a person committed a drug offense that carries a five-year mandatory sentence and that person is convicted of the offense, the judge sentences the individual to five years in prison. Theoretically, the certainty of imprisonment should make the offender think twice about repeating the crime upon release, because he experienced the pains of imprisonment and does not want to endure those pains again. Because the offender perceives a five-year sentence to be a **certain** consequence to committing that crime, he or she would be deterred from committing another drug offense that carries a mandatory minimum. Mandatory minimums ideally promote certainty.

Are Mandatory Minimums Crafted to Minimize Severity?

As discussed above, mandatory minimums clearly are not crafted to minimize the severity of punishment. Upon sentencing the offender will face a lengthy prison term. The experience of imprisonment is supposed to deter the individual from wanting to re-offend. While Beccaria and contemporary deterrence theorists argue for minimum severity of punishment, lawmakers conversely often assume that harsh mandatory sentencing laws will effectively make the offender "think twice" about re-offending.

It's difficult to measure just how much imprisonment would deter an individual from re-offending or committing more serious offenses. Criminologists study who *has not* been deterred, not who *has* been deterred. And it's important to understand that the same sanction (whether it be prison, intensive supervision probation, or another sanction) affects different people differently. While a week long sentence of imprisonment might deter one offender, a yearlong sentence of imprisonment might not deter another.

Are Three Strikes Laws Compatible with the Goal of Specific Deterrence?

Are Three Strikes Laws Crafted to Promote Certainty of Punishment?

Three strikes laws are crafted to teach an offender a lesson. An offender who receives a 25-years-to-life sentence under a three strikes law and serves the minimum sentence should learn that crime does not pay. After losing one's freedom for 25 years and experiencing psychological, physical, and emotional damage while in prison, it is assumed that the offender would not re-offend, if he or she is ultimately released. On paper, at least, three strikes laws entail certain punishment for all offenders who accrue three strikes.

Are Three Strikes Laws Crafted to Minimize Severity?

Three strikes laws are clearly not written to minimize severity. Rather, they maximize severity by requiring lengthy imprisonment terms once an offender is convicted of a third "strikeable" offense. Like mandatory sentencing, three strikes laws assume that the offender will be deterred after serving a harsh punishment. Whether a shorter punishment would accomplish the desired result—desistance from crime—is unclear.

Incapacitation and Sentencing Reforms

The goal of incapacitation involves physically separating the offender from society so that he or she does not have the opportunity to reoffend within society during the period of the sentence. Physical separation from society through incarceration in prison or jail is the most obvious sentence that serves the goal of incapacitation. Incapacitation may also be realized, however, through an intermediate sanction like house arrest.

Do sentencing reforms promote the goal of incapacitation? For the most part, imprisonment is emphasized in mandatory minimum sentencing, in three strikes laws, and to some degree within commission-based guidelines.

Are Sentencing Guidelines Compatible with the Goal of Incapacitation?

As discussed above, sentencing guidelines created by sentencing commissions often list several goals. In virtually every set of guidelines, incapacitation is implicitly or explicitly included as a goal. The Alabama Sentencing Commission suggests that in fulfilling its purposes the commission should be mindful of "protecting the public" (p. 1).

In Pennsylvania, the dominant sentencing goal(s) depend on the location of the grid cell. For offenders who fall in Level 5 (violent offenders and serious drug offenders with a significant criminal history), "The primary purposes of the sentencing options at this level are punishment commensurate with the seriousness of the criminal behavior and incapacitation to protect the public."

At the end of the chapter is a portion of an interview with the Honorable Judge Debra Pezze, Common Pleas Court of Westmoreland County, Pennsylvania. When asked about the worst aspects of the guidelines in Pennsylvania, Judge Pezze responded,

> The bad thing about it is the guidelines do rely too heavily on incarceration. I don't think it's unique to the guidelines. I think somewhere along the way in the United States we have lost our way in terms of incarcerating way, way too many of our citizens (Pezze, 2014, December 22).

Are Mandatory Minimums Compatible with the Goal of Incapacitation?

Mandatory minimum sentences almost always require a prison term (and often a lengthy prison term). As such, persons serving these terms will be physically separated from society, thus incorporating the goal of incapacitation. For example, the harsh federal mandatory minimum prison terms for child pornography offenses were written, in part, to ensure that the offender could not harm children during the term of imprisonment.

Are Three Strikes Laws Compatible with the Goal of Incapacitation?

The sentencing reform for which incapacitation is most clearly articulated is three strikes sentencing laws. The notion that three strikes laws serve the sentencing goals of incapacitation and selective incapacitation have been used to justify their enactment. If one is incarcerated for a long prison sentence, following a conviction for a third serious and/or violent crime, he or she is physically removed from society and cannot commit future crimes in society. Crime is prevented because the offender is in prison and does not have the opportunity to reoffend and inflict more harm on society.

The notion of *selective* incapacitation and the concept of a *career criminal* were introduced by criminologists in the late 1980s and early 1990s. The basic premise was discussed by Blumstein, Cohen, Roth, and Visher (1986) in their book, *Criminal Careers and Career Criminals* and presented in Chapter 1. In this book the authors draw upon research that suggests that a large proportion of crimes are committed by a small percentage of offenders—those deemed "career criminals." Career criminals are those offenders who have a high rate of offending (several hundred crimes per year), commit serious and/or violent crimes, and who have long careers in crime. The policy implications of this body of research suggest that if we can identify those offenders early in their career and incapacitate the few who would be career criminals, then we can efficiently prevent crime. Selective incapacitation rests on the predictive ability of models. It is difficult to predict any human behavior, including criminal behavior. Many have concluded that prediction models are not accurate enough.

Three strikes laws, mandatory minimums, and to some degree, commission-based guidelines seek to separate offenders from society, mostly through incarceration. Because they aim to prevent future crime, they satisfy the utilitarian goal of incapacitation. Whether offenders *would have* committed more crimes if they weren't incarcerated and the types of offenses they would have committed is difficult (if at all possible) to know.

Rehabilitation and Sentencing Reforms

The goal of rehabilitation also seeks to prevent the offender from repeating criminal behavior. The focus, however, is on instilling pro-social values so the offender does not *want* to continue on in crime. Rather he or she is resocialized and/or empowered with tools and opportunities to help him or her lead a crime free life. In a footnote to his article, "The Criminal Law as a Threat System," Ernest van den Haag (1982) noted "While the expected result is the same, 'specific deterrence' is supposed to rely on intimidation or other disincentives while 'rehabilitation' relies on the manipulation of positive incentives" (p. 770).

Are Sentencing Guidelines Compatible with the Goal of Rehabilitation?

When rehabilitation is cited as a sentencing goal in commission-based guidelines, it is almost exclusively for offenders who have committed non-violent, low level offenses and who have little or no prior record. The extent of rehabilitation within prisons is not consistent between states. Some states' correctional systems have more rehabilitation programs available to prisoners than others. Other states lack meaningful rehabilitation programs. Another source of variation is whether participation in rehabilitation programs is mandatory or voluntary.

When asked, "Which of the goals [of punishment] do you *think* should be *most emphasized* in sentencing?" Judge Debra Pezze (2014, December 22) answered, "I just think for everything rehabilitation. I don't think anyone is being rehabilitated when I incarcerate them." Judge Pezze's comments raise the question of whether there can be any realistic hope of rehabilitation within prison walls.

Others states, such as North Carolina, indicate "intermediate punishments" in their grids for mid-range offenders. Programs such as day reporting centers have been developed in some North Carolina counties for repeat offenders who have not been convicted of a violent felony. Day reporting centers epitomize the essence of rehabilitation, by offering the offender a vast number of services and programs which are designed based on the offender's needs.

Another factor affecting how rehabilitation is or is not emphasized within guidelines is whether the system relies on a parole board for inmate release decisions. Some states use a parole board to decide when the offender will be released. In Pennsylvania, for example, offenders sentenced to a state prison term must serve at least half of the maximum sentence. For instance, an offender given a 5- to 10-year sentence could first apply for parole after 5 years. It's up to the Pennsylvania Parole Board to decide when that offender will be released. That decision is based, in part, on evidence that the offender has been rehabilitated.

Other states' commission-based guidelines base the amount of time an inmate will serve in prison largely on a pre-determined formula. North Carolina, for example, has guidelines which allow for a very limited about of earned time (for good behavior) but doesn't have a parole board. The prisoner must serve his or her entire minimum sentence. Time is taken off the maximum sentence only if the inmate earns it.

Therefore, one could conclude that the importance of rehabilitation as a sentencing goal in commission-based guidelines schemes depends on several factors: (1) whether the jurisdiction relies on a parole board for release decisions, (2) what types of programs are available for those sentenced to incarceration, and (3) the extent to which rehabilitation oriented alternatives to prison are utilized by the jurisdiction.

Are Mandatory Minimum Sentencing Laws Compatible with the Goal of Rehabilitation?

Evidence of offender rehabilitation is insignificant to mandatory minimum sentencing practices. Virtually all of these laws require that an entire (and often lengthy) prison sentence be served. The participation by the offender in rehabilitation programs has no bearing on sentence length.

Are Three Strikes Laws Compatible with the Goal of Rehabilitation?

Rehabilitation is clearly de-emphasized in the goals of three strikes sentencing. These laws focus on preventing crime through incapacitation. In a 25-years-to-life sentence, whether an offender takes advantage of rehabilitation may affect when he is ultimately released, but he or she still has to serve a minimum of 25 years in prison before evidence of rehabilitation can even be considered by a parole board.

Beyond Conventional Goals — Another Perspective of What's Behind Sentencing Laws

Some criminologists have suggested that the impetus for modern sentencing policies go beyond the goals which have been conventionally recognized — retribution, general deterrence, specific deterrence, incapacitation, and rehabilitation. They argue that the reasons behind sentencing practices that have resulted in the imposition of lengthy prison sentences and mass incarceration are hardly benign. Instead, these policies and practices have ulterior motives — the disproportionate incarceration of disenfranchised persons — mostly African Americans and/or those coming from low socioeconomic status backgrounds. These are people that have been termed "dangerous" regardless of the nature of their crime.

In *The Warehouse Prison: Disposal of the New Dangerous Class* (2005), John Irwin, a noted criminologist and formerly incarcerated person, described sentencing practices from the 1970s through the 1990s, the resultant increase in the prison population, and the mistreatment of those incarcerated. He suggested that the "punitive penal response" during these decades involved putting hundreds of thousands of people in supermax prisons that functioned as warehouses for people, as opposed to institutions conducive to rehabilitation.

He asserted that this mass incarceration of people into warehouse type facilities was facilitated for the following reasons:

> (1) To divert the public's attention away from other serious social and political problems; (2) to exploit an expedient issue to win elections; and (3) to mount a penal response to control, manage, and dispose of the new dangerous class. This class is largely composed of nonwhite, inner-city youths whose life opportunities had been severely restricted by the economic changes that occurred from the 1970s into the 1990s, and who, it was believed, posed a threat to the lives and property of middle-class Americans. (p. 4)

Irwin's research at the California State Prison in Solano included interviews with prisoners and staff. He describes Solano as a crowded institution that houses up to 6,000 inmates. Notable in Irwin's account is the lack of widespread access by the prisoners to rehabilitative or recreational programs, as well as reduced mobility within the institution. Instead, prisoners are literally warehoused while they serve their sentences.

While Irwin does not claim "harm" to prisoners is a stated purpose, he describes several forms of harm done to inmates through the experience of incarceration. These include (1) inadequate health care for inmates with certain diseases, (2) a cumbersome screening process inmates must go through to access medical care, (3) psychological consequences of long term incarceration, including lack of control over one's life, (4) lack of privacy, (5) damage to sexual orientation, involving celibacy and/or anxiety over prison homosexual relationships, (6) a complex rule system, which many inmates perceive as unfair, and (7) economic exploitation.

Irwin's account of imprisonment at the Solano prison may not be generalizable to all prisons in the United States. It, however, presents a thought-provoking examination into what is going on within the large warehouse prisons which have grown in number in recent years. His account causes one to wonder if rehabilitation is a possibility in an environment that instead of helping equip the incarcerated person with tools and skills to succeed after release seems to dampen his spirit and limit his future success post prison.

By physically separating inmates from society, the warehouse prison seemingly serves the goal of incapacitation. However, Irwin's portrayal of the vast majority of inmates as non-violent begs the question of whether most inmates would pose a threat to society if they were not incarcerated.

Irwin's research raises questions. First, what are the true purposes of harsh sentencing practices that disproportionately impact racial minorities? Second, what can we expect to accomplish by warehousing prisoners? And third, are conventional goals of sentencing (retribution, general deterrence, specific deterrence, incapacitation, and rehabilitation) even relevant today?

Spotlight — Jeff Berryhill Sentenced under Iowa Mandatory Minimum Sentencing Law

The Case

On November 2, 1996, 21-year-old Jeff Berryhill did something that many young males his age have done—he got into a fight over a girl. Jeff found out his girlfriend was spending time with another guy, Randy Jones. Jeff began drinking and went over to Randy's house that night. Jeff found his girlfriend, Amber Baddeley, with Randy. Jeff asked if she would come out to talk. She ignored him.

What Jeff did next changed his life forever. He forced the door open with his shoulder and began arguing. Before he left, Jeff punched his rival in the face. The cut above Randy Jones' eye required several stitches. Jeff was arrested hours later and released by the Estherville, Iowa, police. He knew he would probably be punished but certainly didn't expect that his offense would eventually land him a mandatory minimum prison sentence of 25 years. How could this be?

Assistant Emmet County Attorney Richard Meyer saw things differently than Berryhill and many who learned of the case. Meyer pointed out that Jeff had broken into Jones' dwelling and inflicted "bodily injury." Together, those acts constituted first degree felony burglary. In Iowa, persons convicted of "forcible felonies" were subject to a 25-year mandatory minimum prison sentence (Siegel, 1998).

Jeff was offered a plea bargain that would let him serve a five-year sentence, but he declined the plea deal. He waived his right to a jury trial because law prohibited telling the jury about the potential punishment Jeff could receive if convicted. Instead, Jeff went in front of a judge. The trial took three days and Berryhill was convicted of first degree burglary on November 6, 1997. He learned of the verdict from a phone call from his attorney. Berryhill's parents took him to jail to await sentencing.

Publicity of the case spread through Estherville and beyond. People wrote letters protesting the mandatory minimum sentence Jeff was facing. Many signed petitions in a last ditch effort to spare Jeff the 25-year sentence. People questioned what good could come out of sentencing Jeff to 25 years in prison. Although people believed he should have been punished, they felt that the mandatory prison would be disproportionate to the offense and that it would have deleterious consequences on his life (Siegel, 1998).

Despite these efforts and in accordance with the Iowa law, the judge was required to impose the 25-year prison sentence. The judge said at sentencing that normally he would have discretion and respond in a way that he saw fit. The mandatory sentencing law, however, eliminated such discretion.

Outcry in the community in which Jeff was sentenced ensued. Teachers recalled that Jeff was a model student. His parents were devastated. Even the girl at the center of the altercation did not believe that Jeff deserved the 25-year prison sentence. Amber Baddeley said Jeff came over that night to work things out and that the situation was being blown out of proportion. Although she acknowledged that he deserved punishment, she felt that the actual punishment was way out of proportion to the harm done (Siegel, 1998).

Reporter Terry Moran told Jeff Berryhill's story on the show *20/20*. This coverage caused a huge outcry against mandatory minimums. Berryhill was freed after the story ran. Today, Jeff Berryhill is a successful professional. Moran won the New York Festivals' bronze medal for a human interest story for the work he did on the report (ABC-NEWS, 2009, January 7).

What (If Any) Sentencing Goals Were Served?

Clearly the law under which Jeff Berryhill was sentenced was intended to punish dangerous offenders and like many mandatory minimum laws, send out a message to the general public to "think twice" about committing serious felonies. It was written to serve as a general deterrent. In assessing whether the mandatory minimum served as an effective general deterrent, however, we must consider the nature of the crime. Jeff was under the influence of alcohol when he decided to go the house of his romantic rival. While that is not an excuse for criminal behavior, his judgement was arguably impaired. His crime can also be considered a "crime of passion." Jeff did not take days to plot out the crime, weighing the pleasures and pains associated with committing the offense. He felt another guy was stealing his girlfriend. He acted in a rage that night. Such emotionally charged acts cannot usually be deterred.

Jeff would not have been facing a mandatory minimum for assaulting the romantic rival except for where it happened. The act of punching the other young man was an assault. When he entered someone else's dwelling through a locked door to confront the other guy, however, it became a burglary, which made the criminal offense a "forcible felony." Was the general public aware of this law? Obviously not.

Would a 25-year prison sentence serve the goal of incapacitation? While being behind bars would make it impossible to commit subsequent crimes in the community, one might ask whether Jeff Berryhill would have continued committing offenses in the community. A look at Jeff's criminal history shows that there was none. He had never been in trouble. He played four sports in high school. At the time of the crime Jeff was living with his parents and attending a local community college. He aspired to be a coach and physical education teacher (Siegel, 1998).

Organizations Aim to Challenge and Change Harsh Sentencing Practices

Families Against Mandatory Minimums (FAMM)

Families Against Mandatory Minimums (FAMM) was created in 1991 by Julie Stewart, whose brother was sentenced by a federal court to a five-year mandatory minimum prison sentence (without parole) for growing marijuana in his garage in Washington State. Although Ms. Stewart expected her brother to be punished for the crime, she was unaware at the time of his arrest that he would be charged federally and that his offense was punishable by five years in prison. Upon sentencing, the federal judge said that he felt the punishment was too harsh, but that he had no discretion. The judge was required by federal law to impose the five-year mandatory minimum even though it was the offender's first offense (Families Against Mandatory Minimums 2006; Families Against Mandatory Minimums, 2015, May 26).

On March 23, 1991, 30 family members of persons impacted by mandatory sentencing laws met in Washington, DC, to talk about creating an organization to address the deleterious consequences of mandatory minimum sentencing laws. They created FAMM, a grassroots activism organization to fight these laws and advocate for policy changes. The mission of FAMM, a nonprofit, nonpartisan organization is "fighting for smart sentencing laws that protect public safety. We see a country where criminal sentencing is individualized, humane, and sufficient to impose fair punishment and protect public safety" (famm.org). FAMM's over 70,000 supporters include family members, prisoners, criminal justice professionals (including attorneys and judges), criminal justice researchers, and concerned citizens.

By advocating for sensible state and federal sentencing reform, FAMM helps to do the following:

1. lessen the burden of overcrowded prisons on taxpayers,
2. shift resources from excessive incarceration to law enforcement and other programs proven to reduce crime and recidivism, and
3. mobilize those whose lives are harmed by unfair prison sentences to work constructively for change. (famm.org)

A central activity of FAMM is to educate the public about mandatory minimum sentencing. In 1994, FAMM provided educational materials at concerts, organized a "Justice Day" at the United States Capitol, made media appearances on talk shows, and was featured in articles in *Rolling Stone*, *USA Today*, and *The Washington Post* (Families Against Mandatory Minimums, 2006). FAMM's website presents people's stories—the crimes they committed, their personal characteristics, and the mandatory minimum sentences handed down to them (see *Prisoner Profiles* on famm.org). FAMM shows the human element of these sentences—real people receiving severe punishments, which many argue are disproportionate to their offenses.

FAMM has become a powerful voice in advocating fair sentencing that is proportionate to the offense in various states, as well as the federal system. In 1994, FAMM pushed for the creation and passage of a "safety valve" (detailed in Chapter 6) to decrease the length of incarceration for nonviolent first-time drug offenders in the federal system. In 1998, FAMM successfully lobbied to allow persons sentenced under Michigan's 650 Lifer Law (detailed in Chapter 6) to receive parole and to allow this change to be retroactive. FAMM was also instrumental in 2003 in a more wide-reaching change to Michigan's extremely harsh mandatory minimum sentencing laws for drug offenders.

FAMM has been an effective influence in changing mandatory sentencing policies. Despite the organization's efforts and research findings that fail to establish clear and convincing evidence linking mandatory minimum sentencing with lower crime rates, mandatory minimums are still used by politicians who vow to "get tough on crime."

The Sentencing Project

The Sentencing Project was established in 1986 to "provide defense lawyers with sentencing advocacy training and to reduce the reliance on incarceration." The organization is headed by noted criminologist Marc Mauer and conducts research about the criminal justice system in the United States, publishes reports about topics including recent sentencing policy changes and race and punishment, and advocates for research-driven change. According to the organization's website, "The Sentencing Project works for a fair and effective U.S. Criminal Justice system by promoting reforms in sentencing policy, addressing unjust racial disparities and practices, and advocating for alternatives to incarceration."

The current brochure from The Sentencing Project calls for changes in the way people view crime and punishment in the United States. It promotes the following:

- Justice is fair and equal to all, regardless of race, ethnicity or economic circumstances
- Criminal justice policies are based on facts and evidence
- Sentences become fair and effective and incarceration is used as a last resort
- Penalties that place substantial barriers to an individual's social and economic advancement are restricted
- People leaving prison receive the help that they need to successfully reintegrate into society—thereby making communities safer. (The Sentencing Project, http://www.sentencingproject.org/doc/TSPBrochure.pdf)

The Sentencing Project has been successful in effecting change. This includes shifting public perception from the notion that more incarceration lowers the crime rate to the evidence-based opinion that expanded incarceration has little effect on public safety. The organization has also successfully advocated for changes in federal sentencing policies for crack cocaine.

Stanford Three Strikes Project

The Stanford Three Strikes Project, first discussed in Chapter 6, is the sole legal organization in the United States that is "devoted to addressing excessive sentences imposed under California's three strikes sentencing law" (Stanford Law School). Housed in the Stanford Law School, the project represents offenders who were imprisoned under California's original three strikes law for non-serious offenses. It is staffed mostly by Stanford law students.

The Three Strikes Project staff worked with the NAACP Legal Defense Fund to address the harsh aspects of California's 1994 three strikes law, and their work came to fruition with the passage of Proposition 36 in November 2012. This required the third strike to be a violent offense, as opposed to "any felony." The Three Strikes Project has helped individuals be resentenced and released under Proposition 36.

According to the Sentencing Project website:

> Over 4,000 inmates in California are serving life sentences under the law for non-violent crimes. Project clients have been given life sentences for offenses including stealing one dollar in loose change from a parked car, possessing less than a gram of narcotics, and attempting to break into a soup kitchen. Since the enactment of Three Strikes Reform Act (Proposition 36) in November of 2012, Project staff and Stanford Law students have been working alongside public defenders throughout California to make sure the new law is implemented fairly and consistently. As of August 2013, over 1,000 individuals have been resentenced and released under Proposition 36. (https://www.law.stanford.edu/organizations/programs-and-centers/stanford-three-strikes-project)

The website features a link to "Success Stories" of persons sentenced under the original three strikes laws, the arguably petty offenses that triggered their sentences, and how the Stanford Three Strikes personnel helped them get reduced sentences under Proposition 36.

How Do People Working in the Criminal Justice System View Various Reforms?

Another source of information about the goals of sentencing and the "fairness" of sentencing practices is the perceptions of those who work in the criminal justice system. This author had an opportunity to interview a criminal court judge, Judge Debra Pezze and Chief County Public Defender, Mr. Wayne McGrew, both of whom work in the court system in Westmoreland County in Pennsylvania. The following *Interview* section includes transcripts of the parts of the interviews focusing on sentencing goals of corrections and Pennsylvania's sentencing guidelines.

While we can not generalize the perspectives of Judge Pezze and Mr. McGrew to all who work within the court system in Westmoreland County, or all the court personnel in the state of Pennsylvania, these interviews are quite insightful. Both Judge Pezze and Mr. McGrew share the perception that the Pennsylvania Guidelines put too much focus on punishment and not enough on rehabilitation.

Summary

Oftentimes, crafters of sentencing reforms such as commission-based guidelines, mandatory sentencing laws, and three strikes laws cite multiple sentencing goals of corrections in a single sentencing strategy. Those who promote a reform often state the goals of retribution, general deterrence, specific deterrence, *and* incapacitation are all being met.

Some of these goals, however, are inherently incompatible. Retribution, as a non-utilitarian or backward-looking goal of punishment, seeks to punish the offense in a proportionate and equitable way. It is basically punishment for punishment's sake. Incapacitation, in contrast, is a utilitarian or forward-looking goal which seeks to prevent future crime by physically separating the offender from society so that he or she does not have the opportunity to commit crime during the period of incarceration. If a petty thief has been a serial offender and is predicted to re-offend, it would serve the goal of incapacitation to incarcerate him or her for a long period of time to prevent future offending. A lengthy sentence for a petty thief, however, would not serve the goal of retribution, as petty theft is a relatively non serious offense and a lengthy prison term would not be proportionate to the seriousness (or lack thereof) of the offense.

We examined how each of the three main types of sentencing reforms—commission-based guidelines, mandatory minimums, and three strikes laws—meet or do not meet each of the identified sentencing goals.

An alternative explanation for imposing sanctions for crimes is simply to "warehouse" offenders. From the perspective of criminologist and formerly incarcerated person John Irwin, the purposes of mass incarceration in the United States from the 1970s on served to take the focus away from serious social problems and mount a punitive response to those who are perceived by many to be a "dangerous class" of persons, mostly nonwhite inner-city youths. Irwin characterizes rehabilitation as insignificant to the imposition of a criminal sanction such as prison. He also questions whether any of the conventional goals of corrections are relevant in the present day.

Several social movements and organizations have formed to bring public awareness to the social harms that accompany harsh sentencing practices such as mandatory minimum sentencing and three strikes laws. Families Against Mandatory Minimums (FAMM) seeks to educate the general public about harsh mandatory minimum sentencing laws and has worked to repeal or scale back mandatory minimum sentencing laws in states and in the federal system. The Sentencing Project advocates for research-driven change to make sentencing fair regardless of characteristics such as race or ethnicity. It advocates making incarceration a sentence of last resort. The Sentencing Project also encourages programs that help incarcerated persons make a smoother re-entry back into society upon release. The Stanford Three Strikes Project helped promote the passage of Proposition 36 in California. Its staff has helped individuals be resentenced and released under Proposition 36.

Interviews with a judge and a chief public defender in the state of Pennsylvania suggest that these criminal justice personnel echo the sentiments of these organizations. Both the judge and the public defender see too much focus on incarceration and not enough focus on rehabilitation in the criminal justice system.

Interview

Interview with the Honorable Judge Debra Pezze, Pennsylvania Court of Common Pleas, Westmoreland County, Pennsylvania — December 22, 2014

Questions Focusing on the Sentencing Goals of Corrections in Pennsylvania's Commission-Based Guidelines

LM: First of all, could you describe your experience working in the criminal justice system, including the road you took to being elected as judge?

DP: Yes, I graduated from law school in 1979 and have always at least in some capacity been involved in working with the criminal justice system. I have found it to be enormously challenging and rewarding in a number of different ways. It was certainly not in my plans ever to become a judge. I come from a very working-class family.

I am the first generation in my family that had the privilege of going to college, let alone law school. And I recognize that along with privilege comes obligation. So I have always have worked at least in some capacity in public service.

After two years in law school, I was certified under a Supreme Court rule to practice law for Neighborhood Legal Services and then I went to the Public Defender's Office in Allegheny County and worked part time for the Public Defender's office here while maintaining a private law practice and ultimately, in 1991, was elected to my first 10-year term as a judge in the Court of Common Pleas.

We are judges in general jurisdiction, meaning we handle family, civil, and criminal cases. And initially I did do that . . . I handled all three. But at least for the past 10 years or more, I have handled exclusively criminal cases.

In Pennsylvania, judges are elected and once you are elected to a 10-year term [. . .] you run in what's called a retention election, which is simply in the general election; every ten years there is a question on the top of the ballot: should we keep Judge Pezze another 10 years? So, I have been fortunate enough to have had the privilege of being elected for 2 ten-year terms.

The notion of these 10-year terms and retention elections is to remove us from the political process because obviously a lot of the things I do are not politically popular. And I've said before for a judge to be politically popular we should sentence everybody to the maximum sentence because people love to hear that. The only times people have stopped me on the street and told me what a wonderful job I do is when I've really had to nail somebody. I'm not happy about that. People like to hear that except when it's somebody they know. It's a whole different story when it's someone they know who faces difficulty in the criminal justice system.

You get involved in the criminal justice system, you're in for a world of trouble. Even today, I'm handling mostly guilty pleas, probation violations, and sentencing and just the sheer amount of money and debt that these people bring upon themselves and they have nothing . . . they really have nothing. And I can say that in all my years working in the criminal justice system, and it's been a while now since 1979 at least, and even in law school I worked in some capacity in criminal justice, I count on one hand the number of real serious absolute criminals I've met in my life. It's mostly people overwhelmed with their circumstances and who get into difficulties and situations over their heads. Lots of times it's alcohol or drug abuse involved, if not directly, indirectly in the commission of crimes. It's just people like you and I who just find themselves in situations they can't handle.

LM: How do you incorporate Pennsylvania's Guidelines into your sentencing decisions?

DP: The guidelines are guidelines. I always consider the guidelines. They are the district attorney and the defense counsel compromise in terms of what the person pleads guilty to and the sentence the person receives. And I don't know that I have ever turned down a negotiated plea because when a case comes to me, I know far less about it than the parties. They know the strengths and weaknesses of the case and what they have to compromise. So I respect their judgment on that.

Any guilty plea, plea bargain, is subject to my approval but I give the parties great deference on that because I really believe that this whole system works in our era of mutual respect. Whenever I have a general plea of guilty, and even in a negotiated plea, I ask what the sentencing guidelines are because if they are above or below the guidelines I have to file a written reason why I departed from the recommendations of the Commission on Sentencing. So I have always considered the guidelines in every case that I sentence.

LM: So from a judge's perspective, what do you feel are the best and worst aspects of commission-based guidelines in Pennsylvania?

DP: Well, the best aspect of it is, it assures that people are treated fairly. Everybody is entitled to the same protection under the law. So you can't have one person getting probation and another person doing three years in jail for the same kind of crime with the same kind of background. The bad thing about it is the guidelines do rely too heavily on incarceration. I don't think it's unique to the guidelines. I think somewhere along the way in the United States we have lost our way in terms of incarcerating way, way too many of our citizens.

There just has to be a better way. First off, it's inhumane, and secondly, it's not very cost efficient. It costs so much to incarcerate people. I think we are the only country in the world that does these crazy 40-, 50-, 60-year sentences. What do we accomplish by doing that? This three strikes and life in prison . . . We fill up the prisons with geriatric prisoners who are no threat to society, who have a plethora of medical difficulties. And the cost of it is obscene, but the human cost of it is what really is obscene. You destroy people's lives and futures over some foolish thing that they did when they were 19 years old.

LM: So, when you look at the guidelines, what goal do you think is most empha- sized—retribution, incapacitation, rehabilitation, specific deterrence, gen- eral deterrence, or restitution? Or does is depend in Pennsylvania on what grid cell you land in?

DP: Well, I mean to a certain extent it does depend on that, but at the same time, I'd like to take into consideration all of those factors. I don't hesitate to sen- tence someone outside the guidelines if I deem it would be appropriate. Either way, whether I exceed the guidelines above the top end or go below the guidelines. To be honest, I usually go below. But I may go above if I'm sentencing someone for multiple cases. I give them the guideline range for one case but exceed it because they are being sentenced for multiple cases that run concurrently.

LM: Which of the goals do you *think* should be *most emphasized* in sentencing?

DP: I just think for everything rehabilitation. I don't think anyone is being reha- bilitated when I incarcerate them. Now to be honest, I will put drug addicts in prison for just a short period of amount of time just to get them off drugs. Cause lots of times, there's no other way. People have said to me it was the best thing that ever happened to me—going to prison. Because it gives them a chance to be clearheaded. I don't think any drug addicts want to be drug addicts. I always say they want to stop using drugs, just not necessarily today. But I do think sometimes this testing people, put them back in jail, test them, put them back in jail, it discourages people from seeking treat- ment. I don't want to do that. I think we what we should look toward is rehabilitation.

I don't think people understand the effects their crimes have on victims. Just because they're not thinking about it. If they were considering all these things when they commit the crime, no one would ever commit a crime. But they're not considering that as they go into it and I don't really think that people who say that the death penalty is a deterrent. Are you kidding me? Like who is com- mitting a capital crime and thinks . . . well maybe I will get caught doing this and then if I get caught maybe . . . no one ever thinks that!! Maybe the death penalty would be a deterrent for burglars. Not that I'm suggesting that we have that, but it's certainly not a deterrent for those kinds of crimes. First off, no one ever thinks they're going to get caught.

We're either the most evil people on the face of the earth or we're doing something wrong in terms of incarcerating our fellow citizens.

LM: If there was one change you could make to the commission-based guidelines, what would it be?

DP: It would be less emphasis on incarceration and more emphasis on rehabilitation.

Interview with Chief County Public Defender Mr. Wayne McGrew, Westmoreland County, Pennsylvania — January 14, 2015

Questions Focusing on the Sentencing Goals of Corrections in Pennsylvania's Commission-Based Guidelines

LM: Could you please describe your education and work experience and what drew you to the position of public defender?

WM: Sure, my education is I had an undergraduate degree from Indiana University of Pennsylvania in Finance. I have my law degree from Ohio Northern University Law School. After law school, I practiced for a little bit in Pittsburgh with a small firm and then was accepted into the FBI and went through their academy and became a special agent with the FBI, and I was stationed in New York City.

    Did that for a little over four years. I decided to make a career change, came to Greensburg, back to Westmoreland County. I worked a couple little things, then eventually got in with the District Attorney's Office and prosecuted for about four years there before I went on my own in private practice. I was in private practice for about six and a half years before the commissioners asked me to take over the Public Defender's Office. So in April 2012, I assumed this position as Chief Public Defender for Westmoreland County. So, it's been a windy road.

LM: How do the guidelines themselves negatively affect the defendant?

WM: We have really good judges here, and there are times that I wish the judges would exercise more freedom in their sentencing. The guidelines don't stop them from going outside the standard range. But the judges are required anytime they step out of the guidelines — the standard ranges — they have to put on the record why they went below or why they went above. So, a lot of times they don't want to go outside of them. And I can understand that because there may not be an articulable reason to go above them or below it. But sometimes you just have that right case that the feeling, the hunch, or whatever you want to call it that this person deserves a break and would like to go lower.

LM: Any other ways the guidelines can help the defendant other than that he or she knowing where the starting point is?

WM: That's the biggest one. And I guess in a way because we often, especially in the Public Defender's Office . . . we often see some of the same clients more than once. So you can sit down with them and say what's your prior record score, and they will know it. So that you can look through the guidelines. So, they kind of know going on into the future what they could be facing if they get arrested for something else.

LM: When you look at the guidelines, what goal or goals of sentencing do you think are most emphasized in Pennsylvania's guidelines? Do you think they're most focused on retribution, incapacitation, rehabilitation, specific deterrence, general deterrence, restitution? Or does it really depend on the grid cell that they fall into?

WM: I'm saying it probably is a cross between a few of those terms. It used to be taught or said, if it's not punishment then it's rehabilitation — which I think is not true. There are certain times when it could be rehabilita*tive* because the person gets a chance to get clean off of the drugs. And I keep going back to drugs because that's our biggest contributor to the people in prison right now. It gives them a chance to get clean off drugs. They realize what help that they need. So maybe it's rehabilitative to that person. But as a whole, it's punitive and incapacitative. Just to lock them up for a period of time, so we know at least for this period of time they're not out doing anything or hurting anyone. I think that's in the general sense correct or accurate. Not necessarily correct but accurate to how it happens.

In certain cases they can be rehabilitated, but more as to the drug problem that is what caused them to do the crime. So we got to treat the drug problem. Telling them that it's bad to do the crime . . . you know when they're clean and sober they understand that. They're not having any issues with that. It's the need for the drug, the impulses they can't control—that's what needs to be rehabilitated. And that's what needs to be treated and if you don't that then they're going to come back.

LM: If there was one change you could make to Pennsylvania's commission-based sentencing guidelines what would it be?

WM: I think all and all it's a good thing. In everything you're going to have good and bad. The one thing I would like to see changed is if a judge has been elected by the people and is on the bench and feels it's proper to sentence the person below the guidelines in that particular case . . . I'm not confident that they should be forced or tasked to have to put on record *why* in this particular case this person is eligible to go below the guidelines. Because these are *guidelines* to guide the court and not supposed to be 100 percent strict. And if you've got a good judge, they're not going to be 100 percent strict.

I think that requirement of putting it on the record why you went below or why you went above, and it can't be something as simple as I didn't agree with where the chart said he fell. That's not an acceptable answer. I think if that was taken away so the judges have . . . because I think that restricts some judges. I think they are apprehensive about being reviewed like that. So I would like to see where yes, these are the guidelines. This is where *we*, as a sentencing body, believe that these types of crimes with these types of criminals with this criminal history should fall. But not everybody's the same.

And I point that out because of this. It's a scenario of a guy who's in college. He's partying, he screws up a few times while he's going through school. But he's a kid. That history is going to follow him for life. So now fast forward. Instead of that 19-, 20-, 21-year-old, you have a 55-, 56-, or 60-year-old who gets a DUI. No trouble in between, whatsoever. Maybe DUI isn't the appropriate crime to pick. But anyways let's say DUI.

That history from 40 years earlier still follows him. And still forces him into different ranges on the guidelines. Well maybe this guy really shouldn't have to fall into that higher range. Maybe this guy really should be eligible for that ARD, even though he's been convicted of something in the past.

LM: Interesting. Well thank you very much for participating in the interview. I really, really appreciate it and I think it's going to be great to include in the book your perspectives on it. So thank you.

Discussion Questions

1) Consider the sanction of imprisonment. From your knowledge of the prison system in the United States, answer the following:

   How can it serve the following goals?
   a. Retribution
   b. General deterrence
   c. Specific deterrence
   d. Incapacitation
   e. Rehabilitation

2) Consider the sanction of house arrest. From your knowledge of this sanction in the United States, answer the following:

   How can it serve the following goals?
   a. Retribution
   b. General deterrence
   c. Specific deterrence
   d. Incapacitation
   e. Rehabilitation

3) Why do you think rehabilitation is less prominent than other goals in sentencing reforms? What does this say about the assumptions made about offenders?

4) What sentencing goal(s) of corrections do you feel should be dominant in sentencing offenders? Why?

5) Do you support the work of Families Against Mandatory Minimums? Why or why not?

6) Consider the *Interview* section. Why do you think the judge and public defender believe there is not enough focus on rehabilitation in sentencing offenders in Pennsylvania?

Notes

1. It provided the following scenario to research participants — A "person steals a bicycle parked on the street" and told them that the seriousness of that crime was "10." The respondents were then given descriptions of various crime incidents. If they deemed a crime twice as serious as the bike example, they were instructed to rate it as a "20," if half as serious, a "5," and so on. There was no upper limit and respondents were to answer "0" if they believed the incident shouldn't be considered a crime. It then provided descriptions of other crimes and asked participants to compare them to the seriousness of the bicycle theft. The ratings given by the respondents were combined and a single severity score was developed for 204 items by scaling all responses to the severity of theft of one dollar. The resultant scores ranged from a high of 72.1 for "A person plants a bomb in a public building. The bomb explodes and 20 people are killed" to a low of .2 for "A person under 16 years old plays hooky from school."

2. In Chapter 9 we will discuss evaluation research that explores whether, in practice, mandatory minimum sentencing ensures equal sentencing.

3. van den Haag qualifies his statements concerning general deterrence by stating, "Let me assume finally that, in instances with which I am concerned, the prohibitions of the criminal law are justified, and that the moral or material cost of enforcing them by punishment need not be excessive." (pp. 769–770)

4. It is worth noting that not all legal scholars have agreed that Beccaria's purpose in reforming the legal system was to promote equality. Michael Foucault suggested that Beccaria's reforms actually resulted in greater levels of social control in *Discipline and Punish: The Birth of the Prison*, trans Alan *Sheridan* (1977), pp. 73–103. Foucault questioned the justice and purported "humanity" espoused by Beccaria's suggestions for reform.

5. Note, however, that when the author taught a course in corrections at a university in North Carolina, she used to teach her students the (many) steps of calculating sentences for offenders processed in the state. One of her students, a law enforcement officer, carried the North Carolina Structured Sentencing Training and Reference Manual with him and when he arrested a suspect he referred to the manual, went through the steps (based on the suspect's current arrest offense and what the suspect told him about his prior record) and informed the suspect what type of sentence he or she could receive if convicted of the offense. On a side note, it was quite fulfilling to the author to see her student apply what she taught him in the classroom to the field!

References

ABCNEWS correspondent Terry Moran. (2009, January 7). *ABC News*. Retrieved from http://abcnews.go.com/WNT/story?id=129968

Alabama Sentencing Commission. (2013, October 1). *Presumptive and voluntary sentencing standards manual*. Retrieved from http://sentencingcommission.alacourt.gov /SentStandards/Presumptive%20Manual_2013.pdf

American Bar Association (1994). *ABA Standards for criminal justice sentencing, Third edition: Sentencing*. Washington, DC: American Bar Association.

Beccaria, C., & Voltaire (1801). *An essay on crimes and punishments, translated from the Italian of Beccaria; with commentary, by Voltaire, translated from the French* (Rev. 5th ed). Retrieved from http://hdl.handle.net/2027/njp.32101068978202

Blumstein, A., & Cohen, J. (1980). Sentencing convicted offenders: An analysis of the public's views. *Law and Society Review, 14*, 223–261.

Blumstein, A., Cohen, J., Roth, J. A., & Visher, C. A. (1986). *Criminal careers and "career criminals".* (Vol. 1). Washington, DC: National Academy Press.

Cohen, M. A. (1988). Some new evidence on the seriousness of crime. *Criminology, 26*(2), 343–353.

Cohen, M. A., Rust, R., Steen, S., & Tidd, S. (2004). Willingness-to-pay for crime control programs. *Criminology, 42*, 89–109.

Cullen, F. T., Clark, G. A., Link, B. G., Mathers, R. A., Niedospial, J. E., & Sheahan, M. (1985). Dissecting white-collar crime: Offence type and punitiveness. *International Journal of Comparative and Applied Criminal Justice, 9*, 15–28.

Cullen, F. T., Clark, G. A., Mathers, R. A., & Cullen, J. B. (1983). Public support for punishing white-collar crime: Blaming the victim revisited? *Journal of Criminal Justice, 11*, 481–493.

Cullen, F. T., & Jonson, C. L. (2012). *Correctional theory: Context and consequences*. Thousand Oaks, CA: Sage.

Cullen, F. T., Link, B. G., & Polanzi, C. W. (1982). The seriousness of crime revisited? *Criminology, 20*, 83–102.

Cullen, F. T., Link, B. G., Travis, L. F., & Wozniak, J. F. (1985). Consensus in crime seriousness: Empirical reality or methodological artifact? *Criminology, 23*(1), 99–118.

Durose, M. R., Cooper, A. D., & Snyder, H. N. (2014). *Recidivism of prisoners released in 30 states in 2005: Patterns from 2005 to 2010.* (NCJ Publication No. 244205). Washington, DC: Bureau of Justice Statistics. Retrieved from http://www.bjs.gov/content/pub/pdf/rprts05p0510.pdf

Families Against Mandatory Minimums (2006, Fall). *FAMMGRAM 16*(3). Washington, DC: FAMM.

Families Against Mandatory Minimums (2015). Families Against Mandatory Minimums home page. Retrieved from http://famm.org/

Figlio, R. M. (1975). The seriousness of offenses: An evaluation by offenders and non-offenders. *The Journal of Criminal Law & Criminology, 66*(2), 189–200.

Foucalt, M. (1977). *Discipline & punish: The birth of the prison.* (Trans. A. Sheridan). New York: Pantheon Books.

Geis, G. (1973). Deterring corporate crime. In R. Nader & M. J. Greed (Eds.), *Corporate crime in America* (pp. 182–197). New York: Grossman.

Hawkins, D. F. (1980). Perceptions of punishment for crime. *Deviant Behavior: An Interdisciplinary Journal, 1*, 193–215.

Irwin, J. (2005). *The warehouse prison: Disposal of the new dangerous class.* Los Angeles, CA: Roxbury Publishing Company.

Leeper Piquero, N., Carmichael, S., & Piquero, A. (2008). Research Note: Assessing the perceived seriousness of white-collar and street crimes. *Crime and Delinquency, 54*(2), 291–312. doi: 10.1177/0011128707303623.

Lynch, J. P., & Danner, M. J. E. (1993). Offense seriousness scaling: An alternative to scenario methods. *Journal of Quantitative Criminology, 9*(3): 309–322.

McGrew, W. (2015, January 14). A chief public defender's perspective on Pennsylvania's sentencing guidelines [Personal interview].

Miethe, T. D. (1982). Public consensus on crime seriousness: Normative structure or methodological artifact? *Criminology, 20*, 515–526.

Miller, T., Cohen, M., & Wiersema, B. (1996). *Victim costs and consequences: A new look.* Washington, DC: National Institute of Justice.

Minnesota Sentencing Guidelines Commission. (1982). *Preliminary report on the development and impact of the Minnesota Sentencing Guidelines.* St. Paul, MN: Minnesota Sentencing Guidelines Commission.

Moore, C. A., & Miethe, T. D. (1986). Regulated and unregulated sentencing decisions: An analysis of first-year practices under Minnesota's felony sentencing guidelines. *Law & Society Review, 20*(2), 253–277.

North Carolina Sentencing and Policy Advisory Commission. (2009). *Structured sentencing training and reference manual: Applies to offenses committed on or after December 1, 2009.* Retrieved from http://www.nccourts.org/Courts/CRS/Councils/spac/Documents/sstrainingmanual_09.pdf

Paternoster, R., & Piquero, A. (1995). Reconceptualizing deterrence: An empirical test of personal and vicarious experiences. *Journal of Research in Crime and Delinquency*, *32*(3), 251–286.

People v. Superior Court (Romero), 13 Cal. 4th 497, 917 P. 2 D 628, 53 Cal. RPTR. 2D 789 (1996). Retrieved from http://law.justia.com/cases/california/cal4th/13/497.html

Pezze, D. (2014, December 22). A judge's perspective on Pennsylvania's sentencing guidelines [Personal interview].

Ramchand, R., MacDonald, J. M., Haviland, A., & Morral, A. R. (2009). A developmental approach for measuring the severity of crimes. *Journal of Quantitative Criminology*, *25*, 129–153.

Rosenmerkel, S., Durose, M., & Farole, D., Jr. (2009). *Felony sentences in state courts, 2006 — Statistical tables*. Washington, DC: U.S. Department of Justice, Bureau of Justice Statistics. Retrieved from http://www.bjs.gov/content/pub/pdf/fssc06st.pdf

Rossi, P. H., White, R., Bose, C. E., & Berk, R. E. (1974). The seriousness of crimes: A normative structure and individual differences. *American Sociological Review*, *39*, 224–237.

Roth, J. A. (1978). Prosecutor perceptions of crime seriousness. *The Journal of Criminal Law & Criminology*, *69*(2), 232–242.

Schrager, L. S., & Short, J. F., Jr. (1980). How serious a crime? Perceptions of organizational and common crimes. In G. Geis & E. Stotland (Eds.), *White-collar crime: Theory and research* (pp. 14–31). Beverly Hills, CA: Sage.

Seiter, R. P. (2014). *Corrections*. Upper Saddle River, NJ: Pearson.

Sellin, T., & Wolfgang, M. E. (1964). *The measurement of delinquency*. New York: John Wiley & Sons.

Siegel, B. (1998, February 3). Lovers' spat spins directly into mandatory sentencing laws. *LA Times*. Retrieved from http://articles.latimes.com/1998/feb/03/news/mn-14946

Stafford, M., & Warr, M. (1993). A reconceptualization of general and specific deterrence. *Journal of Research in Crime and Delinquency*, *30*, 123–135.

Stanford Law School. Stanford Three Strikes Project home page. *Stanford Law School*. Retrieved from https://www.law.stanford.edu/organizations/programs-and-centers /stanford-three-strikes-project

The Sentencing Project. The Sentencing Project: Research and advocacy for reform home page. Retrieved from http://www.sentencingproject.org/template/index.cfm

United States Sentencing Commission. (2012). *Report to Congress: Federal child pornography offenses, Executive Summary*. (p. v.). Retrieved from http://www.ussc.gov /Legislative_and_Public_Affairs/Congressional_Testimony_and_Reports/Sex _Offense_Topics/201212_Federal_Child_Pornography_Offenses/Executive _Summary.pdf

Van Den Haag, E. (1982). The criminal law as a threat system. *The Journal of Criminal Law and Criminology*, *73*(2), 769–785.

Von Hirsch, A. (1976). *Doing justice: The choice of punishments*. New York: Hill and Wang.

Von Hirsch, A. (1982). Constructing guidelines for sentencing: The critical choices for the Minnesota Sentencing Guidelines Commission. *Hamline Law Review*, *5*, 164–215

Wolfgang, M. E., Figlio, R. M., Tracy, P. E., & Singer, S. I. (1985). *The National Survey of Crime Severity*. Washington, DC: U.S. Government Printing Office.

9

HAVE THE GOALS OF SENTENCING REFORM BEEN MET? ANSWERS FROM SOCIAL SCIENCE RESEARCH

Chapter Objectives:

- To learn about approaches to evaluating sentencing reforms.
- To comprehend the differences between bivariate and multivariate analyses.
- To differentiate individual level and contextual effects.
- To understand the differences between direct, indirect, and interaction effects.
- To understand what is meant by "sample selection bias" and "the hydraulic effect."
- To assess whether the hydraulic effect is supported by social science research.
- To evaluate whether and how various reforms have met the goals of increasing sentencing uniformity and decreasing disparity and discrimination.
- To consider whether *United States v. Booker* and subsequent decisions have impacted sentencing disparity in the federal system.

Evaluating the Impacts of Sentencing Reforms

Whether sentencing reforms have been successful and what consequences they have had on the criminal justice system and society may seem like straightforward questions. The answers to the questions are, however, quite complex and multi-faceted. In this chapter, we will evaluate the consequences of sentencing reforms through a review of empirical social science research.

We will ascertain whether the purposes of sentencing reforms have been met. Have the three main types of reforms we've discussed — commission-based sentencing guidelines, mandatory minimum sentences, and three strikes laws — done what they said they would do — increase sentencing uniformity, lessen sentencing disparity, and decrease discrimination in sentencing?

Figure 9.1 shows the ideals of various sentencing reforms — how commission-based guidelines, mandatory minimums, and three strikes laws are *ideally* supposed to impact various outcome measures. Commission-based guidelines and three strikes laws have been written to increase sentencing uniformity, decrease judicial discretion, and decrease sentencing disparity. Mandatory minimums were crafted to maximize sentencing uniformity, eliminate judicial discretion, and eliminate sentencing disparity.

Figure 9.1 The Ideals of Sentencing Reforms

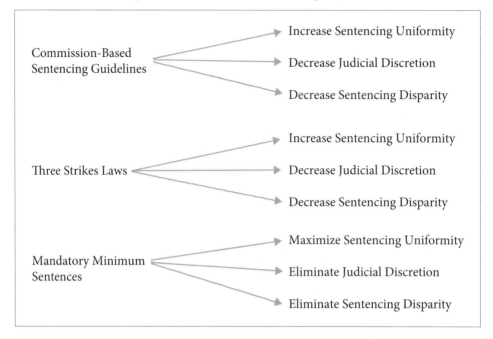

So . . . how do we know if a reform has, in fact, decreased disparity and discrimination and led to more uniform sentencing? Let's explain some terms used in research methods and see how we can get closer to an answer.

Four Approaches to Studying Sentencing Reforms

Four types of social science research can help us understand the nature and consequences of sentencing reform. These are **descriptive, explanatory, evaluation,** and **exploratory** research.

Descriptive Research

According to Chambliss and Schutt (2016), **descriptive research** is "research in which social phenomena are defined and described" (p. 8). Providing descriptive research is a first step in understanding any phenomenon, including sentencing practices. Examples of descriptive research would include a list of mean prison sentences for various offenses or a table listing all states that use a discretionary parole board for release decisions. Descriptive research provides a good starting point for investigating a subject like sentencing reform.

Explanatory Research

According to Chambliss and Schutt (2016), **explanatory research** "seeks to identify causes and effects of social phenomena and to predict how one phenomenon will change or vary in response to variation in another phenomenon" (p. 10). In an effort to understand whether sentencing reforms have led to more equitable sentencing practices, researchers often test whether extralegal and offender characteristics (otherwise known as legally irrelevant variables) influence sentencing outcomes.[1]

Ideally, sentencing reforms are supposed to result in comparable sentences for offenders who have committed crimes with the same *legally relevant* characteristics (for example, seriousness of the crime, extent of injury to the victim, etc.). *Legally irrelevant* characteristics (for example, race of the offender) should play no role in sentencing outcomes.

Social scientists study the relationship between independent and dependent variables. According to Chambliss and Schutt (2016), an **independent variable** is "a variable that is hypothesized to cause, or lead to, variation in another variable" (p. 26). A **dependent variable** is "a variable that is hypothesized to vary depending on or under the influence of another variable" (p. 26).

Sentencing researchers measure the effects of offender and case characteristics on sentencing outcomes. In sentencing research, legally relevant and legally irrelevant case characteristics are the independent variables. The outcomes—which may be the sentence type (prison or not), sentence length, and whether an offender received a sentencing departure are the dependent variables.

For example, a social scientist may look at a sample of offenders sentenced under a commission-based guidelines system and determine through empirical methods whether race affects length of a prison sentence. If a study shows that black offenders receive significantly longer sentences than white offenders (after legally relevant characteristics have been controlled for) then this is evidence that sentences are not equitable.

Two terms are important to our understanding of how sentences are applied. They are **disparity** and **discrimination**. In *Research on Sentencing: The Search for Reform*, Blumstein, Cohen, Martin, and Tonry (1983) distinguished these terms. According to these scholars, "*Disparity* exists when 'like' cases with respect to case attributes—regardless of their legitimacy—are sentenced differently" (p. 8). Sources of sentencing disparity may involve judges who work in the same jurisdiction or among judges across different jurisdictions within a state.

According to Blumstein and colleagues, "*Discrimination* exists when some case attribute that is objectionable typically on moral or legal grounds—can be shown to be associated with sentence outcomes after all other relevant variables are adequately controlled" (p. 8). Sentencing researchers have measured the existence of discrimination based on race, gender, age, and other legally irrelevant variables.

Figure 9.2 illustrates one example of disparity and one example of discrimination. Both examples look at a sample of 100 men convicted of armed robbery with the same legally relevant case characteristics. The top schematic shows that 50 of the men were sentenced by Judge A and 50 were sentenced by Judge B. Judge A imposed sentences between 2 and 4 years, while Judge B imposed sentences between 8 and 10 years. This is an example of sentencing disparity.

The bottom schematic shows a difference in sentence lengths that is linked with a morally objectionable and legally irrelevant variable—race. All 50 white males are given a sentence between 2 and 4 years, while all 50 black males are given a sentence between 8 and 10 years. Since the difference in sentence length is clearly associated with the race of the offender, this is an example of sentencing discrimination.

Figure 9.2 Examples of Sentencing Disparity and Discrimination

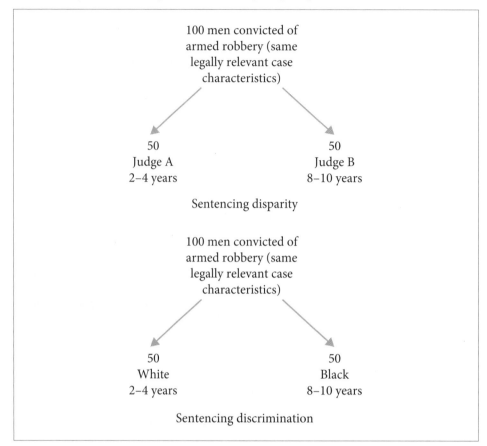

Evaluation Research

Chambliss and Schutt (2016) define **evaluation research** as "research that describes or identifies the impact of social policies and programs" (p. 10). The social policies that we will be studying are the sentencing reforms—commission-based guidelines, mandatory minimums, and three strikes laws. The dependent variables include crime rates and incarceration rates. One example of a question that can be answered using an evaluation approach is, "What impact do three strikes laws have on crime rates?" It is up to social scientists to measure the effect of the law on the rate of violent crimes through quantitative methods. We will look at answers to this question in Chapter 10.

Exploratory Research

Exploratory research is probably the least used in the study of sentencing, but it certainly has its place in furthering the understanding of how sentencing reforms impact offenders and the criminal justice system. Chambliss and Schutt (2016) state that exploratory research "seeks to find out how people get along in the setting under question, what meanings they give to their actions, and what issues concern them" (p. 9).

Conducting open-ended interviews with prisoners about their experience with mandatory minimum sentencing would be an example of exploratory research. Asking judges about how they view sentencing guidelines would be another.

Types of Effects

Figure 9.3 illustrates different types of effects that an independent variable can have on a dependent variable (also known as an outcome measure). The top two models portray **direct effects** of one variable on another. The first shows the effect of the race of the offender on the offender's likelihood of receiving a downward sentencing departure. The independent variable, race, is measured at the *individual level*. This model shows that black offenders have a lower likelihood of receiving downward sentencing departures, compared to white offenders.

The second shows the direct effect of a *contextual level* variable on likelihood of an offender receiving a downward sentencing departure. In sentencing research, a contextual variable measures characteristics of where the sentencing decision was made, i.e., the "context." In this case the measure—the percentage of black residents who live in the county in which the offender is sentenced—is a characteristic of the *county*, not of the individual. This model shows that persons who are sentenced in counties with a higher proportion of black residents have a lower likelihood of receiving downward sentencing departures. Sentencing research may include an examination of various contextual effects including characteristics of a region, county, or court in which one is sentenced on sentencing outcomes.

Whereas race of the offender is an individual level variable, the percentage of blacks living within the county in which one is sentenced is a contextual variable. A statistical model that is trying to assess the effects of race on sentencing outcomes may use one or both of these variables in a single model.

The next two models in Figure 9.3 display **indirect effects**. The first of these shows an indirect effect of an individual level variable—gender—on sentence length. In this example, female offenders are more likely than male offenders to receive bail. Receiving bail release, in turn, is a significant predictor of receiving a shorter sentence length. The effect of gender on sentence length is therefore indirect, and operates through the effect of receiving bail. The next model shows an indirect effect of a contextual variable— whether one is sentenced in a court in an urban area (compared to a court in a rural area). According to this model, persons sentenced in an urban court are more likely to receive bail, which is in turn a predictor of a shorter sentence length.

A third type of effect that is tested by social scientists is called an **interaction effect**. In this case the effect of the independent variable on the dependent variable depends on the presence of another variable. For example, the effect of gender on sentence type (prison or community punishment) depends on race. The model proposes that the effect of gender on sentence type is different for white and black offenders. In this case females who are white are less likely to receive a prison sentence, compared to males. Females who are black are not less likely to receive a prison sentence, compared to males. This suggests that gender interacts with race, so that white women, but not black women, are given a "break" that spares them prison.

Figure 9.3 Examples of Different Types of Effects

Direct Effect Involving an Individual Level Independent Variable

Black Offenders ———————————————————→ Lower Likelihood of Receiving Downward Sentencing Departure

Direct Effect Involving a Contextual Level Independent Variable

Percent of Black Residents Who Live in the County in Which One Is Sentenced ———————————————————→ Lower Likelihood of Receiving Downward Sentencing Departure

Indirect Effect Involving an Individual Level Independent Variable

Female Offenders —→ More Likely to Receive Bail ————→ Shorter Sentence Length

Indirect Effect Involving a Contextual Level Independent Variable

Urban Court ———→ More Likely to Receive Bail ————→ Shorter Sentence Length

Interaction Effect Involving an Individual Level Independent Variable

White Female ———————————————————→ Less Likely to Receive Prison Sentence

Black Female ——————✗——————→ Less Likely to Receive Prison Sentence

Interaction Effect Involving a Contextual Level Independent Variable

Black in Rural County ———————————————————→ Longer Prison Sentence

Black in Urban County ——————✗——————→ Longer Prison Sentence

The last model shows an interaction between a contextual variable and an individual level variable. In this case, black offenders sentenced in rural counties (as opposed to suburban or urban counties) will receive longer sentences than white offenders. In urban counties, however, black offenders are not given longer sentences, compared to white offenders. In this case the effect of race on sentence length is conditioned by a characteristic of the county in which he or she is sentenced.

Ideally, sentencing reforms seek to decrease sentencing disparity and discrimination based on legally irrelevant characteristics. Findings that show that legally irrelevant characteristics affect sentencing decisions challenge whether the goal of increasing sentencing uniformity espoused by sentencing reforms has been met.

Bivariate and Multivariate Research

Another important methodological issue is the difference between bivariate and multivariate analyses. **Bivariate** research presents data about the relationship between two variables, without controlling for the effects of other variables. A table that lists the average prison sentence served broken down by categories of race, which indicates whether the association between these two variables is statistically significant, is an example of bivariate research. It can be a starting point to examining the relationship between race and sentence length.

When one employs **multivariate** techniques, one examines the relationship between the two variables, controlling for other factors. In our example, one might want to control for the seriousness of the conviction offense, whether a weapon was used, and prior record of the offender. Including these variables helps one ascertain if the relationship between race and sentence length persists after these variables are controlled. Multivariate analysis is essential to understanding the relationship between independent and dependent variables. Most studies that we will review employed some form of multivariate analysis.

Two Important Research Issues in Sentencing Research

Before we delve into the studies that assess the outcomes of sentencing reforms, we must first reiterate that the sentencing decision is the last step in criminal case processing before the offender begins serving the punishment. Processing cases through the criminal justice system involves a series of decisions by criminal justice actors. Police officers use their discretion in choosing whether to arrest a suspect. Prosecutors face decisions regarding which cases to prosecute, what charges to bring, and how many counts to charge. Defense attorneys routinely must decide whether they will advise their client to agree to a plea agreement. The actions of criminal justice actors who made decisions earlier in case processing will affect who is ultimately sentenced and the sentence they may face.

Sample Selection Bias

Because prosecutors play a key role in deciding on the number and types of charges that the offender will face, the prosecutor can be seen as a "gatekeeper" of the system. His or her decisions are of great significance to the study of sentencing. Consider a situation in which a prosecutor decides that instead of charging an offender with a burglary that she will charge the offender with an illegal trespass. That offender, who is charged with illegal trespass and later convicted, cannot be punished for the more serious offense, burglary, because he was charged and convicted of a lesser offense.

Discrimination on the part of the prosecutor occurs if he or she systematically lessens the charges for offenders with certain legally irrelevant characteristics, such as gender or race. Let's consider a situation in which the prosecutor lessens the charges from burglary to criminal trespass for most white offenders, but charges most black offenders with burglary. A smaller percentage of white offenders, compared to black offenders, will be convicted of burglary. Even if all of the whites who *are* ultimately charged with and convicted of burglary are given sentences comparable to the blacks convicted of burglary, there is still disparity in criminal justice processing. More whites were given a break earlier, so a smaller percentage of whites, who in reality committed a burglary, will get to the sentencing stage in which the punishment for burglary is handed down. This captures the essence of **sample selection bias.**

There are ways to statistically control for the effects of earlier decision-making to adjust for sample selection bias. Ideally, researchers employ these methods. Many studies, however, just look at the decisions of the judge involving sentencing type (prison or not) and sentence length. Even if studies don't find race to be a significant predictor of sentencing type or length, it doesn't mean that discrimination has not occurred earlier in the criminal justice system.

The "Hydraulic Effect" and Sentencing Reforms

Understanding the "Hydraulic Effect"

Another key (and related) research issue is what criminologists have called "**the hydraulic effect.**" This refers to the notion that reducing or eliminating *judicial* decision-making through restrictive reforms will result in increasing discretion among other criminal justice system actors, namely the *prosecutor* (Alschuler, 1978; Davis, 1969; Greenblatt, 2008; McCoy, 1984; Merritt, Fain, & Turner, 2006; Reitz, 1998; Savelsberg, 1992; Tonry, 1996).

Before modern sentencing reforms, judges exerted oftentimes sizable discretion about the type of sentence they could impose (prison or community based punishment), as well as the sentence length. These decisions have been influenced by many factors, including politics, local and state budgets (which may pay for probation, prison, and jail costs), and prison and jail space.

Another influence on judges' sentencing decisions involves the relationship between the judge and others who work within the courtroom. One might assume that the relationship between the prosecution and defense is purely adversarial — that the prosecution fights to the end to obtain a conviction and the harshest sentence possible, while the defense will not budge or compromise on a plea deal. Research has suggested, however, that there is often collaboration among these actors, referred to as the "courtroom workgroup" (Eisenstein & Jacob, 1977).

According to Eisenstein and Jacob (1977), one characteristic of this courtroom workgroup is that "They are held together by common goals" (p. 20). One of these goals is system efficiency, meaning that cases are handled expeditiously. Another involves preserving group cohesion. Courtroom personnel work together regularly and share some common conceptions of what a fair sentence would be and what the "going rate" (meaning type and length of sentence) is for various offenses (Tonry, 2006).

The concept of the "hydraulic effect" maintains that when *judicial* flexibility is decreased or eliminated, that there must be a concomitant increase in discretion by (an) other component(s) of the criminal justice system in order to avoid tremendous burdens that would likely ensue with an increase in the population under correction supervision.

This shift in discretion is likened to the concept in physics known as hydraulics. McKoy (1984) described this phenomenon as follows:

> An often-invoked simile likens the discretion-ridden criminal justice system to a set of hydraulic brakes. If you push down on one point, the displaced volume of fluid will exert pressure and "bulge out," reappearing elsewhere in the mechanism. Similarly, discretion in the criminal justice system can never be extinguished; it is simply dislodged and shifted to other system parts. (p. 256)

In essence, to keep the "machine running smoothly" there must be movement in discretion from the judiciary, which is constrained by sentencing reforms, to the prosecution. Otherwise, the system will be overloaded — courts would become even more clogged and overcrowding will ensue.

Let's consider a situation in which a state passes a mandatory sentencing law for persons convicted of robbery in the first degree using a handgun. The law requires that upon conviction, that if the crime is committed with a handgun, the offender is subject to an automatic two-year add-on to the prison sentence to that which he or she would receive for the robbery in the first degree. Within this state, the number of cases that meet the legal definition of first degree robbery and in which the suspect uses a handgun remain constant before and after the mandatory sentencing law goes into effect. If one also assumes that the prison beds in that state don't increase or decrease, the concept of system hydraulics would dictate that "something has to give." Under mandatory sentencing, the judge cannot consider the availability of prison space in handing down that term. All persons convicted of a robbery in the first degree who used a handgun in the commission of a crime must get two years in addition to their sentence for the robbery. Because limited prison space (both current and projected) is an issue in this state, the limits on judicial discretion have to be circumvented for the system to keep operating and to avoid backlogs in the court system and overcrowding in the prison system.

The hydraulic effect would mean that the discretion must move from the judge (who is constrained by law to hand down the mandatory two-year add-on) to the prosecutor. Now the prosecutor may choose to charge differently — for example, to change the charge from robbery in the first degree (which in this case would carry the mandatory sentence enhancement) to robbery in the second degree (which does not carry the two-year mandatory add-on prison term).

The discretion that the judge had before the mandatory sentencing law was passed has moved to the prosecutor, who is mindful of relevant issues facing the criminal justice system, such as prison overcrowding and projections of the prison population for years to come. The prosecutor might also consider his or her perception of suitability of the case, in terms of the required sanction. Factors such as prior record, which are ideally are not supposed to affect the imposition of the mandatory two-year add-on may, in fact, affect the prosecutor's discretion in how to proceed with the case.

Research on the Hydraulic Effect and Sentencing Guidelines

Is there evidence of the hydraulic effect subsequent to the adoption of sentencing reforms? Criminologists and legal scholars anticipated a move in discretion from the judge to the prosecutor. Some quantitative research studies have been undertaken to measure whether and how the hydraulic effect has affected sentencing decisions in state and federal courts.

Evidence of the Hydraulic Effect in Minnesota Sentencing Guidelines

Miethe (1987) examined whether there was evidence of the hydraulic effect operating in Minnesota after the state adopted very stringent sentencing guidelines. Minnesota guidelines required that an offender's sentence—whether one went to prison and the sentence length, was to be determined solely on the basis of seriousness of the current offense and prior record. All other factors were prohibited from being considered in sentencing decisions. Miethe suggested that if the hydraulic effect did, in fact, occur, that Minnesota's restrictive sentencing guidelines would be fertile ground, given the significant constraints on sentencing decisions.

Miethe tested the nature and predictors of prosecutorial decision making before and after the guidelines became active. If the hydraulic effect was taking place, several phenomena might occur. One would be that the rates of charge bargaining and sentence negotiations would increase post-guidelines. Another was that the desired goal of sentencing uniformity would decrease as extralegal factors such as race, employment status, and gender of the offender would become more important predictors of charging and plea bargaining practices after the guidelines were put in place.

Miethe's examination of sentencing practices before and after the guidelines were enacted in May 1980 showed few differences in charging decisions and plea bargaining. He also found that the effects of being part of certain social groups that have historically be treated more harshly by the criminal justice system (blacks, the unemployed, etc.) did not differ significantly before and after the guidelines were enacted. There was little evidence that extralegal characteristics became more important predictors of initial charges, dismissal of charges, or sentence negotiations after the guidelines went into effect. He did, however, find some pre- and post-guidelines differences in the effect of some case processing and offense attributes (such as number of alleged offenses) on initial charging decision. Regarding the Minnesota guidelines, Miethe concluded, "the results of this study suggest that the hydraulic displacement of discretion is not inevitable and does not necessarily dampen the success attributed to the primary reform effort" (p. 175).

Evidence of the Hydraulic Effect in Ohio Sentencing Guidelines

Woolredge and Griffen (2005) examined similar questions using data from the state of Ohio, which adopted determinate sentencing guidelines in 1996 under Senate Bill 2 (SB2). They looked at whether there were differences in the likelihoods of first or second degree felony indictments, subsequently dropped charges, reductions in charges, and guilty pleas that involved agreement from prosecutors before and after the guidelines were implemented. Like Miethe, they also looked to see whether the effects of case and defendant attributes on these outcome measures changed after the guidelines were put in place. Specifically, they wanted to see if characteristics that indicated social or economic disadvantage (race, ethnicity, no high school education, and unemployment) affected prosecutorial decision making more after the guidelines were implemented.

Because Ohio's determinate sentencing guidelines were more flexible than Minnesota's, Woolredge and Griffen anticipated similar findings to Miethe's study. As discussed in Chapter 4, the Ohio Criminal Sentencing Commission did not adopt a matrix style grid, but instead set ranges of basic prison terms for five felony levels and indicated ranges of enhancements for repeat violent offenders.

Woolredge and Griffen's analysis of outcomes showed a significant increase in the likelihood of charge reductions among defendants who pled guilty with prosecutorial agreements after the guidelines went into effect. It, however, also showed *no* significant increase post-guidelines in the likelihood of any of the following outcomes: indictment on a first or second degree felony, all charges being dropped, any (but not all) charges being dropped, and those pleading guilty with agreements from prosecutors. They concluded the following: "The finding that charge bargaining actually increased under Ohio's more flexible scheme therefore raises the possibility that even modest shifts in sentencing practices might generate noticeable differences in processing at other decision points within the system" (p. 314).

Regarding the impact of extralegal variables, the researchers found that African Americans experienced a post-guidelines increase in the likelihood of being charged with a first or second degree felony. There were, however, not race differences in the likelihood of all charges being dropped after the guidelines were enacted. There was a significant decrease in the odds of any dropped charges post-guidelines for Mexican American defendants and those who were unemployed. The effects of most extralegal characteristics on the outcome measures post-guidelines, however, were not significant. After examining the impact of seven extralegal variables on the five outcome variables, they found that only four out of the 35 possible relationships were statistically significant. They concluded that Ohio's guidelines scheme did not result in substantive extralegal disparities in the way prosecutors handled the cases, saying, "The few significant differences in extralegal effects that were uncovered in the other model comparisons also did not establish a theme that defendants facing greater racial and economic disadvantages were consistently treated more severely by prosecutors after the implementation of the guidelines" (p. 314).

Evidence of the Hydraulic Effect in District of Columbia Guidelines

More recently, Vance and Oleson (2014) examined whether under the District of Columbia Sentencing Guidelines, discretion moved from the judges to the prosecutors. In August 2004, the District of Columbia adopted a system of voluntary sentencing guidelines in an effort to increase uniformity in sentencing. Prior to that, judges had broad discretion to decide on a sentence outcome within wide statutory ranges.

Using a pre- (2003) and post- (2005) comparison of single-count felony convictions, the researchers found no statistically significant main or interaction effects of the guidelines on charge bargaining. They concluded that there was little evidence pointing to the movement of discretion from the judge to the prosecutor subsequent to the implementation of the sentencing guidelines.

Evidence of the Hydraulic Effect in Federal Sentencing Guidelines

Nagel examined the extent of circumvention of the federal guidelines before and after the *United States v. Mistretta* decision, which upheld the constitutionality of the Sentencing Reform Act. Her 1990 study found some evidence of increased prosecutorial discretion in the forms of charge, fact, and factor bargaining after the guidelines were enacted. She concluded, however, that the guidelines had only been circumvented in a minority of cases that were resolved by guilty pleas.

Nagel and Schulhofer (1992) examined charging and bargaining practices in three districts and showed that there were differences in the nature and extent of plea negotiations and judicial circumvention in each district. They studied individual case files and conducted interviews with judges, prosecutors, defense attorneys, and probation officers in each district. There was a high compliance with guidelines for cases resolved by guilty pleas in District D. District E has high rates of judicial circumvention and a large degree of circumvention, which involved the use of substantial assistance motions to justify downward departures to the guidelines. Nagel and Schulhofer attributed this to resistance to change by the judges, as well as other officials. Findings from District G, which was a high volume district with a high population of drug offenders (factors which might cause one to anticipate greater circumvention), showed a low rate of guideline circumvention.

The authors concluded that a commitment to full compliance to the guidelines by judges, U.S. Attorneys, and federal public defenders varied by district and that this variation explained much of the degree of guidelines circumvention. They found that the *"preferred mode of guideline circumvention"* differed in the three jurisdictions. District E Assistant U.S. Attorneys used guideline-factor bargaining, date bargaining, fact bargaining, and substantial assistance motions to circumvent the guidelines. District G prosecutors used charge bargaining more when deviating from a guidelines sentence. District D prosecutors used 5K1.1 (substantial assistance) motions to a significant degree, when the defendants had not, in fact, provided substantial assistance. They also noted that circumvention was more common when the defendant was facing a mandatory minimum sentence. While Nagel and Schulhofer did not conclude that *all* judicial discretion had moved to prosecutors, they did conclude the following:

> These caveats notwithstanding, we believe that the circumvention we have described is an important obstacle to the success of the guidelines effort. Both the frequency and the extent of circumvention suggest significant divergence from the statutory purpose, as evidenced by large guilty-plea discounts and substantial pockets of uncontrolled discretion.

Schulhofer and Nagel's 1997 study of sentencing data for ten federal districts post-*Mistretta* showed that 20–35 percent of federal cases that were resolved through guilty pleas involved guidelines circumvention or evasion. Their results showed that circumvention was more likely when the case involved drugs or weapons, as compared to offenses such as robbery, arson, theft, and embezzlement. This is because guidelines sentencing in those drugs and weapons cases is anchored by mandatory minimum penalties. They found that in these cases, charge bargaining was the most prominent way to circumvent the guidelines, but that factor bargaining (e.g., the offender's role in the offense) was also used. In addition, "substantial assistance" motions were sometimes used to what Schulhofer and Nagel (1997, p. 1293) refer to as "sympathetic" defendants who had given negligible assistance, assistance that did not impact the case as required by section 5K1.1, or no assistance at all. They also found that the rate of circumvention varied by district. They concluded that mandatory minimums undermine the guidelines process and the goal of sentencing uniformity. They, however, acknowledged that guidelines circumvention does not occur in most cases.

Research on the Hydraulic Effect and Mandatory Minimums

Federal Mandatory Minimum Statutes

Cano and Spohn (2012) tested the assertion that "sympathetic" defendants in federal drug cases were more likely to benefit from guidelines circumvention through substantial assistance departures. As we discussed in Chapter 5, the mandatory minimum statutes are based on drug quantity only, whereas the guidelines would enable the judge to take into account the role of the offender in the crime, or whether he or she accepted responsibility for the crime by pleading guilty. The statutes "trump" the guidelines — meaning that the sentence indicated by the mandatory minimum sentencing laws for drug offenses trump the sentence ranges (and a consideration of offense/offender specific characteristics) indicated by the sentencing guidelines. The mandatory minimums for drug offenses indicate harsher penalties than the guidelines.

A U.S. Attorney may decide to file a motion for a downward departure based on substantial assistance. The sentencing judge may then decide how much to reduce the sentence and is to base this decision on the nature of the defendant's assistance. Consequently, the offender can serve less time than indicated by the sentence indicated by the guidelines. Because the mandatory minimum statutes require lengthy sentences, the downward departures can remove the mandatory minimums that would otherwise be triggered by drug quantity only. Substantial assistance motions, therefore, have the capacity to circumvent mandatory minimum sentences (Kramer & Ulmer, 1996; Mustard, 2001).

Cano and Spohn (2012) examined sentencing of drug offenders in three U.S. district courts in 1998, 1999, and 2000 (when the guidelines were still mandatory, not merely advisory). They sought to understand what factors affected prosecutors' and judges' decisions regarding substantial assistance departures for defendants charged with drug offenses that carried mandatory minimums. Their analysis that controlled for variables such as presumptive sentence and criminal history showed that substantial assistance departures were used to reduce the sentencing for some offenders, but not others. Females, United States citizens, and persons with some college had a higher likelihood of receiving sentencing departures for substantial assistance. Race, ethnicity, employment status, and marital status did not, however, affect the likelihood of a substantial assistance departure. In terms of the sentence reductions, females, United States citizens, employed offenders, and those playing a minor role in the offense had larger sentencing reductions. They also found that sentence reductions varied by the district.

The Impact of Oregon's Measure 11 on Prosecutors' Charging Decisions

In Chapter 6 we discussed Oregon's Measure 11, a mandatory sentencing law that went into effect in April 1995 that aimed to eliminate judicial discretion for a wide range of offenses deemed serious. Measure 11 mandated minimum prison terms ranging from 70 months for assault in the second degree to 300 months for murder. Like other mandatory minimums, prior record level played no role in determining sentence length.

Merrit, Fain, and Turner (2006) noted that decisions of the prosecutors with respect to charging, counts, and plea agreements are less public than judge's decisions. Except in very high profile cases, the public is unaware of prosecutors' decisions or the reasons behind them. They noted a potential role that extralegal factors could play in the prosecution's decision of who gets charged and exactly what charges are brought. If case characteristics such as offender race, offender socioeconomic status, etc. are shown to be linked to charging decisions, then the often stated purpose of sentencing reform — to increase sentencing uniformity and decrease sentencing disparity — has not been met. In essence, discrimination and disparity may still exist in the criminal justice system. The only difference is that instead of it occurring during the sentencing stage, it now happens at the prosecution stage. Defendants who commit "equal crimes" (crimes with the same legally relevant characteristics) may still receive different sentences, because the prosecution charges some offenders with crimes that carry mandatory sentences and lessens the charges for others.

Merritt, Fain, and Turner (2006) detailed two models to describe how mandatory sentencing laws may impact courtroom behavior. The first, the **"simplistic implementation" model**, stirred fears in criminal justice courtroom personnel and criminologists as sentencing reforms grew in scope across the United States. The simplistic model assumes that after a mandatory sentencing law such as Measure 11 is put in place that the percentage of felony cases that would be sentenced post-Measure 11 would remain constant, compared to how those cases would be sentenced before that designation was made to those cases. The impact on prison populations, however, would change. Prior to Measure 11, the bases upon which sentence length were to be determined, according to Oregon's sentencing guidelines, were seriousness of the crime *as well as* prior record. Because Measure 11 dictated that sentence be determined by only seriousness of offense, prior record was insignificant. A simplistic implementation of Measure 11 would mean that more individuals convicted of these crimes would end up in prison, serving lengthy prison terms. Prison populations would rise over time as more offenders were being sentenced to prison and they were being sentenced for longer prison terms.

Conversely, the **"adaptive implementation" model**, acknowledges the process of courtroom system hydraulics and does not predict such a dire situation for the correctional system. This model assumes that prosecutors will use their discretion to select the cases that they deem the most serious and deserving of mandatory sentencing to be charged as Measure 11 offenses. Prosecutors will charge the cases that they do not see as serious enough for sentencing under Measure 11 with Measure 11 *alternate* crimes (for example, instead of charging a defendant with first degree robbery, which is a Measure 11 offense, they would charge the defendant with robbery I attempt — an "alternate" offense). Instead of fully prosecuting all cases that are technically eligible cases to be classified as Measure 11 cases, which would potentially overburden the correctional system (if all of the defendants were convicted), they use discretion early on in the criminal justice processing system to select the cases that they feel are most deserving of mandatory sentencing. In this model, prosecutors would likely secure more convictions through plea bargaining for these "alternate" offenses. Measure 11 "alternate" offenders would likely serve longer prison sentences. Those who are charged and convicted of a Measure 11 offense would serve certain and lengthy prison terms. However, overall fewer offenders would enter prison, compared to the number expected by a "simplistic" implementation scenario.

Merritt, Fain, and Turner (2006) found that prosecutors chose not to charge all defendants who were "on paper" eligible to be charged with Measure 11 offenses as such. Instead, they chose a subset of these offenders for prosecution of Measure 11 offenses, which upon conviction carried mandatory long term imprisonment. They concluded the following:

> Thus our analyses support the statements of Oregon prosecutors, as well as earlier research findings, showing that the proportion of offenders convicted of, and admitted to prison for, M11-eligible offenses decreased whereas the proportion of M11-alternative sentences and admissions increased after implementation of the measure. At the same time, sentence lengths rose within both offense categories, providing further evidence that after Measure 11, rather than being charged with an M11-eligible offense, an offender may be charged with a lesser M11-alternate offense, yet still receive approximately the same sentence that the M11-eligible offense would have drawn before Measure 11. Thus, our findings suggest that passage of Measure 11 affected the "going rate" for both M11-eligible and M11-alternate offenses. (p. 29)

Takeaways from Research on the Hydraulic Effect

A few study results lend support to the assertion that after sentencing reforms were put in place, discretion moved from the judge to the prosecutor. Many, however, show little or no evidence that post-reforms, prosecutorial discretion increased with respect to charges filed, counts filed, etc. Regarding the impact of extralegal variables on prosecutorial decisions, there are some significant findings. If one compiles the "big picture" from the studies discussed above, however, we do not see a clear and consistent pattern that shows extralegal variables playing a greater role in all prosecutorial decisions after reforms have been implemented. The hydraulic effect seems more evident with respect to mandatory sentencing laws, compared to sentencing guidelines.

So why has the research not fully supported the prediction by some that the hydraulic effect would be substantial in sentencing approaches that limit judicial discretion? Miethe (1987) reflected on why the hydraulic effect may not occur or is minimized under Minnesota's guidelines as well as other determinate sentencing practices. He acknowledged that while prosecutors may gain more discretion after sentencing guidelines are put in place that prosecutors are still working within a criminal justice workgroup that includes judges and defense attorneys. The working relationship with these professionals involves shared norms about what are appropriate sanctions for certain offenses, an understanding of how workloads should be managed, and a recognition that there are scarce resources (like prison space). These facts likely minimize the extent to which prosecutors exercise their increased discretionary power.

Miethe commented on other determinate sentencing practices and pointed out the fact that judges do not lose all discretion in many sentencing reform approaches (except for mandatory minimums). Within many guidelines schemes, judges can choose sentence length within a range, albeit a narrow one. This reflection may be even more relevant today with the move from commission-based guidelines being mandatory to them being advisory. As discussed in Chapter 5, the federal guidelines are no longer mandatory. Instead, they are now used as a *starting point* in the process of sentencing federal offenders.

Bushway and Piehl (2007) found more prosecutorial discretion and evidence of the "hydraulic effect" in Washington, a state with presumptive sentencing guidelines, compared with Maryland, which has voluntary/advisory guidelines. In Maryland, they found more judicial discretion at the sentencing stage. They concluded that if one only looks at studies that focus on sentence variation within presumptive guidelines schemes that one may miss significant sources of sentencing disparity. The various results on whether and to what extent the hydraulic effect operates may vary with how "mandatory" the law or guidelines are considered.

Any evidence of the hydraulic effect that shows extralegal variables are significant predictors of prosecutorial discretion that benefit some and hurt others after reforms were put in place signifies a process that is at odds with the goals of reforms. If sentencing uniformity is compromised and if sentencing disparities and discrimination are evident, then the main goals of sentencing reform are undermined. The next section summarizes research on the effect of extralegal variables on sentences in jurisdictions that have adopted various reforms.

Have Sentencing Guidelines Increased Sentencing Uniformity and Decreased Disparity and Discrimination?

The Goal of Sentencing Uniformity

According to Frase (1992–1993)

> Uniformity is achieved when similarly situated offenders receive the same sentence, whether or not that is the "best" (e.g., deserved or most "proportional") sentence. A particularly important subsidiary goal is sentencing "neutrality" with respect to the race, gender, and social or economic status of offenders. (p. 295)

Whether the goal of sentencing uniformity has been achieved by sentencing guidelines can be assessed in two ways. The first way involves measuring the **rates of dispositional (prison or not) departures and rates of durational (length of imprisonment) departures from presumptive guidelines.** The second way is to assess **whether legally irrelevant variables, such as race and gender, affect sentencing decisions after guidelines systems are implemented.** Uniform sentencing should result in few sentencing departures and sentencing practices that are not linked with extralegal factors, such as race and gender.

We will focus (but not restrict) our review of studies to those performed in Minnesota, Pennsylvania, and the federal system after commission-based guidelines were implemented in these jurisdictions.

Evaluations of Minnesota's sentencing guidelines are especially noteworthy since Minnesota was the first state to adopt strict sentencing guidelines. Minnesota's guidelines were designed to target violent offenders and those with longer prior records to receive prison sentences (Daily, 1998; Minnesota Sentencing Guidelines Commission, 1982).

Pennsylvania's presumptive guidelines, which were implemented in 1982, were less restrictive than Minnesota's or the federal guidelines (Ulmer & Kramer, 1996). The current Basic Sentencing Grid indicates a relatively wide range of minimum sentences, especially for serious offenses.[2] The Pennsylvania Commission on Sentencing wanted to leave judges with some discretion, in part to avoid discretion moving away from the judge to the prosecutor. Because Pennsylvania's guidelines allowed relatively more discretion by judges, they could potentially could allow more sentencing disparity and discrimination. The Pennsylvania Commission on Sentencing has collected detailed information on all criminal court cases, and thus provides a rich source of data to assess sentencing practices.

There has been an enormous amount of research on the Federal Sentencing Guidelines. Like the various state sentencing commissions we've looked at, a major aim of the United States Sentencing Commission was to promote sentencing uniformity and decrease sentencing disparity and discrimination.

The Extent of Sentencing Departures

Minnesota Sentencing Guidelines Departures

The Minnesota Guidelines allow defendants falling in "stayed" grid cells to receive any of a variety of sentences, including probation, residential or community treatment, or a twelve-month jail term. Offenders in "executed" grid cells are to be incarcerated in a state facility.

According to the Minnesota Sentencing Guidelines Commission (2014, November),

> "A 'dispositional departure' occurs when the court orders a disposition other than that recommended in the guidelines. There are two types of dispositional departures: aggravated dispositional departures and mitigated dispositional departures. An aggravated dispositional departure occurs when the guidelines recommend a stayed sentence but the court pronounces a prison sentence. A mitigated dispositional departure occurs when the guidelines recommend a prison sentence but the court pronounces a stayed sentence" (p. 23).

These departures are only allowed under a limited range of circumstances, which were specified by the commission and other "substantial and compelling circumstances" (Minnesota Sentencing Guidelines Commission, 1982, p. 13).

The Minnesota Sentencing Guidelines Commission (2014) calculated departure rates over time. **Figure 9.4** shows the overall departure rates (combined dispositional and durational departures) for offenders sentenced in 2013. Seventy-two percent of sentences

Figure 9.4 Overall Departure Rates for Felony Offenders Sentenced in
Minnesota in 2013

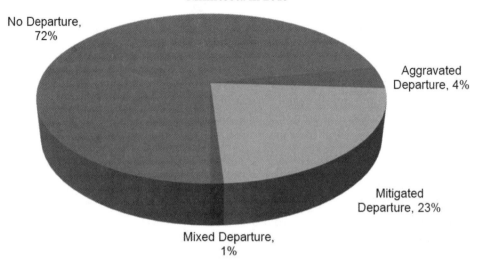

Source: Minnesota Sentencing Guidelines Commission. (2014, November). *2013 Sentencing practices:
Annual summary statistics for felony offenders.* p. 22, Figure 9. St. Paul, MN: Minnesota Sentencing
Guidelines Commission. Retrieved from http://mn.gov/sentencing-guidelines/assets/2013%20
Data%20Report%20Updated_tcm30-31259.pdf

involved no departure, 23 percent involved a mitigated departure, 4 percent involved
an aggravated departure, and 1 percent a mixed departure.

The commission noted that while the judge pronounces the sentence, that other
courtroom actors, including probation officers, prosecutors, and defense attorneys, as
well as victims, will "weigh in" on the sentencing decision. If deemed appropriate, any
or all of these parties may agree that a departure is appropriate. A departure rate of
28 percent might seem high at first glance and provide evidence that sentencing uniformity
has been compromised. The commission (2014, November) noted, however, that only
one or two percent of cases result in appeal (p. 22).

Figure 9.5 shows *dispositional* departure rates only over time, from 1981 to 2013. Aggravated dispositional departure rates have remained relatively stable, hovering between
three and five percent. Mitigated dispositional departure rates have increased overall in
this time period and ranged from a low of three percent in 1981 to a high of 11 percent in
2013 (Minnesota Sentencing Guidelines Commission, 2014, November, p. 23).

According to the Minnesota Sentencing Guidelines Commission (2014, November), a "durational departure" occurs when the court orders a sentence with a duration
that is other than the presumptive fixed duration or range in the appropriate cell on
the applicable grid. An aggravated durational departure occurs when the court pronounces a duration that is more than 20 percent higher than the fixed duration displayed in the appropriate cell on the applicable grid. A mitigated durational departure
occurs when the court pronounces a sentence that is more than 15 percent lower than
the fixed duration displayed in the appropriate cell on the applicable grid (p. 29).

Figure 9.5 Dispositional Departure Rates for Felony Offenders in Minnesota 1981–2013

	1981	1982	1983	1984	1985	1986	1987	1988	1989	1990	1991	1992	1993	1994	1995	1996	1997	1998	1999	2000	2001	2002	2003	2004	2005	2006	2007	2008	2009	2010	2011	2012	2013
Aggravated	3%	3%	5%	4%	3%	4%	5%	4%	4%	3%	3%	3%	3%	4%	4%	4%	5%	5%	4%	4%	4%	4%	4%	4%	4%	4%	4%	3%	3%	3%	4%	4%	
Mitigated	3%	4%	4%	6%	7%	6%	6%	6%	7%	8%	9%	8%	9%	9%	9%	9%	10%	8%	8%	8%	10%	10%	10%	11%	10%	10%	10%	11%	11%	10%	11%	11%	11%
Overall	6%	7%	9%	10%	11%	10%	11%	10%	11%	11%	12%	11%	12%	12%	13%	13%	14%	13%	13%	12%	14%	14%	14%	15%	14%	14%	14%	15%	14%	13%	14%	15%	15%

— Aggravated   ⋯⋯ Mitigated   ▬▬ Overall

Source: Minnesota Sentencing Guidelines Commission. (2014, November). *2013 Sentencing practices: Annual summary statistics for felony offenders.* p.23, Figure 10. St. Paul, MN: Minnesota Sentencing Guidelines Commission. Retrieved from http://mn.gov/sentencing-guidelines/assets/2013%20 Data%20Report%20Updated_tcm30-31259.pdf

Figure 9.6 shows that over time the rate of mitigated *durational* departures has risen pretty steadily from 16 percent in 1981 to 27 percent in 2013 (with a low of 13 percent in 1984 and a high of 30 percent in 2001 and 2002). The rate of aggravated durational departures has fallen over time (Minnesota Sentencing Guidelines Commission, 2014, November, p. 30).

Figure 9.6 Durational Departure Rates for Felony Offenders in Minnesota 1981–2013, Executed Prison Sentences Only

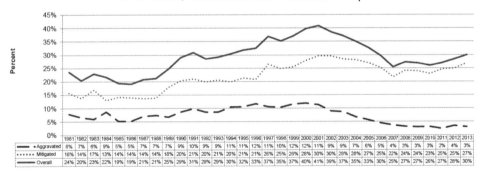

	1981	1982	1983	1984	1985	1986	1987	1988	1989	1990	1991	1992	1993	1994	1995	1996	1997	1998	1999	2000	2001	2002	2003	2004	2005	2006	2007	2008	2009	2010	2011	2012	2013
Aggravated	8%	7%	6%	9%	5%	5%	7%	7%	7%	9%	10%	9%	9%	11%	11%	12%	11%	10%	12%	12%	11%	9%	9%	7%	6%	5%	4%	3%	3%	3%	2%	4%	3%
Mitigated	16%	14%	17%	13%	14%	14%	14%	14%	18%	20%	21%	20%	21%	20%	21%	21%	26%	25%	26%	28%	30%	30%	28%	28%	27%	25%	22%	24%	24%	23%	25%	25%	27%
Overall	24%	20%	23%	22%	19%	19%	21%	21%	25%	29%	31%	29%	29%	30%	32%	33%	37%	35%	37%	40%	41%	39%	37%	35%	33%	30%	25%	27%	27%	26%	27%	28%	30%

Source: Minnesota Sentencing Guidelines Commission. (2014, November). *2013 Sentencing practices: Annual summary statistics for felony offenders.* p.30, Figure 17. St. Paul, MN: Minnesota Sentencing Guidelines Commission. Retrieved from http://mn.gov/sentencing-guidelines/assets/2013%20 Data%20Report%20Updated_tcm30-31259.pdf

Federal Guidelines Departures

As we discussed in Chapter 5, about 46 percent of federal sentences imposed were within the guidelines range in fiscal year 2014. Approximately 2.2 percent of cases were imposed above the guidelines range. About 51 percent were imposed below the guidelines range. Chapter 5 details the ways sentences were imposed outside guidelines ranges.

The Effect of Legally Irrelevant Factors on Sentence Outcomes in Jurisdictions with Sentencing Guidelines

Have sentencing guidelines decreased sentencing disparity and discrimination? A majority of studies have shown that commission-based sentencing guidelines have led to less sentencing variation based on legally irrelevant variables (Tonry, 2014). We will look at literature that has examined the effects of individual level legal and extralegal characteristics. In addition, we will consider the impact of contextual factors on sentencing outcomes.

Legally Relevant Variables

One of the most consistent findings in research on sentencing decisions under the Minnesota and Pennsylvania guidelines is the dominant role that *legally* relevant characteristics, such as offense severity and prior record, play. This is to be expected, as commission-based guidelines systems use these two criteria as the main bases of sentencing within their grids.

Miethe and Moore (1985) and Moore and Miethe (1986) found that after Minnesota's guidelines were implemented, severity of the conviction offense and criminal history were major predictors of the disposition and duration of a prison sentence. Pennsylvania studies showed that offenders convicted of more serious offenses and those who had longer prior records were more likely to receive sentences of prison, and for those who were sentenced to prison these legally relevant variables were linked with longer sentences (Johnson, 2006; Steffensmeier & Demuth, 2001; Ulmer & Bradley, 2006). Kramer and Ulmer (1996, 2002) found that offenders with longer criminal histories and those who committed more serious offenses were less likely to receive a downward dispositional departure and that these legally relevant characteristics were the strongest predictors of departures. Offense severity and criminal history were also the primary predictors of durational departure decisions (Kramer & Ulmer, 1996). Johnson's (2003) study of departure decisions that included offense severity and prior record, however, did not show these factors to dominate sentencing decisions in a predictable way.[3]

Race — Legally Irrelevant

Theoretical Perspectives

The effect of race on sentencing has been theorized and tested in the field of criminology more so than any other extralegal variable. In 1928, noted sociologist Thorsten Sellin discussed how the perception of blacks as having a higher propensity for criminality shapes the way society and the criminal justice system views and treats black suspects and defendants. He suggested that whites are more likely to avoid trial and conviction of an offense compared to blacks. Once convicted, Sellin asserted that black offenders receive harsher sentences in type and length, compared to white offenders.

Sellin offered some explanation for these patterns of differential enforcement of the law. He noted the historically inferior social status of blacks, overt prejudice in society, as well as the decreased likelihood of blacks in obtaining effective legal counsel as reasons why they are at a disadvantage in the criminal justice system.

Criminologists have pointed to social structural factors as explaining the differential treatment of blacks and whites by our criminal justice system. More recently some criminologists have suggested that blacks, and in particular young black males, are seen as a "dangerous class," members of whom have a high propensity for criminal activity (Farley, Steeh, Krysan, Jackson, & Reeves, 1994; Massey, 1993). Stereotypes in society and the media boost these images (Gibbs, 1988). Interviews have suggested that some judges accept these beliefs and that they influence their sentencing decisions (Daly, 1994; Steffensmeier, Kramer, & Streifel, 1993). These perspectives predict that blacks are punished more harshly than whites.

Others have suggested that blacks, Latinos, and immigrants may be perceived as posing a "racial threat," "Latino threat," or an "immigrant threat" (Feldmeyer, Warren, Siennick, & Neptune, 2015). Disparate sentencing may occur in cases in which blacks are viewed as a symbolic threat to the social order. For example, the media linkage of inner city black males and the crack cocaine epidemic in the 1980s promoted the idea that this group is dangerous and may pose a threat if the problem moves to the mostly white suburban areas. This perceived threat may, in turn, prompt actors in the criminal justice system to get tougher on these offenses and the offenders that they deem responsible for such crimes—young inner city black males.

Study Findings

Research on race and sentencing dates back to well before sentencing reforms became widespread in the United States. As such, many early studies examined sentencing decisions that allowed judges wide discretion in the types and lengths of sentences and often found that blacks were sentenced more harshly.

Numerous studies in Pennsylvania after the state's guidelines went into effect have found effects of race and ethnicity on sentencing decisions. Steffensmeier and Demuth (2001) found overall more lenient treatment of white defendants. Research on sentence type and length has shown that blacks and Hispanics are more likely to be incarcerated than whites (Johnson, 2006) and that blacks were both more likely to receive a sentence of incarceration and received longer sentences than whites (Steffensmeier, Ulmer, & Kramer, 1998; Ulmer & Bradley, 2006). Blacks were less likely than whites to receive downward dispositional departures (Kramer & Ulmer, 1996).

Among serious violent offenders, Kramer and Ulmer (2002) found no significant differences in departure chances of whites compared to African Americans, but showed that Hispanics were less likely to receive departures. Hispanic defendants had a higher probability of receiving an incarceration sentence and also receiving longer sentences for both drug and nondrug cases (Steffensmeier & Demuth, 2001). This Hispanic disadvantage may indicate support for the notion of a perception of "immigrant threat" discussed above.

Pennsylvania data lack information on the defendant's socioeconomic status. It is therefore unclear whether race effects would stay statistically significant once socioeconomic status is included in the models. Generally, race is correlated with socio-economic status, with blacks and Hispanics having, on average, lower socioeconomic status, compared with whites.

Research examining federal sentencing data has provided some evidence that blacks and Hispanics receive harsher sentencing outcomes. Studies have shown that racial disparities exist in type of sentence imposed (Jordan & Freiburger, 2015), sentence length (Albonetti, 1997), and likelihood of downward departures (Johnson, Ulmer, & Kramer, 2008). The United States Sentencing Commission (2010, March) found that black male offenders received longer sentences than white male offenders.

Interpreting Studies of Race and Sentencing and the Use of Meta-Analysis

There are some challenges to meaningfully deciphering the results from multiple studies and reaching an overall conclusion of how race affects sentencing. Some studies failed to employ appropriately rigorous methodologies, used imprecise measures of variables, used small samples, and/or failed to test for how social context conditions sentencing disparity. When studies use a variety of more or less appropriate approaches to understanding the effect of race on sentencing, contradictory findings will result (Franklin, 2015; Hagan & Bumiller, 1983; Jordan & Freiburger, 2015; Ulmer, 2012).

One approach to summarizing extant research is through narrative reviews which tally findings from individual studies on race and sentencing. This approach looks at each study and whether the measure of race was statistically significant and reaches conclusions based on the proportion of studies that showed race to be a statistically significant predictor of sentence outcome. A problem with this approach is that when studies employ large samples (which many sentencing studies do) statistical significance is common. Another methodological issue in narrative reviews is that they may not differentiate studies that have varying levels of rigor, with respect to measurement of variables. Given studies of varying rigor equal weight may lead to inaccurate conclusions (Mitchell, 2005).

Mitchell (2005) conducted a **meta-analysis** of 71 studies that have examined the link between race and sentencing outcomes. Meta-analysis is a quantitative approach that provides "effect size" estimates. Meta-analysis determines both the direction and magnitude of an effect found by extant studies. This method controls for methodological rigor and weighs the results of studies with more reliable estimates more heavily. By employing this method, one can more effectively reach conclusions about the overall effect of race on sentencing outcomes from multiple studies.

Mitchell's meta-analysis showed that race has a relatively small, but statistically significant, direct effect on the *probability of imprisonment*. Blacks are more likely to be sentenced to prison than whites. In terms of *length of imprisonment*, the meta-analysis showed relatively smaller effects that are overall statistically insignificant. The race difference that disadvantages black offenders is most notable in cases involving drug offenders.

Mitchell reiterated that blacks are disproportionately represented in the population of offenders incarcerated in the United States. Mitchell, however, concluded that discrimination at the sentencing stage is not the main source of disproportionate minority confinement. He suggested that the decisions that are made earlier in criminal case processing likely involve disparate treatment of whites and blacks and that these decisions contribute significantly to the disproportionate representation of blacks in prisons and jails.

Gender—Legally Irrelevant
History and Hypotheses

Throughout history, males and females have been treated differently by the criminal justice system. Changes in sentencing practices for females have often lagged behind those for males. There was a movement away from rehabilitation as a dominant goal of sentencing for males, as the Reformatory Era (1870–1910) ended. During this time period, however, female "reformatories," which were designed to rehabilitate, rather than to punish, continued to operate.[4] Focus on rehabilitation meant that judges imposed more "indeterminate" sentences on women. Punishment for men was through determinate (fixed) sentencing and it was not unusual for a man to serve a shorter sentence than a woman for the same offense.

The "common knowledge" about the effect of gender on sentencing since the latter 1900s, however, is that most of the time female offenders fare better than male offenders in terms of sentencing and imprisonment decisions. Women are less likely to be incarcerated and if incarcerated, are given shorter sentences (Daly, 1994; Kruttschnitt, 1984). Some have labeled this the "chivalry effect." This is counterintuitive to those who concentrate on the influence of social status on the treatment of offenders by the criminal justice system. If one acknowledges the fact that women have historically been seen as inferior, were once considered property of men, and have historically had fewer rights than men in American society, one would predict that females (like blacks) who occupy a subordinate position in society would suffer more at the hands of the criminal justice system.

Several possible explanations for lenient treatment of female offenders have been put forth. Some reasons for disparate sentencing include the court's consideration of family factors—that women may be pregnant and that women are the primary caregivers of children. A practical matter is that there is less jail and prison space for women. Others have argued that women often commit a criminal act out of coercion by male codefendants. They may also play a minor role in the offense, often acting as accessories, especially in drug trafficking cases (Nagel & Johnson, 1994). In her discussion of transcripts of judges' remarks in sentencing women, Daly (1994) suggested that there should be an examination into how "gendered presuppositions" of women—that they are less likely to be considered hardened offenders, that they are viewed as more likely to be reformed/rehabilitated, and the recognition that female offenders may have also endured victimization, may be reflected in sentencing decisions for female offenders.

In recent years, more attention has been paid to the question of whether there are gender disparities in sentencing. This interest corresponds to the increase in the female prison population. Although women only comprise 7 percent of the prison population, in recent years the rate of growth of female imprisonment per year has been greater than that for males. Female prisoners sentenced to more than a year in state or federal prison grew by approximately 3 percent between 2012 and 2013, compared to a .2 percent increase in male prisoners in this time period (Carson, 2014, September).

Some argue that sentencing reforms that have aimed to increase uniformity are one reason for the increase in the female prison population. Daly and Tonry (1997) described the practice sentencing commissions took when setting appropriate sentence ranges for offenders with the same offense seriousness and prior record. Although reviews of past sentencing practices showed that female offenders were sentenced to lighter terms than male offenders, commissions decided to embrace a "gender neutral" approach to establishing guideline ranges, which used "past average sentences for men or on an average for men's and women's sentences" (p. 205). This standard was then to dictate appropriate ranges for both males and females in an effort to "equalize" sentencing. It thus served to increase sentences for female offenders.

Study Findings

Table 9.1 shows the median time served by offenders who served their sentences in state prisons, broken down by gender (Carson, 2014, September, p. 18). For each crime category and for all individual offenses listed, females served shorter sentences. These are bivariate data and do not, therefore, control for legally relevant case factors.

Gender has been a consistent predictor of sentencing outcomes in multivariate studies done in Pennsylvania. Female offenders typically receive more lenient sentences. Females have been significantly less likely to be incarcerated (Johnson, 2006; Ulmer & Bradley, 2006). Steffensmeier, Ulmer, and Kramer (1998) found that females were less likely to receive a sentence of incarceration and when incarcerated, being sentenced to shorter sentence lengths. Females were more likely than males to receive downward dispositional departures (Kramer & Ulmer, 1996).

Steffensmeier, Kramer, and Streifel (1993) employed multiple measures of offense type and prior record and found that females were less likely to be incarcerated than males, but that there were no gender differences in length of imprisonment. They also found that a higher percentage of female defendants received downward dispositional departures. They reviewed the judges' reasons for departing from the sentencing guidelines and found the following five justifications that favored female defendants: (1) their prior record was comprised of nonviolent offenses, (2) the defendant had mental or physical health issues that would be detrimental to the institution staff and hurt rather than help the defendant, (3) the defendant was caring for dependents or was pregnant, (4) the defendant played a minor role in the offense, and (5) the defendant showed remorse.

Studies examining the sentencing of federal offenders have also shown gender effects. Female offenders were more likely to receive prosecutorial-initiated substantial assistance departures and judge-initiated departures (Cano & Spohn, 2012; Doerner, 2012; Farrell, 2004; Johnson, Ulmer, & Kramer, 2008; Johnson & Betsinger, 2009) and females were less likely to receive an incarceration sentence (Doerner, 2012; Doerner & Demuth, 2014; Johnson & Betsinger, 2009). Starr's (2014) analysis of federal data shows leniency toward females in sentencing but also suggested that much of the gender disparity in sentencing can be explained by differences in charging, plea bargaining, and sentence fact finding. The United States Sentencing Commission (2010) found that female offenders received shorter sentences than male offenders.

Daly and Bordt (1995) conducted a review of 50 data sets gathered in the 1960s, 1970s, and 1980s which had been used in studies that provided information on the relation-

Table 9.1 Median Time Served by Released State Prison Inmates Admitted on New Court Commitments, by Sex and Offense, 2002 and 2012

Most Serious Offense	Released in 2002				Released in 2012			
	Number of Releases	All Inmates	Male	Female	Number of Releases	All Inmates	Male	Female
Violent	82,900	28 mos.	29 mos.	19 mos.	117,400	28 mos.	29 mos.	20 mos.
Murder[a]	4,800	102	103	86	6,900	153	158	103
Manslaughter	2,700	40	41	35	3,200	42	44	35
Rape/sexual assault	17,400	38	38	29	21,800	48	48	29
Robbery	24,000	34	35	20	32,300	34	35	25
Aggravated or simple assault	27,400	18	19	15	43,100	17	18	16
Other violent	6,600	17	17	13	10,100	17	17	14
Property	86,400	12 mos.	13 mos.	10 mos.	111,500	12 mos.	12 mos.	10 mos.
Burglary	31,300	16	17	12	46,200	15	15	11
Larceny	21,300	11	11	9	26,700	11	11	10
Motor vehicle theft	5,800	11	11	8	6,000	11	12	10
Fraud	15,300	10	11	9	17,600	11	11	10
Other property	12,700	11	11	9	14,900	10	11	8
Drug	96,100	14 mos.	14 mos.	11 mos.	105,900	13 mos.	14 mos.	10 mos.
Drug possession	28,200	11	11	9	33,300	10	11	8
Other drug[b]	67,900	15	16	12	72,600	15	16	11
Public order[c]	38,600	11 mos.	11 mos.	9 mos.	71,100	12 mos.	13 mos.	9 mos.
Other/unspecified[d]	2,100	14 mos.	15 mos.	13 mos.	4,200	12 mos.	13 mos.	10 mos.
Total number of releases[e]	317,400		283,700	33,700	413,400		364,700	48,700

Note: Estimates based on prisoners with a sentence of more than 1 year entered prison on a new court commitment. Detail may not sum to total due to rounding and missing offense data. Offense distributions are based on the 35 states that submitted to both the 2002 and 2012 National Corrections Reporting Program (NCRP) data collection, while estimated counts of releases represent data for all states based on NPS. See Methodology.

a Includes nonnegligent manslaughter.

b Includes trafficking, possession, and other drug offenses.

c Includes weapons, drunk driving, and court offenses; commercialized vice, morals, and decency offenses; and liquor law violations and other public-order offenses.

d Includes juvenile offenses and other unspecified offense categories.

e Excludes transfers, AWOLs, and escapes. See Methodology.

Source: Bureau of Justice Statistics, National Prisoner Statistics Program and National Corrections Reporting Program, 2002 and 2012.

Source: Carson, E. A. (2014, September). Prisoners in 2013. p. 18, Table 7. Washington, DC: U.S. Department of Justice. Retrieved from http://www.bjs.gov/content/pub/pdf/p13.pdf

ship between gender and sentencing. They found that about half of the data sets showed that females were given more lenient treatment, one-quarter showed no effect, and one-quarter showed mixed effects. Data sets that included more controls for offense type, offense seriousness, and prior record tended to yield weaker sex effects, however, sex effects did remain. Overall, the differences were larger for the decision of whether to incarcerate, as opposed to length of incarceration.

Bontrager, Barrick, and Stupi (2013) performed a meta-analysis of 58 research studies published since 1991 that yielded 143 unique estimates of the effect of gender on sentencing. While some of the studies used data collected prior to 1980, most used data from the 1980s to 2006. The researchers found that overall 65 percent of the estimates showed that women were given more lenient treatment. Most studies showed that females are less likely to be incarcerated, are given shorter sentences, and receive more downward departures. The more recent studies (2000–2006), however, suggest more "equal treatment" of men and women when it comes to sentencing.

Interpreting Studies of Gender and Sentencing

Daly (1994) cautioned about the interpretation of studies that merely add gender to a model to ascertain whether females are treated differently than men in criminal case processing. She noted the inappropriateness of "add-women-and-stir" approaches that ignore important issues integral to understanding the gendered nature of crime and the system's response to female offenders. Even when studies control for legally relevant characteristics, such as offense seriousness, and assess whether females are given lighter sentences, differences in the nature of the lawbreaking (what caused them to offend, their role in the crime, etc.) may not be factored in to the conclusions.

The ignorance of differences between female and male criminality is also problematic when it comes to calls for "equal treatment." Sentencing reforms that call for sentencing uniformity would, on the surface, mean that the gender differences in sentencing for male and female offenders convicted of the same offense should decrease or disappear. While this may seem to be "fair," it ignores differences in the nature of offending among males and females.

Other Legally Irrelevant Characteristics

Age

Studies using data from Pennsylvania show some evidence that older offenders are more likely than younger offenders to receive downward sentencing departures (Johnson, 2003; Johnson, 2005; Kramer & Ulmer, 1996) and that older offenders are less likely to receive upward departures (Johnson, 2003). Much research has found that older offenders are slightly less likely to receive a prison sentence and/or that if they receive one they serve significantly shorter sentences (Johnson, 2006; Ulmer & Bradley, 2006; Ulmer & Johnson, 2004; Steffensmeier & Demuth, 2001). One study, however, found that age had a curvilinear relationship with sentence severity. Steffensmeier, Ulmer, and Kramer (1998) found that offenders under 21 and those over 50 received the least severe sentences. Those 21–29 received the harshest sentences and after age 30 sentencing severity decreased with age.

Mode of Conviction

Some argue that there is a penalty for going to trial and being convicted of an offense, as opposed to pleading guilty to the offense. This may stem from the perception that pleading guilty indicates acceptance of responsibility and/or remorse. Guilty pleas also enhance organizational efficiency.

Studies in Pennsylvania showed that those convicted by a jury trial were more likely to receive an incarceration sentence and/or receive a longer sentence, compared to those who plead guilty to an offense (Johnson, 2006; Steffensmeier & Demuth, 2001; Ulmer & Bradley, 2006; Ulmer & Johnson, 2004). Serious violent felons who plead guilty were more likely to receive a downward departure, compared to those who went to trial (Kramer & Ulmer, 2002). Offenders who were convicted by trial were less likely to receive a downward departure (Johnson, 2003; Kramer & Ulmer, 1996; Kramer & Ulmer, 2002) and more likely to receive an upward departure (Johnson, 2003).

Individual Level Interactions

Extant research on sentencing under Pennsylvania's guidelines uncovered multiple interaction effects.[5] Some of the most notable interactions involve those with race, gender, and age. Steffensmeier, Ulmer, and Kramer (1998) tested for direct and interaction effects of race, gender, and age in a sample of offenders sentenced in Pennsylvania between 1989 and 1992. The main effects of race, gender, and age were modest in comparison with the interaction effects. Young black males were sentenced more harshly than any other group. Subsequent research showed that young Hispanic males were less likely to receive downward departures (Kramer & Ulmer, 2002) and that young minority males who committed serious violent crimes faced harsher sentences compared to other race/gender/age combinations.

A rather consistent interaction between race and gender has been documented in the literature in recent years that shows that black females are afforded more lenient treatment at the sentencing stage compared to other race/gender combinations (Bloch, Engen, & Parrotta, 2014; Daly, 1987; Koons-Witt, 2002; Kramer & Ulmer, 2002; Kramer & Ulmer, 2009). Young black females were more likely to receive downward departures (Kramer & Ulmer, 2002). This may be due to a perception that black women are mothers who often take on the role of a single parent. Judges may spare black women prison sentences, which would leave their children without a parent.

Contextual Level Sources of Disparity

Pennsylvania's courts provide a good opportunity to investigate contextual effects because they are diverse with respect to size, dominant political affiliation, socio-cultural variables, and dominant crime issues (Kramer & Ulmer, 2002). One of the most comprehensive studies of contextual effects for cases sentenced under the 1997 Pennsylvania Sentencing Guidelines was Johnson's (2005) study on predictors of upward and downward departures. He included measures of county courtroom context (size of court, caseload pressure, violent caseload, trial rate, jail capacity, and county guideline departure rate) and county-level social context (percent black, percent Hispanic, percent unemployed, percent Republican, and percent of a crime-prone age—18–24).

Johnson's research showed several significant contextual effects, including the following: (1) there was significant variation in the rate of departure across courtroom social contexts, (2) being sentenced in a large court increased the odds of downward departure and decreased the odds of upward departure, (3) offenders were more likely to receive departures if they were sentenced in a county that had high departure rates, (4) individuals sentenced in courts with higher caseloads were more likely to receive downward departures, (5) individuals sentenced in courts with high trial rates were more likely to receive upward departures, regardless of whether their case went to trial, (6) offenders sentenced in counties with a larger population of Hispanics were less likely to receive a downward departure, and (7) the effects of individual level characteristics including whether one goes to trial, offense severity, prior record, type of offense, race, and age on likelihood of departure varies significantly by the county in which one's case was processed (showing evidence of an interaction effect). Johnson (2005) concluded that the social context of the court has direct effects on judicial departures and that social context also conditions the effects of several individual level variables on likelihood of departure.

Other studies of sentencing practices under the Pennsylvania Sentencing Guidelines have shown contextual variations across counties and courtrooms. One county level factor of interest is the **percent minority population** within a county. Being sentenced in a county with a larger minority populations did not increase the likelihood one will be sentenced to prison in one study (Ulmer & Johnson, 2004), however, those sentenced in counties with larger percentages of Hispanics received marginally longer sentences in another study (Ulmer & Johnson, 2004). In Mitchell's (2005) meta-analysis of 71 studies, none of the contextual measures of racial threat that he investigated (high proportion black, high black/white poverty ratio, or high crime) showed a clear or significant relationship to effect sizes, however.

County contextual factors, including **percentage urban residents** and **percent Republican**, have also been studied. Some studies have shown that those sentenced in **more urban counties** were more likely to receive a downward dispositional departure (Kramer & Ulmer, 1996), that serious violent offenders sentenced in large urban courts were more likely to receive a downward departure while those sentenced in small rural courts were less likely to receive downward departure (Kramer & Ulmer, 2002; Johnson, 2006), and that those sentenced in large and urban courts were less likely to be incarcerated and those who received incarceration got shorter sentences, compared to those sentenced in medium or small courts (Ulmer & Johnson, 2004).

Offenders sentenced in counties with a high percentage of Republicans were less likely to receive a dispositional departure (Kramer & Ulmer, 1996). Ulmer and Johnson (2004), however, found that political composition of the county was not a predictor of likelihood of incarceration or sentence length.

Those sentenced in courts with **high caseloads** were less likely to be incarcerated (Ulmer & Johnson, 2004; Ulmer & Bradley, 2006) and were sentenced to shorter prison sentences (Ulmer & Johnson, 2004). One notable interaction effect was that the trial penalty was greater for those who were sentenced in counties with heavier caseloads (Ulmer & Johnson, 2004). Those sentenced in courts with **more jail space** were more likely to be incarcerated (Ulmer & Johnson, 2004).

Johnson (2006) examined both county level and **judge characteristics** on individual variations in sentencing. After controlling for individual level sentencing factors, he found that minority judges were less punitive (Johnson, 2006). Judge's gender had minimal effect on sentencing outcome, yet older judges were less likely to sentence offenders to prison and to sentence them to shorter sentences (Johnson, 2006). Johnson's 2014 study showed that offenders sentenced by a minority judge were less likely to be incarcerated. That study also showed that in cases that went to trial, the odds of incarceration were significantly lower if the offender was sentenced by a female judge.

Takeaways from Research on the Impact of Legally Irrelevant Variables on Sentencing under Commission-Based Sentencing Guidelines

Legally relevant variables including offense seriousness and prior record are consistently the strongest predictors of sentence type, length, and whether and what kind of departure is given to the offender. A review of research examining extralegal characteristics on sentencing outcomes, however, suggests that sentencing disparity has lingered. This undermines the goal of sentencing uniformity espoused by sentencing commissions.

Kramer and Ulmer (2002) reflected on findings that some extralegal variables influenced departure decisions among serious violent offenders in Pennsylvania. They, however, offered an explanation that the departures may reflect judges taking into account characteristics of the offense that are not delineated within one offense category. While ten people might be facing sentencing for an aggravated assault that involves "serious bodily injury" the level of injury to the victim may differ in a way that the single category fails to delineate. One may involve stitches to the forehead, while another may involve a gaping wound in the victim's leg that would require surgery and extensive rehabilitation. They asserted:

> Departures reflect the use of discretion to "correct" guidelines. The "corrections" may indicate offense behavior that is less serious than reflected in the guidelines ranking, or factors not considered in the guidelines, but viewed as important to the court at sentencing. (p. 925)

The Honorable Judge Debra Pezze, of the Commonwealth of Pennsylvania, noted in an interview that follows the main text of the Chapter 10, "The guidelines are just that — guidelines. As such, they allow some individualization of sentencing, including sentencing departures, which are subject to appeal" (Pezze, D., 2014, December 22).

The Effects of Recent Supreme Court Decisions on Sentencing Disparity in the Federal Guidelines

Recent research on the Federal Sentencing Guidelines has focused on whether sentencing disparity and discrimination increased after the Supreme Court handed down decisions dictating how the Federal Sentencing Guidelines are to be applied. The Court's decision in *United States v. Booker* (543 U.S. 220 (2005)) directed a move from the *mandatory* application of federal guidelines in sentencing federal offenders to deeming the guidelines *advisory*. In *Rita v. United States* (551 U.S. 338 (2007)), the Supreme Court held that while the guidelines were no longer mandatory post-*Booker*, the guidelines should be the starting point in sentencing. In *Gall v. United States* (552 U.S. 38 (2007)) the Court indicated that the Supreme Court wanted less appellate review and that the appellate court was to review the substantive reasonableness of the sentence imposed under a "deferential abuse-of-discretion" standard.

The United States Sentencing Commission report entitled *Demographic Differences in Federal Sentencing Practices: An Update of the Booker Report's Multivariate Regression Analysis* (2010, March) concluded that after the *Booker*, *Rita*, and *Gall* decisions, sentencing disparity increased. A series of studies and essays in response to this report appeared in the journal *Criminology and Public Policy* in 2011. The contributors voiced differing opinions about the conclusions reached.

Paternoster (2011) agreed with the commission's conclusions and asserted:

> The problem, of course, is that sentences can become more uniform and consistent only at the expense of individual uniqueness and that sentences can be tailored to an individual's unique culpability only by reducing consistency. (p. 1065)

Others, however, disagreed with the conclusion that disparities increased post-*Booker*. Using different methodology than the USSC, Ulmer, Light, and Kramer (2011) analyzed federal sentencing data during four time periods between 2000 and 2009. Among their conclusions was that disparities in gender, race, and ethnicity in decisions about *sentence length* were similar to pre-2003 levels. Albonetti (2011) suggested that one reason disparities in sentencing linked with race and gender might not have increased substantially in all sentencing decisions was that many judges presiding in lower federal courts had always used the guidelines (and never sentenced cases before the guidelines were implemented), and continued to rely on them greatly in sentencing decisions, regardless of the *Booker*, *Gall*, and *Rita* decisions. Others attributed the differences in the results to different methodologies (Spohn, 2011; Engen, 2011).

Have Mandatory Minimum Sentencing and Three Strikes Laws Increased Sentencing Uniformity and Decreased Disparity and Discrimination?

One of the most prominent claims made by advocates of mandatory minimum sentencing and three strikes laws is that they greatly increase sentencing uniformity. Ideally these laws punish all offenders convicted of crimes that trigger the prescribed penalty the same. But do mandatory minimum sentencing laws and three strikes laws impact all offenders in a comparable way? Or do we see race and/or sex differences in the application of these laws?

Race/Ethnicity and California's Three Strikes Law

Figure 9.7 is a bar chart compiled from recent figures showing the percent breakdown by race/ethnicity for four groups: (1) the population of California, (2) the population of felony arrestees in California, (3) the population of California felons sentenced to prison, and (4) the population of those sentenced to 25-years-to-life under California's three strikes law. The largest percentage of California's population (45 percent) is white. The second largest group (33 percent) is Hispanic. Only 6 percent of California's population is black.

When one looks at the percentages of blacks and Hispanics in the other categories, we see disproportionate representation. Hispanics comprise 39 percent of those arrested for felonies and are slightly overrepresented in comparison to the percentage of Hispanics in the general population. Blacks comprise 20 percent of all felony arrestees, which exceeds their representation in the general population by over three times.

When looking at the population sentenced to prison, we see more evidence of disproportionate representation of blacks and Hispanics. Blacks comprise 26 percent and Hispanics 42 percent of those sentenced to prison. This contrasts whites, who comprise only 28 percent of those sentenced to prison.

The race/ethnicity disparity in the breakdown of those sentenced under California's three strikes law is the most marked. Blacks comprise 45 percent of those sentenced under the three strikes law. While blacks are a racial minority in the state of California, they comprise the largest proportion of three strikers.

These figures are descriptive statistics and do not control for the nature of the felonies committed, the strength of the evidence in the case, or information about prior record. Regardless, this comparison casts doubt on the presumption that three strikes laws impact persons of various races and ethnicities similarly.

Disparities in the Application of Federal Mandatory Minimum Sentencing Laws

In 2011, the USSC released a report examining federal cases from fiscal year 2010, entitled *Report to Congress: Mandatory Minimum Penalties in the Federal Criminal Justice System*. This report analyzed data from over 73,000 cases.

In this report, the USSC stated:

> An offender was considered to have been convicted of an offense carrying a mandatory minimum penalty if any statute of conviction in the case contained a provision requiring imposition of a minimum term of imprisonment. This determination was made regardless of whether the offender was ultimately sentenced without regard to the mandatory minimum penalty through operation of the statutory safety valve provision or through a substantial assistance motion made by the government. (p. 120)

In fiscal year 2010, 27.2 percent of the cases involved a conviction of an offense carrying a mandatory minimum penalty. Over three-fourths of the defendants who were

Figure 9.7 Percent Breakdowns in California by Race/Ethnicity

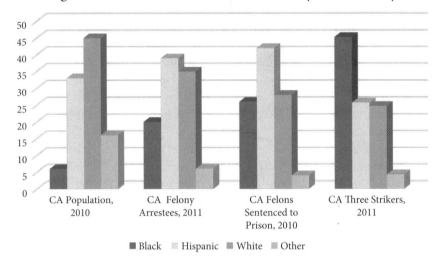

Data compiled for CA Population, 2010, and CA Felons Sentenced to Prison, 2011, from Taylor, M. (Legislative Analyst) (2013 January). *California's criminal justice system: A primer.* p. 39, "Demographics on adults sentenced on felony charges, 2010." Retrieved from http://www.cdcr.ca.gov/Reports /docs/External-Reports/criminal-justice-primer-011713.pdf

Data compiled for CA Felony Arrestees, 2011, from Taylor, M. (Legislative Analyst) (2013 January). *California's criminal justice system: A primer.* p. 23, "Adults and juveniles arrested on felonies, 2011." Retrieved from http://www.cdcr.ca.gov/Reports/docs/External-Reports/criminal-justice-primer-011713.pdf

Data compiled for CA Three Strikers, 2011, from State of California Department of Corrections and Rehabilitation. *Second and third striker felons in the adult institutional population, September 30, 2011.* Table 5, "Third strikers in the adult institutional population by gender, county of commitment, and racial/ethnic group as of March 31, 2011." Retrieved from http://www.cdcr.ca.gov/reports_research /offender_information_services_branch/quarterly/strike1/strike1d1109.pdf

convicted of an offense carrying a mandatory minimum penalty had been convicted of a drug trafficking offense and about twelve percent had been convicted of a firearms offense. Other statutes that carried mandatory minimum sentencing provisions involved child pornography, aggravated identity theft, and violent offenses.

Rates of relief from the mandatory minimum penalty vary by offense type. Over fifty-four percent of drug offenders received relief, compared to 4.2 percent of sex offenders, and 15.4 percent of identity theft offenders convicted of an offense carrying a mandatory minimum (United States Sentencing Commission, 2011, p. 132).

Offenders could be relieved from the application of such a penalty due to substantial assistance or the safety valve. As discussed in Chapter 5, substantial assistance means that the defendant provided information in the investigation or prosecution of another person who has committed an offense. The safety valve allows sentences below the mandatory minimum in drug trafficking cases with certain factors.

Table 9.2 Demographic Characteristics of Federal Offenders, Fiscal Year 2010

	All Offenders	Convicted of a Statute Carrying a Mandatory Minimum Penalty	Relieved of Application of Mandatory Minimum Penalty	Subject to a Mandatory Minimum Penalty at Sentencing
Total (# of offenders)	73,239	19,896	9,291	10,605
Race of Offender (Percent)				
White	27.4	27.4	27.3	27.5
Black	20.7	31.5	23.6	38.5
Hispanic	48.3	38.3	45.7	31.8
Other	3.6	2.7	3.4	2.1
Citizenship of Offender (Percent)				
United States Citizen	55.9	73.6	63.5	82.5
Non-Citizen	44.1	26.4	36.5	17.5
Gender of Offender (Percent)				
Male	87.9	90.3	86.4	93.8
Female	12.1	9.7	13.6	6.2

Source: United States Sentencing Commission. (2011). *Report to Congress: Mandatory minimum penalties in the federal criminal justice system.* p. 124, Table 7-1. Washington, DC: United States Sentencing Commission. Retrieved from http://www.ussc.gov/sites/default/files/pdf/news/congressional-testimony-and -reports/mandatory-minimum-penalties/20111031-rtc-pdf/Chapter_07.pdf

Table 9.2 presents the background characteristics of 73,239 federal offenders in FY 2010. It shows that 19,896 offenders were convicted of a statute that carried a mandatory minimum penalty. Of these, about 47 percent (9,291) were relieved of the application of the mandatory minimum penalty, while 53 percent (10,605) were subject to a mandatory minimum penalty at sentencing (United States Sentencing Commission, 2011, p. 124).

Hispanic offenders comprised the largest proportion of the federal offender population (48.3 percent) and the largest proportion of those convicted of a statute carrying a mandatory minimum penalty (38.3 percent). White offenders were the second largest group in the federal offender population (27.4 percent) while blacks were the third largest group (20.7 percent). However, blacks comprised the second largest group of those convicted of a statute carrying a mandatory minimum penalty (31.5 percent), while whites made up 27.4 percent of those convicted of a statute carrying a mandatory minimum penalty.

When examining who was relieved of the application of the mandatory minimum penalty, one sees that Hispanic offenders comprised the highest percentage (45.7 percent), followed by whites (27.3 percent), and blacks (23.6 percent). The commission explained that this was due to the large number of Hispanic offenders who are relieved through a safety valve.

The last column shows that blacks comprise the largest percentage of those subject to a mandatory minimum penalty at sentencing (38.5 percent), followed by Hispanics (31.8 percent) and whites (27.5 percent). While Hispanic offenders comprised the largest percentage of offenders convicted of an offense carrying a mandatory minimum penalty, black offenders comprise the largest percentage of offenders who are ultimately subjected to a mandatory minimum penalty at sentencing.

In terms of gender, we see that while males constitute 87.9 percent of all federal offenders, they represent 93.8 percent of those who are subject to a mandatory minimum penalty at sentencing. Females comprise 12.1 percent of federal offenders, but only 6.2 percent of those who are ultimately subject to a mandatory minimum penalty at sentencing.

While these figures suggest disparities based on race/ethnicity and gender, bear in mind that these are bivariate statistics that do not take into account the type of offense committed. The commission noted that black offenders who commit drug offenses often have an extensive criminal history or involvement of a dangerous weapon — characteristics that disqualify an offender from the safety valve.

Table 9.3 Average Sentence of Federal Offenders by Demographic Characteristics of Offenders, Fiscal Year 2010

	All Offenders	Convicted of a Statute Carrying a Mandatory Minimum Penalty	Relieved of Application of Mandatory Minimum Penalty	Subject to a Mandatory Minimum Penalty at Sentencing
Total (# of offenders)	73,239	19,896	9,291	10,605
Race of Offender (Months)				
White	49	102	57	141
Black	76	127	81	152
Hispanic	35	87	59	123
Other	45	93	56	147
Citizenship of Offender (Months)				
United States Citizen	62	112	68	143
Non-Citizen	30	80	56	125
Gender of Offender (Months)				
Male	51	108	66	142
Female	25	62	45	94

Source: United States Sentencing Commission. (2011). *Report to Congress: Mandatory minimum penalties in the federal criminal justice system.* p. 139, Table 7-3. Washington, DC: United States Sentencing Commission. Retrieved from http://www.ussc.gov/sites/default/files/pdf/news/congressional-testimony-and-reports/mandatory-minimum-penalties/20111031-rtc-pdf/Chapter_07.pdf

Table 9.3 shows the average sentences of federal offenses broken down by offender characteristics. For each category, black offenders serve a longer sentence. For those subject to a mandatory minimum penalty at sentencing, blacks serve an average sentence of 152 months, compared to 141 months for whites, 123 months for Hispanics, and 147 months for those of other races/ethnicities.

Gender is also associated with sentence length. For each category, males serve longer sentences that females. For those subject to a mandatory minimum penalty at sentencing, males serve an average of 142 months in prison, compared to 94 months for females.

A comparison of the number of males of various races/ethnicities imprisoned over time is informative. The USSC (2011, October) examined the numbers of males by race/ethnicity in federal prisons from 1995 to 2010 and reported that "In each year the number of black male offenders has exceeded the number of any other race/ethnicity in prison. The number of black male offenders in the prison population has grown steadily since fiscal year 1995" (p. 141).

Summary

This chapter has discussed how social scientists go about assessing whether sentencing reforms have met their stated goals. Social scientists can gain some understanding of the impacts of reforms through descriptive, explanatory, evaluation, and exploratory research. Bivariate analyses show the relationship between an independent and dependent variable (such as race and sentence length) *without controlling for the effects of other variables* on the dependent variable. Multivariate analyses indicate the relationship between an independent and dependent variable, while *controlling for the effects of other variables* on the dependent variable. A research may want to know, for example, what effect race has on sentence length controlling for the effect of socioeconomic status on sentence length. A consideration of direct, indirect, and interaction effects was presented. The difference between individual level and contextual level variables was also presented.

Researchers have found some evidence that approaches to curtailing judicial discretion have led to increased prosecutorial discretion, i.e., "the hydraulic effect," especially with more restrictive reforms. This undermines the notion of equal treatment throughout criminal case processing.

Legally relevant variables including offense seriousness and prior record are consistently the strongest predictors of sentence type, length, and whether and what kind of departure is given to the offender. Legally irrelevant variables, however, still affect sentencing outcomes, which suggests that sentencing disparity has lingered. Research from state and federal jurisdictions shows that commission-based guidelines have decreased sentencing disparities to some extent. However, legally irrelevant variables, including both individual level (including race and gender) and contextual level variables (including county and court characteristics) still affect sentencing outcomes. In addition, there is evidence of interaction effects pursuant to guidelines, most notably those involving race and gender. This undermines the goal of sentencing uniformity espoused by sentencing commissions.

A review of mandatory minimum sentencing laws show that these laws are disproportionately applied to racial minorities. The imposition of three strikes laws in California shows that blacks are a racial minority in the state, yet make up the largest proportion of prisoners and offenders sentenced under three strikes laws.

The results of quantitative analyses raise the question of whether sentencing reforms have been completely successful in achieving what proponents have advocated—fairer and more uniform sentences that decrease sentencing disparity and discrimination.

Discussion Questions

1. In assessing whether sentencing reforms have decreased unwarranted sentencing disparity and discrimination, why is it important to look at decisions made by criminal justice actors earlier in case processing?
2. Why has the prosecutor been deemed the "gatekeeper" of cases processed through the criminal justice system?
3. Which type of sentencing reform do you believe has been most effective in decreasing sentencing discrimination **based on race**—commission-based guidelines, mandatory minimums, or three strikes laws? Explain your answer.
4. Which type of sentencing reform do you believe has been most effective in decreasing sentencing discrimination **based on gender**—commission-based guidelines, mandatory minimums, or three strikes laws? Explain your answer.
5. Do you think that sentencing disparity will increase in the federal system post-*Booker*? Why (or why not)?

Notes

1. The terms "extralegal" and "legally irrelevant" will be used synonymously in this chapter.

2. There have been seven editions (and revisions for various editions) of the Pennsylvania Sentencing Guidelines. The grading of offenses and possible minimum sentences have changed, somewhat, over the years. What has stayed constant, however, is the possibility of adding or subtracting to the minimum for the most serious offenses of up to twelve months for aggravating and mitigating factors. Smaller additions and subtractions are also allowed for less serious offenses, based on aggravating and mitigating circumstances.

3. Some scholars would argue that this finding is not surprising in models of sentencing departures. Legal variables, such as offense severity, prior record, and guidelines presumptive sentence, are consistently significant predictors of *whether one receives a prison term* and *sentence length*. Engen and Gainey (2000) contend, however, that for models of *departure decisions*, when presumptive sentence terms are included in the model, legal variables may affect departure decisions in unpredictable ways and that effects of extralegal variables, such as race, ethnicity, and mode of conviction, on departure decisions may be greater.

4. Some would argue, however, that the conditions in women's reformatories were horrific and quite punitive. Rehabilitation involved teaching women how to be "proper" ladies and conforming to traditional gender roles through instruction of how to cook, clean, and mend.

5. It is beyond the scope of this text to discuss all interaction effects discovered by researchers regarding sentencing decisions.

References

Albonetti, C. A. (1997). Sentencing under the federal sentencing guidelines: Effects of defendant characteristics, guilty pleas, and departures on sentence outcomes for drug offense, 1992–1992. *Law & Society Review, 31*(4), 789–822.

Albonetti, C. A. (2011). Judicial discretion in federal sentencing: An intersection of policy priorities and law. *Criminology and Public Policy, (10)*4, 1151–1155.

Alschuler, A. W. (1978). Sentencing reform and prosecutorial power: A critique of recent proposals for "fixed" and "presumptive" sentencing. *University of Pennsylvania Law Review, 126,* 550–577.

Bloch, K. R., Engen, R. L., & Parrotta, K. L. (2014). The intersection of race and gender: An examination of sentencing outcomes in North Carolina. *Criminal Justice Studies, 27*(4), 419–438.

Blumstein, A., Cohen, J., Martin, S. E., & Tonry, M. H. (1983). *Research on sentencing: The search for reform* (Vol. 1). Washington, DC: National Academy Press.

Bontrager, S., Barrick, K., & Stupi, E. (2013). Gender and sentencing: A meta-analysis of contemporary research. *The Journal of Gender, Race, & Justice, 16,* 349–372.

Bushway, S. D., & Piehl, A. M. (2007). Social science research and the legal threat to presumptive sentencing guidelines. *Criminology and Public Policy, 6*(3), 461–482.

Cano, M. V., & Spohn, C. (2012). Circumventing the penalty for offenders facing mandatory minimums: Revisiting the dynamics of "sympathetic" and "salvageable" offenders. *Criminal Justice and Behavior, 39*(3), 308–332.

Carson, E. A. (2014, September). *Prisoners in 2013.* Washington, DC: U.S. Department of Justice. Retrieved from http://www.bjs.gov/content/pub/pdf/p13.pdf.

Chambliss, D. F., & Schutt, R. K. (2016). *Making sense of the social world: Methods of investigation.* Thousand Oaks, CA: SAGE.

Chesney-Lind, M. (2006). Patriarchy, crime, and justice: Feminist criminology in an era of backlash. *Feminist Criminology, 1,* 6–26.

Daily, D. L. (1998). Minnesota sentencing guidelines: A structure for change. *Law & Policy, 20*(3), 311–332.

Daly, K. (1987). Discrimination in the criminal courts: Family, gender, and the problem of equal treatment. *Social Forces, 66,* 152–175.

Daly, K. (1994). *Gender, crime, and punishment.* New Haven, CN: Yale University Press.

Daly, K., & Bordt, R. L. (1995). Sex effects and sentencing: An analysis of the statistical literature. *Justice Quarterly, 12*(1), 141–175.

Daly, K., & Tonry, M. (1997). Gender, race, and sentencing. In M. Tonry (Ed.), *Crime and Justice* (Vol. 22, pp. 201–252). Chicago: University of Chicago Press.

Davis, K. C. (1969). *Discretionary justice.* Cincinnati: Anderson Publishing.

Doerner, J. K. (2012). Gender disparities in sentencing departures: An examination of U.S. federal courts. *Women & Criminal Justice, 176*(22), 176–205.

Doerner, J. K., & Demuth, S. (2014). Gender and sentencing in the federal courts: Are women treated more leniently? *Criminal Justice Policy Review, 25*(2), 242–269.

Eisenstein, J., & Jacob, H. (1977). *Felony justice: An organizational analysis of criminal courts.* Boston, MA: Little, Brown, and Company.

Engen, R. (2011). Racial disparity in the wake of *Booker/Fanfan*: Making sense of "messy" results and other challenges for sentencing research. *Criminology and Public Policy*, *10*(4), 1139–1148.

Engen, R. L., & Gainey, R. R. (2000). Modeling the effects of legally relevant and extra-legal factors under sentencing guidelines: The rules have changed. *Criminology*, *38*(4), 1207–1229.

Farley, R., Steeh, C., Krysan, M., Jackson, T., & Reeves, K. (1994). Stereotypes and segregation: Neighborhoods in the Detroit area. *American Journal of Sociology*, *100*(3), 750–780.

Farrell, A. (2004). Measuring judicial and prosecutorial discretion: Sex and race disparities in departures from the federal sentencing guidelines. *Justice System Journal*, *6*(2), 45–78.

Fazel, S., & Danesh, J. (2002). Serious mental disorder in 23000 prisoners: A systematic review of 62 surveys. *Lancet*, *359* (9306), 545–550.

Feldmeyer, B., Warren, P. Y., Siennick, S. E., & Neptune, M. (2015). Racial, ethnic, and immigrant threat: Is there a new criminal threat on state sentencing? *Journal of Research in Crime and Delinquency*, *52*(1), 62–92.

Franklin, T. W. (2015). Race and ethnicity effects in federal sentencing: A propensity score analysis. *Justice Quarterly*, *32*(4), 653–679.

Frase, R. S. (1992–1993). Implementing commission-based sentencing guidelines: The lessons of the first ten years in Minnesota. *Cornell Journal of Law and Public Policy*, *2*, 279–337.

Gall v. United States, 552 U.S. 28 (2007).

Gibbs, J. T. (1988). *Young, black, and male in America*. New York: Auburn House.

Greenblatt, N. (2008). How mandatory are mandatory minimums? How judges can avoid imposing mandatory minimum sentences. *American Journal of Criminal Law*, *36*, 1–38.

Hagan, J., & Bumiller, K. (1983). Making sense of sentencing: A review and critique of sentencing research. In A. Blumstein, J. Cohen, S. E. Martin, & M. H. Tonry (Eds.), *Research on sentencing: The search for reform* (pp. 1–54). Washington, DC: National Academy Press.

Johnson, B. D. (2003). Racial and ethnic disparities in sentencing departures across modes of conviction. *Criminology*, *41*(2), 449–489.

Johnson, B. D. (2005). Contextual disparities in guidelines departures: Courtroom social contexts, guidelines compliance, and extralegal disparities in criminal sentencing. *Criminology*, *43*(3), 761–796.

Johnson, B. D. (2006). The multilevel context of criminal sentencing: Integrating judge- and county-level influences. *Criminology*, *44*(2), 259–298.

Johnson, B. D. (2014). Judges on trial: A reexamination of judicial race and gender effects across modes of conviction. *Criminal Justice Policy Review*, *25*(2), 159–184.

Johnson, B. D., & Betsinger, S. (2009). Punishing the "model minority": Asian American criminal sentencing outcomes in federal district courts. *Criminology*, *47*(4), 1045–1090.

Johnson, B. D., Ulmer, J. T., & Kramer, J. H. (2008). The social context of guidelines circumvention: The case of federal district courts. *Criminology*, *46*(3), 737–783.

Jordan, K. L., & Freiburger, T. L. (2015). The effect of race/ethnicity on sentencing: Examining sentence type, jail length, and prison length. *Journal of Ethnicity in Criminal Justice, 13*, 179–196.

Koons-Witt, B. A. (2002). Gender and justice: The effect of gender and gender-related factors on the decisions to incarcerate before and after sentencing guidelines. *Criminology, 40*, 297–328.

Kramer, J. H., & Ulmer, J. T. (1996). Sentencing disparity and departures from the guidelines. *Justice Quarterly, 13*, 81–106.

Kramer, J. H., & Ulmer, J. T. (2002). Downward departures for serious violent offenders: Local court "corrections" to Pennsylvania's sentencing guidelines. *Criminology, 40*(4), 897–932.

Kramer, J. H., & Ulmer, J. T. (2009). *Sentencing guidelines: Lessons from Pennsylvania*. Boulder, CO: Lynne Rienner Publishers.

Kruttschnitt, C. (1984). Sex and criminal court dispositions: The unresolved controversy. *Research in Crime and Delinquency, 21*(3), 213–232.

Massey, D. (1993). *American apartheid: Segregation and the making of the underclass*. Cambridge, MA: Harvard University Press.

McCoy, C. (1984). Determinate sentencing, plea bargaining bans, and hydraulic discretion in California. *The Justice System Journal, 9*, 256–275.

Merritt, N., Fain, T., & Turner, S. (2006). Oregon's get tough sentencing reform: A lesson in justice system adaptation. *Criminology and Public Policy, 5*(1), 5–36.

Miethe, T. D. (1987). Charging and plea bargaining practices under determinate sentencing: An investigation of the hydraulic displacement of discretion. *Journal of Criminal Law & Criminology, 78*, 155–176.

Miethe, T. D., & Moore, C. A. (1985). Socioeconomic disparities under determinate sentencing systems: A comparison of preguideline and postguideline practices in Minnesota. *Criminology, 23*(2), 337–363.

Minnesota Sentencing Guidelines Commission. (1982). *Preliminary report on the development and impact of the Minnesota Sentencing Guidelines*. St. Paul, MN: Minnesota Sentencing Guidelines Commission.

Minnesota Sentencing Guidelines Commission. (2014, November). *2013 Sentencing practices: Annual summary statistics for felony offenders*. St. Paul, MN: Minnesota Sentencing Guidelines Commission. Retrieved from http://mn.gov/sentencing -guidelines/assets/2013%20Data%20Report%20Updated_tcm30-31259.pdf

Mitchell, O. (2005). A meta-analysis of race and sentencing research: Explaining the inconsistencies. *Journal of Quantitative Criminology, 21*(4), 439–466.

Moore, C. A., & Miethe, T. D. (1986). Regulated and unregulated sentencing decisions: An analysis of first-year practices under Minnesota's felony sentencing guidelines. *Law & Society Review, 20*(2), 253–277.

Mustard, D. (2001). Racial, ethnic and gender disparities in sentencing: Evidence from the U.S. federal courts. *Journal of Law and Economics, 44*, 285–314.

Nagel, I. H. (1990). Structuring sentencing discretion: The new federal sentencing guidelines. *The Journal of Criminal Law & Criminology, 80*, 883–943.

Nagel, I. H., & Johnson, B. L. (1994). The role of gender in a structured sentencing system: Equal treatment, policy choices, and the sentencing of female offenders under the United States sentencing guidelines. *The Journal of Criminal Law & Criminology,* *85*(1), 181–221.

Nagel, I. H., & Schulhofer, S. J. (1992). A tale of three cities: An empirical study of charging and bargaining practices under the federal sentencing guidelines. *Southern California Law Review, 66,* 501–566.

National Institute of Law Enforcement and Criminal Justice. (1978). *The nation's toughest drug law: Evaluating the New York Experience.* Retrieved from https://www.ncjrs.gov/pdffiles1/Digitization/47795NCJRS.pdf

Paternoster, R. (2011). Racial disparity under the federal sentencing guidelines pre- and post-*Booker*: Lessons not learned from research on the death penalty. *Criminology and Public Policy, 10*(4), 1063–1072.

Pezze, D. (2014, December 22). *Interview with the Honorable Judge Debra Pezze, Pennsylvania Court of Common Pleas, Westmoreland County* (personal communication).

Piehl, A. M., & Bushway, S. D. (2007). Measuring and explaining charge bargaining. *Journal of Quantitative Criminology, 23,* 105–125.

Reitz, K. (1998). Modeling discretion in American sentencing: Some measurement issues with application to preguideline sentencing disparity. *Journal of Criminal Law and Criminology, 25,* 489–500.

Rita v. United States, 551 U. S. 338 (2007).

Savelsberg, J. J. (1992). Law that does not fit society: Sentencing guidelines as a neoclassical reaction to the dilemmas of substantive law. *American Journal of Sociology, 97*(5), 1346–1381.

Schulhofer, S. J., & Nagel, I. H. (1997). Plea negotiations under the Federal Sentencing Guidelines: Guideline circumvention and its dynamics in the post-*Mistretta* period. *Northwestern University Law Review, 91*(4), 1284-1316.

Sellin, T. (1928). The negro criminal: A statistical note. *The Annals of the American Academy of Political and Social Science, 140*(1), 52–64.

Spohn, C. (2011). Unwarranted disparity in the wake of the *Booker/Fanfan* decision: Implications for research and policy. *Criminology and Public Policy, 10*(4), 1119–1127.

Starr, S. B. (2014). Estimating gender disparities in federal criminal cases. *American Law and Economics Review, 17*(1), 127–159.

Steffensmeier, D., & Demuth, S. (2001). Ethnicity and judges' sentencing decisions: Hispanic-black-white comparisons. *Criminology, 39*(1), 145–178.

Steffensmeier, D., Kramer, J. H., & Streifel, C. (1993). Gender and imprisonment decisions. *Criminology, 31,* 411–446.

Steffensmeier, D., Ulmer, J., & Kramer, J. (1998). The intersection of race, gender, and age in criminal sentencing: The punishment cost of being young, black, and male. *Criminology, 36*(4), 763–798.

Tonry, M. (1996). *Sentencing matters.* New York: Oxford University Press.

Tonry, M. (2006). Criminology, mandatory minimums, and public policy. *Criminology & Public Policy, 5*(1), 45–56.

Tonry, M. (2014). Remodeling American sentencing: A ten-step blueprint for moving past mass incarceration. *Criminology and Public Policy, 13*(4), 503–533.

Ulmer, J. T. (2012). Recent developments and new directions in sentencing research. *Justice Quarterly, 29*(1), 1–40.

Ulmer, J. T., & Bradley, M. S. (2006). Variation in trial penalties among serious violent offenses. *Criminology*, *44*(3), 631–670.

Ulmer, J. T., & Johnson, B. (2004). Sentencing in context: A multilevel analysis. *Criminology*, *42*(1), 137–177.

Ulmer, J. T., & Kramer, J. H. (1996). Court communities under sentencing guidelines: Dilemmas of formal rationality and sentencing disparity. *Criminology*, *34*(3), 383–408.

Ulmer, J. T., Light, M. T., & Kramer, J. H. (2011). Racial disparity in the wake of the Booker/Fanfan decision. *Criminology & Public Policy*, *10*(4), 1077–1118.

United States Sentencing Commission. (2010, March). *Demographic differences in federal sentencing practices: An update of the Booker Report's Multivariate Regression Analysis.* Washington, DC: United States Sentencing Commission.

United States Sentencing Commission. (2011). *Report to Congress: Mandatory minimum penalties in the federal criminal justice system.* Washington, DC: United States Sentencing Commission. Retrieved from http://www.ussc.gov/sites/default/files/pdf/news /congressional-testimony-and-reports/mandatory-minimum-penalties/20111031 -rtc-pdf/Chapter_07.pdf

United States v. Booker, 543 U.S. 220 (2005).

Vance, S. E., & Oleson, J. C. (2014). Displaced discretion: The effects of sentencing guidelines on prosecutors' charge bargaining in the District of Columbia Superior Court. *Criminal Justice Policy Review*, *25*(3), 347–377.

Woolredge, J., & Griffen, T. (2005). Displaced discretion under Ohio sentencing guidelines. *Journal of Criminal Justice*, *33*(4), 301–316. doi:10.1016/j.jcrimjus.2005.04.001

10

THE IMPACT OF SENTENCING REFORMS ON CRIME, THE OFFENDER, AND SOCIETY

Chapter Objectives:

- To assess the impact that mandatory minimum and three strikes laws have had on crime rates.
- To gauge how increased incarceration has prevented crime through deterrence.
- To evaluate how increased incarceration has prevented crime through incapacitation.
- To be mindful of the social costs of mandatory minimums and three strikes laws.
- To consider the impact of three strikes laws on women.
- To understand offenders' perceptions of sentencing strategies and sanctions.
- To understand the views of criminal justice actors in Pennsylvania concerning the processing of offenders under Pennsylvania's sentencing guidelines.

Have Mandatory Minimums and Three Strikes Laws Led to a Reduction in Crime?

A major claim made by politicians who have promoted mandatory minimum sentencing and three strikes laws was that they would act as effective deterrents to crime. People would "think twice" about committing a crime if they perceived that a certain and severe penalty would follow the commission of an act sanctioned by a mandatory minimum penalty. Or so the politicians wanted the general public to believe. Let's look to the findings of social science research to assess whether mandatory minimums and three strikes laws have led to a reduction in crime.

Evaluation of the Rockefeller Drug Laws

As discussed in Chapter 6, the Rockefeller Drug Laws enacted severe mandatory minimum penalties for drug offenders. The National Institute of Law Enforcement and Criminal Justice (1978) performed an early evaluation of the effects of the Rockefeller Drug Laws. It sought to assess (1) whether drug users would be dissuaded from using drugs and if drug dealers would be deterred from selling drugs and (2) whether crimes associated with drug addiction, such as robberies, burglaries, and thefts, would decrease after the law was enacted. Their research showed no appreciable or long term effect of the Rockefeller Drug Laws on drug availability and use, sale of illegal drugs, or reduction of crime.

Exactly how the Rockefeller Drug Laws have impacted violent crime is not clear to this day. After the Rockefeller Drug Laws went into effect in 1973, the violent crime rate in the state of New York has fluctuated. It was 741.7 per 100,000 population in 1973. It rose overall throughout the 1980s, peaking at 1,180.9 per 100,000 in 1990. It declined throughout the 1990s and 2000s. By 2013 it had fallen to 389.8 per 100,000 (Federal Bureau of Investigation, Crime Statistics). Remember from Chapter 6 that revisions to the Rockefeller Drug Laws made them *less* stringent over time.

Evaluation of Bartley-Fox

The Bartley-Fox Amendment, adopted in Massachusetts in June 1974, required a mandatory one-year prison term for offenders who were convicted of the unlicensed carrying of a firearm. A short term study of how the Bartley-Fox law affected the workings of the criminal justice system was initiated by the Harvard Center for Criminal Law shortly after the law's passage (Beha, 1977a). Beha (1977b) examined the impact of Bartley-Fox on the possession and carrying of firearms and on crimes committed with firearms. He concluded that the law and the publicity campaign before the law went into in effect resulted in an increase in the compliance of the general public with requirements related to both licensing and firearms identification (FID) card acquisition.

Another goal of the Bartley-Fox law involved reducing violent crimes committed with firearms. Beha's short term study used monthly data from the Boston Police Department from 1972 through the first quarter of 1977 on reported robberies, assaults, and homicides. The results showed that the law had no effect on the level of firearm use in robberies. The use of firearms in assaults declined, but overall assaults did not decline. Beha interpreted this finding as a result of there being fewer "casual carriers" after the law was enacted. Because, unlike robberies, assaults are rarely premeditated, the law may have prevented the use of a gun in situations in which a conflict arose. Firearm homicides also decreased after Bartley-Fox.

Another study published by Pierce and Bowers (1981) investigated the short term effects of the Bartley-Fox law on gun-related assaults, robberies, and homicides. They looked at crimes committed between 1974 and 1976. They found that the Bartley-Fox law decreased the number of gun assaults in Boston and other areas in Massachusetts. During the time assaults committed with guns declined, however, assaults perpetrated without guns increased, which they termed the "displacement effect." According to Pierce and Bowers (1981), ". . . the weapon substitution effect of Bartley-Fox was larger than the deterrent effect—that is, the increase in non-gun assaults more than compensated for the reduction in gun assaults" (p. 129). Pierce and Bowers found that Bartley-Fox reduced gun robberies in Boston. Non-gun robberies increased during the same time frame, however. For homicides, the researchers concluded that the law resulted in a short term reduction in gun-related criminal homicides. There was no evidence that this reduction was accompanied by an increase in non-gun related homicides. Pierce and Bowers

(1981) concluded that the reduction of gun use in the perpetration of the three violent crimes was largely due to the publicity of the Bartley-Fox gun amendment.

Evaluation of Michigan Felony Firearms Statute

The Michigan Felony Firearm Statute mandated a two-year add-on prison sentence to the base sentence of a felony if that felony was committed with a firearm (as opposed to another weapon, such as a knife, club, etc.). It went into effect January 1, 1977.

To ascertain the deterrent impact of the gun law on serious violent crimes, Loftin and McDowall (1981) examined patterns of gun crimes and crimes committed without the use of firearms before and after the law went into effect. Soon after the gun law was passed, violent crime rates went down and many attributed the decrease in crime to the new law. Time series analysis showed several findings to challenge this conclusion, however. The researchers noted that declines in homicide, robberies, and aggravated assaults began five months before the enactment of the Michigan Felony Firearm Law and four months before the publicity campaign began in December 1976. Second, homicide was the only crime for which the change was greater for gun offenses, compared to non-gun offenses, however, Loftin and McDowall's examination of homicide patterns did not attribute this decline to the new gun law. For armed robberies, both gun and non-gun robberies declined in 1977. The levels of gun and non-gun assaults remained essentially stable after the gun law was enacted, although there was a small increase in non-gun assaults.

Loftin and McDowall concluded that

> . . . although the gun law had selective effects on the sanctions delivered by the Recorder's Court, the crime patterns best fit a model in which there were no reductions in serious violent offenses, such as murder, robbery, or assault, which could be attributable to the gun law. (p. 152)

Loftin and McDowall postulated that the potential sanction of a two-year add-on sentence might be too light to serve as a deterrent. They noted that although politically popular, this mandatory sentencing enhancement did not serve as an effective deterrent to the commission of gun crimes. The law served as a potential "easy fix" for gun-related violence. They suggested that effective strategies for decreasing gun violence are likely more complicated.

Three Strikes Laws and Crime

What impact have three strikes laws had on crime? Remember politicians promoting these laws emphasized that their passage would make citizens safer as serious, repeat, and violent offenders would be off the street.

Some anecdotal evidence has suggested that criminals altered their behavior when they became aware of the three strikes penalty in Washington State. A police detective reported that several sex offenders left the state between the time the law first made ballot to the day it was passed by voters. Persons working in Washington's criminal justice system reported that the law influenced offenders to think twice about continuing on in crime. One report suggested that an offender who had committed robberies changed to writing bad checks because he had accrued two strikes and forgery would not be considered a strike (LaCourse, 1997).

Of course, we also must look to empirical research to help answer the question of how three strikes laws have (or haven't) impacted crime rates. Tonry (2009) summarized the findings of 15 empirical studies that evaluated whether California's three strikes laws prevented crime. Each was performed before Proposition 36 was passed in 2012. Thirteen out of the 15 studies showed that California's three strikes laws *failed to reduce serious crime* in California.

One of the most comprehensive studies of the impact of three strikes laws was supported by the National Institute of Justice, and culminated in the report entitled *"Three Strikes and You're Out": The Implementation and Impact of Strike Laws* (Austin, Clark, Hardyman, & Henry, 2000, March 6). The authors examined the impacts of three strikes laws in California and Georgia on the correctional systems and the crime rates in the jurisdictions.[1]

In their analysis of how California's strikes law impacted crime rates, the authors recognized that there was variation by county in how often the law was invoked by the local district attorneys since it went into effect in 1994. They concluded that since crime went down in each county (despite variations in how stringently the three strikes law was invoked) and in the state of California overall, that there was no clear linkage between the adoption of three strikes laws and the crime rate. They reached the same conclusion when they looked only at violent crime rates.

Austin and colleagues also examined Uniform Crime Report data from six states. These included three states that adopted three strikes legislation in 1993 or 1994—California, Washington, and Georgia—and three that did not—Texas, Massachusetts, and Michigan. The latter states had crime rates comparable to the former at the time the former adopted their three strikes laws. For all six states both violent and property crime rates dropped from 1990 to 1997. The authors cautioned that simply examining crime rates does not control for other factors that may affect crime rates. They noted that overall violent crime declined during the 1990s in the United States. But they emphasized that California, the state that had the most stringent laws and the state that invoked three strikes laws in eligible cases to the largest degree, did not experience a lowering of crime rates substantively differently than the other states considered.

Austin and colleagues also interviewed 33 strikers in California. Some felt it deterred crimes because the offender knew that he would face 25 years to life if convicted of a third strikeable offense. Others, however, doubted that offenders perceived they would get caught and that the law had no deterrent effect. Still others were not deterred because they did not understand that a crime such as a petty theft could count as a strike.

Takeaways of the Research Examining the Effect of Mandatory Minimums and Three Strikes Laws on Crime

Michael Tonry (2009) asserted that "The greatest gap between knowledge and policy in American sentencing concerns mandatory policies" (p. 65). Tonry also classified three strikes laws as a type of mandatory sentencing. Research findings from the last several decades support Tonry's claim.

In addition to studies discussed above, the United States Sentencing Commission issued a report entitled *Special Report to the Congress: Mandatory Minimum Penalties in the Federal Criminal Justice System* (1991) that challenged the notion that the "ideals" of mandatory minimums have been realized. This report provided support for the hydraulic effect (that discretion shifts from the judges to the prosecutors), suggested that trial rates increase under mandatory minimum sentencing, showed that the time taken to process a case increases, and revealed that relatively non-serious offenses are punished in a way that is disproportionately harsh. The report also documented the disdain for mandatory minimum sentences by criminal justice actors, including judges, defense attorneys, and probation officers.

Tonry (2009) pointed out that no Western country other than the United States has adopted so many mandatory sentencing laws. Those that have adopted them (Australia, Canada, England and Wales, and South Africa) have less severe mandatory penalties. They prescribe less prison time for even repeat and violent offenses and/or provide the judge the capacity to take into account all the circumstances of the case and adjust the sentence if it is deemed unreasonable.

Even before empirical research studies, there were accounts of persons in eighteenth century England who were attending public hangings for pickpockets, who got their pockets picked at these gatherings (Hay, Linebaugh, Rule, Thompson, & Winslow, 1975). This anecdotal evidence also leads one to question whether severe punishments act as effective deterrents.

Based on research failing to demonstrate a deterrent effect and the monetary and social costs of these sanctions, Tonry (2009) concluded:

> The policy and human rights implications of this two-century-old body of knowledge are clear. Mandatory penalties are a bad idea. They often result in injustice to individual offenders. They undermine the legitimacy of the courts and the prosecution system by fostering circumventions that are willful and subterranean. They undermine achievement of equality before the law when they cause comparably culpable offenders to be treated radically differently when one benefits from practitioners' circumventions and another receives a mandated penalty that everyone immediately involved considers too severe. And the clear weight of the evidence is, and for nearly 40 years has been, that there is insufficient evidence to conclude that mandatory penalties have significant deterrent effects. (p. 100)

Serving Time and Serving the General Public — Is the Public Made Safer by Imprisoning More Offenders?

Sentencing reforms began in the late 1970s and spread throughout the nation at the federal and state levels through the 1980s, 1990s, and 2000s. The prison population has increased due to several factors during this time and harsh sentencing practices have contributed to this increase. Harmon (2013) presented evidence that sentencing reforms, including statutory presumptive sentencing, truth-in-sentencing, and three strikes laws, have led to an overall increase in the prison population, compared to indeterminate sentencing.

The Complex Relationship between Imprisonment Rates and Crime Rates

How May Imprisonment Lead to Less Crime?

What mechanisms may explain the way incarceration can lead to lower crime rates? Stemen (2007, January) argued that policymakers have focused on how incarceration can reduce crime through both incapacitation and deterrence.

It is difficult to disentangle which of these processes associated with incarceration lowers (or doesn't lower) crime rates. If, for example, we see that states with high incarceration rates have lower crime rates, why is that? Is it because dangerous people are now removed from society? Is it because people see that incarceration is a certain consequence to the commission of certain crimes and choose to refrain from the commission of those crimes to avoid punishment? Is it because those who have served a prison sentence felt the "pains of imprisonment" and do not wish to go through that experience again and therefore stop committing crimes after release?

What National Descriptive Statistics Show

As of year-end 2014, the United States imprisoned an estimated 1,561,500 people in state and federal facilities (Carson, 2015, September). The state prison population has quadrupled and there has been a fivefold increase in the number of federal prisoners from 1978 to 2013. Drug offenders comprise 16 percent of the state prison population (Carson, 2014, September). The United States Sentencing Commission reported that 51 percent of federal offenders in prison were sentenced for drug offenses (United States Sentencing Commission, 2015, January).

Much of the monetary cost of harsh sentencing laws is the money that must be spent to house offenders and to build more facilities to combat overcrowding. The Pew Center on the States estimated that total state spending on corrections is approximately $52 billion, most of which goes towards prisons (Pew Center on the States, 2011, April). So, is the cost worth it?

What has happened to the national crime rates from 1978 till the present? Uniform Crime Report data shows that the violent crime rate was 497.8 per 100,000 in 1978. It increased pretty steadily throughout the 1980s and into the 1990s, peaking at 758.2 per 100,000 in 1991. Since 1991, the violent crime rate has dropped to a low of 365.5 per 100,000 in 2014. The property crime rate during this period has followed a similar pattern. In 1978 the property crime rate was 4,642.5 per 100,000. It fluctuated in the early 1980s, rose in the late 1980s and peaked at 5,140.2 per 100,000 in 1991. Since then, there has been a steady decline. The property crime rate was at its lowest point in 2014 at 2,596.1 per 100,000 (Federal Bureau of Investigation, Crime Statistics).

When comparing the patterns of incarceration rates and crime rates over the same time period, one sees that incarceration rates skyrocketed from 1978 to the present and crime rates began to plummet from the 1991 to the present. When campaigning on promises to "get tough on crime," politicians touted harsh reforms as strategies that would effectively reduce crime rates.

Figure 10.1 Hypothesized Relationships between Harsh Sentencing Practices, Incarceration Rates, and Crime Rates

Harsh Sentencing Practices ——▸ Higher Incarceration Rates ——▸ Lower Crime Rates

(Three Strikes Laws,   (Put More People in Prison
Mandatory Minimums,   for Longer Terms)
Truth-in-Sentencing)

Figure 10.1 represents a causal model that politicians cited (without empirical evidence) to gain support for harsh sentencing practices that posits that an indirect relationship exists between an increase in harsh sentencing practices and crime rates. It hypothesizes that an increased use of truth-in-sentencing, mandatory minimums, and three strikes laws would lead to higher incarceration rates, which would, in turn, lead to a decrease in crime rates.

Can we then imply that increased incarceration subsequent to widespread sentencing reforms caused the crime rate to decline? Maybe . . . but maybe not. Let's look at more social science research to answer that question.

What State Descriptive Statistics Show

Twenty years after the 1994 Crime Bill was passed, the Pew Charitable Trusts examined the relationship between incarceration rates and crime rates on the state level in the report entitled *Prison and Crime: A Complex Link* (2014, September 11). For each state, the Pew researchers measured the change in the imprisonment rate from 1994 to 2012 and the change in the crime rate between 1994 and 2012. **Figure 10.2** is taken from this report.

Pew researchers first described figures for the nation and then examined those for each state. They found that since 1994, the nation's imprisonment rate rose 24 percent and the crime rate decreased 40 percent. At first glance, one might be convinced that sentencing reforms that began in the mid-1990s and proliferated over the last twenty years were effective in increasing the imprisonment rate and decreasing crime.

When researchers present the state figures, however, things get a bit complicated. First, in seven states (New York, New Jersey, California, Maryland, South Carolina, Texas, and Nevada) the imprisonment rate actually decreased between 1994 and 2012.[2] The crime rate in each of these states decreased between 27 and 54 percent in this time period. This suggests that for these states as the imprisonment rate decreased, so did crime. This evidence fails to support the causal model in Figure 10.1.

In 43 states, however, the imprisonment rate increased between 1994 and 2012. The increase ranged from 4 percent in Rhode Island to 195 percent in West Virginia. In every state except West Virginia (which had a six percent increase) the crime rate decreased. The smallest decrease was in New Hampshire (-8 percent) and the largest decrease was in Florida (-54 percent).

Figure 10.2 Prison and Crime: A Complex Link

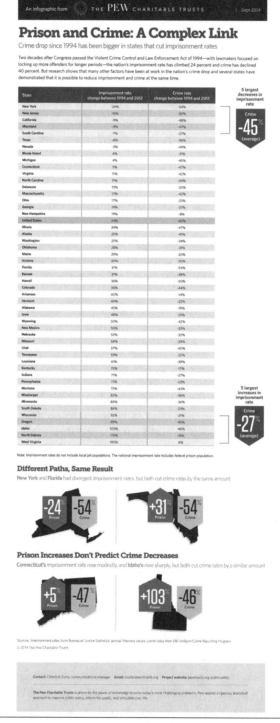

Source: Pew Charitable Trusts. (2014, September). *Prison and crime: A complex link*. Reproduced with permission from Pew Charitable Trusts. Retrieved from http://www.pewtrusts.org/en/multimedia/data-visualizations/2014/prison-and-crime

Pew researchers compared and contrasted the data for New York and Florida. They pointed out that New York had a 24 percent decrease in the imprisonment rate (the largest decrease in the nation) and a 54 percent decrease in the crime rate during the study period. In contrast, Florida had a 31 percent increase in the imprisonment rate between 1994 and 2012 and the same percent decrease as New York, 54 percent, in the crime rate. Pew researchers stated there seem to be "different paths, same result" regarding how crime rates declined in various states.

They also pointed out that in Connecticut a five percent increase in the incarceration rate was associated with a 47 percent decrease in the crime rate. A similar size decrease in the crime rate (46 percent) happened over the study period in Idaho, which had a 103 percent increase in the incarceration rate (Pew Charitable Trusts, 2014, September 11).

While these descriptive statistics are interesting, they fail to adequately explain (1) why we saw changes in the incarceration rates in each state (were they due to sentencing practices or other factors?), (2) what mechanism explains the relationship in 42 states between higher incarceration rates and lower crime rates, and (3) what caused the decrease in the crime rate in the seven states for which the incarceration rate declined.

What Multivariate Analyses Show

Stemen's (2007) review of studies showed that research using national level data has yielded estimates that suggest the strongest relationship between incarceration rates and crime rates, while studies using state and county level data show smaller effects. The most cited estimates of how incarceration affects crime, however, have come from three studies that find that a ten percent increase in incarceration yields a 2 to 4 percent reduction in crime (Levitt, 1996; Spelman, 2000; Spelman, 2005). Spelman (2000) analyzed data from 1972 to 1996 and concluded, "In short, the prison buildup was responsible for about one-fourth of the crime drop. Other factors are responsible for the vast majority of the drop" (p. 123).

Stemen suggested that the cost of achieving the same reduction may be quite different in different states, depending on their existing prison population. He compared the states of California and Nebraska, which had very similar crime rates in 2003 of approximately 4,000 index offenses per 100,000 people in the population. To achieve a 2 to 4 percent reduction, California, which then had a prison population of 162,678 inmates (and a rate of 692 inmates per 100,000 population) would have to incarcerate an additional 16,089 inmates. In contrast, Nebraska, which had a prison population of 3,976, would have to incarcerate only about 400 more people. Stemen estimated the average cost per inmate per year to be $22,650 and concluded that California would have to spend $355 million more than Nebraska to yield the same 2 to 4 percent reduction. He concluded that this strategy may be cost prohibitive in a states like California, which have large prison populations.

And is there such a thing as "too much" incarceration? On one hand, this may be a matter of opinion. Social scientists have looked at this question as well, however. Rose and Clear (1998) found that a sort of "tipping point" existed that showed that once an incarceration rate reached a certain level, the crime rate increased. Liedka, Piehl, and Useem (2006) found that while increased imprisonment over the last 30 years initially reduced crime, the buildup eventually reached a point of declining effectiveness. They found that this happened when the rate of imprisonment reaches 325 per 100,000 people. Because the overall imprisonment rate of sentenced prisoners under the jurisdiction of state or federal authorities was 471 per 100,000 population at year-end 2014 (Carson, 2015 September, p. 7), one might ask if we have reached a tipping point, in which incarceration is failing to meaningfully reduce crime.

Does Imprisonment Deter Crime? A Look at Recidivism Rates

Crime prevention makes imprisonment an appealing practice, especially to the taxpayers footing the bill to build prisons and pay for the operating costs. But does the experience of imprisonment serve as a *specific deterrent*? One approach to understanding whether imprisonment acts as a specific deterrent is to look at recidivism rates of those released from prison. There are several ways to measure recidivism — re-arrest, reconviction, re-incarceration for a new offense, and re-incarceration for a technical violation (for example, failing a drug test or violating another rule while on parole).

Bureau of Justice Statistics Study

A study published by the Bureau of Justice Statistics followed over 400,000 offenders from 30 states, who were released from prison in 2005. It showed that approximately 68 percent of those offenders were arrested within three years of release and almost 77 percent were arrested within five years of release. Twenty-three states provided information on return to prison. These data showed that almost one-half (49.7 percent) returned to prison within three years because they committed a crime or violated parole or probation. Over half (55.1 percent) were re-incarcerated within five years (Durose, Cooper, & Snyder, 2014, July).

This report showed that recidivism rates varied by type of crime, measured as the most serious commitment offense. Property offenders had the highest five year recidivism rate (82.1 percent), followed by drug offenders (76.9 percent), and public order offenders (73.6 percent). Violent offenders had the lowest overall five year recidivism rate (71.3 percent) (Durose, Cooper, & Snyder, 2014, July). Recidivism rates also varied by age of prisoner, race and Hispanic origin of prisoner, and prior record.[3]

The Pew Center on the States Study

In the report, *State of Recidivism: The Revolving Door of America's Prisons*, the Pew Center on the States (2011, April) provided an examination of state-by-state recidivism rates conducted with the Association of State Correctional Administrators (ASCA).[4] Recidivism rates were measured using data from prison systems for inmates released in 1999 (33 states) and 2004 (41 states). Researchers measured recidivism as the percentage of offenders who returned to prison within three years of release. The results showed an overall recidivism rate of 45.4 percent for those released in 1999 and 43.3 percent for those released in 2004.

The Pew Center on the States study also provided the recidivism rate for each state, which revealed enormous variation, not captured by the BJS study. The 2004 release/2007 follow-up data show that Minnesota and California had the highest three-year recidivism rates, 61.2 percent and 57.8 percent respectively. Oregon (22.8 percent) and Wyoming (24.8 percent) had the lowest rates.

The Pew Center on the States study also compared the recidivism rates from the 1999/2002 follow-up with the 2004/2007 follow-up. While the recidivism rate remained relatively stable in some states, the recidivism rate in Utah went down from 65.8 percent to 53.7 percent. Conversely, the recidivism rate went up in South Dakota from 33.7 percent to 45.5 percent.

The Pew Center on the States study offered some explanations for the variations that researchers calculated in state recidivism rates and trends. One involves who is sent to prison. States that send low-risk offenders to prison tended to have lower recidivism rates, compared to states that use incarceration more for dangerous offenders. Another factor that plays into recidivism rates involves how authorities within the state handle technical violations. States with shorter post-release supervision have lower rates of technical violations because these offenders are "at-risk" to violate for shorter periods of time. The caseload of post-prison release programs also plays a role. Supervision agencies with higher caseloads will have less time per inmate to monitor the offender and detect a technical violation. When a technical violation is caught, states also vary with respect to how they handle it. While short imprisonment has been a default mechanism in California, it is rarely used in Oregon (The Pew Center on the States, 2011, April).

Can Incarceration "Backfire" and Increase the Crime Rate?

The figures from the BJS and Pew studies hardly support the notion that the experience of imprisonment serves as an effective specific deterrent. Other studies using multivariate analysis and employing sophisticated statistical techniques have also failed to show that incarceration deters.

Some scholars have raised an alternative to the deterrence argument—that prison produces a **criminogenic effect** (Cullen, Jonson, & Nagin, 2011; Jonson, 2010). Instead of deterring offenders, the experience of imprisonment boosts the offender's involvement in criminal activities. This happens as a result of the severing of prosocial family, peer, and community bonds during imprisonment; socialization with other offenders within the institution; and because of the negative label ex-prisoners experience upon release (Johnson, 2010).

Jonson (2010) performed a meta-analysis of 85 studies to answer three questions— (1) What is the effect of non-custodial versus custodial sanctions on recidivism? (2) What is the effect of sentence length on recidivism? and (3) What is the effect of harshness of prison conditions (as measured by prison security level) on recidivism? Her quantitative review of research showed that custodial sanctions were associated with an 11 percent increase in recidivism and that there was no reduction in future criminal behavior if the individual experienced a harsher sentence as compared to a less harsh sentence. These results supported the argument that imprisonment does not deter future offending. The only finding in her study that supported specific deterrence showed that there was a slight deterrent effect found with longer, as opposed to shorter sentences, which showed that longer sentences were associated with about a five percent reduction in recidivism. Other studies have also failed to find that prison serves a deterrent effect (Freiburger & Iannacchione, 2011; Gendreau, Goggin, Cullen, & Andrews, 2000; Green & Winik, 2010; Nagin, Cullen, & Jonson, 2009; Smith, Goggin, & Gendreau, 2002; Villettaz, Killias, & Zoder, 2006) or that it instead produces a criminogenic effect (Gaes & Camp, 2009).

Cullen, Johnson, and Nagin (2011) concluded that incarceration may have unintended consequences that ultimately make society *less* safe. In their essay, *Prisons Do Not Reduce Recidivism: The High Cost of Ignoring Science*, these researchers likened the use of imprisonment to that of hospitalization. They argued that hospitalization should be reserved for those whose conditions cannot be treated elsewhere. They identified negative consequences of hospitalization, including nosocomial infections and cost. By hospitalizing only those who truly require it, the overall costs of hospitalization can be minimized. The same is true, they argue for incarceration.

Does Prison Help Control Crime through the Incapacitative Effect?

What Social Science Research Has Found

Zimring and Hawkins (1997) suggested that the most effective sentencing policies would incarcerate those who otherwise would be committing the most serious offenses — those involving lethal violence. Given limited correctional resources, the priority should be to incarcerate the most violent offenders and avoid incarceration for non-violent offenders.

Zimring and Hawkins noted that the composition of the California prison population in terms of conviction offense changed from the 1980s to the early 1990s. The authors stated that prisons had already been incapacitating violent offenders in the 1980s. Throughout the next decades, however, prisons began to also incarcerate offenders who had not committed violent crimes. More drug offenders were incarcerated during this time. They argued that the skyrocketing prison population did little to prevent crime, since the violent and dangerous offenders were already being incarcerated.

Bushway and Paternoster (2009) reviewed studies that examined the incapacitative effect of imprisonment. They noted:

> There will always be some benefit to incarcerating an active offender. The exact size of the benefit depends on where the offender fits in the overall offending distribution, where that offender is located on their own "career" path, and the degree to which other offenders replace that offender. (p. 127)

They acknowledged the strategy of selective incapacitation for optimizing crime control and pointed to various risk-assessment tools that have been used by parole boards to help determine when prisoners can be safely returned to society.

What (Other Than Increased Imprisonment) Can Lower Crime Rates?

Increasing Employment

One social cost of mass incarceration and an issue of particular significance to young black male offenders coming from at-risk neighborhoods is the effect of imprisonment on future employability. The Vera Institute of Justice released a report entitled *Reconsidering Incarceration: New Directions for Reducing Crime* (Stemen, 2007). The author of the report succinctly summarized the relationship between incarceration, employment, and income as follows:

> Incarceration creates problems of low earnings and irregular employment for individuals after release from prison by dissuading employers from hiring them, disqualifying them from certain professions, eroding job skills, limiting acquisition of work experience, creating behaviors inconsistent with work routines outside prison, and undermining the social connections to good job opportunities. (pp. 10–11)

In addition to creating barriers to legitimate employment, the experience of imprisonment can create social networks and "opportunities" to participate in illegal activities. Released offenders who become involved in illegal behavior post-incarceration continue to add to the crime problem.

Using state data, Raphael and Winter-Ebmer (2001) found a significant effect of unemployment on property crime rates. They estimated that a one percentage point drop in the unemployment rate causes a decline in the property crime rate of between 1.6 and 2.4 percent. They concluded that a significant proportion of the decline in crime in the 1990s could be explained by the decline in the unemployment rate.

Liedka, Piehl, and Useem (2006) also used state data and found that the unemployment rate was a positive predictor of crime rates. Gould, Weinberg, and Mustard (2002) examined data from a sample of over 700 counties from 1979–1997. They found that declining crime rates between 1993 and 1997 were explained substantially by the decreasing unemployment rate. A 3.1 percent decline in the unemployment rate corresponded with a decrease of 7.5 percent for property crime and 4.0 percent for violent crime. They also showed that a 3.1 percent increase in the wages of non-college-educated men predicted a decrease of 1.7 percent in property crime and 3.3 percent in violent crime. The results of these studies suggest that one effective crime control approach would involve increasing employment opportunities and/or wages for disadvantaged persons.

Increasing Educational Opportunities

More recently, the impact of raising the level of education on crime rates has been examined by social scientists. One study showed that a one-year increase in the average level of education of citizens was associated with a 1.7 percent decrease in the crime rate. The same study showed that a 10 percent increase in graduation rates yielded a

9.4 percent lower Index crime rate. It was calculated that if the high school completion rate was raised by one percent for men aged 20–60 that it would save the United States approximately $1.4 billion (Lochner & Moretti, 2004). Such research findings lead one to consider the potential for prison education programs to reduce recidivism. Research on such programs will be discussed in the final chapter.

Social Consequences of Punitive Sentencing Reforms

Sentencing laws that indicate lengthy sentences obviously affect the individual who is incarcerated. Laws that increase imprisonment impact society as well. Families and communities suffer as a result high incarceration rates. Few would argue against imprisoning serious, repeat, and violent offenders. One could argue, however, that the impact on society of the imprisonment of non-violent offenders, who comprise approximately half of the state prison population in the United States, is profound.

The Attenuation of Informal Social Controls

One social cost of high rates of imprisonment is the negative effect it has on family bonds and a community's capacity for social control. Rose and Clear (1998) suggested that when individual, family, community, and state level controls are weakened or absent, crime flourishes. They argued, however, that state controls (i.e., imprisonment) of an individual may have deleterious effects on the family unit and on neighborhood structures.

Communities with high rates of incarceration (especially for males, who dominate the population of incarcerated persons) are more likely to have high percentages of single-parent families and high rates of births to young single women. Coming from a single-parent household is a risk factor for delinquent and criminal behavior. Children's internalization of pro-social norms may be impeded and parent-child bonds may be weakened because the single parent has less time to spend with the children. Weakened bonds are associated with a higher likelihood of dropping out of school and school failure is a strong predictor of delinquency and criminality. Lack of parental supervision and community supervision is also linked with delinquency. In addition, high rates of imprisonment in a community may encourage resentment towards the legal system.

Children of Incarcerated Persons

At mid-year 2007, over 800,000 of the over 1.5 million prisoners in the United States were parents of children under the age of 18. There was an 80 percent increase between 1991 and mid-year 2007 in the number of children who had a parent in prison. The number of children who had a mother in prison more than doubled in this time period. Offenders convicted of drug and public order offenses were more likely than violent offenders to have children (Glaze & Maruschak, 2008). As we have learned, sentencing practices such as mandatory minimum sentencing often target drug offenders.

So what impact does parental imprisonment have on children? Children whose parents are incarcerated suffer in many ways. Murray and Farrington (2008) found that among a sample of boys studied over time, parental imprisonment in childhood (up to age 10) was associated with higher levels of internalizing problems (e.g., vulnerability to anxiety, phobic fears, and obsessional reactions) and anti-social behavior, compared with children who weren't separated from their parents or children separated from their parents for other reasons. Murray and Farrington (2005) found that parental imprisonment in childhood was a significant positive predictor of boys' antisocial personality and delinquent behavior during adolescence and adulthood. The authors also pointed out other ways parental imprisonment negatively impacts children, including economic loss, school and neighborhood moves, and the negative stigma associated with a parent's incarceration. They suggested that imprisoning parents may contribute to an intergenerational transmission of criminal behavior.

Some researchers have argued that while females comprise less than ten percent of the prison population, maternal incarceration may affect children more than paternal incarceration. Hagan and Foster (2012) explained six reasons why this would be. First, mothers usually spend more time with their children than fathers do and, therefore, they may influence the lives of their children more. Second, when mothers are incarcerated, the children usually don't live with their father. This contrasts with how mothers typically care for the children when fathers are incarcerated. Oftentimes when the mother is incarcerated, the maternal grandmother or other relative of the mother cares for the children (Glaze & Maruschak, 2008). A third hardship involves the location of women's prisons. Because there are fewer women incarcerated in the United States, there are fewer women's prisons. The location of the prison may be hours away from the home where the child is residing, making regular visitation difficult (Glaze & Maruschak, 2008). A fourth reason that maternal incarceration is a particular problem is that children of incarcerated mothers tend to be exposed to more risks within the home environment compared to children of incarcerated fathers (Johnson & Waldfogel, 2004). A fifth adversity concerns the fact that children of incarcerated mothers are more likely to experience events related to the incarceration, like being present at the sentencing, which can result in emotional maladjustments, increased anxiety and depression, and behavior problems (Dallaire & Wilson, 2010). Sixth, teachers see children whose mothers are incarcerated as especially at risk compared with those whose fathers are incarcerated. Differences involve how children of incarcerated mothers are perceived and treated at school (i.e., lower expectations) (Dallaire, Ciccone, & Wilson, 2010).

Hagan and Foster (2012) discussed how "get tough on crime" initiatives that have sent more women to prison have negatively impacted children. The most obvious victim of maternal incarceration is the child who loses his or her mother. Hagan and Foster examined the impact of parental incarceration on children using various outcome measures (GPAs, graduation rates). They also identified how the concentration of incarcerated mothers and fathers in a school could affect children. Their methodologically sophisticated multivariate research identified both individual level and contextual level effects of parental incarceration on children's school performance.

The findings indicated that children whose mothers are incarcerated have *significantly lower GPAs* and that children attending schools with higher percentages of maternal imprisonment have lower high school GPAs. Those whose mother or father is incarcerated have *lower educational attainment* and those who attend schools with higher levels of parental incarceration have lower levels of educational attainment. In addition, both maternal and paternal imprisonment are negative predictors of *whether the child becomes college-educated.* Children whose mother or father was incarcerated are significantly *less likely to be college-educated.* In addition, children who come from schools that have high rates of maternal or paternal imprisonment are less likely to be college-educated. Hagan and Foster term these contextual effects as "negative spillover effects."

Hagan and Foster argued that both federal and state sentencing guidelines curtail judges' discretion to consider the offender's parental responsibilities during the sentencing stage. They challenge the policy which Meda Chesney-Lind (2006) labelled "equality with a vengeance"—in which female offenders are punished "equally," but suffer substantially consequent to furthering the goal of gender neutrality in sentencing. Hagan and Foster (2012) concluded the following:

> We have seen that formal equality can lead to substantive inequality for women and children and that the gendered effects of the logic of judicial neutrality are socially costly not just for the individuals and families, but also for the schools and the communities in which they are located across the nation. (p. 62)

Indirect Ways Three Strikes Laws Negatively Impact Women

One might assume that among adults, mandatory minimums and three strikes laws would affect males almost exclusively. Mandatory minimum laws generally target serious and violent offenses. Since males are much more likely to commit drug, gun, and violent offenses and be repeat offenders, it would seem logical that males would almost exclusively feel the negative effects of mandatory minimums and three strikes laws. Given their shorter criminal careers and the fact that they are less likely to commit the types of crimes that trigger these laws, it would seem to make sense that women are less affected by these sentencing laws.

While fewer women are sentenced under three strikes laws, the passage of these laws has impacted the lives of female offenders, their families, and society in negative ways. Danner (2012) identified three ways strikes laws negatively affect women. First, when money is poured into the criminal justice system, money previously allocated to other government services, such as social services, will be cut or reduced. Such services are targeted for the poor, many of whom are women and children. Second, women are not just more likely to be recipients of social services, but are more likely to work in the social service field. Cutting social services costs jobs for female social workers, case workers, counselors, and support staff. Third, three strikes laws negatively impact families. Imprisoned adults cannot help their families financially or provide emotional support to family members. Incarcerating men for lengthy terms under three strikes laws puts an additional burden on wives, girlfriends, and mothers to provide for their children's economic and emotional needs. When a woman's partner or husband is given a life sentence, the burden of providing all of these needs and raising the children is put on her.

Mental Health Concerns of Incarcerated Persons

Another negative social consequence of incarceration is the impact that imprisonment has on the mental health of the offender. A study examining surveys from 22,790 prisoners from 12 countries found that among male prisoners 3.7 percent had psychotic illnesses, 10 percent had major depression, and 65 percent had a personality disorder, which included 47 percent with antisocial personality disorder. Among female prisoners, 4 percent had psychotic illness, 12 percent had major depression, and 42 percent had a personality disorder, with 21 percent having antisocial personality disorder (Fazel & Danesh, 2002). The same study documented that the percent of incarcerated persons who suffer from mental illness is greater than the percent who suffer from mental illness in the general population.

In addition to pre-existing mental health conditions, the experience of incarceration brings with it extreme stress. The entry into a prison is traumatic, as one's identity is stripped away and in its place, a prison number is assigned and one is separated from family and friends. The environment of prisons itself arguably invites depression. Inmates lack control over their lives, they live in physical conditions that are bleak at best, and they often live in fear of physical and/or sexual abuse by other prisoners and correctional employees.

Some argue that indeterminate sentencing exacerbates the stresses as the inmate does not know when he or she is to be released (Taylor & Williams, 2014). Another perspective, however, suggests that prisoners sentenced under more "truth-in-sentencing" approaches also suffer, knowing that regardless of their actions or behaviors while in prison, their release date is for the most part beyond their control. Regardless of the mechanisms under which the prisoner may be ultimately released, the mental health needs of prisoners are rarely adequately addressed. This neglect affects the offender's well-being while he or she is incarcerated. The lack of mental health treatment also puts offenders in a position of being ultimately released back into society with the same or worse mental health problems.

How Do Offenders View Sentencing Reforms and Criminal Sanctions?

Inmates' Views on Determinate Versus Indeterminate Sentencing

Those most directly affected by sentencing reforms are the offenders sentenced in accordance with them. Larson and Berg (1989) examined the opinions about determinate and indeterminate sentencing from a sample of inmates at a maximum security prison in the late 1980s, when the movement toward more determinate sentencing practices was growing. They sought to understand inmates' perceptions of the strengths of indeterminate and determinate sentencing, as well as how determinate sentencing may or may not deter criminal activity.

According to Larson and Berg (1989),

> Determinate sentencing was defined as presumptive sentencing, that is, sentencing by means of a set of guidelines that specify a certain number of years to be served upon conviction for a given offense and that a judge may slightly increase or decrease in the event of aggravating or mitigating circumstances. (Griswold, 1987, p. 129)

In contrast, the authors stated,

> Indeterminate sentencing was defined as sentencing by means of a minimum-maximum system in which actual number of years served is influenced by rules specifying minimum number of years to be served prior to parole eligibility, the amount of good-time credits that can be earned, and parole board decision making. (p. 129)

A sample of 56 inmates were interviewed. The vast majority of the respondents (87 percent) were serving time for violent crimes.

Inmates' views on replacing indeterminate with determinate sentencing were divided. The largest proportion of inmates were undecided (39 percent) while 32 percent were in favor of the change and 29 percent were opposed to the change. The most common positive quality of determinate sentencing cited by the respondents was "sentence certainty." Many inmates identified the stressfulness of not knowing when they would actually be released by the parole board—a body they felt was difficult to deal with. Inmates identified several weaknesses of determinate sentencing. The most common criticism was that it ignores the individual and sentences the offense. Others anticipated that determinate sentencing would increase the actual time served. Some felt determinate sentencing would reduce incentives for good behavior and encourage bitterness and violence.

Most inmates did not think that determinate sentencing would have an impact on criminal behavior. However, some thought it would increase violence within and outside of prison. Others thought that criminals would be more selective about which crimes they would commit. For example, they might steal less money if they knew that a certain amount of money would trigger a certain punishment.

When asked about the deterrent effect of determinate sentencing, the largest proportion of inmates (41 percent) did not think it would serve as a deterrent. A sizeable proportion (32 percent), however, did feel it would constitute a strong deterrent.

Inmates' Perceptions on the Punitiveness of Imprisonment Versus Alternative Sanctions

In their book, *Ranking Correctional Punishments: Views from Offenders, Practitioners, and the Public* (2010), David May and Peter Wood took an in-depth look at offenders' perceptions of and/or experiences with a variety of custodial and non-custodial sanctions. They noted that offenders' perspectives of sanctions are influenced by length of incarceration sentences, as well as by the conditions imposed in non-custodial sanctions.

Although the offenders did not directly report their perceptions of the sentencing reforms themselves, it is interesting to assess offenders' perceptions of the punitiveness of various sanctions. Sentencing guidelines schemes generally reserve what's thought to be the most severe sanctions for the most serious offenders. Understanding offenders' perceptions of the severity of sanctions may help us understand if the sentences are serving the goals of retribution and deterrence.

Consider a situation of an offender who would rather serve a prison sentence than an intensive supervision probation sentence. Sentencing guidelines, such as those in North Carolina, explicitly reserve prison for the most serious and repeat offenders, while utilizing alternatives to incarceration for more "intermediate" offenders. If offenders perceive intensive supervision probation as more punitive than prison, then the guidelines may not be, in fact, punishing proportionately, at least in the eyes of the offenders. If imprisonment is favored over day reporting, then this casts doubt on the deterrent effect of imprisonment.

Research from Petersilia (1990) showed that given a choice, up to one-third of offenders indicated that they would rather serve a prison term, as opposed to receiving an intensive supervision probation sentence that carried numerous restrictions. When the author of this text began evaluating day reporting centers in North Carolina, criminal justice professionals reported that when given a choice, many offenders would choose a short (six month) jail sentence over a two-year sentence of intensive supervision probation or day reporting. The offenders said they preferred to do a shorter stint in jail rather than be under restrictive conditions that accompanied a lengthier alternative sentence.

May and Wood (2010) emphasized that offenders' perceptions of the punitiveness of sanctions are complex. As we have suggested throughout the text, the experience of a single sanction such as imprisonment may affect different people differently. Females and males may perceive and/or experience incarceration differently (Wood & Grasmick, 1999). The same is true for first-time versus experienced offenders. Crouch (1993) and Wood and May (2003) found that blacks were more likely than whites to choose an incarceration sentence over a community-based sentence. Evidence also shows variation in sanction preference by age, marital status, and offense type (Crouch, 1993; Petersilia & Deshenes, 1994a, 1994b; Spelman, 1995).

May and Wood (2010) described the process of developing "**exchange rate**" measures to ascertain offenders' perceptions of the punitiveness of sanctions. Prisoners were asked about the relative punitiveness of a variety of alternative sanctions compared to imprisonment. According to the authors,

> This method allowed a more sophisticated comparison where offenders chose the amount (in months) of an alternative sanction he or she would endure to avoid a specified length of actual imprisonment. The punishment equivalency between imprisonment and the alternative sanction in question has come to be known as that sanction's *exchange rate*. (p. 16)

The respondents were given descriptions of alternative sanctions including county jail, boot camp, electronic monitoring, regular probation, community service, day reporting, intensive supervision probation, intermittent incarceration, and day fine. They were then asked to consider a set time of imprisonment (usually twelve months) and to say how many months of the alternative they would be willing to do to avoid the twelve-month prison sentence. If, for example, the respondent was only willing to do eight months of the alternative to avoid imprisonment, then the alternative was viewed as more punitive (in the eyes of the inmate) than imprisonment. If the inmate was willing to do more than the twelve months of the alternative to avoid twelve months of prison time, then the alternative was considered less punitive.

May and Wood's research with samples of prisoners confirmed prior research—some inmates preferred prison to alternatives. And like extant research, variation existed that was linked with inmate characteristics. Offenders with more prison experience chose prison. This may be counterintuitive when one thinks of the pains of imprisonment. And it certainly challenges the notion of imprisonment as an exclusive deterrent to offending.

May and Wood conducted interviews with respondents. Respondents who preferred prison to alternatives cited several reasons. These included that alternative programs are difficult to complete, that the rules are hard to follow, that officers try to catch them and send them back to prison, that serving time is easier compared to the alternatives, and that serving time in prison is less hassle because the programs require too many responsibilities.

One noted

> I'd rather go to prison than do probation. It's hard, they come to your house, they belittle you, they degrade you, no matter how good you do, no matter how well you turn your life around. (Respondent #5, p. 45)

Another said

> Well, usually the alternatives are a lot longer and more strict, and you usually end up violating and you end up going back to prison anyway, so it's, in the long run, it's just easier to do your prison time because they make it so difficult. It strings it out longer when you don't do the prison time. (Respondent #14, p. 45)

This body of research is less relevant to assessing the deterrent capacity of mandatory minimums and three strikes laws, as those require lengthy prison sentences, in which no alternatives are possible. It is most relevant to assessing the proportionality of commission-based guidelines that allow judges discretion as to whether to impose imprisonment or alternatives to incarceration. Alternatives to incarceration have expanded over the years. Many commission-based guidelines have incorporated these alternatives into their grids for mid-range offenders.

If the focus of handing down a sanction is retribution, punishment should be proportionate to the severity of the offense. The results of research, however, leave one to wonder what type of sentence (imprisonment or an alternative) is considered more severe. Indeed, it depends on the particular offender's perception of sentencing severity. And this perception varies by offender characteristics. Whether grid cell assignment of offenders to alternative sanctions reflects proportionality is, therefore, unclear.

Evidence shows the most effective deterrent for one offender may not be the most effective deterrent for another. This challenges the set up of many jurisdictions' sentencing guidelines that treat alternative sanctions as "lighter" sentences, compared to incarceration. According to inmates, this is not a universally shared perception. The "pains of incarceration" may not be considered more severe than the negative aspects of sentencing alternatives.

How Do People Working in the Criminal Justice System View Various Reforms?

This chapter provides an additional source of information—how criminal justice professionals view sentencing guidelines in the *Interview* section. The interviewees from Chapter 8, the Honorable Judge Debra Pezze and Chief County Public Defender Mr. Wayne McGrew, both of whom work in the court system in Westmoreland County in Pennsylvania, provide their perspectives on the practice of Pennsylvania's sentencing guidelines. They reflect on whether sentencing guidelines encourage more trials, as opposed to pleas, and identify some ways sentencing disparities may continue to be manifested under the guidelines.

Summary

Evaluations of the impact of reforms on crime rates have shown that the relationship is complex. Crime rates have decreased in the United States as a whole from the time modern sentencing reforms proliferated to the present. Crime rates also decreased in states with indeterminate sentencing and fewer restrictive reforms as well, however. Research suggests that other factors, including decreased unemployment, may have contributed to the decrease in crime from the late 1990s to the present time.

Research shows that while increased incarceration has led to some crime reduction, after a certain point the incapacitative effect is not worth the monetary and social costs of mass incarceration. A body of evidence also casts doubt on the deterrent effect of incarceration. The social costs of incarceration are profound. Children of incarcerated parents suffer in many ways. Communities with high incarceration rates also suffer.

It is important to understand the perceptions of sentencing strategies and sanctions from those who are directly affected by them—the offenders. Offenders' perceptions of the severity of incarceration versus alternative sanctions are not uniform. While some offenders view incarceration as the most severe sanction, others view alternatives to incarceration, which have multiple conditions and restrictions, to be more punitive. The diversity in offender perceptions is linked with gender, race, and career criminality. The ambiguity in perceptions of sanction seriousness raises the question of whether commission-based guidelines produce proportionate sentences. The deterrent effect of incarceration is also questioned.

In the next chapter we will look toward the future of sentencing reforms and assess whether the results of social science research on the effects of sentencing reforms have led to changes in sentencing policies. We will discuss various "evidence-based" practices that have recently been introduced into sentencing and correctional strategies.

Interview

Interview with the Honorable Judge Debra Pezze, Pennsylvania Court of Common Pleas, Westmoreland County — December 22, 2014

Questions about the Practice of Pennsylvania's Sentencing Guidelines

LM: What incentive, if any, does the defendant have to plead guilty under the guidelines?

DP: Well that's a good question because lots of times when the district attorney will make plea agreements they're giving a person a recommendation that's in the standard range of the guidelines. And that's not much of an incentive to plead guilty. Because if you go to trial and get convicted the judge basically has to sentence you within the standard range of the guidelines or provide reasons for going outside that.

        Unless there's something really aggravating about the case that the district attorney's going to cut him a break and give him a recommendation in the standard range, there's no incentive whatsoever and that's what I say to them. If you want to make a plea agreement then you should give them some incentive to plead guilty.

LM: If they're not given a break, from their perspective, take a chance at a trial and possibly be found not guilty?

DP: Absolutely, absolutely, positively.

LM: I understand that someone does a separate presentence investigation, and I guess my question was, do individual factors such as is the person is employed, or if he or she has family responsibilities affect your sentencing decision?

DP: Yes, it certainly does. Lots of times I am of the firm belief that virtually everybody, at least 9.9 out of 10 people, if given the opportunity to live a life of dignity, with a job and a family, will do that. But everybody doesn't have that opportunity. So the fact that somebody doesn't have employment, I certainly don't hold that against them.

        The fact that they have a family, that is a double-edged sword as far as I'm concerned. Because a lot of people will come in here and say I have children to take care of, you're taking me away from my children. I'm not. Certainly I am mindful and sympathetic to the fact that they have children and that their family is going to be punished by them being taken out of the mix but at the same time it makes it worse that they would be involved in that kind of activity. I say to them you're not a single person on whom no one relies. How could you do something like this knowing that the situation you put your family in? So it does in some ways, obviously I don't want to harm the family by my decision but at the same time, this person has completely chosen to disregard their family and again we think all of these things . . . after the fact you know, how could you do this to your family?

Well, if people actually thought that when they were committing crime nobody would do any crime. They do and it's like they say, they become overwhelmed with their circumstances. They just do.

And lots of times, especially now . . . property crimes, drug crimes, we have this horrid, absolutely horrific heroin epidemic in our county. And many similarly situated places, the likes of which I never have seen. Five years ago, I bet you I didn't have 10 heroin cases a year. Now I have 10 heroin cases a day. So people do things that they never in a million years would do because they're sick and they need money to get drugs.

LM: So what kinds of discretion do judges retrain under the Pennsylvania Sentencing guidelines?

DP: Well, I mean, to a certain extent, we maintain complete discretion. If I abuse that discretion then you can take an appeal. But, only if there's an abuse of discretion. Every time I sentence anybody I just made it a habit to place on the record the reasons for the sentence because it is in keeping with the nature of the charges, it satisfies the mandate of the statute.

LM: Do all counties in Pennsylvania have the same sanctions available and if not, is that ideal of sentencing uniformity that's inherent in Pennsylvania's guidelines compromised?

DP: I don't think that they all do and I think that it does compromise that. In the smaller counties that can't afford those kinds of programs they do use jail more. And I don't think it's fair.

LM: That's, I guess, that's common in cities — closer to Pittsburgh and closer to Philadelphia they have more programs but maybe in the middle of the state and rural areas they don't have access to those programs.

DP: Now I will say this. They have really pushed these mandatory courts — drug court, and these specialty courts are very fashionable now. I don't find them particularly useful. Like how do you decide . . . we'll have like 2,000 drug cases and 50 people will be in drug court. They're very effective for the fortunate people who get into them but then what do you say to everybody else? You don't get that break . . . This person's going to get all this treatment and you're going to get nothing? So I think they're expensive in terms of the cost of them in judicial and probation officer resources and if they use up a lot of the limited resources we have and I think these should be spread around.

LM: Any comments or anything you'd like to say about sentencing that I haven't covered in my questions?

DP: I think that I just want to reiterate that I think that our system works in an atmosphere of mutual respect and understanding. Not just for one another but for the people who are involved. For the litigants, for the people who sit on either side of the table. I think if we remind ourselves every day that every person who comes before us is entitled to be treated with respect and dignity and compassion, no matter which side of the table they sit on. And most cases that come before me it's not the defendant saying I didn't do it, it's usually, well I did it but let me tell you what the other guy did first. Now let's put all the cards on the table. Let's tell you everything. And in that atmosphere, if we work in an atmosphere of mutual respect and compassion and understanding, then I think we can get something accomplished.

And I think we need to back off the notion that everybody should go to jail. Really, very few people should go to jail. In my mind, jail should be reserved for violent offenders who can't live in ordinary society. For everybody else, I think there has to be a better way.

LM: Thank you very much for your comments and for your contribution to our criminal justice system.

DP: Thank you for asking me.

Interview with Chief County Public Defender Mr. Wayne McGrew — January 14, 2015

Questions about the Practice of Pennsylvania's Sentencing Guidelines

LM: What effect do you think the guidelines have, if any, on the plea bargaining process?

WM: Well, I think they have some good and some bad influence on plea bargaining. One thing is you can have a chart when you go to a preliminary hearing. I have mine in a book. I can pull it out for the person that I'm representing and I can show them right where their crime that they've been charged with, accused of, will fall into the guidelines — where the prior record score falls in the guidelines and see where the two meet to determine what the standard sentence range would be. So it gives the client a sort of sense of comfort knowing this is where we're starting at *if* I'm convicted of these offenses. So, it gives a little bit of credibility between the attorney and the client.

The problem with it is a lot of times you'll have clients that look at it and say, I know that's the worst I'm going to get, so I might as well go to trial and fight it because you'll have prosecutors that will only give the upper range of the standard sentence. So it has good and bad.

LM: So sometimes the defendant has the incentive to take a chance at a trial?

WM: Sometimes there is. It also depends on the judge you're in front of. And we have great judges in Westmoreland County. Now, obviously, understand that you're writing a book that would be wider than Westmoreland County. But in Westmoreland County we have great judges but every county is going to have judges that have certain personalities. And you're going to get to know those personalities over the years of practicing in front of them. And you're going to know what might trigger a harsher sentence even if it's subconscious in the judge. And if you're doing your job, you convey that to your client, so that they can take that into consideration when they're considering what they want to do.

LM: How do the guidelines themselves negatively affect the defendant?

WM: We have really good judges here and there are times that I wish the judges would exercise more freedom in their sentencing. The guidelines don't stop them from going outside the standard range. But the judges are required anytime they step out of the guidelines — the standard ranges — they have to put on the record why they went below or why they went above. So, a lot of times they don't want to go outside of them. And I can understand that because there may not be an articulable reason to go above them or below it.

But sometimes you just have that right case that the feeling, the hunch, or whatever you want to call it that this person deserves a break and would like to go lower. You don't really have anything to put on the record and I think sometimes they'll get pushed into the standard range, instead of having some flexible freedom in sentencing.

LM: From your experience as a public defender, are extralegal characteristics of the defendants, such as gender, race, socioeconomic status — things that aren't supposed to matter . . . do you feel they're linked with harsher sentences?

WM: In Westmoreland County, no. I can't really speak to that outside of Westmoreland County.

You could always look at numbers and say that the African American male — there's a greater number being prosecuted and put in jail. But, you can also look at the aspect of who's being arrested doing the crimes and what the crime ridden areas are and who makes up those socioeconomic environments. And if you want to take that out of it and just take offender X who happens to be an African American male and offender Y who happens to be a white male, and they've done the same crime, and have the same criminal history. In Westmoreland County, I think they're getting the same treatment, the same sentence without too much variance.

LM: How about something like if they have a family to raise. Can it help them, can it hurt them, or both?

WM: You know what? I'd say both. A lot of our judges will take into account if a person's on the borderline that they would sentence to jail or to probation, and they have the family at home that they're trying to take care of, the sick parent that they're tending to, etc. I think that they'll often take that into consideration and give them house arrest instead of jail time. So I think it would benefit them in that way.

And if you have a person that's committing X crimes and they have young kids at home and say they're accused of selling drugs out of their house and they have needles lying around also, yet they have kids in the house. That might raise the ire a little bit of the judge and maybe there would be a little harsher sentence than if it was just John Doe on the street corner selling a bag of weed.

LM: Interesting. Well thank you very much for participating in the interview. I really, really appreciate it and I think it's going to be great to include in the book your perspectives on it. So thank you.

Discussion Questions

1. How do you think incarceration serves the following goals of sentencing? Does your answer depend on the type of crime the offender was convicted of?
   a. Specific deterrence
   b. General deterrence
   c. Incapacitation
2. If you were to devise an action plan to decrease crime in the United States, what would be your main focus—incarceration, education, or employment? Explain.
3. How might society decrease the social costs of incarceration in the United States?
4. Which (if any) alternative sanction do you perceive to be harsher than twelve months in prison? Explain your answer.

Notes

1. Although Washington had also enacted a three strikes law at the time, the authors chose not to analyze the impact of the law on the outcomes. This is because Washington's three strikes law was narrower in scope and only a small number of offenders had been sentenced under the state's three strikes law, thus it had little impact on the courts and correctional facilities in the state.

2. In 2011, the Public Safety Realignment (PSR) policy took effect in California. It was designed to decrease overcrowding in the state prisons by sentencing nonviolent and less serious offenders to local jail facilities. This explains some of the drop in the prison population in California.

3. A "Prisoner Recidivism Analysis Tool" is available on the Bureau of Justice Statistics website. This interactive tool allows one to input characteristics of the offender (age, race, ethnicity, number of prior arrests, prior imprisonment, sentencing offense, and time served) and then calculates the average recidivism rate for an offender with the selected characteristics. The estimate is based on data from 15 state departments of corrections which participated in a national study of recidivism in 1994 performed by the Bureau of Justice Statistics.

4. The Bureau of Justice Statistics study did not provide state-by-state comparisons. They pooled state data and provided national estimates of recidivism.

References

Austin, J., Clark, J., Hardyman, P., & Henry, D. A. (2000, March 6). *Three strikes and you're out: The implementation and impact of strike laws*. Final Report submitted to the U.S. Department of Justice.

Beha, J. A. (1977a). "And nobody can get you out": The impact of a mandatory prison sentence for the illegal carrying of a firearm on the use of firearms and on the administration of criminal justice in Boston—Part I. *Boston University Law Review*, *57*, 96–146.

Beha, J. A. (1977b). "And nobody can get you out": The impact of a mandatory prison sentence for the illegal carrying of a firearm on the use of firearms and on the administration of criminal justice in Boston—Part II. *Boston University Law Review, 57*, 289–333.

Bureau of Justice Statistics. *Prisoner Recidivism Rates Methods.* Retrieved from http://www.bjs.gov/index.cfm?ty=datool&surl=/recidivism/index.cfm#

Bureau of Justice Statistics. *Prisoner Recidivism Analysis.* Retrieved from http://www.bjs.gov/index.cfm?ty=datool&surl=/recidivism/index.cfm#

Bushway, S. D., & Paternoster, R. (2009). The impact of prison on crime. In S. Raphael & M. A. Stoll (Eds.), *Do prisons make us safer? The benefits and costs of the prison boom* (pp. 119–150). New York: Russell Sage Foundation.

Carson, E. A. (2014, September). *Prisoners in 2013.* Washington, DC: U.S. Department of Justice. Retrieved from http://www.bjs.gov/content/pub/pdf/p13.pdf.

Carson, E. A. (2015 September). *Prisoners in 2014*, (NCJ Publication No. 248955). Washington, DC: U.S. Department of Justice, Bureau of Justice Statistics. Retrieved from http://www.bjs.gov/content/pub/pdf/p14.pdf

Crouch, B. M. (1993). Is incarceration really worse? Analysis of offenders' preferences for prison over probation. *Justice Quarterly, 10*, 67–88.

Cullen, F. T., Jonson, C. L., & Nagin, D. S. (2011). Prisons do not reduce recidivism: The high cost of ignoring science. *The Prison Journal, 91*(3), 485–655.

Dallaire, D. H., Ciccone, A., & Wilson, L. C. (2010). Teachers' experiences with and expectations of children with incarcerated parents. *Journal of Applied Developmental Psychology, 31*, 281–290.

Dallaire, D. H., & Wilson, L. C. (2010). The relation of exposure to parental criminal activity, arrest, and sentencing to children's maladjustment. *Journal of Child and Family Studies, 19*, 404–418.

Danner, M. J. E. (2012). Three strikes and it's *women* who are out: The hidden consequences for women of criminal justice policy reforms. In R. Muraskin (Ed.), *Women and justice: It's a crime* (pp. 354–364). Boston, MA: Prentice Hall.

Durose, M. R., Cooper, A. D., & Snyder, H. N. (2014). *Recidivism of prisoners released in 30 states in 2005: Patterns from 2005 to 2010.* Washington, DC: Bureau of Justice Statistics.

Fazel, S., & Danesh, J. (2002). Serious mental disorder in 23000 prisoners: A systematic review of 62 surveys. *Lancet, 359*(9306), 545–550.

Federal Bureau of Investigation. *Crime Statistics.* Retrieved from https://www.fbi.gov/stats-services/crimestats

Freiburger, T. L., & Iannacchione, B. M. (2011). An examination of the effect of imprisonment on recidivism. *Criminal Justice Studies, 24*(4), 369–379.

Gaes, G. G., & Camp, S. D. (2009). Unintended consequences: Experimental evidence for the criminogenic effect of prison security level placement on post-release recidivism. *Journal of Experimental Criminology, 5*, 139–162.

Gendreau, P., Goggin, C., Cullen, F. T., & Andrews, D. A. (2000). The effects of community sanctions and incarceration on recidivism. *Forum on Corrections Research, 12*(2). Retrieved from http://www.csc-scc.gc.ca/research/forum/e122/e122c-eng.shtml

Glaze, L. E., & Maruschak, L. M. (2008, August, revised March, 2010). *Parents in prison and their minor children.* (NCJ Publication No. 222984). Washington, DC: Bureau of Justice Statistics.

Gould, E. D., Weinberg, B. A., & Mustard, D. B. (2002). Crime rates and local labor market opportunities in the United States: 1979–1997. *The Review of Economics and Statistics, 84*(1), 45–61.

Green, D. P., & Winik, D. (2010). Using random judge assignments to estimate the effects of incarceration and probation on recidivism among drug offenders. *Criminology, 48*(2), 357–387.

Griswold, D. B. (1987). Deviation from sentencing guidelines. The issue of unwarranted disparity. *Journal of Criminal Justice, 6,* 317–329.

Hagan, J., & Foster, H. (2012). Children of the American prison generation: Student and school spillover effects of incarcerating mothers. *Law & Society Review, 46*(1), 37–69.

Harmon, M. G. (2013). "Fixed" sentencing: The effect on imprisonment rates over time. *Journal of Quantitative Criminology, 29,* 369–397.

Hay, D., Linebaugh, P., Rule, J. G., Thompson, E., & Winslow, C. (1975). *Albion's fatal tree: Crime and society in eighteenth-century England.* New York: Pantheon.

Johnson, E. I., & Waldfogel, J. (2004). Children of incarcerated parents: Multiple risks and childrens' living arrangements. In M. Pattillo, D. Weiman, & B. Western (Eds.), *Imprisoning America: The social effects of mass incarceration* (pp. 97–131). New York: Russell Sage Foundation.

Jonson, C. L. (2010). *The impact of imprisonment on reoffending: A meta-analysis.* (Unpublished doctoral dissertation). Cincinnati, OH: University of Cincinnati.

LaCourse, R. D. (1997, January). Three strikes, you're out: A review. *Washington Policy Center.* Retrieved from http://www.washingtonpolicy.org/publications/brief/three -strikes-youre-out-review

Larson, C. J., & Berg, B. (1989). Inmates' perceptions of determinate and indeterminate sentences. *Behavioral Sciences & the Law, 7*(1), 127–137.

Levitt, S. D. (1996). The effect of prison population size on crime rates: Evidence from prison overcrowding litigation. *The Quarterly Journal of Economics, 111*(2), 319–351.

Liedka, R. V., Piehl, A. M., & Useem, B. (2006). The crime-control effect of incarceration: does scale matter? *Criminology & Public Policy, 5*(2), 245–276.

Lochner, L., & Moretti, E. (2004). The effect of education on crime evidence from prison inmates, arrests, and self-reports. *The American Economic Review, 94*(1), 155–189.

Loftin, C., & McDowall, D. (1981). "One with a gun gets you two": Mandatory sentencing and firearms violence in Detroit. *Annals of the American Academy of Political and Social Sciences, 455,* 150–167.

May, D. C., & Wood, P. B. (2010). *Ranking correctional punishments: Views from offenders, practitioners, and the public.* Durham, NC: Carolina Academic Press.

McGrew, W. (2015, January 14). *Interview with Chief County Public Defender Mr. Wayne McGrew* (personal communication).

Merritt, N., Fain, T., & Turner, S. (2006). Oregon's get tough sentencing reform: A lesson in justice system adaptation. *Criminology and Public Policy, 5*(1), 5–36.

Murray, J., & Farrington, D. P. (2005). Parental imprisonment: Effects on boys' antisocial behavior and delinquency through the life-course. *Journal of Child Psychology and Psychiatry*, 46(12), 1269–1278.

Murray, J., & Farrington, D. P. (2008). Parental imprisonment: Longlasting effects on boys' internalizing problems through the life course. *Development and Psychopathology*, 20, 278–290.

Nagin, D. S., Cullen, F. T., & Johnson, C. L. (2009). Imprisonment and reoffending. In M. Tonry (Ed.), *Crime and justice: A review of research.* (Vol. 38, pp. 115–200). Chicago, IL: The University of Chicago Press.

National Institute of Law Enforcement and Criminal Justice. (1978). *The nation's toughest drug law: Evaluating the New York Experience.* Retrieved from https://www.ncjrs.gov/pdffiles1/Digitization/47795NCJRS.pdf

Petersilia, J. (1990). When probation becomes more dreaded than prison. *Federal Probation*, 54, 23–27.

Petersilia, J., & Deschenes, E. P. (1994a). What punishes? Inmates rank the severity of prison vs. intermediate sanctions. *Federal Probation, 58*, 3–8.

Petersilia, J., & Deschenes, E. P. (1994b). Perceptions of punishment: Inmate and staff rank the severity of prison versus intermediate sanctions. *The Prison Journal, 74*, 306–328.

Pew Center on the States. (2011, April). *State of recidivism: The revolving door of America's prisons.* Retrieved from http://www.pewtrusts.org/en/research-and-analysis/reports/2011/04/12/state-of-recidivism-the-revolving-door-of-americas-prisons

Pew Charitable Trusts. (2014, September). *Prison and crime: A complex link.* Retrieved from http://www.pewtrusts.org/en/multimedia/data-visualizations/2014/prison-and-crime

Pezze, D. (2014, December 22). *Interview with the Honorable Judge Debra Pezze, Pennsylvania Court of Common Pleas, Westmoreland County* (personal communication).

Pierce, G. L., & Bowers, W. J. (1981). The Bartley-Fox gun law's short-term impact on crime in Boston. *Annals of the American Academy of Political and Social Science*, 455, 120–137.

Raphael, S., & Winter-Ebmer, R. (2001). Identifying the effect of unemployment on crime. *Journal of Law and Economics*, 44(1), 259–283.

Rose, D. R., & Clear, T. R. (1998). Incarceration, social capital, and crime: Implications for social disorganization theory. *Criminology*, 36(3), 441–479.

Smith, P., Goggin, C., & Gendreau, P. (2002). The effects of prison sentences and intermediate sanctions on recidivism: General effects and individual differences. Ottawa, Ontario, Canada: Solicitor General of Canada.

Spelman, W. (1995). The severity of intermediate sanctions. *Journal of Research in Crime and Delinquency*, 32, 107–135.

Spelman, W. (2000). The limited importance of prison expansion. In A. Blumstein & J. Wallman (Eds.), *The crime drop in America*. Cambridge, MA: Cambridge University Press.

Spelman, W. (2005). Jobs or jails? The crime drop in Texas. *Journal of Policy Analysis and Management*, 24(1), 133–165.

Stemen, D. (2007, January). *Reconsidering incarceration: New directions for reducing crime.* New York: Vera Institute of Justice.

Taylor, P., & Williams, S. (2014). Sentencing reform and prisoner mental health. *Prison Service Journal, 211,* 43–49.

Tonry, M. (2009). The mostly unintended effects of mandatory penalties: Two centuries of consistent findings. In M. Tonry (Ed.), *Crime and Justice: A review of research.* (Vol. 38, pp. 65–114). Chicago, IL: The University of Chicago Press.

Ulmer, J. T. (2012). Recent developments and new directions in sentencing research. *Justice Quarterly, 29*(1), 1–40.

United States Sentencing Commission. (1991). *Special report to the congress: Mandatory minimum penalties in the federal criminal justice system.* Washington, DC: United States Sentencing Commission.

United States Sentencing Commission. (2015). *Quick facts: Federal offenders in prison — January 2015.* Washington, DC: United States Sentencing Commission. Retrieved from http://www.ussc.gov/sites/default/files/pdf/research-and-publications/quick -facts/Quick-Facts_BOP.pdf

Villettaz, P., Killias, M., & Zoder, I. (2006). *The effects of custodial vs. noncustodial sentences on re-offending: A systematic review of the state of knowledge.* Philadelphia, PA: The Campbell Collaboration Crime and Justice Group.

Wood, P. B., & Grasmick, H. G. (1999). Toward the development of punishment equivalencies: Male and female inmates rate the severity of alternative sanctions compared to prison. *Justice Quarterly, 16,* 19–50.

Wood, P. B., & May, D. C. (2003). Race differences in perceptions of sanction severity: A comparison of prison with alternatives. *Justice Quarterly, 20,* 605–631.

Zimring, F. E., & Hawkins, G. (1997). *Crime is not the problem: Lethal violence in America.* New York: Oxford University Press.

The Future of Sentencing in the United States

Chapter Objectives:

- To be aware of recent calls to scale back harsh sentencing practices.
- To gain a perspective of the current status of various reforms.
- To be cognizant of the monetary cost of imprisonment.
- To understand the complexity of public opinion on sentencing and corrections.
- To understand what is meant by "evidence-based" practices regarding sentencing.
- To acknowledge the renewed interest in rehabilitation and assess what impact it might have on sentencing and corrections.
- To gain an international/comparative perspective on sentencing and imprisonment practices.
- To learn the advice of sentencing scholars on future sentencing practices.
- To learn about the experience of imprisonment from an interview with a former inmate at a federal prison for women.
- To consider the future of sentencing in the United States.

Recent Calls to Scale Back Harsh Sentencing Practices

Recent moves to scale back harsh sentencing practices have gained national attention. One of these—former Attorney General Eric Holder's call to reduce mandatory minimum sentences for drug offenders—was discussed in Chapter 6. Let's look at the most recent efforts to attenuate harsh sentencing reforms.

Sentencing Commission Votes to Reduce Sentences for Drug Offenders

In April 2014, the United States Sentencing Commission (USSC) voted unanimously to reduce sentencing guidelines for most federal drug trafficking offenders. On July 18, 2014, the USSC voted unanimously to make the sentence reductions retroactive. This call for sentencing retroactivity means the same sentence reductions would apply to persons already serving time.

Decreasing drug sentences prospectively will reduce the federal prison population by approximately 6,500 over five years. Retroactive application could potentially allow over 40,000 prisoners to be eligible for sentence reductions and save over 80,000 prison beds over time. Because Congress did not block the change, almost half of the federal prisoners incarcerated for drug crimes will be eligible to have their sentences reduced by an average of over two years. This measure was slated to take effect on November 1, 2015, to allow time for each case to be reviewed by a judge. A prisoner would be released at an earlier date than originally indicated by the guidelines only if he or she was deemed to be no risk to public safety.

There was bipartisan support to change policies involving the imprisonment of drug offenders. The USSC held two public hearings and listened to testimony from many individuals, including federal judges, Department of Justice officials, federal public defenders, state and local law enforcement officers, and advocates on sentencing issues. The commission also received over 80,000 letters from the public on the issue and most expressed support for sentence reductions.

The seven commissioners voted to support these measures in an effort to control the costs of federal prisons, decrease the prison population, ensure fair and just punishment, and promote public safety. The Justice Department testified that increases in the prison population that have been seen over time have made prisons less safe for guards and inmates and hindered reentry. It also noted that the Bureau of Prisons budget was over $6 billion, which accounted for 25 percent of the Department of Justice's total budget.

The amendment reduced the sentencing levels associated with drug quantity in the guidelines by two levels. The change lowered the penalties by about 11 months for about 70 percent of new drug trafficking cases. Sentences of about 40,000 inmates who were serving prison terms for drug offenses could be retroactively reduced by an average of 25 months (United States Sentencing Commission, n.d.).

Former Attorney General Eric Holder had originally asked the commission to take a more limited approach that would impact about 20,000 inmates. There were some reports that prosecutors opposed retroactivity in cases with which they had been involved. He, however, lauded the new policy, stating, "This is a milestone in the effort to make more efficient use of our law enforcement resources and to ease the burden in our overcrowded prison system" (Phelps, (2014, July 18).

Justice Department Releases 6,000 Federal Inmates

On October 6, 2015, the Justice Department announced that it was getting ready to release approximately 6,000 inmates from federal prisons. These releases occurred from October 30–November 2, 2015. These releases followed the vote of the USSC detailed above. The releases symbolize a concerted effort to scale back the sentences of nonviolent drug dealers. They also come at a time of bipartisan support to decrease mass incarceration that has disproportionately affected minorities dealing crack cocaine. This release is one of the biggest discharges of inmates from federal prisons in the United States. About one-third of the inmates are undocumented immigrants who will turned over to U.S. Immigration and Customs Enforcement to be eventually deported (Bruer, Perez, & Glover, 2015, October 6; Schmidt, 2015 October 6).

Representatives from the American Civil Liberties Union have praised the decision. Some law enforcement officers, however, have voiced concerns over the release of inmates. Their concerns include the issue that released inmates may not be able to get jobs and that some inmates may come out of prison hardened and will likely reoffend (Schmidt, 2015, October 6). FBI Director James Corney expressed concern about the timing, as murder and violent crime rates have recently surged in some cities in the United States (Bruer, Perez, & Glover, 2015).

Sally Quillian Yates, a Deputy Attorney General with the Justice Department, noted that the drug offenders will have served a large proportion of their sentences and that in addition to federal judges considering each case individually, probation officers will be supervising and monitoring offenders (Bruer, Perez, & Glover, 2015, October 6). The average sentence before release for those eligible for reductions is still considerable— 108 months or 9 years (United States Sentencing Commission, n.d.).

Scaling Back Mandatory Minimums

President Obama Commutes Sentences

On July 13, 2015, President Barack Obama commuted the prison sentences of 46 drug offenders for whom he said the punishment did not fit the crime. Most of these offenders were federal prisoners who were imprisoned for drug offenses and sentenced under mandatory sentencing laws from the 1980s. Thirteen had been sentenced to life imprisonment (Liptak, 2015, July 13).

In a video posted online, President Obama said that the men and women were not "hardened criminals" and stated, "I believe that at its heart, America is a nation of second chances, and I believe these folks deserve their second chances."

Earlier in 2015, Obama commuted the sentences of 22 inmates who were convicted of drug offenses. He has vowed to reform the criminal justice system, with sentencing laws as a major focus. Obama has also voiced support for decreasing punishments for non-violent criminal offenders (Liptak, 2015, July 13). In the video, Obama stated, "Over the last few years a lot of people have become aware of the inequities in the criminal justice system."

Obama proclaimed,

> Right now, with our overall crime rate and incarceration rate both falling, we're at a moment when some good people in both parties, Republicans and Democrats and folks all across the country, are coming up with ideas to make the system work smarter and better.

Bipartisan Calls to Scale Back Federal Mandatory Minimums

Calls from politicians and national leaders to scale back or eliminate mandatory minimum sentences have been made over the last few years. Beginning in the 1970s, both liberals and conservative rallied to "reform" indeterminate sentencing practices and decrease widespread judicial discretion. As we discussed in Chapter 3, the critiques of indeterminate sentencing and reasons behind calls to reform differed. Conservatives pointed to the potential premature release of dangerous felons under indeterminate sentencing. Liberals, however, tended to emphasize racial discrimination and other disparities in sentencing that arose from virtually unbridled discretion inherent in indeterminate sentencing practices.

The recent support for reducing mandatory penalties by both liberals and conservatives also stems from several concerns. Many believe that these penalties are overly harsh and disproportionately affect minority offenders. Some point to the cost of mass incarceration stemming from mandatory minimum sentencing, especially for drug offenders.

Let's look at the calls to reform mandatory minimums from seemingly divergent actors.

Senator Rand Paul (R-KY) stated

> [o]ur country's mandatory minimum laws reflect a Washington-knows-best, one-size-fits-all approach, which undermines the Constitutional Separation of Powers, violates our bedrock principle that people should be treated as individuals, and costs the taxpayers money without making them any safer.

Senator Cory Booker (D-NJ) asserted

> [t]o truly end mass incarceration we need a comprehensive approach. We need to do away with harsh mandatory minimum penalties and the one-size-fits-all approach to sentencing. We should give judges — who are our sentencing experts — more discretion in sentencing.

Senator Dick Durbin (D-IL) noted, "Once seen as a strong deterrent, these mandatory sentences have too often been unfair, fiscally irresponsible, and a threat to public safety."

Former U.S. Supreme Court Justice William Rehnquist said, "Mandatory minimum sentences are perhaps a good example of the law of unintended consequences ... Mandatory minimums impose unduly harsh punishment for first-time offenders."

Grover Norquist of Americans for Tax Reform stated, "The biggest problem from the perspective of the taxpayer, however, is that mandatory minimum sentencing policies have proven prohibitively expensive."

David Keene, former president of the National Rifle Association and the American Conservative Union, reflected on mandatory minimum sentencing as follows:

> Like many conservatives, I supported many of these laws when they were enacted and still believe that, in some narrow situations, mandatory minimums make sense. But like other "one-size-fits-all" solutions to complicated problems, they should be reviewed in light of how they work in practice.

Proposed Federal Legislation

These pleas have culminated in the proposed Justice Safety Valve Act of 2013 (S. 619) and the proposed Smarter Sentencing Act of 2015 (S. 502/H.R. 920). Each act received bipartisan support, but neither has been passed as of press time.

On March 20, 2013, Senator Patrick Leahy (D-VT) and Senator Rand Paul (R-KY) sponsored the **Justice Safety Valve Act of 2013 (S. 619)**. This bill would amend 18 U.S.C. §3553 by adding a subsection that would create a new safety valve for federal mandatory minimum sentences. It would allow the imposition of a sentence below a statutory mandatory minimum in order to prevent an unjust sentence. It would allow sentences below the mandatory minimum if the court finds that the sentencing goals listed in Section 3553 (a) (detailed in Chapter 5) were not fulfilled.

While the current "safety valve" provision allows low-level drug offenders under certain conditions to avoid mandatory minimum penalties, this bill would extend that safety valve to *all* federal crimes subject to mandatory minimum penalties. It would allow a judge to impose a sentence other than the statutorily designated mandatory sentence in certain cases (such as when the mandatory sentence is not necessary to protect public safety). The judge would be required to provide notice to the parties and to state in writing the reasons justifying the alternative sentence.

Senator Leahy commented about the bill the day it was proposed, stating,

> Today I join with Senator Paul to introduce the Justice Safety Valve Act of 2013, which will start to take on the problem of the ever-increasing federal prison population and spiraling costs that spend more and more of our justice budget on keeping people in prison, thereby reducing opportunities to do more to keep our communities safe. This bill will combat injustice in federal sentencing and the waste of taxpayer dollars by allowing judges appropriate discretion in sentencing.
>
> As a former prosecutor, I understand that criminals must be held accountable, and that long sentences are sometimes necessary to keep violent criminals off the street and deter those who would commit violent crime. I have come to believe, however, that mandatory minimum sentences do more harm than good. (Leahy, 2013, March 20)

The Smarter Sentencing Act of 2015 (S. 502/H.R. 920) (SSA) was introduced on February 12, 2015, by Senator Mike Lee (R-UT) with Senator Dick Durbin (D-IL), Senator Ted Cruz (R-TX), Senator Patrick Leahy (D-VT), Senator Jeff Flake (R-AZ), Senator Cory Booker (D-NJ), Senator Rand Paul (R-KY), Senator Sheldon Whitehouse (D-RI), and Senator Christopher Coons (D-DE). Representatives Raúl Labrador (R-ID) and Bobby Scott (D-VA) also sponsored the bill.

It calls for the lowering of penalties for certain non-violent drug offenses. If passed, the bill would lower certain 20-year, 10-year, and 5-year mandatory minimum drug sentences to 10-year, 5-year, and 2-year sentences respectively. It also calls for the reduction of the mandatory minimum life without parole sentence for a third drug offense to a minimum term of 25 years (in the Senate version) or 20 years (in the House version). These provisions would not be retroactive.

In addition, the bill would somewhat increase the use of the existing federal "safety valves" for drug offenses, but would not be retroactive. Whereas the current safety valve can be invoked for federal drug offenders who have no more than one criminal history point (category 1), the bill would allow federal drug offenders with up to three criminal history points (category 2) to be eligible for the safety valve. According to Families Against Mandatory Minimums (FAMM), this bill would prevent old, minor, or misdemeanor convictions for which people did not serve any prison or jail time from disqualifying nonviolent, low-level offenders from receiving a sentence below the mandatory minimum (Families Against Mandatory Minimums, n.d.).

The bill would also make the Fair Sentencing Act of 2010 (FSA) retroactive. As discussed in Chapter 5, the FSA increased the amounts of crack cocaine that would trigger five- and 10-year mandatory minimum sentences for federal crack cocaine crimes and repealed the mandatory minimum for simple possession of five grams of crack cocaine. If the SSA is passed, it would allow federal crack cocaine offenders who were sentenced before August 3, 2010, to make a motion to the court requesting that the SSA be applied to their cases. It would also permit the director of the Bureau of Prisons, the court, or the prosecutor to make such a motion as well. The judge who sentenced the federal prisoner would then decide to grant or deny a sentence reduction and base the decision, in part, on the offender's dangerousness.

The goals of the bill include saving billions of dollars on incarcerating non-violent drug offenders, reducing federal prison overcrowding, and ensuring that the Justice Department can fund law enforcement, victims' services, and reentry programs. The Congressional Budget Office has projected that the passage of the SSA would save more than $3 billion over the next 10 years. The USSC, the U.S. Department of Justice, and the Urban Institute have predicted that the passage of the SSA would also significantly decrease the federal prison population and overcrowding over the next decades. Testimony from the USSC suggests that if the mandatory minimum penalty provisions of the FSA were to be made fully retroactive, 8,829 offenders would likely be eligible for a sentence reduction, with an average reduction of 53 months per offender. The commission estimates that 87.7 percent of the inmates eligible for a sentence reduction would be black (Families Against Mandatory Minimums, 2015, April 9).

In a press conference, Ted Cruz (R-TX) reflected on the SSA and stated:

> The issue that brings us together today is fairness. What brings us together is justice. What brings us together is common sense. This is as diverse and bipartisan an array of members of Congress as you will see on any topic and yet we are all unified in saying common sense reforms need to be enacted to our criminal justice system. Right now today far too many young men, in particular African American young men, find their lives drawn in with the criminal justice system, find themselves subject to sentences of many decades for relatively minor non-violent drug infractions. We've seen the impact of these kind of reforms in the states, the states are laboratories of democracy. My home state of Texas implemented similar reforms and from 2005 the state of Texas has seen a 22 percent decrease in crime and a 12 percent decrease in expenditures on criminal justice. These are basic common sense. It's also a matter of justice. (2015, February 12)

To What Extent Are the Reforms Being Reformed? Sentencing Reform in Context

In light of the president's remarks, the decisions by the United States Sentencing Commission, and bipartisan support for changes to harsh sentencing practices, we must ask the question, "Are sentencing reforms being reformed (again)?" If so, how and to what extent? What is the cost of incarceration in the United States and how do sentencing laws impact the cost? How can we characterize public sentiments toward sentencing practices? How might a renewed interest in rehabilitation and the recent emphasis on evidence-based practices affect sentencing practices? How does the use of incarceration in the United States compare with other countries? What advice do scholars have about sentencing approaches in the future? Will there be sweeping changes in the way citizens are sentenced? What is the future of sentencing reforms?

To help answer these questions, we must look at the cost of corrections, namely the costs of prisons that house persons sentenced to lengthy sentences. We can assess how correctional resources (and lack thereof) may influence future sentencing practices. We need to address public opinion of punishment and sentencing, given that politicians and policymakers are expected to take into account the public's opinion in policy decisions. We must also take a look at a renewed interest in rehabilitation and the new catchphrase—"evidence-based practices"—and how sentencing strategies may be changed to reflect the goal of rehabilitation. We need to understand what noted sentencing researchers suggest for the future of sentencing.

And of course we need to bear in mind that sentencing practices remain different in all 50 states, the District of Columbia, and the federal system. Twenty-one states and the District of Columbia have adopted commission-based guidelines systems. In some cases, states have sought to establish commission-based guidelines, but ultimately decided not to adopt them. In South Carolina, Connecticut, New York, and Maine, for example, sentencing commissions were formed, but they either opted not to create sentencing guidelines, or could not convince the state legislatures to adopt the guidelines that they had designed. In other states indeterminate sentencing has not been challenged.

All 50 states have enacted at least some mandatory minimum sentencing laws. About half of the states have passed three strikes laws, and all have some type of habitual offender statutes.

The Cost of Incarceration

One of the factors fueling the call to reduce sentences for certain criminal offenders is the high cost of corrections, most notably the cost of incarceration. As taxpayers, the general public pays for the costs of corrections. If people are aware of the costs of prisons, they may be more open to sentencing alternatives that save money and may be as or more effective than imprisonment in reducing recidivism.

The question of cost effectiveness is, however, subjective to some degree. Some people might think that imprisonment of certain types of offenders, such as drug offenders, is worth the cost of incarceration. They see these offenders as serious and that offenses such as drug trafficking involve violence and threaten the safety of the general public. Others may feel that certain drug offenders don't pose a safety risk to the general public and that money can be saved by placing such offenders in less costly alternatives to incarceration that take a rehabilitative approach.

Estimating the Cost of Imprisonment

The Vera Institute of Justice's Center on Sentencing and Corrections and Cost-Benefit Analysis Unit worked with the Pew Center on the States to develop a methodology to estimate the full cost of prisons to taxpayers. In 2012, Christian Henrichson and Ruth Delaney authored a report for the Vera Institute of Justice based on this research, entitled, *The Price of Prisons: What Incarceration Costs Taxpayers.*

This report indicated that states' spending on expenditures for corrections almost quadrupled in the past two decades. While most of the costs for state prisons are paid by the corrections department in the state, other departments pay related expenses. It showed that the true cost of corrections includes employee benefits, capital costs, in-prison educational services, and inmate health care costs, all of which are often covered in other state agencies' budgets.

Vera researchers calculated the total taxpayer costs of prisons in 40 states that participated in the study. They concluded that the real price was estimated to be approximately 14 percent higher than what is reported in states' correctional budgets. The total cost to taxpayers was $39 billion, which exceeded the $33.5 billion that was represented in corrections budgets alone for these states (Henrichson & Delaney, 2012).

Costs outside the corrections budget can be divided into three categories: (1) costs budgeted centrally for administrative purposes (employee benefits and taxes, pension contributions, retiree health care contributions, capital costs, legal judgments and claims, statewide administrative costs, and private prisons); (2) inmate services funded through other agencies (hospital care and education and training); and (3) underfunded contributions for retirement benefits (underfunded pensions benefit and underfunded retiree health care benefits). There is significant variation by state with respect to how many and which of these costs apply.[1]

These additional costs outside the corrections department ranged from less than one percent of the total prison costs in Arizona to 34 percent of those costs in Connecticut.

The authors of the report provided the average cost per inmate in each state. This measure is standardized and figures in the comprehensive costs. The average cost per inmate of the 40 states studied was reported to be $31,307 with a low of $14,603 in Kentucky and a high of $60,076 in New York.

The report cautioned against a state-by-state comparison of per-inmate spending. This is because the costs do not reflect how effective the spending is or take into account the collateral costs to society. For example, per-inmate spending is likely lower in states with higher levels of overcrowding. In contrast, states operating under rated capacity may have higher per-inmate costs because although they've reduced their inmate population, they have not reduced the operating capacity to produce savings. Another reason is that the number of low-level offenders varies by state. These offenders are more likely to be housed in minimum- or medium-security facilities, which are less expensive to house offenders, compared to maximum security facilities. In addition, states vary with respect to the extent to which they reimburse jails to house state inmates. Jails usually provide less programming to inmates and thus the per-inmate cost may be less in states that rely more on jails to house state-sentenced inmates (Henrichson & Delaney, 2012).

Strategies to Cut Corrections Costs

The authors of the Vera report suggested a few ways to cut costs while maintaining public safety. The route to reducing prison budgets is to decrease the inmate population, which will in turn reduce the operating costs and related costs. They discussed several as avenues to doing this.

The first is to **restructure sentencing and release policies**. For example, in 2010 South Carolina increased penalties for certain violent offenses but sentences for controlled substance offenses were revised to indicate community supervision, not prison, for some non-trafficking offenses. Some states have revised release policies which have lowered the percent of the sentence that must be served. Mississippi, for example, lowered the percent of time to be served for non-violent offenders from 85 percent to 25 percent. Other states have increase opportunities for "earned time."

Second, specific **recidivism-reduction strategies** have been offered to save the costs of incarcerating recidivists. As we have discussed, recidivism rates are high. Reentry programs and screening tools are being implemented to help corrections personnel identify offender risks and needs. Programs in Oregon and Michigan allow community supervision officers to relay to inmates their expectations upon release back into the community and provide programming for them in the community. In addition, because many parole violations are technical violations rather than new offenses, some states are moving away from incarcerating such violators. Instead, they are putting them on less expensive alternative sanctions, or jailing them for a few days only.

Third, strategies to **increase operating efficiency** have been implemented to decrease prison costs. Cutting staff positions or imposing hiring freezes are approaches that have been used by over 32 states. Most do not cut correctional officer positions because of safety issues. Other ways to increase operating efficiency include the use of video surveillance in prisons and the use of video conferencing for court hearings (which reduces transportation costs). Some states have closed facilities or parts of facilities (Henrichson & Delaney, 2012).

The Cost of Incarcerating Older Offenders

Another key concern regarding cost of imprisonment is the increase in the number of older prisoners, who on average cost more to house. Older offenders often require more medical care. They may suffer from dementia, have limited mobility, and have hearing or vision loss. In the prison setting, the needs of older inmates may necessitate increased staffing and special training (McKillop, 2015 October). Federal facilities that house high percentages of older inmates may spend five times more per inmate on medical care compared to those facilities that house low percentages of elderly inmates ($10,114 versus $1,916) (Office of Inspector General, 2015 October).

In 2014, while the overall prison population in the United States decreased slightly, the number of older inmates grew rapidly. Between 1999 and 2014, the number of state and federal inmates 55 and older increased 250 percent, compared to a growth rate of 8 percent among inmates under 55. Inmates 55 and over represented only three percent in 1999 (43,300) but accounted for ten percent of the prison population in 2014 (151,500) (McKillop, 2015 October).

Continuing to sentence offenders to long prison terms under mandatory sentencing and three strikes laws will result in even higher numbers of elderly incarcerated persons for years to come, absent sweeping changes to such laws. One may ask whether a cost-benefit analysis would justify the long term incarceration of this special inmate population.

A report from the Office of Inspector General (OIG) showed that older inmates commit fewer acts of misconduct while incarcerated and have a lower rate of re-arrest once released. The report suggested that aging inmates could be candidates for early release, which would mean a cost savings. An April 2013 OIG report, however, found problems with the Bureau of Prisons (BOP) compassionate release program. Specifically, it was only being used for inmates with terminal illnesses who have fewer than 12 months to live.

In August 2013, the Attorney General expanded provisions for inmates aged 65 and over to apply for compassionate release as part of the Department's "Smart on Crime" initiative, which in part sought to decrease sentencing disparities and prison overcrowding. The BOP revised its compassionate release policy that day, which expanded provisions for eligibility to older inmates for both medical and nonmedical reasons. Those eligible were to include those inmates 65 years and older who were not convicted on a violent offense and who had served a significant proportion on their prison sentence.

The OIG report used BOP data and estimated that the BOP spent approximately $881 million, or 19 percent of its total budget, to incarcerate aging inmates in FY 2013. It concluded,

> We found that lowering the threshold age from age 65 to age 50 in the revised compassionate release program, coupled with a modest 5 percent release rate for only those aging inmates in minimum- or low-security institutions or medical centers, could reduce incarceration costs by approximately $28 million per year. (p. 47)

The figures on the cost of incarceration in the United States may evoke action to reduce this cost. Revisions to sentencing laws and guidelines that would put fewer people in prison may be an effective way to tackle the problem of costly corrections spending. But would this response meet with public approval?

Public Opinion about Sentencing and Corrections

Changes to sentencing practices that would decrease the number of people incarcerated in the United States would likely come under public scrutiny. Public sentiments about crime issues, including sentencing practices, can affect the actions of lawmakers and politicians who are placed in positions to represent their constituents. Roberts and Stalans (1997) stated, "Public opinion plays an important role in criminal justice policy-making" (p. 6). The authors noted that many judges in the United States face re-election and must, therefore, bear in mind public opinion of them. As elected figures, politicians, prosecutors, and judges do not want to appear "soft on crime."

People are concerned with public safety but as taxpayers, they also want sentencing policies that are cost efficient. So, how do people form their opinions about sentencing practices? From what source(s) do they get the information on the criminal justice system and in particular sentencing?

Only a very small percentage of the general public gets their information about criminal justice issues, such as sentencing, through a college curriculum. The readers of this text are most likely university students studying criminal justice from a social science perspective. The vast majority of the general public, however, has not been taught to apply social scientific methods to evaluating what types of approaches to curtailing crime (including sentencing strategies) are effective. Most people are not aware of research studies that show the social and monetary costs of harsh sentencing practices or that there is little evidence that such strategies are effective deterrents to crime. Simply put, most members of the general public do not have bachelor's degrees, let alone master's or doctorates in the field of criminal justice.

People's perceptions of the criminal justice system may arise from direct or indirect experiences with it. *Direct* experiences include being a crime victim, working with crime victims, witnessing a crime, or volunteering with crime victims. People can also gain knowledge about the criminal justice system *indirectly* by knowing a victim of crime, knowing people who have been involved in the criminal justice system as offenders or professionals, and/or through so-called "common knowledge." The source of "common knowledge" is more often than not the media (Gray, 2009).

The Media's Influence on Public Perceptions of Crime and Justice

The Media's Portrayal of the Crime Problem

Television shows, newspapers, radio, and the internet are all sources of information or misinformation about crime and the criminal justice system. One study found that as many as 95 percent of the public cited the mass media as their primary source of information about issues related to crime and the criminal justice system (Imrich, Mullin, & Linz, 1990). Since that study was done, the internet became a major source of information and the use of social media (which has no requirement to be truthful or accurate) has exploded and become a venue for opinions on criminal justice issues, including sentencing.

News stories involving crimes that are aired usually involve violent, sex, or drug crimes. Most crimes committed in the United States are property offenses, such as larceny theft. These "mundane" crimes rarely make headlines, however, unless they involve a large dollar amount, like in the case of a jewelry or art heist. Who would spend an hour watching a prime time program about how to solve a rash of larceny thefts in an apartment complex? Not exactly an attention grabber!

The general public, therefore, gets a picture of the crime problem in the United States that is skewed. If one only relied on the news or primetime television programs for information about the types of crimes that are most frequently committed, he or she might conclude that most crimes are violent predatory crimes, such as murder, rape, or robbery. Criminal justice students, however, know that these crimes are relatively rare, compared to the number of property crimes committed. If one has an inaccurate picture of the nature of crime in the United States, his or her response on how to deal with "crime problem" will be misinformed and likely quite punitive.

The public is inundated with messages from the media that the criminal justice system is too soft on crime and that victims are failed by the criminal justice system. Perceptions of system leniency may lead the public to call for harsher sentences for offenders (Gray, 2009).

An Australian study showed that the three strongest predictors of punitive attitudes were perceptions of crime levels, education, and reliance on tabloid/commercial media for news. This study showed that those with higher educational levels had significantly lower levels of punitive attitudes, compared with those with less education. Persons who perceived crime levels to be high and those who relied on tabloid/commercial media for news had relatively high levels of punitive attitudes (Spiranovic, Roberts, & Indermaur, 2012).

The Media and the Passage of Three Strikes Laws

According to Grimes (2010), "Social control and punishment take on new meanings in a mass media age: policies about crime and punishment are increasingly shaped by media constructions of social problems that harvest audiences by appealing to fear" (p. 39). Support for the adoption of three strikes laws by the general public in the 1990s grew in part from the media's portrayal of crime, which led to a moral panic (Grimes, 2010). There was national media coverage of the horrific rape and murder of Polly Klaas in 1993 by a repeat violent offender who had been released from a California prison. The media coverage of Polly Klaas's murder gave the public the message that the only way to sufficiently ensure public safety was to increase the sanctions for all violent and/ or repeat offenders. The pressure by crime activists and the general public on politicians to do something about the problem of premature release of dangerous offenders prompted three strikes legislation shortly after the perpetrator was arrested. California passed Proposition 184, the "Three Strikes You're Out" law in 1994. Grimes (2010) performed a content analysis of major newspapers from 1992 to 2005 and found that the frequency of the "three strikes" slogan in headlines increased from 19 in 1993 to 128 in 1994.

Yankelovich (1991) described *public opinion*, which is formed during the early stages of a moral panic or public crisis. In the case of three strikes legislation, there was much support for the passage of such laws at the time of Polly Klaas's abduction and murder by a violent repeat offender. He contrasted this with *public judgment*, which follows after the public is informed about the facts—in this case the way that strikes legislation has been applied to offenders.

Only recently has the media presented stories of real people being sent to prison for life for a third "strike" that was a relatively petty offense, such as stealing golf clubs or stealing less than $250 in video games. Organizations such as the Three Strikes Project feature real life case stories of those persons sentenced under California's original three strikes law. Well publicized cases of California's draconian three strikes laws putting offenders in prison for life for a third non-violent, seemingly "petty" felony offense, as well as the concern of the cost of imprisonment to taxpayers, clearly impacted the general public.

Perhaps the most convincing evidence of the impact of public judgment on policy was when California voters passed California's Proposition 36 in 2012. In this case, the citizens of California became aware of such cases through the media. Over 69 percent voted for Proposition 36, which scaled back California's three strikes law to require the third "strike" to be "serious or violent" and authorized re-sentencing of offenders who were serving life sentences under California's original three strikes law, whose third strike conviction was not serious or violent.

Public Sentiments on Sentencing and Punishment in the United States

Studies performed to gauge public perceptions of various sentencing practices and the appropriate use of imprisonment versus community based corrections have shown that public attitudes regarding the sentencing of criminal offenders are quite complex. Some figures suggest that Americans are quite punitive. Other research has shown that people are open to alternatives to harsh sentencing practices. Listwan, Jonson, Cullen, and Latessa (2008) stated, "In fact, the notion that the public is exclusively punitive is a 'myth'" (p. 426). Cullen, Fisher, and Applegate (2000) suggested that the public's understanding of the severity of various sentences and sentencing alternatives is not fully informed. For example, many people are not aware of alternatives to incarceration, such as intermediate sanctions.

How Punitive Is the General Public?

Cullen, Fisher, and Applegate (2000) raised the question of how punitive the general public really is. They differentiated "global" and "specific" questions that tap public attitudes toward crime issues. They suggested that the results of asking questions in different ways can yield quite different responses.

Global questions are broadly worded and are meant to capture the public's agreement or disagreement with a crime control policy. For example, "Do you support capital punishment?" or "Do you support three strikes laws?" are global questions. Such questions are often asked by large polling firms, such as Gallup or Louis Harris via telephone surveys to representative samples in the United States. The results are often reported by the news media, suggesting that the public is quite punitive with respect to how to deal with criminal offenders.

When asked in a 2015 Gallup poll, "Are you in favor of the death penalty for a person convicted of murder?" 63 percent of Americans were in favor of the death penalty.

This figure was at its lowest (42 percent) in 1966 and the highest (80 percent) in 1994 (Jones, 2014, October 23).

Cullen and colleagues (2000) noted, however, that public opinion for a policy may be different when more information is provided in the question. For example, when people are given more than one sentencing option, the support for the initial option, such as the death penalty, may decline. In this approach, a researcher is trying to capture the complexity of the issue by so-called **specific** questions.

When asked in a 2014 Gallop poll, "If you could choose between the following two approaches, which do you think is the better penalty for murder, the death penalty or life imprisonment with absolutely no possibility of parole?" people's support for the death penalty was much lower, however, they still favored it 50 percent to 45 percent (Jones, 2014, October 23).

Cullen and colleagues (2000) maintained that survey respondents will favor less severe sentencing options when surveys provide detailed information about the offender and the crime and when they can choose from more than one sentence type (imprisonment, intermediate sanctions, community sanctions, etc.). They also noted that surveys should not only ask about what types of punishment the public supports, but should also measure the public's views on more progressive policies, including rehabilitation and early intervention programs. Measuring the public's views on these approaches helps us understand more fully how people feel about the way criminal offenders should be treated by the criminal justice system.

They noted that differences exist in the public's attitudes about three strikes laws when people were asked general versus specific questions. Applegate, Cullen, Turner, and Sundt (1996) found that over 88 percent of a sample of Cincinnati-area residents either "somewhat" (36.3 percent) or "strongly" (52.1 percent) agreed with a three strikes law that would hand down a life sentence of imprisonment to "anyone with two serious felony convictions on their record who is convicted of a third serious crime" (p. 522). The respondents were then presented with a vignette describing various offenses that could invoke the mandatory life sentence under a three strikes law that was at the time pending in the Ohio legislature. It allowed participants to choose a sanction of "no punishment," "probation," and "life in prison." Only 16.9 percent of the respondents chose the life sentence, suggesting that attitudes toward punishment may be less severe than what one might conclude from the global question.

Public Attitudes toward Alternative Sanctions

Public support for alternatives to incarceration, such as intermediate sanctions and restorative sanctions, also challenges the notion that the public is solely punitive. Surveys have shown that people favor locking up people who have committed violent offenses. A body of research also has shown, however, that the American public supports sanctions such as boot camps, intensive probation, and/or house arrest with or without electronic monitoring for nonviolent offenders (Brown & Elrod, 1995; Elrod & Brown, 1996; Senese, 1992). Some studies have shown public support for restorative sanctions, especially for young offenders and non-violent offenders (Huang, Braithwaite, Tsutomi, & Braithwaite, 2012; Moore, 2012, February; Roberts & Stalans, 1997; Roberts & Stalans, 2004). Much of this body of research, however, has come from surveys of respondents from other countries.

A key factor in changing attitudes among the general public involves educating them about alternative sanctions. A study examining the sentencing preferences of a sample of Delaware residents showed that many were open to the use of alternative sanctions for nonviolent offenders. In 1991, the Public Agenda Foundation, a nonpartisan organization, brought together a representative sample of 432 Delaware residents for three-hour sessions to assess their preferences for various sentencing alternatives. Participants first filled out a questionnaire (a pretest) which asked them to choose from one of only two sentencing alternatives—prison or probation, for 23 hypothetical offenders. They were then shown a 22-minute video about the problem of prison overcrowding and were presented with information about five alternative sanctions including strict (intensive supervision) probation, restitution, community service, house arrest, and boot camps. The videos portrayed the benefits and negative aspects of each alternative. The participants then met in groups of 15 people and discussed the issues with a moderator from the Public Agenda Foundation for about 90 minutes. Afterwards, they filled out another questionnaire (posttest), which portrayed the same 23 offenders but this time added the five alternative sanctions in addition to prison and probation from which they could choose (Doble, Immerwahr, & Richardson, 1991).

When given only prison and probation as sentencing options, the Delawareans wanted to incarcerate 17 out of the 23 offenders. After the respondents watched the video and engaged in the discussion, however, the respondents wanted to incarcerate only five of the 23 offenders. Four were violent offenders and one was a drug dealer convicted for a fifth time. In the other 18 cases, the group wanted to use one of the five sentencing alternatives.

Respondents liked the fact that sentencing alternatives gave judges flexibility to make the punishment fit the crime. They viewed the alternatives as appropriately punitive but that they would also serve the community and improve chances of rehabilitation. The Delawareans did not think that prisons kept inmates productively occupied.

Restitution, community service, and boot camp stood out as the alternatives most preferred. Respondents liked the ability to track the offender and that they featured a work component, which allowed the offenders literally to pay back for their crimes. They felt that offenders should be kept busy and believed that working might help offenders acquire job skills and adopt a work ethic.

Studies were also conducted by the Public Agenda Foundation in Alabama (Doble & Klein, 1989) and Pennsylvania (Farkas, 1993) and showed similar results. This body of research had provided evidence that people's impressions of appropriate sentences are malleable.

Public Attitudes toward Rehabilitation

There is also some evidence that the public views rehabilitation as an important sentencing goal of corrections. A national survey conducted in 2001 showed that 55 percent of United States citizens said that rehabilitation should be the "main emphasis" of prisons. The same study showed that 88 percent of people agreed with the statement, "It is important to try to rehabilitate adults who have committed crimes and are now in the correctional system" (Cullen, Pealer, Fisher, Applegate, & Santana, 2002, pp. 136–137).

Evidence that public attitudes can be changed also came from a study of peoples' attitudes towards sex offenders. Kleban and Jeglic (2012) argued that treatment, as opposed to punishment, has been effective in increasing public safety. Their experiment showed that persons who completed an online education module about the benefits of sex offender treatment had less negative attitudes towards the treatment of sex offenders compared to the control group.

While the goals of rehabilitation and punishment may be inherently incompatible (as discussed in Chapter 8) the public seems to want offenders to punished in prison, but also have access to rehabilitation programs within the institution (Cullen, Fisher, & Applegate, 2000; Reynolds, Craig, & Boer, 2009). Contrary to the notion that the American public is wholly punitive, Cullen, Fisher, and Applegate (2000) argued that while support for rehabilitation has declined since its peak in the 1960s, people view treating offenders as an important objective of corrections. This sentiment is especially high regarding the rehabilitative potential for juvenile offenders and at-risk youth (Cullen, Vose, Jonson, & Unnever, 2007; Nagin, Piquero, Scott, & Steinberg, 2006; Piquero, Cullen, Unnever, Piquero, & Gordon, 2010). The way the public views offenders can play a key role in how they may (or may not) be accepted by the community upon release and reintegrated into the community (Reynolds, Craig, & Boer, 2009).

Public Attitudes about Sentencing in Different Countries

So how do public attitudes in the United States match up to those in other countries? Are Americans more or less supportive of punitive sanctions?

A study by Van Kesteren (2009) examined public attitudes toward sentencing across approximately 50 countries using the International Crime Victims Surveys (ICVS) and the European Survey of Crime and Safety (EUICS). Respondents were asked what type of sanction they would consider most appropriate for a recidivist burglar. They were asked to choose one of the following sanctions: fine, prison, community service, suspended sentence, or another sentence. If they chose imprisonment, they were asked what length of time they deemed appropriate.

Community service was the preference of 39 percent of respondents in the 2004/2005 national samples. The percentage choosing community service was lower in the United States. Imprisonment was recommended by 37 percent of American respondents, which was slightly higher than the average. Community service was the preferred sanction in almost every continental European country. Imprisonment was preferred in most developing countries.

Van Kesteren computed a punitiveness score for each country which showed that those in the USA sample had more punitive views on sentencing than average. The percentage of United States respondents who chose imprisonment, however, has declined over several years of administration of the ICVS and EUICS.

Should Public Opinion Impact Policymakers and Policies?

Two opposite viewpoints about the importance of public opinion on criminal justice issues have been expressed in the literature. One is that in a democracy, the public elects officials to represent the people and promote policies that the public favors (Wood, 2009). According to this perspective, political leaders should promote sentencing policies and practices that mirror public opinion.

Cullen, Fisher, and Applegate (2000) questioned this argument. They raised the question of whether public sentiments, especially punitive ones, *should* impact policies on sentencing and corrections in the United States. They asserted

> Public sentiments on policy issues must be accorded some weight in a democratic society, but justifying policies on the basis of what citizens want confronts a dismaying reality: much of the public—in the United States and elsewhere—is ignorant about many aspects of crime and its control. (p. 3)

Evidence-Based Sentencing

So, where might we look to get answers about what sentencing strategies and correctional policies are effective in controlling crime and maximizing public safety? One place is social science research that has evaluated the impact of sentencing policies and correctional strategies on recidivism.

We can look at what researchers have labelled "evidence-based" practices in sentencing and corrections to ascertain how the criminal justice system may promote smart sentencing practices. One might assume that sentencing policies and practices in the United States *have been* informed by evidence-based research. Our discussion throughout the text, however, has shown that in the past, *research has rarely informed sentencing and correctional policies.*

Most would agree that approaches to sentencing and corrections *should be* based on research findings that identify effective strategies in providing uniform sentencing, reducing recidivism, ensuring public safety, and minimizing cost. Let's examine recent efforts that have integrated social science research findings with sentencing and correctional policies.

The NCSC Sentencing Reform Project

In January 2006, the National Center for State Courts (NCSC), with the support of the Conference of Chief Justices and Conference of State Court Administrators, initiated a national sentencing reform project entitled, "Getting Smarter about Sentencing" (Peters & Warren, 2006).

The stated central goal of this project is

> to mobilize the collective energy and experience of the judges and administrators of the state courts under the leadership of the state chief justices and state

court administrators to promote reform of state sentencing policies and practices. (p. 2)

The NCSC identified seven project objectives:

1) To reduce over-reliance on incarceration as a criminal sanction for those not posing a substantial danger to the community or committing the most serious offenses.
2) To promote alternatives to incarceration such as the development, funding, and utilization of community-based alternatives to incarceration for appropriate offenders.
3) To eliminate inappropriate racial and ethnic disparities in sentencing.
4) To promote greater flexibility and judicial discretion in sentencing policy and practice, including repeal of mandatory minimum punishment provisions.
5) To provide greater rationality in sentencing through improved access to and use of relevant data and information in sentencing policy and practice.
6) To promote public safety and reduce recidivism through expanded use of evidence-based practices using programs that work, and offender risk and needs assessment tools.
7) To promote utilization of sentencing commissions and flexible sentencing guidelines systems. (Peters & Warren, p. 3)

The NCSC gave a nine-question survey to chief justices and court administrators in each state in January 2006. Responses were received from 42 states and the District of Columbia and Guam. Respondents identified Objectives 1, 2, and 6 as the most important for their states. It was concluded that these three objectives, along with Objective 5, could most benefit from active involvement from the judges.

The responses from the states indicated a shared perception that incarceration is overused, and that sentencing and treatment alternatives are lacking, especially for drug offenses. The idea of establishing drug courts was raised by the survey participants. Establishing substance abuse and mental health programs was also a commonly cited suggestion. In addition, participants mentioned a wide variety of other alternative sanctions, including but not limited to community service, electronic monitoring, intensive supervision probation, day reporting centers, job training programs, and cognitive-behavioral treatment programs.

Judges identified the importance of relying on sentencing policies and practices that were shown by empirical data to be effective. Judges cited the expansion of evidence-based practices. These include expanding the use of risk assessment tools beyond probation and parole agencies to the courts as well.

When asked "Are there any existing efforts in your state to pursue any of the seven objectives of this national project?" respondents reported efforts in all of the seven objective areas. The efforts that were cited the most were the development of alternatives to incarceration and the promotion of evidence-based practices.

The four specific efforts most commonly cited were (1) the development of problem-solving courts, such as drug courts and mental health courts, (2) the increased use of risk assessment and evidence-based practices, (3) the increased use of alternatives to incarceration, and (4) the continued use of sentencing standards, such as commission-based guidelines, offender scoring, and the monitoring of sentencing statistics, to reduce or eliminate sentencing disparities. Several states had set up task forces to address the NCSC objectives.

The Role of Sentencing Commissions

As early as 1967, in their report, *The Challenge of Crime in a Free Society* (1967), the President's Commission on Law Enforcement and Administration of Justice emphasized the importance of research in informing public policy. One objective of the commission involved the allocation of resources to study each segment of the criminal justice system to ascertain what strategies are effective in controlling crime.

Sentencing commissions provides ideal venues for periodic reevaluation of state sentencing practices and avenues to propose revisions to current practices. Many sentencing commissions have active research components that use social science research to evaluate the consequences of sentencing guidelines. Most notably, the United States Sentencing Commission has a research department that conducts evaluations of the impact of guidelines and guidelines changes on several outcomes including recidivism and the prison population. As discussed in Chapter 5, the USSC considers the federal guidelines to be evolving. Because of this, data-driven research from USSC researchers may prompt review, recommendations to Congress, and ultimately revisions to the guidelines. The Fair Sentencing Act of 2010, for example, reflected earlier recommendations from the USSC. State commissions vary with respect to how much they perform research. Those that do have organized research components can better use evaluations of their guidelines systems to "fine tune" sentencing practices.

How May Reviving Rehabilitation Impact Sentencing Policies?

Penal Harm

In 1994, Todd Clear described "penal harm" as

> ... the essence of the penal sanction—that it harms. It refers as well to its special status as a planned governmental act, whereby a citizen is harmed, and implies that harm is justifiable precisely because it is an offender who is suffering. (p. 4)

Clear identified the indirect consequences of punishments on offenders, including deprivations in prison, medical and environmental threats, and general physical and psychological damage that accompanies prison life. He emphasized that even if prisons were healthy places, however, the sanction would still be harmful, not just because the offender loses his or her freedom, but "because the very content of punishment is harm" (p. 4). Twenty years later, one can still conceptualize punishment in the United States as fostering "penal harm."

Modern Reforms Have Devalued Rehabilitation

We have shown throughout this text that the vast majority of modern sentencing reforms emphasize retribution, deterrence, and incapacitation as appropriate goals of sentencing. As sentencing reforms have spread throughout the United States since the mid-1980s, prescribed punishments have left little room for the expansion of rehabilitative programs, especially for serious/violent/repeat offenders.

No "modern" sentencing reform identifies rehabilitation as the dominant goal. Some sentencing commissions identify rehabilitation as an appropriate goal for some types of offenders—usually nonviolent and/or first-time offenders. A few state guideline systems indicate that some sanctions should promote rehabilitation.

A Revived Interest in Rehabilitation

Only in recent years has the field of criminology begun to take a renewed interest in rehabilitation as a desired goal of sentencing. Many would argue that the idea of rehabilitation is quite appealing. If, through the process of imprisonment, the offender can be rehabilitated and leave prison with the desire and tools to live a productive and crime-free life, then the sanction has resulted in a bettering of the offender and reduced the likelihood of recidivism.

Legal scholars, criminologists, politicians, and community leaders have stressed the importance of empowering individuals with the opportunities and tools needed to live a crime free life after completing their sentences.

Harvard professor Charles Ogletree stated,

> The criminal justice system is devouring our resources; putting people who have committed low-level offenses, who are perfectly capable of being rehabilitated, away for lengthy sentences and turning them into hardened criminals; destroying families and communities; and callously throwing away lives. We cannot afford to continue to invest in such a system. (http://famm.org/sentencing-101/what-experts-say/)

Nathan Deal, the Georgia governor, said,

> Let's get to work on promoting recovery and rehabilitation rather than a system that simply hardens criminals.
> I firmly believe this is a better way to govern our criminal justice system. It's win-win: saving lives and saving money. It's a great change for Georgia. (http://famm.org/sentencing-101/what-experts-say/)

In the research community, criminologists have taken more in-depth examinations of the efficacy of various rehabilitation strategies and programs. The notion that "nothing works," which sprang from the results of Martinson's (1974) article, *What Works: Questions and Answers about Prison Reform* (commonly referred to as *The Martinson Report* and discussed in Chapter 3) has been challenged by criminologists employing more sophisticated methodologies. There is evidence that "something works, sometimes." Whether a treatment/rehabilitation program is effective may depend on factors such as how it is implemented, the characteristics of the offender, program length, and opportunities available after the offender completes his or her sentence.

Cullen and Jonson (2011) recently defined "rehabilitation" as, ". . . a planned correctional intervention that targets for change internal and/or social criminogenic factors with the goal of reducing recidivism and, where possible, of improving other aspects of an offender's life" (p. 295). They noted that rehabilitation can occur with various sanctions, including prison and probation.

Another Look at *The Martinson Report*

We learned in Chapter 3 that *The Martinson Report* represented a nail in the coffin for rehabilitation and sentencing approaches that based the date of prisoner release on evidence that the offender had been rehabilitated. Martinson concluded that there was little evidence that treatment worked better than no treatment. The common "knowledge" for the next decade was that rehabilitative programs did little, if anything, in helping offenders or lowering recidivism.

A careful reading of Martinson's report, however, shows that even he acknowledged several caveats with his conclusion. Methodological issues regarding the studies' designs, as well his narrative analyses of the studies themselves, may have affected his deductions about the lack of efficacy of rehabilitation in lowering recidivism. At the outset of the report, Martinson documented the complexity of reaching conclusions about treatment success or failure with such a diverse population of offenders who were included in his study.

Martinson also noted that his outcome variable, "recidivism" was measured in different ways in the various studies. "Recidivism" may include "failure measures" such as arrest rates or parole violations, or it may mean "success measures," such as satisfactory completion of a community based sentence, like probation or parole release.

Another issue that Martinson brought up in his analysis of studies was ambiguity in the way treatment programs were carried out. If they weren't implemented in the way they were supposed to be, lack of success might not have to do with the failure of the program, but rather in not implementing the program correctly.

The issue of offender amenability was also brought up by Martinson in his discussions of individual counseling programs. He documented that this treatment may have worked for some individuals better than for others. Another issue that could explain the lack of success of some individual counseling programs involves the level of the therapist's skill.

Martinson admitted, "It is possible that some of our treatment programs *are* working to some extent, but that our research is so bad that it is incapable of telling" (p. 49). Regardless, he reached the bold conclusion that in his review of the over two hundred studies that there was no sure way to reduce recidivism through rehabilitation programs.

Recent Evidence of the Effectiveness of Some Rehabilitation Programs

Even when punitive models dominated corrections soon after *The Martinson Report* was released, some researchers, including Paul Gendreau and Robert Ross (1979, 1987), continued to explore whether and under what conditions rehabilitation could occur. Their conclusions included the finding that behaviorally oriented programs (a type of program that Martinson did not include in his analysis), including those with incentive systems and behavioral contracts, were effective in lowering recidivism.

In addition, Gendreau and Ross found that programs that emphasized the addressing of "criminogenic needs" were most successful. Criminogenic needs means characteristics of offenders that research had shown to be linked with recidivism, like antisocial attitudes and those characteristics that could be changed through programming. Gendreau and Ross's research also showed some contingencies under which treatment worked and noted that some offenders are more or less amenable to specific types of treatment. They showed, for example, that those offenders who were deemed "high risk" received greater benefits from treatment and that offenders with lower intellectual capacities did better in programs that involved structured learning.

Gendreau and Ross also raised the importance of considering the issue of **therapeutic integrity**. This basically means that the program was based in theory and implemented in the way it was designed to be implemented. For example, if a program based on anger management techniques was designed to have participants meet four times a week with a trained psychologist and a limit of ten participants, but the program actually included 20 participants, only met once a week, and its leader was a staff member and a high school graduate, then the effectiveness of that program cannot meaningfully be assessed.

Gendreau and Ross (1987) concluded, "In summary, it is downright ridiculous to say 'Nothing works'" (p. 395).

More recently, Cullen and Jonson (2012) addressed the evaluation research that has been conducted on the efficacy of rehabilitation programs and come to a much more positive conclusion than Martinson did back in 1974. They differentiated **narrative reviews** from **meta-analyses** (as we did in Chapter 9) and showed that both approaches suggest that some rehabilitation programs do "work" to lower recidivism under certain circumstances. They emphasized the special importance of meta-analysis in challenging the many critics of rehabilitation, as it takes a quantitative approach to measuring treatment effects.

Remember that narrative reviews are qualitative approaches that involve reading multiple evaluations of rehabilitation programs and coming up with a conclusion based on how many studies found evidence of rehabilitation. Martinson's study is one example of a narrative review. Another narrative review by Palmer (1975), which reanalyzed Martinson's data, however, came up with a different conclusion. It was noted that of the 231 studies on rehabilitation that Martinson reviewed, that 82 had recidivism data. Among those 82 studies, 39 (or 48 percent of the 82 studies) showed that participation in treatment lowered recidivism. Cullen and Jonson illustrated the very different conclusions than those Martinson and Palmer reached. Labeling Martinson a "half-empty reviewer," Cullen and Jonson (2012) stated "Martinson concluded that since no one type (or modality) of program could be shown to work all or most of the time, *nothing works* in correctional treatment" (p. 156). They contrasted this with Palmer's "half full" review that concluded that treatment works about half the time.

Cullen and Jonson (2012) suggested that the appropriate next step to understanding the effectiveness of rehabilitation programs was to see which programs worked for which offenders under what circumstances. And they noted the importance of evaluating more recent programs.

Meta-analysis, which essentially involves the computation of the statistical relationship treatment has with recidivism, has become the preferred technique in ascertaining the rehabilitative effect of programs. According to Cullen and Jonson (2012),

> The relationship between the treatment intervention and measure of recidivism is called the *effect size*. What a meta-analysis does is to compute the relationship between the treatment variable and recidivism for every study in the sample of studies being reviewed. When this is done, the researcher comes up with the *average or mean effect size*. This is treatment's batting average (so to speak). Moreover, this average effect size is a number, which is usually expressed as a correlation coefficient (Pearson's r). p. 160

In their review of the results of meta-analyses of treatment programs, Cullen and Jonson separated the studies into those which combine various treatment strategies and those that include only certain program types. The former strategy yields an "overall effect size"—the effect of treatment (undifferentiated by type) compared to no treatment. Extant research suggests an effect size of $+.10$, which essentially means that the recidivism rate for those who don't receive the treatment (called the control group) would be 55 percent, compared to the recidivism rate for those who participated in the treatment, which would be 45 percent. Therefore, this suggests that treatment programs (as a whole) reduce recidivism by about 10 percent. This contradicts Martinson's (1974) conclusion that many interpreted as "nothing works." Some would label a 10 percent reduction modest, however.

When one calculates effect size by type of program we see some different results that help us understand what types of rehabilitation programs show the most promise for a reduction in recidivism. Many studies have shown that *cognitive behavioral programs* are very effective at reducing recidivism. Appropriate cognitive behavioral programs aim to help offenders see what issues got them into trouble, to set goals, and to devise better solutions to their problems and carry out more pro-social behavior. Cullen and Jonson's arguments, supported by both narrative reviews and meta-analyses, clearly challenge the notion that "nothing works" and put the burden on the critics of rehabilitation to produce a meta-analysis showing otherwise.

How Can a Renewed Interest in Rehabilitation Affect Sentencing Practices?

So how can we reconcile a renewed interest in rehabilitation with current sentencing and correctional practices? As we have discussed, prison practices across the nation have deemphasized rehabilitation and the empowerment of the offender over the last forty years. Prisons have been used more to "warehouse" prisoners, than help reform them. Harsh sentencing laws have sent more people to prison for longer terms of confinement.

If rehabilitation continues to gain support from policymakers and the general public, might there be a push to re-examine sentencing practices so that they are more compatible with a rehabilitative approach? Can a renewed interest in rehabilitation and attention to the importance of assisting prisoners re-enter society prompt changes in current sentencing policies, laws, and practices? Could evidence that various rehabilitative efforts do, indeed, work sway criminal justice decision makers to "reform the reforms"? If so, would we see less emphasis on incarceration and more emphasis on sanctions that identify rehabilitation as a primary goal?

The answer is "maybe." Certainly we saw modern sentencing reforms stem in part from the change in emphasis from rehabilitation to retribution, deterrence, and incapacitation. Is there a cyclical pattern? Will rehabilitation become the dominant goal of sentencing again? Only time will tell. And if rehabilitation does become recognized as a primary goal of corrections, will sentencing policies and practices change to be more in sync with this goal? They would certainly have to.

Political pressures were one source of change in reforming sentencing practices beginning in the late 1970s. The "get tough on crime" sentiment ignited harsh reforms across the nation. Sentencing laws would have to change to be in alignment with the rehabilitative ideal. Changes in mandatory minimum sentencing laws would have to come from the legislature. Changes in three strikes laws could come from the legislature or ballot measures. Changes in commission-based guidelines would come from sentencing commissions. Changes in sentencing practices may decrease how many people would be sent to prison. The extent to which offenders would have access to an array of rehabilitation programs would also have to increase.

The Growing Interest in Reentry Programs in the United States

What Is Offender Reentry?

The interest in **offender reentry**—helping offenders make a smooth transition from prison back to society upon release through programming—has grown recently. Many efforts have been made to research the offender reentry process and to evaluate reentry programs. Offender reentry is indeed a "hot topic" in the field of criminal justice today and one that emphasizes the importance of treatment and rehabilitation.

Reentry programs seek to empower the prisoner who is approaching his or her release date in a variety of ways. Designers of these programs acknowledge that the artificial prison environment that offenders must become used to hampers their capacity to reintegrate back to society upon release and live a crime-free life. Many also argue that prisons are "schools for crime" and that prisoners learn how to be better criminals after spending time with other more seasoned offenders. Their fellow inmates teach them tricks of the trade (e.g., seasoned burglars teach other prisoners techniques to become better burglars and evade apprehension). Reentry programs vary in content, but include helping the prisoner be more hirable upon release through job training programs, providing them transitional housing, giving them access to psychological support, and providing them with employment resources upon release.

How Imprisonment Impedes Reentry

The ideas that prisoners become socialized into an artificial society with its own values and leadership structure and that this assimilation impedes successful release are not new. Donald Clemmer discussed these ideas in a series of articles beginning in the 1930s and authored a book entitled *The Prison Community*, which was first published in 1940. In his 1950 article, entitled *Observations on Imprisonment as a Source of Criminality*, Clemmer stated ". . . American prisons contribute in some degree to the criminality of those they hold" (p. 311).

Much of Clemmer's writing occurred during a time when rehabilitation programs were expanding in prisons. The 1940s ushered in a greater focus on rehabilitation in prisons in the United States, compared to previous years. Despite this emphasis, Clemmer detailed the prison culture and highlighted how the assimilation process through which the inmate adopts new values and norms of prison hinders the process of reentering society when he is eventually released.

Clemmer (1968) coined the term "prisonization" to describe how inmates specifically adopt in varying degrees the "folkways, mores, customs, and general culture of the penitentiary" (p. 299). Clemmer asserted that all men who enter prison undergo prisonization to some degree. The new inmate is stripped of his status as a free man and a prison number replaces his name. He becomes a member of a subordinate group (the prisoners) and the warden is superior. He learns prison slang. He learns the rules of the institution. The inmate learns to distrust the corrections officers. In essence, the inmate learns through socialization the formal rules of the institution and the informal rules and values of the institutional culture from other inmates.

Sentencing Approaches and Reentry

As we have detailed, sentencing approaches used in various states and the federal system vary considerably. One source of variation involves how the ultimate length of the sentence is determined. In some jurisdictions, the offender must serve at least 85 percent of his or her sentence (as dictated by truth-in-sentencing laws or according to some commission-based guidelines, such as those in North Carolina). Others allow limited "good" time or "earned" time based on positive behavior. In other states that retain indeterminate sentencing, however, the length of the sentence is determined by the discretionary parole board and may amount to only one-half or even one-third of the maximum sentence pronounced by the judge at sentencing.

Regardless of the process employed to determine when the offender will be released, reentry programs help ease the transition from prison life to life on the outside. Whenever one is approaching release, efforts to boost one's successful reentry can be introduced. Evidence suggests that such efforts can maximize inmate success upon release. Over time, reentry programs can alleviate monetary and social costs associated with recidivism.

No sentencing strategy is specifically prohibitive of the establishment of reentry programs. The establishment of these programs, however, requires government funding. Just as sentencing policies are influenced by the public and elected officials, so would be the establishment of programs that are designed to help the offender.

In 1950 Clemmer argued, "Prisons and prisoners are what they are because of what they have been in the past, and because of the mood and temper of society concerning them" (p. 314). This quote is as applicable today as it was 65 years ago.

The *Interview* section at the end of this chapter features an interview with "Serena," a woman in her fifties who was sentenced to a five-month prison sentence for embezzling approximately $68,000 from a bank where she worked as head teller. "Serena" reflects on her crime, her experience being processed in the federal system, and her experiences at Alderson Federal Prison for Women, including the separation from her child.

Consistent themes in her interview include how institutionalization damages incarcerated women, the lack of opportunities, and the absence of reentry programs available to those about to be released. This interview is informative in understanding what goes on within prison walls as well as what does not happen in preparing the women to leave prison and re-enter society. Sadly, her responses to interview questions are quite reminiscent of what Clemmer detailed about the prisonization process for men in the 1950s. The call for reentry programs is loud and clear from those incarcerated, as well as academics and politicians. Whether and how they will be integrated into sentencing is yet to be seen.

An International Comparison

Spotlight — Sentencing and Incarceration in Germany and the Netherlands: A Cross National Study

Background

Lengthy sentences contribute to the sizeable United States prison population. In addition to significant monetary correctional costs, the social costs of incarceration, as detailed in Chapter 10, are also profound.

The Prison Law Office, which is based in California, created the European-American Prison Project, which was administered by the Vera Institute of Justice in an effort to educate state-level policymakers about systems in European countries.[2] A goal was to stimulate reform efforts in the United States that could apply strategies that work in these countries to various states' correctional systems.

In February 2013, participants visited Germany and the Netherlands. Delegates, all of whom were "stakeholders" in their states' correctional systems, were selected from Colorado, Georgia, and Pennsylvania. The participants in each state "team" included corrections directors, legislators, judges, prosecutors, and public defenders. They toured prisons and talked with corrections officials and inmates to understand and appreciate the differences between these correctional systems and those in the United States.[3]

The Vera Institute of Justice detailed this innovative program in their report, entitled *Sentencing and Prison Practices in Germany and the Netherlands: Implications for the United States* (Subramanian & Shames, 2013). This section highlights the background, findings, and implications of this report.

Findings

Many Northern European countries have lower incarceration rates and rely more on non-custodial sanctions, especially for non-violent crimes, compared to the United States. **Figure 11.1** illustrates the differences in incarceration rate for Germany (79/100,000), the Netherlands (82/100,000), and the United States (716/100,000) at the time the report was published.

Figure 11.1 Comparison of German, Dutch, and American Incarceration Rates

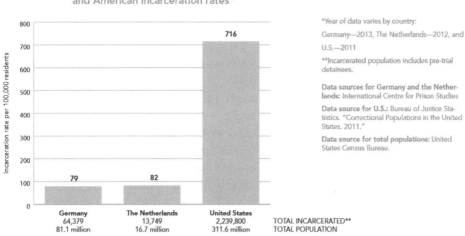

Source: Subramanian, P. & Shames, A. (2013, October). *Sentencing and prison practices in Germany and the Netherlands: Implications for the United States.* p. 7, Figure 1. Retrieved from: http://www.vera.org/sites/default/files/resources/downloads/european-american-prison-report-v3.pdf

Reproduced with permission from the Vera Institute of Justice.

The goals of rehabilitation and resocialization are prominent in both the German and Dutch systems. There is more of a focus on retribution and incapacitation in the United States compared to these countries. Prominent themes in Germany's Prison Act include empowering the prisoner to lead a crime-free life and establishing an environment in prison that is as similar as possible to life in the community in order to promote smooth reintegration upon release. The Netherlands 1998 Penitentiary Principles Act similarly focuses on re-socialization of prisoners within the prison environment with a minimum of restrictions and an emphasis on forming and maintaining relationships with others. These principles can be labeled "normalization" (Subramanian & Shames, 2013, p. 7).

The sentencing practices in these countries complement their goals of corrections. Indeterminate sentencing is practiced. As discussed earlier, rehabilitation as a sentencing goal of corrections is compatible with the practice of indeterminate sentencing. Subramanian and Shames (2013) stated, "With offender rehabilitation and resocialization the primary goals of corrections, conditions of confinement—in particular, treatment and disciplinary approaches—are less punitive and more goal-oriented" (p. 9).

Indeed, in both countries, incarceration is used less often and prison lengths are shorter. Even for serious crimes such as burglary and aggravated assault, many offenders are diverted from the criminal justice system and often receive suspended sentences, community service, and/or fines. In Germany in the year 2006, 75 percent of prison sentences were for one year or less and 92 percent were for two years or less. Most prison sentences under two years were suspended. In the Netherlands in 2012, 91 percent of sentences were for one year or less and 95 percent were for two years or less. This contrasts with the average sentence length in the United States, which is about five years. The mean time served in the United States is over two years.

While incarcerated, prisoners in the United States experience harsher conditions compared with those imprisoned in the Netherlands and Germany. Prisoners' accounts of their incarceration in these European countries suggested that the stated goals of rehabilitation and resocialization were indeed emphasized in practice. The act of confinement—separating the offender from society—is considered a distinct punishment in and of itself in these countries.

The goal in these European countries is to prepare prisoners to live productive and crime-free lives upon release. The daily regimen and loss of control over their lives that prisoners experience characterizes United States' prisons. In contrast, in these European countries, prisoners' control over their daily lives is maximized, as they can decide what to wear, what to eat, and even how to decorate their cells. Privacy is valued and guards knock before coming into one's cell. Meaningful work and education programs are available. Both Germany and the Netherlands offer some prisoners the chance to spend time outside of prison either on the weekends or other leave time for the purpose of maintaining relationships with their families and easing into reentry. A German prison allows mothers to parent their children up to age three. Re-socialization and reintegration are viewed as paramount concerns.

Corrections staff training is extensive and involves a social work approach. In Germany, corrections staff use positive reinforcement and rarely use solitary confinement. Disciplinary measures more often involve monetary and property restrictions and taking away leisure activities. In the Netherlands, inmates can appeal administrative decisions to a review board or courts and can be awarded damages.

The physical characteristics of the facilities also differ. Prisons in Germany and the Netherlands boast wide hallways, an abundance of windows, and comfortable temperatures. This contrasts the "warehouse" image of many prisons in the United States.

Takeaways

The impact of the information gleaned from the communication with representatives from the correctional systems in Germany and the Netherlands was considerable.

The teams identified four key areas that they wanted to further explore with relevant parties in their states.

The first was to expand disposition and sentencing options. Delegates from the three states expressed a desire to devise approaches to reducing the number of persons incarcerated. This includes the development of diversion programs in Pennsylvania. The judges were interested in increasing the availability of specialty courts, such as drug and veteran courts.

The second area identified was the focus on normalization. Participants suggested several efforts that could be made, especially for low-level offenders. These include allowing inmates to have more personal property, clothing choices, and increasing inmate pay. One conclusion was that state and federal prison systems need to better prepare their prisoners to reenter society and avoid re-incarceration.

The third area identified was the development of mother-child units, like the one participants visited in Germany. In the United States, most mothers who have their children in prison are separated from them. The development of such units could help strengthen the mother-child bond and potentially lower recidivism risk.

The fourth area deemed important by delegates of the three states was to update the Mental Health Procedures Act in the states in order to provide needed mental health services in an effective manner. This has not been updated since its passage in 1979. The group from Pennsylvania also decided to review its use of solitary confinement.

Key concepts stressed in Germany and the Netherlands, such as diversion, rehabilitation, and "normalization" seem relevant and important takeaways to incorporate into the correctional systems in the United States. A nationwide review of solitary confinement practices, including a consideration of the deleterious effect of long term solitary on the mental and physical health on inmates, seems warranted.

Many states are taking a second look at their sentencing policies. Since 2005, 27 states have taken part in the **Justice Reinvestment Initiative**. This is a federally funded and data-driven program with the goals of reducing corrections spending and reinvesting the money in efforts to maximize public safety and empower neighborhoods. Addressing the monetary and social costs of imprisonment and incorporating lessons learned from other countries can lead to smarter sentencing practices in the United States.

The Advice of Scholars

So what advice do noted criminologists and legal scholars give regarding sentencing practices? What strategies do they put forth to further the goals of sentencing uniformity and fairness? How do they suggest the United States move away from mass incarceration, which has been a consequence of harsh sentencing practices for the past last thirty-five years?

In 2014, the scholarly journal *Criminology & Public Policy* featured a series of essays by nationally recognized scholars in the field of sentencing. Each author reflected on the state of sentencing in the United States and made suggestions for the future of sentencing practices. Let's look at the views of these noted scholars.

In the lead article, *Remodeling American Sentencing: A Ten Step Blueprint for Moving Past Mass Incarceration*, Michael Tonry (2014) presented many suggestions for state sentencing practices. Tonry stated, "A just system of American sentencing would incorporate the best features of the indeterminate systems that existed in all 50 states and the federal system from the 1930s to the mid-1970s and of the short-lived sentencing reform period that immediately followed it" (p. 511).

He cited three characteristics of indeterminate sentencing, espoused in the *Model Penal Code* (American Law Institute, 1962) that he labelled admirable — **individualization of punishment, humanity** (in effect, addressing the needs of offenders), and **parsimony** (minimizing the severity of the sanction) — and argued that these elements promoted just sentencing. He acknowledged the problems of indeterminate sentencing, including lack of fairness, lack of transparency, and lack of accountability. He asserted that parole and sentencing guidelines helped address these concerns and promoted two other requirements for just sentencing — **proportionality** and **regularity** (consistently applied standards).

Tonry offered suggestions for sentencing that would replace the existing practices that have led to high imprisonment rates, high monetary costs, high social costs, and what he labelled "widespread injustice" (p. 513). The ten steps are as follows:

> *First, three-strikes, mandatory minimum sentence and comparable laws should be repealed.*
>
> *Second, any three-strikes, mandatory minimum sentence, and comparable laws that are not repealed should be substantially narrowed in scope and severity.*
>
> *Third, any three-strikes, mandatory minimum sentence, and comparable laws that are not repealed should be amended to include provisions authorizing judges to impose some other sentence "in the interest of justice."*
>
> *Fourth, life-without-possibility-of-parole laws should be repealed or substantially narrowed.*
>
> *Fifth, truth-in-sentencing laws should be repealed.*
>
> *Sixth, criminal codes should be amended to set substantially lower maximum sentences scaled to the seriousness of the crimes.*
>
> *Seventh, every state that does not already have one should establish a sentencing commission and promulgate presumptive sentencing guidelines.*
>
> *Eighth, every state that does not already have one should establish a parole board and every state should establish a parole guidelines system.*
>
> *Ninth, every state and the federal government should reduce its combined rate of jail and prison confinement to half its 2014 level by 2020.*
>
> *Tenth, every state should enact legislation making all prisoners serving fixed terms longer than 5 years, or indeterminate terms, eligible for consideration for release at the expiration of 5 years, and making all prisoners 35 years of age or older eligible for consideration for release after serving 3 years. (p. 503)*

Tonry is clearly emphatic about doing away with, or at the least scaling back, mandatory sentencing and three strikes laws. Tonry emphasized that commission-based guidelines have been shown to be effective. He strongly suggested that this is the route for jurisdictions to take to ensure fair and just sentences that decrease sentencing disparities and discrimination. He favors the adoption of parole guidelines to help parole boards in making release decisions.

Regarding his suggestion to reduce imprisonment, Tonry acknowledged the challenges. He concluded that "Unwinding mass incarceration will be much harder than creating it was. Little will happen unless powerful groups want it to happen and are willing to spend political capital to make it happen" (p. 527).

Cassia Spohn (2014) echoed many of Tonry's sentiments. She stated,

> Michael Tonry's (2014) proposals for "remodeling American sentencing" are principled, evidence-based, and feasible. They are essential if we are to reduce the number of men and women locked up in our nation's prisons and to decrease the collateral consequences that imprisonment has for them, their families, and their communities. (p. 539)

Spohn raised the question of whether the adoption of a sentencing commission in every state would, in fact, lead to lower incarceration rates. She noted that while presumptive guidelines have reduced sentencing severity in some states, that in others such guidelines have led to more severe sanctions. This is because some states' guidelines greatly restrict judges' discretion in considering personal circumstances.

Spohn relayed a slightly more optimistic view of what has been done to reform the harshest sentencing practices. She cited Congress's consideration of legislation to reduce prison overcrowding and that some states are changing their response to non-violent and drug offenders and revising mandatory sentencing practices. Spohn also pointed to the decriminalization or legalization of marijuana in some states as evidence that politicians and the public are rethinking their stance of the harmfulness of some drugs.

Stephen Raphael (2014) offered general support for Tonry's suggestions but questioned whether reducing the prison population by half by 2020 can be achieved without increasing crime rates. He suggested that strategies to revise and refine police practices to *prevent* crime may be effective and necessary steps to avert a rise in the crime rate that could occur with the release of so many prison inmates.

Gerald Lynch (2014), who is a judge of the United States Court of Appeals, Second Circuit, generally supported Tonry's suggestions, but like Spohn, he questioned Tonry's assertion that sentencing commissions that produce presumptive guidelines would function in a way to reduce the prison population. He noted the following:

> Commission and guidelines systems have many advantages, especially with respect to predictability and equity in sentencing. But guidelines and commissions do not inherently lead to reducing (or increasing) prison populations. That depends on the substance of the guidelines. In the federal system, harsh mandatory guidelines were a significant factor in dramatically increasing sentence lengths. (p. 562)

Lynch pointed out two additional concerns. First, Tonry's ten-step blueprint calls for reductions in the prison, but not the jail, populations. Lynch suggested that this population, which is comprised of those awaiting trial as well as those serving shorter sentences, is also too big and should be reduced. Lynch also raised the issue of the institutionalization of the mentally ill. He noted that due to deinstitutionalization of the mentally ill in the 1960s and 1970s, prisons now house the largest proportion of institutionalized mentally ill persons in the United States. He emphasized the importance of providing enough funding for mental health in the United States if the prison population is to be reduced.

Jeremy Travis (2014) focused his essay on the practical issue of political mobilization to effect the changes that Tonry put forth. While he acknowledged some calls by some conservatives and liberals to reduce the prison population and revamp harsh sentencing practices, he asked, "On what basis, one might wonder, can we imagine that the politics of crime would change sufficiently so that our elected legislators would affirmatively vote to reduce—significantly, not at the margins—the use of prison as a response to crime?" (p. 570).

He argued that governors and legislators as well as elected prosecutors and judges must promote changes in sentencing and the goal of reducing incarceration. Because in many states the governor appoints members of the parole board and sets parole board policies, Travis suggested that he or she could impact policies of the parole board, including early release, work release, and compassionate release for sick or older inmates. A "brave governor," Travis suggested, could publicly promote different approaches to reform sentencing within his or her state in a way that would be acceptable by the general public.

Travis suggested that prosecutors should make public statements that acknowledge how current sentencing strategies and incarceration policies disproportionately impact minority communities. He pointed to how judges successfully pushed for drug courts and other specialty courts in recent years with concrete results. He highlighted the importance of these actors in changing public opinion about these issues.

Anthony Doob and Cheryl Marie Webster (2014) provided an international perspective in their discussion of how Finland and the Canadian province of Alberta successfully reduced their imprisonment rate substantially. The main motivation for the reduction in Alberta was to save money that could be spent on other programs. A two-thirds reduction in Finland, however, took 40 years.

The researchers emphasized that each state and the federal system all have different policies concerning imprisonment. They presented data showing that imprisonment rates vary greatly in the 50 states. They stated, "We simply suggest that high imprisonment in the United States not only is related to other punitive criminal justice policies but also is embedded in social values (e.g., how much the least paid workers in the state should make)" (p. 556). They reflected on the fact that overall, countries that have lower rates of income disparity and that have more robust social welfare programs have lower imprisonment rates. They argued that prison policies across the 50 states represent different cultural values and may not be easily changed.

What Is the Future of Sentencing Practices in the United States?

Calls to Reform the Reforms

Years ago, liberals and conservatives agreed that unbridled judicial discretion was unacceptable. They called for more structure in sentencing. Today, liberal and conservative politicians, other community leaders, the United States Sentencing Commission, and organizations including Families Against Mandatory Minimums and The Sentencing Project have made efforts to scale back, reduce, or eliminate the practice of mandatory minimum sentencing, which is arguably the most draconian sentencing "reform" in the United States. It is unusual for liberals and conservatives to agree on any criminal justice issue, but we have seen that both sides have again made collective calls to reform sentencing practices.

What the future holds will be at the hands of the politicians, policymakers, Congress, and voters. The way in which policymakers understand and apply evidence-based practices in sentencing and corrections will play a key role in sentencing practices across the nation. Social science research shows promising sentencing strategies in terms of lowering recidivism, protecting the public, serving victims' needs, and cost effectiveness. Whether those sentencing approaches are ultimately adopted, however, will be determined by the actions (or inactions) of those making or revising sentencing laws and policies. The time frame is unclear, but the interplay of researchers and policymakers is key to "reforming the reforms."

Recent events suggest that communication between researchers and practitioners is happening. Research suggests that the general public is receptive to trying evidence-based practices, including alternative sanctions that would maximize public safety, decrease recidivism, and cost less money. It seems then that the public would approve of sentencing practices that move away from long mandatory penalties to those that maximize rehabilitation.

The Continuum of Judicial Discretion in Sentencing Practices

The amount of discretion afforded to judges through various sentencing practices in the United States can be viewed on a continuum. **Figure 11.2** illustrates the level of judicial discretion of three sentencing approaches in descending order — indeterminate sentencing, commission-based guidelines, and mandatory minimums.

On the top is indeterminate sentencing, which affords the judge wide discretion. The judge can choose the type and length of sentence and individualize sentencing to the specific offender. The judge's discretion is constrained only by broad statutes.

On the bottom of the continuum, we see mandatory minimum sentencing. Judges lose all discretion at the sentencing stage. If an offender is convicted of a crime that carries a mandatory minimum, the judge must impose that sentence.

The middle ground of sentencing practices in terms of judicial discretion is the use of sentencing guidelines. Guidelines schemes vary considerably, depending on how strin-

Figure 11.2 Continuum of Amount of Judicial Discretion in Different
Sentencing Approaches

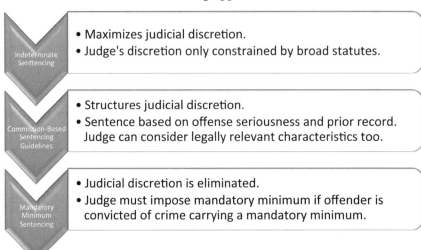

Indeterminate Sentencing
- Maximizes judicial discretion.
- Judge's discretion only constrained by broad statutes.

Commission-Based Sentencing Guidelines
- Structures judicial discretion.
- Sentence based on offense seriousness and prior record. Judge can consider legally relevant characteristics too.

Mandatory Minimum Sentencing
- Judicial discretion is eliminated.
- Judge must impose mandatory minimum if offender is convicted of crime carrying a mandatory minimum.

gently they are applied, but they seek to structure, rather than eliminate, judicial discretion. Commission-based guideline approaches rely on the intersection within a grid of offense seriousness and prior record level to form the basis of the sentence or sentence range. The narrow ranges within a sentencing grid allow some judicial discretion. Aggravating and mitigating factors also play a role in a more individualized sentence. So while sentencing guidelines structure judicial decision making, they also allow judges to consider legally relevant variables in their sentence.

When safety valve exclusions are allowed, mandatory minimums allow a little judicial discretion. Three strikes laws allow virtually no judicial discretion, but as we have seen in California, some judicial discretion may occur with respect to whether prior offenses are counted as strikes.

Variation in Sentencing in the United States Will Likely Persist

A prominent feature of sentencing in the United States is the variation in sentencing practices across all 50 states, Washington, DC, and the federal system. There is no dominant model of sentencing in the country. States that have retained indeterminate sentencing may vary in terms of ranges of sentences for the same offense. The indicated sentence range for the same offense may also vary when one compares sentencing grids among states with commission-based guidelines. As we saw in Chapter 9, even within a state that has sentencing guidelines, there are differences in the type and length of sentence by county and/or court characteristics. And within a single state, there may be multiple approaches to sentencing, which depend on the type of crime and prior record. A state with sentencing guidelines may also have mandatory minimums for certain offenses and habitual offender or three strikes laws for others. This is true also in the federal system, in which the statutes always "trump" the guidelines.

Trends in Sentencing in the United States

So what is the "ideal" approach to sentencing? The answer is that it depends on who you ask and where you are asking the question! What goals are deemed most important? Decreased judicial disparity? The maintenance of judicial discretion? Increased sentencing uniformity? Getting tough on certain offenses? As we have seen, multiple (and sometimes inherently contradictory) goals have been cited concurrently by sentencing commissions and legislators.

There is currently no sentencing strategy in the United States that is uniformly considered to be the best. Each of the fifty states, Washington, DC, and the federal system all have a unique mix of sentencing approaches within their jurisdictions. This makes the study of sentencing complicated. Every sentencing approach discussed in this text has critiques. It is unlikely that sentencing commissions will be abandoned and that all states will revert back to indeterminate sentencing. Those states that have retained indeterminate sentencing, however, will likely continue to do so.

We began the book by illustrating how an offender with a conviction for an offense could potentially receive very different sentences depending on where he committed the crime. This variation will no doubt continue. While this may seem inherently unfair, it highlights the value placed on local values and customs in establishing sentencing policies and law. Indeed, there is no one process of punishment in the United States.

Summary

There have been recent moves to scale back harsh mandatory minimum sentencing practices. These efforts have had bipartisan support. Like the move from indeterminate sentencing to more determinate sentencing practices beginning in the late 1970s, the endeavors to ease draconian sentencing practices have been launched by both liberals and conservatives. While liberals tend to emphasize the injustices of what they perceive as grossly disproportionate sentences, conservatives focus on the high cost of incarceration as a reason to ease mandatory minimums and three strikes laws.

Public opinion on sentencing practices and corrections is complex. People want to be safe and the media has fueled the perception that the only answer to ensuring public safety is through incarceration. However, research suggests that public opinion is malleable. When people are presented with information about alternatives to incarceration and that they may save money, they are open to them.

Recent "evidence-based" research regarding sentencing and corrections has led to a revived interest in rehabilitation. Offender reentry programs that empower the offender and decrease recidivism have become popular in many jurisdictions. The increased value placed on helping the offender may, in turn, affect future sentencing practices and the goals that are emphasized.

An international comparison of sentencing goals and approaches to corrections shows that the United States is quite punitive, compared with other Western industrialized nations. The interaction between practitioners and scholars of European countries may lead to a reconsideration of the predominant focus of punishment in the United States.

Within the United States, the fifty states, the District of Columbia, and the federal system all have different sentencing approaches. Even within a jurisdiction, there may be multiple sentencing approaches (i.e., sentencing guidelines, as well as mandatory minimum sentencing laws). The study of sentencing is complex due to this variation. It highlights the premium placed on local control.

Future sentencing practices are likely to be informed by social science research that shows what sentencing practices are effective in reducing crime and saving money.

Interview

Interview with Former Inmate at Alderson Federal Penitentiary for Women, "Serena"— August 29, 2015

Serena is a woman in her fifties who agreed to be interviewed about her experiences being processed in the federal system for bank embezzlement of approximately $68,500 about 10 years ago. She served five months at Alderson Federal Penitentiary for Women. The opinions expressed are those of "Serena" and do not represent those of any personnel of the federal system, Alderson management or staff, or the Federal Bureau of Prisons.

LM: Could you tell me a little bit about the nature of your offense?
Serena: My offense was embezzlement. It was stealing money from a bank I worked for.
LM: Over how long did that occur?
Serena: About a year.
LM: Could you tell me a little bit about how you were apprehended, about your defense attorney, a little bit about the processing of the case before it went to sentencing?
Serena: Yeah, the crime itself, I had a bad gambling problem. And so, I kept going to the track and I was taking money from the vault. And the last six months it was more survival. I knew I had stolen the money and I kept going over stealing more trying to get the money back—thinking I could put it back. And the last night that I gambled I had taken five thousand dollars. I lost it in 2 hours. I didn't have 50 cents in my pocket and I actually was going to commit suicide.
        And instead, I went into the bank the next day and turned myself in.
LM: So you did go to trial?
Serena: No, when it went to trial, it wasn't a jury trial, it was the judge. And I went in front of the judge for sentencing. Then I pleaded guilty.
LM: Now tell me a little bit about your defense attorney. Was he a public defender?
Serena: He was a public defender.
LM: Did he explain to you how you would be sentenced if found guilty under the federal guidelines?

Serena: Yes. We went into his office about 15 minutes before going in front of the judge. We walked in; the first thing he wanted to know was directions to the racetrack. The second thing he wanted to know was if I could get him tickets for the horse races. Then he started to tell me a story about this other guy who stole all this money and finally we said, "Are we going to talk about my case? We go in front of the judge soon."

So he got a booklet out. It was the federal guidelines. My case was cut and dry—I confessed. So it wasn't much defense I guess. And I got two points against me for being in a trusted position. I did get points off for turning myself in and showing the bank how I did the crime.

LM: What was your position at the bank?

Serena: I was head teller. I spent hours with the bank helping them so this could not happen again to them.

LM: What was your sentence minimum and maximum according to the guidelines?

Serena: According to the guidelines when we went into court it was five months to 18 months.

Note: Serena was sentenced to five months.

LM: What impact did it have on your son?

Serena: It was devastating. It was absolutely devastating. He was still in school. He was 16. He had an abusive father. I knew I was always more or less the protector between them. Which had a lot to do with everything that was going on at the time. And I knew that I was going to have to leave him unprotected for five months.

L.M.: So, you went to Alderson. Can you tell me a little bit about it and I guess my main question is, did they get you help you needed for your gambling addiction—which you say is the underlying problem of your offense?

Serena: No, there's no help in there for gambling. Gambling isn't considered in their eyes in prison an addiction. They did have AA classes in there and NA classes in there. But nothing for gambling. I guess cause you were physically not messing yourself up. You weren't physically ingesting something.

LM: So could you talk for a little bit about your experience at Alderson . . . the conditions, the nature of the offenders there . . . because I think people don't realize who makes up the federal prison population.

Serena: Everybody calls it "Camp Cupcake." And everyone thinks that since Martha Stewart went there it was a camp for the rich offenders . . . that it is a white collar camp. While in reality, there was only about 60 white collar people in there. The rest were drug offenses. There was people who was murderers in there.

LM: How many inmates were in there?

Serena: Way more than they were allowed. There was probably 1,150 when I was in there. The ones that was in there for murder, they had gotten down to camp status. They start out in maximum security, then they do so many years good and then they get put down to camp status.

The conditions in Alderson. Actually it looks like a college campus. No wonder people think it's so great. But it's not. It's a prison. No matter how you put a bow on it, it's a prison. You lose your freedom when you walk in that gate. You get treated like a piece of garbage and there's no privileges.

Now when I went in they put you through a two-week orientation.

LM: Did they just teach you the rules of the place?

Serena: Yeah, it was basically trying to weed you into the prison system. We were allowed to mingle with the other prisoners. We were allowed to walk on the campus. But it was more or less, our day was teaching us how to survive Alderson. Teaching us the rules.

LM: What helped get you through every day?

Serena: You had to change. You had to become a prisoner when you went in there. I went in there. I had never been in crime, had never been behind a crime scene. To me, you know, that wasn't my life. For most of the women it was. That's the only life they had ever known. When you go in there, you have to become hard and you have to become hard really quick. If not, you become a target.

And the camps you got more freedom. You can walk around more, so more things can happen in the camps than can happen [elsewhere].

And I was there the day a girl got beat with rocks, and I still to this day don't know if she went out of there alive or not. Three girls jumped her and beat her with rocks and socks. And nobody's seen a thing.

LM: How were you treated because you were a white collar offender by staff?

Serena: My main counselor that was supposed to help me get into the prison system and get used to it, she hated me. She told me the first day "I can't stand you." She says "I hate you." She says, "You white collar people come in here and you think you're so much better than anyone else in here." She said at least they have an excuse. Meaning because they were on drugs and everything. They accepted that addiction, but not anything else. She said just stay out of my way till you're out of here.

LM: So she was staff supposedly helping you and telling you to get away from her?

Serena: I never saw her again till the end. You got your good and your bad in prison. Same with the guards. You got your guards that are fair, that are good to you and then you have your guards that aren't. We had one that called us names . . . I mean bad names. They would moo like cows to us and come around in the middle of the night and would poke you and hold the flashlight in your face and wake you up. Very degrading. And there's nothing that's not degrading in prison.

LM: Today you're a successful businesswoman. Why do you think you succeeded while so many offenders don't and return to prison?

Serena: I think a couple reasons. One, I had a lot of support. When I did this I turned myself in. I took responsibility for what I did and people knew me and knew that something had to happen in my life. When I came out I had a lot of support and that makes a world of difference.

A lot of the women in there didn't have that coming out. They were from the streets coming in and they were going back to the streets. And once they're out of prison they don't care what happens to them. They just get put back in the same lifestyle they came from.

LM: If you had one suggestion . . . or maybe two about the federal system . . . meaning from the time you turned yourself in to processing through serving time at a federal institution, what would be your suggestions?

Serena: I think the breakdown comes once you're in and getting out of prison. There's a major breakdown for women.

They don't make preparations for these women getting out. You know there's women that are in there and they become "institutionalized," they call it. They've been in there for years. That's the only life they know. And as long as they're in those walls, they're safe. They're getting three meals a day. They have somewhere to sleep.

Now they're coming out and they have nowhere to go. They have no family left. Everybody's abandoned them. They have no family. They're homeless. And they put them in a halfway house but they're only in the halfway house for so long and then they're gone. Eventually they got to go into the real world and there's nothing there for them.

And that's why they start fights and they do things before they get out to get a longer sentence to stay in. I mean I seen this happen a couple of times in there where women purposely started a fight with somebody or did something so that they could add to her sentence. So she wouldn't be leaving prison.

LM: What do you think the federal prison system does? What should they do to help that transition?

Serena: There's got to be more help out there for them. Whether they have more counselors, more people helping them get jobs. You know . . . that's the breakdown. They get out and they go back to the life they came from. They're going right back into the same life because they know nothing else.

LM: And did you get to see your son? Did you choose to?

Serena: No. I did not have my son come down there. I did not want him to see me in there. That was just something I chose. He had enough to deal with without having to deal with seeing his mother behind bars.

I did get to talk to him on the phone daily and I wrote to him letters.

When I went to prison, I wasn't the victim. My family was. I did that to them.

But there's got to be something to help them. To get transportation so their kids can see them. These women are in there for a year or two . . . they can't lose contact with their kids.

LM: Any other comments about your experiences that you want to share?

Serena: I think the system breakdown like I said was it's coming out. Ones coming out of prison. It's getting the ones that are so institutionalized not so afraid of the outside world again.

Discussion Questions

1. There have been recent bipartisan calls to scale back harsh sentencing practices like mandatory minimum sentencing. What do you think accounts for support by both Democrats and Republicans to reduce these penalties?

2. What monetary costs, other than those discussed in the chapter, do you be-
    lieve stem from mass incarceration?
3. What features of the correctional systems in the Netherlands and Germany
    do you believe should be integrated into American correctional systems?
    Why?
4. Do you think that the general public would support Michael Tonry's *Ten
    Step Blueprint for Moving Past Mass Incarceration*? Which parts do you think
    would yield the most support? Which parts do you think would get the least
    support? Explain your answer!
5. After reading this book, what sentencing approach do you think is the most
    ideal? Did your opinion change from what it was at the beginning of the text?

Notes

1. Henrichson and Delaney (2012) noted that even these expenditures don't account for all the costs associated with incarceration. Indirect costs, including those of social services, child welfare, and education, are paid by other agencies. In addition, the social costs of incarceration (detailed in Chapter 10) are excluded from their cost calculations.

2. According to its website, http://www.prisonlaw.com/about.html, the Prison Law Office is a non-profit public interest law firm that provides free legal services to California state prisoners and focuses on issues involving conditions of confinement. A small staff of attorneys in the organization "represents individual prisoners, engages in class action and other impact litigation, educates the public about prison conditions, and provides technical assistance to attorneys throughout the country."

3. There are some hindrances to direct cross-national comparisons, which include variations in defining and classifying crimes, as well as different approaches to measuring incarceration rates and recidivism rates. Despite these differences, an appreciation of the differences in core goals in the German and Dutch systems with those in the United Sates is relevant.

References

American Law Institute. (1962). *Model penal code — Proposed official draft*. Philadelphia, PA: American Law Institute.

Applegate, B. K., Cullen, F. T., Turner, M. G., & Sundt, J. L. (1996). Assessing public support for three-strikes-and-you're-out laws: Global versus specific attitudes. *Crime and Delinquency, 42*(4), 517–534.

Brown, M. P., & Elrod, P. (1995). Electronic house arrest: An examination of citizen attitudes. *Crime and Delinquency, 41*(3), 332–346.

Bruer, W., Perez, E., & Glover, S. (2015, October 6). Roughly 6,000 federal inmates to be released. *CNN*. Retrieved from http://www.cnn.com/2015/10/06/politics/federal -inmates-bureau-of-prisons/

Clear, T. R. (1994). *Harm in American penology: Offenders, victims, and their communities*, Albany, NY: State University of New York Press.

Clemmer, D. (1950). Observations on imprisonment as a source of criminality. *Journal of Criminal Law & Criminology, 41*(3), 311–319.

Clemmer, D. (1968). *The prison community*. New York: Holt, Rinehart and Winston.

Commonwealth of Pennsylvania v. Newman, 2014 PA Super 178 No. 1980 EDA (2012).

Cruz, T. (2015, February 12). Sen. Cruz: Smarter Sentencing Act is common sense. Retrieved from http://www.cruz.senate.gov/?p=press_release&id=2184

Cullen, F. T., Fisher, B. S., & Applegate, B. K. (2000). Public opinion about punishment and corrections. In M. H. Tonry (Ed.), *Crime and justice: A review of research, Volume 27*. Chicago, IL: University of Chicago Press.

Cullen, F. T., & Jonson, C. L. (2011). Rehabilitation and treatment programs. In J. Q. Wilson & J. Petersilia (Eds.), *Crime and public policy* (pp. 293–344). New York: Oxford University Press.

Cullen, F. T., & Jonson, C. L. (2012). *Correctional theory: Context and consequences.* Thousand Oaks, CA: Sage.

Cullen, F. T., Pealer, J. A., Fisher, B. S., Applegate, B. K., & Santana, S. A. (2002). Public support for correctional rehabilitation in America: Change or consistency? In J. V. Roberts and M. Hough (Eds.), *Changing attitudes to punishment: Public opinion, crime, and justice.* Cullompton, UK: Willan.

Cullen, F. T., Vose, B. A., Jonson, C. L., & Unnever, J. D. (2007). Public support for early intervention: Is child saving a "habit of the heart"? *Victims and Offenders, 2*(2), 109–124. doi:10.1080/15564880701263015

Doble, J., Immerwahr, S., & Richardson, A. (1991). *Punishing criminals: The people of Delaware consider the options.* New York: The Public Agenda Foundation.

Doble, J., & Klein, J. (1989). *Punishing criminals: The public's view — an Alabama survey.* New York: The Public Agenda Foundation.

Doob, A. N., & Webster, C. M. (2014). Creating the will to change: The challenges of decarceration in the United States. *Criminology & Public Policy, 13*(4), 547–559.

Elrod, P., & Brown, M. P. (1996). Predicting public support for electronic house arrest: Results from a New York county survey, *American Behavioral Scientist, 39*(4), 461–473.

Families Against Mandatory Minimums, (2015, April 9). *Frequently asked questions about S. 502 / H.R. 920, The Smarter Sentencing Act of 2015.* Retrieved from http://famm .org/the-smarter-sentencing-act-faq/

Families Against Mandatory Minimums, (n.d.). *S.502/H.R. 920, The Smarter Sentencing Act.* Retrieved from http://famm.org/s-502-the-smarter-sentencing-act/

Farkas, S. (1993). Pennsylvanians prefer alternatives to prison. *Overcrowded Times, 4*(2)1, 13–15.

Gendreau, P., & Ross, R. R. (1979). Effective correctional treatment: Bibliotherapy for cynics. *Crime and Delinquency, 25*(4), 463–489.

Gendreau, P., & Ross, R. R. (1987). Revivification of rehabilitation: Evidence from the 1980s. *Justice Quarterly, 4*(3), 349–407.

Gray, J. M. (2009). What shapes public opinion of the criminal justice system? In J. L. Wood & T. A. Gannon (Eds.), *Public opinion and criminal justice* (pp. 49–72). Portland, OR: Willian.

Grimes, J. N. (2010). The social construction of social problems: "Three strikes and you're out" in the mass media. *Journal of Criminal Justice and Law Review, 2*(1/2), 39–55.

Henrichson, C., & Delaney, R. (2012). *The price of prisons.* New York: Vera Institute of Justice. Retrieved from http://www.vera.org/sites/default/files/resources/downloads /price-of-prisons-updated-version-021914.pdf

Huang, H., Braithwaite, V., Tsutomi, H., Hosoi, Y., & Braithwaite, J. (2012). Social capital, rehabilitation, tradition: Support for restorative justice in Japan and Australia. *Asian Criminology, 7*, 295–308.

Imrich, D., Mullin, C., & Linz, D. (1990). Sexually violent media and criminal justice policy. In R. Surette (Ed.), *The media and criminal justice policy* (pp. 103–123). Springfield, IL: Thomas.

Jones, J. M. (2014, October 23). Americans' support for death penalty stable. *Gallup Politics.* Retrieve from http://www.gallup.com/poll/178790/americans-support-death-penalty-stable.aspx

Justice Safety Valve Act of 2013, S. 619, 113th Cong. (2013–2014). Retrieved from https://www.govtrack.us/congress/bills/113/s619

Kleban, H., & Jeglic, E. (2012). Dispelling the myths: Can psychoeducation change public attitudes towards sex offenders? *Journal of Sexual Aggression, 18*(2), 179–193.

Leahy, P. (2013, March 20). Bipartisan legislation to give judges more flexibility for federal sentences introduce . . . Bill would expand 'safety valve' to all federal crimes. Retrieved from http://www.leahy.senate.gov/press/bipartisan-legislation-to-give-judges-more-flexibility-for-federal-sentences-introduced

Liptak, K. (2015, July 13). President Barack Obama commutes sentences of 46 drug offenders. *CNN Politics.* Retrieved from http://www.cnn.com/2015/07/13/politics/obama-commutes-sentences-drug-offenders/

Listwan, S. J., Jonson, C. L., Cullen, F. T., & Latessa, E. J. (2008). Cracks in the penal harm movement: Evidence from the field. *Criminology and Public Policy, 7*(3), 423–465.

Lynch, G. E. (2014). Ending mass incarceration: Some observations and responses to Professor Tonry. *Criminology & Public Policy, 13*(4), 561–566.

Martinson, R. (1974). What works? Questions and answers about prison reform. *The Public Interest, 35*, 22–54.

McKillop, M. (2015, October 7). Number of older prisoners grows rapidly, threatening to drive up prison health costs. *The Pew Charitable Trusts.* Retrieved from http://www.pewtrusts.org/en/research-and-analysis/blogs/stateline/2015/10/07/number-of-older-prisoners-grows-rapidly-threatening-to-drive-up-prison-health-costs

Moore, E. (2012, February). Restorative justice initiatives: Public opinion and support in NSW. *Crime and Justice Statistics Bureau Brief, Bureau of Crime Statistics and Research*, Issues Paper no 77, (pp. 1–12).

Nagin, D. S., Piquero, A. R., Scott, E. S., & Steinberg, L. (2006). Public preferences for rehabilitation versus incarceration for juvenile offenders: Evidence from a contingent valuation. *Criminology & Public Policy, 5*(4), 627–651.

Office of the Inspector General, U.S. Department of Justice. (2015, May). *The impact of an aging inmate population on the Federal Bureau of Prisons (Evaluation and Inspections Division 15–05).* Retrieved from https://oig.justice.gov/reports/2015/e1505.pdf

Palmer, T. (1975). Martinson revisited. *Journal of Research on Crime and Delinquency, 12*(2), 133–152.

Peters, P. W., & Warren, R. K. (2006). *Getting smarter about sentencing: SCSC's Sentencing Reform Survey.* National Center for State Courts. Retrieved from http://www.ncsc.org/~/media/microsites/files/csi/gettingsmarter_sentencingreformsurvey_finalpub.ashx

Phelps, T. M. (2014, July 18). Federal government moves to reduce sentences of 46,000 drug offenders. *Los Angeles Times*. Retrieved from http://www.latimes.com/nation /nationnow/la-na-drug-sentences-reduced-20140718-story.html

Piquero, A. P., Cullen, F. T., Unever, J. D., Piquero, N. L, & Gordon, J. A. (2010). Never too late: Public optimism about juvenile rehabilitation. *Punishment & Society, 12*(2), 187–207.

President's Commission on Law Enforcement and Administration of Justice (1967). *The challenge of crime in a free society*. Washington, DC: Government Printing Office.

Raphael, S. (2014). How do we reduce incarceration rates while maintaining public safety? *Criminology & Public Policy, 13*(4), 579–597.

Reynolds, N., Craig, L. A., & Boer, D. P. (2009). Public attitudes towards offending, offenders, and reintegration. In J. L. Wood & T. A. Gannon (Eds.), *Public opinion and criminal justice* (pp. 166–186). Portland, OR: Willian.

Roberts, J. V., & Stalans, L. J. (1997). *Public opinion, crime, and criminal justice*. Boulder, CO: Westview Press.

Roberts, J. V., & Stalans, L. J. (2004). Restorative sentencing: Exploring the views of the public. *Social Justice Research, 17*(3), 315–334.

Schmidt, M. (2015, October 6). U.S. to release 6,000 inmates from prisons. *The New York Times*. Retrieved from http://www.nytimes.com/2015/10/07/us/us-to-release-6000 -inmates-under-new-sentencing-guidelines.html?_r=0

Senese, J. D. (1992). Intensive supervision probation and public opinion: Perceptions of community correctional policy and practice. *American Journal of Criminal Justice, 16*(2), 33–56.

Smarter Sentencing Act of 2015, S. 502, 114th Cong. (2015). Retrieved from https://www .govtrack.us/congress/bills/114/s502/text

Spiranovic, C. A., Roberts, L. D., & Indermaur, D. (2012). What predicts punitiveness? An examination of predictors of punitive attitudes towards offenders in Australia. *Psychiatry, Psychology and Law, 19*(2), 249–261.

Spohn, C. (2014). Twentieth-century sentencing reform movement: Looking backward, moving forward. *Criminology & Public Policy, 13*(4), 535–545.

Subramanian, P., & Shames, A. (2013, October). *Sentencing and prison practices in Germany and the Netherlands: Implications for the United States*. Retrieved from http:// www.vera.org/sites/default/files/resources/downloads/european-american-prison -report-v3.pdf

Tonry, M. (2014). Remodeling American sentencing: A ten-step blueprint for moving past mass incarceration. *Criminology & Public Policy, 13*(4), 503–533.

Travis, J. (2014). Assessing the state of mass incarceration: Tipping point or the new normal? *Criminology & Public Policy, 13*(4), 567–577.

United States Sentencing Commission. (n. d.) *Profile: Sensible sentencing reform: The 2014 reduction of drug sentences*. Retrieved from http://www.ussc.gov/sites/default /files/pdf/research-and-publications/backgrounders/profile_2014_drug _amendment.pdf

Van Kesteren, J. (2009). Public attitudes and sentencing policies across the world. *European Journal of Criminal Justice Policy Research*, *15*(1/2), 25–46. doi:10.1007/s10610-009-9098-7

Wood, J. (2009). Why public opinion of the criminal justice system is important. In J. L. Wood & T. A. Gannon (Eds.), *Public opinion and criminal justice* (pp. 33–48). Portland, OR: Willian.

Yankelovich, D. (1991). *Coming to public judgment*. Syracuse, NY: Syracuse University Press.

INDEX